DICTIONARY OF CHILDREN'S FICTION FROM AUSTRALIA, CANADA, INDIA, NEW ZEALAND, AND SELECTED AFRICAN COUNTRIES

DICTIONARY OF CHILDREN'S FICTION FROM AUSTRALIA, CANADA, INDIA, NEW ZEALAND, AND SELECTED AFRICAN COUNTRIES

Books of Recognized Merit

ALETHEA K. HELBIG
AND
AGNES REGAN PERKINS

GREENWOOD PRESS
Westport, Connecticut • London

Library of Congress Cataloging-in-Publication Data

Helbig, Alethea.
  Dictionary of children's fiction from Australia, Canada, India,
New Zealand, and selected African countries : books of recognized
merit / Alethea K. Helbig and Agnes Regan Perkins.
    p. cm.
  Includes index.
  ISBN 0–313–26126–1 : (alk. paper)
  1. Children's stories, Commonwealth of Nations (English)—Bio-
bibliography. 2. Children's stories, Commonwealth of Nations
(English)—Dictionaries. 3. Authors, Commonwealth of Nations—
Biography—Dictionaries. 4. Children's stories, African (English)—
Bio-bibliography. 5. Children's stories, African (English)—
Dictionaries. 6. Bibliography—Best books—Children's stories.
7. Authors, African—Biography—Dictionaries. I. Perkins, Agnes.
II. Title.
PR9084.H45 1992
823.009′9282′09171241—dc20   91–35234

British Library Cataloguing in Publication Data is available.

Library of Congress Catalog Card Number: 91–35234
ISBN: 0–313–26126–1

First published in 1992

Greenwood Press, 88 Post Road West, Westport, CT 06881
An imprint of Greenwood Publishing Group, Inc.

Printed in the United States of America

CONTENTS

PREFACE

The *Dictionary of Children's Fiction from Australia, Canada, India, New Zealand, and Selected African Countries: Books of Recognized Merit* contains 726 entries on such elements as titles, authors, characters, and settings based on 263 books by 166 twentieth-century authors. Like its four companion volumes on American and British fiction for children, it is intended for the use of everyone who is concerned with children's literature in any way: librarians, teachers, literary scholars, researchers in comparative social history, parents, booksellers, publishers, editors—those to whom literature for children is of vital interest professionally or personally. Periodic updates of these books are underway.

A reference book dealing with fiction from those countries which, along with the United States and the British Isles, publish and give awards to books for children in English is especially appropriate at this time. Diversity of cultures has become a strong interest in schools and the subject of much scholarly study. Fiction receiving critical acclaim in emerging countries makes a fascinating comparison to that coming from countries with longer histories of publishing for children. Several countries whose literary traditions developed later than that of the United States or Great Britain have recently found their own voices, in some cases highly sophisticated. Many of these books are not widely known outside their own areas.

This *Dictionary* brings together in one volume a representative sample of those books that critics have singled out as the best. We, as Americans, were pleased to become acquainted with these books and hope that others, regardless of nationality, will be equally enthusiastic about them and excited to discover literary traditions for children that they may not have known existed.

Not all countries that publish books for children in English include original fiction in their lists. Where English is not the first language, textbooks usually take precedence, followed by collections of folk tales or hero tales from oral tradition. Even in some of those countries where fiction is published, there is such a small output that awards are not given or there is no mechanism for honoring the better books. The award lists we have used from the various countries are not entirely parallel, but are as similar as we could determine, mainly from library associations or government sponsored groups. Ordinarily, only awards given to published books are included, but in a few cases the procedure for selection is different and required a slight change in our criteria. In India, for instance, the Children's Book Trust gives prizes to manuscripts in a contest, then prints the winners and honor books as it can. As in our previous *Dictionaries*, we have not included translations, books with awards given by strictly regional groups, or those issued by organizations to their members only. We have also excluded books chosen by children, since children as a whole are unsophisticated readers and have limited critical experience.

Because our study is of fiction and not of illustration, we have not included stories in picture book form, since the texts of such books can seldom stand alone and their analysis requires a consideration also of the illustrations. Somewhat arbitrarily, we have set 5,000 words as a minimum; most books must be at least that long to develop a story that can function on its own. Books of more than 5,000 words are included, even if the illustrations are very prominent.

Collections of short stories also require a different sort of analysis and plot summary from novels and are not included, even if technically they are fiction. Retellings from oral tradition appear if the material has been developed like that in novels, as in James Houston's *Tikta' liktak*.

In our author entries, we have focused on what in the author's life is most relevant to children's literature and to the particular books in this *Dictionary*. Although several other published sources give biographical information about authors, none considers all the authors whose books are in this study. Having the information in the same volume is not only of convenience for researchers; it is of particular value for those areas where libraries are on limited budgets and do not own the other publications. Moreover, a large percentage of these authors are unknown outside their countries, yet are making significant literary contributions.

In presenting our entries we have tried to follow an arrangement that will be convenient for a variety of users. Entries are of several types:

A. Title entries. These consist of bibliographical information, including the American title if it is different from the original; the publisher; the sub-genre to which the work belongs; a plot summary incorporating the plot problem (if any), significant episodes, and the denouement; a brief literary critical evaluation; names of sequels, if any; additional entries not mentioned in the summary, if any; and awards and citations in abbreviated form. A list of the complete names of the awards and citations appears in the front matter. Entries vary in length. The number of words in an entry does not indicate the importance or quality of the book, since plots can be summarized more briefly and critical judgments stated more succinctly for some books than for others. Most readers will be acquainted with the terms we have used for sub-genres, but a few terms may need some explanation. By realistic fiction, we mean books in which events could have happened some time in the world as we know it, as opposed to an imaginary or fantastic world, and not necessarily that the action is convincing or plausible. Historical fiction includes those books in which actual historical events or figures function in the plot, as in *Rebels Ride at Night* by John F. Hayes and *Ghamka Man-of-Men* by Eve Merchant, or in which the specific period is essential to the action and in which the story could not have occurred in any other time, as in *The Treasure Box* by Sarojini Sinha and *The Parkhurst Boys* by Margaret Beames. Books that are merely set in a past time, like Eleanor Spence's *Lillipilly Hill*, we have called period fiction. Although all plots are driven by problems, we have used the term "problem novel" in its more recent sense to refer to those stories where social, physical, or psychological concerns dominate, as in Patricia Wrightson's *I Own the Racecourse!* and *Always Ask for a Transfer* by Vancy Kasper.

B. Author entries. These consist of dates and places of birth and death, when available; education and vocational background; major contribution to children's literature; significant facts of the author's life that might have a bearing on the work; titles that have won awards; frequently titles of other publications, usually with brief information about them; and critical judgments where they can safely be made.

C. Character entries. These include physical and personality traits for important, memorable, or particularly unusual characters who are not covered sufficiently by the plot summary, and focus on such aspects as how they function in the plot, how they relate to the protagonist, and whether the characterization is credible and skillful. Characters are classified by the name by which they are most often referred to or by the name by which the protagonist refers to them, e.g., the despot, Aunt Nan Henry, Mrs. Angela Chase, Nunganee. The name is also cross-referenced in the index under the most likely possibilities. If the character's surname does not often appear in the story, it will usually not appear in the index; when it is included, it is usually as a family name: Whitburn family, Brary family, and so on. If the plot summary gives all the significant information about characters, as with many protagonists, they are not discussed in separate character entries. All major characters, however, are listed in the index.

D. Miscellaneous entries. These include particularly significant settings and elements that need explanation beyond mention in the title entry.

Every book has title and author entries. When a book has different original and American titles, the complete entry appears under the original title, but the book is also listed under the American title, with a reference to the original title. Entries are in alphabetical order for convenience. Asterisks indicate that the item has a separate entry elsewhere in the book. Accompanying entries do not duplicate one another. While a book's title entry gives the plot summary and a critical assessment, other entries provide additional information to give a more complete understanding of the book.

A list of awards and their abbreviations appears at the front of the *Dictionary*. A list of books and authors by country is in the back of the volume as well as a list of the books classified by awards. The index includes all the items for which there are entries and such elements as cross-references, major characters for whom there are no separate entries, specific place settings, settings by period, and such matters as themes and subjects, books of first-person narration, unusual narrative structures, significant tone, authors' pseudonyms, illustrators, and genres.

The number of books included in the *Dictionary* from each country varies widely. The largest representation comes from Australia, which has a long history of publishing for children and of giving awards to outstanding books. Canada, also, has been publishing for children for a long time, but lists of runners-up or honor books have not always been kept so that, although there are more Canadian awards, the total number of books included is not as great. Countries like Nigeria and South Africa have far fewer, since publishing children's fiction in English is more recent there, and giving prizes for such books is limited to the last few years.

The literary quality of the books also varies greatly. While it is difficult and perhaps unfair to judge from this obviously small sample, some generalizations can safely be made since these books have all been critically acclaimed. Books from Nigeria display a sometimes charming verve but are less polished in style and plotting. They are varied in subject matter with a strong didactic strain. With a few notable exceptions, those from India are adventure-mysteries dealing with such problems as poaching, jewel theft, and international smuggling. Although full of exciting action, they seem to have little beyond place names to distinguish the part of the world where they are set. The several award-winning books from South Africa are, on the whole, more sophisticated in style and structure. Most are concerned with such contemporary social problems as poverty and the homeless.

Many of the earlier books from Australia were family or adventure stories, reminiscent of those published in the United States at least ten years earlier. Historical fiction has always played a strong role, dealing especially with the settlement of Australia and the pioneer experience. Beginning in the late 1970s, Australian writers for children seem to have found distinctive voices and are producing books skillfully written and full of interesting ideas and action. Throughout these books, both early and recent, runs a strong sense of place, an appreciation for the physical elements of the country and, even in books set in cities, a good feel for how the setting influences the action. Particularly notable is a strong interest in the culture of the Aborigines and sympathy for their plight. On the whole, Australia has a large volume of good books for children.

Canadian authors, too, have long shown interest in indigenous people, including books from as early as the 1950s like Kerry Wood's *The Great Chief*, and more recently, Jan Hudson's *Sweetgrass* and in other historical fiction like Janet Lunn's *Shadow in Hawthorn Bay*. Adventure stories also stand out, for example, those by Roderick Haig-Brown, Farley Mowat, and especially James Houston. L. M. Montgomery's *Anne of Green Gables*, published in 1908, has influenced domestic girls' stories throughout the English speaking world and has retained its popularity, while *The Incredible Journey* by Sheila Burnford, published in 1962, is outstanding among animal stories. Only recently, however, have Canadian writers of problem novels, fantasies, and domestic adventures emerged from the shadow of their British and American counterparts (Janet Little being a notable exception). The past decade has seen the appearance of Kevin Major, Cora Taylor, Monica Hughes, and Brian Doyle, among many accomplished writers.

One of the most pleasant surprises in our research for this *Dictionary* was the discovery of the high quality of the books from New Zealand, both realistic fiction and fantasy. Only a few, like those of Margaret Mahy, have been republished in the United States, but the award winners are consistently well written, interesting novels. Even as far back as 1945, with Stella Morice's *The Book of Wiremu*, and 1958, with Maurice Duggan's *Falter Tom and the Water Boy*, the books have individuality, varied subject matter, subtle humor, and distinctive style. More recent books have kept this tradition.

As with the companion volumes on American and British children's fiction, we ourselves have read every book included in this *Dictionary* and have done all the research and writing in this volume. As university teachers of literature for children and young adults for twenty-five years and as people trained in the study of literature as literature, we are dedicated to the idea that books for children must be judged by the same criteria as those for adults, keeping in mind, of course, that children are the intended audience. Our critical comments, therefore, judge each book as imaginative literature, not on other values, regardless of the country of origin or the particular emphasis of the award for which it was chosen.

We have had some valuable assistance from a variety of sources, making it possible for us to secure all but a few of the books we needed. We wish to acknowledge the help of Eastern Michigan University with leaves and grants and to express our appreciation to the Eastern Michigan University Library and the Ann Arbor, Michigan, Public Library for the use of their extensive collections. Specifically, we thank Marcia Shafer, formerly of the Ann Arbor Public Library Youth Room, and her staff for their aid; Brian Steimel and Thomas Staicar of the Interlibrary Loan Department of Eastern Michigan University Library for their help in obtaining obscure books; Meena Khorana of Coppin State College in Baltimore who generously loaned us books from her own collection and directed us to the Children's Book Trust of India; and Ian McLean of Punchbowl Elementary School Library in New South Wales, who on his own time found sources for the last books we needed from Australia and New Zealand which we had been unable to get elsewhere and sent a number of them to us at his own expense. Other people who helped us with lists and leads include Barbara Garner, Janet Lunn, Jay Heale, Manorana Jafa, Mabel Segun, and Osayimwense Osa.

AWARDS AND CITATIONS

Aust. Bk. of Year Com.

Australian Book of the Year Commended

Aust. Bk. of Year Highly Com.

Australian Book of the Year Highly Commended

Aust. Bk. of Year Winner

Australian Book of the Year Winner

Aust. Jr. Bk. of Year

Australian Book of the Year Junior Book Award

Books Too Good

Children's Books Too Good to Miss (1963, 1966, and 1979 editions, not limited to U.S. writers)

Boston Globe Honor

Boston Globe-Horn Book Honor Book (not limited to U.S. writers)

Boston Globe Winner

Boston Globe-Horn Book Award Winner (not limited to U.S. writers)

Can. Bilson

Geoffrey Bilson Award for Historical Fiction for Young People (Canada)

Can. Bk. of Year Runner-Up

Canadian Library Association Awards Book of the Year for Children Runner-Up

Can. Bk. of Year Winner

Canadian Library Association Awards Book of the Year for Children Winner

Can. Council Hon. Ment.

Canada Council Children's Literature Prizes Honorable Mention

Can. Council Winner

Canada Council Children's Literature Prizes Winner

Can. Ebel Runner-Up	Max and Greta Ebel Memorial Award for Children's Writing (Canada) Runner-Up
Can. Ebel Winner	Max and Greta Ebel Memorial Award for Children's Writing (Canada) Winner
Can. Gov. General's Hon. Ment.	The Governor General's Literary Award (Canada) Honorable Mention
Can. Gov. General's Winner	The Governor General's Literary Award (Canada) Winner
Can. IODE Natl.	National Chapter of the Imperial Order of the Daughters of the Empire (Canada)
Can. Ruth Schwartz	Ruth Schwartz Children's Book Award (Canada)
Can. Young Adult Runner-Up	Young Adult Canadian Book Award Runner-Up
Can. Young Adult Winner	Young Adult Canadian Book Award Winner
Carnegie Com.	Commended for the Carnegie Medal (not limited to British writers)
Carnegie Winner	Carnegie Medal Winner (not limited to British writers)
CBT of India	Children's Book Trust Prize for Fiction and Science Fiction (India)
Child Study	Child Study Children's Book Committee at Bank Street College Award (formerly called Wel-Met)
ChLA Touchstones	The Children's Literature Association Touchstones (not limited to U.S. writers)
Cont. Classics	Contemporary Classics list published by *Horn Book* (not limited to U.S. writers)
Fanfare	*Horn Book* Magazine Fanfare lists (not limited to U.S. writers)
Guardian	Guardian Award for Children's Fiction (not limited to British writers)
IRA	International Reading Association Children's Book Award

Jr. High Cont. Classics	Junior High Contemporary Classics list published by the American Library Association *Booklist* (not limited to U.S. writers)
Lewis Carroll	Lewis Carroll Shelf Award
Nigerian Ife	Nigerian Ife Bookfair Children's Book Competition
Nigerian Natl. Council	National Council for Arts and Culture, First Prize, English Language (Nigeria)
Nigerian CLAN First Prize	Children's Literature Association of Nigeria
Nigerian CLAN Hon. Ment.	Children's Literature Association of Nigeria
N.Z. Esther Glen	Esther Glen Award (New Zealand)
N.Z. Govt. Short List	New Zealand Government Publishing Awards, Book of the Year Short List
N.Z. Govt. Winner	New Zealand Government Publishing Awards, Book of the Year Winner
Other	The Children's Rights Workshop Other Award (not limited to British writers)
Poe Nom.	Nominee for the Edgar Allan Poe Award Best Juvenile Mystery Category (not limited to U.S. writers)
Sanlam	Sanlam Prize for Youth Literature (South Africa)
Young Africa	Maskew Miller Longman Young Africa Award (South Africa)
Young Observer	Young Observer Teenage Fiction Prize (not limited to British writers)

DICTIONARY OF CHILDREN'S FICTION FROM AUSTRALIA, CANADA, INDIA, NEW ZEALAND, AND SELECTED AFRICAN COUNTRIES

A

ADAM WEBB (*Rebels Ride at Night**), Toronto lawyer who works closely with the wealthy leaders known as the Family Compact but whose sympathies are secretly with the organization of workers and settlers called the Reformers. At first seeming cold and supercilious, he shows himself to be quite a different character after he confides his dual role to Frank Sanford. Adam deeply loves his son, Clifford, and at Frank's urging lets Clifford know of his involvement with the rebel group. When he learns of plans to disrupt Reformer meetings and kill the leader, William Lyon Mackenzie*, he sends the boys north with a warning, but he never comes out openly for the Reformers. Frank is able to tear the page containing Adam's name from Mackenzie's list of supporters before it falls into the hands of the police, so he is never known to belong to the group and evidently continues his profitable law business without disturbance. The ethics of his position are not questioned in the novel.

ADVENTURE ON GOLDEN LAKE (Sinha*, Nilima, ill. Mrinal Mitra, CBT, India, 1986), novel of adventure and mystery set in Kashmir, northern India, involving the kidnapping of two English girls and their rescue by a quartet of Indian youngsters. While hiking to the village of Aru, the Mehta children, Nina, 12, and her twin brothers, energetic Anaud and thoughtful Ajit, 14, are overtaken by a blizzard but are invited to share the shelter of a cave by two English girls, Ann Brown and Jane Philips, medical students on vacation. They arrange to meet again at the houseboat *Rosebud* on Dal Lake in Srinagar, to which the girls will be returning after their extended Himalayan hike. On the agreed day, the Mehtas, who also are vacationing on a Dal Lake houseboat, get Rashid, 11, the son of their boat owner, to take them to the *Rosebud*, only to find it apparently deserted. The owner, a surly man named Gulam Kadir, tells them that the girls never returned from their hike, but Ajit recognizes a blue anorak and the camera that Ann let him examine lying on the divan. When they confront Kadir with this information, he angrily tells them to go. Rashid, however, introduces them to a dwarf named Cuhotu who lives near the *Rosebud* and who assures them that the girls did return but had disappeared by the next morning. Wanting to get evidence before they alert the police, Anaud and Cuhotu return to the *Rosebud*, enter through a window, and find the camera in a cupboard. As they leave, Kadir sees them. After a disaster nearly fatal to Anaud, when Rashid's little boat is rammed by a *shikara*, a canopied gondola, containing Kadir and two confederates, they enlist Cuhotu to watch Kadir's movements. When he reports that the boat owner goes out at the same time every day, they follow him, with Nina, whom he presumably will not recognize, going first and her brothers trailing further behind. Kadir enters a tumbledown cottage. Anaud impulsively follows, is caught by the three from the shikara and a younger, blond man, and is locked in their boat. Shortly afterward, with Nina creating a diversion by pretending to be lost, Ajit enters the cottage, where he, too, is caught. Thinking it is the same boy, the men this time lock him in the attic, where he finds Ann and Jane. They explain that by agreeing to deliver some papers for the blond man, whom they met on their hike, they have inadvertently become involved in an international espionage ring and are being held until they give up the papers, which Ann cleverly hid. Nina, in the meantime, has met up with Rashid and, together with Cuhotu, they rescue Anaud. The four then storm the cottage, tie up the blond man who is now alone, free Ajit and the girls, and, each running in a different direction, throw off the pursuing boatmen and make their way to the Parimahal, a ruin overlooking Dal Lake where Ann hid the papers. The spies give chase but the youngsters, the girls, and Cuhotu outwit them and arrive at the police station with the evidence. The lively if implausible plot uses the conventions of mistaken identities, foreign spies, and wild chases. The book is more interesting for its setting, making extensive use of local color and giving a sense of the beauty of Kashmir. Characters are mostly types, with the twins broadly differentiated by their opposite personalities and Rashid by his cleverness, but none of them is developed. English idiom is sometimes strange, particularly the frequent use of "reach" without an object to mean "arrive." CBT of India, Second Prize.

AGNES BRARY (*Snow Apples**), grudging, embittered mother of the narrator, Sheila. Occasionally, the girl she used to be shows through her humorless exterior, when her husband buys a used piano and she sits playing half the night and when Sheila and her brother Tom give her a correspondence course in poetry, in which she shines, even writing and selling a couple of poems. At the same time, she resents Sheila's opportunity to graduate from high school, having left school after fourth grade herself, and she tries to block Sheila's ambition to train as a nurse. Even her great gesture of selling the piano to pay Sheila's tuition turns out to be false, since Tom gave her the tuition money for Sheila from his own earnings before the piano sale. The most complex character in the book, she is interesting but not sympathetic.

AGNES MACKENZIE (*Going to the Dogs**), Billy Mackenzie's vitriolic mother. She thoroughly dominates her husband, Alex*, who masochistically appears to enjoy her abuse and even tries to curry favor with her by abusing the children verbally and psychologically. She appears to feel a sexual love for Billy and resents Anne, her daughter, so much that she denigrates her at every opportunity. Her main pleasures are television news programs, which she watches all day long, cigarettes, and tea. She also resents Poppy* Richardson, because Poppy is Billy's girl, and calls her a whore. Her spying on Billy and Poppy leads to Billy's leaving home. Agnes is presented as a modern maternal type, exaggerated to advance the plot, and is a foil for Poppy's meek and obsequious mother, another type.

AIDAN WILMOT (*Lillipilly Hill**), bookish eldest child, who, disappointed that his plans to enter Rugby have been disrupted by the family's move to Australia, is determined not to like the new life or to make friends with any of the other youngsters at Barley Creek School. His superior attitude makes him unpopular and the butt of taunts and pranks, but because he disdains violence, he does not respond, thereby making himself even more disliked. Clay* Stewart's love of the outdoors makes Aidan look around and begin to appreciate Australia for the first time. Aidan treats his younger sisters, especially Harriet, with scorn, but in the first real crisis after he has met Clay, he calls on Harriet to help him. He is a complex character, for whom sympathy grows in the story.

ALDOUS, ALLAN (1911–), born in Leederville, a suburb of Perth, Western Australia; dramatist, lecturer, broadcaster, novelist. He attended a state school and Christian Brothers' College in Perth. He worked as copyholder [*sic*] and proofreader on *The West Australian* and in 1935 won a one-act playwriting contest conducted by the Perth Repertory Club. He married and sailed for London, where he worked as proofreader at a typesetting house and sold articles and stories, and had three plays produced by the British Broadcasting Company's overseas service. When World War II broke out, he was classified as "domiciled," which meant that he was not allowed to return to Australia with his wife and daughter. He enrolled in Civil Defense, was transferred to the National Fire Service, and eventually joined the Allied Invasion Forces pay corps. In 1943 he returned to Australia, where he transferred to Army Education, organizing drama groups in New Guinea and Bougainville until his discharge in 1946. Since that time he has been a free-lance writer, lecturer, and broadcaster. Among his best-known books for young people are the several McGowan books, starting with *McGowan Climbs a Mountain* (Oxford, 1947), based on his mountaineering experience in the British Isles. Two of his novels for young people were commended for the Australian Book of the Year award, *Kiewa Adventure** (Oxford, 1950) and *Doctor with Wings** (Hodder, 1960), both realistic adventure stories more notable for evoking a strong sense of place than for convincing characterization or plot. *Doctor with Wings* is set in Northern Territory, mostly in Alice Springs, and is concerned with the Australian Flying Doctor Service that provides emergency medical service to isolated settlements over a vast area. *Kiewa Ad-*

venture, which involves a mystery, is set in the Kiewa Valley of New South Wales.

ALDRIDGE, (HAROLD EDWARD) JAMES (1918–   ), born in White Hills, Victoria, Australia; journalist, war correspondent, and novelist, known primarily as a writer for adults. He attended the London School of Economics and Political Science and Oxford University and wrote for London papers. During World War II, he free-lanced as a correspondent in Finland, Greece, the Middle East, and Russia for the Australian Newspaper Service and North American Newspaper Alliance. Injured in the Syrian campaign, he was invalided home to Australia and also wrote for *Time* before returning to the front. He completed his first novel while a correspondent, *Signed With Their Honour* (Little, 1942), about the Royal Air Force in Greece and based on his war experiences there. After becoming a free-lance writer in 1944, he published more than two dozen novels, several books of travel and observation, plays, television scripts, and short stories. Among the best known of these is *A Sporting Proposition* (Little, 1973), which was made into the film *Ride a Wild Pony*. For a teenage audience he wrote *The True Story of Lilli Stubeck** (Hyland, 1984), the growing-up story of the invincible daughter of a ne'er-do-well Victoria family during the Depression that was Australian Book of the Year for young readers, and *The True Story of Spit MacPhee** (Viking, 1986), a Guardian winner, about a male counterpart of Lilli. Substantial and naturalistic, both books excel in depicting small town society. For children he also wrote *The Flying 19* (Hamilton, 1966).

ALEX (Duder*, Tessa, Oxford, 1987; *In Lane Three, Alex Archer*, Houghton, 1989), realistic girl's growing-up novel of friendship, swimming as a sport, and death, set in New Zealand in the mid– to late–1950s. In lane three, competing against her arch-rival in the crucial race to determine who will represent New Zealand at the 1960 Olympics in Rome, star swimmer Alex (Alexandra) Archer, almost sixteen, describes the race as it proceeds and reflects on the six years of hard training that got her there, concentrating on the events of the last year. Tall, muscular, hard driving, a fine student who also excels in piano, ballet, and field hockey, Alex puts in long hours at practice and on schoolwork. She is encouraged by her supportive middle-class family, but her three younger siblings sometimes think she gets too many favors. Auckland's best hope for a medal, she falls second to Maggie Benton, newly arrived from Singapore. Maggie's highly directive mother keeps a firm hold on all aspects of Maggie's life and career, as well as an apprehensive eye on Alex. In addition to determination, Maggie has financial resources that Alex's more modest circumstances cannot match. The year leading up to the finals holds problems as well as joys and challenges for Alex: gossip about her femininity; the need to determine her priorities, particularly after she sustains a leg injury playing hockey; sorting out her feelings about Andy* Richmond, a studious and ambitious young man who becomes her sweetheart, confidant, advisor, and dearest friend; learning to understand and appreciate Maggie, whose cool ability she comes to admire and whose superiority she eventually acknowledges; and hardest of all, coping with Andy's death. For weeks after he is struck by a car, Alex suffers nightmares, and inwardly she vows two gifts to his memory, to sing a Noel Coward song he loved in the school year-end revue and to beat Maggie in the finals. She accomplishes both and is gratified to discover that both girls will go to Rome. In taut present tense, Alex describes the big race in short italicized prologues to each of the sixteen chapters and in an epilogue. These passages provide most of the novel's tension. The chapters in which she speaks in past tense tell how she came to be in lane three swimming against Maggie. The reader gets to know Alex well through her observations about situations and the important people in her life. Scenes are well fleshed: the school musicals, races, a dance, an evening with a drunken friend of Andy, training, going for a swim to relax the night before the big contest. This engrossing and substantial book is strongest for the picture it gives of the world of competitive swimming, its characterization of Alex as a many talented young woman as well as a gifted and dedicated athlete, and its convincing presentation of the thoughts and feelings of an intelligent, sensible, and serious young woman as she comes to terms with defeat and the loss of the young man she hoped to marry. N. Z. Esther Glen; N. Z. Govt. Winner.

ALEX KENDALL (*The Year of the Currawong**), Alexander, named after Alexander the Great by his father, a history professor. Treasurer of the Currawong Mine Preservation Society, Alex is a peaceable, bookish boy, who nevertheless likes adventure. He takes the dare of a local youth to spend the night in the Silver Bell, the supposedly haunted, abandoned hotel, and thus encounters the Swagman*. Much of the story is told from Alex's viewpoint but not by him. Alex is more fully rounded than is the usual mystery story protagonist.

ALEX MACKENZIE (*Going to the Dogs**), Billy Mackenzie's wimpy father. The manager of the local Hudson's Bay Company store, he provides adequately for the family but has few pleasures except Kiwanis and watching television. Billy despises him for his weakness. Alex is a type figure, exaggerated for the plot, and serves as a foil for Poppy* Richardson's over-organizing father.

ALF (*Family at The Lookout**), retarded nephew of Miss Elsie Howe, proprietor of the general store. With great pride, Alf makes the deliveries for the store and takes care of the old horse, Jip. He repeats frequently what his aunt has said, that he ''was born to drive Jip.'' When the bush fire threatens, he is delighted to drive ''to rescue the Major and the little pups and the big dogs.'' As the threat becomes more serious, his aunt sends him to drive Jip to a safer area. He is an example of a polite, useful young man, even though, as his aunt says, he is ''a little simple.''

ALL THE PROUD TRIBESMEN (Tennant*, Kylie, ill. Clem Seale, Macmillan, 1959; St. Martin's, 1960), realistic novel set among a small community of Melanesian islanders between northern Australia and New Guinea. When unpleasant, patronizing Dr. Mason, government scientist, informs the people of Firecrest Island that their volcano, Old Faithful, will soon erupt and the island sink into the sea, the islanders put little stock in what he says, since a previous prediction did not come true. After the men set out on their annual visit to the pearl diving grounds, violent tremors shake the island and even create great cracks in the church walls. Miss Alice Buchanan, the islanders' respected and beloved white teacher, sends her ward, Kerri*, 13, who tells the story, and Alu, a venerable former diver, to fetch the men back to evacuate the people. When the evacuees are just five miles offshore, the volcano explodes with a huge lava flow, and the entire island is engulfed by the sea, causing a tidal wave of such proportions that it almost swamps the frail luggers. In spite of tumultuous seas and at the command of Miss Buchanan, who is determined that the islanders continue to live as traditional an existence as possible, they make for Malu, an island thought cursed because of pagan ceremonies once held there and now occupied by Dr. Mason. Although uneasy about landing there, though they remind themselves they are now Christians and no longer believe in the old tales, the islanders respond to her strong leadership and set about making new homes. They meet powerful opposition from Dr. Mason and his retainers. Approached by little Patty, the doctor's strong-willed daughter, who says her father is ill and even tried to kill her, Miss Buchanan hurries to the doctor's house, where she learns that he has been behaving strangely ever since he fell and hit his head while examining some rock paintings. She administers morphine and has Kerri radio for help. When Kerri rescues Patty from a crocodile, Dr. Mason changes his mind about allowing the islanders to stay. Old Alu, however, says the sacred objects left by the old worshippers must be destroyed, and Kerri perilously climbs down a rock face to the once holy cave to do so. He falls ill of exhaustion from the feat, and, while he recovers, the island commissioner arrives. A council decides the islanders will stay on Malu, and the government will assist them in resettling with equipment and stock. It is also decided that the government will send Kerri to school to Queensland, Miss Buchanan feeling it is vital that he gain a white education in order to help his people. Although the island elders are almost indistinguishable, Dr. Mason is a chauvinistic type who changes predictably, Miss Buchanan the good, all-wise white lady, and Kerri the worthy lad who will guarantee their future. Some incidents are too convenient. The plot has a strong initial problem that develops into a continuing one that sustains attention. Kerri's personal concern, whether or not he should try for a scholarship, is well knit with the main plot and resolved credibly. The book is most memorable for its clear and affectionate picture of the warm, gracious, hospitable islanders and its strong contrast between their beliefs and ways and those of the whites from the outside world with whom they come into contact. Aust. Bk. of Year Winner.

ALL WE KNOW (French*, Simon, Angus, 1986), novel of family and school life in Sydney, Australia, in the late twentieth century. Arkie (Arkravi) Gerhardt, 12, goes through her sixth-grade year observing a number of different, mostly non-traditional families. Of these her own family, with her high-school music teacher mother, Susan, her little brother Jo (Joachim), 8, and her stepfather, Michael Byrne, a high-school English teacher, is one of the strongest and most loving. Although she considers loud, brash Sean Taylor the biggest pain in her class in school, she feels some compassion for him when his parents have a wild physical fight, witnessed by most of the neighbors. Again, with her best friend, Kylie Bethel, Arkie witnesses a less happy family when her friend's father comes to take Kylie out between his allotted monthly visits, Kylie's mother refuses, and a nasty argument ensues. Most difficult is the situation of Ian Koh, a waif-like boy in her school class who is Jo's best friend. Ian, when he isn't at Arkie's house with Jo, spends his evenings sitting on the steps of the pub, waiting for his mother. A strange child, he is shunned by most of his classmates. Twice Arkie's family takes a long day's trip into the country to stay with Carol, who was Susan's best friend at boarding school, and her husband John and their baby, Rhys. There they meet the Arcana family, a widow and her five sons who live in a converted double-decker bus. Arkie finds out, accidentally, that the boys keep a sort of shrine to their father's memory in a cave, with his motorcycle helmet and other memorabilia. She takes one of their pictures on the first trip, meaning to return it when they go back, but finds that their mother has remarried, their bus is gone, and the cave is bare. When they return, Michael's dog Headley, for whom Kylie was supposed to be caring, has disappeared. After Ian does not return to school, Arkie puts two and two together, and she and Michael go to Ian's apartment where they find the boy has been keeping Headley for company, his mother having been gone for a couple of weeks. Michael is especially gentle with Ian, and Arkie realizes from what he has said, much he has not said, and some old pictures left in her desk, that he, too, was an abused child. Welfare workers come and take Ian into care, and the whole family is sad and feels vaguely guilty that it could not do more for the boy. All this is played out against a background of raucous twelve-year-old school taunts and insults and the near worship of the whole class for their unconventional teacher, Mr. Clifton, who wears an earring, fills the classroom with artwork and caged mice, and makes even math interesting. At Arkie's home, the background is her mother's piano on which she is constantly composing, mild squabbling with Jo, and the high-spirited banter between Susan and Michael. Arkie comes to see the grown-ups as individuals. In the end she even writes a tentative letter to her real father in Perth, who sends her birthday cards but whom she hardly remembers, enclosing her picture and asking for one of him. School scenes and dialogue ring true, with humor and gritty details, and the point of view of teachers is especially well expressed. Arkie is a bright, realistic child, the other characters are well drawn and individualized, and the overall tone is affectionate. Aust. Bk. of Year Winner.

ALMOST-MOTHER (*Sweetgrass**), Bent-over-Woman, Sweetgrass's step-mother, a Blackfeet Blood. She is presented as typical of Blackfeet women in that she is modest, homeloving, family oriented, and hardworking. She tends to lose her composure, however, a deplorable trait in her culture.

ALWAYS ASK FOR A TRANSFER (Kasper*, Vancy, ill. Glenn Priestley, Schoolhouse, 1986), realistic sociological problem novel set in a contemporary, unnamed, probably Canadian city. Since their abusive, alcoholic father assaulted their mother so severely she landed in General Hospital, Willy*, 14, and Laura*, 10, have been farmed out to a series of foster homes. Now with Dino* Bazos, an elderly pizza shop owner, and his wife, Yota*, Greek immigrants, Laura is optimistic, but Willy is bitter, worried that their father will somehow trace them, and sure that the Bazoses will exploit them for work as the other foster parents have. He is amazed when Dino insists that Willy put in only limited hours at the pizzeria, pays him well, and urges him to excel at his studies and play basketball. Both children are amazed also when Dino and Yota include them in their social life, give them considerable freedom, and respect them as human beings. Just when they feel accepted, a serious problem confronts Willy: his father arrives. He accosts Willy, ironically as the boy is on his way to bank his pay, takes the money, and demands all future earnings. Willy keeps silent, for fear the Bazoses won't want the children of a drunken extortionist. Laura and the Bazoses, however, think it is strange that Willy never seems to have any money. Then Willy arranges for his best school friend, Karl, a topnotch basketball player and smooth talker, to help at the pizza shop. Soon Dino misses supplies, and Willy suspects Karl, but out of loyalty says nothing. Things come to a head when one busy night Yota suffers a heart attack and Dino leaves the boys in charge. When he returns, he discovers cash missing. Karl accuses Willy, Dino believes him, and Willy flees. Apprehended by the police when he breaks the glass of a city transfer booth, Willy names Dino as his father, and Dino rescues him. The truth then comes out: Karl stole the money. Dino and Willy are reconciled, and the children's future with the Bazoses seems secure. The plot is overforeshadowed, and some events, like Willy's fracturing the glass in the booth with his fist without sustaining any injury, seem unlikely or strained. Karl and Willy's father are conventional, transparent figures, and the Bazoses are sentimentalized, but Willy is likeable and realistic for his sincerity and perse-verance, and strong-minded Laura is especially winning. Much of the dialogue and many of Willy's frequent ruminations seem to voice the thoughts of the author or a social worker, being either exceptionally mature and knowledgeable or in language not quite right for even a bright early teenager. The book has a didactic attitude that fortunately is relieved by the fast-moving sequence of events. Structure and vocabulary are not difficult and well within the scope of middle and later elementary readers. The result is an interesting look at life for foster children. Can. Ebel Runner-Up.

ANDERSEN, DORIS (1909–   ), born in Tanana, Alaska; Canadian librarian and writer. She grew up in Victoria, British Columbia, and was educated at the University of British Columbia and the University of Washington. She served as a librarian in Seattle, Ottawa, and Vancouver and was lecturer in children's literature at Capilano College in North Vancouver. Late in her career she began writing novels for children about Native Americans in Canada. Her extensive research and generous use of cultural detail produce strongly realistic pictures of life in both pre- and post-contact times. *Blood Brothers* (Macmillan, 1967; St. Martin's, 1967) tells of the friendship between a Norwegian and a Native American youth. In *Slave of the Haida** (Macmillan, 1974), which was runner-up for the Canadian Library Association Book of the Year for Children, Kim-ta, a Salish boy, is kidnapped and enslaved by marauding Haida. Andersen's novels tend to be conventional in plot and stereotyped in characterization, but move along well and present sympathetic and authentic if simplified views of their times. She has also written several books of history and biography, including *Evergreen Islands: The Islands of the Inside Passage, Quadra to Malcolm* (Gray's, 1979); *Ways Harsh and Wild: Adventure and Hardship during the Yukon Gold Rush* (J. J. Douglas, 1977); *The Columbia Is Coming!* (Gray's, 1982); and *To Change the World: A Biography of Pauline Jewett* (Irwin, 1982).

AND TOMORROW THE STARS (Hill*, Kay, ill. Laszlo Kubingi, Dodd, 1968), historical novel based on the life of John Cabot*, fifteenth-century English explorer, who claimed the northern Atlantic coast of North America for the British crown. Born in Genoa about 1451, young Vanni (Giovanni) Caboto is more interested in boats and fishing with his old friend, Emilio, than in his father's spice-trading business. At about nine, however, he is sent to Venice to live with his humorless, wealthy Uncle Luigi Romano, who has lost his wife and only child during a plague and is willing to adopt a prospective heir. Although he suffers under his uncle's severe and conventional regime, Vanni makes a number of friends—Fra* Andrea, a Franciscan pharmacist with a remarkably advanced attitude toward science and learning who becomes his tutor; Michiele, the pharmacist's apprentice, a friendly boy whose secret desire is to be a barber; and Guido Pestrelli, a gondolier with whom Vanni becomes involved in a smuggling ring when he gets a little older, sneaking out at night for the adventure until he is nearly murdered for his knowledge and Guido deserts him. Since his uncle has discovered his absence, though he ascribes it to amorous not illegal adventures, Vanni is sent for punishment to work as a *grommet* or apprentice aboard the *Santa Lucia*, a trading vessel bound for Constantinople. At first he is made uncomfortable by the smarmy, probably homosexual interest of the steward, Scalzi, and the resentment of the other grommets, but the trip is a marvelous experience for him. Among other people, he meets Amerigo Vespucci from Florence, whom he does not much like, and Fra Andrea's friend, Ibn Haud, a scholar in Alexandria, but his most important friend is Gabriel Duchesne, a ship's officer, to whom he trades tutoring in reading for Gabriel's knowledge of the sea. As a result of these trips, he understands the importance of the spice trade and is inspired to seek a way to Asia by sailing west. The rest of the book deals with his adult life, including his two voyages to the New World with Gabriel as shipmaster and pilot and Michiele as doctor, on the first of which he claims Canada for the British. On the second, he sails down the coast expecting to reach Cathay (China) and Cipango (Japan). Finally, they run into the Spanish, who maintain that the English are trespassing on their territory, and Cabot realizes that what they have found is not Asia but land lying between two oceans, a wholly new land. With a ship badly damaged by worms, supplies low, and dissension among those aboard, the book ends with Cabot heading into a storm exhilarated by his realization. Historical notes at the end give little information on the man and his voyages on which the book is based. Cabot's ship never returned from the voyage, though some of his small fleet may have. The youth of Cabot in Italy and his travels in the Mediterranean show thorough research and bring the period to life in a lively story. By contrast, the major voyages to North America make slow reading and, although full of the intrigue of the rival nations, are not nearly as interesting, nor does the adult Cabot seem as real a character as the spirited boy. Can. Bk. of Year Winner.

ANDY RICHMOND (*Alex**), eighteen-year-old boyfriend of star girl athlete Alex Archer. Also a swimmer, he encourages Alex in training and aspiring to study law. His love for Alex helps her cope with catty remarks that question her sexual orientation.

ANGELITO (*Detour to Danger**), ten-year-old gypsy orphan whom Nando Herrera finds living in the back rooms of his great-great-aunt's decaying villa in Andalusia. The very small, thin boy is terrified of the neo-Nazis who occupy the villa next door and who have deliberately run down the gypsy cart and killed all the rest of his family. Angelito, himself, and the chicken he was holding on his lap, were thrown clear and overlooked by the killers, who seem to have been motivated by prejudice against gypsies and fear that the family, who sometimes lived in the deserted villa, might have learned too much of their secret plans. After one of the leaders also kills Anton, the chicken, Angelito says he must avenge his family. When the two men responsible for the "accident" are both killed at the festival, Nando is left with an uncomfortable suspicion that the boy might have persuaded some other gypsies to help him to get revenge, though it is also possible that the two Nazis, who were rivals for position in the group, caused each other's deaths. Angelito is extremely clever and, once he decides Nando is a friend, devoted. In the end, Nando takes Angelito to Catalonia, where his warmhearted Scottish mother takes the boy in and plans to educate him.

ANGEL SQUARE (Doyle*, Brian, Groundwood/Douglas, 1984; Bradbury, 1986), lighthearted, episodic, realistic novel of family, neighborhood, and school life with detective story aspects set for a few days in December, 1945. Tommy, perhaps twelve, who tells the story, lives with his big, bluff Dad*, his fussy Aunt Dottie, and his retarded older sister, Pamela ("She's M.D.," Mentally Deficient) on Cobourg Street, a mixed, working-class neighborhood in Lower-town, Ottawa, Canada. Although Tommy is "not anything," he attends York School on Angel Square, where the Jewish youth study. The French Canadians (the Pea Soups) and the Irish Catholics (the Dogans) attend other schools on the square. Tommy describes with relish the frequent fights in which the boys of the three groups engage. His best friend and cohort in brawls is Jewish Sammy Rosenberg, who figures strongly in the book but does not appear until the very end. Three interwoven stories unite Tommy's often amusing, sometimes poignant recollections: his need to make money for Christmas; his infatuation for classmate Margot Lane; and his efforts to discover who beat up Sammy's father, a night watchman in a streetcar barn. All the strands revolve around his liking for "The Shadow," a historical radio show featuring super-sleuth Lamont Cranston, which is also Tommy's nickname. Tommy has several odd jobs, singing in the Episcopal choir, serving as altar boy at the Catholic church, helping at the synagogue, being stock boy at Woolworth's, among others and manages to accumulate enough money not only for nice gifts for his family but also for a rather lavish present for Margot. Throughout the year, he has also for every holiday and even slightly significant occasions sent her a card signed "The Shadow," thus far without response or sign of recognition. Because of Aunt Dottie's remark that Mr. Rosenberg is the victim of religious prejudice, Tommy, Dogan Gerald Hickey, and Pea Soup CoCo Laframboise decide to ferret out the criminal. Their quest leads them to a local feed and seed store, then to the streetcar barn, where they encounter Fleurette Featherstone Fitchell, Tommy's boy-crazy classmate, necking with Lester Lister. Through them they discover a significant clue, a comic book bearing the initial "L," which they eventually trace to Mr. Logg, a piggy-eyed, scruffy car barn mechanic who collects comics. On his own, Tommy bravely visits Mr. Logg in his apartment, ostensibly to sell him comics. He finds evidence (an anti-Jewish poster, a feed bag) that may implicate Mr. Logg in the assault, reports to the policeman who is moonlighting as the Wool-worth Santa, writes notes signed "The Shadow" directing suspicion toward Mr. Logg, and distributes them in the neighborhood. The neighbors decide Mr. Logg is guilty and applaud The Shadow, though they don't know he's Tommy. All the children do, of course, and when Tommy delivers his Christmas gift to Margot, she thanks him as The Shadow and compliments him on his courage. Tommy's Christmas turns out to be special in another way, too. Sammy Ro-senberg returns from the hospital in Toronto with the news that his father is going to be all right. There is a very large cast of characters, most of whom the reader never gets to know. Tommy's peers are distinguished by one, or possibly two, features: Gerald Hickey "knows about" Pamela, which is a good thing, Tommy thinks, because Gerald will see to it that she is safe; CoCo speaks with a thick French accent and is reputed among the boys to be a good detective; Margot is not only beautiful but smart enough to play things cool; and Fleurette is the "easy" girl. Tommy is round and likeable. Although he sometimes compromises between right and wrong, mostly he appears as earnest, intelligent, persevering, and ready for fun and fights. Although some incidents are overdrawn, like the one in which Dad's friend Frank* crashes through the house, undone by his overzealous efforts not to offend Aunt Dottie, others are truly hilarious, like that in which Mr. Blue Cheeks, the English teacher, struggles with Tommy over grammar. Situations sometimes seem contrived, the conclusion is abrupt and rushed, forcing the reader to reread, and there is very little physical description. Best are the intimate tone, light, conversational style, the accurate self-revelation, the warm, witty humor, the keen sense of the forties period, and the theme of religious tolerance presented in the comic context. *Up to Low** is a companion novel. Can. Council Hon. Ment.

ANGUS (*Wild Man of the Woods**), old Indian who carves masks and hangs them in the woods to ward off evil spirits. He tells Stephen and Louie the story of how Bighand killed Crooked Beak long ago, thinking that he was being attacked and knocking the other Indian so that he fell and hit his head on a stone. Bighand was sent away and when he returned his people were all gone. Later old Mrs. Riley, who runs the campground on the lake, tells enough of Angus's past arrest and imprisonment for manslaughter so it is clear that the story was autobiographical.

ANNE OF GREEN GABLES (Montgomery*, L. M., Page, 1908), classic realistic, girl's growing-up novel set in the rural area of Avonlea on Prince Edward Island, Canada, in the early 1900s. Marilla* and Matthew* Cuthbert, a brother and sister of almost sixty who operate their family farm of Green Gables, request the orphanage to send them a boy to help with chores and by mistake receive a girl, impulsive, grandiloquent, imaginative, red-haired Anne* Shirley, 11. Although Matthew loses his heart immediately to the thin, drably clad child, Marilla insists that Anne be sent back to the orphanage until she discovers that Anne will then become the hired girl of sharp, touchy, demanding Mrs. Bluett and decides to keep her. Since events are loosely connected, the book takes on the effect of an episodic novel, but the strongly drawn, engaging protagonist and three main story strands unify it: Anne's adjustment to living with the Cuthberts and her adventures in the neighborhood; her close and unswerving friendship with Diana* Barry, a neighbor girl her age; and her unyielding animosity toward schoolmate Gilbert Blythe. Marilla begins immediately to try to make hoydenish Anne into her idea of a young lady. Matthew has agreed to allow Marilla to have her way, though he secretly prefers Anne just as she is, impulsive, romantic, and bubbling over with energy. Anne's strong personality resists modification, however, and she soon gets into trouble. Notable examples involve busybody Mrs. Rachel Lynde and Marilla herself. When Mrs. Rachel comes to inspect Anne and remarks pointedly in front of the girl that she is "terrible skinny and homely," Anne flies into a temper. Marilla sends her to her room until she apologizes, and at Matthew's suggestion, Anne does so, in a highly dramatic expression of regret that satisfies Mrs. Rachel and ironically amuses Marilla. When Marilla's heirloom amethyst brooch comes up missing, Marilla assumes Anne has stolen it and orders her to her room until she confesses. Though innocent, Anne is afraid she will miss the Sunday School picnic and owns up to the theft, again in an elaborate discourse, but shortly afterward Marilla discovers the brooch stuck in a shawl. Anne gradually sheds her wildness and gains self-control though she never loses her strength of mind, lively imagination, and ready tongue. In other episodes, on the first day Anne attends Sunday School, she creates a stir because she has decorated her plain hat with real buttercups and roses. At school, when Gilbert Blythe calls her "carrots" and she breaks her slate over his head in retaliation, the teacher makes her stand before the class the rest of the afternoon to punish her for her fit of temper. The next day her humiliation continues; when she and other pupils are late for school after the noon recess, the teacher singles out Anne for punishment and makes her sit with Gilbert, whom Anne now regards as her archenemy. Anne gathers up her things and storms out in righteous indignation, vowing she'll never return. She soon also gets into trouble with Diana's mother. At tea, she accidentally serves Diana currant wine instead of raspberry cordial, and Diana goes home drunk. Diana's friendship denied her, Anne decides she may as well return to school. Mrs. Barry relents, however, when Anne saves the life of her little girl, Minnie May, ill of croup. After that Anne's association with Diana flourishes, and the two girls become "bosom friends." They play about the countryside, Anne giving romantically descriptive names to many places, like Violet Vale, Lover's Lane, and Willowmere, that reflect her deep love of the outdoors and her fanciful nature. She attends a "concert" (a program of recitations and short dramatizations) with the Barrys and stays overnight with Diana, inadvertently creating another ruckus when she suggests they race down the hall and jump into bed and they leap right on top of old Aunt Josephine who has come unexpectedly to spend the night. Anne also gets into trouble when she walks the ridgepole of the Barry house on a dare, falls, and breaks her ankle. Anne, Diana, and several other girls from school form a writing club and sometimes dramatize pieces. Anne plays Elaine in Tennyson's "Lady of the Lake," drifting down the lake in a flat-bottomed dory, which gradually sinks from leaks. She is rescued by Gilbert, to her mixed feelings of gratitude and chagrin. He asks to make up, but she adamantly refuses. Anne also has adult friends in the community. She becomes particularly close to Mrs. Allan, the minister's wife, and to the new teacher, Miss Stacy. Anne and Gilbert lead the school in scholarship, a strong rivalry developing between them. Miss Stacy encourages them and several other students to try for the Queen's Academy and acquire teacher's credentials and gives them special instruction. Anne passes the entrance exam with the highest score of any student taking the test. At Charlottetown, she works hard, as does Gilbert, and both take honors in the spring exams, Gilbert winning the school medal and she a scholarship to Redmond College. Higher education does not lie in Anne's immediate future, however. Matthew has a heart attack and dies, and Marilla, whose sight has been failing, decides to sell Green Gables. Believing her duty lies with Marilla and Green Gables, Anne foregoes college to accept the teaching position at Avonlea (her own school), which Gilbert, who had been hired for the post, gives up for her convenience. Anne is grateful and tells him she'd like to make up, and the expectation at the conclusion is that the two may eventually discover a romantic interest in each other. The strong characterizations of Marilla, Matthew, Diana, and, in particular, Anne draw attention away from the generous amounts of sentimentality and moralism. The passages that describe the region capture the area's natural beauty and appeal strongly to sight and smell. Details of everyday life give a clear social sense, making this a fine period piece as well as an always interesting story of how a strong-minded, intelligent girl grows into a useful, contributing adult. Much humor comes from Anne's naive expressions of her love for life and Marilla's contrasting practical adult way of perceiving the world. This book is the first in a series that features one of the best-known and most memorable heroines in literature for the young. ChLA Touchstones.

ANNE-MARIE CHARBONNEAU DUCHARME (*Let It Go**), mother of Lance* who left him and his father when the boy was five to rejoin the band she had sung with before marriage, which is now headed for Nashville. Daughter of a Cree woman and a part-Indian drifter who abandoned the family, she took care of her younger siblings while her mother worked from the time she was eight, hating the small town in northern Saskatchewan and escaping in fantasy as she listened to the local radio and sang the country songs it featured. At fourteen she won a school talent show and was asked to sing with a small-time band that played at rough bars and dances. At fifteen she escaped the town in reality with Mike Ducharme, a part-Cree rodeo rider from northern Alberta. By the time she was seventeen, she was married and a mother, and Mike had settled down to manage Silverwinds Ranch near another small town. When Jerry, the band manager, tracked her down and asked her to rejoin him, she left Mike and five-year-old Lance and the restrictive small-town life she had always hated. Now a newly discovered star in Nashville, she comes back to Alderton, wanting to talk to her son and determined to seek his custody. When she sees his drawing of an eagle, she realizes that she must give Lance his freedom, and she lets him go back to the ranch, taking with her only his drawing.

ANNE SHIRLEY (*Anne of Green Gables**), orphaned protagonist of a classic girls' growing-up novel. Anne's parents were teachers who died of fever when she was three months old. Anne was taken in first by their housekeeper and her husband, with whom she lived until she was eight, and then by a woman with eight children, among whom were three sets of twins. After two years with this family, she was sent to an orphanage. She has had very little schooling but can read well and knows many pieces of poetry by heart. When she arrives at Green

Gables to live with Matthew* and Marilla* Cuthbert, Anne is a thin, little redhead of eleven, dressed in a "very short, very tight, very ugly dress of yellowish gray wincey." She longs for a permanent home, and Green Gables and the Avonlea environment appeal strongly to her romantic beauty-loving eyes. At first Anne's impulsiveness, strong will, ready tongue, and lively imagination get her into trouble in particular with prim and proper Marilla, whose sometimes overly rigid expectations are tempered by warmhearted, reasonable Matthew. The first couple of years that Anne spends at Green Gables, which make up most of the novel, are a rich source of domestic adventures and lighthearted humor as Anne settles in at the Cuthbert household and learns what Marilla expects of her and as she makes friends with Diana* Barry, establishes herself among the young folk of the region, and adapts to school. Firmly, roundly, and dynamically drawn, Anne is one of the best-known and most loved heroines in literature for children.

ANNE TIPPETT (*The Feather Star**), independent, willful waif and village pest, who frequently interjects herself into whatever at the moment seems most interesting and can be identified by the red hat she always wears. Light-fingered, she is something of a human pack rat, collecting items usually of little value to anyone but herself. She owns Queenie, a big, white cat with one green and one blue eye, which causes the book's most comic scene and leads to its major problems. Her tendency to help herself to things not hers causes a major problem, too. A well-realized figure, Anne catches and holds the reader's attention.

ARKWRIGHT (Steele*, Mary, ill. author, Hyland, 1985), comic talking animal novelette set in recent years on the coast of Australia. On his last voyage after a lifetime at sea, old salt Captain Chilblain looks forward to settling down with a pet, something different, however, not the usual dog or cat or parrot. In South America, he encounters a Giant Anteater who agrees to be his companion. The captain takes Arkwright (self-dubbed in memory of Noah, who was the first ark wright), a creature "most handsome" with a "thick grey fur coat . . . , dashing side-stripes, and a huge bushy tail," around the horn and back to Australia. After a ticklish time at customs, they settle down in an "old-world cottage" with a view of the ocean in the sleepy village of Candlebark uphill from the seaside township of Tumbalunda. At Arkwright's suggestion, Captain Chilblain names his place Nozama (Amazon backwards), because the little river and garden out in back remind the anteater of his homeland. They are happy in retirement, in spite of the Captain's haphazard housekeeping, and they make friends in the neighborhood. Arkwright busies himself in the back, ripping up the ground for ant-snacks, while presumably preparing the area for a garden. Two related problems crop up. The first grows out of a public demonstration against spraying the ants that infest the local Bowling Club. With the help of neighbors Norm Woollybutt, his wife, and Nelson, their son, Arkwright organizes an ant-control squad consisting of himself and eight local echidnas, chief among them bristly Ethel.

The next and more serious problem arises when entrepreneur Hogarth P. Wanderlust decides to develop the area as a theme park for tourists, the Candlebark Safari Park, featuring Arkwright and the echidnas and eventually other wild creatures. Arkwright engineers an attack of the dreaded Anteater Blotch. Mr. Wanderlust thinks they are all ill and departs quickly, leaving the captain and Arkwright to enjoy their retirement. The raucous tall tale pleasingly strains belief at every point. It has no serious purpose, though it takes a few gentle swipes at contemporary do-gooders and quick-money makers. Humor of dialogue, some of it insult (''Noah was the first arkwright, stupid''), of situation (hilarious scenes where Nelson and his friend bathe Arkwright), of concept, and of wordplay combine with many black and white comic illustrations for a happy romp that projects the kind of exaggerated amusement that under-twelves particularly favor. Aust. Jr. Bk. of Year.

AROUND NIGERIA IN THIRTY DAYS (Onadipe*, Kola, Natona, 1981), realistic novel of the adventure-travelogue type set in the 1970s in Nigeria. When Mr. Kalio, popular young teacher of geography and physical education in a private boys' school in Lagos, delivers an impassioned lecture on the importance of knowing their country and devoting effort to its betterment, he so inspires four close friends of twelve and thirteen, Audu Yahaya, son of the Assistant Inspector General of Police, Laolu Olaku, son of a lawyer from Ibadan, Nkem Obina, son of a wealthy businessman and politician, and Tolu Allen, son of a university teacher, that they form a ''Supreme Expedition Council'' and plan a trip for their next holiday to ''see the country and to know Nigeria and Nigerians'' firsthand. Although Tolu breaks a leg and cannot participate, the other three set out in high spirits, with Laolu serving as recorder of their adventures. The trip takes them around their homeland from the capital northward along the Niger River, northwest to Sokoto, then through the northern Muslim section to the northeast to Maiduguri, southward almost to the Cameroun border, and then home via Port Harcourt and Benin City. They travel by train, taxi, and mostly truck, stopping mainly at the capitals of the nineteen states of the Nigerian Federation, visiting places of historic importance and scenic interest, and gaining limited information about them. Along the way they have some terrifying experiences and many happy ones and encounter some villainous sorts and many people of good spirit, at the end satisfied that they have achieved their objective. At Ibadan, they take a side trip to Oyo, the ancient town of the Oyo Alafin empire where they visit the palace, one of the proudest sites of the Yorubas, and in the north they view the great Kainji Dam and impressive Bussa Falls. At the sleek modern city of Kaduna they are terrorized by a villainous cab driver, and later a truck they ride in bursts into flames. They are usually badly treated by subordinate policemen, who regard them as potential thieves or nuisances, but police officials adopt a different attitude, being of a higher moral caliber evidently, and also soon becoming aware of Audu's father's position. Thenceforth they keep a protective eye on the boys and occasionally rescue them from tight situations, for example, when the youths are captured by smugglers pretending to be Christians at worship. In other adventures, the boys are attacked by angry villagers who blame them for the death of a donkey, encounter road blocks and lions, attend a Muslim service, stay at a chief's house, sleep in workers' barracks, in friends' houses, in a dope house, and in a hotel where carousing goes on all night long, and are entertained by a poor elderly Ibo woman who laments the country's social and economic deterioration. At Benue River, they are surprised when the greedy, disagreeable man who ferries them across the river in his leaky boat turns out to be a biology teacher teasing them. They return right on schedule to Lagos where they are greeted by a band, reporters, and photographers, a rousing welcome arranged by Mr. Kalio, who has been kept apprised of their progress by Laolu's regular reports home to Tolu. Incidents are numerous and move without causal relationship to one another or suspense and are insufficiently developed to be memorable. Characterization is sparse, and the boys are almost indistinguishable from one another except in broadest outline. The style employs many interesting expressions, some of them common English idioms that take unexpected turns. Moralistic and encouraging comments appear frequently, along with some pessimistic ones to the effect that Nigeria is rapidly declining morally, statements made by Laolu or by adults the boys encounter, but on the whole the tone is upbeat. The book succeeds admirably in what are probably its two main purposes: adventure, of which there is enough for at least two books, and creating a sense of the vastness, diversity, and potential of the large, emerging nation. A map would be a welcome aid. Nigerian CLAN First Prize.

ASH ROAD (Southall*, Ivan, ill. Clem Seale, Angus, 1965; St. Martin's, 1966), realistic novel set in the Prescott district of Australia among the foothills near Tinley, presumably about the time the book was written. The story follows a large cast of characters as a forest fire approaches and engulfs the area. Three city boys, Graham*, Harry, and Wallace, all about fifteen, are camping, on Ash Road, where one of their classmates has a summer home, as their eventual destination. By accident, Graham spills the methylated spirits for their camp stove and starts the tinder-dry brush and forest burning. Panicky, unable to put out the fire, they flee over the hills the six or seven miles to Ash Road, hoping to give the appearance of having spent the night at the home of their friend's family, the Pinkards. Ash Road, at the head of a valley, is a dead-end lane with half a dozen families scattered along it: the Pinkards, who are still in the city; the Tanners, now housing only Grandpa* Tanner; the Buckinghams, with three children, Pippa, about 14, Stevie, 9, and Julie, 5; the Fairhalls, an older couple with their visiting grandson, overprotected Peter, 13 or 14; the Georges, a raspberry farmer who drives his daughter, Lorna, 14, and her older brother, John, mercilessly to make their marginal farm pay; and the Robertsons, a couple with a young baby. When the news of the fire comes, Bill Robertson collects Mr. Buckingham and other local men to go help fight it. John George deserts the raspberries to race off on his motorcycle to his fire brigade. Mrs. Robertson leaves her baby and Mrs. Buckingham leaves her youngest, Julie, with Grandpa Tanner, and they join Gran Fairhall and other women driving to the nearest town to help house and feed evacuees from the fire area. Lorna continues to pick the already spoiled raspberries in the blazing heat until her father collapses beside her, evidently a stroke victim. When the three city boys who started the fire appear, dirty and exhausted, she commandeers them to carry her father to his ancient car, then cannot find the keys. Stevie and Pippa have joined the scene. Gramps Fairhall, determined to take Peter back to the city away from danger, at last gets his car started and is intercepted and, with difficulty, convinced that he must take Mr. George to the hospital with Harry and Wallace to help. After a harrowing ride, through road blocks and along a forest road with the fire bearing down upon them, Gramps wrecks the car. The fire skips past them and the boys carry Mr. George, using the car seat for a stretcher, only to find the town deserted and to realize that their patient is dead. Meanwhile, Grandpa Turner, experienced in fire and the harsh country, has fastened the Robinson baby in a basket and strapped Julie to a chair and let them both down the well, resigning himself to death but hoping to save the children. As the fire approaches, Lorna finds Graham, and together with Pippa and Stevie they stand under the sprinklers in the carrot patch. The three women, realizing finally that the fire is going to hit Ash Road, try to get back from town, eventually abandoning the car and running up the road. When Peter discovers that his grandmother, unable to keep up with the others, has been left behind, he runs toward the fire and manages to drag her to the Tanners' potato patch, away from the brush. Just as it seems as if they will all die in the inferno, a freak of the overheated air and the moisture it has drawn up starts a sudden downpour, and Ash Road is saved. The action shifts from one of the large number of characters to another, each of whom has his own problem. The author does a remarkable job of keeping the various concerns clear and urgent. The sense of the landscape and the hot, dry conditions of the countryside is strong and convincing. The characters often seem overwrought, however, especially before the danger is imminent, and the adults particularly are inclined to make too many foolish decisions under pressure to be entirely believable. Aust. Bk. of Year Winner.

AUNT BELINDA WEBSTER (*The Brown Land Was Green**), John Webster's sister, who reluctantly emigrates to Australia to care for his family. In the early part of the novel, she is an unsympathetic figure, complaining, prim, always concerned with appearances. She has a little money of her own, which she holds in reserve, intending to use it to pay the fare back to England, when, as she hopes, John comes to his senses. Later, she mellows and even develops an interest in Bill* Everard. She gives John the money to use to stock his acreage. Although Belinda changes suddenly, her dynamism is not inappropriate.

AUNT GEMMA SWALES (*What's the Matter, Girl?**), Anna Swales's sharp-tongued, plain, religious, self-righteous aunt, Uncle* Arion's younger sister of sixteen. Gemma has a suspicious nature and when she accuses Anna of an unnatural love for Arion, Anna loses her temper. Gemma is a foil for Arion and for Anna herself.

AUNT ISABEL CANNON (*Come Danger, Come Darkness**), often called Aunt Isa, mother of Cousin* Flora and aunt of Otter and Paddy Paul Cannon. She suffers from rheumatics and seems weak willed and fussy but can show considerable spunk, especially where Flora is concerned. She insists that Flora have greens to maintain good health, and thus the boys discover that Isak* plans to escape. Aunt Isa also insists that Dr.* Butler treat Flora, not Dr. Fitch, Dr. Butler's superior, since she rightly regards Fitch as ignorant and incompetent. Hence Butler is able to influence Major Cannon to allow Otter to study medicine.

AUNT LEAH (*Corner Store**), plump, good-humored wife of Papa's* brother, Uncle Dave. She is Becky's* favorite relative and is understanding, bringing a book for the tenth birthday party, while Aunt* Sadie brings an undershirt. She has also arranged that a cousin get a slightly flawed coat, a second, at half price for Becky's gift from her parents. It is Aunt Leah who produces Miss Sylvia* Cohen as a candidate for Papa's new wife. She tries to explain to Becky that Mama wanted Papa to marry again, and she says that Mama will always be in her heart, a statement that causes imaginative Becky to believe that her tension cramps must be caused by Mama, who has somehow slipped a bit and is now in her stomach.

AUNT LIZZIE KLASSEN (*Days of Terror**), sister of Peter's* mother. Her husband is wantonly shot by bandit anarchists simply because he owns property. Her two sons are killed when her house is burned, and she is found wandering, half out of her mind. Brought to the Neufelds, she has the clothes on her back and a few other small possessions, among them, a silver samovar and, ironically, a medallion her husband had received from the Czar. Considered by the doctor to be too frail to emigrate, she nurses Katya through the measles and later dies in her sleep. She is one of the most interesting figures in the novel.

AUNT NAN HENRY (*The Root Cellar**), always busy, pregnant mother of four sons. She is a writer and the sister of Rose Larkin's deceased father. Aunt Nan welcomes Rose and treats her like a member of the family, but, because Rose has never had the experience of living in a real family situation, the girl feels intimidated and overwhelmed by the boisterous, casual, outspoken Henrys. When Aunt Nan finds the complaining note Rose writes to another aunt, she is so shocked by Rose's selfishness and ingratitude that she falls and must spend the rest of her pregnancy in bed. Rose feel guilty about what happened and assumes more responsibility about the place. Aunt Nan is a sympathetic figure, a foil for Rose's dead grandmother.

AUNT SADIE (*Corner Store**), Papa's* older sister, who bosses him and his family and has few kind words to say of anyone. Becky* dislikes her and despises her loutish husband, Uncle Morris. When Mama is having a troubled pregnancy, Aunt Sadie scolds her for not heeding the doctor's warning that she should have no more children and for not visiting the doctor when she has pains and swollen legs. After Mama's death, Aunt Sadie comes frequently to the home behind Papa's store, bringing food but criticizing the children, the housekeeping, and Papa himself so much that they find it hard to be grateful. Her candidate for a new wife for Papa is grotesque, a *shvartz yor* he complains. She is furious when he likes Aunt* Leah's candidate better and huffily ignores the family for a while, but once it is clear that Papa is going to marry Sylvia* Cohen, Aunt Sadie takes over, sets the date, insists the wedding be at her house, and makes all the arrangements. Sylvia coolly lets her except in one matter: she firmly says that both Becky and her brother will be part of the ceremony, and Aunt Sadie backs down.

B

BAILLIE, ALLAN (1943–   ), born in Prestwick, Scotland; Australian journalist, novelist, and editor. His family emigrated to Australia when he was seven, settling in Melbourne, where he later attended the university. He was a reporter for the Melbourne *Herald/Sun* and has been editor for papers in London and Sydney, the Australian Broadcasting Company, and John Fairfax and Sons, Publishers, in Sydney. He has traveled extensively gathering material for his books. His first novel, *Mask Maker* (Macmillan, 1975), for adults, concerns a renegade teacher in the Laos mountain war and opium trade. His second book, *Adrift* (Nelson, 1984), a survival fiction for children, won the Kathleen Fidler Award from the National Book League. Highly commended for the Australian Children's Book of the Year was *Little Brother** (Blackie, 1985; Methuen, 1988), the dramatic account of a war-refugee boy's harrowing search for safety and his lost brother. Incidents reflect Baillie's observations of family hardships and disruption during the Cambodian War. *Riverman* (Nelson, 1986; Blackie, 1986) is an adventure novel set among lumbering operations on the Gordon and Franklin rivers. Baillie's other titles for young readers include *Eagle Island* (Blackie, 1987), *Drac and the Gremlin* (Viking, 1988), a picture book, and *Megan's Star* (Blackie, 1988).

BALDERSON, MARGARET (1915–   ), born in Sydney, New South Wales, Australia; librarian and novelist. She attended high school in Sydney and worked there as a librarian and a house mistress in a girls' school. Her best-known book, *When Jays Fly to Barbmo** (Oxford, 1968; World, 1969), arose from her experience as a resident worker in Norway, where she lived for some time in Tromso, the largest town north of the Arctic Circle. Set during the Nazi occupation in World War II, it is about a girl who makes an arduous journey to find her Lapp grandfather, having newly discovered her relationship to the nomadic people. It was commended for the British Carnegie Award and won the Australian Children's Book Council Book of the Year Award. She also published *A Dog Called George** (Oxford, 1975), a warm and funny pet story set in Canberra,

Australia, which was highly commended for the Book of the Year Award, and a picture book, *Blue and Gold Day* illustrated by Roger Haldane (Angus, 1979), set on the Australian coast. Her books have received critical praise for their ability to invoke a strong sense of place. Although she has traveled to India and Greece as well as northern Europe, she has made her home in the coastal town of Shoalhaven Heads, Australia.

BARNEY AND THE EELS (Somerset*, David, ill. Ernest Papps, Price, 1981), humorous, realistic, episodic novel of the Henry Huggins variety set during one year in the 1970s in the seaside town of Morristown, N.Z. The story is built loosely around the efforts of Barney Valentine, about eleven, to capture the wily old eel that dominates the silent pool on elderly Jake Hathaway's farm in the gorse-clad hills above town. Failing to catch the wily one, he pulls in another for an assignment for his student teacher, but when the eel rises up and pokes his nose in the face of regular teacher, Mr. Downes, Mr. Downes drops the aquarium, the classroom is a mess, and Barney is bawled out and told never to bring an eel again. Then bossy, know-it-all Skinny Rogers fashions a gaff with a barbed hook, but the wily eel eludes them again, the barb lodges in Barney's ankle, Skinny goes to pieces, and Barney bravely and coolly removes the hook by himself. Two episodes involve Barney's tree house, built because Bitzer, his dog (called so because he consists of bits of various breeds), chases an opossum up a tree that has old lumber near it just right for the purpose. He is helped by Fast Car Reid (aka Wendy Lowell), a classmate nicknamed for a race driver because she is so slow at doing her classwork. After the tree house is finished, Fast Car runs away and lives in it when Mr. Downes pressures her to finish her social studies project. For three days she stubbornly refuses to come home, until her little brother throws a fit because he misses her so much. Then Barney decides to camp out in the tree, too. His first night a clever old tramp named Skipper also moves in. Skipper stays the night but leaves early in the morning before Barney wakes, taking with him Barney's gear and the five dollars the boy earned watching old Jake's cows. Barney's dad insists he dismantle the tree house to satisfy the Lowells, but Barney discovers Skipper is living in it and holds off. Unsure what to do, he notices one day that Jake is burning the gorse. Realizing Skipper is in danger, he races to warn him, reaching the old tramp just in time. Later, Barney and Fast Car paddle air mattresses down the Awaroa River gorge behind Jake's house, looking for eels, find ones too big to catch, then spot a huge, antlered stag, which Bitzer bravely drives away. In April a Maori friend, Tama Waitoa, and his father show Barney and Fast Car how to trap migrating eels by digging channels between the river and the sea. Fast Car displays talents of which Barney was unaware when she prepares the eels for dinner, a meal the elder Valentines do not appreciate as much as the children anticipate. The final chapter finds Barney and old Jake spending the night by the pool with a special eel-catching pole and bait of three-foot-long worms. Barney's patience and persistence are rewarded when he hooks the creature, but he so admires the fish's size and pluck that he releases it. Morning finds him walking home content with life and pleased with his world. The narrative is exaggerated but not impossible and laced with humor that is less contrived and dependent on situation than in most books of this genre. Descriptions of the hillside, pool, and river reveal an appreciation for wild nature. The school scenes lack conviction, but the pool and river action episodes are lively with detail and are suspenseful. Although the parents and teachers are types, Barney and his child and adult friends reveal distinct personalities. N. Z. Govt. Short List.

BASSER, VERONICA, born in Victoria, Australia; teacher, writer of poems and stories for children. She attended Star of the Sea Convent, Elsternwick, moved to Sydney, and became a teacher in New South Wales until her marriage. Her first published work is *Glory Bird* (Sands, 1947), a story for young children. Among her other works are *The Martins of Montrose* (Aust., 1948) and two animal stories, *Ponny the Penguin** (Aust., 1948) and *Bright-Eyes, the Glider Possum* (Aust., 1957), both of which were chosen by the Education Department of New South Wales as school readers. She has also published a book of verses for children and has written plays and poems for *The School Magazine*.

THE BATES FAMILY (Ottley*, Reginald, Collins, 1969; Harcourt, 1969), novel of family life of drovers, those who herd sheep and cattle for hundreds of miles from property to property or to railway yards in the Australian outback, presumably in the mid-twentieth century. Albie and his twin sister, Linda, 17, are the eldest of the eight Bates children who, with their parents, live in the Northern Territory with no fixed roots. They rely on their string of horses and the jobs they get from the big cattle and sheep stations moving stock or, in droughts like that which is devastating inland Australia, cutting scrub, low branches and leafy boughs, to feed stock and checking gullies and the dwindling waterholes, where cattle and horses frequently get mired down, to save as many of the weakened animals as possible. Albie, whose hip was injured when he was dragged by a bolting horse, is frequently in pain but does not let that interfere with his many hours of backbreaking work in the relentless sun, and Linda, who is so close to her twin that she almost feels his pain with him, is torn between her desire to do more than her share to spare him physically and her realization that she should let him carry his own weight and some of hers, too, a psychological need for the crippled boy at least as pressing. Before the drought breaks, the twins have tried to save a number of mired horses and cows, mostly without success, while Mervyn, 15, Pru, about fourteen, and the four younger siblings, spend long days cutting scrub and helping around the camp that is their temporary home. Then the sky opens and pours torrents for days. Although Mr. Bates rigs tarps to ward off the worst of the water, none of them can sleep dry. The four oldest children ride out to round up their horses before they get stranded in the flood, while the other four help their parents move the camp to higher ground. Of their thirty horses, six have died, but the youngsters are able to save the rest.

Twice the twins and Pru save headstrong Mervyn from the results of his own impulsiveness. Later, Albie is almost drowned when they rig a line for their father's return after he has gone to the station house to get supplies and has had to swim his horse across a flooded billabong. The station owner hires Mr. Bates and his older offspring to join in a roundup of the brumbies, the wild horses, which are invading his land from the ranges and consuming the scarce feed. Albie, Linda, and Pru are all in the long line of riders driving the brumbies toward the station yards when a young stallion turns the herd and, unable to crash through the line where the twins ride, leads the whole group over the edge of a chasm to their deaths. The whole family is relieved when Mr. Bates decides to move on into sheep country, where he thinks they will have a good chance of a droving job while their own horses recover from the effects of the drought. Less a plotted novel than a series of incidents, the book is held together by the family's strong unity and stoic supportiveness in their terribly difficult and precarious life. Focus is mainly on the twins, with their unusual closeness of understanding and their responsibilities as the eldest of the offspring. The vast, almost barren wilderness where the family lives and works and the extreme weather conditions that determine life are as strong in the story as the people themselves. A note says that, although the book is fiction, it is based on a real family. Aust. Book of Yr. Com.

BEAKE, LESLEY (1949–   ), born in Scotland; South African teacher and free-lance writer. Her novel, *The Strollers** (Maskew, 1987), about street youth in Cape Town, received the Maskew Miller Longman Young African Award and the Sir Percy Fitzpatrick Award. Previously she published the historical novel, *Detained at Her Majesty's Pleasure* (Tafelberg, 1986). Her other published books include *Traveler*, *A Cageful of Butterflies*, *Merino*, and *Rainbow*, all published by Maskew Miller Longman in 1989. Owner of a research agency, she makes her home in Hout Bay, Cape Town.

BEAMES, MARGARET, born in England; New Zealand author of novels for children and radio and stage plays. A primary teacher, she moved to New Zealand in 1974 and published her first book, *The Greenstone Summer* (Stanmore, 1977) four years later. Her historical novel *The Parkhurst Boys** (Mallinson, 1986), about convict youths from Parkhurst Prison on the Isle of Wight remanded to New Zealand as apprentices in the nineteenth century, was named to the New Zealand Government Short List of best books for children. Married and the mother of two, she tutors dyslexic children.

BEATIE BOW (*Playing Beatie Bow**), Beatrice May Bow, 11, of Sydney, Australia, in 1873. She is a small, pale child with very short hair that is furry because it is just beginning to grow out after being cut off while she was ill with typhoid fever. She apparently has inherited just enough of the Tallisker Gift* to enable her to peer into the Sydney of one hundred years hence. Beatie is fierce and hot tempered and resents being denied further schooling because she is a girl. Abby encourages her to go to the teacher of her older brother, Judah, and request more instruction than she can get in Ragged School. Abby later learns from Robert Bow that Beatie became a famous classics scholar and headmistress of a school near where Abby's apartment house stands. Apparently Beatie was also formidable as an adult, and the school children developed a scary game about her, the one the neighborhood children are playing when Abby first sees Beatie and which Beatie is watching them play. Beatie maintains the records in the family Bible by which Abby learns what happened to the Bows and Talliskers. Beatie is a strongly realized figure, with Granny* Tallisker one of the most interesting characters in the novel.

BECKY DEVINE (*Corner Store**), Rebecca, perceptive and imaginative but naive Jewish girl in Winnipeg of the 1930s who, in the year between her tenth and her eleventh birthday, loses her mother, gains a stepmother, and finally comes to terms with the change. When Mama tells her a baby is growing inside her, Becky figures out how babies are started—by kissing, she is sure—and since the baby must come out through the navel, it must be kissing on the navel, an idea that fills her with revulsion. She bosses her brother, Saul, whom she calls Simply Simon, without realizing that her behavior is much like that of Aunt* Sadie, her father's older sister, who bosses Papa in a way Becky resents. Although she knows about death and, after Mama dies, is told that she has been buried, Becky really believes that her mother appears and talks to her and is causing a series of minor accidents to the old maids who are brought by relatives as prospective new wives for Papa*. Through her troubled year, she writes compulsively in her "scribblers," writing tablets from Papa's store. When she finally resolves her fears and admits she loves Sylvia,* her stepmother, Becky burns all her scribblers and starts her story afresh in a bound book of blank pages, a gift from Sylvia for her eleventh birthday.

BEETLES AHOY! (Jackson*, Ada, ill. Nina Poynton, Paterson, 1947), nature studies slightly fictionalized, dealing with flora and small fauna in southwestern Australia, set evidently in the World War II era, since blackouts are mentioned. John, 10, and Molly, who seems to be slightly younger, of Perth meet their new neighbor, Mr. Jones, an older man with a long beard, who they decide must be a professor. He invites them to see his collection of butterflies and beetles and encourages them to make their own collections. Soon they are working on their cigar-box museum, with advice and information from the Professor, as they call Mr. Jones. In twenty-two short chapters, he tells them about insects and bugs; fungi; frogs, snails, slugs, and spiders; shells, mollusks, and sharks; seaweed, sponges, coral, sea eggs, and starfish; bluebottles or the Portuguese Man-o'-War; flowers and leaves; birds; ancient plants and animals; flies; ants; and lizards and snakes. He advises them about different ways of preserving or recording their finds. Occasionally he tells them an Aborigine story about some natural phenomenon. There is no attempt at plot or character development, beyond portraying Molly as slightly squeamish about worms. Most of the information is given in dialogue and is interestingly written despite its obviously didactic purpose. Except for a few, the pieces were originally broadcast in a series of Nature Studies for School Children by the Australian Broadcasting Commission, a fact that helps account for their uniform length and structure. Aust. Bk. of Year Highly Com.

BEHIND THE WIND (Wrightson*, Patricia, Hutchinson, 1981; *Journey behind the Wind*, Atheneum, 1981), fantasy set in Australia based upon Aborigine beliefs about earth-spirits and, like its predecessors, *The Ice Is Coming** and *The Dark Bright Water*, improvising upon the hero-quest pattern of oral tradition. Wirrun, an Aborigine youth educated in white schools but very close to his heritage, has been living off the land in northeastern Australia with his water-spirit wife, Murra*, whom he married in *The Dark Bright Water*. He still possesses the power stone that protects him and enables him and Murra to fly on the wind. When Ko-in*, the man of the mountain, summons him because great trouble threatens the land, twice, once before he and Murra leave and once on the journey, Wirrun spies in the undergrowth a malevolent, red-eyed, shapeless creature he knows must have something to do with the trouble. Along the way he learns from People (Aborigines) of the mysterious death while prawning of expert Aborigine fisherman, Jimmy Ginger. Then late one afternoon in a storm Murra's water-dwelling Yunggamurra sisters call her home. While Wirrun sits in bitter loss, Ko-in appears and upbraids him for conduct unbecoming a hero, urges him to seek out and slay the evil creature that is bringing death to humans and earth-things alike, a creature born in the west now come east bringing his evil with him. Ko-in's dog, huge, black Jugi, bears Wirrun swift as the wind to Mount Conner in central Australia, where Wirrun tells his friend Tom Hunter details of the death of their mutual friend, Ularra, in *The Dark Bright Water*. Wirrun is then carried to the far southwest by various earth-spirits, where he tricks and captures a cold-spirit, the Noatch, and is informed by other spirits, the Jannocks, that the dread spirit of death, called the Wulgaru, lives in the north. Borne there by more spirits, Wirrun goes into a trance during which his spirit searches for the death-being. Next, his yearning for Murra takes him to her country where he hopes to join her, even if in death, but when he finds her, she rejects him because he comes in revenge not love. Resigned to his loss, he continues his search for the death-spirit, assisted with food and supplies by an Aborigine named Derby, sends his own spirit out of his body in a vain search for the Wulgaru, decides to return to the scrub area and wait for the creature, and is attacked by vicious cold from which happily the power stone protects him. Knowing it will be a battle to the death to render the clever, leather-winged, green-glowing horror powerless, he again seeks Murra's help. He asks her to guard his body while his spirit lies on the grave platform. In a dreadful scene, the spirits of the dead mill about Wirrun's spirit, dancing and howling, but since

Wirrun is facing the Wulgaru, though he gives his life, he triumphs, and the Wulgaru must capitulate and agree to leave People and spirits alone. Wirrun enters legend as Hero, the Ice-Fighter who, though he died, conquered death. The descriptive prose reveals genuine affection for the land and its ancient heritage. Atmosphere rather than action produces the book's effect, and the plot pattern repeats that of the two earlier books about Wirrun. As in the previous books, there is a certain frustrating obscurity about the style, whose hints and allusions contribute to mood but inhibit comprehension and make Wirrun's conflict, which is in large part with self, hard to follow. The numerous spirit-beings are inadequately differentiated, and they and incidents come to seem repetitive and trite. By the time Wirrun meets the Wulgaru, the reader scarcely cares any more. Aust. Bk. of Year Com.

BEL BEL (*The Silver Brumby**), a creamy brumby (wild horse), mother of Thowra, also a creamy. She is the leader of the little band that consists of herself and Mirri and their two sons, Thowra and Storm*. She knows that creamies are especially prized by stockmen, because she herself has been the object of many drives, and she takes pains to teach her son survival skills. When she gets old, she goes off alone to the mountains and dies there. She is presented as sturdy, brave, and wise, the worthy mother of a stalwart son.

BENNETT, JACK (JOHN BAILLIE) (1934–   ), Australian author of novels, non-fiction, and books for children. His *The Lieutenant** (Angus, 1977), a historical novel based on the open-boat journey of Captain Bligh and eighteen men after the mutiny on HMS *Bounty* in 1789, was originally published for adults, but it was commended for the Australian Book of the Year for Children. A different sort of sea survival story is *The Voyage of the Lucky Dragon* (Angus, 1981), a novel published for adults but often read by young people. In it a young Vietnamese boy tells of the perils and hardships his family endure as boat people, journeying to Indonesia, Singapore, and finally to Australia to find political asylum. Among his other books are *Gallipoli* (Angus, 1981), a novel based on the screenplay by David Williamson, which in turn was based on a short story by Peter Weir. Bennett is editor of *The Earth Beneath Me: Dick Smith's Epic Journey Across the World* (Angus, 1983), a non-fiction work about flying to Australia by helicopter. For children he wrote *Matilda Goodbucket* (Angus, 1984), a brief book illustrated by Trush Hart.

BENNY GOLIGHTLY (*An Older Kind of Magic**), sober, shy boy who helps to save the local botanical gardens from commercial development. Benny is good with magic tricks and on the night of the comet, conjures up a Pot-Koorok, an Australian indigenous being. When Rupert and Selina* take Benny on a tour of the Department, the office building in which they live, they overhear plans for making part of the gardens into a parking lot. This leads to the eventual saving of the gardens. Benny is a foil for the more self-assured Selina and Rupert.

BHATT, KAVERY RAGUNANDAN, born in Palangala, Kodagu district, Southern India; surgeon and author. She was graduated with honors from St. John's Medical College and was sponsored to the University of Liverpool, England, for surgical training. She became a Fellow of the Royal College of Surgeons of England at the early age of twenty-four and returned to India with her husband, also a Fellow of the Royal College of Surgeons, where they work together in underserved rural areas. Starting about 1983, Dr. Bhatt has published a large number of stories for adults and young people, as well as award-winning novels for children. *Once Upon a Forest** (CBT, India, 1985), a group adventure novel set in the Palali Game Reserve, won the Children's Book Trust first prize and the UNICEF Award. Among her other award-winning books for children are *Cuckoo Clock* (CBT, India, 1985), *School Upon a Hill* (CBT, India, 1988), and *Kitty Kite* (CBT, India, 1985). Her play for children on the environment, *Listen to the Mountain* (CBT, India, 1989), won the World Wildlife Fund Award. Many of her works have been translated into Hindi.

BHATTY, MARGARET R., free-lance writer who has made her home in Nagpur, India. Her articles and stories have appeared in many newspapers and magazines. She won first prize in the fiction category of a contest sponsored by the Children's Book Trust of New Delhi in 1983. Her winning entry was *Kidnapping at Birpur** (CBT, India, 1985), a fast-moving detective story concerning the abduction of a wealthy, crippled Indian boy and his friend. She has also published *Traveling Companions* (Thomson, 1982), a circus story set in India, and the non-fiction *An Atheist Reports from India* (Am. Atheist, 1987).

BILL EVERARD (*The Brown Land Was Green**), gentle, responsible, resolute drover on Kammoora sheep station. He is an obvious foil for Benjamin Jones*, and the Websters like him immediately. Though innocent, he was transported to Australia as a convict, served his time, and, discovering he loved the beautiful land, elected to remain. He held odd jobs in various places, developing a sympathy for the blacks (Aborigines) and eventually taking a position at Kammoora. He is the only person on the station who dares to stand up to Jones, who respects him in spite of his background.

BILL GRANT (*The Feather Star**), youth who wants to become a fisherman. Intelligent and sensitive, he likes poetry, which he quotes unselfconsciously to Lindy Martin, and helps her see the symbolism of the feather star. He is a type but suits the story.

BILL MACLEOD (*Bush Holiday**), bully son of Jock Macleod of Tangari, an Australian ranch in the outback. He dislikes tenderfoot Martin and torments him, once, for example, with his bullwhip. After Martin saves Bill from the falling gum tree, he gives Martin a rifle. Bill earns money by trapping rabbits with ferrets. Like the other characters, Bill is a clear type and an obvious foil for the polite, reserved, earnest Martin.

BIRTLES, DORA (TOLL) (1903? 1904?–), Australian novelist and writer of non-fiction. For adults she published *North-West by North: A Journal of a Voyage* (Cape, 1935), a book of personal observation and experience during a trip aboard the cutter *Skaga* from Sydney to Singapore; *Australia in Colour* (Sandy, 1946), a book of travel and description; and *The Overlanders* (Shakespeare, 1946), a novel inspired by a film of the same name. For young readers she has written *Pioneer Shack** (Shakespeare, 1947), in which a family down on its luck redeems a parcel of land lost from its possession and builds a house on it, which was commended for the Australian Book of the Year Award, and *Bonza The Bull* (Aust., 1950).

BLACKBIRD (*Pastures of the Blue Crane**), the term the people of northern New South Wales call the South Sea Islanders brought to Australia to work on the banana plantations.

THE BLIND WITNESS (Dutta*, Arup Kumar, ill. Mrinal Mitra, CBT, India, 1983), realistic detective novel set about the time the book was published in an unnamed city in India. When Mr. Gopalan, the tenant upstairs, is shot and killed, only the blind schoolboy Ramu can identify his murderers. He knows they are two men, one tall and muscular and named Boka, the other thin and quick and called Ranga. When the police ignore Ramu, he enlists the help of a classmate, Sunil, in contacting a private detective, Mr. Om Prakash, to investigate the death of the man who had been Ramu's friend and to whom Ramu had taught Braille. To the boys' surprise and disappointment, Prakash angrily turns them away. Coincidentally soon thereafter, the same two men break into Ramu's apartment. Ramu evades them by hiding on the ledge outside, then persuades Sunil to accompany him to the police station. Mr. Cyrus Lalakaka, superintendent of police, and Mr. Anil Chaudhuri of the Central Bureau of Investigation listen attentively and inform Ramu that Gopalan was an undercover policeman who had infiltrated a gang of international antique smugglers. They conclude that Prakash is somehow associated with the gang. When Ramu tells them that he taught Gopalan Braille, Lalakaka realizes that Gopalan had recorded his report to the police in Braille and produces the manuscript. Ramu's translation reveals that the brains of the gang is Hari Singh, who heads a string of presumably legitimate business enterprises and also Hind Exports, which is apparently a front for the smuggling. The police then set a trap for the criminals, using Ramu and Sunil as bait. The plan goes awry, and the boys are kidnapped. They cleverly stall for time by pretending to be ignorant of Gopalan's work, then inadvertently give themselves away. Taken by Singh's henchmen to a warehouse to be killed, they break away during a power failure, hide, and are rescued by police in the nick of time, having been traced by an electrical device planted on Ramu, and the smugglers are apprehended. Incidents, characters, and language are stock for the genre, as are the melodrama and sensationalism. A heavy emphasis on the capabilities of the blind gives a didactic flavor to the book. Except for his sightedness, Sunil is almost indistinguishable from Ramu. Only the occasional Indian words, the names, and characteristic turns of phrase serve to identify the setting as Asian. The main item, the plot, moves very fast, action is abundant, and suspense is high and well maintained. The result is an always interesting, lively, if conventional, mystery intended purely as escapist entertainment for middle and later elementary readers. CBT of India, Second Prize.

BLUE ABOVE THE TREES (Clark*, Mavis Thorpe, ill. Genevieve Melrose, Lansdowne, 1967; Meredith, 1968), historical novel of the opening of the Great Forest in South Gippsland in Victoria, an area of extremely rich soil but so dense with vegetation that no one lives there, until the government opens it to home-steaders in the late 1870s. While the two eldest sons of English immigrant William* Whitburn's three sons and three daughters share his enthusiasm for developing their 320-acre selection, pretty Clarissa*, 17, leaves for Melbourne as soon as she can. Patient Sarah*, William's wife, loyally makes a home and tempers her husband's severity with the children. Although Simon*, 13, from whose vantage point events are seen, is dutiful and freely contributes his labor, he longs to become a surveyor, encouraged by Old* Jesse, the father of the local innkeeper, and by Sarah. Clearing land is brutally hard, and maintaining the rude hut takes its toll on Sarah who also bears three more children. Since they need cash for food and stock, William and the boys hire out to clear land for other settlers. Although the work is unrelenting and William is an unyielding taskmaster, good times occur, like socials at the Petersons' home after they get a piano. William, however, begrudges Simon time to visit the lyrebirds the boy has discovered by the creek, and he is furious when Simon buys a rocking chair for Sarah with the pound he earns showing Mr.* Ronald Drew over the adjacent selection. After the Peterson men help the Whitburns burn off the area they have struggled to clear, William plants English grass seed, and, on the strength of the coming crop, buys seven Ayrshires. Caterpillars devour the grass two years in a row and the Whitburns' hopes for prosperity. Another setback comes when William breaks a leg, and they almost lose a selection because William tarries filing for it. The family persists and eventually wins out, mainly because of William's dogged will to succeed and the boys' compliance with his wishes. William mellows, even allowing Simon's lyrebird area to remain intact and agreeing that the boy may study with Mr. Drew to sit for the University matri-culation exam. Simon's chance for an engineering degree comes from an un-expected source, Cousin Mildred in Melbourne, who is so impressed by the boy's diligence and achievement on the exam that she offers to pay for his education. The book then skips ahead to Simon's return from Melbourne, just in time to help the men fight a raging grass fire. He is gratified that William puts as much effort into saving the lyrebirds as the house. The end finds Simon at age twenty-five, still happy with surveying and looking ahead to marrying Miranda Peterson. The most interesting figure in this rich, substantial novel is William, the hard-driving father, whose pride and determination might have destroyed the family but are fortunately toned down by the good sense, love, and quiet assertiveness of his wife and the understanding and respect of his children. Simon is also a complex figure, and Sarah wins attention, too. Most other characters serve the plot or are flat foils: giggly Hilda; earnest Betsy; single-minded, hardworking Andrew, the eldest son; Old Jesse; Darby Peterson, who holds singalongs and lobbies for a school and church; and Mr. Drew, who encourages Simon but is not successful with his own selection, among many others. Outstanding is the picture of the brutally hard lives of the Great Forest pioneers—their reliance on the family for physical labor, their isolation and consequent gratitude for helpful neighbors, the immensely hard work involved in clearing the dense, three-layered forest, the constant need for cash, the beauty of wild nature, the tenacity of the area to remain wild, the simple recreations, and the harsh austerity of the settlers' lives. Aust. Bk. of Year Com.

BLUE FIN (Thiele*, Colin, ill. Roger Haldane, Rigby, 1969; Harper, 1969), realistic adventure novel set in Australia in the mid-twentieth century, of a boy's efforts to prove himself to his father in the dangerous and demanding life of a tuna fisherman. Snook (Steven) Pascoe, 14, is a weedy, awkward boy, poor at schoolwork, with no mechanical aptitude and with a history of rheumatic fever. Although he wants more than anything to be part of the crew of *Blue Fin*, his father's tuna boat, he is seldom allowed aboard. On a rare trip during which he has been useful as a chummer, tossing scoops of bait overboard to excite the fish and start them biting, Snook is knocked overboard in a race to dock first. Although he is saved, Snook's father is furious at him and doesn't let him forget the incident. Mr. Pascoe has been suffering a bad season and two of his crew members have been injured, but he treats Snook's offer to help crew with scorn. Thinking it over, however, he decides to take on Snook as a chummer over the Easter holiday, since he badly needs one good catch before the tuna season is over. When they have only half a load and need a full load to ward off financial disaster, they stay on despite radio warnings of rough weather. After they run into a school of smaller tuna, they are so busy pulling them in that they do not see the funnel cloud, a waterspout or tornado at sea, until Snook looks up and yells, giving his father just enough time to unbuckle his safety belt and scramble off the poling rack. Snook is knocked down the open hatch onto the brine tank below and comes to choking in the escaping ammonia gas from the freezer compressor. He finds his father unconscious at the foot of the companion ladder and, by tying a rope under his arms and taking a hitch around a stanchion, hauls him up into the fresh air. The boat is stripped of almost everything, her instruments and the engine are dead, water is three feet deep in the engine room, and no sign remains of the other crewmen. When his father regains consciousness briefly, Snook discovers he has a broken leg and probably a broken shoulder and ribs. On his own, Snook proves that though he may be clumsy and not very strong, he has tremendous persistence. He tends to his often delirious father, pumps the water out of the boat, shifts the tuna, fifteen tons, from the useless tank on the starboard side to the port tank, which is still working, sets a signal flag and lantern, despite the wildly rolling boat, and, when his father wakes clearheaded enough to give him directions, repairs the fuel line and starts the engine. Although they have only a vague idea of their position, Snook sets a course and maintains it in the bitter cold of the wrecked wheelhouse. After four days he sights land and later in the day is spotted by the *Petrol*, which escorts them home. Then, when it seems as if they will arrive in triumph, the *Blue Fin* runs out of fuel and wallows toward the rocks. Bernie Lloyd, a big man in the *Petrol* crew, jumps to the *Blue Fin*, picks Mr. Pascoe from his bunk, ties a rope around him, and swings him to the *Petrol* deck, with Snook grabbing a rope and jumping after him. Snook watches the *Blue Fin* crash into the rocks and the tuna, which he has spent grueling hours shifting, pour out into the sea. The boat is insured, his father survives a successful operation, and Snook overhears him bragging to the nurse about his son. The boy realizes that he has finally achieved status in his father's eyes. The father-son conflict is predictable and the characterization standard for the genre. Snook is more competent in the emergency than is easily believable. Scenes of tuna fishing are very effective, and the struggles to pump out the boat, shift the tuna, and get the *Blue Fin* sailing again are memorable. Aust. Bk. of Year Highly Com.

BOB REGAN (*Take the Long Path**), husband of David's mother, Joy*, revealed to be the boy's stepfather. A bigoted Irishman, Bob is antagonistic toward his Maori neighbors, partly because in the past he bought a piece of land adjoining his farm, only to have the Maoris prove it is tribal land. More recently, he has tried to rent grazing rights, but his offer was rejected. He also is jealous of his wife's first husband, a Maori, and bullies her son, who has been brought up to think Bob is his real father. He insults his Maori neighbor, Henare Waka (whom he calls Henry Walker, refusing to pronounce the name correctly), but needs his help with the shearing. When David saves Henare's son, Hemi*, from a sudden freak wave, the Maoris pay their debt by allowing Bob to graze his sheep on their land rent free.

BODGER (*The Incredible Journey**), Ch. Boroughcastle Brigadier of Doune, old white English bull terrier. A natural clown, Bodger is confident, people loving, comfort loving, and inclined to be lazy and manipulative, but he is fond of the other two animals and bows to the retriever's terrible longing to find his home and master again. When they must cross the river, he is reluctant and, finally persuaded by the retriever to try, is a poor and fearful swimmer, but he is delighted with himself when he makes it. By the time they reach their destination, he has hardened up and arrives thin and tired but relatively fit. He is the most developed character in the book.

BONNY BENEDICTA (*Memory**), mixed-blood (Oriental, Maori, and white), Janine* Dart's best friend. Bonny, Janine, and Jonny Dart used to play a make-believe game in which Bonny wore a flowing gown and was the Pythoness from ancient Greek mythology. During one such game Janine fell to her death from a cliff. Now a serious university student, Bonny contrasts not only with Jonny but also with her adopted sister, Samantha, a Maori activist leader.

A BOOK DRAGON (Kushner*, Donn, ill. Nancy Ruth Jackson, Holt, 1987), inventive fantasy chronicling six centuries in the life of a dragon in which he finds and protects his treasure—and possibly saves the whole world from destruction. Nonesuch, a young dragon during the War of the Roses, lives with his grandmother in a cave above the village of Serpent Grimsby on the south coast of England. By this time, dragons have lost their fiery breath and seldom attack men, being suspicious of a species that kills but does not eat its own kind. After her son, Greedyguts, the father of Nonesuch, is killed by a small, neat man in black armor, the grandmother becomes strangely silent and disappears for longer and longer times down the passage at the back of the cavern. When she does not return, Nonesuch follows her until the passage becomes a volcanic fissure, so hot that his paws are deformed by his own weight, and he realizes that she has traveled to the molten lava, the source of dragon strength, from which she might someday emerge, grown enormously larger and fiercer, and destroy the world. Nonesuch returns to the cave and carries the treasure down the passage to a point too hot for humans, then seals up the cave mouth with boulders and flies away. During this period he has eaten little and soon discovers that he has grown smaller. Experimenting, he learns that his metabolism has changed, probably because of exposure to great heat, so that he can vary his size by eating or abstaining. Being smaller, he is more alert and nimble, and he deliberately shrinks. Without a treasure, however, he feels incomplete. Smaller than a bird now, he is blown in a storm to a stone rib in a stained glass window and follows a bat through a crack into the nave of a church and finds the scriptorium, where Brother* Theophilus is copying and illuminating a Book of Hours. The gentle monk sees Nonesuch and paints a small dragon in the vines bordering one page. Nonesuch overhears a plot by the loutish son of a stone mason to steal the locked box in which Brother Theophilus keeps the unbound pages of his manuscript, because the boy thinks it must contain the gold the monk uses in his paintings. Determined to protect the book, which has, of course, become his treasure, Nonesuch, now shrunk to insect size, hides between the pages. The thief, unable to pick the lock, is tricked by another thief in a low tavern, who hides the box in a cellar, and is caught and hanged for another theft before he can retrieve it. In the centuries that follow, Nonesuch learns to read from a literary rat, lives in an eighteenth-century chemist's laboratory, sleeps for many decades in a Scottish farm storeroom, and is still in the box when it is auctioned off to an elderly New England book dealer. Throughout this time, the box is never opened, though Nonesuch has gnawed a way to get out. Occasionally, he sees his grandmother, now become a sort of spirit dragon, visible only in fire. The book dealer, Mr. Samuel Gottlieb, has a small shop perched on a hill above the harbor. He has guessed that such a well-made box must contain something of value and is appropriately impressed and fascinated by the Book of Hours when Bartholomew Sacco*, neighboring shoe- and key-maker, has picked the lock for him. For some time Nonesuch lives happily in the bookshop, seen only by Professor* Ash, an alcoholic who frequents the place. A threat to this happy existence appears in the form of Mr. Brian Abercrombie, a wealthy and unprincipled developer, who sees the site as ideal for a luxury hotel. He tries to pressure the owners to sell, first by offers, then by threats and harassment. Nonesuch, horrified at the prospect of fire, which seems to be next on the list, deliberately starts eating, devouring small creatures and working up to prize sheep on the estate next to that of Mr. Abercrombie. Grown to some twelve feet long, he catches the developer on his evening walk and finishes him off, cashmere sweater, Rolex wristwatch and all. During the following days, he stays on a small deserted island, until he is small enough to return to his beloved book. His devotion to this treasure, he suspects, will keep his grandmother from exercising her power to destroy the universe. Although the story ranges widely in time and space, it is held together by the personality of Nonesuch, who is naive but steadfast, and by a tone of light amusement. The claim of cosmic importance is never pressed. Descriptions make the Book of Hours a fascinating masterpiece; the medieval theme is charmingly echoed in the illustrations, which include enlarged and decorated initial letters, intricate borders, and occasional tiny figures at paragraph openings or along the running heads of pages. Can. IODE Natl.

THE BOOK OF WIREMU (Morice*, Stella, ill. Nancy Parker, Angus, 1945; Paul's, 1946; Phoenix, 1958), brief, episodic story of a young Maori boy who lives with his uncle on the Waitukituki River in New Zealand. Because his parents have too many children, Wiri (Wiremu) has been given to his uncle, Hori, who has none, and they live happily with his big brindled pig dog and his black and white cat in his whare, a house made of slabs from an old sawmill, roofed by a piece of iron fallen from a passing wagon and fastened with nails that Hori has taken from the shed of Mr. Waterford, a kind man who, Hori says, would surely be glad to give them if he knew. The Waterfords figure frequently in the lives of Wiri and Hori. Mrs. Waterford gives them cut down clothes for the boy and gets Hori to plant her sweet potatoes, and she sees that they have food to take home or a good meal eaten with the workmen so that they never go too hungry. When Mrs. Waterford's nephew, Anthony, a spoiled little city boy, comes to visit, she turns him over to Wiri, so that soon he forgets to whine for his blue train left at home and has a marvelous time around the farm, playing in the river, and hunting for pigs. In other episodes Wiri visits his grandmother, who washes him in a warm spring and tells him the story of how her husband was chosen, or perhaps a legend of a beautiful girl with her name; neither of them seems to make a distinction between the two. Once Wiri, fishing for eels with a string held in his hand, catches a fourteen-pound trout, which an Englishman who is fly-fishing buys from him. Later, when they see in a magazine Mrs. Waterford has given them a picture of the man posing with his catch from the Waitukituki River, Hori laughs and laughs and pastes the picture on their wall, which is papered with other magazine pictures that have taken his fancy. And so they live, taking what they are given and giving what they have, or meaning to give what they have, "which is the Maori way." It is a simple, warm story with an affectionate tone and sly touches of humor, giving a tolerant picture of a way of living and an attitude about life very different from the usual Western stories of trauma and achievement. It uses many Maori words and turns of English phrase and provides a glossary at the end. N. Z. Esther Glen.

BOORI (Scott*, Bill, ill. A. M. Hicks, Oxford, 1978), fantasy in the hero tale pattern leaning heavily on Aborigine myth and traditions, set in Australia before the coming of the white man. Budgerie, a wise old man of the People, who live between the east coast and the mountains, following directions from Ganba, the chief of the spirits, goes apart and makes a man from clay, whom he calls Boori. For three years he teaches Boori all that it is necessary to know, especially the Law of the People, and before he dies he predicts that Boori must succeed at two tasks, to win the friendship and service of the spirit chief of the dingo people and to obtain the magic spear of Melong, chief of the water spirits. After Budgerie's death, Boori goes for the first time to the camp of the People, where he must prove himself by traveling south with his Jaree*, his personal spirit companion that lives in a leather bag carried around his neck, find the man of the southern tribe who is holding the mullet by a spell, and by magic force him to let the fish go on their usual migration. Then Boori leaves the tribe to explore and learn about the world. On the western side of the mountains, he is imprisoned in an egg of magic by old bad Bookal, a Goundir or magician cast out from his tribe. When even his Jaree cannot penetrate the smooth grey walls of shell, Boori sings a deep magic to call Perentie, the iguana-man spirit, who has power over eggs, and who appears as a tiny, fiery lizard and agrees to help Boori break the spell if he will then travel to Perentie's land and accomplish a task for him. On the long journey to the desert land of Perentie, Boori overcomes a number of obstacles. When he reaches his destination, Perentie enlists his aid against the Puk-wudgies*, who are stealing the opals that contain the fire of the spirit's power from the hills of the desert. Seeing that he must have the aid of Dingo*, spirit chief of the doglike people, Boori sets Jaree to spy and learns of a secret waterhole that is essential to Dingo's power. He calls up the water spirits of the coast to make a binding spell to keep Dingo from his well and, when challenged, fights a duel with Dingo in his man-shape in which both of them are wounded and that ends with Dingo pledging his help and grudging friendship. He cleverly tricks the Puk-wudgies and forces them to return the opals to Perentie's hills. Then he travels home with Dingo, who now has become his true admirer and friend. Back among the coastal people, they learn that some of their tribe have been stolen by Melong, evidently in angry retaliation for Boori's having summoned him to hold Dingo's well. Boori frees the captives and tricks Melong into throwing his spear, which always finds its target and returns to the hand of the thrower. With powerful magic, Boori keeps the spear from striking him and turns it to his own use. In retaliation, Melong devastates the coast with a terrible storm and puts a water spell on the whole area, which prevents the People from lighting any fires. With Dingo and Jaree, Boori travels to the tallest peak in the great range west of the coastal plain and there, with proper incantations, casts the spear of Melong at the setting sun and catches the returning coal in his bare left hand, nursing it in the pile of tinder and kindling to give fire back to the People. Upon returning, he is acclaimed by the People, who suggest that he travel far north to a very wise man, who may be able to heal his left hand, and with Dingo and Jaree he prepares to set out on this new journey. Told with dignity and respect, the story emphasizes various beliefs and patterns of Aborigine life, in particular the ideas that any breaking of the Law, however inadvertent, must be punished and that one must pay for and strive to undo any harm brought through one's actions, however unforeseen or incidental to what one set out to do. The deep belief in the many forms of magic that control the Aborigine life is convincing in the context, and the events are both strange and interesting to western readers. An author's note at the end points out that, though many of the included stories and elements are from the oral tradition, the events and plot are fictional. Aust. Bk. of Year Highly Com.

BOY ALONE. See *BY THE SANDHILLS OF YAMBOORAH*.

BRANDIS, MARIANNE (1938–   ), born in the Netherlands; Canadian college teacher and novelist. Her family emigrated to Canada when she was a child. After attending the University of British Columbia and St. Francis Xavier University, she earned her B.A. and M.A. degrees from McMaster University. From 1964 to 1966 she was associated with the Canadian Broadcasting Company and since 1967 has taught English at Ryerson Polytechnical Institute in Toronto. Her published novels for older children and young people include *The Tinderbox* (Porcupine's Quill, 1982) and its sequel, *The Quarter-Pie Window** (Porcupine's Quill, 1985), both substantial historical novels about the settlement of York, now Toronto. The second of these, seen from the vantage point of a girl in her early teens, won the Canadian National IODE Award and the Canadian Young Adult Award. Among her other books are *This Spring's Sowing* (Harrap, 1970; McClelland, 1970) and *Elizabeth, Duchess of Somerset: A Novel in Two Volumes* (Porcupine's Quill, 1989).

BREAD AND HONEY (Southall*, Ivan, Angus, 1970; *Walk a Mile and Get Nowhere*, Bradbury, 1970), boy's growing-up novel set in a small coastal town in Australia early in the last third of the twentieth century, dealing with one day on which the boy gains self-confidence. On Anzac Day, dedicated to those lost in various wars, Michael Cameron, 13, expects to attend the parade and celebration with his grandmother, who lost her husband in World War I, two sons in World War II, and a grandson in Vietnam, and who has made a wreath to place on the monument. Michael wakes early and exuberantly rolls naked in the dewy grass, although the girl next door, Jillian Farlow, 11, once saw him doing this and her mother has complained to his father, clearly intimating that Michael is depraved. This time he is not observed, but he can't wake his deaf grandmother, so he starts off for the parade alone in the rain. On the way he is nearly hit by the Farlow car, containing Jillian, her parents, and her brother Ray, who used to be Michael's best friend. They stop to give him a ride, and Mrs. Farlow uses the opportunity to be highly unpleasant under the pretext of worrying that he will catch cold. Escaping from them, Michael edges into the crowd, only to see Bully Boy (Bruce) MacBaren and his sidekick, Flackie (Warren) Flack, who never lose an opportunity to torment him, bearing down on him. He escapes to the beach, where he blows his nose on his shirt tail, only to discover that he is being watched by a small girl who introduces herself as Margaret Hamworth, 9 1/2. Margaret talks constantly in a combination of naive and grown-up chatter, explaining that she is a witch, has a magic ring, and can turn herself into a cat. Michael is both annoyed with and attracted to her. When he tells her to leave and she starts around a dangerous point, he belatedly rushes after her, slips, and falls into the water. She drags him out by the hair and insists on giving him mouth-to-mouth resuscitation. She has hit him on the nose, which bleeds for the rest of the story. Then she takes off all her clothes except her shoes and her panties because the sea water makes her itch. Embarrassed and angry, Michael tries to force her to dress, and she slips, hits her head, and he actually has to save her. His relief that she is all right is short-lived because he sights Bully Boy, Flackie, and Ray coming to find them, the first two sent by Margaret's father, the drummer in the Salvation Army band from the city, and Ray sent by his mother who nosily wants to be sure Michael goes home to take care of his cold. Michael tries to run and pull Margaret along with him, fails to get away, and is humiliated by their remarks. When Bully Boy goes off with Margaret and Flackie says something nasty, Michael turns on him and to the surprise of both of them and of Ray, beats him up. His triumph seems futile, however, because Margaret doesn't observe it. He makes his way home, having lost his shirt and shoes, and is in the shower when his grandmother wakes. Unaware that he has been out, she bemoans the fact that they have slept in and missed the parade. With new maturity, he tells her they will go and put her wreath on the monument anyway. The book seems to be making satiric comments on the attitudes toward the memory of the war dead, the scientific outlook on life that denies the imagination (as exemplified by Michael's absent father who doesn't understand him), and the hypocrisy of a propriety that labels natural feelings as depravity. It also details how difficult it is for a lonely thirteen-year-old boy to sort out his emotions and to find his position among his peers. Since everything is seen through

Michael's perceptions and his thoughts are centered on his own problems, none of the other characters is developed. The tone conveys his confusion but starts on such a high pitch that his thoughts and actions seem frenetic and become so wearying long before the end that it is hard to keep any patience for or interest in the protagonist. Aust. Bk. of Year Winner.

BREAKING UP (Willmott*, Frank, Collins, 1983), realistic novel of a disintegrating family in Melbourne, Australia, told in diary entries written by the elder son, Mark Wheeler, 14, dated from March 2, 1981, to January 23, 1982. Mark's parents, Alec and Jackie, have bought a decrepit old house, and the whole family spends a great deal of time and exerts much effort in fixing it up. In the school Mark attends, Alec is an unconventional teacher, devoted to his students and willing to put in long hours and much emotional energy helping with their numerous personal and family problems. Jackie has also been a teacher, now working part time in fabric design, and like her husband is a former rebel but with a much more relaxed and level-headed attitude. Mark's younger brother, Andy, 11, is asthmatic, a strange, self-contained boy, very close to his father. Mark gradually becomes aware that one of Alec's students, Lesley Anherbrat, a girl more mature than the others, is "rapt in" his father, a fact well known around school and even by Andy. At one point Mark, determined to confront her, goes to her house in a run-down district and is scared off by a brutal-looking man who says he is her uncle. The growing uneasiness Mark feels between his mother and Alec comes to a head the week when Alec's division has been on a school camp, and he fails to return. At school Mark learns that after Lesley's uncle came to camp threatening everyone, Alec left a day early, taking Lesley in another teacher's car. He ends up in the hospital, badly injured in what Mark assumes was an automobile accident, although his smashed nose, broken ribs, and generally bruised and mauled look seem to indicate that he was beaten up. When he is able to return home, he announces that he is not going back to teaching. After a restless recovery, he takes a job as a delivery man, quits it, starts washing dishes in a cafe, then suddenly leaves for Queensland. A visit by police and scraps of conversation Mark overhears make him think that Alec is in trouble for having sex with a minor, and he is actually relieved, though slightly shocked, when Jackie says that Alec was concerned for Lesley, who was being abused by a relative, but she doesn't think Alec was making love to her because he always told her when he had been unfaithful. About a month later, Alec returns for a joyful homecoming, which is soured when the boys realize that he is not planning to stay at home. In the next three months they gradually come to terms with the new arrangement, although the explanations that Alec is a restless spirit and needs to learn about himself don't make sense to Mark. He is unenthusiastic about his mother's return to teaching and the man she starts to date, but he begins to accept the situation. The difficulties of Mark's parents are paralleled by Andy's development of nightmares and sleepwalking and his greater dependence on his older brother. The diary entries also relate many incidents of school life. For example Mark's friend Billy, who steals anything he comes across and is expelled from school for talking back to a teacher with foul language, turns out, when Mark hunts him up at his home in a housing project, to be the competent and loving caretaker of four younger siblings and the defender of his mother against her drunken and abusive husband. Although the problem has been handled in many other books and is predictable, good characterization of all the major figures makes this novel rise above the average. The hurt both the boys and their mother feel is strongly evoked, and even the actions of their father, with his strong enthusiasms but lack of perseverance, are understandable. Mark's voice is well sustained, though he is rather too good at quoting dialogue for the entries to be convincingly from a diary. Aust. Bk. of Year Com.

BRINSMEAD (BRINSMEAD-HUNGERFORD), H(ESBA) F(AY) (1922–), born in the Blue Mountains of New South Wales, Australia, and acclaimed for her more than a dozen novels for children and young people. Her parents were missionaries in Indonesia, who returned to Australia where her father homesteaded a farm and operated a sawmill and mail run in the remote Blue Mountains. The youngest of five children, Brinsmead was educated at home by her mother and through correspondence. She went to high school at Wahroonga near Sydney, had some teacher training at Avondale College, and worked for two years as a governess in the western sheep country and in Tasmania, hoping eventually to get a job in radio. Her first book, *Pastures of the Blue Crane** (Oxford, 1964; Coward, 1966), a girl's growing-up story with color prejudice and intergenerational aspects, was named Australian Children's Book of the Year. *Season of the Briar* (Oxford, 1965; Coward, 1967), a novel set in Tasmania, came next, followed by *Beat of the City* (Oxford, 1966; Coward, 1968), which won special mention for the Book of the Year Award. It is a realistic sociological problem novel involving both "street" and "straight" youth in Melbourne, an urban setting with which she seems less comfortable. Her most highly regarded books take place in imaginary Longtime* in the Blue Mountains and draw heavily upon her family history: *Longtime Passing** (Angus, 1971), the first in the series and a Book of the Year Winner, is the broad-canvas story of the Truelances, Blue Mountain pioneers, as told by the youngest child, a girl named Teddy. Its companion for a younger audience, *Once there was a Swagman** (Oxford, 1979), is set during the Great Depression and was highly commended for the Book of the Year Award. Others in the series are *Longtime Dreaming* (Angus, 1982) and *Christmas at Longtime* (Angus, 1984). Most of her writing is for teenagers, but *Time for Tarquinia* (Hodder, 1982), set in ancient Etruria, is also for younger readers. Critics have praised her fluid, vigorous, storytelling style and warm tone and her ability to evoke setting, especially in the Longtime books, and to realize her main characters.

BROCHMANN, ELIZABETH (1938–   ), born in the Alberni Valley of Vancouver Island, British Columbia, Canada; teacher and writer. The valley in which she was born and grew up is the setting for *What's the Matter, Girl?** (Fitzhenry,

1980; Harper, 1980), which received honorable mention from the Canada Council. A girl's growing-up story, it describes life in a close-knit family as its members await the return from World War II of an uncle whose mind is gone. Brochmann received her teaching certificate from Victoria College in 1968. She taught in the Indian village of Fort Nelson in the Canadian North, in Nova Scotia, in Ghana, and in the West Indies, where she also was a volunteer worker with the mentally ill. She has taught continuing education writing classes at the University of British Columbia and at Langava College. She draws upon personal experience for her stories, some of which have been aired by the Canadian Broadcasting Company. She has also published *Nobody Asked Me* (Lorimer, 1984). She has lived in North Vancouver.

BRON LORENNY (*Devil's Hill**), a fearful, overly conscientious child of about eight, younger sister of Sam*, Badge's cousin. Her main duty in life has been to keep tabs on her sister, Sheppie*, to whom she is devoted. Bron is mature for her age in doing chores, but extremely fearful in unfamiliar situations and terrified of snakes. She finds the cow pat that puts the Lorennys on Brindle's trail. She is an interesting, credible character.

BROTHER THEOPHILUS (*A Book Dragon**), gentle monk at the Abbey of Oddsfields who is copying and decorating a Book of Hours intended for a part of the marriage portion of Lady Blanche, the youngest daughter of Hungerford Castle. Brother Theophilus sees Nonesuch, the dragon shrunk to insect size, and carefully paints him into the border of the page he is working on. On subsequent pages, he adds at least one dragon, sometimes just a wing or a tail emerging from the shrubbery, sometimes a full portrait in gleaming colors and gold ground fine, at the same time talking to the tiny dragon, which perches on his lamp and appears to listen but does not answer. At night the monk locks the unbound pages into a box bound with iron bands and stapled to the wall. After the box, containing the book and Nonesuch, is stolen by Hubert, the stone mason's fat elder son, Brother Theophilus, grieving over the loss, makes other books but paints no more dragons. Since moveable type has already been discovered, Brother Theophilus is one of the last to copy and illuminate books by hand, and his Book of Hours is one of the last of the beautiful books produced.

BROWN, JAMIE (1945–   ), born in Brantford, Ontario, Canada; playwright and novelist. He received his B.A. degree from the University of Waterloo in 1968. From 1974 to 1977 he was a consultant to the National Film Board of Canada and from 1979 to 1985 was a lecturer in creative writing at Concordia University in Montreal. In 1978 his screenplay, *The War is Over*, was nominated for the Canadian Film Award from the Canadian Film Academy, and he has written several other screenplays. His first juvenile novel, *Super Bike** (Clarke, 1980), won the Young Adult Award. Based on his own experience as a motorcycle racer, it is about an unhappy teenager who gains self-esteem and a better relationship with his stepfather through repairing and racing a classic model motorcycle. Among his novels for adults are *Stepping Stones* (Clarke, 1975), *So Free We Seem* (Clarke, 1976), and *Shrewsbury* (Clarke, 1977). He has also published a non-fiction book, *The Lively Spirits of Provence* (Clarke, 1974). Brown, who married a television producer and has three children, has made his home in Quebec.

THE BROWN LAND WAS GREEN (Clark*, Mavis Thorpe, Heinemann, 1956), historical novel of the settlement of the Australian interior. Fleeing the English Depression of 1844, widower John Webster, a carpenter, and his family sail to Melbourne in the Province of Port Phillip (later Victoria), Australia, in August (the spring). From Melbourne they sail to Portland Bay (modern Portland). There he accepts a position as a craftsman on Kammoora sheep station, which lies seventy miles inland in the Wannon Valley and is owned by Mr.* Archibald Blake of Melbourne and managed by Benjamin Jones*. John's contract specifies ownership of one hundred acres and the cottage on it in five years in return for his and his family's labor and two pounds a week in wages. In spite of what they know will be a hardscrabble existence, the Websters are in high spirits: steady Andrew, 15, who longs to be a farmer; rambunctious, impulsive William, 10, who wants to become a drover and is eager to see blacks (Aborigines), and strong-minded, spunky Henrietta, 14, from whose vantage point events are seen. Aunt* Belinda, John's maiden sister, however, has misgivings and came along only because her brother needs her help, especially with fractious, eighteen-month-old Edward. The journey inland over the deeply rutted track is difficult with the heavily loaded bullock supply wagon and the drays but accomplished with few untoward events. Second in command is quiet, capable Bill* Everard, the drover of the bullock team, whom the family immediately likes, but they soon discover that Jones has a fanatical fear and hatred of blacks. To their chagrin, the house promised them turns out to be a tiny wattle-and-daub hut amid lonely she-oaks about three miles from Kammoora, but they make the best of it, and later, at Jones's suggestion, John builds a house of stone. Andrew and William herd sheep, Henrietta conducts school for the station children, and Belinda cares for them all. One day, when Edward wanders off, Henrietta finds him with some black children minded by a girl named Mundowie, who is a little younger than Henrietta. When Jones finds out, he organizes a troop to hound the blacks, and despite Bill's warning that the Border Police will object, attacks their village, killing some and scattering the rest. In retaliation, the blacks set grass fires, and while taking water to the fighters, Henrietta and William discover Mundowie lying wounded in the brush, load her on their horse, and take her to She-oaks, where they nurse her in the duck shed. John returns from fire fighting with a broken leg, and when William carelessly mentions where Mundowie is, Jones furiously orders the Websters to be off the station within a week. To make matters worse, the family discovers that the contract is missing. Without telling anyone, in the middle of the night Henrietta takes William and rides thirty miles to the coach station, from which with the help of the kind and amiable coachman they travel the two hundred miles to Melbourne. There Henrietta locates Mr. Blake and tells him her story. He accompanies them to Kammoora and straightens out matters. He fires Jones, also in trouble with the Border Police because of his treatment of the blacks, but suggests that the police drop charges and allow Jones to return to England. Bill is made manager, and he and Aunt Belinda, between whom a romance has developed, plan to marry. Henrietta and her family look forward to a fine future on their own land in the country they have come to love, an area that is usually brown but which the spring rains turn to a vibrant and welcoming green. Characters are stereotypes, events the conventional ones of pioneer stories, problems overforeshadowed, and some incidents unconvincing or overly fortuitous, like that in which Henrietta follows Jones and his men on the night trip to kill the blacks and another where William is bitten by a snake and a black happens to be near and sucks out the poison. Best are the action scenes and the clear and affectionate descriptions of the land. The historical information is well integrated with the story, and the author obviously sympathizes with the indigenous people in their fruitless struggle against unscrupulous and greedy whites. Aust. Bk. of Year Highly Com.

BRUCE MARTIN (*To the Wild Sky**), twin of Jan*, an uncomplicated boy, friend of Gerald* Hennessy, eager to attend the birthday house party. In the crash, he is the only one injured, an ankle evidently badly sprained, though he thinks at first it is broken. Although he milks this injury for sympathy, he is the only one to concentrate on the sensible project of forming a large SOS with stones on the beach. Later, he is the one who pushes the idea of building a raft and actually thinks they should set off that night. While he is often annoyed with his twin, Jan, he defends her against Gerald after Gerald has knocked her down.

BRUJA VIEJA (*Tal and the Magic Barruget**), old woman of Ibiza who keeps house for Tal and his artist father. Her name literally means ''Old Witch,'' and there is a nice ambiguity about whether she really is a person of unusual powers or just a superstitious old woman. She knows how to trap the Barruget, seems to remember just where the black bottle will be, and advises Tal about the incantation he makes up to get the Barruget back in the bottle. She seldom tells the boy directly how to proceed, but through enigmatic statements maneuvers him to use his own initiative. Her timelessness is suggested when she tells Tal, ''I've never known a better boy across all the centuries and all the lands.''

BRUNO GUNTHER (*The Sun on the Stubble**), bright but naive Australian farm boy, youngest son in a large family of German extraction. Well-meaning but hapless Bruno gets into one predicament after another, often running into the wrath of his irascible father when he least expects it. With his next oldest brother, Victor, he sleeps in a room built over the fruit cellar, where they enjoy a kind of frontier freedom from the rest of the household and can listen to the weekly radio thriller on Victor's crystal set. Bruno also enjoys the independence of roaming the hills to tend his trapline. Because the farm cannot absorb all four boys and Bruno has always done well at his lessons, his parents decide that he must attend high school, which means leaving home at twelve to live in Adelaide, a prospect which fills him with dismay but which he cannot argue with Dad*.

BUCKLEY HUON (*Cannily, Cannily**), father of Trevor, a large, genial, bearded man, who has chosen the life of a migrant worker for the adventure and experience it offers. Although he and his wife, Kath*, let Trevor make his own decisions, Buckley comes to his son's defense when Mr. Fuller, the coach, is holding a sort of court martial in front of the team. Both parents are aware of Trevor's unhappiness and realize that he must be having trouble with the teacher, but until they read his story, they do not know of his longing for the stable home on the coast that he remembers from his early childhood. Buckley has retained his attachment to the home, too, as evidenced by the surfboard that he has carried on the top of his van throughout years of living in inland areas. He is a compassionate, understanding father.

BUFFIE, MARGARET, born in Winnipeg, Canada; teacher, novelist. Her first novel was *Who is Frances Rain?** (Kids, 1987), a time-slip fantasy in which the setting alternates between the present day and the youth of the protagonist's grandmother. It won the Canadian Young Adult Book Award and was a runner-up for the Canadian Book of the Year Award. She has also written *The Guardian Circle* (Kids, 1989). Buffie has made her home in Winnipeg.

BULSARA, C(AVAS) N(OWSHIRWAN) (1927–), businessman, and writer. His first story, *Robin and the Hawk** (CBT, India, 1982), won second prize in the Children's Book Trust all-India contest for children's literature. A story of anthropomorphized birds, in which a young robin helps drive off a hawk that has been terrorizing a community of birds, it is highly illustrated by Jadish Joshi. A sequel, *Return of the Hawk*, also won second prize in the fiction category of the 1983 Children's Book Trust contest but was not immediately published.

THE BUNYIP HOLE (Wrightson*, Patricia, ill. Margaret Horder, Angus, 1957), realistic family novel set for the period of one week in the mid–1950s in the rugged North Coast country of New South Wales just south of Queensland, Australia. When the "Gastric" (flu) hits the teacher of their one-room country school and they receive unexpected holidays at Easter, the four Collins children, Ken, 12, Val (Valery), 11, Binty (Herbert), 8, and Joan, 6, decide to clear out the pool at the foot of the waterfall on the mountainside above their house. They also clean and fix up the humpy (hut) that stands on the route to the falls and then camp out there for a couple of days. Two city boys about Ken's age, Joe and Bob, rowdies staying with a farm family over the ridge, harass them by fouling the pool with stones, broken bottles, and tin cans. To keep the boys from returning and trashing the humpy, the children rig up Horrible Harry, a ghost with a glowing face made of a sheet stretched over cans to guard the humpy path. Then Homer, their mixed-breed dog, turns up missing. Binty finds a note from the two boys (whom the children refer to as Ring-tailed Bandicoots) demanding five bob (shillings) ransom. Positive that the loss of Homer is his fault, Binty places three bob, a flashlight bulb (all he has that might suit), and an IOU at the designated place, without telling the others, then hunts for Homer on his own. Having left an explanatory note with Joan to be given to Ken and Val at sundown, he climbs a hill the children investigated earlier. He discovers Homer confined to a shed on the farm over the ridge, releases the dog, and almost gets away without incident except that Homer barks. With the rowdies in hot pursuit, Binty scrambles through the trees and brush with the dog and takes precarious refuge on a narrow ledge about ten feet down a cliff overlooking a chasm called the Bunyip Hole. Joan having given Ken and Val the note as instructed, they search for Binty and come upon the participants just as Binty blows the family bugle (carried with him just in case) in the old song "Cookhouse Door," a melody distorted by the echoes and Homer's howl into an eerie, hollow moaning sound that spooks the Bandicoots and attracts his siblings. Ken engineers a daring rescue with the others' help. The Bandicoots are further frightened by encountering Horrible Harry and flee home. The next day the Collins children tramp uphill and over the ridge to pay off Binty's IOU, a matter of grave concern to him, the others making up the remainder of the money he insists he owes the rowdies. They pay up just as the two boys are about to leave for the Brisbane bus, their holiday over. The Collinses return to the hut to eat a hearty lunch and pack up for home, Binty having earned a new nickname, Bunyip. This is a rousing children-on-their-own adventure in the Arthur Ransome vein, exciting if unlikely, a mild thriller that pits good country youth against city bullies. Adults are very much on the fringes, and the children are types. Ken is the almost all-knowing patriarch of the group, the one who usually takes charge, while Val fills the maternal role of caretaker, peacemaker, and housekeeper. Joan is chattery and inquisitive, the one they all protect. Binty, the most fully characterized and the only dynamic figure, is dreamy and inept, often abstracted, diffident, and less able in school than the others, the one Ken especially feels he needs to bring up to be a man and often calls "son." Not unexpectedly, Binty grows in self-esteem and courage through his adventures in retrieving Homer. The descriptions of the terrain are vivid and clear and project a genuine love for wild nature, and the careful detail with which the author lays out their preparations for cleanup and camping, among other situations, make the incidents completely convincing. The bunyip is an Australian legendary composite creature. Aust. Bk. of Yr. Com.

BURNFORD, SHEILA (1918–1984), born in Scotland, died in Hampshire, England; scriptwriter, journalist, novelist. She was educated in Edinburgh, Yorkshire, and Germany, and she came to Canada in 1948 with her husband and children. Her best-known book has become an animal classic, *The Incredible Journey** (Little, 1961; Hodder, 1961), a story of two dogs and a Siamese cat who make their way home across Northern Ontario, surviving many difficulties along the way. Although the book has been criticized as sentimental and anthropomorphic, it maintains a surprisingly objective viewpoint, ascribing to the characters very few emotions that could not be observed and, in spite of the multiplicity of their problems, no actions that are not possible. It has received numerous honors, being named a Junior High Contemporary Classic and to the Lewis Carroll Bookshelf, included in *Children's Books Too Good to Miss*, listed by *Choice* magazine as a basic children's book for an academic library, and winning the Canadian Library Association Book of the Year Award. Burnford's only other book for children, *Mr. Noah and the Second Floor* (McClelland, 1973; Gollancz, 1973; Praeger, 1973), is a fable-like ecological novel that has not been as popular. Early in her writing career, Burnford turned out scripts for a puppetry group in Port Arthur, Ontario, and sketches about Canadian life for British periodicals. She also wrote a novel for adults, *Bel Ria* (Joseph, 1977; Little, 1978), and three books of non-fiction, *The Fields of Noon* (McClelland, 1964; Little, 1964; Hodder, 1964), a book of autobiographical sketches, *Without Reserve* (McClelland, 1969; Little, 1969; Hodder, 1969), about the Indians of Ontario, and *One Woman's Arctic* (Hodder, 1972; Little, 1973), about the Eskimos with whom she lived for some time.

THE BUSHBABIES (Stevenson*, William, ill. Victor Ambrus, Hutchinson, 1966; Houghton, 1965), adventure novel set in Kenya in the mid-twentieth century when new African nations were replacing white employees with natives. Game Warden ''Trapper'' Rhodes and his family, who have grown up in Kenya, departing from Africa must leave behind their many pets, but Rhodes gets a game permit for Kamau, the bushbaby that belongs to his daughter Jackie, 13. As they board the freighter at Mombasa, Jackie realizes that she has left the permit behind, and she impulsively slips off the ship and finds Tembo* Murumbi, her father's headman and longtime family friend and servant, who has accompanied them on their railroad journey to the coast and now is mournfully playing his harmonica on the wharf. She enlists his aid to take Kamau back to the Place of the Hippopotamus where he was born and will have a chance to survive. She persuades Tembo that they will go first to the family vacation cottage at Vipingo and get help from the neighbor, Major Bob. Unfortunately, Major Bob has gone to Nairobi, and as she goes to the post office to wire the ship, she overhears an Indian policeman exhorting the villagers to help find and arrest the bad man who has kidnapped the white girl, Rhodes. She insists that she and Tembo start immediately the hundred miles to Ndi, where they both have friends who will clear up the misunderstanding. As they travel through the bush, following the old slave trail on Jackie's map, marked, Tembo knows, by lines of mango trees, they are beset by many dangers, both natural and human. Drought has dried up their possible river route and has forced elephant herds into a move, followed by the pygmy elephant hunters and the large predator animals. A shoot-on-sight order is put out against Tembo. An archeologist family friend, Professor "Cranky" Crankshaw, hunting pygmy poachers with his sailplane, is signaled down by Tembo, refuses to listen to Jackie's explanations, and tries to arrest Tembo, but he and Jackie escape and resume their journey. Fire, set by the Masai to bring on new grass, threatens them, and the storm that follows creates a flood. When at last they reach the railway station at Ndi, it has been cut off from the outside world by downed telegraph lines and track washouts, but Gideon, the African stationmaster, rigs a hot bath for Jackie, then takes them to the washout to try to warn a freight train approaching from the other side. Although wires and tracks are down, a water pipe, supported on separate pylons, is still standing. Fastening a message and a fishing line onto Kamau's harness, they put him into the broken end of the pipe and allow his natural curiosity to cause him to drag the line through. There it can be attached to a rope, pulled back, and used to stabilize a rubber raft to cross the flooded piece of track. Jackie's father, on the other side, reads the message, forgives his daughter, is grateful to Tembo, and promises Kamau will go with the Rhodes family when they leave again. Although the motivation for the journey, analyzed separately, is somewhat unconvincing, in the context of Jackie's passionate feelings for Kamau and her confidence in Tembo it seems plausible. The journey through the bush is tense and fascinating, full of understanding of animals and conditions of the country that cause Jackie and Tembo difficulties and make their survival possible. Throughout there is an appreciation of the wisdom and devotion of the African man and mutual respect for the abilities of the two cultures. Although Jackie is never aware of the sexual implication assumed by the authorities in her association with the African man and the idea is never exploited, it is clear that Tembo understands the problem and its dangers to him. Fanfare.

BUSH HOLIDAY (Fennimore*, Stephen, ill. Ninon MacKnight, Doubleday, 1949), realistic novel of domestic adventures set on a ranch in the Australian bush shortly after World War II. Since the death of his pilot father in the war, polite, earnest Martin Haddon, a Boston youth of about twelve, and his mother have been living in Melbourne with her brother. Because Fred is so irascible, Mrs. Haddon arranges for Martin to live with the affable rancher Jock Macleod and his family at Tangari on the Yedda River, a three-hundred-mile train ride into the mountainous outback. When the story opens, Martin is on the train, where he makes friends with hefty, loquacious Mr.* Jo Creasey, of jovial personality and questionable morality, who drops in and out of the story. Martin immediately takes to the towering, laconic, white-haired, Scots-dialected Macleod, a widower, his patrician sister, invalid Aunt Jeannette, and especially his daughter, lively Penny*, who is Martin's age, but Martin gets off on the wrong foot with his son, Bill*. He soon comes to love the rough, forested area. He shares the bunk hut with Bill and the eccentric, old prospector Uncle* Luke, and he becomes friends with Old* Marjorie, the equally eccentric cook. The book ambles along, and most interest centers on Martin's becoming familiar with his new environment with feisty Penny's help. Two concerns gradually develop: Martin's relations with Bill and Martin and Penny's hope that Mr. Macleod and Mrs. Haddon will marry. The boys' relationship takes a turn for the better when, while the three children are ferreting rabbits, Martin warns Bill about a falling gum tree and probably saves his life. At the end, they are reconciled through two unrelated events. Bill respects Martin's ability to live off the land when he gets lost in the mountains, and later, during a forest fire, Bill appreciates Martin's bravery and perseverance in saving Tangari. The other concern is resolved through Penny's hobby of collecting beetles and butterflies (activities described in some detail which, like ferreting, might offend some readers). The children find a new species of beetle, which they show to Steve Duke, the rancher at Twenty-Mile, an amateur but knowledgeable entomologist. He turns out to be a friend of Martin's dead father. The book's conclusion finds Steve Duke and Mrs. Haddon planning to marry. Martin will continue to live in the bush he has come to love, and Penny will have the companion for whom she has longed. Interspersed are scenes involving Uncle Luke and Mr. Creasey. Although Martin too readily accepts being sent to the bush, doesn't seem to miss his mother, or be concerned about what is happening to her, or even wonder whether he will ever see her again, he is a likeable boy and remains an interesting if static protagonist. Characters are types or oddballs but suit the plot, which contains consistently entertaining adventures, especially when Martin is lost in the bush. The ending is pat and overforeshadowed but satisfying for the kind of book, which the author intends to be a domestic adventure story rather than problem realism. Appreciation for the beauty of the remote, rugged area comes through strongly, and much use of Australian terms, interesting in themselves, supports the setting well. The sequel is *Bush Voyage**. Aust. Bk. of Year Com.

BUSH VOYAGE (Collins*, Dale, ill. Margaret Horder, Heinemann, 1950), realistic holiday adventure novel, sequel to *Bush Holiday**, set on the *Bunyip*, a small paddle steamer, that sails the Murray River from New South Wales into South Australia. Martin Haddon, here presented as an earnest, reliable London youth of about twelve recently emigrated to Australia, and his chum, Penny* Macleod, spirited daughter of the widower owner of the outback ranch Tangari, who met in the first book, accept the invitation to go adventuring with their old friend, Mr.* Jo Creasey. Apparently no longer in trouble with the law, he is still garrulous, portly, jovial, and addicted to the sweets he carries in his copious pockets. Mr. Creasey has sold his store in town to ease his "itchy foot" and bought the *Bunyip*, a floating store. The children accompany him in his old Ford, Lysbeth, on a long day's trip overland and embark in high spirits. They happily explore the cabins just their size and make friends with the crew: lean, bewhiskered old river salt, Cap'n Puddifoot, who tells them stories about whaling and the history of the Murray River and old Australia; John-Willy, genial Aborigine cook; pleasant Tom Burton of the engine room; and big, burly John Smith, really Patsy Ballarat, one-time Australian heavyweight champion, now able seaman and assistant storekeeper, obviously disguised in an old hat with attached whiskers, Jo says, to elude his admirers. The episodic plot meanders along with much conversation, generous details of place, costume, and incident, and some action. The children are marooned on an island by a sudden fog. Martin visits a town where he discovers Dingo Peters, a blind musician and composer, and persuades Steve Duke, his stepfather, to help Dingo get his compositions published. Penny wins the donkey riding contest at a rodeo, and Martin becomes jealous when a telegram delivery boy takes a shine to Penny. Martin also rescues Mr. Creasey's termagent older sister when she falls overboard. Two interesting but low-keyed mysteries provide unity. To whom does the baby girl belong that they find on Penny's bunk and who has chewed up the note telling who she is? Will Patsy find the man for whom he is searching, Mike Halloran, and for whose crime of murder Patsy was convicted and is now on the run? The children solve both problems. They encounter a recluse, notice he has a scar of the sort Patsy has described his adversary as having, and lure him to the *Bunyip*, where Patsy captures him. The mystery of the baby is solved when the children are taking her out in a baby carriage and are spotted by a detective. They learn she was kidnapped by her ne'er-do-well father and abandoned on the *Bunyip* just before he was killed in an accident. Story's end finds Mr. Creasey and the baby's mother planning to marry and Steve Duke arriving to fly the children to the two-thousand-acre sheep station of a friend for more adventures. Most characters are types or peculiar, but Martin and Penny are likeable and interesting if a shade too capable and fortunate. Some local dialect contributes to the setting and adds spice, and there is humor. The ending seems rushed and too fortuitous, and coincidence abound, but the entertainment value is high, and the result is a fine example of unreal realism. Aust. Bk. of Year Highly Com.

BUTLER, SUZANNE (SUZANNE LOUISE BUTLER PERRÉARD)
(1919–   ), born in London, England; Canadian teacher and novelist for adults and children. She attended private schools in England and France, St. Clement's School in Toronto, and Provincial Normal School in Victoria, B.C. After teaching for a year in Victoria, she taught at The Study, a private girls' school in Montreal from 1942 to 1949. She then served as secretary for the Association of Canadian Clubs National Office in Ottawa, Ontario, until 1953. She moved to Switzerland, where she opened and operated a nursery school in Geneva. Most of her books are novels for adults, among them *My Pride, My Folly* (Little, 1953), *Vale of Tyranny* (Little, 1954), and *Portrait of Peter West* (Little, 1958). Of her juvenile novels, *Starlight in Tourrone** (Little, 1965) was named to the Fanfare list by the editors of *Horn Book*. It tells how six determined French children inspire the disheartened inhabitants of their village to revive the exciting pre–World War II custom of marching through the village to re-enact the Nativity story on Christmas Eve. This short novel is most notable for its picture of the

ways and attitudes of children. In *The Chalet at Saint-Marc* (Little, 1968), also for a juvenile audience, four children trapped by avalanches must cope when a neighbor becomes ill.

BY THE SANDHILLS OF YAMBOORAH (Ottley*, Reginald, ill. Clyde Pearson, Deutsch, 1965; *Boy Alone*, Harcourt, 1966), boy's growing-up novel set in the early 1930s in Yamboorah, a cattle station near the desert edges of South Australia. A boy, whose name and age are never given but who must be between ten and fifteen, works as a wood-and-water joey on the big ranch, without parents, relatives, or other youngsters. Although the cook, Mrs. Jones, has a soft spot for him, the closest to a friend he has among the humans is dour old Kanga*, the dogman, who handles a pack of dogs to rid the range of rabbits, dingoes, and feral dogs. When Kanga's bitch, Brolga, has puppies, the boy is delighted, but since the dogman has bred her only to raise one pup to be his new lead dog, he kills all but the best of the litter and makes the boy bury them. For the next two months, the boy has the companionship of Brolga and the pup, which he names Rags. Then Kanga comes back from roaming the range with his dog pack and takes Brolga, though the boy begs him to leave her longer. When he returns without Brolga and says that she just stopped eating and died, the boy, in a desperate effort to save Rags, sets off across the sandhills with the pup. The adventure is doomed by the sheer size of the desert, of which he has no clear idea, by his ill-fitting boots, and by a camel that they stumble upon and that smashes the water bucket. Too exhausted to turn back, they stagger on to a lone, leafless desert tree, where they collapse in the spare shade of the trunk. There Kanga finds them. As they ride back, the boy and the dog on the horse behind Kanga, they meet other riders from the station who have been out searching for them. Although a new "king" dog is essential to Kanga's continued work and with Brolga dead he has no bitch good enough to breed, he gives Rags to the boy. Into this bare plot are woven episodes of a bull chasing the boy during the branding roundup, a wind-and-dust storm of tornado force, and a day off when the boy meets an Aborigine who shows him a valley full of feeding kangaroos. Under their rough exteriors a number of the men are concerned for the boy—the unnamed boss; Ross, the overseer; Yabba, an itinerant worker or swagman; even some of the Aborigine workers. Although nothing is told of the boy's past life, he is shown to be sensitive and loving. The strongest feature of the story, however, is the picture it gives of the hard work and the life on the isolated ranch and of the desolate land's beauty. Aust. Bk. of Year Highly Com.; Lewis Carroll.

C

CABOT, JOHN (*And Tomorrow the Stars**), born Giovanni Caboto, historical Genoese explorer who reached North America and claimed it for the British in 1497. Always fascinated by ships and the idea of new lands, the boy is inspired to study mainly to find out about navigation and to check the widely differing theories of the size of the earth. Pictured as a lively boy who suffers under the restrictions of his grim uncle, Vanni is bright but, as a youth, reckless. He is past forty before his plan to sail west, seeking the Spice Islands, is put into effect. On his second voyage to North America, his ship is lost, but his son, Sebastiano, who was supposed to be on one of the other ships in his small fleet, lived to make other major discoveries.

CALLIE'S CASTLE (Park*, Ruth, ill. Kilmeny Niland, Angus, 1974), short realistic novel of family life. Though the story is set in Sydney, Australia, in the 1960s or early 1970s, the plot involves a timeless concern: the need of the eldest child for space, both literal and metaphorical. Ever since the family moved to the top floor of the big old Victorian house overlooking the harbor, Callie (Carol) Cameron, 10, has been increasingly in conflict with her family, though she knows they love her: her mother, Heather Beck; her stepfather, Laurens*, a painter and paperhanger; her half-siblings, Dan, 6, finicky since the flu; naughty Gret, about five; and little Rolf, 3. Even her teacher, Mrs. Wheeler, has "turned sour," and she has quarreled, quite unreasonably she knows, with her best friend, Frances. The last straw comes when she returns home from school one day to find that Dan has spitefully allowed the younger children to mess up her things. She flies into a fury and runs away to Grandpa* Scotty Cameron, who gives her tea, brings her home, and confides to Heather that what Callie, who shares a room with Gret, really needs is a place of her own. A former builder, he surveys the house, paying particular attention to the decorative cupola with four oval windows and a time- and weatherworn rooster weathervane. He discovers that the entrance to it is through a small, nailed trapdoor in the ceiling of the cupboard at the top of the stairway landing. The whole family fall in love with the tiny hideaway, which they discover previous generations of children had enjoyed, too, but Grandpa informs Callie that it's her "castle," and that she doesn't have to share it unless she wants to. Even Heather feels excluded and tries to insinuate herself into the renovation project. Dan, spoiled since his illness, organizes the children into an attack, and when Callie repulses them, they tumble down the ladder, provoking still another family crisis. This time Laurens comes to the rescue. He sells his veteran Cadillac, which he had been refurbishing to show, for money for a staircase. Since there is just enough room for a tiny spiral one that only children will be able to negotiate, the renovation must be finished before the "fairy staircase" is installed. Callie invites the grown-ups, including Mrs. Wheeler, to visit, and then the ladder is removed and the staircase fitted into place. Callie's school friends visit, including Frances, with whom Callie makes peace. Her new sense of satisfaction motivates her to think about Dan differently, and she decides that, when she is too big to fit the stairway, Dan will be old enough for a castle of his own, and she will give it to him. The story captures with startling clarity and occasional poignancy and humor the pressures of young, working-class family life and the special need of the eldest for identity and distance. Although the plot is slight, the book draws strength from its rich characterizations and its warm, affectionate, understanding tone. There is a strong visual aspect to the narrative, and scenes are vivid and clearly realized, giving a keen sense of lived experience. The style is distinguished by interesting images ("getting Dan and Gret away to school was like getting Hannibal's army over the Alps") and extensive dialogue, which sounds as if it is being spoken by real people. Aust. Bk. of Year Highly Com.

CAMERON (*Shantymen of Cache Lake**), leader of the union and the strike in the logging camp after the death of Angus Bains. A thoughtful, patient man, he is at first too unassertive to be effective and keeps counseling delay in contrast to hothead Tim McGuire, but after the collapse of the log chute that kills Tim, Cameron grows in authority and is spokesman during the second strike. When he and the Bains youngsters start to walk to Ottawa, he realizes that his leg has been fractured in a chute collapse and he becomes so discouraged that without John* and Meg* he would have died on the trail. Back in the camboose, with his leg splinted by Mrs. Ferguson and the men solidly unified behind him, he becomes a strong leader. He is a major figure in the completion of the chute and the log drive during the spring flood.

A CANDLE FOR SAINT ANTONY (Spence*, Eleanor, Oxford, 1977; Oxford, 1979), school novel of a close friendship between two schoolboys set in Sydney, Australia, sometime after World War II. Tall, blond, athletic Justin Vincent, 15, son of a well-off Sydney businessman, spoiled, self-important, ambitionless, Protestant, attends exclusive Bayside College for boys. Newly enrolled in January is Rudi Mayer, also fifteen, a scholarship student, slight, dark, quiet, serious-minded, bright, hoping to become a doctor, Catholic, an emigrant from Austria with his family when he was seven. The two boys meet in Fraulein Neuhaus's German conversation class, where German-speaking Rudi is the assistant. Taking an immediate dislike to Rudi because he is so different from the Bayside boys and especially from Justin's crowd, Justin tries to bully him, and, when Rudi refuses to grovel, abruptly stops the hazing, impressed by the other boy's grit. The two strike up a friendship that deepens as the weeks pass. They visit each other's homes and spend so much time together that their closeness provokes jibes of "fairies." When they learn there is to be a class trip to Vienna in early September and Rudi will go on reduced fees as assistant, Justin decides to go, too. His father agrees provided he gets 70 percent or better on his exams that spring. With coaching from Rudi and much hard work, Justin passes handily. Rudi works extra hours at a milk bar for spending money, and the two depart happily for a fortnight's vacation. All goes well, though Greg, one of Justin's "old" buddies, is jealous. They enjoy Vienna and are delighted to be included in a special side trip to the Vienna Woods. There they discover and clean up a small, ruined chapel, which they are certain was dedicated to Saint Antony, who, Rudi says, was the first Christian monk, the one to whom he offered candles to insure Justin's success on the exams. One day, just before they leave for home, Rudi and Justin go to the little chapel, where a sudden storm catches them. While they sit huddled there, Rudi suggests that they remain in Europe and says he loves Justin. The remark is overheard by Greg who reports it to the other boys. Rudi is deeply hurt that his expression of simple and honest affection is misinterpreted as homosexual love and runs away. He is found at the home of a friend but refuses to return to his family in Australia and later enrolls in a school in Austria that will prepare him for medical school. Justin is too close to his family to remain with Rudi in Vienna as Rudi hopes. He returns to Australia, but the experience has matured him. Only Rudi and Justin are multi-dimensional characters, and events proceed pretty much as expected. The novel attempts to examine contemporary attitudes toward expressions of affection. The story moves slowly, since the author must show the "naturalness" of the relationship between the boys, the point evidently being that a close association between two boys need not have homosexual connotations. Justin's acceptance of Rudi seems sudden, given the ferocity of his earlier antagonism and his character as presented, and his intense dedication to his studies after his previous playboy behavior is not convincing. There is a kind of deviousness about Rudi that lessens the reader's liking for him and works against the theme. Except for Justin's mother, whose intelligence comes out gradually, the adults are shallow. References to Saint Antony help to unify the story. Aust. Bk. of Year Highly Com.

CANNILY, CANNILY (French*, Simon, Angus, 1981), boy's growing-up story set in a small sawmill town in Australia in the late twentieth century. Although he is used to traveling with his cheerful parents in their van and living in the caravan or house trailer as they go from one fruit-picking job to another, Trevor

Huon, 11, always dreads starting at a new school. Since his father, Buckley*, has decided to switch back to an earlier skill of bricklaying, at this school there are no other picker children, and Trevor starts alone in a room with a scornful teacher, Mr. Fuller, and a crowd of hostile boys. Mr. Fuller proves to be a sarcastic drill-sergeant type, devoted to his Club Under Twelves Australian-style football team, which has won the district competition for two years and is well on its way to a third title. Trevor's seatmate, Martin* Grace, the biggest boy in the class and almost a year older than the others, makes derogatory remarks and faces at Trevor. Sizing up the situation, Trevor sees that football is the key to acceptance, and he invents a past team and experience when he applies to join the Under Twelves. He is soon putting in grueling hours at practice three times a week, with Mr. Fuller shouting abuse, all to be the third reserve and sit on the bench at the weekly game. Nevertheless, he perseveres, growing more determined as the others heap scorn on him, for his clumsy playing as well as for his unusual clothes, long hair, and home in a caravan park. Gradually Martin begins to talk to Trevor and pries out the admission that he's never played on a real team before. Trevor's mother, Kath, and Buckley innocently admit to another parent that Trevor has had no previous experience. At the next practice, in a freezing rain, Mr. Fuller assembles the team and announces that one of them is a liar and asks how they shall punish him. Martin weakly defends Trevor, but before the kangaroo court goes further Buckley strides up, tells Mr. Fuller firmly what he thinks of his coaching tactics, and the practice breaks up in a new downpour of rain. Because Mr. Fuller now expects him to quit, Trevor stubbornly continues. Mr. Fuller is clearly never going to let Trevor play, unless three players are injured, making a third reserve absolutely necessary, and Martin, now Trevor's supporter, intends to see that it happens. With strong-arm tactics he persuades the rest of the team, and, secretly sick of Mr. Fuller's bullying, they agree. At the next game a minor player fakes an injury, then Martin lets himself be mauled and taken out, but with the team losing, the plan seems about to fail until the lead player actually is injured. With no alternative, Mr. Fuller sends Trevor in, and he makes a couple of fair plays and one bad one just before a torrential downpour causes the referee to call the game. That night Buckley and Kath admit that they have read a story that Trevor has written for school, beginning with his early memories of a real home on a beach, and telling about living in caravan parks, starting new schools several times a year, and being treated as stupid because he is different. His parents realize that the life they love is hard on their son, and Buckley says that he's done enough bricklaying, that they'll leave at midweek and head for the coast. Before the family leaves town, Martin asks Trevor to write him a letter, an idea that has never before occurred to Trevor. Although the novel is obviously about prejudice against anyone who is different, it does not seem written to thesis, but rather to explore the feelings of one child caught in an awkward situation who retains his individuality by staunchly refusing to conform to expectations. Mr. Fuller is drawn as a thoroughly unlikeable teacher, but considering the avidness of small-town sports fans, his character is believable. The title wrongly implies that Trevor consciously manipulates events, whereas he mostly endures them. Perhaps ''Stubbornly, Stubbornly'' would be more appropriate. Aust. Bk. of Year Com.

CAP'N ELIJAH WILSON (*The River Kings**), hot-tempered but kindly captain of the aging riverboat *Lazy Jane* on Australia's Murray River. Cap'n Elijah is tolerant of the eccentricities of his crew but irate at the thieving ways of Red Morgan, the Murray pirate, and thereby brings about the end of his own boat and his river career when Morgan sets the *Lazy Jane* afire in revenge. Though preoccupied with worry over his debts and the deteriorating condition of the old boat, Cap'n Elijah keeps a watchful eye on Shawn, writes to the boy's mother to assure her that he will get good treatment, and pays him a decent wage, which he insists be sent home.

CARCOOLA (Handford*, Nourma, Dymock's, 1950), realistic novel of family and neighborhood life, set on a sheep station in Australia from autumn to spring shortly after World War II. Active, energetic AnnAnne and Dimity Bell, twins about fourteen, who have been in boarding school in an unidentified city, and their capable, widowed stepmother, Lucy, take the Monday mail plane over the mountains to join Lucy's son, red-haired Andrew Garrick, 24. Having recovered from traumatic experiences as a Japanese prisoner of war by vacationing in sheep country, Andrew has just bought a small sheep station in the outback, using the proceeds from their comfortable town house. They discover that the station is small and the cottage needs cleaning and fixing, but they settle in with excitement and a will, name the place Carcoola, which means gum tree, and learn as they go, fortunate to secure the help of a knowledgeable but touchy elderly handyman, Mr. Mac, whom Lucy charms into helping her by pretending she's an incapable female. A continuing problem revolves around whether or not they will be able to make a living because of the steadily worsening drought. Another concern is the hostility of their neighbor, Robert Macairn. The proprietor of a large sheep station called Coonundra, Mr. Macairn resents Andrew's getting a veteran's privilege to buy land adjacent to Coonundra, which Macairn had hoped would go to his son, who was killed in the war. Right away, Rory Pepper, 13, the son of one of Macairn's hands who was also killed in the war and now the sheepman's ward, pulls spiteful tricks: he steals the girls' clothes while they are skinny dipping in the Carcoola waterhole; he shifts sheep from paddock to paddock to block the road when he knows Andrew will be driving by in his jeep, Waltzing Matilda; and he once tries to mire the jeep in mud. The first trick ironically starts a friendship between Lucy and Hope, Macairn's eighteen-year-old daughter, when Hope comes to apologize. Ranch responsibilities bring Hope and Andrew together and they gradually become friends. When Andrew, who had played polo before the war, learns that Bright Blaze, Hope's horse, won't be entered in the big local race because women are barred from riding and no station hand is available, he offers to ride for her. Macairn rejects the idea outright at first but changes his mind after a conversation with Andrew about a chap named Pepper in Andrew's base hospital. The man turns out to be Rory's father, not dead after all but repatriated as an amnesiac. Mr. Pepper's memory is restored when he is brought back to Coonundra and sees Rory. After a terrible storm destroys many of Andrew's sheep and his hay crop, Macairn offers Andrew a job as the ranch boss. Andrew refuses, but this action further impresses Macairn and he says that Andrew may ride Bright Blaze. Although Rory remains resentful throughout the book, he comes around when the storm-swollen creek sweeps the twins downstream toward the river and he is instrumental in their rescue. At the end, the two families are friends, Andrew is practicing for the race, and Andrew and Hope plan to marry. Although characters and incidents are conventional, the twins are not individualized, and luck and coincidence abound, the carefully calculated pace, generous action, vividly drawn scenes, lively dialogue, a little mystery, a pleasant romance, and especially the amiable tone and clear sense of sheep-ranching life from mostly the proprietor's point of view make for entertaining reading throughout. Sequels. Aust. Bk. of Year Com.

CARLETON JENNER (*Last Chance Summer**), Englishman who runs a group home for troubled boys on his farm near the Alberta badlands. Enthusiastic and somewhat naive, Carleton is often mimicked and ridiculed by the boys for his British speech and his optimism, but he is a realist and understands them better than they suppose. One of the boys rightly explains to another that although he seems tough he has a soft spot in his heart, especially for new boys. When he is accused by Vilda*, the cook, of selfish pride in wanting to handle everything by himself, he realizes some truth in what she says and takes steps to get help.

CAROL BANCROFT (*To the Wild Sky**), poised, attractive schoolmate of Gerald* Hennessy, much admired by all the boys. Although her mother is socially ambitious for her, she keeps their secret shame very quiet, an Aborigine great-grandmother on Carol's father's side. After the plane crash, Carol tries to get away by herself to see whether her Aborigine blood will give her insights that will help save them, and she discovers the ruins that make them think they are on Molineaux Island. Carol very much admires Gerald and does her best to encourage him until he says something she takes as derogatory to blacks. Then she snaps back and walks off, leaving him confused and deflated. She and Jan* Martin act as direct foils for each other.

CASE, DIANNE (1955–   ), born in Woodstock, Cape Town, South Africa; bookkeeper and writer. She won the Adventure Africa Award with her novel *Albatross Winter* (Maskew, 1983). Her second novel, *Love, David** (Maskew, 1986), about a black family living in the Cape Flats shantytown, won the Young Africa Award. Case is married, with three daughters, and lives in Lansdowne, Cape Town.

THE CATALOGUE OF THE UNIVERSE (Mahy*, Margaret, Dent, 1985; Atheneum, 1986), lighthearted, realistic psychological problem novel set for three days in a contemporary, unidentified city probably in New Zealand. Tall, beautiful, romantic Angela May, 18, and her mother, Dido*, live a hand-to-mouth existence. Dido has often told Angela her fairy-tale story: Angela is the child of a passionate love affair and is illegitimate only because her father was prevented from marrying Dido by the obligations of a wife and children but has occasionally given her financial assistance. Angela has grown increasingly curious about her father, who she has discovered from papers in her mother's files is Roland Chase, a wealthy businessman. She has located his elegant home and the downtown office of his flourishing import business. Angela's closest friend is short, plain, diffident Tycho* Potter, also eighteen, who has been in love with Angela almost since they began school but has been too shy to declare his feelings. A brilliant boy, he compensates for his inferiority complex by excelling at school. He particularly enjoys reading the ancient Greek philosophers and studying astronomy. On the last day of school, Angela asks Tycho to accompany her to the inner city, where she takes him to an exclusive coffee shop across from her father's business. An expensively dressed man enters, his coppery red hair and sharp widow's peak the duplicate of Angela's, but when Angela confronts him, he deliberately ignores her. Angela informs Tycho that this man is her father and that her previous attempts to force a dialogue were also unsuccessful. The next day in Chase's office he admits that she may indeed be his daughter, but he says he feels no obligation to her or her mother, never gave them money, and has no family of his own—in short, Dido's story has been a lie. Angela leaves his office hurt by his callousness and angry at her mother. Tycho sensibly reminds her that she still is what she has always been, a child of love, and forcefully declares his affection for her. She pays no attention, however, and goes off by herself to a low-life bar. She deliberately invites seduction, but, because she has drunk too much, she vomits all over herself, and the man leaves before anything happens. In the middle of the night Angela shows up at Tycho's house, having slept off the liquor, and declares she loves him. With an understanding she has never before shown, she places on the floor the book about the stars and planets she gave him for his birthday, *The Catalogue of the Universe*, so that he can stand on it and be nearer her height. They kiss and make love. The next morning, on the way to Dido's house, they see a terrible automobile accident. Tycho bravely pulls a man from the car before it explodes, and reporters interview him. Angela forgives Dido for her deception, and both Angela and Tycho have discovered new resources in themselves and possibilities in their friendship and are content with their world as it is. The accident seems unnecessary to build up Tycho's self-esteem, since he wants Angela's love more than the approval of other people, and the uncomplicated plot has held the attention well enough. More significant than the plot, however, is the psychology of the two main characters. Much pleasure comes from Angela's and Tycho's inner thoughts, and also from the witty conversations between the teenagers and between them and their parents. Characterizations are bold and fresh, and even the minor characters are individualized and assume more than a utilitarian dimension. Mrs. Potter is overly maternal, conventionally middle class, and disapproving of Angela because she thinks the girl is not good enough for Tycho though ironically she gives him little credit for his intellect. Her counterparts are Mrs.* Angela Chase, Angela's wealthy and snobbish grandmother, and Dido May, unconventional, independent, and loving. Mr. Potter appears seldom but significantly as the father who has spoiled his daughter to her detriment and that of his family, and Tycho's brother, Richard, is Tycho's foil, a glib, flamboyantly dressed modern youth more interested in conforming than in developing his abilities. The Potter and May establishments are also obviously foils. There are some overtly funny scenes, but most of the humor grows subtly out of the conversations, characters, and situations, and there is considerable poignancy in Angela's and Tycho's circumstances. This is a rich and absorbing novel about two young people who discover that being different is not only acceptable but valuable. Fanfare.

THE CATS (Phipson*, Joan, Macmillan, 1977; Atheneum, 1976), nightmarish adventure story set in the mountains of central Australia in recent times, involving a botched kidnapping. When their parents win a large sum in the lottery, Jim, 15, heedlessly spreads the news. That afternoon, he and his brother, Willy, 14, are abducted by an older boy, Socker, 18 or 19, and his sidekick, Kevin. When Socker speeds toward the ranges, Willy acts strangely relieved, and Jim, used to interpreting his strange brother to others, remembers that Willy sometimes takes off for several days on his bicycle, exploring the mountains alone, at ease there as he never is among people. After a long and difficult trip, during which a storm blocks their return route, they reach a deserted house that smells like a zoo where Socker plans to leave the brothers with Kevin while he crosses the river in a place he has scouted below and phones for ransom from the boys' father. When his plans go awry, Socker becomes furious, jumps in the car without unloading the groceries, and rattles off down the road toward the river. Jim recognizes Kevin's need to be bossed, butters him up skillfully, and soon he and Willy are untied, having possession of his rifle, and are in charge, but they dare not start back over the long trail where there is no water. Socker eventually returns on foot, having discovered, as Willy predicted, that he could not cross the rain-swollen river. He has also fallen in and lost the car keys. In the night Kevin's hand is bitten by something that he insists was a snake. The bite, however, looks more like that of an enormous cat. After another day without food, just as they are starting for the car, a large kitten crawls from under the porch. In fury, Socker picks it up by the hind legs and smashes it against the edge of the step. Outraged, Willy strides off ahead out of sight of the other three, who trudge on, with an uncomfortable sense of being followed. In a deepening fog, they lose their way and soon they are surrounded by the largest cats Jim has ever seen. Just as they attack Kevin, Willy reappears, and the animals vanish into the mist. Willy, now clearly the leader, quietly tells Jim that the cats have never known anyone but him, and now they have been hurt by a human. The next morning, though Willy warns him, Socker again tries to cross the river. Kevin is ill from his infected hand. Willy knows another possible place to cross the river, on a fallen log. He and Jim discuss going on their own, but they are reluctant to leave the older boys helpless. They shut Kevin in the car and hunt for Socker, finding him surrounded by cats, trying to beat them off with a stick. Jim rushes in just as they pull Socker down, drives them off, and holds them at bay until Willy comes quietly, making soothing noises, patiently talking to the animals and stroking them until they relax and back off. The brothers make a rough stretcher and drag Socker through the night back to the car, with the cats pacing threateningly beside them. Just as the sun breaks, they reach the car, and the cats disappear. Willy bargains with Socker: he and Jim will not tell about the kidnapping if Socker will not tell about the cats, so no one will come and destroy them. The brothers find the log, inch their way across, get to an isolated farm, and call their parents. They invent a story of being lost and meeting accidentally with Kevin and Socker. Police rescue the older boys. The book ends with an extract from a Sydney newspaper describing the giant cats, descendants of domestic pets gone wild, discovered roaming central Australia, breeding in fantastic numbers and killing off the natural wildlife. A thriller that becomes a survival story, its growing intensity is well sustained to the very end. The changing dynamics of the group are skillfully handled. Characterizations are interesting of forceful, truculent Socker, resentful of anyone better off in society, whom Jim cannot help but admire; weak, sniveling Kevin, whom they can scarcely even pity; and strange, self-absorbed Willy, who proves to be the strongest of them all. Aust. Bk. of Year Com.

CHADWICK, DORIS, born in Newcastle, New South Wales; Australian teacher, editor, historical novelist. She attended schools in Grafton and Newcastle and, briefly, in Queensland. In 1920 she was graduated from the University of Sydney with honors in English and history, and received her diploma of education in 1921. After two years as a high school teacher, she joined the editorial staff of *School Magazine*, where she served for thirty-eight years as assistant editor and editor. Her best-known novel, *John of the "Sirius"** (Nelson, 1955), started as a story to accompany an eight-section feature in comic-strip form published in the magazine, for which she read diaries, dispatches, and memoirs of naval and marine officers in the First Fleet, the eleven vessels which brought the first settlers to New South Wales. She then expanded the material to a full-length novel, followed by two sequels, *John of Sydney Cove* (Nelson, 1957) and *John and Nanbaree* (Nelson, 1962).

THE CHANDIPUR JEWELS (Sinha*, Nilima, ill. Jagdish Joshi, CBT, India, 1981), mystery novel set in Chandipur in northeastern India in modern times. Sunil, 10, his brother, Praveen, 12, and their older sister, Sarika, probably thirteen or fourteen, travel from their home in Patna City to their grandfather's home, the palace of Chandipur, next to the old fort. They have been summoned by their dying grandfather, who disowned their mother, his only daughter, for marrying out of her Rajput caste. They are met at the station by their grown-up third cousin, Rakesh, who belongs to the branch of the family that still lives in the fort, and his Alsatian, Rex. Although they are apprehensive about meeting their grandfather, who was *zamindar* or Raja sahib in the old days and who was known to have a fierce temper, they find a frail old man, helpless in bed, who weeps at Sarika's resemblance to her mother. He whispers to Praveen directions to find in the Red Room his papers, which will lead them to the family jewels, and warns him to proceed in secret, since others want the treasure, too. He also says something about green eyes, but faints before he can finish. Inadvertently Sunil, a lively, thoughtless child, tells Rakesh that they are looking for the treasure. The head servant's daughter, Munia, gives them a tour of the house, ending with the single room on the roof, which they find locked. Though married, Munia has not yet gone to live with her husband's family. She is no older than Sarika, still child enough to hitch up her sari and scramble up the wall and through the skylight to open the door from the inside. They discover that the ceiling, much of the furniture, and the carpet are red. As Praveen and Sarika search the room, someone approaches and unlocks the door. They hide, but after shuffling through papers in drawers, the person leaves without their discovering who it was, and they continue their work, coming by accident upon a statue of Ganesh, with beautiful green eyes of jade. When they press one, the head comes off, and they find a will and a sealed envelope addressed to them, containing two keys and directions for finding the jewels in the Bridal Chamber, which is in the fort. The next day they visit the fort, meet Rakesh's family, including an old aunt who tells them about the lavish past, and Rakesh gives them a tour, which includes the Bridal Chamber, but they can think of no way to return to continue their search. Munia, in gratitude to Sarika, who begins to teach her to read, shows them her secret cave in the garden, which is really the end of an underground passage into the fort. Their grandfather's doctor waylays Sunil, offers him chocolates, and pumps him for information. The next day Praveen and Sarika go through the tunnel and find the Bridal Chamber, where they are accosted by two men who chase and capture them, truss them up, and lock them in a small room. After a series of rescues and recaptures, during which they find the jewels, the villainous doctor and his henchmen are tracked down and captured by Rakesh and Rex. The children's parents, alerted by a telegram that the three are missing, arrive, and there is a loving and tearful reconciliation between the grandfather and his daughter. The novel is aimed at middle readers, with a conventional plot of no great complexity and no attempt at subtlety of characterization. It gets its main interest from the setting, with its exotic names and history of past glories. The writing is competent. Sequels. CBT of India First Prize.

THE CHANGEOVER: A SUPERNATURAL ROMANCE (Mahy*, Margaret, Dent, 1984; Atheneum, 1984), mystery of the supernatural with girl's growing-up story aspects covering about a week's time in a middle-class suburb of a New Zealand city in the 1980s. Plain, intelligent Laura Chant, 14, lives with her divorced mother, Kate*, a bookshop manager, and her little brother, Jacko, 3. Laura is mostly satisfied with her life, except that she regrets her plainness and is a little afraid of the changes her body is experiencing. She also fears the "warnings" that occasionally come to her. One of these occurred just before her father walked out and again when Sorry* Carlisle, prefect and model student, arrived in school eighteen months earlier. Only Laura recognizes him as a witch. One school day, after Laura collects Jacko from his sitter, the two visit an antique shop where the owner, disagreeable Carmody Braque, rudely stamps Jacko's hand with his own picture. Jacko complains of persistent pain. Coincidentally, that evening Kate arrives home with a new man friend, Chris Holly, a Canadian librarian, of whom Laura immediately feels jealous. Although the stamp disappears, Jacko has a bad night and the next day worsens. Laura fears witchcraft, especially when she detects in his room the same peppermint odor she smelled in Braque's shop. She consults Sorry, who lives with his mother and grandmother, Miryam* and Winter, also witches, in the old Carlisle mansion. Sorry suggests that Braque is a lemure, a wicked spirit of the dead who maintains his life by absorbing the energy of a living person whom he has managed to get into his power. Sorry says that Laura can save Jacko's life only by forcing Braque to let the child go. While Jacko is in the hospital, where doctors despair for him, Laura stays with the Carlisles, who persuade her to undergo a "change-over," that is, to go through the ritual to become a witch. A long passage describes the rather intricate ritual that the three Carlisles conduct and recalls descriptions of rites of passage of primitive societies. Laura then quite boldly seeks Braque, tricks him into extending his hand to her, marks it quickly with a stamp bearing her own likeness, and, with him thus in her power, causes him to fade away, leaving only a pile of clothes around a rotting mass of leaves. Jacko recovers quickly. Laura feels more content with herself, is less afraid of her changing sexuality, and discovers that she is no longer resentful of her mother's relationship with Chris. She and Sorry agree to put their own budding romance on hold, at least until both have finished school. Laura and her family are thoroughly likeable, but the Carlisle women seem shallow and made to order. The author's original concept, suspenseful plotting, touches of humor, snappy dialogue, engaging, realistic main characters, and literate, imagistic style give the book distinction. The carefully worked out details about witchcraft hold the reader's attention and contribute to the suspense. Laura's feelings about her mother's boyfriend seem legitimate, and Sorry's levelheadedness is a refreshing feature. Laura's evolution into a young lady from a petulant child and Sorry's gradual acceptance of his own ambivalent nature are completely believable. Boston Globe Honor; Carnegie Winner; Fanfare.

CHAPMAN, JEAN, born in Sydney, Australia; writer of books and radio scripts, mostly for younger children. She grew up during World War II and attended the National Art School, but she did not start writing until 1953, for her own daughter, and later for her son. Many of her stories were accepted for the Australian Broadcasting "Kindergarten of the Air" and by the *New South Wales School Magazine* for primary school children. For twenty years she wrote scripts for the Australian Broadcasting Commission's educational programs and has been a children's literature advisor. Three of her books have won commendations for the Book of the Year Award: *Tell Me Another Tale* (Hodder, 1976), *The Sugar Plum Christmas Book* (Hodder, 1977), and *The Wish Cat** (Angus, 1966), which is a brief, amusing story of a cat that joins a family and, with some difficulty, trains all the members to treat it as it thinks it deserves. Among her numerous other books are collections of stories: *Tell Me a Tale* (Hodder, 1975), *Tales to Tell* (Hodder, 1978), and *Supermarket Thursday* (Nelson, 1977); her non-fiction works include: *Sun, Wind, and Coral: Australia's Great Barrier Reef* (Wentworth, 1972); and her picture books include: *Dilly Dally Man* (Angus, 1975) and *The Great Candle Scandal* (Hodder, 1982). Her husband, an engineer, often helps with mechanical facts for stories. Some of her books have been translated into German and Danish.

CHARLEE (*The River Kings**), Chinese cook aboard the *Lazy Jane* riverboat on the Murray River in Australia. Something of a stereotype, Charlee speaks in a kind of pidgin English, is superstitiously afraid of bunyips, and when roused goes berserk with his cleaver. Usually he is kindly, offering hot black tea as solace to any crew member who needs comfort and soothing his own fears by shutting himself in the galley and peeling potatoes.

CHARLIE WATERS (*The Nargun and the Stars**), described as "the exact picture of what an Australian country man is supposed to be." Tall, thin, laconic, he is proud of his sheep run and works hard to keep it up. He slowly makes friends with Simon Brent, wisely allowing the boy to adjust to his new circumstances in his own good time. He early enlists the boy's help in simple chores about the place, and they grow together through their efforts to deal with the destructive Nargun.* Charlie is a distinctive figure, no mere type.

CHAUNCY, NAN (CEN BERYL MASTERMAN) (1900–1970), born in Middlesex, England; Australian writer who three times received the Australian Children's Book of the Year Award and is credited with making Australian children's literature more realistic and with developing appreciation for the Aborigines' vanished way of life. Her father, a civil engineer, emigrated with his six children to the remote and secluded one thousand acre valley in Tasmania near Hobart where she grew up, spent most of her life, and found the material for her best-known books, those about the warm, close, hardscrabble Lorenny family. These form a trilogy that revolves around the youngest child, Badge. They are particularly notable for their appreciation of the bush terrain and wildlife. *Tiger in the Bush** (Oxford, 1957; Watts, 1961) and *Devil's Hill** (Oxford, 1958; Watts, 1960) were both named Australian Children's Book of the Year, and *The Roaring 40** (Oxford, 1963; Watts, 1963) was highly commended for the award. She also received the Book of the Year Award for *Tangara** (Oxford, 1960; *The Secret Friends*, Watts, 1962), a fantasy-adventure novel of the friendship between a white girl and an Aborigine girl. Commended for Book of the Year were *High and Haunted Island** (Oxford, 1964; Norton, 1965), a mystery, adventure, and survival story set at a religious colony made up of Circlists, and *Mathinna's People** (Oxford, 1967; *Hunted in Their Own Land*, Seabury, 1973), an ambitious historical novel covering the 150 years from first arrival of the whites in Tasmania until the extinction of the Aborigines. Among her other books are *Half a World Away* (Oxford, 1962; Watts, 1963), about her English childhood, *They Found a Cave* (Oxford, 1948; Watts, 1961), filmed in color in her home valley, and *A Fortune for the Brave* (Oxford, 1954; Watts, 1961), which describes the houseboat on which she and her brother lived briefly near Windsor Castle. After her marriage, she and her husband settled in the Tasmanian valley of her childhood, making it into a wildlife sanctuary. Long active in the Girl Guides, Chauncy edited their journal, contributed to wildlife magazines, and wrote for the Australian Broadcasting Company. Among her other honors were the Boys Club of America Award for *Devil's Hill* and election to the Hans Christian Andersen Honors List for *Tangara*.

CHESS KENDALL (*The Year of the Currawong**), Charles Edward, named for the Young Pretender of England by his history professor father. General helper in the Currawong Mine Preservation Society, he affects the story several important times. Not always obedient, he goes into the mine alone, though he knows it is strictly forbidden, and finds the tin box containing the deed. Chess first makes friends with Pat Vane, who helps to keep the area from being developed and losing its rural flavor. Unable to go to school because he has cut his thumb severely, Chess sees the man fencing the mine, and thus the children become involved in trying to find out who really does own it.

CHILDREN OF THE DARK PEOPLE, AN AUSTRALIAN STORY FOR YOUNG FOLK (Davison*, Frank Dalby, ill. Pixie O'Harris, Angus, 1936), fantasy set in primitive Australia in the period following the early white settlement, probably in the very early nineteenth century. Two young Aborigine children, Nimmitybel, a girl who seems to be about ten, and Jackadgery, a boy slightly older, are lured into taking a canoe down river from the camp of their people by a wicked witch doctor, who by magic changes their river into a mountain range so that they cannot find their way back. He then pursues them, planning to put them permanently in a place from which they cannot return. They are aided, however, by various spirits of the bush, including the Spirit of the Billabong (or pool), Donna-Buang, who is the spirit of the snow mountain, the Spirit of the Caves, Grandfather Gumtree, Mickatharra, who is the boy of the Brumbies or wild horses, the Spirit of the Plains, and the Imp of the Willy-willy or wind funnel. All advise them to find Old Mr. Bunyip, the spirit that watches over all the planets and animals of the bush and who will know their way home. Throughout their travels they have various encounters with the witch doctor, who hinders them by the use of his magic hat. Finally, when word has reached Mr. Bunyip of their plight, he appears and directs them back to their canoe, and they return to their village where the elders in solemn meeting listen to their stories and to that of the witch doctor, who returns with an invented tale, and decide that the children are blameless and that the witch doctor has been rightfully punished by the elements. Although the author obviously finds the Aborigine culture interesting and worthy of respect, the story is a curious mixture of primitive lore and the attitudes of English fairy tales. Some of the language is out of place and out of date: the children collect wild game and grubs "for tea," and babies are referred to as "piccaninnies." As a novel, the story lacks any adequate motivation for the main villain and has little tension, since whenever the children are in a difficult situation, some spirit appears to aid them. The book is an interesting example of the difficulty of fusing two cultural traditions, an earnest but clumsy attempt. Fanfare.

CLARISSA WHITBURN (*Blue Above the Trees**), eldest daughter in the large Whitburn family of the Great Forest of South Gippsland in Victoria. Clarissa resents the wilderness. To get money to go to Melbourne, she sews for the wife of the local innkeeper. She returns to the Great Forest in a couple of years, after an unfortunate love affair never described, and later marries a neighbor boy. She is a dynamic character, whose behavior the reader both deplores and applauds.

CLARK, CATHERINE ANTHONY (SMITH) (1892–1970), born in London, England; columnist for the Nelson, British Columbia, Canada, *Prospector* and novelist for children, mainly of fantasies set in the Rocky Mountains that are strong in local color and among the first to incorporate beliefs of indigenous Canadian peoples. Educated at the Convent of Jesus and Mary in Suffolk, she emigrated to Canada in 1914, married, and lived on a ranch in British Columbia. Critics have noted that Clark's novels employ the same basic structural pattern: a boy and slightly younger girl pursue a quest that leads them into a fantasy world whose well-being is restored through their efforts. An example is *The Sun Horse** (Macmillan, 1951), her best-known book and winner of the Canadian Library Association Book of the Year Award. A boy and girl search for the girl's lost father, who disappeared while seeking a fabled palomino stallion, are drawn into a fantasy world hidden in the mountains, and there they recover a powerful Love Magnet needed to destroy a terrible Thunderbird. Her other titles include *The Golden Pine Cone* (Macmillan, 1950), in which children must restore a magical cone to is rightful owner; *The One-Winged Dragon* (Macmillan, 1955), which combines Chinese and Native American lore; *The Silver Man* (Macmillan, 1958), about restoring an Indian chieftain to his tribe; *The Diamond Feather* (Macmillan, 1962), involving a search for a lost prospector; *The Hunter and the Medicine Man* (Macmillan, 1966), about an evil medicine man; and a historical novel, *The Man with the Yellow Eyes* (Macmillan, 1963), involving prospecting in British Columbia.

CLARK, JOAN (1934–   ), born in Liverpool, Nova Scotia, Canada; teacher, writer for children. She received her B.A. degree from Acadia University in 1957 and later studied at the University of Alberta. She has taught in Sussex, New Brunswick, in both Edmonton and Calgary, Alberta, and in Dartmouth, Nova Scotia. Her writing career began after her marriage to an engineer and the birth of the first of their three children. In her first novel, *Girl of the Rockies* (Ryerson, 1968), she traces the parallel developments of a bear cub and the girl who keeps it as a pet. Her *Wild Man of the Woods** (Penguin, 1985) won the Canadian Book of the Year Award. It is a story set in the Alberta mountains about a boy tormented by bullies who finds his solution in the masks carved by a reclusive Indian. Some critics have found more successful her related novel, *The Moons of Madelaine* (Viking, 1987), whose main characters are the sisters of the boys in *Wild Man*. Set primarily in Calgary, it is a fantasy quest story with elements of Greek mythology. Among her other books is a first-person novel, *The Hand of Robin Squires* (Clarke, 1977), which concerns the mysterious "money pit" on Oak Island, Nova Scotia. In her fiction, Clark is usually concerned with the modern problems of young people paralleled either in reality with the use of symbols, or in fantasy by mythic or folkloric stories. She has also published picture books, including *Thomasina and the Trout Tree* (Tundra, 1971), illustrated by Ingeborg Hiscox, and stories in magazines, including *Canadian Fiction*, *Waves*, *Dollhouse Review*, *Journal of Canadian Fiction*, and *Wascana Review*.

CLARK (LATHAM), MAVIS THORPE (1912?–   ), born in Melbourne, Victoria, Australia; author of nearly two dozen novels of historical and contemporary realism mostly for teenagers as well as textbooks and non-fiction for young readers and biographies for adults. She wrote her first book, *Hatherly's First Fifteen* (Oxford, 1930), while attending Methodist Ladies' College in Melbourne. It was published in serial form by *Australasian* and then as a book when she was eighteen. After her marriage, she wrote short stories, articles, and radio plays. Her first book of historical fiction was *The Brown Land Was Green** (Heinemann, 1956), a story set in Victoria in the 1840s for which she got information from her Aunt Martha who died at age ninety-two and whose parents pioneered there. The book was highly commended for the Australian Children's Book of the Year Award. Also commended was *Blue Above the Trees** (Lansdowne, 1967; Meredith, 1968), a vividly detailed historical novel about the difficulties faced by homesteaders in opening the dense forested area of South

Gippsland in Victoria in the late 1870s. She won the Book of the Year Award for *The Min-Min** (Lansdowne, 1966; Macmillan, 1969), which is set among a community of fettlers (railroad workers) on the transcontinental railway in the western desert outback. Other titles are *Gully of Gold* (Heinemann, 1958), about the Victoria gold rush, *Pony from Tarello* (Heinemann, 1959), about horse competitions and station life, *Nowhere to Hide* (Lansdowne, 1969), set during World War II, *The Sky Is Free* (Hodder, 1974; Macmillan, 1976), set in the opal fields, and *Solomon's Child* (Hutchinson, 1982), in which a teenager must face her parents' divorce. Clark's publications for adults include *Pastor Doug* (Lansdowne, 1965), a biography of Sir Douglas Ralph Nicholls, the first Aborigine to be made a Knight of the British Empire, and *Jane and Betty Rayner, Strolling Players* (Lansdowne, 1972), about the beginnings of the children's theater movement. Most of her novels have an Australian background, and she has traveled extensively collecting materials for them. She has also written under the name Mavis Latham.

CLAY STEWART (*Lillipilly Hill**), boy of sixteen or seventeen who has been living for more than a year in a cave on Maloney's Hill when Aidan* Wilmot stumbles onto him in the night. The son of a ne'er-do-well Englishman of a good family and a half-Aborigine woman, he has left home after his father deserted the family and his mother got a job in a hotel where Clay cannot keep his beloved dog, Patchy. It is through Patchy that he is drawn to live again among people; when the dog breaks a leg, Clay brings it to Lillipilly Hill, hoping to get treatment for it. In the story he functions as an Australian role model for Aidan, but he is not very convincing.

CLIMB A LONELY HILL (Norman*, Lilith, Collins, 1970; Walck, 1972), realistic survival novel set in the barrens of New South Wales, Australia, in the late 1960s. The story begins as Jack* Clarke, 14, and his sister, Sue*, 12, awaken after their Land Rover utility vehicle has been wrecked in a desert ravine. They are bruised and battered from the accident, and their driver, jovial Uncle Bert Clarke, is dead, impaled on the broken steering shaft. The narrative then slips back to the children's dismal life with their alcoholic father and their joyful preparations for a Christmas holiday jaunt to prospect in some almost forgotten gold diggings with itinerant mechanic Uncle Bert. Past the Darling River, the second day out they turn off on an almost trackless line that stretches toward rocky outcroppings Bert calls mountains, the tire blows, and they crash into a stump and down into the cutaway. Knowing it will be days before they are missed, the children close the truck as a kind of coffin for Bert, carefully gather together the gear, and move it from the truck to a shaded gully. In the process, a water drum falls on Sue's instep, injuring it enough so that walking is painful. Precious water is lost; only a couple of days' supply remains. The children realize that they must go to the hills where Bert said water can be found. Jack assumes leadership, a novel experience for him, and after rechecking their supplies and retaining only the barest essentials, climbing a tree to survey the route, and fashioning a crutch of sorts for Sue, they begin their journey at mid-afternoon, being careful to keep the sun directly ahead. They arrive at the foothills on the third day, after a slow, frustrating, and, for Sue, very painful trip, a little drunk on the last of their fluid, some beer. Jack discovers a secluded pool to which he carries and drags Sue. Under a sort of overhang decorated with Aborigine drawings they make camp. Their main problems are securing food and keeping a fire going. Jack learns to use Bert's rifle, but mostly he runs down or snares small game like lizards and snakes, and Sue maintains the fire with wood Jack scrounges. About two weeks later a plane flies over, spots their fire, and the book ends with their knowing that rescue is imminent. The narrative projects a vivid picture of the vastness and barrenness of the terrain in which the children are marooned, and the author makes their desperate plight convincingly real by judiciously reminding the reader of the desert, the hot sun, and the lack of water and wildlife. The area is so realistically depicted that it almost becomes an animated antagonist. Sue's injury seems an unnecessary complication, but her disability adds to Jack's responsibility, and he emerges with an enhanced self-image, which had been much damaged by life with an alcoholic. The interaction between the youngsters has the feel of real life, just enough bickering for realism, and captures convincingly their thoughts about each other and about their father, often the butt of town jibes that have wounded their psyches considerably. Ironically, life with father has prepared them for this ordeal and made them better able to fend for themselves. Occasionally the point of view strays from that of the children, and the author's voice can be heard commenting or explaining, for example: "Already the sharp edge of horror had been slightly dulled, and there was even a certain exhilaration in the Robinson Crusoe–like adventure of the situation. To be responsible for their own survival, without adults, and without help, was part of the universal dream of childhood." On the whole, however, skillful characterization, a suspenseful plot, and a keenly realized setting make for a top-notch adventure story in which inward and outward problems are carefully knit. Aust. Bk. of Year Com.

CLIVE SCOTT (*The Min-Min**), earnest, naive schoolteacher, whose first teaching post is the one-room school at the fettler (worker) settlement on the Trans-Australian Railway where Sylvie* and Reg* Edwards live. He has expended considerable time, energy, and money to enrich the learning experiences of the intellectually impoverished children and is disillusioned and angry when the school is vandalized and his new record player broken. His decision to leave is partly responsible for Sylvie's running away. At the hearing, he is praised for trying to upgrade these children's education.

CLIVE TREVOR (*Good Luck to the Rider**), smaller of the twin brothers of Barbara Trevor. Clever and sometimes a bit mean, Clive makes fun of her clownish looking horse and suggests Rosinante for its name, realizing that Bar-

bara does not know the Don Quixote story. When Barbara's school friend, Will*
Stockton, visits, he meets his match in her clever insults, much to the amusement
of his twin, George*. Clive is really more interested in machinery than in horses.

COCKY'S CASTLE (Syred*, Celia, ill. Astra Lacis Dick, Angus, 1966), realistic
family novel with mystery aspects set near Bowral in the Southern Highlands
of New South Wales, Australia, for about a year beginning in June or July in
the 1960s. When elderly Aunt Pen decides to sell the family homestead known
locally as Cocky's Castle because she can no longer afford to maintain it, two
sets of brothers and sisters (cousins), the Crathie children, decisive leader Simon,
16, and maternal, conciliatory Linda, 14, and the Smeaton children, sturdy,
uncomplicated Barry, 14, and Fran, 12, set out to save it. About one hundred
years old, the rambling Victorian house was built by their ancestor Jonathan
Penrith and called Cocky's Castle because Jonathan was a small farmer, or
cocky, and because a large gable protrudes from one side of the upper story,
giving it the appearance of a fortress. Slight, imaginative, artistic Fran, from
whose point of view most events are seen, comes up with the idea for retaining
it: fix it up and enter it in an Australian historic homes contest. Capable, fond
Ken Smeaton, her father, a builder, helps and advises the children who work
very hard every spare moment on the house and yard. They luckily get materials
inexpensively at an auction and some castoffs from the adults that stretch the
meager $14 that is all Aunt Pen can spare. Some disquieting events take place.
Two escaped convicts hide in the house, and much of the children's hard work
is wrecked in the struggle to recapture them and must be repeated, and one day
Fran discovers an antique dealer named Mr. Terrence upstairs going through an
old photo album. Help also comes from an unexpected source: bouncy red-haired
Chris Weatherby, about Fran's age, the daughter of the gentleman farmer who
has bought Binnil House, the other part of the Penrith estate, who wishes to buy
Cocky's Castle from Aunt Pen, and for whom Mr. Smeaton is doing some work.
Chris assists in the refurbishing and becomes close friends with Fran. While
investigating the cellar of the old cheese house on the Binnil property, Fran
discovers a trunk full of paintings done by Jonathan Penrith. The pictures come
to Aunt Pen in an unexpected way. One rainy night Fran discovers Mr. Weatherby
pinned under his Land Rover down by the steadily rising creek and rescues him.
In appreciation, he sends the trunk of paintings to Aunt Pen. After Christmas,
the children learn that Cocky's has won second prize, a mixed victory, since
the $100 and plaque do not help Aunt Pen much, and she puts the house up for
sale again. A motel company makes a firm offer, but just before Easter Fran
awakens one night to see a rosy glow on the horizon: Cocky's is on fire. Aunt
Pen is safe, but the old house is destroyed. The insurance money enables Aunt
Pen to buy a little cottage not far away, however, and Mr. Weatherby buys the
land and deeds the wild hill next to the house to the state as a nature preserve.
Jonathan's paintings are exhibited in Sydney and acclaimed for their historic
value. Although the main plot concerns keeping the old house in the family, the

book is also about warm, supportive family life and a girl's growing up. Fran, a tag at the beginning, learns to assert herself and gains a friend independently of her sibling and cousins. The details of the renovation are consistently interesting, and as the work goes on, the characters of the four children gradually become known. Mr. Terrence provides a little tension but disappears from the story, the Weatherbys are stereotypes, and Mr. Weatherby's accident and rescue are too convenient. The Penrith clan is convincing, and the interpersonal family relationships seem accurate. The descriptions of the things they do together, their conversations, and their banter and bickering reflect real family situations. Food comes into the story often, and there is a deep appreciation for the beauty of the Australian countryside and the wildlife, especially the birds. Aust. Bk. of Year Highly Com.

COLIN KERR (*To the Wild Sky**), brightest of the youngsters on the ill-fated flight to Gerald* Hennessy's fourteenth birthday party. He is also well mannered, a quality that parents appreciate more than his contemporaries do. Early in the flight he is airsick, ruining the coat of his good suit, and in his humiliation he collapses and falls asleep, so he doesn't know what happens and is of no help during the flight, but after the crash he takes the lead in getting the others to shore and dives back into the plane to save Gerald. He also manages to strong-arm his younger brother, Mark*, who is afraid of water and by literally bashing his head forces Mark to shore. As the plane lists, however, his clothes are washed away and the next morning he is so appalled at being in his underwear in front of the girls that he hides until Carol* Bancroft lends him her pink slacks. After unsuccessfully trying to spear fish, he collects a heap of cockles, their first real possibility of food. He generally makes the best decisions.

COLLINS, (CUTHBERT) DALE (1897–   ), born in Sydney, Australia; novelist, journalist, and travel writer, known mainly for his adult books recording life aboard ship and his crime stories. He joined the staff of a Melbourne paper at age fourteen, where he showed such promise that he soon became drama and special events writer for the Sydney *Bulletin* and other papers. After accompanying a Chicago millionaire on a 35,000 mile voyage by yacht around the world, he recorded their adventures in *Sea-Tracks of the Speejacks around the World* (Heinemann, 1923; Doubleday, 1923). He then lived in London where he turned to novels, publishing *Ordeal* (Heinemann, 1924; Knopf, 1924), a sea story that he subsequently dramatized and produced, and several others. He traveled extensively, continued to publish novels until World War II when he served as a press censor, returned to Australia, and published another dozen books for adults. Under his own name and using the pseudonym Stephen Fennimore, he wrote an equal number of adventure novels for youth. The most critically acclaimed are *Bush Holiday** (Doubleday, 1949), a lively ranch story published under the name Fennimore, and its sequel published under his own name of Collins, *Bush

*Voyage** (Heinemann, 1950), about a trip down the Murray River on a store boat. Exuberant in the Arthur Ransome holiday-adventure mode, they were commended for the Australian Book of the Year Award. Other titles for young readers include *Shipmates Down Under* (Holiday, 1950) and *Storm over Samoa* (Heinemann, 1954).

COLLURA, MARY-ELLEN LANG (1949–   ), Canadian teacher and novelist. Her first book, *Winners** (Western, 1984; Dial, 1986), a contemporary problem novel concerning an orphaned Blackfoot youth sent to live with his grandfather on the reservation near Calgary, received the Canadian National IODE Award and the Canadian Young Adult Award. The book excels in its depiction of the impoverished lives of the prairie Indians and in its revelation of the disparaging attitudes of the whites toward them. A part-time high school English teacher, she lives with her husband and sons on a small farm near Parksville, British Columbia. She has also published *Sunny* (Irwin, 1988) and a study guide for grade seven of Native American communities as presented in *Winners, Sweetgrass** (Tree Frog, 1984; Philomel, 1980) by Jan Hudson* and *Brothers of the Heart* (Scribner, 1985) by Joan Blos.

COME DANGER, COME DARKNESS (Park*, Ruth, Hodder, 1978), historical adventure novel set for several weeks in 1838 on Norfolk Island off southern Australia, on which are confined the ''vilest [convicts] in the penal colonies.'' After their soldier-father dies in India, Otter (Octavius) Cannon, 13, and his brother, Paddy (Patrick) Paul, 7, are sent by their mother to live with his brother, Major Daniel Cannon, the commandant of Norfolk Island, to be trained as soldiers in the family tradition. Paddy Paul likes the idea and arrives in high spirits, but Otter, on whom the book mainly focuses, is increasingly unhappy and determined to become a surgeon. He soon comes to grips with Uncle Daniel over his ambition but is encouraged by the new physician assigned to the colony, Dr.* Butler. His second problem concerns a young prisoner, Corny* Stack, once the groom at Otter's father's estate in Ireland. Otter decides to free the youth, who he is sure is innocent, and determination and chance aid his enterprise. By luck he finds a whaleboat, and, while out hunting for greens to prevent scurvy, he happens on a hollow tree containing useful supplies secreted there by the boys' tutor, Isak*, a fat trusty whom they thought too fainthearted to plan an escape. Swearing Paddy Paul to secrecy with a ''dreadful oath,'' Otter takes advantage of a birding expedition to get the two men away, then finds to his dismay that they are unable to manage the boat on their own and leaps in to pilot them to New Zealand. The expedition goes awry in the fog, and they smash on nearby Phillip Island, where they are taken prisoner by two escaped convicts, Willy Willy, a vicious bushranger, and Twig, a one-eyed gypsy (both typical villains). When Isak and Corny foil the convicts' attempt to barter Otter for their freedom, Willy Willy leaps from a cliff to his death in the sea, Twig is seized, and the others are rescued by a boat from Norfolk Island. Major Cannon recommends that Corny's and Isak's sentences be commuted, and upon the suggestion of Dr. Butler, who has observed that Otter has skill with healing, agrees to allow the boy to study medicine. Though it often projects the melodramatic tone of a pirate or desert isle adventure and many events are conventional, the book moves fast and is constructed with greater finesse than most adventure stories, interlacing characters and events with precision. Most of the large cast are clear types to aid the plot, but some stand out: snobbish Cousin* Flora Cannon, who brings about Otter's rescue; Lady* Kezia Butler, the doctor's wife who cleverly pries the tale of Otter's schemes out of Paddy Paul without compromising his oath; Aunt* Isabel Cannon, seemingly fluttery but set on the best possible life for Flora; and Major Cannon, stern but just and a loving and devoted husband and father. Best is the picture of life on the island, isolated, harsh, and lonely even for the soldiers and officers. The convicts are regarded as scarcely human, the dregs of society, and are brutalized as part of their sentence. A few are more fortunate because they have needed skills, like Isak and on occasion Corny, but most exist mainly on hominy and scroungings and are angry, hostile, and hopeless. Floggings, maimings, and deaths from poor treatment and malnutrition are common. Although the abundant adventure keeps the book from sounding morally didactic, Otter's ambition and the strong part Dr. Butler plays in the resolution show the author's sentiments: the system of transporting twice-convicted men was horrible and ill became a civilized nation. Aust. Bk. of Year Com.

CORNER STORE (Kaplan*, Bess, Queenston House, 1975; *The Empty Chair*, Harper, 1978), girl's growing-up novel of a Jewish child in Winnipeg, Canada, in 1937 who, after the death of her mother, resists and finally accepts her new stepmother. The narrator, Becky (Rebecca) Devine, 9, is thrilled when Mama tells her that she is soon to have a baby, which Becky is sure will be a girl. Though she finds Simply Simon, as she calls her younger brother Saul, often a trial and squelches him whenever possible, she is sure a sister will be blond and lovable and, most of all, devoted to her. She doesn't worry much when Aunt* Sadie, her father's acid-tongued older sister, berates Mama for not seeing a doctor. Becky is more concerned when Papa*, who has a neighborhood store behind which they live, drives away his customers by his bad temper, is critical even when she improves her grades, and doesn't seem to have enough money to replace her outgrown coat. She is deliriously happy when for her tenth birthday Mama has the relatives, Aunt Sadie, Aunt* Leah, and their husbands, for a little party and gives her a coat, a second procured at half-price by a cousin, but still a new coat, red with a fur collar. That very night Papa rouses her to say she must care for Saul while he takes Mama to the hospital. They wake to find the relatives again gathered and to learn that both Mama and the baby are dead. In an effort to hang on to Mama, Becky keeps her wooden spoon and her apron on her bed, and Simply Simon hauls Mama's chair upstairs to Becky's room so that Uncle Morris, whom they both despise, won't sit on it. Later, Becky is sure she sees Mama and hears her say she'll come back as soon as they let her. In the next weeks Becky clings to that memory and has dreams in which Mama appears and tells her the baby is growing. She is outraged when a neighboring widow dolls herself up and coyly buys a single egg, obviously using the occasion to court her father, and when the relatives all propose to find him a new wife. She takes him at his word that he is not interested in marrying again. There follows a parade of old maids escorted by Aunt Sadie and various cousins. When Aunt Leah's choice, Miss Sylvia* Cohen, arrives, Papa acts quite differently toward her, and Simply Simon traitorously falls under her charm. She is no beauty, but she is sweet, gentle, and clever, has been a schoolteacher, and is independent and sure of herself, so that the courtship inexorably moves toward marriage. In the following months, Becky is torn between her loyalty to Mama's memory and her growing attraction to Papa's wife. Sylvia, as they call her, certainly manages Papa in a most remarkable way. Becky is afraid that Mama is angry with her for feeling friendly toward Sylvia and is creating her stomach cramps, coming in nightmares with a knife in hand, causing Papa to break his leg, making Sylvia sick in the mornings, and finally, after Becky has tried to shut her out, waiting outside her bedroom window and tapping on the glass. After Papa scolds her severely for leaving her light on at night, Sylvia questions her gently, and Becky pours out the whole story. Together, they discover that the tapping is caused by a wire, left loose when the new phone was installed, swinging against the glass. The next day Papa, still walking with a cane, takes Becky to the cemetery, where he shows her Mama's grave in the snow and she is able to weep and believe at last that her mother is really dead and at peace. That night Sylvia tells her and Simply Simon that she will have a baby in the spring, a girl, Becky is confident, and Becky decides that, so the baby will not be confused, they should stop calling her Sylvia and change to Mummy. The main strengths of the book are characterizations, clearly drawn of even many minor figures, and the picture of life in the Jewish community of mostly poor first- or second-generation immigrants in a Canadian city of the 1930s. Descriptions of holidays and occasional Yiddish words add flavor in an unselfconscious way, and a glossary is provided. Some of the scenes, particularly the visits of Papa's suitors, are very funny, and Becky has a convincing narrative voice. Can. Council Hon. Men.; Can. Ebel Runner-Up.

CORNY STACK (*Come Danger, Come Darkness**), former groom at the Cannon family farm in Ireland, convicted innocently and transported to the Norfolk Island penal colony off southern Australia. Corny is melodramatically described as ''pale [and] spindle-shanked'' and with ''skeleton hands.'' Though usually abject in spirit, he shows courage and ability in the whaleboat, but his foolish argument with Isak* results in the loss of the compass. Corny is a type figure but still one with whom the reader sympathizes.

COUSIN FLORA CANNON (*Come Danger, Come Darkness**), cousin of Otter and Paddy Paul Cannon. At first she seems a prissy snob, but later she confesses that she acted that way because she was afraid that the boys would look down on her as countrified. She is really an agreeable and clever child. She informs her father that Otter is behind the convicts' disappearance and suggests that Lady* Kezia might be able to get Paddy Paul to tell what Otter is scheming. Thus Otter is rescued. She is a type figure but an attractive and appropriate one.

COUSINS-COME-LATELY: ADVENTURES IN OLD SYDNEY TOWN (Pownall*, Eve, ill. Margaret Senior, Shakespeare, 1952), historical novel for middle-grade readers, set in New South Wales, Australia, in 1832. Ned Fraser and his sister, Emily, arrive with their parents in Sydney and stay temporarily with their cousins, Lucy and Tom Fraser. As they are being shown the sights of the town, they stop at the bird shop of Ben Bolton where they meet Joe, a young convict now on a ticket-of-leave, having served most of his sentence and been assigned to Bolton because he is so good at working with birds. Joe, who was transported after being wrongly accused of poaching, will be free on his birthday in a couple of weeks, and Tom knows that Bolton expects to make him a partner in the shop as a gift. Among other birds, they are shown a macaw, which Joe is keeping for ne'er-do-well Cuppy Hicks. Later the boys overhear Cuppy threatening Joe, saying that he will accuse Joe of having stolen his bird unless he cooperates in his scheme. The next morning the children learn that both money and jewels have been taken from the house of wealthy Mr. Lord, and they rush to the scene of the crime. Too small to push through to the front of the crowd, Emily wanders off to watch wallabies playing in a yard, where she meets and talks with Sir Richard Bourke, the governor, and also overhears Mr. Lord telling Bourke that he suspects Cuppy Hicks of the robbery. When the children inform Joe of this development, he is very worried because he saw Cuppy at the shop about midnight and fears he will be implicated. Soon they learn that Joe has run off, shortly before a constable comes to take him for questioning. Throughout the rest of the book the children attempt to find Joe and persuade him to return, having the assurances of their fathers and Ben that they will testify in his favor and, after a visit by Emily and Lucy to the Bourke house, that the governor will listen to his side of the story. Among others, they ask Biliwah, an Aborigine boy, to watch for Joe. Ned and Tom visit a friend, George MacDonald, who lives on a farm up the Lane Cove River. There they suspect Joe may be hiding out nearby because the farm dogs are disturbed at night and vegetables are missing from the garden, but they do not see him until a bush fire threatens a nearby farm and Joe appears to help fight the flames with the others. They try to persuade him to come back to Sydney with them, but after the fire is controlled he disappears again. Biliwah finally brings word that Joe is at the whaling station, where preparations are being made for the next trip to the Antarctic. In his canoe, Biliwah takes the two boys to the station, where they find Joe acting as the cook. Even the news of the governor's possible help does not persuade him to return with them, so great is his fear of the chain gang. When the three boys start back, a wind upsets the canoe, and they cling to it as a rescue boat sets out, manned by Nobby, a ship's carpenter Ned knew on their voyage to Australia, and Joe. When they land in Sydney, the girls and other friends are waiting for them, and Nobby and others forcibly escort Joe to Bourke's office, where Emily and Lucy tell the story. Before His Excellency decides Joe's fate, Bolton appears carrying the parrot cage, which, upon a suggestion from Nobby, he has discovered has a false bottom in which Cuppy has hidden the stolen jewels. Joe is freed and becomes a partner at his birthday celebration, which they all attend. The main interest in the book is in the scenes of Sydney and the surrounding area, which are described in interesting detail, with the predictable plot acting as a vehicle to allow the children to explore the area. Although the age of the young people is never given, the boys seem to be in their early teens and the girls a little younger. Though not highly developed characters, they are well differentiated and often bicker like normal siblings. Aust. Bk. of Year Highly Com.

COWLEY, (CASSIA) JOY (SUMMERS) (1936–   ), born in New Zealand; scriptwriter and novelist. She attended girls' high school in Palmerston North, Wellington, New Zealand, and became an apprentice to a pharmacist. In 1970 she married Malcolm John Mason, and she has three children. Her fable-like novel of a deaf-mute in the Figi Islands, *The Silent One** (Whitcoulls, 1981), was the Book of the Year Award winner of the New Zealand Government Publishing Award. Among her other books for children is *The Ducks in the Gun* (Doubleday, 1969), which was a Junior Literary Guild selection. Her novels for adults include *Nest in a Falling Tree* (Doubleday, 1967), *Man of Straw* (Doubleday, 1970), *Of Mice and Angels* (Doubleday, 1972), and *The Mandrake Root* (Doubleday, 1975). She has also published stories in New Zealand literary periodicals and school readers and has been a writer of radio scripts for the New Zealand Broadcasting Corporation.

THE CROOKED SNAKE (Wrightson*, Patricia, ill. Margaret Horder, Angus, 1955), domestic adventure novel with mystery and detective story aspects set in August in the mid–1950s in and around the village of Tarrawong in southeastern Queensland. The secret Society of the Crooked Snake consists of six school children from about ten to twelve years old, all amateur photographers: serious, assertive John Fenton, the captain, and his younger brother, quiet loyal Roy; Jenny Conway, the secretary, and her younger brother, impulsive Pete; and the lively, red-haired twins, Spike (Isabel) and Squeak (Caroline) Kemp. The members meet in an old quarry in the hills overlooking the village and later in the Fenton's toolshed, where they hold secret meetings to discuss their plans and fix up a darkroom for developing film. The children early come into conflict with four older boys, who on one occasion harass them in the hills with rifles they are too young to have and purposely leave paddock gates open to get them in trouble. Under strict orders from Parents (the children's term) to stay away from the big boys, they keep tabs on the D.P.s (Dangerous Persons) anyway. As a holiday project they decide to make a photographic survey of the flora, fauna, and industries of their region. They pool their money for film, plan the project carefully, and ride their bikes about the area, taking pictures of cattle yards, cattle drives, miners, and the like. Early one morning, while accompanying old Mr. Robertson on his cream lorry, they discover a wildlife sanctuary about three miles away cross-country and decide to take snapshots there. To their horror, they find that they have been trailed by the D.P.s, who shoot some birds and animals. "Declaring war" on the D.P.s, they lure them to the sanctuary, so that they can be caught in their illegal activity. In a series of fast-moving, action-filled scenes, Squeak and Pete pretend to take pictures of the boys with their rifles after they have shot a pigeon. While the D.P.s chase them to a rock fortress the society has rigged up and try to get the camera, John and Roy find and hide the rifles. They fetch old Mr. Berry, the former warden of the sanctuary who lives near by, and the D.P.s are seized. The children never learn whether or not they are punished, but the boys' parents take them firmly in hand, and they never bother the society again. At a special school assembly, the society members are awarded prizes of new cameras for their fine survey. This engaging story for younger readers features natural dialogue and an evenly complicated plot. Although the members of the society get along too agreeably to be completely convincing, most incidents seem acceptable. It does not seem likely that the older boys, and even the members of the society, should not have been aware of the sanctuary before this, however. Characterization is shallow, the members of the society are almost indistinguishable from one another, and the D.P.s are clearly types. As the children gather material for their album, the reader gains a limited sense of the economy and physical appearance of the region, but the author avoids didacticism. Aust. Bk. of Year Winner.

CUCULANN (*The Druid's Tune**), legendary, noble champion of ancient Ulster, called the Hound of Ulster, with whom Rosemary and James Redding associate while they are in ancient Ulster. Cuculann is presented as a mighty warrior, finely trained and eager for combat, proud, strong, quick witted, loyal, completely dedicated to the cause, and always concerned about honor. He readily accepts Jim as a companion-in-arms, trains him to fight, and trusts him implicitly. He and Jim have good times chatting and playing games, like chess, but Cuculann has trouble understanding why Jim lacks such practical knowledge as cooking. In battle, a black frenzy comes upon Cuculann, which is expended only when he has annihilated the enemy confronting him. Mighty and imposing as he is, the children often address him as Cucu.

THE CURSE OF THE TURTLE (Roy*, Thomas, Bodley, 1977; Collins, 1978), realistic novel of suspense in a family and community setting in northern Australia in the late 1940s. Events take place during about two years in the life of earnest Jimmy (James) Brent, 13, the only child of Mary and Jack* Brent, owners of a cattle ranch that has been in the family for three generations in the wild, drought-ridden Cape York Peninsula. Jimmy's best friend is Tajurra, son of

Tajalli*, the leader of the Oonas, the local tribe of Aborigines to whom the
Brent property once belonged and to whose god, Oona, the great turtle, it is
sacred. The Aborigine name for the area, Oonaderra, "land of the turtle,"
testifies to their hereditary ownership. After Tajurra makes Jimmy his blood
brother, the Oona youth informs him that a curse haunts the region and threatens
to destroy every living thing in it unless the Brent house is moved. After the
mercy killing by the tribe of aged Tirkalla*, Tajurra's grandfather, the man who
instituted the curse, a very severe drought sets in and lasts for many weeks.
When the Wet (rainy season) finally comes, the Oonas leave for their annual
walkabout. Convinced that Jimmy needs more than a correspondence school
education and fearful that he is becoming too Aborigine in thought and behavior,
Jack takes him to boarding school in Brisbane. Except for the Christmas holidays,
Jimmy stays there until called home by Jack's accidental death. Jimmy finds his
mother facing financial ruin from an even more severe drought, which mysteriously afflicts only Oonaderra. When just a few inches of water remain in the
household tanks, Mort Chandler, the mailman, arrives on one of his infrequent
rounds. He suggests looking for underground water and divines a stream not far
away. Through strenuous digging, Jimmy, Tajurra, and Tajalli bring in a strong
artesian well. Jimmy's mother decides to move closer to the well, thus terminating
the curse and repairing the strained relations between the Brents and the Oonas.
Tajalli exorcises the devils from the old homesite, and all ends well. Most
characters are flat, and motivations are flimsy and not always logical. Jimmy
tells the story as an adult looking back on what happened. Now the owner of
the ranch, he relates too dispassionately the events of these months so significant
for these people with conflicting yet interdependent lives. As a result, the events
that lead to the righting of an old and festering wrong are less interesting than
the picture of life in the Cape York region, where everyone depends on the
annual Wet. The ranchers are isolated from white civilization and must rely on
the Aborigines for labor; yet they look down on them. The Aborigines are
sympathetically and colorfully drawn, and Jimmy's visits to their camp give the
reader fascinating views of customs and ceremonies. Through Jimmy's conversations with the Oonas, in particular Tajurra, the reader learns something about
the Aborigines' beliefs, values, attitudes toward the whites and each other, and
closeness to the earth and the weather. They are shown as a sensible, dignified
people whom the whites should respect as positive, contributing human beings.
Aust. Bk. of Year Com.; IRA.

THE CURSES OF THIRD UNCLE (Yee*, Paul, Lorimer, 1986), historical
novel of mystery and adventure in the Chinese community of Vancouver, B.C.,
Canada, in 1909. On the fourteenth birthday of Lillian Ho (whose Chinese name
is Ah-Lai), her father, Ho Jin Chong, leaves on mysterious business, as he has
often done before. This time, however, he does not return to their clothing-
factory home where all the family members and several single Chinese men

work and live. For five months Lillian, her pregnant mother, her three younger sisters, and Blind-Eye, father's friend who lost his sight and lives with the family, barely make do until Third Uncle, father's no-good younger brother, announces that he has sold the sewing machines and will send Mama and the girls back to China. This idea terrifies Lillian, who knows that girls are considered liabilities and even sold in China when families are in difficult financial circumstances. When Lillian overhears Third Uncle boasting to friends that he has lots of money, she assumes that he has stolen it and searches his room. She finds a letter to her from her father, hidden in the lining of a suitcase. It instructs her to pick up a package containing a very valuable notebook from the railway station counter. The ticket to retrieve the package, however, is gone. When Lillian is chosen by the mission to escort a young woman newly arrived from China with her baby to Revelstoke, some four hundred miles northeast, Blind Eye tells her to look there for a healer called Cariboo Wing. After a long walk through the snow in the mountains, Lillian finally stumbles into his cabin as he is treating a seriously ill man. She is commandeered into using her young strength in the Hay-Gung ceremony that harnesses and directs life forces. Cariboo Wing tells her that her father has been collecting money for the revolution against the Chinese Empire, idealistically wanting to reform China under Sun Yat Sen so that his children can be proud to be of Chinese ancestry. The notebook contains the names of all those who have contributed to this cause in British Columbia and would be of great value to the spies of the Empire. She returns to Vancouver to work as a maid at the household of the Bells, who are well meaning but have many racial and class prejudices. On Christmas evening she slips out of the house to try to see her mother, who is very ill. She sees Third Uncle bargaining with some men, admitting that he has sold information about Ho Jin's whereabouts and arguing about a price for the notebook. After treating her mother with Hay-Gung, Lillian rushes to the Athletic Club where Dr. Sun, campaigning for his cause, is preparing to talk. Despite great difficulties, she gets his support for her plan to unmask Third Uncle. When Dr. Sun in his speech holds up a notebook and praises Ho Jin Chong as a martyr, Third Uncle rushes out. Lillian follows him, sees him stabbed by an Empire agent who thinks he has been betrayed, and, crouching by him, demands to hear the whereabouts of the notebook before she gets help. At her home, Dr. Sun himself arrives to present money collected for the family at the meeting. Lillian leads him to the shrine in the back of the factory workroom and reaching behind it finds the notebook Third Uncle, dying, has admitted to her he hid there. Action in the novel is exciting, if not entirely plausible, but the main interest lies in the pictures of the Chinese communities of Vancouver and Revelstoke, and in the tension between the Canadian-bred girl and her traditional Oriental parents. While Third Uncle is a stock villain and most of the lesser characters are merely functional, Lillian and her angry, worried, overworked mother, who hides her love for her daughters behind verbal abuse, are strongly drawn and memorable. Can. Council Hon. Men.

CUT CHEEK (*River Runners**), Naskapi medicine man (shaman), who performs the shaking tent ceremony for attracting game. He is presented as a greedy, mean fake (though the characters do not recognize him as such). Later almost dead of starvation, he is rescued by Andrew Stewart and his Indian friends. He is a type figure, right out of a conventional Indian adventure story, a quite unsympathetically depicted Indian among otherwise very likeably drawn Native Americans.

D

DAD (*Angel Square; Up to Low**), also known as Tommy, son of Old Tommy and father of Young Tommy. A great talker, he is always ready with a Mean* Hughie story about his boyhood neighbor on the Gatineau River. Dad is a powerful man, whose physical strength rivaled that of Mean Hughie when they were boys and when they both worked on the dam. Temperamentally, however, he is very different, a good-natured, easygoing fellow, putting up tolerantly with his drunken friend, Frank*, cleaning up after him and happily cooking up a big stew so that Young Tommy can ask Baby Bridget over for dinner. In town, he seems to have been equally tolerant of his fanatically clean sister, Dottie, who keeps house for him and Young Tommy. But with a wink at his son, he ditches on the streetcar the bottle of Lysol that she has given them to wash the berries they pick. He has a minor role in *Angel Square*.

DAD GUNTHER (*The Sun on the Stubble**), Marcus, German-Australian farmer and father of four sons and two daughters. High-tempered and volatile, Dad is inclined to shout first and think later. Even when his plans backfire, as when he shoots the galvanized water tank as full of holes as a colander when trying to catch thieves who are stealing logs from his woodpile, he never admits that he is wrong. When Bruno* wants to spend the first of his reward money for capturing the sheep stealers on a hot-water heater for the family, Dad is touched, but he insists on being the one to try it out, at first being unable to light it, then scalding himself in the first shower, and finally refusing ever to use it again. A big, strong man, he is more bluster than force, and although the boys know enough to keep quiet and walk carefully when he is angry, they also hold their sides laughing after they are out of earshot when things go wrong.

DALLAS, RUTH (RUTH MUMFORD) (1919–), born in Invercargill, New Zealand; poet and author of books for children. She is best known for her series about a nineteenth-century family of four children and their widowed mother, who is the settlement nurse, starting with *The Children in the Bush* (Methuen,

1969), followed by *The Wild Boy in the Bush* (Methuen, 1971), *The Big Flood in the Bush* (Methuen, 1972), and *Holiday Time in the Bush** (Methuen, 1983), all told from the point of view of the youngest child, eight-year-old Jean. The fourth of these was named to the New Zealand Government Publishing Award short list. Dallas began her writing of prose for the school journals, to give New Zealand children some reading material about their own country, and many of her works, including her animal novel, *A Dog Called Wig* (Methuen, 1970), are written in a simplified, easy-to-read style. *The House on the Cliffs* (Methuen, 1975), however, is for older children. It is a story of a friendship between an eccentric old woman and two schoolgirls. *Shining Rivers* (Methuen, 1979) is a historical novel set in the goldfields of Otago in the 1860s. Dallas has also published a number of books of verse.

DANCING IN THE ANZAC DELI (Wheatley*, Nadia, ill. Waldemar Buczynski, Oxford, 1984), mystery and adventure novel based on a screenplay, set in Newtown, Sydney, Australia, in the period of its publication. It is a sequel to *Five Times Dizzy**. The smashing of the front window of the Anzac Delicatessen, owned by Baba, Georgis Nikakis, from Crete, is the first terrorist act by the Munga, the Greek-born enforcer for a local underworld boss. Marika Nikakis, about twelve, who lives upstairs with Baba, Mama, her little brother, Costa, and her paternal grandmother, Yaya, does not understand what is putting lines in Baba's face. Marika and her friends, the three Wilson children, sneak out at night in dark track suits and into a warehouse yard, hoping to get and sell some empty beer cans they have spotted there. The underworld boss, referred to as the Red-Headed Man, and the Munga are in a building on the lot, drinking beer and talking about how to pressure Nikakis into giving up his building, which the boss wants for his refrigerator business, a front for illegal activities of various kinds. Alerted by the noise, they chase the children but trip on the cascading cans, and the children escape and are escorted home by Kyrios Graham, the local alderman, who is out jogging. Then the Red-Headed Man leases the Haunted House, a derelict building that the children have used as a clubhouse. Used refrigerators are set up in the yard, and the children's belongings are dumped in the alley. They retaliate ineffectively by picketing and by circulating petitions, but Alderman Graham harasses the gangsters more when he gets the city to close off the block "for repairs." These activities are interspersed with stories told by Yaya, who speaks no English, translated by Marika for the other children while they take Yaya's goat, Poppy, to the park to graze. She tells them how during the Nazi attack on Crete, her own skinny, crippled Yaya beat a paratrooper unconscious with her cane and how the members of the Resistance helped English and Australian soldiers over the White Mountains to boats for Africa. Then Poppy disappears, kidnapped by the Munga. Ridiculed by his boss for taking the goat instead of more drastic action, the Munga fire bombs the shed at the back of the Anzac Deli, and all the neighbors gather in the middle of the night to help and to watch the firemen. Just as the fire is extinguished and dawn breaks, the Red-Headed Man and the Munga drive into the alley. All the neighbors, fed up with their terrorism, encircle them and are held off from attacking only by the wheel-wrench the Red-Headed Man swings around him. He does not notice Yaya climbing on his truck with a board, which she swings down upon his head, battering him as her Yaya battered the paratrooper. Then she places the curse of the Evil Eye on the Munga, so scaring him that he leaves forever. The crowd hoots at the Red-Headed Man, destroying his reign of fear. From a number of clues, Marika realizes where Poppy must be hidden among the other goats at the agricultural college farm. When she brings the goat back, the barkeeper across the street plays Greek music on his loudspeakers and brings out glasses of ouzo, Baba and Mama chop cheese and salami and set out trays of olives, and all the neighbors dance through the deli and around the streets in a big celebration. The Wilsons' grandfather, arriving just then with the parents, turns out to be one of the Australian soldiers helped by Yaya. The novel proceeds in a series of scenes, lively but not entirely realistic, reflecting its source in a movie for children. The most interesting character, and the only one really developed, is Yaya, in her traditional black dress of the Cretan grandmother, her dependence on Greek, her understanding of her goat, the children, and the situation, despite the language barrier. Glimpses of the Greek-Australian ethnic group are the best part of this otherwise lightweight book. Aust. Bk. of Year Com.

THE DANGEROUS COVE (Hayes*, John F., Copp, 1958; Messner, 1960), historical adventure novel set in Newfoundland in 1676, dealing with the conflict between the settlers and the Devon fishermen who control the ports during the fishing season. Hunting for his lost dory, Peter Thistle, 15, comes upon a boat containing two men, one dead and the other, a boy his own age, close to death from exposure. He drags the boy ashore, dresses him in his own dry clothes, warms him by a fire, and eventually learns his story: he is Tom Thorbourn from Boston, where he has been living with his Uncle Spencer and has been impressed into the crew of a Devon ship. He escaped with a seaman named Santos Largo, but Largo was killed, and Tom nearly died before reaching Treshaven's Cove. The two boys become immediate friends, and both are disappointed when Peter's father, John Thistle, decides Tom is well enough to walk to St. John's, where he may find passage on a ship for Boston. When the boys arrive in the town, they discover the Devon captain, the first to arrive in port for the season, who, by law, becomes the Fishing Admiral, is Hans Grobber, the same man the boys have earlier discovered ripping off panels from the cabin of the *Berbice*, a pirate ship seized and kept by the men of Treshaven. Although the fishing admirals often have abused the local people, Grobber goes further, burning and pillaging, with an edict from the king to drive the settlers from Newfoundland. Peter and his uncle are taken prisoner and escape only with Tom's help. Knowing that Treshaven is next on Grobber's agenda, the boys rush back and arrive exhausted but in time to warn the community to set the boom across the entrance to the cove, a chain attached to floating logs by which they can slow a ship until the treacherous current catches and wrecks it. As they struggle to set it, Grobber's ship arrives and in the ensuring turmoil, Peter is captured. He manages a daring escape. Later, when his father is taken hostage, Peter and Tom engineer his escape, too. All the women and children have retreated inland, taking with them the livestock and supplies that the Devon captains need during the season. When Peter joins them, he discovers in the knapsack that originally belonged to Largo a letter from his brother, who had been pirate captain of the *Berbice*, telling where he has hidden the directions to the treasure from Grobber, the mutinous mate. Just before Grobber leaves with the *Berbice* as well as his own ship, Peter's father has gone to St. John's and persuaded the authorities of Treshaven's grievances and has enlisted the help of Spencer Thorbourn, Tom's uncle, who has come with an armored ship seeking his nephew. With his help, after a couple of other daring escapes, they defeat Grobber, find the treasure, and decide to go with Spencer to England to plead the case of the Newfoundland settlers before the king. Despite the inclusion of Newfoundland history, the story has no feeling of having occurred in the seventeenth century. The dialogue generally sounds like that of the mid-twentieth century: "Mother sure knows how to feed a fellow!" Characters are not developed and the number of escapes and daring rescues strains credulity, but the fast pace and continual action help obscure the implausibility of the plot. Can. Bk. of Year Winner.

DANIEL BLACKWOOD (*The Seventh Pebble**), older brother of Rachel. When home from boarding school, he spends much of his time hunting rabbits until he meets Maeve Connell, to whom he is immediately attracted. His mother promptly arranges a party for him to which local "acceptable" girls are invited. He gets into a terrible fight with Billy Finch over Maeve that is the talk of the community youth. Later, he informs Rachel that Maeve is pregnant, which provokes Rachel's innocent comment that since Maeve isn't married she couldn't be. Daniel is a well-mannered boy who decides to follow his father into medicine in view of the coming war.

DARKIE JOHNSON (*Spear and Stockwhip**), part Aborigine youth, who participates in the cattle drive. At first Darkie often seems sullen and aloof, suspicious of the other boys because he appears to anticipate discrimination, but as the trip continues he relaxes. He contributes to their success because he knows some Aborigine and is fluent in sign language. Sensing that the boys are prejudiced against Darkie, Chikker tells the patently didactic story of the bravery of Darkie's half-Aborigine father, Nigger, in World War I, when he was cited for a Victoria Cross but was never granted it because he was an Aborigine. Later Nigger became a top stockman and was killed in a stampede while saving another man's life—Chikker's.

DARKNESS UNDER THE HILLS (Scott*, Bill, ill. A. M. Hicks, Oxford, 1980), fantasy of the hero-quest type, sequel to *Boori**, continuing the adventures of this Aborigine youth in the major mission for which he was created, to defeat the evil spirit called Rakasha that has entered the land of the People in the north and is destroying or subverting all good figures in an effort to control their world. A message comes to Boori from Ganba, the greatest spirit, that a terrible evil has come upon the land, and he travels north with Dingo*, the shape-changing spirit of the dog people, and Jaree*, his personal companion spirit, who rides through the day in a leather bag at Boori's throat and guards his camp at night. He is also looking for a great healer named Kolonga, who is said to have power to restore the use of his injured left arm and hand. Word of his coming and his mission is sent ahead by the elders of his tribe through mind-power. After an encounter with a treacherous ghost, they pass the boundaries of their own land, and Boori is challenged and taken as a prisoner to the elders, to whom he proves his identity and with whom he helps retrieve two children who have been stolen by the evil power. Gratefully the elders furnish a guide through their land and the companionship of their Goundir, or wise magician, to help find the mountain where Kolonga dwells. Climbing this great stone outcropping with Dingo in his man shape, Boori encounters a surly old man who turns out to be a shade taking the shape of the true healer, whom they find imprisoned by magic in a cave and whom Boori, himself a powerful Goundir, frees. Then Kolonga, with the help of the local Goundir, heals Boori's arm in a ceremony that is dangerous to his spirit and physically excruciating but successful, At the next boundary, Boori meets two young, newly initiated warriors, the cousins Bororen and Benaraby, who first capture him, then become his guides to the northern border of their land. Traveling in the barren land to the north of this river, Boori comes across the trail that Dingo identifies as that of a great dog spirit, a discovery that infuriates him because he is assigned to be the spirit of dog among the People. At a sacred place of the Kangaroo Dreaming, they find a Goundir, Gogango, badly wounded by this dog, which he describes as all black, waist high to man, and totally evil, the chief servant of Rakasha. After Boori treats his wounds and finds him food, Gogango tells him the story of Rakasha's coming and how he and one other Goundir, Goovigen, are the only men still standing against this evil power, each protected in a sacred place of his own skin or totem group. Finding his own sacred place of the eagle-hawk, Boori coordinates the magic of the three Goundirs and destroys Rakasha. Dingo dies of wounds he receives in killing the great black spirit dog. Exhausted, Boori is given a choice by Ganba to return to the Cave of Honey and live in honor or to go the campfires of the sky. He chooses the latter, and three new stars appear, two bright ones for Boori and Dingo and one little spark for Jaree. Although carrying on the story from the earlier book, this novel is more cohesive and conventional than the first, following the traditional hero pattern more closely. Much of the action depends upon the ability of the old men and the Goundirs to send thoughts by telepathy, a system that seems logical and possible in the context of the story's culture. Although Rakasha is never identified clearly, he seems to be an Oriental evil power, having been driven out from a northern land and being described as having eyes that slant. Great respect is shown for the customs and beliefs of the Aboriginal people. Aust. Bk. of Year Highly Com.

DATTA, ARUP KUMAR. See DUTTA, ARUP KUMAR.

DAVE LORENNY (*Devil's Hill*; Tiger in the Bush*; The Roaring 40**), strong, patient, resourceful father of Badge, Iggy*, and Lance, husband of Liddle-ma*, and uncle of Sam*, Bron*, and Sheppie*. His great pleasures are prospecting, tramping through the bush, and devouring the few newspapers the family acquires. He and Badge are close and often go for jaunts in the forest. He recognizes that Sam is spoiled and needs to be helped to develop a sounder sense of values. He also takes pains to explain to Badge why he gives Badge the duties he does— because he cannot rely on Sam to do them but knows that Badge will always come through. Dave is a convincing character and a good foil for his less practical, more opportunistic brother, Link.

DAVISON, FRANK DALBY (1893–1970), born in Genferrie, a suburb of Melbourne, Victoria, Australia; died in Melbourne; farmer, businessman, novelist, short story writer. He spent his boyhood in the Elsternwick-Gardenvale district, where he attended Caufield State School, and his middle and late teen years in America, where his father's business took the family. At the outbreak of World War I, he shipped across the Atlantic, helping care for a load of Canadian broncos, and enlisted in the British Cavalry. After the war he returned to Australia and farmed in Western Queensland until driven off by drought. For two years he worked for a monthly magazine published by his father in Sydney, then went into business. During the Depression he wrote *Man Shy* (Aust. Authors, 1931; *Red Heifer: A Story of Men and Cattle*, Coward, 1934), a novel about "scrubbers," domestic cattle gone wild, that grew out of his Queensland experience, printed it himself, and with his brother hawked it door to door in Sydney until a publisher who had previously rejected it published it. *Children of the Dark People** (Angus, 1936) is a fantasy featuring two Aborigine children, one of the earliest attempts to incorporate elements from the Australian oral tradition into stories for children. After World War II, he rewrote a story about a wild dog that he had first written during his years in America as a ballad, incorporating much of his Queensland experience, and it was published as *Dusty* (Angus, 1946), winning the novel competition sponsored by the Melbourne *Argus*. Among his fiction for adults is *Wells of Beersheba* (Angus, 1933), which was based on a World War I cavalry incident and was later reprinted in *The Road to Yesterday* (Angus, 1964), a collection of short stories by Davison. An earlier collection was *The Woman at the Mill* (Angus, 1940). His last published novel was *The White Thorntree* (Nat. Press, 1968; Ure, 1970), a two-volume work about the Australian culture's attitudes toward sex in the 1920s and 1930s, a novel whose frankness was ahead of its time. He is best remembered for his animal stories and praised by critics for his "ability to get within the mind and motivations of an animal without sentimentality or even unjustifiable anthropomorphizing."

DAY, DAVID (1947–), Canadian poet and writer known mainly for his books for adults. His numerous publications include *A Tolkien Bestiary* (Ballantine, 1979); *The Doomsday Book of Animals* (Viking, 1981), an encyclopedia of three hundred species; *Castles* (Allen & Unwin, 1984; Bantam, 1984), an anthology of folklore about castles; *Eco-Wars* (Key, 1989), about environmental protection; and several books of poetry, among them *Many Voices* (J. J. Douglas, 1977), an anthology of contemporary Canadian Indian poetry. For children he wrote *The Emperor's Panda** (McClelland, 1986; Dodd, 1987), a mythical fantasy set in ancient China that tells how a poor but virtuous shepherd boy becomes the emperor of all China with the help of the magical and very wise Master Panda. Lively and witty, it was runner-up for the Children's Book of the Year of the Canadian Library Association and received honorable mention from the Canada Council.

DAYS OF TERROR (Smucker*, Barbara Claassen, Clarke, 1979; Herald, 1979), historical novel about events leading up to the emigration in the early 1920s from the Ukrainian steppes to Canada of German-speaking Mennonites to escape persecution during the Russian Revolution. While most episodes are based on actual happenings and a few minor figures really lived, the focus is on the fictitious Neufeld family, Father (Gerhardt), Mother, Peter*, 10, little Katya, and the eldest, Otto, perhaps seventeen, of the village of Tiegen. The villagers are descendants of persecuted Swiss and Dutch Mennonites who in 1805 were invited by Empress Catherine II to settle in Russia. They prospered and grew numerous until at story's start they consist of forty-one small settlements. Their good fortune contrasts sharply with the poverty of the Russian peasants who live around them and sometimes work for them. The book opens at harvest in 1917, and Russia is involved in World War I. Since Mennonites practice non-violence, even to the extent of not owning weapons, Otto has been doing his military service as a Red Cross worker and has been mustered out. The joy of his safe arrival at the train station is tempered by surprise and fear when bystanders jeer and call them spies. As events soon show, this is just the tip of the iceberg of the hatred and violence the Mennonites will experience during the next few years. Otto, who is in much of the book a main source of information about the outside world, explains that the Russians consider the Mennonites foreigners, since they continue to speak German, and that his people have become scapegoats for the Russian war defeats. After the Czar is deposed, the prisons are opened, and bandits ravage the countryside in droves. The first time they come to Tiegen, Otto and Peter put on the Indian costumes Uncle Jakob has sent from Nebraska and frighten them away. In February, 1918, Uncle Herman, an estate owner, is wantonly slain, and Aunt* Lizzie comes to live with the Neufelds. Tanya, the Russian maid, is taken away by her family because it is no longer safe for her to serve the Neufelds. More bandits come, and then soldiers, all raiding for food, clothing, blankets, anything of any value, until the Neufelds can barely manage to exist. Peter and Katya hide in the barn each time the raiders arrive.

The new government closes the church, and the ruling elder, Peter's Grandfather Penner, is taken hostage. A Soviet takes over, a council of five workers and peasants, illiterate Bolsheviks, haughty and cruel. Days and nights of violence and chaos ensue. The village food supply dwindles rapidly, since the little they do manage to grow is soon stolen. When the Bolshevik government negotiates a separate peace with Germany, giving the Ukraine to Germany, Mennonite hopes rise, only to be shattered shortly when the Germans lose the war. Father, staunchly non-violent, is shocked to learn that Otto, who has gone away to school, has joined a resistance group, the Mennonite Defence Unit, and the family again fears for his safety. Peter first begins to feel that Father considers him a man when Father confides that the Mennonites plan to leave Russia. The hardships and terror continue for months. Drought strikes, then famine, and the people resort to eating mice, crows, and wheat stretched by being mixed with dust. Many, Russians and Mennonites, die of starvation and then typhus, an epidemic spread by the raiders. Relief comes from the North American Mennonites. Mackenzie King, prime minister of Canada, invites them to emigrate, and plans for that are finalized. Months pass, however, before departure, and tension grows. The examining doctor refuses to allow Aunt Lizzie to leave, and Katya falls ill with measles and must stay behind with Lizzie until she is well. The rest of the family make it to Latvia, then Canada, and Otto emigrates through Holland to Nebraska, just a few of the approximately 20,000 altogether who move to North America. After Katya arrives in Canada, the Neufelds settle in Manitoba. The story of the Mennonites' numerous hardships is occasionally ironically amusing, mostly horrifying, leaving the reader with a sense of outrage at how a people so peaceloving, generous (they share readily and often with their Russian neighbors), religious, self-sufficient, and industrious can be so cruelly treated out of envy and ignorance. Most characters are types, and some scenes stand out, for example, at the railroad station and during the bandits' early attacks. Events become repetitious, however, and the conclusion is cluttered with incidents and information. On the whole, the writer appears caught up with the historical facts and is better at conveying them than at telling a story. Historical figures briefly seen are P. C. Hiebert, North American relief worker, David Toews, a Canadian leader of the mass migration, and Makhno, a Ukrainian anarchist bandit. Can. Council Winner; Can. Ruth Schwartz.

DEAR BRUCE SPRINGSTEEN (Major*, Kevin, Doubleday, 1987; Delacorte, 1987), epistolary novel revealing a young Canadian teenager's turmoil after his parents' separation and his gradual coming to terms with that problem and with his own social and school problems during a period of about seven months. In April, Terry Blanchard, 14, starts writing to his idol, rock star Bruce Springsteen, first just a fan letter, and continues, without ever getting an answer, as a way of expressing and organizing his own troubled life. The reader learns that Terry's father, a musician, left the family about six months before the first letter, that his mother works as a nursing assistant, that he has a sister, Amanda, 10, and that he is considered a difficult student by most of his teachers, particularly his sarcastic math teacher, Jenkins. As the school year ends, his good relationship with his mother deteriorates, he acquires a friend named Sean who shares his interest in music, and he makes some agonized attempts to date a girl named Kristy. Terry is attracted to Springsteen's music partly because it is his one genuine connection with his father. During the early summer months Terry manages to buy a used guitar and amplifier and toys with the idea of giving a concert for charity, inspired by a Live Aid tape. When his mother brings a friend named Nick home to dinner, Terry is deliberately rude to him. In August his mother tells him that she and his father are getting a divorce. After mulling this over for some time, Terry hitchhikes to Callum, 150 miles away, where he suspects his father is staying, and tracks him down through a bar named BJ's to the slovenly apartment, where he is living with a woman named Charlene. His father takes him to a practice of his new band, the Backstreets, but after a couple of days Terry decides to go home and leaves a note, for he is unwilling to say goodbye in front of Charlene. His father follows him to the bus depot, where they have a confrontation and reach a sort of understanding, with Terry taking the baseball cap that has always been his father's favorite and promising to send a new one in return. Terry's return marks an upturn in his relationship with his mother and in his life generally. He accepts Nick's invitation to go canoeing and duck hunting, and he tells his mother that he has no real objection if she wants to marry the man. With encouragement from the music teacher, Kirkland, he and Sean decide that their charity performance will be a lip-sync concert with the money going to a local family whose home was burned. Suddenly his phone is ringing off the hook with calls from girls wanting to do Madonna or Cyndi Lauper or the Pointer Sisters. After school starts again, they get the backing of the principal, hold auditions, and put together a program. His father writes, as he has promised, and Terry answers with a long letter about the concert plans. The performance is a great success and through it he becomes acquainted with Joanne, a girl he has long admired. His last letter, dated October 30, recognizes that his need to talk to someone is no longer pressing and that it is time to stop the one-sided correspondence. The voice of the adolescent, while consistent, becomes tedious, and the plot is predictable. Terry is the only developed character, and though his parents are believable, Amanda, Sean, and the high-school girls are cardboard figures. Throughout, Terry comments on various records and songs by Springsteen and compares them to the work of other musicians, elements that probably appeal to the teenage audience at the moment but may make the novel rapidly out-dated. Can. Young Adult Runner-Up.

DE HAMEL, JOAN (LITTLEDALE POLLOCK) (1924–), born in London, England; language teacher and novelist. She was educated at schools in London and Switzerland, and at Shrewsbury and Lady Margaret Hall, Oxford, taking honors in modern languages. She served as assistant mistress at St. Nicholas

School in Herfordshire and head of languages at Francis Holland School, London. Since marrying and emigrating to New Zealand, she has made her home in Dunedin, where she has been a lecturer in French at Teachers College. She has five sons. Her first novel, *"X" Marks the Spot* (Lutterworth, 1973), which she illustrated, is a story of three children surviving a helicopter crash in the bush of Fiordland, New Zealand. *Take the Long Path** (Lutterworth, 1978) is a more complex novel of a boy who discovers that Maori traditional beliefs have a strong effect on his life. It received the Esther Glen Medal.

DESAI, ANITA (1937–), born in Mussoorie, India; novelist for both adults and children. She was graduated from Delhi University, is married, and has four children. Her novel, *The Village by the Sea** (Heinemann, 1982; Allied, 1983) is a quiet, evocative story about a poor family in modern India. It won the prestigious Guardian Award for Children's Fiction. Most of her novels for adults are set in India and explore relationships between family members, among them *Cry the Peacock* (P. Owen, 1963), which uses stream-of-consciousness imagery of a woman who is slowly disintegrating psychologically; *Where Shall We Go This Summer?* (Vikas, 1975), about alienation and lack of communication in married life; and *Fire on the Mountain* (Harper, 1977), a story of a reclusive old woman and her great-granddaughter. *Bye-Bye, Blackbird* (Hind, 1967) concerns an Indian immigrant in England who struggles with the alien culture. Among her books for children are *The Peacock Garden* (India, 1974) and *Cat on a Houseboat* (Orient Longmans, 1976). Desai has also published short stories in many periodicals, including *Harper's Bazaar, Writer's Workshop*, and *Envoy*.

THE DESPOT (*The House that was Eureka**), Nanna Oatley, landlady to Evie*, mother of Nobby*, and grandmother of Noel*. Having suffered a stroke, she is bedridden and apparently unable to talk, though Noel is sure she can move about and speak if she wants to. She orders her timid daughter, Noel's mother, and Noel about by writing on a soft, erasable slate, then angrily ripping the transparent sheet up to make the message disappear. Her fierce independence has grown to cantankerous bullying over the years. When the Cruise family cannot pay the rent in 1931, she will listen to no pleas and calls the police to enforce the eviction. The pickets and the children jumping rope to mocking verses force her to stay inside, even though she has nothing to eat, but she will not listen to Nobby's arguments on behalf of the Cruise family, and when the police come she lets them in so they can cross the scullery roof and enter the upstairs of the Cruise house, thereby overcoming the defenders. After Nobby leaves she destroys his letters to Lizzie and keeps the ones from Lizzie she has promised to send on to her son. After the re-enactment of the Eureka House eviction, when she finally rises from her bed and speaks to comfort Evie's terrified little sister, the despot is able to tell Nobby that she is sorry. She also relents enough to allow Ted to pay the rent by making repairs on her houses while he is out of work. She is a disagreeable but pitiable and believable character.

DETOUR TO DANGER (Wuorio*, Eva-Lis, Dell, 1981) mystery set in a village
of Andalusia, Spain. On his holiday from school in England, Nando Herrera
(Fernando Vermontes y los Rios, Duke of Herrera), 16, is asked by his Scottish
mother's Great-Aunt Jane to "stop by" Andalusia to check on her villa, where
her "Second Sight" tells her something odd is going on. Though it is far out
of his way home to Catalonia, he agrees and hitchhikes, saving the expense
money she has sent him for sailing gear. He finds the villa in a shambles, windows
broken, doors gone, rubbish in the main rooms, and a dormitory-like row of
cots upstairs. He also finds a little gypsy boy, Angelito*, about ten, and his pet
chicken, Anton, living in the back rooms. Angelito tells him of the "Dark Ones,"
the black-clad men who come to the villa next door, some of whom sleep in
this house, and who have meetings and singing in the caves behind the garden.
The boy is terrified of the Dark Ones and attaches himself gratefully to Nando.
To call his aunt and report, Nando goes to Malaga, where he meets his Andalusian
friend, Ana-Maria, who has followed him and is dressed like a hippie. He also
encounters some men he has seen watching him on the ferry from Dover, an
ill-assorted group that has attracted Ana-Maria's attention by giving Aunt Jane's
villa as their address. They hire Nando and the girl to work for them and give
them directions to the village. There Angelito takes them to the caves where
they discover swastikas and portraits of Hitler. At first, Nando hopes they are
filming a movie, but he soon realizes that they are neo-Nazis, planning some
violent demonstration in two day's time. From friends Ana-Maria gets the shocking news that her brother Diego has joined the Fascist group. In a series of
complications, the Nazis kill Anton, and Nando is captured, escapes, is recaptured, and becomes convinced that they plan to kill the young king, Don Juan
Carlos, who has brought democracy to Spain, and to seize power. He is also
aware that they plan to have him at the scene when the king lands his plane and
to make it seem that he has carried a bomb to assassinate the king, a plausible
scheme since many of the noble families were pro-Fascist in the Franco days.
At the crucial moment, Diego tackles the terrorist with the bomb and runs with
it into the fields where it explodes, killing only him, while Nando runs the other
way to clear the airstrip of the "goats" that have wandered out onto it, actually
Angelito, Ana-Maria, and children they have recruited dressed in goat skins,
who have come in an attempt to rescue him. Another of Ana-Maria's brothers,
alerted earlier by Diego, arrives to take over the clearing and repair of the house,
while Nando flies with the grieving girl and Angelito to his mother's home.
With its red-haired hero as first-person narrator, the story is believable and fast
paced and deftly includes a good feeling for the Moorish setting and for recent
Spanish history. The heroics of Nando are not beyond those possible for a boy
his age. Poe Nominee.

THE DEVIL HOLE. See *THE OCTOBER CHILD.*

DEVIL'S HILL (Chauncy*, Nan, ill. Geraldine Spence, Oxford, 1958; Watts,
1960), realistic novel of family life set in the mid–1900s in the Tasmanian bush.
Earnest, naive Badge (Brian) Lorenny, 11, his capable perceptive mother, Liddle-

ma*, and his patient, resourceful father, Dave*, lead an isolated, austere, but quite satisfying existence in a rugged, forested region across the Gordon River from the farm of Dave's brother, Link. Badge has mixed feelings about starting school, since he will have to go to live with Uncle Link and his family. He looks forward to the company of Sam*, Link's son his age, but resents and fears Sam's superior attitude. Quite unexpectedly Uncle Link shows up at The Wire, the metal bridge that spans the Gordon River, with not only Sam, but also fearful Bron*, about eight, and strong-willed Sheppie*, 5. He leaves them with Dave and Liddle-ma, since Aunt Florrie must have an operation. Dave receives them hospitably if a bit reluctantly. A strong sense of family loyalty and neighborliness precludes refusal, but food is hard to come by, and the family cow has just died in an accident. Still, Dave and his family make the best of the situation, and all the characters change credibly as a result of the next few weeks' experiences. The plot involves two intersecting story strands: the relationship between Sam and Badge and recovering Brindle, dead Bow'ra's feral heifer calf. As the need for milk is critical, they close the cabin and hunt for Brindle, camping at night and making a slow and laborious way on foot over ridges and streams and through the trees, carrying their necessities and having small adventures. One day while the others are scouring the valley overlooked by the mountain called Devil's Hill, Badge and the girls explore a tunnel that leads through the mountain and come upon Brindle's bush home and brand-new calf. Characters are drawn with skill and subtlety. Round and dynamic, they change believably in their relationships with one another and to their circumstances. Sam, who at first downgrades bush life and takes advantage of Badge, comes to appreciate the value and satisfaction of helping in a common cause. Badge realizes that he has important skills and knowledge and looks forward with more confidence to school. The deceptively simple plot moves at a leisurely pace for the most part, and interest focuses mostly on relationships. Action scenes are vivid and carefully placed, and the unschooled speech supports the setting, which is vivid with concrete and figurative details and skillfully integrated into the plot. The result is a story of unusual conviction and impact and seemingly without artifice. The title refers to a bear-like Tasmanian mammal, which in the story has lairs on the mountain of the cave. *Tiger in the Bush** and *The Roaring 40** are also about the Lorennys. Aust. Bk. of Year Winner.

THE DEVIL'S STONE (Frances*, Helen, Omnibus, 1983), novel consisting of two interlocking suspense stories, one set in 1851–1852, and other in 1981–1982. The action in both occurs on the same farm in a remote valley in the Tiers range at the edge of the Adelaide plains in South Australia. The stories involve two generations of the Tregarren family, the first the people who pioneered the region and the second their descendants of one hundred thirty years later. The two stories are told in alternating third-person omniscient chapters and occasional flashbacks and selections from old diaries are included in the modern portions. Irish Ma* and Cornish Father Tregarren and their children, red-haired twins, vivacious Emma Rose and reticent Lauralei, 11, and their toddler son, Patrick, set up housekeeping in the remote valley in 1851. The girls take to the area, seeing in it great possibilities for adventure, in particular on the stony mountain overlooking their farm. They soon discover two caves, a larger one with exotic Aborigine drawings on the walls, among them a giant spiral snake, and the other a tiny one higher up that they dub the Crow's Nest. The first major trouble strikes in the winter of 1851 on the way back from a trip to sell gum logs in Adelaide. In early evening, as they are crossing the ridge, they rest briefly before descending into the valley. A sudden avalanche sweeps down, killing the hired man and maiming the bullock team so badly that Father shoots the animals. The need for money takes Father to distant gold fields, and for more than a year the girls and Ma struggle to survive alone. One day in 1852, the girls go to the ridge to scout for the man who is to bring them a new supply of flour. When a sudden fog envelopes them, Emma Rose slips into the Crow's Nest, and a day and a half later a black man brings her home, but Lauralei is never seen again. Developing concurrently is the story of the family of Jim Tregarren, who is a direct descendant of Patrick of the historical family. Jim's twin daughters, Emma and Leigh, are the counterparts of their ancestor aunts in age and personality. Emma is outgoing and assertive and Leigh imaginative and cautious. One morning, the route of the girls' school bus is blocked by a stone so immense that it must be blasted out of the way. An Aborigine schoolmate of the girls says that it has come down from the crag where devils dwell. Grandpa Tregarren, who believes in the Aborigine tales, says that the crag has always meant trouble for the Tregarrens. The family discovers in a diary Emma Rose left a reference to a "devil's stone" falling from the sky in 1880. The girls also find in the big cave, where they sometimes play, another diary that their great-great-great-aunts left, which Leigh especially finds interesting. As the days pass, other mysterious happenings occur. While Leigh is certain the answer to their difficulties lies in the diaries and ponders them, painstakingly deciphering the old-fashioned handwriting, Emma seeks a natural explanation. She cajoles and bullies Leigh into accompanying her to the ridge, where the girls are caught in a sudden, violent rainstorm and take shelter in the big cave. An earthquake dislodges boulders that seal them into the darkness. While the Tregarrens organize a search, Emma finds Leigh unconscious in the dark and manages to rouse her. As tremors continue to shake the cave, a girl they recognize as Lauralei appears, a happy, laughing child dressed in old-fashioned clothes and surrounded by light. Beckoning to them to follow her, she takes them through a narrow, winding tunnel gradually upward until they arrive safely in the Crow's Nest on the peak. Emma and Leigh clamber out into the morning, and just before they rejoin their anxious family, Leigh sees a vision of two red-haired girls seated on a bullock wagon, one of whom raises her arm to wave at them. Questions linger in the reader's mind. What is the significance of the devil's stone? If Lauralei can lead the modern girls to safety in the Crow's Nest, why could she not have escaped the same way in her own time? Would not the black man who found Emma Rose have known of the connecting tunnel and brought Lauralei out, too? How did she die? Why should these modern troubles suddenly begin in 1982? In spite of these and other plot problems and the book's clumsy structure, suspense is high, increasing steadily throughout, and the climax is very tense. The two sets of twin girls are interesting and likeable, and Ma Tregarren, the pioneer mother, is an unusually well-drawn figure. The historical parts are filled with local color and fascinating details of Australian settlement life and are clearly the book's best features. The members of the pioneer family speak in Cornish and Irish dialect, which adds to the sense of time and place and helps to distinguish them from the modern family. Aust. Bk. of Year Winner.

DEVLIN, ABRAHAM (*The True Story of Lilli Stubeck**), reporter for *The Sentinel* in St. Helen with whom Lilli Stubeck runs off after Miss* Dalgleish dies. Kit* Quayle describes him as "something of a [physical] freak" and an object of town ridicule. He is a Utopian preacher who often puts his little wooden box on the pavement outside the photography shop where Lilli works for a while. Devlin moves in and helps care for Mrs.* Stubeck and Jackie*.

DIANA BARRY (*Anne of Green Gables**), daughter of a farmer. While Diana's imagination is not as keen as Anne* Shirley's imagination and she is not as daring and outgoing as Anne, Diana also loves adventures and make-believe games. Diana's parents decide not to send her to Queen's Academy for advanced schooling, and the year Anne spends there is their first extended time apart. Anne's deep friendship with Diana is one of the book's strongest points. Their conversations seem genuine, and their imaginative play and closeness to the near exclusion of other friendships seem typical of their age, the circumstances, and the characters as presented.

DIDO MAY (*The Catalogue of the Universe**), mother of illegitimate Angela May. Dido concocted the romantic tale about her ill-fated love affair with Angela's father because, when she was in the hospital having Angela, the attendants told her it is important for children to feel loved and wanted. When Roland Chase, Angela's father, learned that Dido was pregnant, his family shipped him off to Australia, and his mother, Mrs.* Angela Chase, gave Dido money for an abortion. Dido used the money for things for Angela and then supported herself and Angela by working in a variety of low-paying jobs, gradually accumulating enough money to buy the rustic house they now occupy and to enroll at the university. Although unconventional in her way of life, Dido has made the best of the situation. She is sturdy, calm, and reasonable and has raised Angela with love and good sense. She is one of several contrasting women in the novel.

DINGO (*Boori**; *Darkness under the Hills**), spirit chief of the dingo people, a shape-changer who appears most often as a big yellow dog but also in his man shape. He is cunning, tireless, and brave, and he often tempts humans to try to catch him, taunting them when they fail. In a duel, Boori, though badly wounded, manages to pin one of Dingo's feet to the ground and so compels him to listen and, by talking respectfully, gains his aid. Dingo soon becomes an enthusiastic follower of Boori, appearing sometimes as a dog, sometimes as a man in their later adventures. In *Darkness under the Hills* Dingo is Boori's constant companion and frequently by his special senses makes the difference between success and failure. Boori chooses to go to the campfires of the sky partly so that he can join Dingo there.

DINNY O'BRIEN (*Lillipilly Hill**), tough little village girl who drops out of a tree, almost onto Harriet Wilmot, on whom she has been spying out of curiosity. Dinny later befriends Harriet when the Wilmot children start school at Barley Creek. Dinny is the oldest of a large family of O'Brien children, whose father works five miles away in the sawmill and whose cheerful mother keeps haphazard house on very little income. Practical, hardworking, unsentimental Dinny is a foil for Harriet in the way she is raised, but they share a spunky attitude and a spirit of adventure.

DINO BAZOS (*Always Ask for a Transfer**), elderly Greek immigrant, foster father and owner of a pizza shop. Dino is a supportive and loving husband, conservative, hardworking, and traditional in his views about the roles of men and women. Although a type figure and sentimentalized, he suits the plot, and his becoming less chauvinistic seems reasonable.

DISPLACED PERSON (Harding*, Lee, Hyland House, 1979; *Misplaced Persons*, Harper, 1979), science fiction fantasy set in Melbourne, Australia, in the late twentieth century, involving a nightmarish experience that a teenager shares with a girl about his age and an older man. Told in the first person, presumably on two tapes of a compact cassette recorder, by Graeme Drury, 17, the story starts when he realizes that people are beginning to ignore his presence, as if they cannot see or hear him. At first he can make himself noticed by shouting or touching the person, but gradually that power disappears as also color and sound are disappearing from the world around him. His own parents do not seem to notice him, nor does his girl friend, though he sleeps on the bed with her and watches her dress. Terrified, Graeme tries traveling, but the greyness seems to be everywhere. Food has become tasteless and sensations like cold and heat do not affect him. Gradually he loses tactile contact with the world around him, as if a viscous substance he calls "the interface" prevents him from touching anything directly. When he hears a recorder playing "Greensleeves," he eagerly follows the sound and discovers a shabbily dressed man, perhaps sixty, Jamie Burns, who takes him to a derelict house that, like Jamie, retains its color and odors. There Graeme meets Marion*, a girl Jamie found sobbing hysterically and has sustained by scrounging for things that have "come through," as they say, and can be recognized by their color and other sensory properties, like the old house and occasional cans, bottles, and other food items in the supermarkets and shops they haunt. Their biggest problem is having no water. Marion discovers and shows Graeme a small rock pool that has come through at the edge of the sea. Although it is not deep enough for swimming, they wash and Graeme wades. They return to the house to find Jamie, who was once a university music teacher but became an alcoholic, very upset because the bottle of Drambuie that he had been saving has disappeared. Later Jamie complains of the dark moving in around him and a feeling of something stirring outside, and the next morning he is gone. When they try to return to the pool, they realize that it, too, is gone. That night Marion feels the dark approaching her, and she and Graeme try to ward it off by talking and singing into a compact tape recorder that they have found. Marion tells him about her past, and they sleep in each other's arms in front of the fire, using the last of their small supply of wood, but in the morning Graeme wakes to find himself alone. As he tells the story into the tape recorder, he feels and sees the dark crowding in around him. He gives Jamie's explanation for their experience: the world is run not by a benevolent god, but by some bureaucratic force as an experiment, and occasionally when some cosmic filing clerk makes an error or misplaces someone or something, that person or thing falls into Limbo, as they call their condition. The last chapter is told by Graeme, who has found himself back in his own house having completely forgotten his experience. Little or no time seems to have passed during the days he thought he was gone. He has found, however, a cassette tape recorder in his pocket and listened to the astonishing story in his own voice, with a scrap of a song sung by him and a girl. He has also found a faded rose and a piece of paper saying, "Marion. Remember me." A tone of mounting horror keeps the story seeming plausible despite some rather undefined concepts. The characters are more than stock figures: Jamie has quirks and failings that make him more than the stereotypical keeper who aids the young; Marion has a spiky personality that only partly hides her fear. The romance that develops under these strange conditions is restrained and believable, and it keeps the novel from seeming as monochromatic as Limbo is. Aust. Bk. of Year Winner.

DOCTOR WITH WINGS (Aldous*, Allan, ill. Roger Payne, Brockhampton, 1960; Criterion, 1961), realistic novel of the Australian Flying Doctor Service, based in Alice Springs, Northern Territory, in the mid-twentieth century. When David Locke, 16, first arrives at "The Alice," he can see nothing attractive in the sprawling, raw looking community so different from his native Edinburgh, and, with all the young people away at boarding school, he is lonely. His father, however, is enthusiastic about his new job in the medical group that services by air the widely separated cattle stations and missions. On a drive his family picks up a boy about David's age, a surly kid with a "slum accent" who seems secretive about why he is alone on the road without even a water bottle, a condition that could lead to certain death in the arid climate. He gives his name as Bert Wilson from Melbourne and is annoyed when Dr. Locke reports him to Tom Bigsby, the local constable. Although not sure he likes Bert, David hangs around and helps at the garage where Tom gets the boy a job and becomes rather unwillingly his confidante, learning that Bert's real name is Kiddle, that he was involved with two other boys in stealing and wrecking a car, and ran away when he saw a policeman talking to his brutal father. His ambition is to get a job at a cattle station and learn to ride horses and "all that." David gets a chance to accompany his father in the little airplane that makes emergency flights and helps get a badly injured man into a body splint and onto the aircraft. The station owner, Andy Mackay, suggests that David stay over a week, since Mackay will be driving into Alice Springs then and can bring him home. At first David is fascinated with all he sees, but his enthusiasm wanes when he learns from the radio conversations, which are a major part of the ranch life, that Bert has been traced and has hitchhiked out of Alice Springs on a truck, stolen the driver's rifle, and headed out alone, evidently not too far from where David is. That night, sleeping on the screened veranda, he hears someone outside and discovers Bert, who threatens him with the gun, thinking that David has betrayed him, then insists that David come with him and carry the water and food he has stolen. Although a newcomer in the area, David has a better idea than the Melbourne slum boy of how impossible is his plan to cut across country to the Barkly Highway, some hundred miles over rough terrain in searing heat, but Bert refuses to listen to reason and threatens to shoot him if he raises the alarm. They walk all night, and before midday David gives out, exhausted, with blistered feet. Bert divides the water and food and goes on alone. After a long rest, David starts to walk back and is discovered by Tom Bigsby in his Land Rover. Tom leaves him to wait for Mackay, who is coming with horses, while he goes on to try to follow Bert. With David on an extra horse, he and Mackay come up to the Land Rover. It is mired deep in sand and Tom is bleeding from a rifle shot in the shoulder, with Bert sitting beside him, shading him with a branch. Mackay won't listen to his explanation that he did not shoot Tom, but since the man obviously needs medical attention he sends David riding back the twenty-five miles to the station while they dig out the vehicle. Unused to riding, David falls off some three miles from the station and staggers on, finally collapsing within sight of the buildings, barely able to get his message across before the radio switches off for the day. When he wakes, his father has arrived and operated on Tom, who is able to confirm Bert's story that the gun went off by accident. Mackay offers Bert a job. The plot is really a vehicle to tell about the history and operation of the Flying Doctor Service, which is a lifeline for most of the isolated settlements in the huge, nearly empty area. Dialogue is inclined to be static, with long speeches about the area and the traditions of the territory, and the characters are underdeveloped and predictable. The setting, however, is well realized; a reader gets a feeling for the heat, the vast, nearly arid stretches, and the strange beauty of the place. Aust. Bk. of Year Com.

A DOG CALLED GEORGE (Balderson*, Margaret, ill. Nikki Jones, Oxford, 1975), animal story of an Old English sheep dog that attaches itself to a boy in Canberra, Australia, in the 1970s and is the catalyst for marked improvements in his life. Bespectacled Tony Brent, 10, is the despair of his teacher, Dillweed (Mr. Dill), butt of his classmates' jibes and humor, and a concern for his parents. He seems unable to get to school on time, incapable of concentrating on schoolwork, uninterested in improving his limited reading ability, and fascinated only by airplanes and models of aircraft, which he builds with skill. He insists on taking the long route to school along the bypass, a wide strip between the backs of houses and cow pastures set aside for a highway extension, which he calls the runway where he can zoom along, pretending he is a Spitfire shooting down Messerschmitts over France. There one foggy morning, he runs into a large, furry dog, white in front with a black rump, which follows him to school with embarrassing results and is waiting for him when he walks home. His mother, an understanding woman, points out that this is a well-kept dog of an expensive breed, not a stray mutt, and that, while he can keep it until they can locate its owner, he mustn't get too attached to the animal. Nevertheless, Tony is jealous when the dog pays attention to his brothers and sister, and he scornfully rejects their suggestions that it be named Fluffyfeet or Mop or Powder-puff, insisting that the dog's name is George. His mother prevails over the objections of his father, who is taking night classes and has little time for his son, but she firmly sees that Tony take responsibility for the dog, cleaning him up, feeding him, and taking him for a walk on the runway after school each day. George is a natural ham, playfully extroverted. Tony, who has always been solitary, surprisingly finds himself drawn into conversations with a wide variety of people who stop to admire the dog. The mother of a sick schoolmate persuades him to bring George to see her bedridden son, and Tony makes his first real friend his age. After some weeks they discover that George belongs to an old man who is in the hospital with a heart attack. Reluctantly Tony visits to tell him that George is all right and finds a lively, bearded fellow named Hob* (Mr. Hobson), bored with confinement. When Hob is finally able to pick up George, Tony is crushed that the dog is wildly excited to see his master again, and he rejects the gift Hob brings him of a brick of clay. Eventually, out of loneliness and curiosity, Tony goes to Hob's house and is greeted enthusiastically by George. Hob, who is a potter, lets Tony putter in his workshop and after a few days proposes a deal: if Tony will take George out for exercise, Hob will teach the boy to make things of clay, and they will share the dog, half and half. By the end, Tony has found friends, has a new interest at which he is skillful, has an improved relationship with his father, and realizes that half of a dog like George, friendly to all and undemanding, is better for him than the devoted, well-trained, one-man dog he once desired. Tony changes predictably but believably. The story is conventional in plot but written with humor and sharp observation of character. There are some very funny scenes, in particular when George visits the classroom and when Tony takes him to obedience school. The parents, especially Tony's mother, are well-drawn, interesting characters. Aust. Bk. of Year Highly Com.

THE DOLL (Taylor*, Cora, Western Producer Prairie Books, 1987), fantasy
of a Canadian ten year old who, through the intermediation of a doll, returns to
the time of her great-great-grandmother's journey with her family to a homestead
near Fort Carlton, north of Saskatoon, Saskatchewan. Meg, recovering from
rheumatic fever at the home of her grandmother, Grace Cameron, sleeps with
the "Invalid Doll," Jessie, a china-headed antique that has been passed down
through the family from her great-great-grandmother and is kept carefully in the
cedar chest except when one of the children is ill. One night, she finds herself
crossing the prairie as part of a pioneer family consisting of the parents, two
older brothers, serious Archy and teasing Geordie, and a younger sister, Lizzie,
not yet three. Meg herself is Morag, a ten-year-old who has been ill from a fever
on the trip and is still weak. At first Meg thinks she has been dreaming of a
strange camping trip, but when night after night she slips back into the past she
comes to accept and even welcome her place in the Shearer family, since in her
present-day life her parents are contemplating divorce, a fact that they do not
realize she knows. As Morag she helps gather eggs from the hens they have
brought in crates, quiets and leads the cow, Evangeline, who has just dropped
a calf, names the new heifer Buttercup, minds her little sister, crosses the South
Saskatchewan River on a flat ferry, picks saskatoons, and makes scones with
the berries, substituting pebbles in the ones for teasing Geordie. In more dramatic
episodes she rescues Lizzie from a badger and from a prairie fire. This last occurs
when the family is within a few miles of Fort Carlton. Seeing the fire advancing,
the boys herd the cattle into a boggy area while Mother madly drives the Red
River cart on ahead and Father puts both girls in the back of the wagon and
whips the oxen toward the fort, which is protected by a wide plowed firebreak.
The jolting knocks Morag's precious doll out of the back, and Lizzie either falls
or jumps out to retrieve it. Morag leaps out to rescue her. Intent on reaching
the fort, neither parent notices the incident. Knowing she cannot beat the fire to
the plowed strip, especially with Lizzie in tow, Morag heads for a ravine, which
fortunately has some muddy water at the bottom, where the girls lie with mois-
tened strips of Morag's petticoat covering their faces. The fire passes over and
a heavy rain follows. In the darkness Morag does not dare leave the ravine, but
she shelters Lizzie as best she can against a large rock that retains heat from the
sun and fire. Her fever returns, warming the toddler. The next morning rescuers
discover the girls from Lizzie's wailing, but Morag is unconscious. Geordie
finds Jessie and tucks the doll in beside Morag on the cot at the fort, and they
exchange fond insults in Morag's brief conscious moments. In present-day life
Meg looks through family albums with her grandmother, who remarks that Meg
looks just like Morag in the photograph taken before the family started west.
She learns that Lizzie was her grandmother's grandmother and was the owner
of the doll, Morag having died of a recurrence of rheumatic fever before the
family reached their homestead. Meg also finds that she can face her parents'
separation and continue loving both of them. Just how the experience with the
pioneer family makes this adjustment to reality possible is not clear, and the

conclusion seems forced. Individual scenes, however, are strong, particularly of the pioneer period where they give a sense of the physical setting. The fantasy element is strengthened by the reaction of the grandmother's cat, which hisses and bristles at the Invalid Doll until the end, when Morag is dead, after which he curls up happily on the bed between Meg and Jessie. Can. Ruth Schwartz.

DOROTHY MALONE (*The True Story of Lilli Stubeck**), Lilli Stubeck's only close girl friend in St. Helen, daughter of the local car dealer. The two girls have a long and satisfying relationship, starting when Lilli first comes to school and is Dorothy's seatmate. Characteristically, Lilli accepts her help of school supplies but expresses no thanks. She seems to feel that all such gifts are her due. A sweet, gentle girl, Dorothy eventually becomes a nun. She tells Kit* Quayle some of the things he puts in his story about Lilli.

DOUGLAS MARINER (*The October Child**), youth who loyally pitches in to help with his autistic younger brother, Carl. Douglas wants to become a music teacher, like Daniel Mead, the young music instructor whose normal baby, Chantal, just Carl's age, serves as an effective contrast to Carl. Douglas enrolls at Daniel's music school, where he receives not only instruction but also moral support. Douglas is sometimes angry about Carl, and sometimes he feels overwhelmed and neglected because of Carl, but he is mature for his age and adjusts to Carl's demands better than do his siblings. He is the only developed figure in the novel.

DOVEY TALLISKER (*Playing Beatie Bow**), Dorcas, kindhearted, sweettempered, self-effacing, lame girl, who takes care of Abby Kirk while Abby recovers from the blow on the head she suffers when Samuel* Bow knocks her down during one of his "spells." Dovey becomes Abby's friend, tells her about the family Gift*, and marries Judah Bow. Abby sees their wedding in a vision after she returns to modern Sydney. Judah later dies at sea, and Dovey, the child of Dovey and Judah, and Granny* Tallisker all die of smallpox. Dovey's nickname aptly describes her character.

DOYLE, BRIAN (1935–), born in Ottawa, Canada; journalist, teacher, and writer of amusing contemporary sociological problem novels for teenaged readers. He earned a degree in journalism from Carleton University, worked for some years for the Toronto *Telegram*, then returned to Carleton for a B.A. in English. He taught English in high school and served as chair of the English Department at Glebe Collegiate in Ottawa, the school he himself had attended. His first novel, *Hey, Dad!* (Groundwood/Douglas, 1978), developed from notes he and his daughter recorded during a family trip. More about the same characters appear in *You Can Pick Me Up at Peggy's Cove* (Groundwood/Douglas, 1979). While critics deplore his loose plotting and use of contrivance, they praise his effective first-person narration, rich characterizations, fresh dialogue, highly engaging tone, wit, and deft touch with comic and slapstick humor, which both relieves and supports the very serious themes, such as the transience of time and religious intolerance. His third novel, *Up to Low** (Groundwood/Douglas, 1982), ranked as one of his best, was Book of the Year of the Canadian Library Association. It uses the journey structure both symbolically and literally to convey the important themes of maturation and joy of life. Its companion, a "prequel" according to Doyle, *Angel Square** (Groundwood/Douglas, 1984; Bradbury, 1986), received Honorable Mention from the Canada Council. Amusing and lively, it confronts the social and humanistic problems of ethnic prejudice within the framework of a boy's growing-up story. Both books are based on his memories of his own childhood and project an effective nostalgic tone. *Easy Avenue* (Groundwood/Douglas, 1988) is about a high school boy torn between loyalty to his friends and the desire to belong to a "better set."

DR. BUTLER (*Come Danger, Come Darkness**), young surgeon (physician) at the Norfolk Island penal colony. Dr. Butler opposes the harsh policies of his superior, Dr. Fitch, toward the convicts, insisting that they be treated humanely, that they suffer from scurvy because of their inadequate diet, and that Cousin* Flora, Major Cannon's daughter, needs greens, too. When Major Cannon discovers that Dr. Butler is noble, the heir to an earldom in England, he thinks better of the young surgeon, of medicine as a vocation, and of Otter's ambition to become a doctor. He then listens to Dr. Butler's urgings to allow the boy to pursue a medical career.

THE DRUID'S TUNE (Melling*, O. R., Kestrel, 1983; Penguin, 1984), fantasy novel of time travel and adventure that improvises on the "Tain Bo Cuailnge," the Irish national epic also known as "The Cattle-Raid of Cooley." Two modern-day siblings from Toronto, Canada, Rosemary, 17, and James, 15, Redding, are sent for the summer to the home of their mother's brother, Patsy Donovan, a farmer in Ballinamore, Northern Ireland. They are immediately intrigued by the peculiar behavior of Peter* Murphy, 21, the aloof, gray-eyed farmhand who plays and sings a haunting tune on a mandolin. One night shortly after they arrive, they follow Peter to Lake Drumoor in the hills overlooking their uncle's farm and observe him in a strange ritual. They fall asleep and awaken to find themselves in ancient Connaught, where they encounter a contingent of cavalry under the command of young Maine, one of Queen Maeve's seven sons. Maine is immediately attracted to Rosemary, who returns his interest, and ushers them to his mother's encampment. The children discover that Peter is a priest of the ancient order of Druids and is known to the Connaughtmen as Peadur Murrich. They also learn that Maeve and her husband, King Ailill, are preparing to attack Ulster for the Ulstermen's greatest prize, the Brown Bull of Cuailnge, to match a mighty one they already possess, Finnbennach the White. While Rosemary becomes friends with Finnebar, Maine's lively and congenial sister, and the romance between Rosemary and Maine quickens, Jim is assigned to Fergus mac

Roich, a dissident Ulsterman in service to Maeve. Fergus trains Jim to fight and to drive his chariot. As the huge army moves slowly eastward, it is harried by Cuculann*, Ulster's greatest companion, the other Ulstermen having been rendered powerless to fight by an old enchantment. One day Jim encounters Cuculann, is impressed by the sturdy, solitary youth so outnumbered in his defense of his country, and joins him. Most of the rest of the novel revolves around Cuculann's exploits in resisting the invaders. Days pass as he meets and defeats in hard-fought single combat several of Maeve's mightiest champions. Matters come to a head when Rosemary is accused of treachery because Jim has joined Cuculann and is tied to a pillar while the hero and Maeve's men battle around her, Cuculann in his characteristic, unrestrained battle frenzy. Peter intervenes just before the hero slays her, the madness rendering him incapable of distinguishing friend from foe, and Rosemary, Jim, and Peter are returned to the Donovan farm. When they have been home about a week, they decide to go back to Ulster with Peter. They arrive to find Cuculann dying of wounds, absorb his pain, and thus save his life. Rosemary and Jim then join the youth troop of Ulster, a little army made up of children, which is soon annihilated by Maeve's forces, but Rosemary's and Jim's lives are spared. Rosemary becomes Cuculann's charioteer and Jim his fighting companion. They witness the terrible single-combat battle in which he slays Ferdia, his best friend, whom the devious Maeve has incited against the hero. After a homecoming feast at Dun Dealga, Cuculann's house, Peter transforms the children into ravens with a spell. In that form flying high in the air above Ulster, they witness the great struggle on the Plain of Meath between the two armies and between the Brown Bull and the White Bull, which ironically slay each other. Some time later in modern Ireland, the two again discover Peter by Lake Drumoor, radiant and surrounded by a "faint music." He says he is now a Harper, evidently having acquired the peace and position he had been seeking, and in the lake he shows them a panorama of "countless worlds and races" tied together by similar needs and emotions, among them Maine pining for Rosemary and Cuculann bound to a great stone in his death agony. The images fade, and Peter disappears, leaving the children standing alone, mystified yet curiously satisfied. The plot occasionally violates logic. For instance, reason dictates that the newly arrived children be terrified when confronted by Maine's war party, yet Rosemary responds immediately to his blandishments. The apparent themes are several: one finds one's self in helping others, past and present are inextricably bound together, war is wasteful and futile, growing up brings problems—these seem both obvious and ironically anomalous. Peter's mystical search for self is labored, and the plot seems overly complicated. Involving youths from the present in past dilemmas is a convenient device for helping modern readers to identify with the protagonists but creates other narrative problems. For example, Jim becomes adept with weapons and chariot much too quickly. The novel does, however, show the importance of war as a sport and the value placed upon honor in that early period. Irish legends told by various characters explain events and contribute depth. Scenes stand out:

Cuculann and Jim play a kind of chess involving poetry making, an incident that becomes amusing when Jim relates a scurrilous modern verse that tickles Cuculann's funnybone, and Maine and Rosemary leap over the fire in a fertility ritual at the festival of the full moon. Maeve is appropriately blowsy and arrogant, Maine is a handsome lover and sturdy fighter, Rosemary and Jim mature predictably, Peter remains too obscure and distant for sympathy, and Cuculann is the most interesting figure. Can. Young Adult Winner.

DUDER, TESSA, New Zealand novelist, whose own experiences inspire her writing. A pianist, her music and her musical family provided the material for *Jellybean** (Oxford, 1985; Viking, 1986), about a girl whose mother, a world renowned cellist, has little time for her and who wants to become a conductor. It appears on the New Zealand Government Short List of books of the year. A championship swimmer, Duder's own competitions gave her background, characters, and episodes for *Alex** (Oxford, 1987; *In Lane Three, Alex Archer*, Houghton, 1989), in which a fifteen-year-old girl competes for a place on the New Zealand swim team for the 1960 Olympic Games in Rome. Duder set records for the butterfly and medley and also won a silver medal at the 1958 British Empire Games. *Alex* was New Zealand Children's Book of the Year and won the Esther Glen Medal. *Night Race to Kawau** (Oxford, 1982), a dramatic sailing adventure story, was also named to the New Zealand Government Short List for its year. A former reporter and now a full-time writer, she has lived in Pakistan and London and makes her home in Auckland.

DUGGAN, MAURICE (NOEL) (1922–1974), born in Auckland, New Zealand; advertising writer, author of short stories for both adults and children. He was educated at the University of Auckland and worked at a large variety of factory and clerical jobs, proofreading and book reviewing, before working in advertising. Only two of his books were published for children, *The Fabulous McFanes and Other Children's Stories* (Cape Catley, 1974) and *Falter Tom and the Water Boy** (Paul, 1957; Faber, 1958; Criterion, 1958), a charming brief fantasy about an old sailor's adventures under the sea with the "water boy," a sort of eternal child spirit of the ocean. It won the New Zealand Esther Glen Award. Duggan also wrote five books of short stories for adults, among them the posthumously published *Collected Stories*, edited by C. K. Stead (Auckland, 1981).

DUNHAM, (BERTHA) MABEL (1881–1957), born in Harrison, Ontario, Canada; teacher, librarian, and writer of novels and non-fiction. Her reputation in children's literature rests on her one book for young readers, *Kristli's Trees** (McClelland, 1948), which was named Book of the Year by the Canadian Library Association. A quietly amusing, episodic novel of Mennonite family life, it tells of the everyday problems and simple adventures of an earnest, mischievous, little boy growing up in a small, isolated, tightly cohesive community. Dunham attended school in Berlin (now Kitchener), Ontario, taught school from 1898 to

1904, received her B.A. from Victoria College at the University of Toronto in 1908, earned her degree in library science from McGill University, and joined the Berlin Public Library, which she served as director from 1908 to 1944. She also lectured in library science at Waterloo College (now the University of Waterloo), Ontario, from 1932 to 1945. Her novels for adults, which include *The Trail of the Conestoga* (Macmillan, 1924), *Toward Sodom* (Macmillan, 1927), and *The Trail of the King's Men* (Ryerson, 1931), and her non-fiction works revolve around the emigration of pro-British Mennonites from Pennsylvania to the Waterloo area as a result of the American Revolution and draw upon her own family records.

DUSTY MEREWETHER (*Pastures of the Blue Crane**), Ryl* Merewether's grandfather, a crusty, opinionated, seedy man, who grudgingly puts up with his granddaughter's efforts to remake Geebin Farm. Dusty had had a falling out with his son, Ryl's father, over the son's marriage during World War II to a part South Sea Island girl and was unaware of Ryl's existence until the reading of his deceased son's will. An interesting figure who changes believably as a result of his experiences with Ryl and the people of the region, Dusty becomes more likeable as the story progresses.

DUTTA (DATTA), ARUP KUMAR (1946–), born in Jorhat, Assam, India; teacher, journalist, and novelist for adults and children. After acquiring a university education, he taught English in a college in Jorhat for more than fifteen years before becoming a full-time writer. He has received three awards in the Children's Book Trust of India competitions. *The Kaziranga Trail** (CBT, India, 1979; as Datta), an exciting detective story in which three resourceful schoolboys bring a ring of rhinoceros poachers to justice, won first prize. He received second price for *Trouble at Kolongijan** (CBT, India, 1982), in which villagers foil a plot to destroy their dike, and for *The Blind Witness** (CBT, India, 1983), in which a blind boy helps police capture an international smuggling ring. *The Kaziranga Trail* was filmed as *Rhino* and translated into several languages. In addition to short stories and serializations, his publications for young readers include *The Lure of Zangrila* and *Revenge* (both CBT, India, 1986) and *The Poisoned Pool* (Ratna, 1990), a sequel to *The Kaziranga Trail*, about fish poaching. His books have been praised for their authenticity and careful attention to details of time and place, as well as for their action-filled plots.

E

EDIE WATERS (*The Nargun and the Stars**), Australian farm woman who is "stout on top, with skinny legs," and has a creamy complexion and quick, gray eyes. Both she and her brother, Charlie* Waters, are nervous about having orphaned Simon Brent come to live with them, and Edie tries too hard at first to make Simon feel comfortable. She gradually grows to understand the boy, and he to understand and appreciate her, particularly through their mutual efforts to save Wongadilla from the Nargun*. She is an attractive, well-drawn figure with a personality all her own.

EDWIN TRUELANCE (*Longtime Passing**; *Once there was a Swagman**), dutiful father of Mark*, Patsy*, Boo, and Teddy* and loving husband of Letty*. A long, lean man, intellectually and physically active, Edwin is somewhat impractical yet resilient and persistent enough to overcome his problems. Edwin is the most interesting figure in *Longtime Passing*, a complex, vital man, of greater depth than reported. Undeveloped, for example, is his inability to communicate with Mark. Edwin appears briefly at the beginning of *Once there was a Swagman*, as he leaves to peddle a new kind of kerosene lamp called the Eladdin.

EKWENSI, CYPRIAN (ODIATU DUAKA) (1921–), born in Minna, Nigeria; pharmacist, broadcaster and publisher, chemist, novelist, short story writer. He attended Achimota College, Ghana, and Ibadan University, then did further study at Chelsea School of Pharmacy, London, and the University of Iowa. His varied and distinguished career has included college teaching in both chemistry and pharmacology, broadcasting for both the Nigerian Broadcasting Corporation and for an independent Biafran radio station, serving his country in the Federal Ministry of Information, the Bureau of External Publicity, and as consultant to the executive office of the president. He has also been managing director of two different publishing companies. Most of his novels and short stories for adults are set in modern Nigeria, the best known being *People of the City* (Dakers,

1954; revised, Heinemann, 1963), a story of a crime reporter who succumbs to the evils of city life in modern Lagos. For young people he has published more than a dozen books, the first being *Ikolo the Wrestler and Other Ibo Tales* (Thomas Nelson, 1947). Two feature an adventurous Nigerian boy, *Samankwe in the Strange Forest* (Longman, 1973) and *Samankwe and the Highway Robbers** (Evans, 1975), which won the Children's Literature of Nigeria first prize. Both are fast-paced action stories for beginning readers of English. He has also written plays and scripts for radio and television, and stories and articles for a number of African and British magazines. In 1969 he won the Dag Hammarskjold International Prize for Literary Merit.

ELDEST NARGUN (*The Ice Is Coming**), a monster of rock that lives off the Victoria coast in southern Australia. In early times it defeated ice-spirits known as Ninya and drove them northward. From Ko-in*, the man of the mountain, Wirrun learns that "Narguns are born from the fire deep in the earth, and because this is the Eldest it has the power of First Things." Since it can call up fire, it is a particularly powerful enemy of the Ninya. The People (Aborigines) also avoid it because from time to time it crushes and eats one of them. The Eldest Nargun is held in much awe.

ELEANOR, ELIZABETH (Gleeson*, Libby, Angus, 1984; Holiday, 1990), sociological problem novel set in Australia one hot, dry spring in 1960, in which entries in her grandmother's diary facilitate a young girl's adjustment to a new home and school. The story begins *in medias res*. The Wheeler family is moving from an unspecified city to the farm in the bush where Mum grew up. Eleanor, 12, from whose perspective events are seen although she does not tell the story, is particularly apprehensive about the move. Her brothers, Ken, 13, and Bill, 6, find plenty about the new place to occupy their time and fit in right away at school. Eleanor's first day at school is rotten: she finds the girls unfriendly and the teacher's voice strident, and a bully, Danny Stewart, grinds her hand into the playground grass. She resists settling-in activities at home, though comments about relatives who lived in the old house do occasionally pique her curiosity. Life becomes more interesting when she discovers the old, boarded-up schoolhouse out in back that her grandmother, Elizabeth Walters, and her siblings attended. Poking about, Eleanor finds in an old chest a carefully wrapped packet containing the diary Elizabeth received from her grandmother on her thirteenth birthday in September, 1895, sixty-five years earlier. Eleanor reads it avidly, every chance she has. She is especially intrigued by two items; Elizabeth's "special place," a cave about a half hour's walk away from the farmhouse by the creek, and Elizabeth's growing attachment to Edward Walters, her handsome, fifteen-year-old cousin. By the creek one day with Mum, Eleanor thinks she spots the special place, identifying it by landmarks Elizabeth has mentioned, but she keeps her suspicions to herself. Shortly thereafter, a bush fire breaks out while she, Ken, Bill, and a neighbor boy, Mike Turner, also thirteen, are fishing by the dam. Eleanor leads them along the creek to the cave, where the children hide the rest of the afternoon and all night while the fire rages. In there Eleanor stumbles upon what she realizes later is her grandmother's locket, a gift from Edward. While recovering from the ordeal, Eleanor reads more entries in the diary about Elizabeth and Edward. She discovers that, though Elizabeth dreaded going to a neighborhood party her mother insisted she attend, she had enjoyed herself thoroughly that night in Edward's company. To mark that occasion, Edward had given her the little silver locket. Eleanor tells Mum about the locket and diary. Mother and daughter are saddened when Mum pulls out from old family photos one they realize must be Edward. It shows a young soldier in uniform, and on the back appear two inscriptions: ''To Elizabeth, All my love, Edward. South Africa, 1900,'' and underneath that: ''Vale Edward James Walters (1880–1901).'' Edward apparently died in the Boer War. Eleanor returns to school the next day feeling a stronger sense of self-worth and is hailed as a heroine for saving the boys and herself from the fire. The girls rally around her and beat up Danny, and Eleanor knows she has been accepted. When she visits the old schoolroom after school, she finds a blank diary awaiting her, a gift from Mum inscribed ''for a new start.'' Though Elizabeth's diary is too polished in style, too detailed, and too carefully organized to be convincing as a diary, Eleanor's and Elizabeth's stories dovetail nicely, each supporting the other. The fire is a bit too convenient, though it has been foreshadowed by frequent mention of the hot, dry weather and the building of a firebreak, but it does contribute tension to what is otherwise a slow narrative. Except for the diary entries, which are interspersed throughout the main story, the narrative focuses tightly on Eleanor and includes only what she herself knows, hears, or thinks, giving the effect of first person. Because Eleanor is a child and looks at things as a child, there is another level of appreciation for the more experienced or astute reader. Since Eleanor herself does not seem to know, the reader never finds out where the Wheelers have been living or why they have moved to the farm. Sentences are short, often only fragments, and the reader must stay alert. Conversation is lively and typical, and the adults are sympathetically and believably drawn. Family relationships ring true, and the school scenes also seem typical if harsh. Descriptions of the bush carry a strong appreciation for the beauty of the region. Aust. Bk. of Year Highly Com.

ELEPHANT ROCK (Macdonald*, Caroline, Hodder, 1983), time-slip fantasy set in New Zealand, in which a 1980s girl experiences some of the scenes of her dying mother's youth. Twelve-year-old Ann has spent the last four years in an exciting whirl of travel throughout Europe and other parts of the world with her laughing, evidently carefree mother, also named Ann. Now they have returned to the New Zealand coastal village, to the same house in which her mother spent vacations when she was Ann's age, to await her death, evidently from cancer. Stella, a carping, disapproving distant cousin, has come to help out, and Grandad, mother's father, an understanding widower now married again, lives nearby, visits daily, and plans to take care of Ann after her mother dies. One day, escaping the sadness of the cottage, Ann walks near the Maori settlement by the river and meets a strange old woman, who seems to know her. While climbing the huge elephant-shaped rock that is partially submerged at high tide, Ann has the first of a series of strange experiences in which she sees the cottage as it was twenty years before and seems to be dressed in unfamiliar clothes and wearing her hair short, as her mother did at her age. She soon realizes that she is becoming, for short periods, her mother as an adolescent. Many of these times she is accompanied by Jenny, the Scotch terrior of her mother's youth. These experiences coincide with her mother's "bad turns," during which she seems to lose consciousness but wakes feeling better than she has for weeks, even able to talk a little again. Although they never actually discuss it, Ann thinks her mother also realizes that she is reliving some of her past in Ann's person. One night Ann, evidently her mother somewhat older, finds that she is sneaking out to meet a boy at the Surf Club dance. She realizes, thinking it over afterwards, that her mother is deliberately showing her Allan, her father, as an attractive boy, not the successful businessman who cared little for his family and now has a wife and baby in a second marriage. From Grandad she learns that the old woman was a local character, known as a fortune teller and healer, who would be well over one hundred years old if she were still alive. Still, Ann sets out to find her, hoping she may produce some cure for her mother. In her persona as the earlier Ann, she visits the old woman, only to be told to travel and do the other things she longs to do soon because she will not live long. When she runs home, rejecting that prediction, she finds that her mother has died a few minutes earlier. Because the experiences produce no miraculous healing, only short periods of slight improvement in the mother, the fantasy has a modest quality. Ann does, however, know her mother better by the end of the narrative and has at least a slight understanding of her father. The novel's strength lies in its evocation of Ann's distress at her mother's condition, her annoyance at bossy Stella, and her mixture of fear and excitement when time slips back twenty years. N. Z. Govt. Short List; N. Z. Esther Glen.

ELIZABETH KENDALL (*The Year of the Currawong**), named for Elizabeth I of England by her history professor father. Plump, unathletic, not good at any one thing like her brothers and sister, she is president of the Currawong Mine Preservation Society. She discovers that the local silver mine is rumored to hold a hidden treasure. She also makes friends with the neighbor Pat Vane, a young housewife who is a potter, and becomes interested in pottery, in particular in what might be done with the distinctive clay that lies near the mine. Thus she draws Pat into the plans for preserving the mine and developing community spirit. Elizabeth grows more self-assured as the novel progresses.

ELLA TRUELANCE (*Longtime Passing**), eldest daughter of Edwin* and Letty* Truelance, for whose health they move to the mountains when she is three. The fresh air and simple nourishing soups Letty feeds her (ironically, about all Letty knows how to cook) soon build her up, and she speaks for the first time in her life. Overjoyed, Edwin gets out his cornet and plays the Doxology, whose melody conveys his happiness and gratitude throughout the hills.

THE EMPEROR'S PANDA (Day*, David, ill. Eric Beddows, McClelland, 1986; Dodd, 1987), fantasy of the fairy-tale type. Dutiful, orphaned Kung the Fluteplayer lives a humble but satisfying life with his Uncle Latzu, who keeps sheep, in Sung Wu, a "slightly enchanted realm to be found along the legendary Silk Road of the West which led to the Imperial City" in ancient China. One day from the west appear three black-cloaked, armed, bejeweled travelers. They enlist Latzu's aid in carrying what they claim is an important message for the Emperor. When Latzu fails to return, Kung goes in search of him. On the way he meets Lord Beishung, the Master, or Great, Panda, who rules the Sleeping Bamboo forest and gives Kung a ring of invisibility, and Sheng, the Eagle Lord of the Dragon Pass, who informs him that the travelers are evil wizards. He tells Kung that the wizards used Latzu to secure a powerful white pearl from an Ice Dragon and then went on to the Imperial City, where they now plan to sell Latzu into slavery. In the Imperial City, Kung joins a troupe of traveling players who perform for the Emperor and attracts the attention of the princess, who helps Kung find and free Latzu. Then two more interlocking and even more formidable problems face Kung. The wizards secure the black pearl of great power by killing a Fire Dragon, and the Emperor promises his daughter in marriage to whoever brings him the Master Panda to add to his large collection of magical animals. Realizing that the wizards will try to use the pearl to capture Panda and gain control of the kingdom, Kung rushes to help his friend and is captured by the wizards, who use him to blackmail Panda into surrendering. Remembering Panda's advice to "overcome evil with reason, not with force," Kung uses his invisible ring to take the white pearl from the wizards. With it he breaks the power of the black pearl, and the pearls and the wizards disappear in a whirlwind. Surprisingly, Panda then volunteers to join the Emperor's zoo, thus enabling Kung to win the princess and succeed to the throne. The plot cleverly elaborates upon conventional folkloric material and moves at a fast pace with a swirl of activities that follow in rapid succession without much causal relationship but with so much action and intrinsic interest that one must read carefully to catch essential elements. Told stories interrupt the action and make the pace uneven but contribute important information and add to the sense of ancient times and significant events. Characters are stock or types, except for self-assured, decisive, all-wise Panda, who functions as the ageless force by which all things are set to rights. The tone is romantic and melodramatic, and there are occasional touches of humor, some situation comedy, and some wordplay ("Doing battle with the Panda is the worst thing in the world for wizards. . . . It's what the Yellow Emperor used to call *Panda-monium*"). Vivid descriptions of the countryside, the city, and the troupe in concrete terms ground the story in reality and offset the fairy-tale atmosphere, giving the story a legendary quality. The story offers an explanation for the dot and swirl Chinese Yin-Yang emblem, the two dots being the pearls and the lines representing comets from the great whirlwind. The numerous black-and-white illustrations are also romantic and stylized and make this a very attractive book. Can. Bk. of Year Runner-Up; Can. Council Hon. Ment.

THE EMPTY CHAIR. See *CORNER STORE*.

ERASMUS WATERMEDICINE (*Winners**), the big, stubby gap-toothed, weather-beaten Indian cowboy who helps Jordy adapt to life on the prairie and appreciate his cultural heritage. He makes the Hallman Cup Ride possible for Jordy. On the night before the race, he sleeps in the mare's stall and foils an attempt to drug the horse. He is a stereotypical figure but fits the story.

ERNIE RYAN (*Fire in the Stone**), son of a drifter who has been stranded on the Australian opal fields for five years. Though considered much like his father, Ernie has some of the strong will of his mother, who deserted the family some years before. He is also devoted to Willie* Winowie, his Aborigine friend, and fiercely resents the way these native people are forced to live.

EVANS (*The Racketty Street Gang**), Australian soldier who became friendly with Mr.* Smertzer, Anton's father, when Evans was a prisoner of war on Crete during the German occupation of that island during World War II. When Evans escaped from the prisoner-of-war camp through a tunnel the prisoners constructed, Mr. Smertzer had a chance to shoot Evans but didn't. Evans refuses to acknowledge he knows Smertzer when the two meet in the bank where Evans has taken a job as floor cleaner because he plans to rob the bank. Later, at the showdown in the tunnel, he does admit that he knows Smertzer and can testify that Smertzer is innocent of the war crimes of which he is accused. Evans is one of the more developed characters in the novel.

EVERS, L(EONARD) H(ERBERT) (1926–), Australian writer whose *The Racketty Street Gang** (Brockhampton, 1961), a boy's detective story set in a working-class section of Sydney, won the Australian Children's Book of the Year Award. His other novels include *Pattern of Conquest* (Currawong, 1954), *Long Under Darkness* (Currawong, 1957), and *Fall Among Thieves* (Currawong, 1968).

EVIE (*The House that was Eureka**), passive, unhappy modern teenager, who spends much of her time caring for her younger half-sisters and doing housework. She is constantly hectored by her stepfather, Ted, for not having a job. She realizes that she has caused much of the antagonism between herself and Ted, but not until she has had the terrifying experience of merging with Lizzie Cruise is she able to feel strong emotion and to make tentative peace offerings to her stepfather. As she shares the nightmarish time-slip experience with Noel* Cavendish, they are drawn together and in the epilogue they are close friends, with Evie working in a music store and Noel going to school but frequenting the store afterward to walk home with Evie.

THE EXQUISITE BALANCE (Sengupta*, Poile, ill. Mrinal Mitra, CBT, India, 1987), science fiction novel with mystery story aspects set in the 1980s in an urban apartment house complex called Phul Vihar in India. When a mysterious stranger speaking in a voice that "sounded like countless bells ringing" tells Mrs. Inder where she can find the forty rupees she thinks her maid has stolen, Subir, 13, and his friend Harish set out to learn his identity. They soon discover that he is a friend of a new tenant, Professor K, a renowned physicist, writer of science fiction, and authority on outer space. Unknown to the children, the mysterious man is Hru, a spaceman sent by his Elders to investigate conditions on earth. Since he has lost the small shiny stone that functions as his "travel bud," he cannot return to his own dimension. Also unknown to the children, the stone is in the possession of Suprabha, Subir's twin. She picked it up in the apartment house yard, where Hru lost it on arrival, just before she suffered a sprained ankle, which has confined her to her room. Then an acquaintance, jealous, spoiled Aparna, steals the stone, which she thinks is just a pretty bauble, and Hru's situation becomes extremely dangerous because he cannot tolerate earth's heat much longer. By deduction Suprabha learns that Aparna has the stone, and, Hru having cured her sprain, wrestles the bud away from Aparna, thus making it possible for Hru to return to his planet. Brief italicized introductions in Hru's words begin each chapter. The bulk of the story, however, is in omniscient third person, presenting both Suabir's and Suprabha's points of view. In addition to the mystery, which employs conventions of the genre, the book has another main interest, discrimination against girls. Suprabha's anger against her twin, who refuses to allow her to play his games, insisting they are too dangerous for girls, her mother's sympathy and description of faded hopes, and Hru's description of his non-sexist planet form a didactic sequence unskillfully melded with the problem of the stone. Subir's change of heart and decision to allow Suprabha to play football, for which she has longed, is awkwardly accomplished. The dialogue is bookish, and Indian terms and modes of expression are prevalent and provide much of the story's appeal. The plot moves fast, and there is always something happening to hold the reader's attention. The children are lively and, though types, suit the plot. CBT of India, Second Prize.

F

FALSE FACE (Katz*, Welwyn Wilton, Groundwood/Douglas, 1987; Mc-Elderry, 1988), fantasy novel of magic and the supernatural set for two weeks in the late twentieth century in a middle-class neighborhood in London, Ontario, Canada. Laney McIntyre, 13, has an uneasy relationship with her divorced, money-oriented mother, Alicia, who owns and operates an antique shop. Alicia, who was trained as an archaeologist, often disparages her ex-husband, archaeologist Dr. Ian McIntyre, complains that Laney is irresponsible and thoughtless, and seems to favor her witty, pretty, and popular older daughter, Rosemary, 16, perhaps because Laney resembles Ian. Trouble follows for the McIntyres after Laney's dog, Hambone, digs up Iroquois Indian artifacts in the bog that borders the marsh across the street. Tom* Walsh, a classmate whose Iroquois father is dead and who has an uneasy relationship with his white mother, takes the pipe Laney finds to the Indian museum, but Laney shows the miniature false face mask to Alicia. Alicia immediately recognizes its great value and insists on preserving it with chemicals and offering it for sale, even though she knows she is breaking the law. She also extracts a promise from Laney not to tell Ian. Tom finds another mask, a full-face one of the extremely powerful Iroquois god Gugawara, whose strength the miniature mask can temper. It also disappears. Laney soon discovers that she can use, at least to some extent, the mini-mask's power, when, in a moment of anger, she makes Rosemary sick to her stomach. She also has terrifying dreams involving Indian curing songs and dances. She suspects her mother may have the large mask when her mother's main competitor falls ill and closes his shop and Hambone, whom her mother dislikes, becomes sick. She investigates her mother's shop workroom, Tom secretly trailing her and spying, finds the mask, and almost succumbs to its angry power. Laney tries to warn her mother of the mask's capability for destruction, and her fears increase when she overhears a phone conversation that indicates that Alicia has decided not to sell the large mask. Laney and Tom go to Alicia's store in the middle of the night to tie the little mask to the large one in order to temper the large one's power, but things go awry. Bicycling home by herself, Laney is stopped by police who take her to her father. Ian discovers the mini-mask in her bag, and the story comes out. The showdown with Alicia occurs ironically on Halloween at the McIntyre home after Alicia, also ironically, brings the mask home from the store, even wearing it at the door like a treat-or-tricker. When Alicia tries to destroy Ian with the mask, Tom suggests that Laney will the ownership of the mini-mask to Alicia in order to diminish the large mask's strength. Laney does so, and Alicia breaks down and surrenders both masks to Dr. McIntyre. He gives them to Tom, who returns them to the bog. The book moves slowly while the author establishes the youths' somewhat parallel family situations and their growing friendship. The pace picks up and suspense tightens after the youngsters discover Alicia has the large mask and the mask begins to express its anger. The events are stereotypical, the climax and conclusion seem strained and rushed, Alicia is one-dimensional in her shallowness, greed, partiality toward Rosemary, and antipathy toward Laney, and Dr. McIntyre is too obviously her antithesis. Laney grows in self-confidence as expected, and Tom learns that as he has been suffering from the prejudice of his schoolmates so also he has been rejecting his mother because she is white. Best are the anthropological details about the masks and the legal and moral aspects involved in keeping them. Can. Ebel Winner; Can. Gov. General's Hon. Ment.; Can. Young Adult Runner-Up.

FALTER TOM AND THE WATER BOY (Duggan*, Maurice, ill. Kenneth Rowell, Paul's, 1958; Criterion, 1959), brief fantasy of a sailor who, in his old age, has a marvelous adventure under the sea. Called Falter Tom because of the way he walks with one stiff leg acquired in a whaling accident, he tells the village young people stories in his Irish brogue, of which they rightly believe only a small portion. Every day he walks in his halting way out to the promontory that forms one arm of the bay and stands staring out over the sea, with the salt wind in his face. One morning he climbs slowly down the steps cut into the cliff to the little patch of sand uncovered by the tide and sees what he thinks is one of the village lads. He calls that it is a dangerous place to swim and orders him to come in at once. He is answered by a bubbling laugh, and then he sees a green boy with copper-colored hair and slanted eyes lying in the shallows smiling up at him. He says he is a water boy who would drown in the air, and he persuades Falter Tom to put one leg into the water and to count to twenty, though the old man thinks it is a daft thing to do. When he draws his leg out, it is completely dry. The next day, Falter Tom walks in up to his neck and returns dry again. To be able to breathe under the water, the boy tells Falter Tom to bring a charm that is "part of a fish and a piece of gold kept all for luck" and to not eat or drink or speak to anyone after midnight. The old man discovers a fine gold chain attached to a whale's tooth set in gold stuck in the lining of his sea chest and remembers he once wore it for luck. After one unsuccessful try, Falter Tom is very careful to follow instructions, and coached by the boy, he leaves his cap on the rock, fastens the chain around his wrist, looks directly into the path of the sun, repeats the charm, and sinks backward under the water, breathing as he does so. To his surprise, it is quite easy. The boy laughs merrily to see Falter Tom try a slow breast stroke and shows him how to swim like a fish, directing him to "fall through the water," to "throw his head away" and dive after it with his body. With a little practice, Falter Tom learns to swim in this fashion, and they glide off like strong, quick fish. The boy tells him that he is not young, but old, perhaps as old as the sea itself, and the only one of his kind. He refers frequently to "them," the sea kings to whose cave they are headed. They pass ancient galleys, pierced for oars, fast sailing ships, and rusting tramp steamers lying on the bottom. At one wreck, Falter Tom gasps to see heaps of ancient coins, and scraping his hand across the bars of gold, he unknowingly loses his charm. Almost at once he has difficulty breathing. The boy drags him to the surface and then to a rock in the sea, where he leaves him, soaked to the skin and shaking with cold, while he tries to find the charm. Falter Tom has resigned himself to death when the boy finally returns with the charm and takes him to shallow water where he can warm himself again. When at last they come to the Cave of the Voices, the home of the sea kings, Falter Tom is commanded to make a choice: if he wishes to stay in the sea, he will continue forever, growing no older, but he can never go back to the land; if he wishes to return to land, the water boy will take him to his own bay, but he will forget his adventure and have no explanation for the time that has passed. He has the time of three tides to make up his mind. Instead of agonizing over the decision, he takes a nap and wakes to see the boy smiling at him. He opts for life in the sea, and the green boy shouts for joy. In the meantime, a lawyer has come to the village with news of an inheritance due the old man, but the postmaster says he has disappeared and is believed to have drowned. The simple story is made convincing by the characterization of practical Falter Tom, who accepts the enchantment in a very matter-of-fact manner, and by strong descriptions of their journey through the sea. Although the book is brief, it is not directed especially toward young children, having interesting turns of phrase and bits of action to appeal to older readers as well. N. Z. Esther Glen.

FAMILY AT THE LOOKOUT (Shelley*, Noreen, ill. Robert Micklewright, Oxford, 1972), realistic family novel set in the Blue Mountains of New South Wales, Australia. When an uncle, a famous ornithologist and painter of birds, dies, he leaves his twenty-five-room home, The Lookout, in Gully Heights to Bill Weatherall, father of Mark, 12, Lindy (Belinda), 10, and Butch (Bruce), almost two. Because of a family quarrel, Bill, also an artist, has never met his uncle, but he moves his family from Sidney to The Lookout, where they find circumstances strange. The house is on an almost impassable track, its rooms are full of stuffed birds, and Miss Caroline Hatch, the curious, reserved former housekeeper who now lives in a nearby cottage, alternates between shyly friendly overtures and open hostility. They meet other local characters: Frederick Abernathy, the fat, lazy taxi driver and postmaster; Dorothy and Dimity Gray (Dotty and Dim), middle-aged twins who run a milk bar; Call-Me-Jack Johnson, the butcher; Elsie Howe, who runs the general store, and her simpleminded nephew, Alf*; and Major* Caldwell, a stiff-necked Englishman who disapproves of both artists and foreigners. The first-person narrator, Mark, quickly makes a friend of Joss Vermeer, a recent immigrant from Holland, and the two boys and Lindy set out to explore the Gully, a deep ravine overlooked by The Lookout. In the small creek at the bottom, Lindy slips and badly sprains her ankle. Before Joss can summon her father, Major Caldwell arrives with his bulldog, Nelson. With their shirts and a couple of saplings, they make a stretcher and carry Lindy up the steep trail, a grueling effort for both Mark and the elderly man. Mark's persistence and rapport with Nelson impress the major, and he offers the boy one of the pups of Nelson and Emma, his female bulldog whose litter is about ready to be weaned. At the major's out-of-the-way house, Mark picks out the strongest pup, which he names John Bull. Because Lindy falls in love with the runt, the major gives it to her as well, and she names it Major. When they first arrive at The Lookout, the studio is locked, and Miss Hatch says that she has mislaid the key. A letter from the uncle's publisher arrives saying that some dozen or more paintings are missing from a manuscript, and Joss and Mark, after some spying around, suggest that Miss Hatch has them and is forging duplicates. Before this problem is resolved, a bush fire threatens the area. Bill joins the voluntary firefighters. Their mother, with Butch, Lindy, the puppies and kittens, and Joss's mother and little sisters all take refuge in the railroad subway in the village. Mark and Joss, after going with Alf to get Major Caldwell, join him and Miss Hatch in trying to save The Lookout. Just as they are on the point of exhaustion, the firefighters arrive, then the rain. Later they discover that the small suitcase entrusted to Mark by Miss Hatch has all the missing illustrations, and they realize that in her devotion to the deceased uncle she was simply trying to conclude his last work for him. When Bill says he will complete the illustrations, she decides to go live with her sister, and the major, whose house has burned down, will live in her cottage. Characters are one-dimensional, but the eccentric locals are interesting. The mystery of Miss Hatch and the paintings is contrived, and the bush fire too readily resolves all the other conflicts. The strongest aspect of the novel, as with much Australian fiction, is the vividly evoked setting. Aust. Bk. of Year Winner.

THE FAMILY CONSPIRACY (Phipson*, Joan, ill. Margaret Horder, Angus, 1962; Harcourt, 1964), realistic family novel set on a sheep ranch in central western New South Wales, Australia, near Bungaree in the mid-twentieth century. When Mrs. Barker suddenly becomes ill and the doctor advises rest and an operation, her children are worried and feel guilty, since immediately preceding her illness she had organized and managed a party for their friends. Lorna, 14, and Edward, a year or two younger, are due to return to boarding school, so they make a pact with Belinda, 10, and Robbie, 9, that they will earn all the money they can to help pay for their mother's operation. Jack, 20, out of school and helping his father on their sheep station, is too preoccupied with the drought and too adult to be included. Fanny, a self-absorbed toddler, is too young. Each pursues money in his own way. Belinda sees a new baby-clothes shop in Bungaree and knits a sweater to sell there. The proprietor kindly shows her that it is too full of mistakes, but she suggests that she will buy some baby nightgowns if Belinda will sew them. Diligently, she spends every spare minute sewing, strains her eyes, and her glasses are an added family expense. With her earnings, she buys lottery tickets and almost immediately regrets it. Robbie hunts for gold in an old mine tunnel, which caves in on him. He is nearly killed but is rescued by Jack. Genuinely scared, he turns his attention to trapping rabbits and is outraged when his father sends his skins along with those caught by the hired man to town for sale with no intention of letting him have the profit. Lorna learns that her roommate's sister, Jill, who lives in Sydney, needs help with her three children and applies for the job during the holidays, even though she is homesick and wants to return to her family. She does a fine job until she is asked to take the children to the zoo, when they take the wrong bus. She gets the children home eventually by taxi, very cold, wet, and late. Edward can think of no money-making scheme until vacation and fears he may have to sell his well-trained sheep dog, Brigalow. He finds a job as assistant to a drover who is taking cattle from the worst of the drought-stricken area to the hills, where they can find some feed. All goes well until the nearly starved cattle break through a fence and one group stampedes back to the bush. With Brigalow, Edward follows them and, when he can't head them back, stays with them through the night, even though a much-needed rain soaks him. He manages to drive them back to the road the next day. Though sworn to secrecy, a friend tells Jack of the conspiracy. He pays Robbie for his rabbit skins. To everyone's astonishment, Belinda wins fifteen pounds in the lottery, so they proudly give their savings to their mother. The pride and joy of the occasion is almost spoiled by their sudden realization that they have left Fanny in Bungaree. They discover that she has been going from house to house begging, having overheard the older children's plan to help their mother. Although somewhat slow paced, the story delineates the personalities of the individual children well and gives a sense of the life and work on a none-too-prosperous ranch in an inhospitable part of the country. Too often feelings and assessments of the characters are told rather than shown, but the adventures are plausible and the misunderstanding of the children's motives by the parents keeps some tension in the plot. Sequel is *Threat to the Barkers**. Aust. Bk. of Year Winner.

FAR FROM SHORE (Major*, Kevin, Clarke, 1980; Delacorte, 1980), realistic novel of a Newfoundland, Canada, boy's troubled year with his family deteriorating and his personal life in a downward spiral, in the late twentieth century. Told in brief chapters, the story alternates from one character to another, each speaking in first person, but the protagonist is clearly Chris Slade, 15, at the opening a likable, good-natured boy given to high spirits and horseplay. On

Christmas Eve, his sister, Jennifer, 16, cooks dinner and coerces Chris into helping decorate the tree, trying to recapture the holiday spirit of past years, but their father, Gord, arrives late and very drunk, a frequent condition since he lost his job some months earlier. His wife, a long-suffering but resentful woman, gets Chris to help her put him to bed and cleans up after him silently when he is sick, but Jennifer speaks up, and before Christmas is over, he has hit her in the face and started drinking again, and Chris has gone to stay with his friend, Steve Tomkins. In the next months, Gord leaves to find work in Alberta, the mother takes a job in a diner owned by Frank Osmond, Jennifer renews her determination to leave their small town of Marten by going to college, and Chris, having lost his girl friend, Monika, starts drinking more frequently and socializing with an older, wilder crowd until one morning, after a night when he passes out from a combination of alcohol and marijuana, he is charged with vandalism, the school windows having been smashed the night before. His father phones and berates him, and his mother, torn by her worry over Chris and her growing attraction to Frank, tries to keep him busy painting the kitchen. Then Rev. Wheaton, for whom Chris used to serve as altar boy, asks him to be a counselor at church camp. Chris jumps at the chance to get out of Marten. At first he does well. Wheaton asks him to try to cheer up a homesick eleven-year-old boy named David Morrison, and Chris makes some headway by taking him out in a canoe and helping him to overcome his fear of the water by teaching him to float on his back. The senior counselor in charge of the canoes, a self-important college boy, berates Chris for taking a canoe without asking special permission and scornfully tells him to let the swimming instructor teach David so his swimming technique isn't hurt by a wrong start. Although the boys in David's cabin nickname Chris "Beefbrains" and begin to idolize him, he is upset by the unjust criticism and succumbs to the pressure of his roommate to smoke some marijuana in the middle of the night. The next morning, still high and his judgment impaired, he takes David in a canoe out onto the pond, even though the wind is strong. The boat capsizes, and with great difficulty Chris saves David, who has hit his head and must be taken to the hospital. Wheaton drives Chris home in disgrace. While Wheaton tells Mrs. Slade the story, Chris goes to the bathroom and sees the reflection in a mirror of Frank Osmond, who is hiding behind the door to the spare room. Putting two and two together, Chris blunders out of the house, wanders around in shock, and some six hours later goes to see his old friend, Steve, who welcomes him. His father returns from Alberta, takes Chris fishing, and goes with him to court, where he pleads guilty, though he genuinely believes he did not damage the windows. He must pay his share of the damages. His mother has second thoughts about divorcing Gord and agrees that if Gord can't find work near home, she will go to Alberta with him. Chris decides to give school another try, and with Susan, a girl he has long admired, and Steve supporting him seems ready to make a go of it. A letter from David shows that Chris made lasting headway with the boy, and he considers asking him to Marten for a visit. As a picture of a family going to pieces and beginning to pull itself together again, the novel is convincing, but its main power comes from its portrait of Chris, an adolescent full of confusion and resentment, surly one minute, naively charming the next, cynical and idealistic by turns, almost adult and still a child. The pressures of teenaged life in a small town in the late twentieth century are well handled. Can. Young Adult.

FATCHEN, MAX (1920–), born in Adelaide, South Australia; journalist, writer of verse and fiction. He spent his early life on a farm at Angle Vale, north of Adelaide, and was educated at Angle Vale Primary School and Gowler High School. During World War II he served in the Australian Air Force. Afterwards he worked for the Adelaide *News and Sunday Mail* until 1955 and then as writer and literary editor for *The Advertiser* in Adelaide. He has published several books of verse, for both children and adults, and his topical verse has appeared frequently in both *The Advertiser* and in the *Denver Post*. His first novel, *The River Kings** (Hicks, 1966; St. Martin's, 1968), set in South Australia's pioneering days, was inspired by a trip in an old paddlesteamer on her last voyage from Berri to Mannum in South Australia and by a subsequent visit to the United States, where he visited New Orleans and learned much about riverboating on the Mississippi. *The River Kings* has been translated into Swedish and serialized by the New Zealand Broadcasting Corporation. Its sequel is *Conquest of the River* (Hicks, 1970; Methuen, 1970). *The Spirit Wind** (Hicks, 1973; Methuen, 1973) is a historical novel of a boy who jumps ship in Australia and is saved by friendship with an old Aborigine. Both it and *The River Kings* were commended for the Australian Book of the Year Award. Other titles by Fatchen for young people include *Chase Through the Night* (Methuen, 1977), *The Time Wave* (Methuen, 1978), and *Closer to the Stars* (Methuen, 1981).

FAVILLE, BARRY, New Zealand teacher, broadcaster, and writer. He teaches English at Taupo-nui-a-Tia College and has worked in broadcasting as a scriptwriter and producer. His biography, *Cook's First Voyage to New Zealand* (School Publications Branch, Dept. of Education, 1969) is one of a number of his writings for the *School Journal*. His first novel, *The Keeper** (Oxford, 1986), is a futuristic fantasy set about five generations after a nuclear holocaust has annihilated the population of the northern hemisphere and left small, isolated settlements in New Zealand. It won the New Zealand Government Publishing Award. A later novel for young people, *The Return* (Oxford, 1988), is set at Wilkes Beach, a small settlement on the eastern coast of the North Island of New Zealand.

FAVOURITE CHILD (*Sweetgrass**), Blackfoot Blood girl. Her dominant characteristics are her garrulousness and giggling. Because she is gossipy and outgoing, Sweetgrass and the reader learn essential information. Favourite Child survives the smallpox epidemic.

THE FEATHER STAR (Wrightson*, Patricia, ill. Noela Young, Hutchinson, 1962; Harcourt, 1963), realistic novel set somewhere in Australia in the mid-twentieth century. The Martins—father, mother, fun-loving Chris, 7, and sensitive, self-conscious Lindy, 15—vacation at a seacoast village while Mr. Martin recovers from an unspecified illness. Taking care of her younger brother brings Lindy into contact with some of the youth of the community. Fleece* (Felice) Bates, whose family runs the local grocery and variety store, and Bill* Grant and Ian* Hull, who gather bait to sell to vacationers. Almost always underfoot is an unsupervised urchin Chris's age, little Anne* Tippett, a snooper and collector often accompanied by or searching for her misused and hence fractious cat, Queenie. Anne and Chris soon make friends, and thus Anne becomes an added responsibility for Lindy, who is mostly good-natured about taking her on. Much of this almost plotless book concerns Lindy's problems with keeping Chris and Anne in line, her exchanges of confidences with Fleece, who wants to become a model, her encounters with the boys, some embarrassing, others pleasant, and her typically ambivalent adolescent behavior toward them, herself, and her parents. In one episode, she enjoys an early evening fishing expedition with the youths in which she, the neophyte, makes the only catch. While exploring the fractured sea wall, she discovers a beautiful feather star (which Bill explains is similar to a starfish). Anne's cat proves responsible for the only real problems. Queenie attacks the feather star, breaking it, but Bill reassures Lindy that the creature can regenerate itself and become several of its kind. More serious trouble follows when Anne helps herself to a black chiffon nightgown that Fleece has sewn and cherishes. After Anne and Chris dress Queenie up in the gown, the frightened, annoyed animal escapes, races through the local bar, nightgown trailing, and finally seeks refuge under the bed of old Abel—a Bible-quoting, irascible recluse who lives in a tumbledown shack down the dune near the shore—arousing his ire. When Abel complains that Lindy stole a piece of blue glass he uses as a blade sharpener and Lindy later discovers that Anne has taken it and retrieves it, she is faced with a dilemma. Morality wins out. But when Abel takes the now broken glass, utterly without grace and flings the pieces into the sea, reviling Lindy, Lindy realizes that he himself is responsible for his isolation. She sees that one's behavior affects the attitudes and behavior of others toward one. The rest of the Martin seashore holiday passes uneventfully, and once home, summer people and events fade from memory. Developing interpersonal relationships, building trust, and coming to terms with life's small problems form the core of the novel, and the author's sufficiently descriptive style realizes the setting and incidents well. Although the book starts slowly, events are seen convincingly from Lindy's point of view, and her easily hurt feelings, shyness, and occasional overreactiveness seem appropriate for a sheltered girl of her age and background and are sympathetically handled. The tone is non-didactic, but the feather star is an obvious symbol: life goes on. The teenagers occasionally seem a little young for their ages, but this is not a disturbing element in the book, and the parents are portrayed with unusual sympathy for a sixties novel.

This is a pleasing, believable story of one family's holiday. Aust. Bk. of the Year Com.

FEBRUARY DRAGON (Thiele*, Colin, Rigby, 1965; Harper, 1966), family novel of a bush fire that destroys the Pine family's home and much of the rural community between Summerton and Upper Gumbowie near the South Australian border, presumably in the 1950s or early 1960s. The Pine family lives at Bottlebrush Barn, a farm not far from the country store run by Mr. Billings, known as Old Barnacle. The three children, Resin (Melton), 12, Turps (Crystal), 10, and Columbine (Colin), 6, ride the school bus driven by their favorite teacher, Mr. Harvey, whom all the children call Miss Starvy and refer to as Starvy. The first four-fifths of the book is an almost episodic account of life on the farm and at school. The children are delighted by the romance between Starvy and their other teacher, Miss Lemmen, their wedding and reception in Gumbowie Hall, and their move into Humpty Doo, a cottage at the edge of the Big Scrub near Bottlebrush Barn. They collect pets to join their old cat, Puss'll-do, and Woppit, a dog half kangaroo, half kelpie: Gus, a large goanna that wanders in from the scrub and is never really tame, Pinch, an opossum that they find in the pouch of a mother killed on the road and raise on a bottle, and Turp's beloved pony, Ginger. When Mrs. Pine's sister and her family visit from Summerton, the opossum, terrified by the unfamiliar crowd and Aunt Hester's dramatic gestures, runs up her leg and clings with all his sharp little claws, an incident their aunt never lets them forget. Resin and his friend, Burp (Bert) Heaslip, ride along on their first spotlight hunt, when the men from neighboring farms chase and shoot down foxes at night with a spotlight mounted on the cab of the Pine's truck. They attend the annual Gumbowie Show, a fair where both the humans and the family pets win prizes. Throughout there are mentions of fires and scenes of the Emergency Fire Service displays of firefighting technique, and after Christmas the drought makes all the men tense and alert, but danger does not threaten until Aunt Hester takes some visiting friends from the city for a "chop" picnic at Rowett's Reserve and ignores the ban on fires. She douses the fire with water from the billy and goes off with self-righteous remarks about safety, but she fails to turn over the log and see the coals still glowing on the underside. The next day a gusty wind whips up a scatter of sparks, ignites the tinder brush in the reserve, and soon the Big Scrub is flaming. Most of the men rush off to join the firefighters. School is dismissed early, and Starvy, trying to get the bussed children home, almost runs into the fire. Abandoning the road, he heads for the fallow paddock recently plowed beside Heaslip's dam and, when a tire bursts, ends up with the bus in the pond but all the children safe. The fire, however, has destroyed Humpty Doo, Bottlebrush Barn, and a number of other homes. Old Barnacle has been killed in his store and, heartbreaking to Turps, Ginger has died in the stable because the girl had forgotten to let her out before school. Mrs. Pine doesn't tell them that Puss'll-do was shut in the house. As they view the terrible devastation, Pinch skitters from the cover of an underground water tank, where he has been hanging, and onto Resin's shoulder. Aunt Hester and her husband arrive and insist that the family come and temporarily stay with them in Summerton, but she bridles at the sight of Pinch. Resin firmly announces that he won't come if Pinch can't, and Mr. Pine, already planning to head for Adelaide to get a job as soon as possible, says he will shut the opossum in his truck cab for the night. The novel has a strange structure. The easygoing domestic adventures proceed in a pleasant, often amusing way throughout most of the story. Then there occurs a sudden shift to the dramatic and tragic fire. The children are well differentiated and life in the rural area is pictured in an interesting and realistic way. Scenes of the fire are vivid, as are those of the later blackened, devastated area. Aust. Bk. of Year Highly Com.

FENNIMORE, STEPHEN. See COLLINS, DALE.

FINKEL, GEORGE (IRVINE) (1909–1975), born in South Shields, County Durham, England; naval officer and author of fiction and non-fiction for adults, older children, and teenagers, which were published while he lived in Australia. After attending the Royal Air Force and Royal Navy training schools, in 1940 he was commissioned as a qualified aeronautical specialist by the Royal Navy. After the war, he transferred to the regular Navy as a lieutenant commander, left the service in 1950, and emigrated with his wife and children to Australia, but he was recalled as a training officer in the Korean War. In 1958, he again left the Navy, moving to the University of New South Wales as a planning engineer. Although he wrote official publications for the Navy during World War II, his literary career began in 1962 with an adventure novel, *The Mystery of Secret Beach* (Angus, 1962), and more than a dozen novels of adventure, historical fiction, and fictionalized biography and a dozen books of non-fiction on specialized topics for the South Australian Education Department came out over the next fifteen years. Two of his books were commended for the Australian Children's Book of the Year Award: *The "Loyall Virginian"** (Angus, 1968; *The "Loyal Virginian,"* Viking, 1968), a historical novel about the involvement of a young mid-seventeenth-century Virginia planter and trader in the English Civil War, and *James Cook, Royal Navy** (Angus, 1970), a biographical novel of the youth and early voyages of the famous eighteenth-century circumnavigator and map maker. In both books, characterization is less memorable than detail of period and story. Other novels are *Watch Fires to the North* (Viking, 1967), based on the legends of King Arthur, and *The Peace Seekers* (Angus, 1970), about voyages of exploration to North America.

FINN'S FOLLY (Southall*, Ivan, Angus, 1969; St. Martin's, 1969), realistic problem novel set in a mountainous area 180 miles from Melbourne, Australia, in the period contemporary with the writing, detailing happenings in a few hours of the night when an accident occurs on a remote road. In the Shaw family, Max, 15, Brenda, 14, and Tony, 11, have become used to having their lives revolve around the problems of David, 9, a severely retarded mongoloid child who must be watched constantly so that he will not run away. When Mrs. Shaw leaves their isolated lakeside cabin shortly after midnight to pick up her husband at the nearest railway station, she wakes Max to tell him that he is in charge. In the meantime Alison McPhee and her father, riding in his big transport truck, have finally realized that they are lost in the fog on an isolated road unsuitable for vehicles that large. A macho, attractive man in his early forties, he has raised Alison since her mother left when she was four and has sent her to a posh boarding school, but on vacations she travels with him. He has made a wrong turn when trying to find the home of a bar friend, Fred Finn, where he has expected to stay during the fog. As he tries to edge the big truck around a hairpin turn, a car hits the truck and it goes over the edge, crashes down the hillside, and scatters its load of drums containing cyanide and other dangerous chemicals. Realizing that the crash they hear must be their parents, since the area is otherwise virtually deserted, Brenda and Max take the only flashlight and try to find the site of the accident, leaving David in Tony's care. Brenda slips on white pellets, panics when she sees the drum marked "cyanide" burst open beside the road, and heads back with the flashlight to change her clothes and wash, while Max stumbles on in the fog, now beginning to lighten as moonlight penetrates. Eventually he discovers his parents' car smashed beyond any possibility of survivors, and he finds Alison and her father inside the crushed truck cab. She is still alive but pinned and unable to move; her father is dead. Max is able to reach one arm into the cab and touch her hair, a communication that thrills them both. They have an idyllic romantic interlude, unable to see each other's faces but feeling deep love and commitment. In the meantime, Tony, who really loves David more and understands him better than any of the others, has the hyperactive child in bed with him and, holding him firmly, begins to drift off to sleep when their nearest neighbor, Frank Fenwick, breaks the door down and rushes in, shouting that he will shoot, thinking he is facing some threat to defenseless Mrs. Shaw and her four children. In the confusion David runs out and disappears in the fog. After they all hunt frantically, Fenwick finds David, bitterly cold and unconscious in his pajamas and bare feet, lying in a pile of cyanide. Phyllis Fenwick, a disagreeable, self-centered actress who doesn't like children, warms the child and insists that her husband try to find the accident to see if there are survivors. Reluctantly, he does, realizing from the name he has seen on the drums scattered around the road that the trucker was Phyllis's first husband and that Alison, whom he finds with Max, is her daughter. He sends Max back to take charge of his siblings, while he plans to get help, take care of Alison, and arrange that the poison be cleaned up before it contaminates the reservoir. Max and Alison realize that they will probably never see each other again. The tension of the accident is strong, but it is made less effective because the story starts on too frantic a note. Max's initial fear at being alone with the younger children is unreasonable, and Brenda's frenetic goading and sniping at him before they hear the crash makes their real apprehension about the accident less convincing.

Scenes of the various characters blundering around in the fog are vivid. The most interesting questions of the plot, however, are left unanswered: How will the Shaw youngsters get along and cope with David? Will Alison and her mother accept each other? Did McPhee really have an acquaintance named Freddy Finn? If so, did Finn really have a place in the mountains? If it is invented, was it invented by Finn or by McPhee, who may have seen the article in a theater magazine about "Phyll's Folly," the Fenwick place? If this last is the case, was it a conscious effort to get Alison to her mother or an unconscious memory that got mixed with some drunken invitation from a barroom friend? While an open ending may be intended, so many loose strands make the story unsatisfying. Aust. Bk. of Year Com.

FIRE IN THE STONE (Thiele*, Colin, Rigby, 1973; Harper, 1974; Penguin, 1981), mystery and adventure novel set in the opal fields of South Australia, six hundred miles northwest of Adelaide, midway between Port Augusta and Alice Springs, in the last third of the twentieth century. Ernie* Ryan, 14, lives in the rough town with his feckless father, Robbie, in a dugout that protects them somewhat from the extremes of temperature, wind, and dust. His friend, Willie* Winowie, with the other Aborigines, lives in a run-down reserve. Ernie's mother having left some years before and his father being often absent or drunk, the boy is frequently on his own and spends his spare time noodling (looking for opals in waste heaps) with Willie's people or exploring the abandoned mines near his home. After he finds opal at the end of a seam of patch he has been following, he gathers as much as he can in his pockets and boots, hides most of it in a can under his bed, and registers the mine in his own name. When he returns, he discovers the can stolen and his find in the mine cleared out. He sells the few pieces he has been carrying with him to a Japanese buyer for sixteen hundred dollars and starts a bank account. He keeps the bank account secret from his father, but he does tell him that he has registered the mine. Robbie insists that he have at least two companions when he goes into the mine again. Ernie persuades Willie and Nick Andropoulos to be his partners, and they do some exploring but find nothing of value. In an almost unrelated episode, the three boys go camping in the Breakaway, an area of deep erosion and wild beauty. When, as a result of their horseplay, Nick is badly injured, Willie and Ernie get him on an improvised stretcher up the ravine, then ten miles toward home before a rare passerby picks them up. Nick recovers, Ernie is briefly a hero, and Willie is mostly ignored. Robbie discovers Ernie's bank passbook, forces him to sign over the money, then takes off prospecting or on a spree. News of a rich find brings foreign buyers, and the boys near the entrance to Ernie's mine watch a German buyer take off in his private plane with two suitcases of valuable opal, then, obviously with engine trouble, head back toward the field and crash. They rush up and drag his body away just before the plane bursts into flames, but Willie sees another man near the plane in the smoke. The boys realize that this is a thief who must have taken his loot into the mine, and they stake out the entrance until they see Dosh Dobruzza, a drifter Ernie has already suspected was the thief who took his find, emerge after dark. After a series of exciting developments, Dobruzza is arrested and held on suspicion of theft. The boys take the opportunity to search the mine and realize that the opal is buried in the floor under rubble. Ernie starts to dig, hits a booby trap, and an explosion brings down rubble that blocks the entrance. He finds Willie unconscious but still alive. With great difficulty Ernie digs a way out and pulls Willie after him. Nick, unhurt, has been trapped in another passage. Willie is flown to the hospital in Adelaide. The three boys share a ten thousand dollar reward for finding the opal. Worried about Willie, Ernie starts to hitchhike to Adelaide, since he is on his own now and doesn't know that Willie died that morning. There are a number of loose ends. Since the fame of their exploits spreads rapidly, there is no explanation of why Robbie doesn't return to claim Ernie's new fortune, nor is there any explanation of how Dobruzza manages to be at the scene of the crash so promptly, though it is suggested that he tampered with the plane. There is an attempt to explore the discrimination against Aborigines and the deplorable conditions of their lives and to cross the color barrier in the friendship of Ernie and Willie, but the camping episode, brought in to strengthen this tie, seems extraneous and excessive. The strongest feature of the book is the setting and the feel it gives for the barren but beautiful land and the rough but hardy life of the opal miners. Aust. Bk. of Year Com.; Fanfare; Poe Nom.

THE FIRST WALKABOUT (Tindale*, Norman B. and Lindsay*, H. A., ill. Madeleine Boyce, Longmans, 1954), historical adventure novel based on archaeological discoveries about prehistoric migrations into Australia from the north during the last Ice Age. Events of thousands of years are telescoped into several generations and epitomized by the experiences of the family of Gunju, a group of Negritos, the little dark men who were among the earliest of several groups of Australian Aborigines. The original home of the Negritos is in the forests of southeast Asia, where they live in skillfully constructed tree houses for protection from the fearful jungle beasts and subsist by hunting and gathering. A peaceful people, they flee from the taller, aggressive, more technologically advanced Hunting Men on hastily constructed rafts, island hopping for many months until they reach northern Australia. Under Gunju's leadership, they gradually move into the continent, using whatever resources the immediate area offers in the way of food, surviving plagues of mosquitoes, terrible storms, scorching heat, and bitter drought, and retreating from their dreaded enemies, who also move southward from Asia. Gunju grows up, marries, and has a son, Pek, a bright, curious lad who discovers how to capture the emu and to shock fish into insensibility with a certain seed pod, and other similar advances. He falls in love with pretty Liliri, whose uncle has promised her to another man. Pek and Liliri run away, and in an exciting flight they are relentlessly pursued by the warriors of the tribe, who track them expertly and will put them to death if they catch them. The two cross the desert, surviving by drinking water Pek discovers inside a species of frog. With other outcasts, Pek and Liliri eventually make a home in what is now Tasmania. The poorly paced, undeveloped plot has some exciting moments, but it mostly serves as a way of conveying information about the early history of Australia. The descriptions of the ways and problems of these primitive people as presented seem reasonable and have greater interest than the meager story. Gunju and Pek are the only figures that are developed to any extent, representing two different types of tribal leaders. Aust. Bk. of Year Winner.

FIVE TIMES DIZZY (Wheatley*, Nadia, ill. Neil Phillips, Oxford, 1982), domestic adventure novel set in the Newtown suburb of Sydney in the early 1980s. Although she has been in Australia only three years, Marika Nikakis, 10 or 11, speaks English fluently and understands the culture, but her grandmother, Yaya, who has followed recently from Crete, cannot adjust to a life so different and seems to be growing old and listless, living only in memories of her Greek friends and her goat, Poppy. Marika's father, Baba, and her mother are so busy with their store, the Anzac Deli, behind which the family lives, that they do not notice Yaya's unhappiness or the way Marika is excluded from the fun of the neighborhood young people led by Patricia and Rowley Wilson, both about her age. Marika has an inspiration: Yaya must have a job to keep her busy. After searching the help wanted ads in vain, Marika asks Baba for advice, but she gets no encouragement. What sort of job could Yaya, unable to speak English, unfamiliar with city life, still wearing the black dress and head covering traditional for older women in Crete, find, especially when men born in Australia are out of work? Besides, Marika knows, Baba wants very much to be just like the Australians and is not eager to have his mother noticed by the neighbors. Marika helps in the store and is on very good terms with many of the neighborhood adults, including Mrs. Wilson, Mr. MacKenzie (or Mr. Mac, as he is generally called), and the Professor, a thin, bearded man who is writing a book. Mr. Mac tries to bring her and Patricia Wilson together by getting them both to help him feed the thirteen puppies for which his greyhound bitch cannot supply enough milk, a job even Yaya is drawn into and at which she is especially good. Mr. Mac says regretfully that the pups would do better on goat milk, and Marika has her second inspiration: Yaya needs a goat and could sell the milk. Each time an idea for Yaya hits Marika, she feels as if she is dancing the Cretan *Pentozalia*, the Five-Times-Dizzy-Dance that spins so fast it takes the breath away. Marika finds an ad in the newspaper for nanny goats for one hundred dollars, but when she suggests it to Baba he is angry. Does she know what hay would cost in the city? Does she want to add to the debt he owes for the store, the truck, and the refrigerator? Marika's next inspiration occurs when she sees the Professor cutting his grass with lawn shears. He needs a goat! When he listens seriously, as he always does to her concerns, he helps her organize the Newtown Goatmower Roster Service Incorporated: Excellence Guaranteed. She calls at every house with a lawn, explaining her service and emphasizing the cleanliness of her goat and the good supervision her grandmother will provide, and some people sign up for the service. Her problem then is to get money for a goat. Help comes from an unexpected source, the Wilsons, whose mother points out that the way to make money is to have a fete. Soon all the Wilsons and Marika are busy working on booths and cleaning up the derelict Haunted House for a spook house. Mama firmly quells Baba's opposition, and he becomes involved in the preparations, as do Mr. Mac and the Professor. The fete is a great success. At its height, Baba arrives with a goat and presents it to Yaya, who finds herself the center of affectionate attention. The story has charm mainly because of the mutual concern and love between Marika and her grandmother, who worries because the girl is excluded by the other youngsters and spends so much time working in the store. Ethnic Greek details add interest and, although all works out a little too neatly to be believable, it makes a satisfying novel for middle-grade readers. The sequel is *Dancing in the Anzac Deli**. Aust. Bk. of Year Com.

FLEECE BATES (*The Feather Star**), Felice, pretty, spunky, responsible girl, who works regularly and competently in the family variety store. She aspires to become a model, but later she thinks she may become a seamstress instead. The black nightgown she sews produces the story's main problem. Like Lindy Martin, she gains in resiliency and comes to appreciate her mother more, especially after she and Lindy overhear Fleece's mother give old Abel a good dressing down about his attitude toward the children and not paying for merchandise.

FLETCHER, JANE ADA, born in Victoria, Australia; writer and teacher. Fletcher grew up in Queensland, where her father, a widely known naturalist, was agricultural editor of the *Queenslander* for many years. She taught in bush schools in Tasmania, and, having inherited a love for nature from her father, she did field work in natural history and Aborigine remains that resulted in books of nature stories and articles. She also wrote supplementary school readers, contributed stories to the *School Paper*, was a founding member of the Royal Ornithological Union, and contributed to its magazine, *The Emu*. She is best known for her popular *Little Brown Picaninnies of Tasmania* (Sands, 1949), which was highly commended for Australian Book of the Year.

THE FORBIDDEN BRIDGE (Roland*, Betty, ill. Prudence Seward, Bodley, 1961; ill. Geraldine Spence, McGraw, 1965), short novel of family and farm life set at Cromarty, a large Australian sheep ranch near Nagambie, Victoria, evidently in the mid-twentieth century. Jamie (given the last name of Kendall in later books of the series), 7, is lonely since he and his mother have come to live at the home of his Uncle David McBride after the death of his father. His cousin, Malcolm McBride, 13, treats him with scorn. His mother is very busy helping his grandmother, who is in poor health, and running the house for Aunt Marion, who is an invalid confined to a wheelchair. Old Ned, the yardman, is not unfriendly but taciturn by nature. The only nearby children are the numerous Pinkertons, who live in a ramshackle house across the river, reached only by the railroad bridge, which Jamie is forbidden to cross by himself. His best diversions are playing with his cocker spaniel puppy, Fran, which he loves dearly, and sometimes riding his cranky pony, Jock. For some days he has been watching the Pinkertons build a humpy, a makeshift shelter, on their side of the river, and he gets his mother to agree that she may take him across the bridge and let him play with them, then sleep in the humpy. That night, however, his grandmother has one of her "bad turns," and his mother is too busy to pay any attention to him, except to warn him to play very quietly that day. He wanders down to the river, where the Pinkertons call to him to come over for a party they are having in the humpy. When he says he is not allowed, they taunt him as scared, a " 'fraid cat," and chickenhearted. Eventually, he puts his ear to the rail to be sure no train is approaching and, with Fran, dogtrots across to be welcomed by the Pinkertons. After a fine party of sticky cakes and toffee, he realizes it is getting late and hurries back to the bridge. Halfway across, he calls to Fran to hurry and sees the train approaching. Panicky, he catches his foot, falls, and stumbles on blindly until someone grabs him up and jumps over the side of the bridge. After a minute of blackness, Jamie wakes to see that it was Malcolm, now white and unconscious on the ground near him. To his horror, he sees Aunt Marion, leaning on old Ned, trying painfully to stagger toward her son. Thinking Malcolm must be dead and Fran, too, Jamie runs away until he falls and sobs himself to sleep. He is wakened in the dark by Fran's warm tongue licking him, and then Uncle David comes hunting for him with a flashlight. When he starts to sob again, Uncle David picks him up and comforts him, assuring him that Malcolm has a sprained ankle but is not dead and that Fran lay flat and let the train thunder over her. Although Uncle David points out that it was very wrong to cross the bridge by himself, he is gentle and, when he sees Jamie limping, gives him a ride on his back to the house. The story is intended for early readers, with simple style and brief chapters, but it deals in a sensitive way with the loneliness and guilt feelings of a child. Adults are kind if not totally understanding, and Malcolm's treatment of his little cousin as a nuisance and pest, yet someone to be rescued, is realistic. Sequels. Aust. Bk. of Year Com.

FOWLER, THURLEY, born in Griffith, New South Wales, Australia; author of novels of family life for children. *The Green Wind** (Rigby, 1985) is the story of an eleven-year-old girl whose family lives on a farm much like that on which Fowler grew up. It was winner of the Australian Book of the Year Award. An earlier novel, *Wait for Me! Wait for Me!* (Rigby, 1981), won first prize in the Rigby 1980 Anniversary Literary Contest. It is about a skinny ten-year-old boy who tags along with his three older brothers, all accomplished athletes. More recent titles include *Am I Going With You?* (Hippo, 1986) and *A Hippo Doing Backstroke* (Hodder, 1988). Fowler is married to an aeronautical engineer, has three children, and has made her home in suburban Melbourne.

THE FOX HOLE (Southall*, Ivan, ill. Ian Ribbons, Methuen, 1967; St. Martin's, 1967), short, contemporary realistic novel set mostly in a former gold mining region of southeastern Australia. One Friday afternoon diffident Ken, 10, takes the train from Melbourne to spend a "beaut" holiday weekend with his country relatives: Uncle Bob, his mother's brother; Auntie Kath; and their children, Hugh, 11, Joan, 10, and Francie, 6. When Ken changes from the train to the bus, however, the trip turns sour, and he suffers various mishaps. When he arrives at the bus stop where his cousins eagerly await him, he is tired, distraught, and close to tears. His discomfort increases during the evening. His cousins noisily vie for his attention, and Hugh and Uncle Bob tell a "beaut" (in Hugh's opinion) story about two Chinese miners who were found murdered at their mine shaft near Desmond Creek, which lies at the bottom of the hill where Uncle Bob's house stands. When Ken and Hugh leave to spend the night in a tent down by the dam on the creek, an outing that Hugh has arranged as a special treat, Ken is afraid to sleep out but too intimidated to protest. When he finally falls asleep, he has a terrible nightmare. He awakens early in the morning, creeps out into the forest, still nervous, and spies a fox slinking across a clearing with one of Joan's bantams in his mouth. He screams for help and pursues the fox into a dense tunnel of blackberry bushes, where he gets stuck fast on the thorns. Hugh is terrified when he discovers that Ken is caught in what the local children dread and call the gully or the Fox Hole. Sensing Hugh's terror, Ken struggles even harder to free himself, the ground gives way beneath him, and he falls through a rock-lined shaft, landing about thirty feet down in what seems to be damp humus or thick mud. He is bruised, battered, and terrified, with the story of old murders very much on his mind. Up above, his relatives carry on variously about the calamity. Uncle Bob, to whom the story interest shifts, cuts the berry bushes down as fast as he can, slashing furiously, old tensions between himself and his disparaging, judgmental sister (Ken's mother) adding force to his blows. With a rope he lowers a torch (flashlight) to Ken, who soon calls up that he sees gold in the rock. While ironically the usually muddled Hugh keeps his mind on the problem of rescuing Ken, gold fever consumes Uncle Bob, who insists that the news of gold in the shaft must not leak out until he has had time to get a license to work the lode. He descends into the shaft to look for himself, almost oblivious to Ken huddling there choking back sobs of fear and pain because his chest hurts. Suddenly, memories of an orphan boy he saw crouched in a fox hole during the Korean War flash through Bob's mind, and, conscience stricken, he realizes that Ken suffers from broken ribs. He calls up to Joan to phone for the police, telling her that it is only fool's gold, a lie that he realizes will cost him a fortune. Waiting down in the shaft with his uncle's arms tight around him, Ken feels a surge of love for the man and promises he'll always keep the secret. Characterizations are strong, with Uncle Bob, Hugh, and Ken the best drawn. The other figures are less well fleshed, but good contrasts. Joan is mainly seen as practical, a miniature of her mother; Francie is portrayed as a willful child, who, as the youngest, feels she must shriek her observations and desires in order to get attention. Though Ken's mother never appears in the story, she is deftly sketched through his memories as hypercritical, status conscious, and over-directive. Some subtle humor derives mainly from the interaction of the characters and from the children's uninformed, naive, romantic way of looking at things. Although the book holds the reader's interest, problems arise with both tone and substance. The mood starts on a peak of apprehension: the three siblings are veritable hellions, and there are allusions to some terrible, probably unpreventable catastrophe that happened one time at their place. The focus then moves to Ken's travel problems and his anxiety during the evening, making much of his distraught state of mind and doing it sympathetically and convincingly. When the high point of the story arrives, however—Ken in the shaft—it seems anti-climactic. Moreover, shifting from Ken's predicament in the shaft to Uncle Bob's moral struggle interjects a new complication with undertones of long-standing family problems that are not developed. The discovery of the gold is overforeshadowed, and the double meaning of the title seems labored. Aust. Bk. of Year Com.

FRA ANDREA (*And Tomorrow the Stars**), Franciscan monk who tutors young Vanni Caboto (John Cabot*) and inspires him to study so that he can learn enough to voyage in exploration. Inspired himself by a pure love of learning, Fra Andrea is wise enough to lure the boy into studying with tales of Marco Polo and other explorers. When Vanni is in trouble with his unsympathetic uncle, Fra Andrea suggests that he be put to work on a sailing vessel, a "punishment" that he knows will delight the boy. Fra Andrea has a true scientist's attitude and frequently urges his pupils to see for themselves and not to trust to other people's reports. Far more than his dour uncle, Fra Andrea becomes a father figure for the lonely boy.

FRANCES, HELEN. See GRANGER, HELEN, and PEARCE, FRANCES.

FRANK (*Angel Square; Up to Low**), friend and drinking pal of Dad*, Young Tommy's father, who buys a new Buick for the forty-mile trip to Low and pretty much wrecks it by bumping into things and scraping against things all the way there. Most of the people they stop to see, and have a drink with, on their journey suggest that Frank should sign the pledge, and the other listeners say, "I'll believe that when I see it." After he has dropped his outboard motor into the lake, made a terrible mess of the cabin, and collapsed his tent, Dad and several of his brothers take him by force to Father Sullivan, who gets him into his office by banging his knuckles with a rock when he braces himself in the doorway. Frank emerges with the signed paper, pledging not to drink liquor, wine, or beer again. He studies his situation for some time and discovers a loophole: liqueur is not included. He buys a case of creme de menthe and soon is staggering about as usual. He is a caricature, treated humorously, but he also serves to point out the tolerance of Dad's view of the world.

FRANK BRARY (*Snow Apples**), irresponsible father of the narrator, Sheila*. At fifty-five, some fifteen years older than Sheila's mother, Agnes*, he has lied about his age to get into the air force in World War II, and his allotment checks have given the family its first steady income. Even while awaiting discharge in Vancouver, he has been living with other women, and after he goes to work in the mines he marries again, without having divorced Agnes. He tells Sheila that he and her mother were never actually married, a story she doubts. A man of quick temper, he has once threatened to beat Sheila until she can never have children because she talked back to him, but she turns to him when she is pregnant, and, obviously having been through this experience before, he buys some capsules that he calls Brown Bombers, which make her violently ill and induce an abortion. Although he has never supported the family adequately nor been faithful to his wife and is pressuring her to turn her land over to him, he tells Sheila that her mother broke his heart when she said that they were through, a statement that astonishes her. She concludes that her mother has done everything for him except the one thing he requires, that she fuss over him and pretend he is perfect.

FREEMAN, BILL (WILLIAM BRADFORD) (1938–), born in London, Ontario; Canadian sociologist and writer. He dropped out of high school and spent three years wandering across Canada and London, England, working at a variety of jobs. He then returned to earn his B.A. degree from Acadia University in Wolfville, Nova Scotia, and his M.A. and Ph.D. degrees from McMaster University, in sociology and economic history. These interests are reflected in his series of novels starring Meg Bains, set in the 1870s, each dealing with labor-management relations in various Canadian industries, in which the feisty girl and her brothers help the underdog workers to attain some measure of economic justice. The first, *Shantymen of Cache Lake** (Lorimer, 1975), set in a lumber camp in eastern Ontario, won the first Canada Council Award, and for the five related novels Freeman received the Vicky Metcalf Award. They have been praised for their faithful depiction of the work in the camp, aboard ships and fishing boats, and in a clothing factory and for their concern with the exploitation of the ordinary workers. He has also published two works of social history for adults, *1005: Political Life in a Union Local* (Lorimer, 1982), a history of local 1005 of the United Steel Workers of America, and *Their Town: The Mafia, the Media, and the Party Machine* (Lorimer, 1979), an expose of Hamilton, Ontario, written with his wife, Marsha Hewitt*.

FRENCH, SIMON (1957–), born in Sydney, New South Wales, Australia; teacher, youth worker, novelist. He grew up in Blacktown, a western suburb of Sydney, attended Marayong Public School, Blacktown High School, and Mitchell College, where he earned his teacher's diploma in 1979. He started his first novel, *Hey Phantom Singlet* (Angus, 1975), a story about school life, while he was in high school, and it was published just before his seventeenth birthday, being cited for Special Mention for the Book of the Year Award. His second novel, *Cannily, Cannily** (Angus, 1981), about the son of migrant workers, was commended for the Book of the Year Award, and a third, *All We Know** (Angus, 1986), was winner of the award. Although all three are notable for realistic pictures of home and school life, they show a steady progression of skill in the handling of structure and plot. French taught Infants' School in New South Wales from 1980 to 1984 and served as a youth worker from 1984 to 1987. He has also worked as a library clerical assistant, a fruit picker, and in pre-school child care.

FRYER, JOHN (*The Lieutenant**), carping, disgruntled sailing master who almost incites a second mutiny against the captain. He questions the captain's judgment, refuses orders to do work that he thinks is not part of his job, and grumbles about everything. He backs down at a showdown with the captain on Sunday Island, when he sees that he doesn't have the backing of enough of the crew and that the captain is absolutely sincere when he says he will kill him for any more insubordination.

FYFE MACPHEE (*The True Story of Spit MacPhee**), half-mad old recluse watch and clock repairer, grandfather of Spit* MacPhee. Mr.* Quayle tells the "true story" of Spit and Fyfe at Spit's custody hearing. Fyfe, a proud and self-sufficient emigrant from Scotland, came to St. Helen after the death of his son in a fire and set up housekeeping in an old boat boiler he painted red and green and enlarged with a wooden addition. Shortly thereafter Spit and Spit's mother, Mary, moved in. After the death of Mary, who had been horribly disfigured in the fire, Fyfe and Spit live alone in the old boiler. Fyfe occasionally suffers fits brought on by a terrible head injury he sustained during World War I and which was repaired with a metal plate. A raucous but admirable old man, Fyfe is respected in the town although he is also sometimes ridiculed. Spit loves him dearly.

G

GALAHAD SCHWARTZ AND THE COCKROACH ARMY (Nyberg*, Morgan, Groundwood/Douglas, 1987), comic fantasy set recently somewhere in the Latin American jungle and then in a North American city called Glitterville. When his Nobel-prize-winning scientist parents leave the jungle by balloon to bring rain clouds to the Sahara and fail to return on schedule, their son, Galahad, 11, flies to Glitterville where his grandfather Schwartz lives. He finds the balding, orange-haired, green-eyed old fellow (a typical Schwartz in appearance) living in a dingy, rundown apartment house, which is infested with cockroaches and other vermin, and supporting himself by playing the guitar and singing cowboy songs on street corners. He shares his sparsely furnished rooms with a wheelchair-bound blind man named Wheels, and their friend and cook is Slim, who runs the tattoo parlor downstairs and who calls the boy Galley Head. Also downstairs is an exterminating establishment run by a small, unsavory character named Creetch, whose right-hand man is the giant Angel. Before long, Galahad discovers that by using their exterminating spray cans Creetch and Angel can make people disappear, too, but at first no one believes him. One day while exploring the public library, which is underground, Galahad finds a tunnel in which he encounters Quig, his former butler and an Indian medicine man, who teaches him to speak with animals. The mayor of Glitterville, an ineffectual administrator who performs comic routines on television, announces that there will be a parade, with three million dollars going to the best entry. Galahad organizes his human friends and his animal and insect friends to present a superb float. But before he receives the award, Creetch takes over the town, his hoodlums threatening everyone who opposes him with instant obliteration, and the city seems doomed. Since Creetch wants to learn how Galahad can communicate with animals, Galahad lures him and his minions to a barge in the river, where they are beset by millions of insects, including an army of cockroaches. After that, incidents happen thick and fast for a rousing, rushed climax. The upshot is that the villains' disappearing spray loses its effectiveness at the critical moment. Their barge breaks loose and is carried out to sea, but Galahad swims to shore. Slim, who had turned traitor, sees the error of his ways, is given the three million dollars, runs for mayor, and is elected, and the city returns to normal. The Schwartz parents arrive having succeeded in making the Sahara bloom, and they, Galahad, and Wheels repair to the jungle, leaving Grampa Schwartz to the guitar and street singing he loves. Though less than a hundred pages long, the story is jam-packed with incidents. The characters and action are exaggerated for effect, like a cartoon, and some elements are tenuously connected, like a surrealistic painting, with the result that the comedy often seems strained. Although some might read social comment here and there, the book's main intention is to provide fast-moving and undemanding entertainment. Can. Gov. General's Winner.

GEE, MAURICE (GOUGH) (1931–), born in Whakatane, New Zealand; highly acclaimed novelist for adults, who has also written several fantasies for children. The best known of his children's books are the "O" trilogy, the first of which, *The Halfmen of O** (Oxford, 1982; Merrimack, 1983), received the New Zealand Children's Book of the Year Award. It and its successors, *The Priests of Ferris** (Oxford, 1984) and *Motherstone** (Oxford, 1985), both of which were included on the short list for the award, are action-filled, dramatic good-versus-evil adventures, tinged with the comic and set on a planet reached through an abandoned gold mine. For children he also wrote the fantasies *Under the Mountain* (Oxford, 1979), which was serialized for television, *The World around the Corner* (Oxford, 1980), and *The Fire-raiser* (Penguin, 1986), which was also a televised series. After earning degrees from Avondale College and the University of Auckland, he studied further at Auckland Teachers College. He worked at teaching and odd jobs for ten years, earned a degree in library science, and served as a librarian in Napier and Auckland before turning to full-time writing in 1976. He published his first novel for adults, *The Big Season* (Hutchinson) in 1962, and since then he has received many honors for his work, including the prestigious James Tait Black Prize and the New Zealand Book Award, among others, for *Plumb* (Faber, 1978). His collection of short stories, *A Glorious Morning, Comrade* (Auckland, 1975), and his novel *Meg* (Faber, 1981; St. Martin's, 1982), both for adults, were also New Zealand Book Award winners. He has written many plays for television and films and contributed to periodicals and anthologies.

GEORGE STRONG (*The Secret Family**), widowed father of Ariel, who, insensitive and busy with his own concerns, leaves her almost entirely in the care of the grumbling housekeeper, Mrs. Murphy. When he does have an engagement to take her to dinner, he forgets and leaves her waiting for hours, while he has steak, then takes her home without anything to eat. Prodded by Mrs. Murphy, who, despite her crochety temper, is protective of Ariel, to pay more attention to his daughter, he sends her to have golf lessons, planning to fit her in along with his Saturday morning game, thereby losing no extra time to fathering. In the middle of their regular game, which Ariel never protests although she finds it boring, he suddenly announces that he is planning to be married again, but tells her nothing about her prospective stepmother.

GEORGE TREVOR (*Good Luck to the Rider**), larger and quieter of Barbara's twin brothers. George is sympathetic toward his younger sister and agrees to help bring home the colt she has found, even though he doubts that his father will allow Barbara to raise such an unpromising stray. Throughout George is supportive to Barbara and friendly to her school chum, Will* Stockton.

GERALD HENNESSY (*To the Wild Sky**), son of a man who inherited an eight-hundred-square-mile Crown leasehold and is one of the wealthiest sheep raisers in Australia. Gerald is good looking, well mannered and intelligent, but he is not as confident as he appears. When Bert, the taxi driver, baits him, he is edgy and becomes upset. Although he has bragged that he can fly a plane, he has never landed and knows little about the instruments, so he alone realizes how desperate their situation is when their bush pilot dies in the air. On the beach, Gerald is dismayed to realize that he is not the leader and that the others do not automatically take his advice to stay at the crash site.

GHAMKA MAN-OF-MEN (Merchant*, Eve, Tafelberg, 1985), boy's growing-up story set on the southern shores of Africa in the late fifteenth century, near what is now Mossel Bay, South Africa. Ghamka is the son of Attaqua, leader of his clan of the Khoi-Khoin people, who have lived in peace for several years in an area occupied by Obiqua's clan, having been driven south by a cattle sickness. When the weather becomes too wet and the cattle, on which the Khoi-Khoin depend, are ill from foot rot, Obiqua does not honor his promise to let Attaqua's people graze their herds on higher ground. He attacks their village, hoping to take the remaining cattle for himself. In a battle witnessed by Ghamka and his cousin, Xhan, from high in a tree, Attaqua wins by cunning planning, although he and Xhan's father, Khori, are both wounded and a number of their warriors are killed. Rather than stay in the place of death, Attaqua leads his people westward, stopping at what seem likely sites but each time moving on again because of the nearness of the Khoi-San, the bush people who steal cattle, or leopards that kill their sheep. At last they find a home on the banks of a great ocean bay, where they have a good spring of fresh water and high, dry grazing land. One day Ghamka sights two small spots approaching across the water. As they come near, he sees that they are like two bulging huts of wood. Logs are let down their sides, and men sit on them and push them through the water with branches. The man in charge, who has skin as pale as milk and strange, light eyes, makes signs that Attaqua's people do not understand, and he makes marks on the sand, "Bartolomeu Dias." When the strangers return the next day, Attaqua's men are ready to fight them but hold off until the milk-skins take on fresh water. Fearing that their spring will dry up, the natives throw rocks and spears and are appalled that the strangers turn and kill Ni-qua, the best herdsman and special friend of Ghamka, with a crossbow. The strangers leave, and, when they return a month later, Attaqua's people stay in their village. In the next ten years, Ghamka grows up, passing the tests of manhood and assuming a more important role in the clan. His rivalry with Khan sometimes flares into open antagonism, but gradually each follows his own path, Khan becoming a skilled hunter like Khori, Ghamka learning how to make policy and lead men wisely, like his father. When the thunderbirds come over the water again, Ghamka goes with his father to the shore to meet the strangers. This time their leader is a dark-haired man who does not seem to be laughing at them and gives his name as Vasco da Gama. With him they trade cattle and sheep for pretty beads and some of the precious stone to heat in the fire and then pound into hard spear heads. After a month, the strangers, like the ones before them, take water from the spring. When Attaqua tries to stop them, they shoot cannons from the ships and raise a cross on the shore. After they leave, the people destroy all signs of the strangers and move inland. The next spring Ghamka marries a girl from a distant Khoi-Khoin village and goes to live with his wife's people until their first child is born, after which he will return to take his father's place in his own clan. The story also tells of the rivalry between the two medicine men, Khetsi, a magician priest, and Gai-Aob, a healer and herbalist, and includes interesting characters like Noni, Ghamka's understanding mother, and Haru, his wise grandfather. Although the life of Attaqua's people is largely speculation, their story is interesting and plausible and is treated with dignity. A historical author's note gives facts of the early Portuguese explorations and what anthropologists know of the Khoi-Khoin of the period. Descriptions of the setting are memorable. Sanlam.

GIBBIE BOW (*Playing Beatie Bow**), Gilbert, a spoiled, disagreeable boy of almost ten, son of Samuel* Bow. The family caters to him since he has been slow to recover from typhoid fever, and they do not expect him to live much longer. Sulky and demanding, he continually whines and badgers for favors of one kind or another, insists the others wait on him, and spouts pious sentiments to get his way. Abby Kirk rescues him from the fire Samuel accidentally sets, thus ironically perpetuating the Tallisker family Gift* through Gibbie.

THE GIFT (*Playing Beatie Bow**), special power handed down through the Tallisker clan and inherited by Granny* Tallisker. It originated when Granny's seventh grandmother, Osla, was taken by elves. Osla returned from Elfland with a child about to be born. With that child came the Gift, the ability to see the future, to heal, and to use secret wisdom. A prophecy goes with the Gift; it states that whenever the Gift is about to die out, a stranger will come to keep it going. The stranger can be identified because he or she will have something belonging to the Talliskers. Because Granny feels her gift waning and because Abby is wearing the crocheted collar Granny plans to make, Granny is certain that Abby is the promised stranger who will make the Gift strong again.

GISELLE MARTIN (*The Sun Horse**), at eleven the youngest child in the French-Canadian family whose father disappeared while seeking the legendary palomino Sun Horse. Because she misses him so much, is worried about her careworn, overworked mother, and is concerned because her brothers can't manage the ranch, she and Mark* Gunning decide to search for Mr. Martin. Giselle is spirited, intelligent, and adventurous but inclined to become anxious and nervous under stress. The talking bat bites her, thus putting a mark on her that is recognized by the other magical bats of Forgetful Valley, which then help her and Mark defeat the terrible, vicious Thunderbird. She has dimension as a character but is not memorable.

GLEESON, LIBBY (1950–), Australian novelist whose sociological problem novel for girls, *Eleanor, Elizabeth** (Angus, 1984; Holiday, 1990), was highly commended for the Australian Children's Book of the Year Award. Eleanor, 12, is unhappy when her family moves to the bush farm of her grandmother, Elizabeth, until she discovers Elizabeth's diary in the old boarded-up schoolhouse and the past sheds light on the present. The story reveals Gleeson's skill with dialogue, family relationships, and setting. She has also written *I Am Susannah* (Angus, 1987; Holiday, 1990), a mystery in which a girl seeks the truth about the strange new resident of her best friend's old house. A former high school teacher, Gleeson lives in Sydney.

GLEN DYNON (*Pastures of the Blue Crane**), unsteady, fun-loving son of the druggist in the little town near Geebin Farm. He squires Ryl* Merewether to dances and takes her surfing. He evidently looks down on the South Sea Islanders (blackbirds*), and while he is aware that Ryl has South Sea Island blood through her mother, he dates her and regards Perry* Davis as a rival for her affection. An argument between him and Ryl leads to the disclosure of Ryl's ancestry. He is a conventional, utilitarian figure.

GOAT (*Last Chance Summer**), nickname for Greg Land, at fourteen the oldest boy on the Jenner farm, already seeming in some ways like an old man, shut in emotionally and more weary than angry. He resents Marl for causing him to expose himself to caring for someone else, but he seems impelled to protect the younger boy on several occasions. At Ryerson, the reform school where Goat was sent at age eleven for breaking and entering, he fought so often that he was placed in "closed custody," confined alone to a locked room all the time that he was not in class. Abused as a young child, his body is so covered with scars that he keeps his shirt or his pajamas buttoned to his throat even in the Badlands heat so that no one can see what he considers his shameful condition. Although Marl is the protagonist, Goat is the most memorable character.

GOING TO THE DOGS (McRae*, Russell, Viking, 1987), realistic psychological problem novel that examines contemporary small-town youth culture in the northern Ontario, Canada, mill town of Nugget. The episodic account of an adolescent in rebellion against parents and society starts in Billy Mackenzie's nineteenth year, just before he drops out of school. The story then traces his increasingly turbulent adolescence mainly through his relationships with the most important people in his life, his best friend, Rocky* Barbizan; his younger sister, Anne; his parents, Agnes* and Alex* Mackenzie; and his girlfriend, Poppy* Richardson. Popular Billy is an honor student and a sports star and dates the prettiest girl around. Increasingly antagonistic toward adults and manipulative, he yearns for freedom, which he feels depends upon money (from thirteen on he has various jobs, from working in a gas station to the local mill) and also seeks through alcohol and drugs. Rocky Barbizan, who drops out of school when the coach catches him with drugs, deals drugs, providing Billy first with marijuana and then harder stuff. The two get stoned regularly, in this condition having long discussions in which they roundly condemn society. Anne, the most significant person in Billy's life, commits suicide at fifteen. Before that, beginning when she is nine and Billy is twelve, she and Billy get stoned in Billy's room every Tuesday night, their parents' night out. In long, bitter talks, they dissect their family, Anne quite thoroughly devastating any childish illusions Billy harbors about the Mackenzie home being a happy one. Both Billy and Anne detest their parents, Agnes for her castrating ways and Alex for being a wimp. After Anne's death, Billy has little to do with his parents, deliberately keeping their relationship as impersonal as he can. Sexually active as he enters his teens, he starts dating and having sex with Poppy at sixteen, and the fondness he feels for her grows into genuine love. When Poppy discovers that she is pregnant the September both begin grade thirteen, the book moves to a climax— Billy's confrontation with his family—after which he leaves home. A showdown with the Richardsons soon follows. He and Poppy leave school and head for Toronto, where they hope to complete their education on savings he has accumulated and the bonds her family has set aside for her. The language is earthy and explicit, and some scenes are graphically vivid. Although Billy's point of view remains central and the result is a searing indictment of life in a small town and of contemporary family life in particular, the book also reveals how shallow even the so-called best of the younger generation, youth like Billy, can be. To them, life appears dismal, stifling, meager, worthless—drugs pervade school and community, power-hungry teachers enforce traditional and outmoded rules and are narrow minded and generally ignorant both of real life and their subjects, the police employ Fascist tactics, family life is cruel and abusive because parents seek to control each other out of the lust for power, and youth are pawns, who either simply capitulate and become clones of their parents or maintain some measure of individuality by turning to alcohol or other drugs, the late-night social scene, and sex. Especially imaginative ones like Billy are the most hurt because they are the most susceptible. The dialogue is extensive and realistic. Especially memorable scenes include Billy and Rocky evading a police net late at night, Billy and Anne raking their parents over the coals in Billy's room, Billy's mother verbally and psychologically abusing her husband, and Billy using sex to get his way with his teachers. The Mackenzies and the Richardsons typify married couples, the first set wife dominated, the latter husband dominated, and Poppy is a sweet, somewhat naive and trusting young woman who learns to make up her own mind. Rocky Barbizan seems fake, from his name to his job with an international drug dealer for whom he transports drugs by air and with the proceeds buys a dazzling silver Porsche. Plain, obese, mother-hated and mother-hating, super-intelligent Anne captures the reader's emotions even though many of her conversations with Billy ring false in the psychological conclusions and the experiential impressions they convey. Billy is both revolting and winning, revolting for his grossness, self-destructiveness, judgmental attitude, and self-righteousness, and sympathetic for carefully considering the situation with Poppy and deciding that they can have a good life together. Evidently he learns that freedom can be dearly bought and carries with it certain obligations. There are a few lighter passages, and the book moves fast, but on the whole the tone is bleak and pessimistic. Can. Gov. General's Hon. Ment.

GOLDEN (*The Silver Brumby**), beautiful creamy tame mare Thowra lures away. She never learns brumby ways, and, when about to give birth, she returns to the security of the corral, from which Thowra must recapture her. Golden is beautiful and sweet tempered, but she lacks the self-confidence and toughness of the wild horses and is most notable for her beauty. She is a foil for Mirri and Bel* Bel, the mother mares.

THE GOLDEN BUDDHA (Joshi*, Niharika, ill. Subir Roy, CBT, India, 1982), realistic detective novel set in recent years in northern India among Tibetan settlements and in adjacent Tibet. It involves the recovery of a priceless Tibetan idol. Although the characters and incidents are fictitious, they have their source in the flight from Tibet into India of the Dalai Lama and his followers after the Chinese absorbed their homeland. The story begins some twenty years after the emigration with an old, one-eyed lama in a Tibetan community in Miao, India, a small town on the borders of Assam and Arunachal Prades. Swearing his friend to secrecy, the dying carpet maker divulges that he is Tashi Tsering, the former head priest and keeper of the Royal Museum at Lhasa. Before leaving his homeland, he hid the museum's most sacred possession, a Golden Buddha, to keep it from falling into the hands of bandits. He gives his friend an exquisitely decorated prayer wheel, which he says contains the secret to where the Buddha lies, and tells him to order his crippled son to take the wheel to the Dalai Lama at McLeodganj. As it happens, Phunsok Dorje, the nephew of the now deceased head bandit, has been living at McLeodganj as one of the lamas and caring for the Dalai's orchid garden. He chances to glimpse the prayer wheel, recognizes it, and kills the youth, dumping his body into the river. Most of the rest of the book tells how, ironically, he convinces the crippled youth's father to help him in his quest for the Buddha and describes the details of his search. His journey of several weeks, making use of a map he finds inside the wheel, takes him by plane to the village of Tuting just outside Tibet and on foot through dense jungle and precipitous terrain. Skillfully avoiding the police and border authorities, he arrives at Gelling inside Tibetan territory, where through deduction he finds the idol in a cave of blue stones. On his return, he cleverly attaches himself to an anthropological-archaeological party, one member of whom has an interest in orchids, and hides the Golden Buddha at the bottom of a bag of rare orchids. He is unaware that Detective Inspector K. D. Rao is on his trail. K. D. makes connections with the scientists, and the bandit is apprehended by chance at Tuting. He is discovered hiding in a hedge, sniffed out by Chili—the Lhasa apso dog that he had earlier booted out of his way—belonging to a child with the party. Despite numerous clichés (''K. D.'s voice was hard as steel'') and many awkward expressions, the entertainment value is high for the intended audience of middle-grade readers. The pace is swift, the sense of place strong, and the tension well sustained. The characters are the familiar good-bad types of the genre, the children, Pinku and Ranjat, local officials, and scientists are choral figures and difficult to tell apart, and the author makes generous use of coincidence and detective story conventions. Although there are frequent scene shifts from the bandit to ''good guys'' and back again, the moves are accomplished with skill, and the otherwise uncomplicated linear plot remains clear. The most arresting figure is the old lama, whose story, which introduces the book, grabs the reader's attention. Some characters appear in *The Mystery of the Fake Arjuna**. CBT of India, Second Prize.

GOOD LUCK TO THE RIDER (Phipson*, Joan, ill. Margaret Horder, Angus, 1953; Harcourt, 1968), horse story set at Tikera sheep ranch in the Bungaree district of Australia in the mid-twentieth century. When Barbara Trevor, 12, finds a foal whose mother's shoulder has been broken in a storm, she does not protest her brother's shooting the mare, but she insists on bringing the colt to the home ranch, even though her sister, Sheila, 17, and her twin brothers, George* and Clive*, about fifteen, object that its sire is probably inferior stock and, moreover, it is a ludicrously marked creature with a white blaze lopsided to give its face a clown-like appearance. Her sheep-rancher father is less than enthusiastic, but her mother, knowing that this means much to the indecisive, timid girl who has been sick often, sticks up for her. Although she must go away to boarding school for the first time only weeks after the find, she spends as much time as possible with the colt and dreams about him when she is away. Boarding school is bewildering to her at first, but she makes one good friend, Will* (Willhelmenia) Stockton, a practical, self-possessed girl from North Queensland. At the suggestion of sharp-tongued Clive, who likes to play jokes, she names her colt Rosinante, not realizing the implications of the name. Mr. Trevor has his wise horse breaker, Mike, train the colt, and by the time he is a two-year-old, Barbara, who has been afraid to ride the pony, Ting-a-ling, which her father bought for her, is riding the very large Ross with confidence. When Will comes for a holiday, they discover that Ross is a natural jumper, and

Barbara decides to enter the children's hunt class at the Bungaree horse show. Though her family is astonished, she trains her horse with determination and rides well to win the blue ribbon. In a story almost without conflict or tension, the main focus is on Barbara's gaining confidence in herself through her devotion to her horse. Unfortunately, too much of this is told in the wise comments of the parents to each other about her, and not enough is shown through Barbara's own perceptions and actions. The sense of locale at the ranch (but not at school) is strong and makes a more lasting impression than the slight story. Aust. Bk. of Year Winner.

GRAHAM (*Ash Road**), the one of the trio of city boys camping on holiday who actually starts the destructive fire. Graham is slightly younger and smaller than the other two and has old-fashioned, very straight-laced parents, and he has been surprised that they allowed him to be part of the outing. In the end, after hysterically hiding and nearly being killed by the fire, he is persuaded by Lorna George that it will be easier and better to confess to his accident and to face the consequences than to continue running.

GRAMPS SWALES (*What's the Matter, Girl?**), grandfather of Anna Swales and father of Anna's Uncle* Arion, Aunt* Gemma, and about a dozen other children. German born, he and Gran* emigrated to western Canada. He likes to pinch Gran's fanny and tends to be earthy in speech. The reader gathers that time has mellowed him and that he has become more indulgent toward his family. He regrets signing the papers that allowed Arion to enlist in the army during World War II; yet he felt keenly the community's suspicion directed toward him because of his ethnic background. He is one of the most interesting figures in the book.

GRANDMOTHER (*Sweetgrass**), Sweetgrass's Blackfoot Blood grandmother, a stubborn, outspoken, old woman. She was once a warrior, like many Blackfoot women of her generation. She is tough, decisive, and resourceful, traits that show up well during the Assiniboin attack, when she and not Almost-Mother* plan their escape. Grandmother is away—living with other relatives—during the smallpox epidemic but dies of the disease anyway.

GRANDPA SCOTTY CAMERON (*Callie's Castle**), Scots-born grandfather of Callie Cameron. Although his son, Callie's father, died in an automobile accident when Callie was a year old, she suddenly yearns deeply for him and runs away to Grandpa, a substitute for the father she never really knew. Grandpa is a retired builder who works as a handyman for a local business and lives in a tiny cottage rent-free in return for doing yard work. For some time he has not had much contact with the Beck-Cameron household, but he soon realizes that Callie needs his support. He is the chief force behind fixing up the cupola, Callie's "castle," and he encourages Callie to stand up for herself against the lively and often pushy younger half-siblings. He is a laconic Scot but is never dour or standoffish, and the other children love him, too. He loves his ex-daughter-in-law and has a lot of respect for Callie's stepfather, Laurens* Beck. At first it seems that he will be just another type, but the author soon gives him an attractive individuality.

GRANDPA TANNER (*Ash Road**), oldest inhabitant of the road, a lonely man, very fond of the neighboring Buckingham children. When the fire approaches, with cool courage and presence of mind, he ties the Robinson baby in a basket and Julie Buckingham, 3, into a chair and lets them down the well, expecting that he will be killed but that in investigating his remains searchers will find the children. At the last minute he covers the well, after instructing Julie to call out, "Here I am, everybody. Down the well." He then soaks a blanket and crawls under it. The sudden rain saves him.

GRANGER, HELEN, born in Beechworth, Victoria; Australian author with Frances Pearce* under the pseudonym Helen Frances of *The Devil's Stone** (Omnibus, 1983). A substantial novel both of historical fiction and contemporary realism set against Aborigine beliefs, it was named Australian Children's Book of the Year. After several years of traveling and working in Europe, Granger married an American whom she met in Crete. They lived on the west coast of the United States before moving to Australia in the late 1970s and settling in the Adelaide Hills. The area provides the setting for *The Devil's Stone*.

GRANNY TALLISKER (*Playing Beatie Bow**), resolute old woman who emigrated from the Orkney Islands to Sydney, Australia, in the 1870s to care for her dead daughter's family. She rules the house firmly and kindly and possesses the family Gift* of healing, second sight, and wisdom. She is convinced that Abby Kirk is the stranger of the family prophecy, the one who will keep the Gift in the family. The crocheted collar Abby finds in Natalie Crown's mother's rag bag and affixes to the green velvet Edwardian dress she wears as an affectation bears an Orkney pattern and is handwork that Granny makes.

GRAN SWALES (*What's the Matter, Girl?**), grandmother of Anna Swales and mother of Anna's Uncle* Arion, Aunt* Gemma, and about a dozen other children who have survived from her original seventeen. Born in Flanders, Gran married Gramps*, a German, against her family's wishes and emigrated with him to Canada. Aunt Gemma and Arion are Gran's favorites among her offspring, and she doesn't seem to feel that there is anything wrong with showing favoritism. Gran is impatient and often expresses her feelings in her "sharp bird's tongue." When Anna moons for Arion on Gran's front porch, Gran, who dislikes idleness, dumps potatoes and toothpicks in Anna's lap and tells her to at least keep occupied by making potato men. Gran is one of the most fully realized figures in the novel.

GRAVES, RICHARD H., Australian writer who received a commendation for Australian Children's Book of the Year for *Spear and Stockwhip: A Tale of the Territory** (Dymocks, 1950). This mystery-adventure of the western novel type in which five youths escort a herd of 2,400 Herefords one thousand miles from eastern New Queensland to pasturage in the Northern Territory is filled with action and conflict and evokes a good sense of the region. Graves also wrote the Bushcraft Handbook series that includes *Bush Aircraft* (Dymocks, 195–?), *Bush Hutmaking* (Shakespeare, 1952), and *Knots and Lashings* (Shakespeare, 1952).

THE GREAT CHIEF: MASKEPETOON, WARRIOR OF THE CREES (Wood*, Kerry, ill. John A. Hall, Macmillan, 1957; St. Martin's, 1958), fictionalized account of the life of Maskepetoon, historical chief of the Cree Indians of Alberta, Canada, set mainly in the first half of the nineteenth century. About two-thirds of the novel is devoted to the early years in which Maskepetoon establishes himself as a mighty war chief. The story starts while he is in his teens, bitter and angry because his father, Redpine, a leader in Chief Two-Dogs's band, refuses to let him embark on the war path until he has satisfied his vision quest. Under the instruction of the wise, peace-loving medicine man Kukaku the Crow, whose daughter, Pa-pee, the youth much admires, he goes for a six-day quest to Sunset Hill, the highest of the Medicine Lodge Hills. On the last day he has a vision in which he sees his tribesmen facing the Blackfoot in battle and himself on a hill watching them, his arm greatly enlarged and outstretched between them, painful with bullet and arrow wounds. The vision pleases Kukaku, who bestows on the youth the name under which he becomes famous, Maskepetoon, meaning wounded or broken arm, and he obscurely remarks that the youth will understand the vision's significance when he knows why he tried to stop the battle. Still determined to kill enemies, the boy sets out alone and single-handedly kills three Blackfeet, traditional enemies of the Cree, returning with their horses and plunder. He offers Kukaku the horses for Pa-pee, but Kukaku refuses. Angry at being rejected, he does more such feats of bravery against the Blackfeet, but with no success at winning Pa-pee. He marries Menish, ironically a pacifist, who becomes the mother of his only son. As the years pass, Maskepetoon becomes known for his prowess in hunting as well as in battle, and Menish adds many feathers to his eagle headdress, though always sadly when they symbolize fallen foes. His fame spreads, and his fighting force swells to fifty warriors. His attitude toward fighting changes one day, however, when outside Rocky Mountain House trading post he is challenged to a duel of knives by a young Blackfeet. He defeats the man handily, but spares his life because he feels sudden sympathy for the man's wife and small child, seeing the little family as the mirror of his own. He travels widely and even accompanies a white trader named John A. Sanford to Washington, where he receives a medal with Andrew Jackson's image on it. Another turning point in his life comes when he takes a bullet in the arm and his best friend, At-Toos the crippled arrow-maker, falls from a Blackfoot arrow while the two are out hunting buffalo. The meaning of the vision suddenly comes clear. After another Blackfoot raid kills nineteen Crees, including Chief Two-Dogs, he accepts the chieftainship but with the proviso that he will no longer lead war parties. Kukaku approves and gives him Pa-pee in marriage. (She and their child later die in a smallpox epidemic.) From this point on, Maskepetoon works as zealously for peace as he previously did for success on the war path. He becomes firmly of the mind that the Indians must stop killing one another in order to preserve what is left of their culture in the face of the white advance, but his words mostly fall on deaf ears. In 1869, when he is an old man, a messenger comes to his camp with the news that the Blackfoot have raided a Cree camp near Fort Edmonton. He takes his Hudson's Bay Company flag, the banner under which he has ridden on many a peace mission, and goes alone to the Blackfoot camp. As he tries to dissuade the chief from further hostilities, he is killed by a bullet from behind, assassinated by an enemy he never sees and by a weapon he has urged the Indians not to adopt for warfare. Characters are flat types, depicted only in general terms, and most are only names. Plot development is hampered by the tragic facts, and the tone frequently becomes informational and sounds like a textbook: "Each adult buffalo provided a hundred pounds of dried meat; also fresh delicacies of tongue, heart, kidneys, and liver. . . . Tough meat from old animals was kept in the dry state and called 'jerky.' " As a novel, the book is mainly memorable for several dramatic scenes, particularly those in which Maskepetoon spares the life of his dueling opponent and where he shakes hands with his son's murderer, practicing the forgiveness he preaches, and for the clear sense it gives of the Indians' way of life at the time of first contact with whites. The first part of the book, which is the more fictionalized, is the more interesting; the last part reads almost like a history book outline of this valiant leader's ill-fated attempts to promote peace and save his people. Can. Gov. General's Winner.

GREAT-GRANDMOTHER SCHOLAR (*The Haunting**), 88, the matriarch of the "papery" Scholar clan, Barney Palmer's dead mother's family. She has sharp, unfriendly eyes and a fetish for neatness, and no one in the family dares cross her. She herself was born a witch, hated her ability, suppressed it, and kept it secret. She was determined that the similar ability of her son, Great-Uncle Cole, be suppressed and that he be an ordinary, well-behaved boy like his brothers. Mrs. Scholar represents domineering parents.

GREENER, LESLIE (1900–1974), born in Capetown, South Africa; Australian archaeological artist, teacher, and author. He was a graduate of the Royal Military Academy at Sandhurst, England, and a student at Academie Julien, Paris, and at the University of London. After serving as a career officer in the British Indian Army, he taught art and French at Victoria College, Alexandria, Egypt, and then became a member of the University of Chicago Oriental Institute Expedition, Luxor, Egypt, as an archaeological artist. On this experience are based a number of his books, including *Wizard Boatman of the Nile* (Harrap, 1957), *High Dam over Nubia* (Viking, 1962), and *The Discovery of Egypt* (Cassell, 1966; Viking, 1967). For several years he worked for Associated Newspapers in Sydney, Australia, then served with the Australian Army, was taken prisoner in Malaya (now West Malaysia), held by the Japanese for three and a half years, and after the end of World War II, returned to his newspaper work in Sydney. From 1949 to 1954 he was the director of adult education in Tasmania, Australia. Then he again joined a University of Chicago expedition as an artist. He wrote books and scripts for both radio and television, mostly on archaeological subjects. His novel, *Moon Ahead** (Viking, 1951), though a departure into science fiction space travel, starts and ends at an archaeological site in Australia.

THE GREEN LAUREL (Spence*, Eleanor, Oxford, 1963; Roy, 1963), a pleasing, uplifting, encouraging realistic novel of family and community life with girls' growing-up story aspects, set in New South Wales, Australia, not long after World War II. For years Lesley Somerville, 11, and her sister, Rae, 10, have traveled with their parents throughout the countryside, living in a tent and attending school irregularly. Their father, John, operates a train concession for small children at fairs and carnivals. High-spirited, confident, athletic Rae enjoys the nomadic life, but less self-assured Lesley longs for roots, like those of the green laurel in a poem by Yeats, and yearns to go to high school and eventually study architecture. When John falls ill of some unexplained respiratory ailment, the family settles for a year in Dragon Bay on the coast not far from Sydney. The girls make friends with Meredith* and Richard* Brent, a well-off sister and brother from Sydney, whose father is an engineer and who are vacationing at a nearby hotel. When rowdies disrupt the concession and damage the train, John overexerts himself and faces an indefinite period in a veterans' hospital in Sydney. The family sells the train and moves its few belongings to a duplex in low-cost housing on the outskirts of Sydney intended primarily for immigrants. Since she had eagerly anticipated living in a house, Lesley is disappointed by the bleakness of the neighborhood and feels unwanted. Although she eventually makes friends among the settlement youth and even is invited to join a club called the ''Blackbutt Hill Outcasts'' led by a youth named Steve*, pursues her interest in drawing, and continues her friendship with the Brents, she realizes that she may not pass the exams for high school and feels even more rootless than ever. John suggests that she enter a house design contest and writes also to the school headmaster suggesting that he organize the youth in establishing a library for the settlement. Lesley rises to the occasion, showing unexpected qualities of leadership, and spearheads the effort, even locating the culprits responsible for vandalizing the place once it is opened. The end finds her with third prize in the contest, and for the first time she feels like part of a community. Though extensive and idiomatic, the dialogue often seems false. The characterization is minimal, and, except for Rae, who is round, and Lesley, who is also dynamic, all the figures are types or one-dimensional. Lesley is a likeable protagonist, and it is easy to sympathize with her efforts to find a place both literally and figuratively. The plot moves unevenly, and some incidents seem concocted. The themes of love of family, neighborliness, cooperation, perseverance, growth through involvement, facing issues, and parental responsibility are clear and really too many for the plot to bear. Everybody behaves too decently, or comes around too readily, for credibility. Although the author is never moralistic or preachy, she seems ever-present and obligated, for example, to point out Lesley's growth instead of letting readers arrive at their own conclusions about her. Aust. Bk. of Year Winner.

THE GREEN WIND (Fowler*, Thurley, Rigby, 1985), story of family life in a fruit-growing community north of Sydney, Australia. Centered on bright, sharp-tongued Jennifer, 11, it traces the development of the four Robinson children during 1948, a year of hardships and discovery for all of them. Unlike pretty, artistic Margaret, 13, and self-confident Richard, 10, red-haired Jennifer is isolated by her prickly personality and her secret desire to write. Alexander, 8, also lives in a private world where his best friends are animals, mostly the chickens that he cares for devotedly and whom he entertains with his harmonica. Although the electric line has finally reached their farm, their father, who suffers mentally from having been a prisoner during World War II, lacks the money to have it installed. Jennifer's great desire to have a best friend seems to be fulfilled when a new girl, Beverley Martin, comes to school, but Beverley's visit to the Robinson farm is disastrous. When Jennifer returns to school a week later after she and Richard have stayed out to help pick grapes, Beverley has spread word of the Robinson farm's deficiencies and is now best friends with Linda Grey. The other main concern in Jennifer's life is the inexplicable interest shown her by Raymond Bradley, a boy Margaret considers her own property. He confides in Jennifer that he writes poetry and asks to see some of her writing. Although at first reluctant, she finally gives him a piece—which she started in her secret copybook—titled "The Green Wind," in which she develops an idea about the feel of spring. When Linda and other girls in her class taunt her about green winds and pink frosts, she feels betrayed and at the first opportunity pushes Raymond off the edge of the bridge into deep mud. Only after Richard's teacher tells her that she recognized that his composition was not his own work but read it to the class as an example of imaginative writing does she realize that her brother has swiped a piece of her copybook and is to blame. She retaliates by letting the air out of Richard's bike tires and keeping the valves, so he has to walk home in the rain and collapses on the porch with a serious case of diphtheria. While he is in the hospital and they pick oranges on the quarantined farm, Jennifer suffers from guilt until her gentle father points out that they are all blaming themselves. Only Alexander, who sends his beloved harmonica to the hospital for Richard, is free of self-blame. At the end of Jennifer's last term in primary school, the Robinson farm at last has light at the push of a switch, a symbol of better things to come. In Jennifer's own life, the end of the year is rocky. She rescues Alexander from a crowd of older boys by charging into the group swinging her school bag wildly, driving off most of them and giving Raymond, who had mistakenly thought Alexander killed the dead ibis he is cradling, a black eye. In an essay contest sponsored by the local newspaper, two outstanding entries are named, Jennifer's and Linda Grey's, but the prize is given to Linda, whose father helped write hers. In the end, however, Jennifer triumphs. Raymond has secretly sent her essay to the Sydney newspaper along with one of his poems, and there on the children's page is "The Green Wind" by Jennifer Robinson. His own work has won nothing, but he is delighted for her and shyly asks if he may come see her in the afternoon. A secondary concern is the relationship between Richard and his father, whom the boy scorns for his lack of spirit. When he stops the ice-cream man's runaway horse, risking injury and possible death to save the man, Richard begins to see that he is no coward. The characterization, rather than plot, theme, or style, is the main attraction of the novel. Both parents are well drawn, the efficient, non-emotional mother and the gentle, disturbed father. The four children are perhaps too firmly differentiated, but Jennifer, in particular, is an interesting and believable girl, struggling to control her temper and still assert himself. Minor characters fare less well. Raymond is too forebearing to be entirely convincing, and Linda and Beverley are stock types. Aust. Bk. of Year Winner.

GREENWOOD, TED (EDWARD ALISTER) (1930–), born in Melbourne, Victoria, Australia; illustrator, teacher, writer. He was graduated from Melbourne Teachers' College with a Primary Teaching Qualification in 1949 and from the Royal Melbourne Institute of Technology with a Diploma of Art in 1959. He taught in primary school in Melbourne in the late 1940s and early 1950s, and he was a lecturer in art education at Melbourne Teachers' College from 1956 to 1960 and at Toorak Teachers' College, Toorak, Melbourne, from 1961 to 1968. He has served as deputy chairman of the Community Arts Board of the Australia Council for the Arts and has been a writer, illustrator, and craft reviewer for the *Age* newspaper. His illustrations for *Sly Old Wardrobe* by Ivan Southall* (Cheshire, 1968; St. Martin's, 1970) won the Picture Book of the Year Award, and *Joseph and Lulu and the Prindiville House Pigeons* (Angus, 1972), which he both wrote and illustrated, was commended for the Picture Book of the Year, as was also *Terry's Brrrmmm GT* (Angus, 1975), which in addition won the Visual Arts Award for illustration for the Australian Council for the Arts. Although he started as an illustrator and then wrote picture books, he has written longer books, including *The Pochetto Coat** (Hutchinson, 1978), a novel entirely in dialogue in which an old clown on the skids tells stories to the bear trainer's daughter, giving her courage to follow her own heart's desire to be a clown. It was commended for the Australian Book of the Year. Other titles of longer books by Greenwood include *The Boy Who Saw God* (Hutchinson, 1980), *Ginnie* (Kestrel, 1979), and *Marley and Friends* (Hutchinson, 1983).

GUARDIAN (*The Guardian of Isis**), the large and shining robot that directs affairs on Isis for the Lady Olwen*. Although a machine, he has strong emotions and is protective of Olwen, whom he loves dearly. He also has genuine concern for the residents of Cascade Valley, to whom over the years he has given important technology. Until Jody arrives at Bamboo Valley, the Guardian is unaware that the items have not been used for the intended purpose. Neither he nor Olwen knows, until Jody tells them, that the President has set himself up as the absolute ruler of the area and has banned technology. Although a familiar science fiction type, the Guardian is less exotic and gimmicky than most of his kind.

THE GUARDIAN OF ISIS (Hughes*, Monica, Hamilton, 1980; Atheneum, 1982), novel of science fiction set in the twenty-second century on the planet Isis in the galaxy of Ra. Descendants of emigrants from Earth several generations earlier, the now approximately eight hundred people of Isis live a semi-paranoid existence in secluded Cascade Valley. They have reverted to a primitive agricultural state and are governed by a tyrant, President Mark London, who insists that they abide by certain legends and taboos to maintain the status quo. Jody N'Kumo, probably in his early teens, always in trouble, and a Third, that is, a member of the third generation and hence a worker, is perceived by his elders as an irresponsible dreamer and by the President as a potential threat because he asks questions. To Jody's surprise, he is chosen, presumably by the Guardian*, the god of Isis, as a Bearer for the spring Thanksgiving Day ceremony, the annual celebra' on of the arrival on Isis. Though the office is an honor, the four Bearers also face great danger, since they must carry an offering of food up the mountain to the room behind the waterfall that plunges into the valley. Jody suspects that, although presumably he was chosen by the Guardian, the President may really have picked him in hopes he will fall to his death. The next morning, while near the cascade, he notices a strange red flash on the hilltop, climbs to investigate, and discovers a black-and-white stick with a red flag attached to it. When he takes this to the President and also tells the leader he is certain the river is rising dangerously, the President says that he must keep vigil in the Sacred Cave of the Guardian and ignores his fears about the water and his questions about the stick. In the cave, Jody observes objects considered magic but which the reader recognizes as modern technology—a computer, radio, and laser—replaces a "magic wand" (fluorescent tube) with another, and floods the place with light. The deed infuriates the President, who tries him before the Council of Seven. In spite of the valiant efforts of Jody's aged, lame Grandfather, an original inhabitant, a Councillor, and a long-time foe of the repressive President, Jody is exiled for sacrilege. He bravely ascends the tabooed mountain, trudges for many days over extremely rough terrain, and, when almost completely spent by physical hardships, lack of food, and rarefied air, crosses a divide into a broad, green, bamboo valley. There he encounters a strange, spiny, friendly beast, called Hobbit, and its master, a bright and shining, larger than life, man-like being, whom he recognizes as the Guardian and who Jody later learns is a robot brought from Earth. The Guardian takes him to a large palace inside a mountaintop, where he meets the Lady Olwen* Pendennis, the white-haired, green-skinned Keeper of the Isis Light, the beacon that both led the people to Isis and warns others away. He likes and respects her and recognizes her innate goodness. The descendant of the original couple sent from Earth to prepare the area for occupation, she tells him the story of the planet's development and leads him to see that the President has distorted truth to gratify his desire for power. Jody learns that he has been able to reach this valley because his skin is black and hence he was able to withstand Ra's rays. (It is unclear how many of people on Isis are black.) Since Olwen and the Guardian are not gods but helpers, they have not intervened to change the socio-political structure in Cascade Valley, hoping that with time the people will depose the tyrant and restore their previous democratic system. The Guardian and Olwen tackle the problem of the rising water, however, knowing it was caused by a recent minor earthquake. The Guardian and Jody plant explosives where the river is blocked, and the water gradually recedes. Jody is returned to his valley in the Guardian's floater (air ship), and, somewhat wiser about human nature and more confident of himself, he looks forward to helping his people to a better way of life. As with most science fiction, the plot receives the emphasis and moves with well-calculated suspense. The characterization is minimal, most leading figures being well-known types, sociological themes are pronounced, and the ways of Cascade Valley are well drawn. That the people should have lost their heritage and history and given up their independence so completely in only a couple of generations is not entirely plausible. The conclusion is reasonable, given the circumstances, and Jody is a convincing and likeable protagonist. He grows and changes about as much as can be expected within a couple of weeks. The President, Grandfather N'Kumo, and Olwen are obvious foils, and the story of their relationship with one another is told to Jody in detail appropriate for one of Jody's age to know and adds an interesting dimension. Occasional melodrama mars the impact of the usually dispassionate, objective tone. Presumably the title refers to the shining robot, not to Jody. The book is the second in a series that includes *The Keeper of the Isis Light* and *The Pedlar of Isis*. Can. Council Winner.

GUNN, JOHN, Australian author of *Sea Menace** (Constable, 1958), which won the Australian Library Association's Book of the Year Award. It is a novel set in 1807 about immigrants who encounter pirates off New South Wales and Tasmania, an action-filled adventure full of captures and daring escapes.

H

HAIG-BROWN, RODERICK (LANGMERE) (1908–1976), born in Lancing, Sussex, England; very highly regarded Canadian writer of the mid-twentieth century noted in children's literature for his adventure and animal novels. He came to North America in 1926 and worked as a logger, fisherman, trapper, and guide in Washington State and British Columbia. He became a full-time writer in 1934, publishing altogether some thirty books of fiction and non-fiction, mostly for adults on outdoor subjects. In addition, he made films, broadcast and moderated television programs, and contributed many articles to anthologies and widely circulated periodicals. He was also distinguished for his record of public service; among other positions he acted as provincial magistrate and judge for thirty-five years in British Columbia, a major in World War II, and chancellor of the University of Victoria in British Columbia. Of his half-dozen novels for young readers, he received the first Canadian Library Association Children's Book of the Year Award for *Starbuck Valley Winter** (Collins, 1944; Morrow, 1943), about a boy who spends the winter trapping on Vancouver Island to get money for a boat. Its sequel, *Saltwater Summer** (Collins, 1949; Morrow, 1948), received the Governor General's Award. Details of landscape and outdoor life, obviously based on experience, give his adventure novels conviction. He won the Book of the Year Award again for *The Whale People** (Collins, 1962; Morrow, 1963), a historical novel set on the west coast among the Nootka Indians. For young readers he also wrote *Ki-Yu: A Story of Panthers* (Houghton, 1934), a realistic animal novel that pits panther against hunter, a biography of George Vancouver, and non-fiction works about the history of British Columbia. A much honored writer, he won the Vicky Metcalf Award for his entire body of works for young readers and received an honorary doctorate from the University of British Columbia.

THE HALFMEN OF O (Gee*, Maurice, Oxford, 1982: Merrimack, 1983), otherworld fantasy in which a schoolgirl of twelve and her boy cousin become involved in a desperate struggle to defeat the evil Halfmen of the planet O. Nick

(Nicholas) Quinn and his family of Auckland, New Zealand, customarily spend January holidays at the farm of their Ferris relatives by Lodestone Creek in a lonely, gold-prospecting corner of southern New Zealand. Susan Ferris has been quiet and standoffish since birth, when her parents discovered that she had an odd birthmark on the inside of her wrist. This summer, a disagreeable, scruffy old prospector named Jimmy* Jaspers forces her to inhale yellow, carbide-smelling fumes from an old whiskey bottle that cause her to do his bidding and lures her into an antique mine shaft. Nick finds the discarded bottle, inhales, too, and follows them. The two children soon discover themselves in O, a planet somewhere in the Milky Way, that has fallen into the clutches of evil Otis Claw, tyrant ruler of the Halfmen, to whose minion, Odo Cling, Jimmy delivers Susan. Treated cruelly by Cling and his Deathguard, Susan is rescued by Nick and the Woodlanders of Wildwood, small, wiry, tough man-like beings with woolly faces and merry eyes. The Woodlanders Brand and Breeze take the children to their leader, Marna, a healer and herself a Halfie, who tells them how O fell into the control of these wicked beings. In an ancient time, the Halfmen's great ancestor, Freeman Wells, created the Motherstone, laying upon it two stone Halves and placing Humankind into balance between good and evil, and thus the situation has remained for eons. In Marna's generation, her husband, also named Freeman Wells, the guardian of the stone, had as a pupil Otis Hand, who became wicked and wrenched the Halves apart, maiming his hand into a Claw and earning his new name. By upsetting the balance of the universe, Claw created the Halfmen, or Halfies, in whom either good or evil predominates, and he made himself ruler over the wicked Halfies who now control O. Freeman salvaged the Halves and hid them, instructing the keepers to give the pieces only to the one who bore a special Mark. Wells then entered Earth through the mine shaft and marked Susan, thus designating her the one to restore O to balance, and then he was killed. Susan and Nick, with the help of the Woodlanders and Jimmy, who has seen the error of his ways, spend the rest of the book carrying out Susan's mission. They follow a tortuous route through mountains and over chasms to the land of the Birdmen, who help her recover one of the Halves from a cave on the mountaintop, and then to the land of the Stonefolk, who assist Susan down into the terrible Throat of the world to recover the remaining Half. All the while they are pursued by the dreaded Odo Cling, his hooded, red-eyed Deathguards, and his ferocious Bloodcat. When finally, after a terrible struggle involving a long climb over a slippery dome of force, Susan places the Halves on the Motherstone, Claw's power is broken, and the Halfmen fall into excru-ciating pain as good drives out the evil within each, and they and O are slowly restored to normalcy. Jimmy Jaspers elects to remain in O, and Susan and Nick trudge home to discover that only a couple of hours have elapsed in Earth time. None of the characters has much individuality. Jimmy Jaspers is the most fully drawn, and even he is a caricature. The book is all plot with the well-known conventional incidents of the Tolkienesque good versus evil folkloric, otherworld novel. Coincidences are numerous, high suspense and action are continuous, and the pace is frenetic. Details are left unjustified. It is never clear, for example, why Susan should have been chosen to be the deliverer, how the Halves and the Motherstone function to keep things in balance, or why, once she discovers that her birthmark can be used as a weapon, she doesn't use it more often. As a heroine she is a relatively passive, suffering figure, whose inability to take control of situations serves to build up the awfulness of the Halfies. The comedy lessens the book's credibility, and Gee overwrites most scenes in clichés, with the result that the book projects the sensationalism of a television cartoon: "He snarled back at his men . . . their red eyes shining with hatred." Though the intended audience is probably later elementary and junior high readers, primer-like language is the rule: "Dale and Verna led them. These two had been good friends to Susan. She felt lonely to see them go. But Breeze and Brand were left. And Nick was there. . . . " *The Halfmen of O* is one of a series about the land of O that includes *The Priests of Ferris** and *Motherstone**. N. Z. Govt. Winner.

HALVORSON, MARILYN (1948–), born in Olds, Alberta, Canada; cattle rancher, teacher, writer. She was graduated from the University of Alberta and has taught at the Sundre school, which she once attended. Although set in the modern west of ranches and rodeos, her novels are primarily about personal relationships within troubled families. *Cowboys Don't Cry* (Clarke, 1984), which won the Clarke Irwin/Alberta Culture Writing for Youth Competition, is about the estrangement and eventual reconciliation between a hot-tempered teenager and his alcoholic father, a rodeo clown. *Let It Go** (Clarke, 1985) concerns two boys, one unappreciated by his policeman father and the other living happily with his ranch manager father until his mother, a country-western singer who abandoned the family, returns. It received an honorable mention from the Canada Council. Its sequel, *Nobody Said It Would Be Easy* (Clarke, 1987; *Hold On, Geronimo*, Delacorte, 1988), is a survival novel featuring the same two boys and a girl cousin stranded in the wilderness after a plane crash. A more recent title is *Bull Rider* (Collier, 1989). Halvorson's novels have been praised for their strong characterization.

HANDFORD, NOURMA (1911–), Australian journalist and writer of fiction for adults and children, whose first short story was accepted for publication by the *Queenslander* magazine when she was sixteen. She attended Brisbane High School for Girls, left school at seventeen, held a succession of jobs, married at twenty, and became the mother of two boys and a girl. She contributed short stories to various magazines, held a variety of positions, including fashion writing and copywriting, and became a public relations officer for one of Sydney's large department stores. Later she joined the staff of *Woman's Day* as features consultant and public relations officer. Her "Carcoola" books for young girls became very popular. They include *Carcoola** (Dymock's, 1950), which was commended for Australian Children's Book of the Year, and several sequels, for which her childhood holidays on a large sheep station provided the background. She came from a family that for many years owned and edited the first newspaper in Warwick, Queensland.

A HANDFUL OF TIME (Pearson*, Kit, Penguin, 1987; Viking, 1987), realistic psychological problem novel with time-travel fantasy sections set one recent summer at a lake near Edmonton, Alberta, Canada. Her mother the prominent television news anchor Ruth* Reid and her father the noted journalist Harris Potter, Patricia Potter, 12, is sent to stay for the summer with her mother's sister and her family, the Grants, at the Reid family cottage while her parents work out the details of their separation. Plain, shy, awkward Patricia, an only child, gets along badly from the start with the active, outgoing Grant children, who call her Potty. She especially has trouble with bossy, strong-willed Kelly, who disparages and patronizes her. Kelly, a girl a year younger than Patricia, is the leader of the pack of cousins that also includes Patricia's mother's brother's children. One afternoon Patricia takes refuge in the old guesthouse, called La Petite, finds under the floorboards a gold watch inscribed to her grandmother, winds it, and is transported back to the Reid cottage thirty-five years earlier the summer her mother was twelve years old. This happens on several occasions, with no lapsed time in the modern dimension, and Patricia soon develops a close emotional bond with her mother as a girl, though she never participates in the action of the earlier dimension. Beautiful, intelligent, determined, Ruth is patronized by her two older brothers, psychologically unsupported by her patriarchal father, and berated and harangued by her mother, Pat*, who disciplines her for doing things the boys are allowed or even encouraged to do but that the family considers inappropriate for a girl. Ruth becomes moody and resentful, adopts a "Some day I'll show them" attitude, and hides the watch she knows her mother cherishes. Back in the modern dimension, things come to a head when Pat makes a brief visit, now an imperious old lady called Nan. When Nan grills her about her parents and harshly criticizes Ruth's way of life, Patricia unexpectedly and strongly asserts herself in her mother's defense. The impending divorce has been kept secret from the cousins, who now sympathize with Patricia, and for the first time she feels that she is a part of the group. After Nan leaves, Ruth arrives. Patricia realizes that seeing her mother as a child has given her insights into her mother's behavior as an adult and chooses to live with Ruth after the divorce. The book concludes with Patricia telling her mother about finding the watch and their decision to return it to Nan at her home in Calgary on their flight back to Toronto. The two time periods are skillfully melded, each shedding light on the other and both contributing to the revelation and development of Patricia's character. The pleasures of lake life are strongly depicted in both dimensions. The male figures are types necessary for the plot and choral, and the women dominate the book. Aunt Ginnie, much the youngest of the Reid siblings, is loving, cheerful, and maternal. She apparently turned out as Nan thought a girl should, with a husband and a large family. Kelly is a modern

Ruth, but she fortunately has an understanding mother and in addition is the eldest, which gives her an advantage that Ruth did not have. Their foils are sad, hurt Ruth, forever still in the process of finding herself, and fearsome Nan, still trying to run the family and make the girls over into her mental image of what girls should be. Patricia grows convincingly in self-confidence, changing believably through both her past-time and her present-time experiences. There is a very strong sense of family stresses and strains in both dimensions, revolving mostly around Nan, and even though Patricia rises too rapidly in the esteem of her cousins, the story succeeds in being a non-didactic representation of how difficult it is for women to live their lives as they wish in accordance with their capabilities and how, ironically, their own mothers perpetuate and even encourage repression and stereotyping. Can. Bk. of Year Winner; Can. Ebel Runner-Up.

HARDING, (JOHN) LEE (1937–   ), Australian author of science fiction novels and short stories for both adults and young people. His disturbing science fiction fantasy, *Displaced Person** (Hyland, 1979; *Misplaced Persons*, Harper, 1979), won the Book of the Year Award. Among his other books are several in the Listen and Read Series, published by ABC Radio, among them *Journey into Time* (1978) and *The Legend of the New Earth* (1979). *Rooms of Paradise* (Quartet, 1978) is an anthology of science fiction stories edited by Harding. He has also published more than forty science fiction short stories, which have been translated into nine languages. Other books by Harding include *The Web of Time* (Cassell, 1980) and *Waiting for the End of the World* (Hyland, 1983). He lives in the mountains near Melbourne.

HARDY (*Shantymen of Cache Lake**), brutal foreman at the lumber camp, the main reason the workers feel compelled to organize a union. A man of great size and enormous physical strength, he bullies everyone in the camp and, as most of them suspect, killed Angus Bains to rid himself of a strong leader and organizer, then placed the body under a fallen tree to make it look like an accident. His insistence that the workers build the log chute from the top down, instead of constructing a firm base and building upwards, is a major grievance and causes the collapse that injures several men and kills Tim McGuire. He breaks up the first strike by threatening the men with guns and driving them out to camp in the bitter cold, but when he tries the same tactic in the second strike, the men are solidly unified, and he dares not face the anger of some forty lumberjacks so far from police or army backing. He is a stock villain but important to the story, the main vehicle for plot complications.

HARI (*The Village by the Sea**), second in the poor village family of Thul, one year younger than Lila.* In the city he is at first terrified, but when, by good luck and the kindness of a stranger, he lands at the Sri Krishna Eating House, he works as he has not at home and saves all his meager wages to take back to his family. Clearly a bright boy and more given to emotional swings than Lila, he hates his father whose drinking and debt have almost ruined them, nearly gives way to despair and homesickness in the city, and responds eagerly to the friendship and education offered by Mr. Panwallah. Although Lila has kept the family alive and saved her mother's life while he is gone, it is Hari's plans and training that offer hope for the future.

HARRIS, CHRISTIE (LUCY IRWIN) (1907–   ), born in Newark, New Jersey; very highly regarded Canadian writer for children, especially noted for her retellings of stories from Northwest Coast Native American oral tradition. In 1908, her family moved to a British Columbia farm. She received her teaching certificate from Provincial Normal School in Vancouver, B.C., and taught until her marriage in 1932. While her children were young, she turned to writing, doing scripts for the Canadian Broadcasting Company, and for six years she was women's editor of *British Columbia News Weekly*. After moving to Prince Rupert on the Northwest Coast in 1958, she began to study the Indian culture and west coast history that she later drew upon for her writing. She has published some twenty books of historical and realistic fiction, fantasy, retellings of Native American myths and legends, and other non-fiction works for children and young people and has won many awards. Of her retellings, the collections of stories about Mouse Woman, a *narnauk* or spirit who can appear as either a mouse or a tiny grandmother, are considered especially spirited and faithful versions of the original stories. The first of these, *Mouse Woman and the Vanished Princesses* (McClelland, 1976; Atheneum, 1976), won the Canadian Library Association Book of the Year Award. Also highly regarded is *The Trouble with Princesses* (McClelland, 1980; Atheneum, 1980), which won the Canada Council Prize. Her interest in Native American life is also reflected in the novel *Raven's Cry** (McClelland, 1966; Atheneum, 1966), another Canadian Library Association Book of the Year Award winner. It traces the decline of the Haida nation through several generations of chiefs. About the opening of the West are *Cariboo Trail* (Longman, 1957), which was first written as a radio script, *West with the White Chiefs* (McClelland, 1965; Atheneum, 1965), and *Forbidden Frontier* (McClelland, 1968; Atheneum, 1968), all historical novels. Other books relying on Native American legendary material are *Sky Man on the Totem Pole?* (McClelland, 1975; Atheneum, 1975) and *Mystery at the Edge of Two Worlds* (McClelland, 1978; Atheneum, 1978). She fictionalized her own children's experiences in her contemporary novels *You Have to Draw the Line Somewhere* (McClelland, 1964; Atheneum, 1964), *Confessions of a Toe-Hanger* (McClelland, 1967; Athenuem, 1967), and *Let X Be Excitement* (McClelland, 1969; Atheneum, 1969), books she has termed "case histories." Among her other honors are the Vicky Metcalf Award for the entire body of her work and induction into the Order of Canada.

HARRY BURNEY (*Tiger in the Bush*: The Roaring 40**), Henry Burney, the "hatter," or "old bloke gone bush" (one who has deserted civilization for life alone in the Tasmanian outback), long-time friend of Dave* Lorenny. Harry is described as "a tawny frogmouth of a man," tall and thin, who can appear and disappear at will in the rocks and gullies, "his untidy hair . . . like gray feathers against the sky. . . . " His main role in *Tiger in the Bush* is helping Badge trick the American zoologists out of finding the Tasmanian tiger. In *The Roaring 40*, he suffers some sort of attack, perhaps a stroke. Seeing in Dave's newspaper the picture of his boat that he thought wrecked off Port Davey and lost at sea, the *Thora Ann*, refurbished and called the *Roaring 40*, was too great a shock for the old recluse. Ned*, the wild boy found at Port Davey, is his nephew. Harry is important in both books, but the reader never gets to know him well and sees him mostly through Badge's eyes.

HATFIELD, WILLIAM (ERNEST CHAPMAN) (1892?–), born in England; sign painter, stockman, writer. At nineteen, he left England, made his way to Adelaide, surviving mostly by repainting store and hotel signs. From there he went to Cordillo Downs, a sheep station in the northeast corner of South Australia, and thereafter he wandered about rural Australia, breaking horses, droving, kangaroo shooting, living for periods with the aboriginal people, taking on any job available in out-of-the-way places (from cooking to bookkeeping), all the while getting to know some of the older people who remembered the early days in the outback. *Ginger Murdoch* (Angus, 1932), based on a tough character he met in South Australia, and *Wild Dog Frontier** (Oxford, 1951), a story of stock ranching in the Channel Country of southwest Queensland, employ much of the bush knowledge he acquired in his travels. *Barrier Reef Days* (Cumberlege, 1949) is set on Green Island, off Cairns. *Buffalo Jim* (Oxford, 1938) is based on his experience of cooking for drovers, of the gold strike in the Granites in 1932, and of buffalo shooting near the Adelaide River, in the Northern Territory. Among Hatfield's other writings are *Sheepmaster* (Angus, 1931) and *Desert Saga* (Angus, 1933).

THE HAUNTING (Mahy*, Margaret, Dent, 1982; Atheneum, 1982), fantasy of magic and ghosts with mystery story aspects in a family setting, which takes place recently in a contemporary city of undisclosed location. Shy, withdrawn Barney Palmer, 8, whose real name is Barnaby, is the youngest in his close-knit family, which includes his often absent father, John, Claire, his warm, understanding, and affectionate stepmother, and his two older sisters, aloof, silent, fanatically neat Troy*, 13, and bossy, garrulous, self-assured Tabitha*, about ten, an aspiring writer. Events start when Barney has a vision on the way home from school one Friday afternoon of a ghostly child in a blue velvet suit, who announces mournfully that Barnaby is dead and he feels lonely. Terrified, Barney assumes that the vision foretells his own imminent demise and is greatly relieved to discover when he gets home that his Great-Uncle Barnaby Scholar on his dead mother's side has passed away. That evening, Barney again hears the ghostly voice, and the next day, when the family visits the Scholar relatives to pay respects, still another haunting occurs, this time one that Tabitha observes.

Family conversations reveal the startling information that the Scholars have a skeleton, a black sheep relative, Great-Uncle Cole, who had supernatural powers that brought him into conflict with his imperious mother. Cole ran away while still quite young and is presumed to be dead. The hauntings continue, leaving Barney pale and wan. He confides in Tabitha that he is convinced that Cole intends to take him away, and Tabitha consults Great-Uncle Guy, a pediatrician, who says he thinks Barney is a Scholar magician—there has been one in every generation; Cole was the one in his time—and the family has discovered that Cole is still alive and had been in contact with Great-Uncle Barnaby. The mystery intensifies, and the climax occurs when Cole arrives at the house to claim Barney as friend and associate in dead Barnaby's place. A battle of wits and magical powers ensues, and, when the Scholars also arrive, the conversation becomes quite acrimonious as old hostilities surface. When, to put a stop to the arguments, Barney offers to accompany Cole, surprisingly Troy speaks up. She reveals the shocking information that it is she and not Barney who is the magician in their generation and that she has inherited her special powers from Great-Grand-mother* Scholar. The old woman loathed her talent, had submerged it, and was determined to make Cole over into her image of what a young man should be. Barney is delighted to be completely ordinary, and Cole and Troy become friends. For the first time in his life, Cole has a family that appreciates him for what he is. The characters are well drawn, and Barney is a convincing and winning protagonist. That the Palmers should be unaware of a black sheep in the family seems unlikely, however, and Troy's change in personality is altogether too sudden, dramatic, and felicitous, but these shortcomings fade in view of the skillfully sustained atmosphere of light suspense, the moments of comic relief, the richness of the underlying ideas, the deft psychological touches, and the accuracy and inventiveness of the diction. Although an artful mystery on the first level, this is primarily a story of family relationships and suggests that people cannot be made over and that it is important for all members of the family to be loved and appreciated for what they are, themes that emerge gradually without explicit statement. Carnegie Winner; N. Z. Esther Glen.

THE HAUNTING OF FRANCES RAIN. See *WHO IS FRANCES RAIN?*

HAYES, JOHN F(RANCIS) (1904–1980), born in Dryden, Ontario, Canada; journalist, artist, historical novelist. He went to work early in a variety of jobs—salesman, musician, lumberman, steel worker—and later was educated in night classes at the University of Toronto. He entered the publishing business as a copy and layout man and eventually became an executive in one of Canada's largest newspaper organizations. Although he considered writing a hobby, he published eleven substantial novels as well as short stories for young people and a number of books for adults. *A Land Divided** (Copp, 1951), a story of the removal of the Acadians in 1755, won the Governor General's Literary Award, as did *Rebels Ride at Night** (Copp, 1953), a novel about the revolt in Toronto led by William Lyon Mackenzie* in 1837. Also honored was *The Dangerous Cove** (Copp, 1958), on the conflict in late seventeenth-century Newfoundland between the settlers and the Devon fishermen over control of the ports. It was the winner of the Canadian Library Association Book of the Year Award. Among the other novels by Hayes for young people are *Buckskin Colonist* (Copp, 1947), about the Selkirk settlers, *Treason at York* (Copp, 1949), about the war of 1812, *Quest in the Cariboo* (Copp, 1960), about the British Columbia gold rush, *Flaming Prairie* (Copp, 1965), about the Riel Rebellion, *The Steel Ribbon* (Copp, 1967), about the building of the Canadian Pacific Railway, and *On Loyalist Trails* (Copp, 1971), about the Loyalist emigration to Canada. The novels seem somewhat old-fashioned, with similar manly teenage protagonists, strong father figures, and improbable plots, but they are historically authentic, fast paced, and exciting.

HEBE'S DAUGHTER (Syred*, Celia, Hodder, 1976), romantic period novel beginning in 1786 about the varying fortunes of Elizabeth Pollard, called Liz, statuesque, red-haired daughter of beautiful London actress, Hebe Jacobs. Liz grows up in Essex at Harry Pollard's estate, Polstead, which she loves dearly and which she confidently expects some day to inherit. Since Harry and Hebe love parties and high living, Polstead is always on the edge of financial ruin, and Liz early learns to work along with the servants to run the household. Left orphaned and almost penniless at age sixteen, she is claimed by her mother's sister, Nancy Hitchens, and Nancy's husband, Fred, an avaricious draper also involved in smuggling and fencing stolen property. Uncle Fred appears suddenly, strips Polstead of anything that could be sold, and takes Liz with him to his shop in Rag Lane in London, where termagent Nancy works her like a slave, then to Ironlatch farm near Hastings on the coast of Sussex, where for some time she works as a housekeeper for Jake Hallam, a smuggler, and where she makes friends with Jem* Fletcher, Hallam's self-pitying stepson whose ambitions parallel Liz's. He yearns to own the inn that had belonged to his dead father, while she is determined to reclaim Polstead. These are only the first of many harrowing adventures that Liz undergoes before returning to Essex. Shipwrecked and cast ashore in Normandy, she is rescued and taken to the village of Esterel. As Babette la Rousse (Babette the Redhead) she slaves for some months as a servingwoman in the village inn and befriends a thin, pale, mistreated scullery lad of about eight called Petit-Jean*. When the French Revolution breaks out and the inn is besieged by angry landless villagers (for some of the book's most vivid scenes), she flees with Petit-Jean by fishing boat to England. Back in Essex, she is astounded to learn that relatives from Jamaica have appeared, claimed Polstead, and sold it. When she protests, they inform her that Harry Pollard was not her father. She goes to see her grandmother Jacobs, who owns the Gamecock inn in Blackfriars and who tells her that her real father was a waterman (sailor) from Rye named Charlie Duff. She ends up in Hastings where

blames Hemi and calls him an insulting name. Hemi walks away with dignity. He doesn't blame David for his father's bigotry but tells his own people that David saved him.

HEWITT, MARSHA (1948–), historian, teacher, author. With Claire Mackay* she coauthored *One Proud Summer** (Women's Press, 1981), a historical novel based on the 1946 strike of the workers of Valleyfield, Quebec, against Montreal Cotton, which won the Ruth Schwartz Children's Book Award and received honorable mention for the Canada Council prize. She is also the coauthor, with her husband, writer Bill Freeman*, of *Their Town: The Mafia, the Media, and the Party Machine* (Lorimer, 1979), an expose of Hamilton, Ontario. Hewitt has taught Canadian labor history and religion in Montreal.

HIGH AND HAUNTED ISLAND (Chauncy*, Nan, ill. Victor Ambrus, Oxford, 1964; Norton, 1964), realistic adventure novel with mystery and survival story aspects. In the early 1960s, the yacht *Timmari* plies a vacation course down the rugged, windblown, island-strewn east coast of Tasmania. She carries as passengers her owner, Australian millionaire P. G. Ironn and his son, Rusty (Roger), about eighteen, and Mr. Ironn's old friend, John Roxtell, and John's son, Otter (Timothy Ottis), a little younger than Rusty, and as cook, inscrutable, irritable Jake. Questions arise: why is Mr. Roxtell so interested in Port Davey, a remote harbor facing Antarctica? Why does Jake become more agitated the further south they go, and especially when they draw near Haunted Island, once called Reef Island, an area of sudden storms and supposedly untoward happenings? The answer to the first question comes when Mr. Roxtell tells how his sister, Tess, then about Otter's age, was presumably lost at sea in World War II while traveling from boarding school to a friend's house for Christmas. Exploring the beach at Port Davey, the boys find an old vinegar bottle containing a page from Tess's composition book on which appear the words "Reef Island." This much of the novel is told in the first six chapters, the next dozen go back twenty years to follow Tess and Vicky Kroom, typical boarding school girls in their late teens, as they prepare for the trip and board ship. Off Port Davey, their vessel is accosted by Germans, and by sheer luck the girls reach shore near Port Davey. They scrabble for existence for some time in an exciting, suspenseful, and well-drawn part of the book. The girls are found by Circlists, an eccentric religious sect that shares possessions and labor, eschews money, and uses the circle as their symbol. The Circlists take the girls, prisoners really, to Reef Island, on whose elevated promontory they have built an almost self-sufficient colony. The girls gradually join Circlist activities and eventually marry. When the Circlists' ship sinks on a trip to New Zealand and one of the few remaining residents, a youth called Jacob, disappointed at losing Tess's hand, goes off in their only boat, the girls and their families are marooned. The narrative now skips ahead to the *Timmari*, where Jake, really the Circlist Jacob, prompted by the message in the bottle, acknowledges his part in the strange events, and the *Timmari* sails to Haunted Island. The Roxtells are reunited with Tess, now a widow with a daughter named Anni, and meet Vicky and her family. Jacob (Jake) "asks" for Tess, she consents, and they are married. Some of the survivors choose to remain on the island, others to accompany the *Timmari* to Australia. As a result of his adventure, Rusty feels more mature and knowledgeable about the world and is determined to return to the island and Anni. Though conventional in incident and characters and overforeshadowed, the story keeps up a good pace. While Rusty and Otter are hardly distinguishable from one another, spirited, adaptable Vicky and less resilient Tess seem better drawn and more convincing. Scenes in school, on ship, and on shore involving them carry a conviction lacking in other passages. The Circlists' culture is revealed in tantalizingly superficial strokes, and it does not seem logical that search crews would not have tried harder to find the girls. If they had and if alert, they would surely have found the bottle and gone on to the island. Nor does it seem logical that the Roxtells would have waited all this time without searching for the only sister and daughter in the family. Style projects a deep appreciation for the beauty and magnificence of the coast and sea. Aust. Bk. of Year Com.

HILL, DEIRDRE, born in Northbridge, a suburb of Sydney, Australia; author of articles, stories, and novels for young people. She attended business school and worked as a stenographer for a firm producing radio serials. During World War II she joined the Women's Australian Royal Air Force and served in the meteorology section. After her marriage in 1946, she contributed stories and articles to women's magazines, and she became seriously interested in writing in the early 1960s when she was left to support her four children. Her first novel, *Over the Bridge** (Hutchinson, 1969), in which a young boy saves his favorite trolley car from the scrap heap, is set in Northbridge. It was commended for the Australian Book of the Year Award. More recently, Hill has been secretary to the headmaster of a large boys' school in Sydney.

HILL, FITZMAURICE (1898–   ), born in Kew, Victoria, Australia; Australian novelist and writer of radio scripts. He served with distinction in both world wars, rising to the rank of lieutenant colonel in the Royal Australian Corps of Signals. A series of broadcasts for the Australian Broadcasting Commission about Australian history led to his novel, *Southward Ho with the Hentys** (Whitcombe, 1953), dealing with the earliest settlement in Victoria. It was highly commended for the Australian Book of the Year Award and won first prize in the Victoria Centenary Literary Competition. A second book, *By Their Endeavours* (Whitcombe, 1956), contains one-act plays of pioneer men and women of Australia. Many of his radio plays have also been broadcast by the British and Canadian broadcasting commissions and some of them have won prestigious awards.

HILL, KAY (KATHLEEN LOUISE) (1917–   ), born in Halifax, Nova Scotia, Canada; writer best known for her retellings of Native American legends. After attending schools in Halifax, she became a court reporter and then a scriptwriter for radio and television. A series based on the trickster-hero Glooscap led to her first book, *Glooscap and His Magic: Legends of the Wabanaki Indians* (Dodd, 1963). This was followed by two other volumes, *Badger, the Mischief Maker* (Dodd, 1965) and *More Glooscap Stories* (Dodd, 1970). *And Tomorrow the Stars**, her biographical novel based on the life of the explorer John Cabot* won the Canadian Library Association Book of the Year Award. A second somewhat fictionalized biography, *Joe Howe: The Man Who Was Nova Scotia* (McClelland, 1980), tells of the life of a nineteenth-century statesman. She also wrote a number of dramas, including a three-act comedy, *Three to Get Married* (Samuel French, 1964) and *Cobbler, Stick to Thy Last* (Dramatic Publishing, 1967), which was produced in Ottawa at the National Arts Centre in 1969. In 1971 she received the Vicky Metcalf Award, given for a "body of work inspirational to Canadian Youth."

HOB (*A Dog Called George**), Marmaduke Eldridge Hobson, 79, owner of the Old English Sheepdog, George, that Tony Brent finds and cares for. In the hospital, Hob is a trial to his nurses because he is lively when he is supposed to rest quietly. He persuades Tony to bring him a model airplane to assemble because he doesn't care much for books. In subsequent visits, Tony learns that he has been a flyer, sailor, sheep shearer, manager of a pub, diver for abalone, and had various other occupations, but was injured in a sawmill accident and has become a potter. In a book on pottery, Tony's mother learns that he has a distinguished record, with numerous exhibitions, and to Tony he remarks that he learned too late what he was really good at doing. Sorting through junk, he tosses out the Distinguished Flying Cross he received in World War I. He teaches Tony not only how to handle clay but also that patience is needed to do good work. By example, he encourages an accepting attitude toward George, so that the boy appreciates the dog's friendliness and good humor and no longer wishes for a disciplined pet. Bearded and shaggy, Hob looks something like George.

HOLD FAST (Major*, Kevin; Clark, Irwin, 1978; Delacorte, 1980), realistic novel about the trauma a Canadian boy suffers when, after his parents' death, he must leave his small, coastal Newfoundland town of Marten and go to the city to live with relatives he does not know. Michael, 14, the narrator, starts the story with the funeral for his mother and father, killed in an automobile accident, at which he bolts to keep from breaking down in front of the crowd. Although he tries to comfort his brother, Brent, 7, by assuring him that they will team up and stick together, he is shocked to learn that his Great Aunt Flo, who lives with Grandfather, will take in Brent but that he is to go to St. Albert to live with Aunt Ellen and Uncle Ted. Everything is difficult for him. Aunt Ellen, whose only interest is in keeping their suburban tract house spotless, is obviously afraid of her husband. Uncle Ted, at first trying to be friendly, proves to be an unreasonable tyrant. Marie, 16, is disaffected but thoroughly cowed, and Curtis, whose room Michael must share and who is his age, refuses to speak to him until his placement test puts him in the high track with Curtis in math and science, proving to the bookish boy that he is not stupid. Michael is very homesick, mostly for his grandfather, who used to take him squid jigging and into the woods, and also for Brent and his friends in Marten. At school, his rural speech and friendly manner are hilarious to a group of city boys led by Lewis Kenston, who calls him a "baywop" and mocks him, and they have a minor skirmish, which is broken up by the English teacher. He gets to know a girl named Brenda from Simond's Bay, who comes into town to stay with an aunt and goes out to a movie with him, then for a long walk. When he comes in very late, he has his first real confrontation with Uncle Ted, who threatens to beat him, as he would beat Curtis, but backs down when Michael challenges him to try. When Kenston starts to taunt him about Brenda, Michael knocks him backward over a desk where he hits his head on the floor and is taken to the hospital with a concussion. The attitudes of the principal, who suspends Michael for a week, and of both his aunt and his uncle, who will not accept his account of the incident, infuriate Michael, but Curtis sticks up for him, and when Michael starts making preparations to run away, Curtis decides to go with him. Knowing that they will be sought first in Marten, they plan to go to a National Park, closed for the winter, camp out there for a while, then move on to Aunt Flo's house. They hitchhike, then help themselves to a Volkslaufe parked at the airport by the last person to give them a ride, a woman who will be in Europe for two weeks. At the National Park they hide the car out of sight, find one rest room open, and spread their sleeping bags in the utility room that opens into it. Though it snows and is bitterly cold, they manage for several days. Mostly they are bored with almost nothing to take up their time. By mutual consent, they take the car back to the airport, hitchhike to Marten, and arrive to find Aunt Flo frantic with worry and Grandfather very ill. Michael is able to talk with him for awhile before he dies. Aunt Ellen and Uncle Ted, somewhat chastened, arrive, and Curtis stands up to them for the first time, then goes back to St. Albert, hoping for a more reasonable life. Michael stays with Aunt Flo and Brent, planning to be a real companion to his little brother. Although the escape and period in the National Park are well worked out, the main interest is in the way the school and Uncle Ted are viewed by Michael, a boy who has been independent both in action and in thought and who is continually astonished at the different expectations for him in the city. His voice, in rural Newfoundland dialect, is believable, and his frustration is very well evoked. Curtis is less convincing, although when he finally makes the break from home, he interestingly is far less cautious than Michael and less worried about the crimes of car stealing and snaring rabbits in the park. Can. Bk. of Year Winner; Can. Council Winner; Can. Ruth Schwartz.

THE HOLE IN THE HILL (Park*, Ruth, Ure, 1962, Macmillan, 1962; *Secret of the Maori Cave*, Doubleday, 1964), mystery of adventure and suspense set in New Zealand in the mid-twentieth century, involving the discovery of an ancient Maori sacred cave. Brownie Mackenzie, 14, and her brother Dink, 12, from Australia, go to camp at Three-Mile Farm, which her father has inherited from Great-Uncle Angus, while he confers with lawyers in Auckland. At the farm they find everything orderly though spare. They are surprised by a big Maori boy who has come over to feed the dog, Chicken, and who introduces himself as Tom Te Taniwha, 16, of the family that formerly owned the land. Although he is friendly and attractive, he lets them know that there was a feud between Uncle Angus and his grandmother, the matriarch of the family. That night Brownie and Dink are terrified by a weird moaning whistle. The next day, Tom pretends ignorance of the sound, and, angry, Brownie distrusts him but agrees to go to the neat, well-painted Maori farm because Tom's grandmother wants to make an offer for Three-Mile Farm, which Brownie's father plans to sell. To their surprise, she is a well-traveled, cosmopolitan lady. She offers twice what the farm is worth. They jump to the conclusion that the terrifying night noise is created by the Maoris to scare them off and decide to explore the farm carefully to see what might be worth the money Tom's grandmother is offering. As Dink pushes ahead, he suddenly disappears, having fallen down a hole shaped like an inverted funnel. Brownie hurries back to the house for some rope, catching sight of Tom as she runs and twisting her ankle badly when she slips. With great pain, she limps back to Dink with a rope. As soon as he is out, he tells her excitedly that the pothole leads to a huge cave. In the next two days they discover another entrance and explore the cave, followed by Tom who has overheard their conversation. When their exit is cut off by rising water in an underground river, they team up and for many weary hours hunt for another exit. Suddenly, they come upon a huge figure carved of wood, the Guardian, Tom says. He decides that he must reveal the Maori mystery to the Mackenzie children, and he leads them past the figure into a room that contains priceless Maori artifacts, including the boat in which the first Maoris arrived in New Zealand. Tom knows of these things from the traditions of his people, but the way into the cave has been lost for generations. Finding that the way out from the treasure cave is halfway up the cliff above the Maori farm, they retrace their steps part way and eventually come to the same pothole Dink fell into earlier. There above them they find Mr. Mackenzie, Tom's grandmother, and the storekeeper searching for them. It is agreed that the artifacts will be kept for the Maoris, who will allow scientists to examine them, and that if Mr. Mackenzie opens the rest of the cave to visitors, he will wall off that part so that it will not be desecrated. The strange noise is caused by wind howling through the cave. The plot is knit together reasonably, but the supposed threats of the Maoris are never convincing, and the story strains for suspense until they are lost in the cave, then their journey becomes absorbing. The characters are developed only as much as is necessary for a mystery of this type. Aust. Bk. of Year Com.

HOLIDAY TIME IN THE BUSH (Dallas*, Ruth, ill. Gary Hebley, Methuen, 1983), realistic family novel set near the town of Greenbush, New Zealand. Jean, 8, tells of events that take place at the end of the school year and during Christmas holidays in 1890. When Mr. Clark, the teacher at the little country school, announces a pet parade for the year's end, the children look forward with anticipation to winning in the different categories. Jean's sister Helen, 9, enters Hokey Pokey, the family cow, and her older sister, Sophie, 13, enters Samuel, the rooster. Considerable excitement ensues when Samuel gets loose and is chased by another contestant, a dog, into the schoolhouse, which is left a shambles, and then flies up onto the roof. He is rescued by Jean's brother, Robbie, 10, who dislodges the gutter and drainpipe in the process. Jean enters Spud, her beloved dog. When she bathes him, she accidentally rinses him with water containing starch, and his hair stands up so stiffly it amuses the judge. The only one of the family that wins a prize is Robbie, who had planned to enter his big black spider, Scary. When Scary turns up missing, he enters Marmaduke, the classroom moa, instead. Marmaduke is a five-hundred-year-old skeleton, whose bones Robbie found in a cave and helped assemble. The entry is declared legal, and Robbie takes first prize for most unusual pet. The children's next adventures revolve around Christmas, which Mother, who came from Scotland, finds strange since it occurs during the summer months in the southern hemisphere. A visitor, bashful young Barney, arrives on horseback with strawberries for dessert, and also, to the children's great joy, with a leg of lamb, which saves Samuel the rooster from the cook pot. The children have a happy time on Christmas Eve preparing the dinner for the next day and hanging their stockings. Christmas morning they find gifts of clothes and toys, even though times are hard since Father died and Mother doesn't make much as a seamstress. After breakfast Helen notices that the chimney is on fire. Mother sends Sophie for the fire fighters, who soon put it out with wet sacks. After church, the family enjoys a fine dinner on a white, starched tablecloth with a vase of red roses as a centerpiece and brightly colored crackers by each plate. As a special holiday surprise, Mother arranges for them to attend the regatta at Bluff Harbour on New Year's Day. She makes new dresses for the girls, and the family packs a picnic basket the night before. After a quick breakfast, they walk to Greenbush and board the train. They stroll the sandy beach, wade in the waves, and collect shells. A big wave knocks Helen over, drenching her new dress; Jean gets lost in the crowd gathered to watch the races and is returned by a big gentleman with whiskers; Sophie loses her new sun hat to the wind; and Robbie disappears. He returns hours later with several big fish that he caught from a boat in the harbor. He had tried to ask permission of Mother to go on the boat, but at the time they were out hunting for him. At the end of the day, they walk back to the railroad station, board the train, and return home hot, sandy, sunburned, and sleepy but very happy after a perfect day at the seaside. The adventures are the simple ones that might occur in any family of lively youngsters. The children are almost indistinguishable from one another, and the style and the vocabulary easy enough for early readers to handle: " 'No! No! No!' she said, 'You must not kill Samuel! I won't eat Samuel. I won't eat any Christmas dinner.' " Although the dust jacket indicates that the time is the 1890s, the story projects little sense of the times. Advertised on the jacket as A Read Aloud Book, this is one of the Bush Children series. N. Z. Govt. Short List.

THE HOUSE THAT WAS EUREKA (Wheatley*, Nadia, Viking, 1985), fantasy set in two time periods, May, 1931 and May, 1981, dealing with parallels in the unrest of the unemployed in a working-class district of Sydney, Australia. The title is an allusion to the Eureka Stockade of 1854 when miners at Ballarat, protesting unjust fees, fought off armed police and troops and, despite the death of thirty men, forced adoption of the first civil rights laws in Australia. Action centers on two attached terrace houses, into one of which Evie*, 16, has just moved with her mother, her stepfather, Ted, and her three young half-sisters. In the adjoining house lives Noel* Cavendish, 15, with his timid, fussy mother and his grandmother, Nanna Oatley, "the despot*," who owns both dwellings. She has suffered a stroke and is bedridden, unable to talk. Evie, whose room is the old scullery attached to the rear of the house by a breezeway, starts to have what at first seem to be dreams and gradually pull her into the personality of Lizzie Cruise, the girl who lived in the house fifty years before, a period during which unemployed workers were evicted for non-payment of rent, leaving half the houses empty while shanty towns sprang up at the city's edges. Inside the door of a triangular cupboard built across one corner of her room, where a water heater once stood, Evie finds a heart, within which is scratched the message, "I love N 4 Ever," with a date which at first seems to be in May, 1981, but she later realizes is 1931. One night, unable to sleep, she starts to clear out the cupboard and, trying to dislodge the old stovepipe at the top, finds a gun which Noel, who has pulled out loose bricks from the scullery in his house and crawled through to her closet, takes from her. He then disappears through the hole again. The story moves back and forth from the time of Evie and Noel to the earlier period of the Cruise family, in which Lizzie and the boy next door, Nobby, friends since early childhood, are torn between antagonism and love. The Cruise men, unable to pay the rent, and their friends decide to make a stand against eviction, and they barricade the house, leaving only one small opening in the dining room window through which Nobby, as the smallest male, can squirm to be their runner, bringing supplies and carrying out chamber pots and messages. To take this position he has had to defy his mother who owns the houses and has called the police to throw out the Cruise family. Lizzie nails a sign to the front of the house saying "Eureka Stockade." Evie, in the 1980s, is experiencing a similar love-hate relationship with Noel. Though she has been unemployed and on the dole since she left school, Evie doesn't realize that Ted, too, has lost his job and that his constant abusive nagging at her is partly caused by worry that his family will be evicted. Mostly to deflect Ted's hectoring, Evie starts going to the CYSS center, a government-sponsored youth club where job announcements are posted. She becomes acquainted with Roger, a young man preoccupied with video taping, on whom she develops a crush, and Sharnda, who wrote her college thesis on the so-called riots of the unemployed in the depression of the 1930s. When they learn that she lives in the house where the 1931 clash between police and tenants occurred, they decide to re-enact and video tape the incident. The two stories merge on the night of the re-enactment, which is the anniversary of the actual night when armed police stormed the barricaded house. Noel, also Nobby, crouches on the balcony pointing the gun at the tough kids acting as cops, not realizing that it is still loaded with a single bullet Nobby put in fifty years before. Just as Noel is pulling the trigger, the barrel is knocked upward by Nobby, now an old man, who has returned and taken a room nearby after fifty years of wandering in the outback. Together Noel and Nobby run, as Nobby did fifty years before, through the breezeway to the scullery and shove the gun back into its old hiding place in the cupboard where Evie, merged with Lizzie, has been crouching. The incident has also shocked the despot into moving and talking. Real police break up the simulated attack, which has become a near riot, Noel's mother is amazed and pleased to find Nobby, the brother her mother (married and widowed again) never mentioned to her. The complex time-slip plot is effective mostly because the nightmarish tone is well sustained as the modern young people feel their identities slipping away and in the confrontation scenes with the police. Characters are rounded and differentiated: Evie is passive and rather sullen, Lizzie is fiery and emotional, Noel is talkative and ironic, Nobby is self-doubting. The despot, both mothers, Ted, the Cruise men, and even the younger sisters are also well drawn, though Sharnda and Roger are functionary stock figures. Aust. Bk. of Year Com.

HOUSTON, JAMES (1921–   ), born in Toronto, Ontario, Canada; highly acclaimed artist, illustrator, author, screenwriter, glass designer, and promoter of Inuit (Eskimo) culture. Houston studied at the Ontario College of Art from 1938 to 1940. After serving in the Toronto Scottish Regiment from 1940 to 1945, he returned to his art training but yielded to wanderlust and sketched among the Swampy Lake Cree for some time. A chance encounter in the Arctic with a bush pilot who offered him a ride into the Far North completely changed Houston's life. He spent the next twelve years, until 1962, in the Arctic, where he lived among the Inuit, learned their language and about their culture, and served as administrator of West Baffin Island. He was impressed by the Inuit sculptures and was instrumental in arranging commercial outlets for their work among friends, at the Hudson's Bay Company store, and in the United States. He also trained Inuit printmakers and arranged shows for them, thus starting an artistic tradition for which the Inuit are now renowned. After he left the Arctic he moved to the United States, where he accepted a position as design director with Steuben Glass in New York. Another chance encounter changed his life again. His writing career began when he met Margaret McElderry, an editor at Harcourt, while visiting a mutual friend. That meeting resulted in his first children's book, *Tikta'liktak** (Longman, 1965; Harcourt, 1965). He has since published some two dozen books, most of them stories of high adventure and survival often set in extremely hostile terrain and employing the journey structure. He has been honored with three Book of the Year Awards from the Canadian Library Association, for *Tikta'liktak*, *The White Archer** (Longman, 1967; Harcourt, 1967), both sometimes classified as retellings rather than fiction, and *River Runners** (Atheneum, 1979; Penguin, 1981). *Tikta'liktak* is the tense account of an Eskimo youth's efforts to survive when carried away by an ice floe. *The White Archer* tells of an Eskimo youth's determination to avenge the deaths of his parents and the kidnapping of his sister. In *River Runners*, a white youth and a Native companion survive a long and harrowing winter in the interior. *Akavak* (Longman, 1968; Harcourt, 1968), another story of humans against nature, concerns a boy's travels over hazardous terrain to take his dying grandfather to visit his brother. Houston has published other novels and retellings for young readers, compiled Eskimo poems, and written novels for adults, as well as screenplays, and other non-fiction. He has also illustrated many books by other writers. His most acclaimed book has been *Tikta'liktak*, which has won almost a dozen prizes, been translated into twenty-five languages, and been made into films. Critics count him among the major writers of adventure stories for young readers and praise his ability to catch in words and his accompanying black-and-white illustrations the starkness and power of the Arctic landscape and the ways and strength of the people who live there.

HUDSON, JAN (1954–   ), born in Calgary, Alberta, Canada; attorney and novelist. She began writing *Sweetgrass** (Tree Frog, 1984; Philomel, 1989) while working toward her B.A. degree from the University of Calgary and her law degree from the University of Alberta. She has spent most of her life in Alberta. *Sweetgrass* takes place in the early nineteenth century, concerns a fifteen-year-old Blackfoot Blood girl whose parents are choosing a husband for her, and focuses on the lives of Native women at the height of the Blackfoot confederacy. A girl's growing-up story, it is generous with details of everyday life and attitudes toward and of women. The book was discovered by a Tree Frog Press editor while judging Alberta Culture's first writing contest for young people. After publication, the novel won the Canada Council Award and the Canadian Literary Association Book of the Year Award and was runner-up for the Max and Greta Ebel Memorial Award. *Dawn Rider* (Harper, 1990; Philomel, 1990) tells of a Native American girl's efforts to persuade her people to accept the horse.

HUGHES, MONICA (1925–   ), born in Liverpool, England; prolific, versatile Canadian author best known for her science fiction novels for young people. Her family moved to Cairo, Egypt, before she was a year old but returned to the British Isles six years later. She was educated at a private school, served in the Women's Royal Naval Service in World War II, worked as a dress designer in London and Zimbabwe and as a bank clerk in Zimbabwe. She moved to Canada in 1952 where she was a laboratory technician for the National Research Council in Ottawa, Ontario. She began to write, married Glen Hughes, a civil servant, and became a Canadian citizen. The family settled in Edmonton, Alberta, and, the children in school, she returned to writing. She has since published some twenty novels and won the Vicky Metcalf Award for her total body of work. Some of her books are adventures based on Canadian history, like her first novel, *Gold-Fever Trail* (LeBel, 1974), and *The Treasure of the Long Sault* (LeBel, 1982). Some focus on minorities, like the Inuit in *Ring-Rise, Ring-Set* (Watts, 1982; MacRae, 1982) and the Hutterites in *Beyond the Dark River* (Hamilton, 1980; Athenuem, 1981). Others are contemporary problem stories like *The Ghost Dance Caper* (Hamilton, 1978) and *Hunter in the Dark** (Clarke, 1982; Athenuem, 1982), which many critics consider her best work and which illustrates the literal and symbolic journey structure she often employs. Winner of the Canadian Young Adult Award and the Canada Council Award, it is about a youth with leukemia, who goes alone into the woods on what may be his last hunting trip. Her Isis trilogy has received critical attention, the second of which, *The Guardian of Isis** (Hamilton, 1981; Atheneum, 1982), won the Canada Council Award. It postulates a rigid, futuristic society in space that has reverted to a primitive agricultural state. Companion books are *The Keeper of the Isis Light* (Hamilton, 1980; Atheneum, 1981) and *The Isis Pedlar* (Hamilton, 1982). Critics praise her as an intelligent and daring writer who confronts her protagonists with significant social and personal problems that are resolved in innovative, interesting, and exciting plots. Among her other science fiction books are *Crisis on Conshelf Ten* (Copp, 1975; Atheneum, 1979), set in an undersea society, *Earthdark* (Hamilton, 1977), set on the moon, *Beyond the Dark River* (Hamilton, 1979; Atheneum, 1981), about nuclear survival, and *Devil on My Back* (MacRae, 1984; Atheneum, 1985) and its sequel, *The Dream Catcher* (MacRae, 1986; Atheneum, 1987), which deal with the dangers respectively of a conformist and benevolent society. Other titles include *Log Jam* (Irwin, 1987; Stoddart, 1989), *The Promise* (Methuen, 1989; Stoddart, 1989), *The Refuge* (Doubleday, 1989), and *Little Fingerling: A Japanese Folktale* (Kids, 1989).

HUGHIE (Martin*, David, ill. Ron Brooks, Nelson, 1971; St. Martin's, 1971), realistic sociological problem novel set in the town of Merringee, New South Wales, Australia, in the 1960s, a story of friendship between two youths, one white, the other black, and racial discrimination against Aborigines. Hughie Jollet, 13, corkscrew-haired Abo schoolboy, son of a Town Council roadman, and red-haired Clancy Folger, 14, white son of the local newspaper publisher, have been "cobbers," best pals, since early childhood. Hughie admires Clancy's ability as a swimmer, which is widely recognized as championship in quality, and takes pride in his own ability as an artist, but he has little hope that he will ever be able to rise above his father's station in life. Ironically, on the very day the town turns out for the funeral of Hughie's little cousin, Chrissy, who died in the local Abo swimming hole in Colemans Creek, Hughie learns that he has won an artist's kit, one-half of first prize in a Sydney department store contest, for his painting of Merringee. A further irony is that the painting consists of an aerial view of the town's pride, a new Olympic pool, which is closed to Abos. Then Clancy stops coming to the creek hole. Uncle Nelson, local Abo leader, says it's because the Abo Rainbow Serpent (mythological figure) lives there. Hec Allen, Clancy's swimming coach, says it's because the Folgers won't let him, and Mr. Jollet says it's because Hughie's black. The two boys decide to tackle the problem of discrimination against Abos by printing and distributing posters advocating opening the pool to everyone, but Mr. Folger catches them in his printshop and tears up the posters. Then Hughie goes to Mr. Ern Kaufman, local manufacturer of butter, who donated the land for the pool, hoping he'll back the cause, only to get brushed off with the usual glib, evasive, biased talk. Next, Hughie, Clancy, and Harriet, Clancy's sister, "point the bone," that is, try to hex, Mr. Kaufman. The freezing mechanism goes off in his factory, liquefying gallons of butter, but Hughie feels the bone pointing has really failed because Mr. Kaufman doesn't open the pool and Hughie's little sister, Susan, almost dies after being bitten by a snake that comes out of the creek. Discouraged, Hughie runs away into the bush, where he meets some timbermen, one of whom gives him a lift to Sydney. After a narrow escape from prejudiced policemen, he locates his cousin, Greg Hinley, Merringee's pride because he is a top university student. It turns out that Greg is the center of a mixed racial group of guitar-playing, liberal, activist hippies. They adopt Hughie's cause, and seventeen of them arrive in Merringee for a Freedom Sing-out at the pool during the district championship swimming meet. Petitions in favor of opening the pool to everyone are circulated and garner a substantial number of signatures, and a Sydney newspaper headlines the story, but the local swimmers do badly, and, when the students launch into "We Shall Overcome," the crowd turns ugly. The appearance of dignified, old Uncle Nelson puts an abrupt stop to the fighting and the demonstration. Clancy wins the freestyle preliminary but disappears mysteriously before the finals. Harriet begs Hughie to find him, and Hughie traces him to the creek swimming hole, but Clancy refuses to return to the meet. The book ends as he strips for a plunge, shortly to be joined by Hughie. The conclusion is abrupt and puzzling, since events are seen from Hughie's point of view and Clancy doesn't tell Hughie why he won't finish. Hughie thinks he will in his own good time. In any event, the conclusion commendably avoids easy solutions. It appears to offer little hope for improving race relations and economic and social conditions for the Abos and to suggest that friendships can continue in spite of circumstances over which individuals have no control. Though motivations are not always clear, the author realizes scenes well, some obviously didactic: Hughie's harrowing experiences with the biased policemen in Sydney; Mr. Kaufman condescendingly explaining to Hughie why Abos can't use the pool (most Abos are "respectable," of course, but——; Abos don't really want to use the pool, because they'd be just "too embarrassed"); Hughie's mother, who works for Mr. Kaufman, hooting with laughter over the spoiled butter, though she knows she'll be the one who has to clean up the mess; timberman Joe Louis telling the sad story of his father, champion boxer who, because an Abo, was never given the chance to fight for the big title—scenes vividly drawn in town, country, school, home, at the creek, at the pool. Most episodes have Hughie at their center, and occasionally they are from the standpoint of the author as observer. In a few places, however, the author intrudes, and the tone becomes overtly instructive and moralistic, for example, ''That's right: they would have kept him out, because it was out of bounds to him and all like him. Forbidden to Aborigines!'' Although the book keeps the attention and the racial problems persist, tone and substance date the book, leaving it important as an artifact. Aust. Bk. of Year Com.

HUNTED IN THEIR OWN LAND. See *MATHINNA'S PEOPLE.*

HUNTER IN THE DARK (Hughes*, Monica, Clarke, 1982; Atheneum, 1983), realistic novel with problem story aspects, which pits human against nature and physical circumstances and also against other humans and self. The story takes place over about three days' time in the 1970s in the forest of Swan Hills just northwest of Edmonton, Alberta, Canada, and about a year previously in flashbacks. Mike Rankin, 16, runs away from home to go hunting alone. He hopes to bag a white-tailed deer for the trophy head, which to him symbolizes the glory and value of life. He has purchased part of his equipment on the sly with the help of schoolmate, Doug O'Reilly, and Doug has loaned him the O'Reilly four-wheel-drive Toyota. The two boys have been planning this special trip for some months. As Mike sets up camp, battles a sudden life-threatening snowstorm, and stalks his deer, he looks back upon the events of the year that brought him to this solitary camp. Shortly after his fifteenth birthday, he falls ill during a basketball game, is hospitalized for tests and then for drug therapy that brings acute discomfort and eventually causes his hair to fall out. Because he must spend his weekends in the hospital for more tests and therapy, his social life almost ceases, his girl friend breaks off their relationship, and he feels isolated by the pain and circumstances. He knows that he must have some terrible illness, but not until he courageously pursues leads in the library can he put a name to it, and only after a forced, frank discussion with his doctor, Jim Gage, does he know for sure that he has fatal leukemia. Mike's other great burden is his parents, who refuse to acknowledge openly the likelihood of his death and become extremely protective. By smothering him with love and refusing to let him participate in activities even when he feels good, they make him feel even more isolated and miserable. When in March he is again hospitalized, and his days are particularly bleak with pain and depression, Doug sneaks into the hospital the mule deer trophy head he bagged the previous fall just after Mike fell sick. This inspires Mike to fight back and the boys to plan Mike's trip for the fall, when Mike is again in remission. Doug's cheery attitude and the doctor's calm encouragement help Mike see that it will be by living life as fully as possible that death will be made acceptable. He sneaks away from home for one last chance to do what a normal, life-loving boy might do. When the time comes to dispatch the magnificent white-tailed deer he sights, he has come to realize how precious life is and the potential for glory and wonder that it offers. He is content to hold it in his gaze and never tightens the trigger. All characters except Doug and Jim Gage are faceless, and even they exist more for the parts they play than as distinctly realized human beings. The dialogue often sounds forced. Imagery of light and dark supports the theme well if a little too obviously. The author's skill in showing Mike as a decent, typical youth in spite of his indulged upbringing, her ability to create tension, her masterful interweaving of the two survival stories, and her talent for giving just enough information about the disease, its symptoms, and the therapy to orient the reader and make the situation real without lapsing into morbidity, coupled with her ability to make the camping trip thoroughly credible and her consistently objective yet sympathetic tone convey the sense of Mike's ordeal without making this into a treatise on the horror of leukemia. Can. Council Winner; Can. Young Adult Winner.

I

IAN BRITTON (*Sea Menace**), cousin of Paul Harris who with him is traveling to New South Wales when they are shipwrecked, are captured by pirates, and have a series of escapes and near escapes. Ian is an extremely strong young man with a placid disposition and great devotion to his mild, decent father. During one of their imprisonments, he is able to get out of their place of confinement by breaking out the planks in the deck that forms the ceiling. In the final adventure, only Ian, by walking day and night, arrives at Sydney in time to warn the settlement of the pirates' plan to capture it.

IAN HULL (*The Feather Star**), football hero in the seaside village and close friend of Bill* Grant. Ian is inclined to be abrupt and less understanding than Bill and hopes some day to become a scientist. He makes a scarecrow of Fleece* Bates's black nightgown, which helps Fleece to see the funny side of the episode but which upsets Abel, who feels it is intended to mock him. Thus Lindy Martin's problem with returning the blue glass is increased.

THE ICE IS COMING (Wrightson*, Patricia, Hutchinson, 1977; Atheneum, 1977), fantasy improvising on Australian Aborigine folklore about earth spirits. In the far north of Australia, the Mimi*, a shy and fragile rock spirit, is snatched by a hostile wind and carried south to central Australia, where live rebellious ice beings called Ninya. Angry at being defeated eons ago by the Eldest* Nargun, a powerful fire spirit, the Ninya capture the Mimi and frost the region. The scene shifts to a young man of the People (Aborigines), Wirrun, who lives among whites but has stayed close to his ancient heritage. While camping in the interior, he sees an unseasonable frost, reads a series of newspaper reports about similar phenomena in eastern Australia, and decides to solve the mystery. He travels to a mountain in New South Wales near one of the frost sightings and encounters various spirits, among them Ko-in*, the man of the mountain, who helps him to obtain a stone of power, tells him to summon Men of the People to sing the Ninya powerless and back to their homes, orders Wirrum to journey to the far south and warn the Nargun of this danger, and instructs the Mimi, who has escaped from the Ninya and been blown to the mountain, to go along. On his long quest, Wirrum barely keeps ahead of the Ninya, who travel underground by secret passages. He goes on foot, by train, and, empowered by the stone, by wind, sometimes alone, sometimes with the Mimi clinging to the opossum-cord that binds the power stone bag to his belt, she on the lookout for ice and he guarding the power. Along the way he meets some hostile, some helpful earth-things, among them the little, dark, man-like Wa-tha-gun-darl, the bird-like Yauruks, the fierce, little Nyols, the formidable Bunyip, and the Yabon, a shape-changing creature who appears in the form of a dog. Wirrun discovers that the Ninya have outdistanced him and are already coating the coast with frost. Since the Men of the People from the interior have not yet arrived, Wirrun seeks help from a nearby community of People to maintain bonfires throughout the night and to locate the Eldest Nargun. In an exciting climax, the Ninya attack on the Eldest Nargun, who has been worn down to the size of a pebble by wind and waves, is repulsed by the combined efforts of various earth-things, particularly the Yauruk, who bring whales to break up the ice, and by another younger and very powerful cave-dwelling Nargun. His task completed, Wirrun arranges for the Mimi to ride home with him and the Men of the People from the interior, who have by this time arrived, but she has gained confidence in her ability to care for herself and decides to seek her own way home. The Mimi stands out and provides levity for this predominantly serious story, and it is easy to admire the noble and resourceful Wirrun. The book relies heavily on coincidence and has many underdeveloped creatures and incidents, particularly in the middle portions, where interest flags accordingly. The author creates setting and at-mosphere remarkably well—the sense of a great malevolent evil in an Australia peopled by personified elemental forces of nature. Humor also comes from the depiction of the spirits as native tribesmen and from satire on the Happy Folk, the whites of the coastal cities. Sequels are *The Dark Bright Water* and *Behind the Wind**. Aust. Bk. of the Year Winner.

IGGY LORENNY (*Tiger in the Bush*; The Roaring 40**), Isobel, brash, strong-willed daughter of Dave* and Liddle-ma* and older sister of Badge*. She enjoys outings in the mountains, especially with Lance, her elder brother, whom she adores, to Badge's chagrin, is not afraid of hard work, and likes people. She is a managing sort, almost a schemer, but never with mean intentions. For example, when she decides that she wants to go to school in Hobart, where Lance is, she achieves her objective by knitting to pay her expenses. She tends to be loud and over-assertive, but she is warm and true blue at heart.

IHAKA AND THE PROPHECY (Orwin*, Joanna, ill. Robyn Kahukiwa, Oxford, 1984), boy's growing-up story set from spring to late fall nine hundred years ago by Delaware Bay near Nelson, New Zealand. An extended family of Maori heed the last words of their late elder to join their kin across Raukawa

(Cook) Strait to "renew the strands of the net that bind us to Hawaiki," their common ancient homeland across the sea. Their highly respected *tohunga*, or craftsman in wood and stone, aged Paoa, whose apprentice is young Ihaka, is to direct the enterprise. Ever mindful of Maori custom, he asks permission of the forest god, Tane, to fell two large trees to make a twin-hulled canoe. Then, under the leadership of Tokatu, Ihaka's father, the men paddle to the quarries on Rangitoto (D'Urville Island) for a special stone for more adzes, which Paoa and Ihaka then construct for felling and hollowing out the trees. Ihaka, whose mind is always full of pictures of things to create, is pleased when Paoa compliments him on his work. Felling the trees is very difficult, but the men labor diligently. They ring and bring down first one, which the boys then top, and then the other. Disaster strikes when the second falls, accidentally injuring Paoa, but Ihaka saves the day when he thinks quickly and picks up the ritual chant the old man was uttering. Paoa never recovers from the wound, and though his mind is clear, he tires easily and is often weary. Paoa, Ihaka, Tokatu, Mawera the headman, and a couple of other men undertake the skilled work on the canoe, Paoa with a special adze made of a hard black stone. Paoa also lays out the sides of the canoe. By the midsummer the work has progressed to the point that Paoa says the trees must be pulled to the shore. Since they need more manpower for this, they ask help from Tikitu's group across the bay. After the tremendous task of dragging the two huge trees down the hillside to the coast is accomplished, a great feast is held. Since Ihaka has distinguished himself in behavior and craft, he is initiated into manhood during the festivities. As a special honor, Paoa hangs a bird pendant about his neck. Ihaka also asks pretty young Hinewai, of Tikitu's group, to marry him. When the canoe is launched, a great storm whips the lagoon. Paoa, now very tired, has been watching the launch from a bed on the shore. The men help him to his hut where he dies. They bury him with his tools, retaining only the black adze as a reminder of his greatness and the prophecy. The book sees ancient Maori life almost completely from the male point of view, women appearing only as mates, cooks, or in vague behind-the-scene tasks. The potential for excitement is rarely exploited, and characters are minimally developed and easily recognized types. Numerous Maori words explained in a glossary add some needed zest, and the role of religion comes through strongly. The details of canoe building are fascinating and far more interesting than Ihaka's personal story. The book is the sequel to *Ihaka and the Summer Wandering*. N. Z. Govt. Short List.

THE INCREDIBLE JOURNEY (Burnford*, Sheila, ill. Carl Burger, Little, 1962), realistic animal story of two dogs and a cat who make their way home across some two hundred fifty miles of Canadian wilderness in the mid-twentieth century. John Longridge, a writer who lives by himself in an isolated house, has been caring for the pets of the Hunter family, while Jim Hunter, an English professor in a northwest Ontario university town, teaches for nine months in England and takes his wife and his son, Peter, 11, and daughter, Elizabeth, 9, with him. Longridge's nearest neighbors expect to care for the animals while he vacations with a brother at Heron Lake, but through a mix-up they think he has taken the dogs and cat with him. Shortly after Longridge drives away, the younger dog, Luath*, a red-gold Labrador retriever, decides to start for home, leading Bodger*, the old white English bull terrier, and Tao*, a wheat-colored Siamese cat. At first Bodger, aging and out of condition, finds the going hard, and both dogs are very hungry, but the cat hunts expertly and seems untired by the trek, eventually supplying the bulldog with essential food. The cat also rescues Bodger from a bear cub, which playfully jumps on the exhausted dog, and bluffs the mother bear into taking her cub and departing. The animals have several encounters with humans, a group of Ojibways, men at a lumber camp, and a half-mad hermit. When they steal a chicken from an isolated farm, Bodger, by nature a fighter, rescues the retriever from the attack of the farm collie. Luath, having been bred and trained to retrieve game undamaged, is nearly starving before he begins to hunt for food. When he attacks a porcupine and gets quills in his nose, he suffers greatly and half his face becomes infected. Yet he retrieves a duck for a hunter, who extracts the festering quills, cleans up the infected face, and gives him his first real meal since the journey's start. The man's wife has already welcomed old Bodger, and that evening the cat, having learned to open doors at home, expertly lifts the latch on the stable where they are shut, and they escape. Tao has a couple of adventures by himself, being hit by a floating log as they cross a river, washed far down the stream, and pulled out, stone deaf, by a Finnish girl who adopts him with love. When his hearing returns, he starts out after the dogs, catching up with only one real difficulty, a threat by a lynx. By this time Longridge has returned, realized that the animals must have started for home, and through diligent inquiry managed to trace them part of the way. Reports of Luath's emaciated condition and the rigors of the last fifty miles through rough, uninhabited country make him give up hope, and he must greet the returning Hunters with this news. He and the Hunters are at their summer home at Lake Windigo when Elizabeth hears a bark. Their father's whistle is answered by joyous barking, but before the retriever can race the last piece of his journey, Tao hurtles down the trail and lands at their feet, and soon also comes Bodger, as fast as his short bulldog legs can carry him. Though, as in most stories of pets, there is a strong appeal to sentiment, the novel makes a great effort to keep the point of view objective, not crediting to the animals any thoughts, skills, or emotions that cannot be observed and mostly not humanizing them in other ways. Their adventures are detailed plausibly and are neither too numerous nor too fantastic. The human characters, however, are cardboard figures, purely functional. Books Too Good; Can. Bk. of Year Winner; Jr. High Cont. Classics; Lewis Carroll.

IN LANE THREE, ALEX ARCHER. See *ALEX.*

I OWN THE RACECOURSE! (Wrightson*, Patricia, ill. Margaret Horder, Hutchinson, 1968; *A Racecourse for Andy,* Harcourt, 1968), realistic, sociological problem novel set in a working-class area of Sydney, Australia, in the 1960s.

Blond, spike-haired, blue-eyed Andy Hoddel, 12, is different from the boys he associates with, Mike and Terry O'Day, Joe Mooney, and Matt Passan. "Something happened" when Andy was five, and now he lives "behind a closed window" and must go to a separate school. Andy cannot understand the game the boys play in which they pretend they own all the most valuable public properties in Sydney. One Saturday evening, feeling lonely and isolated, he goes off by himself to a cliff overlooking the Beacham Park Trotting Course, the local horse- and dog-racing track. He thrills to the noise and excitement of the crowd and the color and drama of the races. Poking about the deserted track the next day, he encounters a bent old man in faded green pants and a baggy gray jacket scavenging for bottles. The tramp "sells" the track to Andy for three dollars. When Andy takes the boys to his private vantage point, proudly shows them the place he "owns," and assures them he really does own it by explaining how he exchanged money for it with an old tramp, they react variously but mostly with horror about the tramp's morality and the potential damage to Andy's ego when he learns the truth. They try to convince him of reality as they see it, but the attitude of the track employees complicates their efforts. When the men discover that Andy thinks he owns the place, they adopt him as a kind of mascot. They greet him warmly and address him as "owner" or "boss," and concessionaires give him free bags of chips. Andy helps groundsman Bert Hammond weed flower beds and even makes friends among the horse and greyhound drivers. Trouble begins when Joe's birthday comes. To surprise Joe and also to liven up the track, Andy decorates the older grandstand with discarded colored streamers he has found in an alley. When the decorations please the crowds, he decides to continue sprucing up the place, by, among other things, painting the bandsmen's benches. The paint, however, is old and tacky and leaves white stripes on their trousers. Bert astutely suggests that Andy may try more "improvements" and tactfully suggests that Andy check with him first. Andy, however, has had the wit to report to Bert that two suspicious-looking men offered him two dollars to give "aniseed" to a certain horse before a race. This stands the boy in good stead when the racing committee meets to discuss what to do about him. The situation is resolved when Bert and the committee "buy" back the track from Andy for ten dollars. Andy is happy because he has realized what he recognizes as a tidy profit, and the race track operators are pleased because they have solved their dilemma without alienating park employees or hurting Andy's feelings. The author draws the racecourse in such clear and thrilling detail that the reader can easily understand how a child like Andy would be both excited and perplexed by what was happening. The normal boys are barely individualized and serve the plot and as foils for Andy, but Andy is drawn with the complexity of the mentally handicapped and is dynamic. His retardation (the word is never used) is revealed without sentimentality and didacticism through his thoughts and behavior and through the reactions of others toward him. Some humor comes from the boys' attempts to explain and reason with Andy and from Andy's perfectly logical defense, in particular since the track men straightfacedly accept him as the "owner." The relationship between Andy and the normal boys is warm and kind, and their concern for his feelings seems completely genuine. Aust. Bk. of Year Highly Com.; Fanfare.

ISAK (*Come Danger, Come Darkness**), educated trusty convict who serves as tutor on Norfolk Island. At first the boys think he is a fat, frightened sycophant who curries favor at the expense of self-respect, though they recognize his ability as a teacher. Later they discover that his toadying is just an act, that he is using the folklore-encrusted story of an escaped convict to aid in his own planned flight, and that he is desperate, resolute, and daring. In the whaleboat, he loses his nerve, however, and then gets into an argument with Corny* Stack, and the result is that the compass falls overboard.

THE ISLAND OF FISH IN THE TREES (Wuorio*, Eva-Lis, ill. Edward Ardizzone, Nelson, 1962; World, 1962), brief story of one day's adventure for two little girls on one of the Balearic Islands in the Mediterranean off the eastern coast of Spain set in the mid-twentieth century. Belinda, pre-school age, whose doll, Maria-Carmen, has lost her head and whose mother has a toothache, sets off to find Señor el Medico. Before she can leave the house, her little sister, Lucy, possibly two years old, joins her. In the village, Belinda remembers that the last time her mother took her to the doctor, they went on a bus, so she gets on the bus to join the market people at the port. There her friend Pedrito offers to row them to Lobster Pot Bay, since the doctor has gone to the Windmills above that bay, and Pedrito's mother gives them breakfast and a golden baby goat, which they name Oro. And so they go on. At each place they are treated kindly by the islanders, given food and an animal Lucy admires—a puppy, a kitten, finally a donkey. When they at last catch up with the doctor, he gets them all a ride home in a rickety truck and then fixes Maria-Carmen's head. They return to find that islanders have reported their progress to their mother all day and have even brought the visiting dentist to care for her tooth. A simple, warm story, it gets most of its charm from sticking to the point of view of little Belinda, to whom the long mission of mercy seems perfectly logical. Ardizzone's illustrations are mostly double-page spreads in muted colors depicting island life with detail and affection. Fanfare.

IT HAPPENED ONE SUMMER (Phipson*, Joan, ill. Margaret Horder, Angus, 1954; *Six and Silver*, Harcourt, 1971), holiday adventure set in Sydney, Australia, and the Karkoo Ranges of New South Wales, presumably in the 1950s. The novel can be divided into three major episodes. In the first the Steadman family, Jack, 16, Pat, 13, little Billy, and their parents, come from a farm near Talia in the Northwest to the seaside for the first time. Every day on the beach by their vacation cottage they see a crowd of well-tanned, stylishly dressed young people, expertly swimming and body surfing. Jack, who swims fairly well, resents their greater expertise and confidence. Pat, who swims very little, admires them and wishes to become acquainted. When the youngest one, Tess Moorland, makes the first overture and offers to teach her, Pat is pleased and she tries doggedly under Tess's demanding direction. Jack responds less graciously and has a series of humiliating disasters. He tips over the boat when they go sailing and develops a cramp while diving, so that he must be rescued by Tess and her older sister, Mary. When Pat asks Tess to come home with them for the last two weeks of vacation, Jack is not pleased, but at their sheep ranch the tables are turned and Tess is the greenhorn, falling off the pony Billy usually rides and becoming so sore that she can hardly walk. Nonetheless, she shows her determination and is such a good sport that Jack is not too upset when Pat asks her to join them on a planned expedition to Mount Calca with some of Jack's boarding school friends. This camp-out takes place the next spring. After much discussion and pruning of the equipment lists, they set off with Jack, now seventeen and a legal driver, taking the two girls and his border collie, Silver, to the home of the Felton boys, near Kullaroo. There they are joined by Dick Felton, 16, and very bright Mick, 13, and are driven up into the mountains where they are joined by their guide, Ted, and his packtrain. They make an arduous climb and camp near the peak of Mount Calca. For a couple of days all goes well. Then Silver fails to return to camp and no amount of calling and whistling brings back the sheep dog. Ted organizes them each to search in a different direction, to go for a prescribed length of time, then turn back. He is doubtful about sending Tess alone because she is a city girl, but the others vouch for her good sense. When they all return except Tess, worried Ted sets off to find her. He meets her returning with Silver, whom she has freed from a rabbit trap, but in doing so she has snapped the trap on her own hand, has been unable to free it, and has had to dig up the trap and carry it with her as she stumbles back in pain. Fortunately her hand is not broken, and Silver is not seriously injured. The novel has pleasant descriptions of life at the seaside and on the sheep ranch and of the mountain trip, but it is unfocused, without any well-defined central conflict or resolution. The point of view in the first episode is Pat's, but it shifts to be mostly Tess's in the rest of the book. The characters are not well developed: the two girls are almost identical and the three boys are differentiated only by Jack's concern for his dog and Mick's intelligence. The title is a puzzler: action takes place over one summer and the next spring. The American-British title is not much of an improvement, since it ignores the first two-thirds of the novel. Aust. Bk. of Year Highly Com.

J

JACK BRENT (*The Curse of the Turtle**), father of Jimmy Brent and owner of the family cattle ranch in Oonaderra in northern Australia. Jack is presented as reflecting the prevailing Australian attitude toward the indigenous people. A stern, taciturn man, he despises the blacks and treats them like ignorant children. He dies when a tank of carbolic acid falls on him while the whites are disinfecting the cholera-stricken Aborigine camp.

JACK CLARKE (*Climb a Lonely Hill**), youth marooned with his sister, Sue*, in the Australian desert. Although the school clown (his way of coping with jibes because his father is often drunk), Jack is a stickler for rules and propriety. These characteristics, plus his ability to escape into an interior world to blot out hurtful outward circumstances, enable the children to survive. At the end Jack decides that he wants to do more with his life than become a stockman. Jack is a likeable, well-drawn figure, a foil for Sue and dynamic in his own right.

JACKIE STUBECK (*The True Story of Lilli Stubeck**), younger brother of Lilli Stubeck. Handicapped because he has only three fingers on each hand, he still scavenges and thieves with ease. Lilli depends on him to augment her slim salary after Mrs.* Stubeck falls ill. Once while stealing chickens, his leg gets caught in a trap and Lilli calls on Kit* Quayle to help him out.

JACKSON, ADA (ACRAMAN), Australian author of natural science books, including *Beetles Ahoy** (Paterson, 1947), a slightly fictionalized series of nature studies originally written for the Australian Broadcasting Commission and produced as a radio series for children. The book was highly commended for the Australian Book of the Year Award. She also wrote *Sea Shore, Swamp, and Bush; Exploring Nature's Mysteries* (Robertson & Mullens, 1941).

JACOB TWO-TWO MEETS THE HOODED FANG (Richler*, Mordecai, ill. Fritz Wegner, Knopf, 1975), fast-moving comic fantasy in which characters, incidents, tone, and atmosphere suggest Saturday morning television cartoons. Jacob Two-Two, the youngest of five children in an English family, tolerates what he sees as injustices from siblings and parents and has developed the habit of repeating every statement to get attention. When he is sent to the greengrocer for two pounds of firm, red tomatoes and repeats himself as usual, the grocer pretends to be insulted and frightens the boy, who races away in terror to Richmond Park. He flings himself down on the grass to compose himself and soon notices fog coming in. Apparently a dream sequence ensues during which Jacob is tried in a court of law for insulting a "big person." Justice Rough sentences him "for his own good" to two years, two months, two weeks, two days, two hours, and two minutes in the darkest dungeons of the children's prison. Two children, O'Toole and Shapiro (actually Jacob's brother and sister), clad in superman-like costumes, their shirts emblazoned with the words "Child Power," burst into the courtroom and vow to release Jacob and avenge him against the judge. At the island prison, Jacob Two-Two must operate the machine that makes the fog that shrouds the prison whose warden is the dreaded Hooded Fang. Jacob, who refuses to quail before the ostensibly vicious Fang, soon notices that after every visit Fang makes to his cell, candy bars appear. Deducing the monstrous warden is really a softy and threatening to expose his tender heart, Jacob blackmails him into carrying a message outside that enables Shapiro and O'Toole to rescue Jacob and two hundred other imprisoned children. Jacob Two-Two soon finds himself back in Richmond Park, where he awakens to discover his family searching for him. Characters and incidents have the one-dimensionality of the comic book, the atmosphere is grossly slapstick, events tumble after one another in rapid succession, the extensive dialogue makes generous use of insult and crude witticisms, and the satire is heavy handed and aimed at children as well as adults. Can. Bk. of Year Winner; Can. Ruth Schwartz.

JAMES COOK, ROYAL NAVY (Finkel*, George, ill. Amnon Sadubin, Angus, 1970), biographical novel of the youth and early voyages of historical James Cook (1728–1777), explorer, map maker, and circumnavigator. Even as a boy of eleven on his father's Yorkshire farm James dreams of sailing to far-off, unknown lands. At age seventeen Cook meets Henry Walker of the Walker ship line, an encounter that leads to a coveted apprenticeship on the *Freelove*. When the tallyman (accountant) suffers an accident, James takes over, an opportunity that soon leads to a promotion. He conducts himself well, studies in his free time, and is made an Able Seaman in 1852 at age twenty-four. Four years later he joins the Navy, one step ahead of the press gang, serving as commander of a sloop consort to the *Eagle*, a warship commanded by Captain Hugh Palliser, whose friendship and respect for James prove of advantage to the younger man many times in the future. The scenes in which the *Eagle*, chiefly through James's skillful handling, captures a French frigate are vividly described. Further distinguished service against the French and high political connections elevate James to the rank of master and second-in-command on the *Pembroke*, also under Hugh Palliser. Soon dispatched to the New World, the *Pembroke* sees service against the French at Louisbourg and Quebec with General Wolfe, who appears briefly in the story. James now begins the navigational charts for which he becomes famous, mapping the coastal waters and the St. Lawrence River. Upon his return to England, he marries. Fairly well off from booty and publications, he owns a house near London where he spends his winters with his growing family and prepares charts for the British Admiralty. In 1769, at age forty-one, he is commissioned the commander of the *Endeavour*, which is to sail to the South Seas to investigate the lands charted by Dutchman Abel Tasman and named New Zealand and to determine if a continent lies there. The last half of the book details his three-year voyage around South America and across the Pacific, focusing mainly on the events that occur in New Zealand, off Australia, and in the Dutch East Indies. He stops frequently for supplies and to allow his passenger, the brilliant young naturalist, Joseph Banks, to collect specimens. After sailing around both New Zealand islands, he surveys and takes possession of the east coast of Australia for England, naming it New South Wales and naming Botany Bay in honor of Mr. Banks. The voyage becomes increasingly hard, and by the time the *Endeavour* reaches Cape Town twenty-eight of ninety-four men have died. The ship is so battered that James must drop out of the convoy, finally reaching the Thames in July, 1771. In reward for his discoveries and good leadership, James is promoted to commander, a commission that is brought to him in a cameo appearance by James Boswell. An appended "Historical Note" says that Cook made two more voyages to the South Seas, on the second of which he met his death from natives in Hawaii. His family was granted a coat of arms to honor his achievements. The book is filled with a vast amount of fascinating information about ships, battles, current affairs, exploration, and history, all carefully compiled and affectionately related. These same details, however, often impede the story's flow. Cook is the best-drawn figure, the model officer. Mr. Banks, the other character mentioned frequently enough to have personality, is presented as another type, the youth born to enough means to be a gentleman scholar but who uses his wealth and position to get his way and is seldom circumspect. A few other famous figures also appear briefly, and the passages describing the deliberations of the Lords of the Admiralty are intriguing for their insight into the times. Although occasionally tedious, this rich and substantial book paints a clear picture of an exciting period and of the man who did much to shape it. Aust. Bk. of Year Com.

JAMIE'S DISCOVERY (Roland*, Betty, ill. Geraldine Spence, Bodley, 1963; Scholastic, 1963), brief novel for younger readers involving a lost dog and the discovery of a cave with Australian Aborigine paintings, sequel to *The Forbidden Bridge**, and set about one year later, presumably in the period of its publication. Since the death of his father, Jamie (in a sequel surnamed Kendall), 8, and his mother have lived at Cromarty, the two-thousand-acre grazing property in the Goulburn Valley of Victoria belonging to his Uncle David McBride. Also resident are his grandmother and his Aunt Marion, an invalid confined to a wheelchair. Jamie's best friends are the Pinkertons, a large family living in a tumbledown shack across the river, now spanned by a foot bridge Uncle David has built. With his cocker spaniel, Fran, and Len Pinkerton's big dog, Joker, the two boys fish for yabbies (crayfish) in the waterhole near the Cromarty boundary fence. When it is time to go home, Joker is with them, but Fran is nowhere to be found. She does not return that night, and the next day Uncle David takes Jamie to check the fence near the waterhole and finds a place where the rabbits have broken through, large enough for Fran, whose hairs are caught in the mesh, but not for Joker. Though they call and hunt beyond the fence, they see no trace of Fran. Everyone is very kind to Jamie, but they give him little hope that Fran will return, saying she has probably run into a snake or followed a rabbit into a hole where she is stuck. Len comes that evening with the news that a swaggie (tramp) has been seen down at Kelly's Crossing and suggests that he might have taken Fran. Jamie rides his pony, Jock, bareback to the crossing. sneaks up on foot, and sees an old man sitting by his campfire, talking and singing to himself. Jamie goes quietly back to his horse and rides home in the dark. After a week, Mr. Pinkerton agrees to take the boys back to the waterhole, where he is going to mend the fence, and let them have one more look. They separate, and after a long search, Jamie decides to take a shortcut to the tree where they have agreed to meet. He hears a whine from a crevice in the rocks, frantically signals Len, and together they search for another opening. Jamie worms his way under a rock ledge and shouts to Len that there is quite a large cave, then becomes quiet. Len hurries off to summon his father. When they return, they find boy and dog sitting on the rocks, and Jamie explains that a rock slide had blocked Fran's return route, and as he tried to get to her, it gave way and he was knocked out. He is still dizzy and confused, but he is sure there were drawings on the walls and a pool of water on the floor. The next day Mr. Pinkerton and Uncle David take them back, clear out the fallen debris, and discover extensive Aborigine drawings. Fran, having had water during her imprisonment, soon recovers. The style is simple, but not of primer quality, and there is enough plausible action to keep a reader's interest. The characterization is minimal but adequate. A sequel is *Jamie's Summer Visitor**. Aust. Bk. of Year Com.

JAMIE'S SUMMER VISITOR (Roland*, Betty, ill. Prudence Seward, Bodley, 1964; McGraw, 1967), sequel to *The Forbidden Bridge** and *Jamie's Discovery**, set again at Cromarty, a big sheep ranch in the Goulburn Valley of Victoria, Australia, in the mid-twentieth century. Jamie Kendall, now nine, is gloomy when he learns that a girl is coming from Sydney to visit for Christmas vacation, the daughter of a beautiful friend of his mother. To Jamie's surprise, Nola, 10, turns out to be a plain child with glasses and braces on her teeth. Unfortunately, she is scornful of almost everything at Cromarty. When Jamie and his friend,

Len Pinkerton, are at the swimming hole in the river with all the Pinkerton siblings, Nola humiliates them by doing a skillful Australian crawl with ease out to the barge, where only the strongest swimmers venture, then taunting them to follow. Jamie and Len manage to splash and dog-paddle their way to the barge, where she condescends to give Len instructions. Jealous and left out, Jamie starts back, gets caught in the current, and panics, flailing wildly and yelling for help. Nola expertly tows him to shore, then goes back to help Len. She agrees not to tell Jamie's mother, but his dislike of her grows. She doesn't care for his precious cocker spaniel, Fran, or the calves and lambs and prize Merino rams that make up much of Jamie's life on his Uncle David McBride's farm. He first feels sympathy for Nola as they ice the Christmas cake and she confesses that she's never had a real, homemade Christmas cake or a pudding with favors baked in it. She also proves to be a clumsy rider and afraid of horses, even of Jamie's old pony, Jock. She sticks doggedly to learning to ride, however, as Jamie is determinedly trying to improve his swimming. They are out riding together, with Jamie ahead. He leaves Nola struggling to close the gate between two paddocks, one containing sheep sorted out for sale. That afternoon, Uncle David, furious, demands to know who left the gate unbarred so that the sheep mingled and had to be resorted. Nola begs Jamie not to tell on her, and he stays silent even when Uncle David says he must be punished by staying home while they all go to the annual Christmas Eve celebration in the nearest town, Nagambie. Just before they are to leave, Nola breaks down, weeping and confessing that it was she who left the gate unbarred and admitting that she didn't confess earlier because she was afraid of being sent away, as her mother has sent her to boarding school and left her with friends for holidays to get her out of the way. Uncle David relents, they have a grand celebration for Christmas Eve, and the next day Nola gets the boomerang in her slice of plum pudding, meaning to her delight and also to Jamie's that she will return to Cromarty. The novel, like its predecessors, is brief and simply written, intended for younger readers. The psychology, though obvious, is sound, and the changing attitudes of the two main children are convincing. Aust. Bk. of Year Highly Com.

JANINE DART (*Memory**), child tap-dancing star of television commercials. Although Janine died before the novel begins, she has great importance, since Jonny Dart feels responsible for her tragic death. He has also felt inferior to her in talent because she was older than he and hence more adept and also because she was a striking blonde and his hair was dyed to match hers so that they would be more photogenic. Bonny* Benedicta informs him that Janine's death was accidental and that he was also thought very talented. Thus Jonny is freed from his troubled past and enabled to embark on a more productive future, perhaps in dancing.

JAN MARTIN (*To the Wild Sky**), Janet, twin of Bruce*, who has been asked to Gerald* Hennessy's birthday house party partly because her brother and Gerald are friends and partly because Gerald's mother wanted another girl in the group besides Carol* Bancroft. Jan, who thinks she is homely and awkward, is uneasy about the trip and refuses at the last minute to go but is forced by her mother to be part of it. On the plane she is airsick, but after they crash she has presence of mind and with Colin* Kerr manages to rig a rope to shore and to resuscitate Gerald after Colin drags him from the plane. She has little sympathy for Bruce, thinking, with some justification, that he is faking his injury. Because she is religious, she is chosen to give an elegy for the dead pilot and finds herself tongue-tied. Her on-again, off-again quarrel with Carol is one element that keeps the group from any effective cooperation, but her knowledge of history places them on Molineaux Island and she eventually makes the fire that might save them.

JAREE (*Boori**; *Darkness under the Hills**), also called Jun Jaree, personal companion spirit to Boori, who lives in a small leather bag worn around his neck. Appearing usually as a spark, Jaree is a minor fire spirit, and he is most useful as a spy, watching those who threaten Boori, gathering information from other spirits, warning of trouble, and advising his human friend. Although devoted to Boori, he is impertinent and often critical of him, and he is quarrelsome with Dingo*, though they come to respect each other. Inclined to brag and occasionally to be tripped up by his self-promotion, Jaree provides some comedy in the predominantly serious stories. At the end, he becomes a star, along with Boori and Dingo, a tiny one dancing ahead of the other two in the sky.

JARL HANSEN (*The Spirit Wind**), Norwegian orphan who has shipped for South Australia aboard the old *Hootzen* and jumps ship to escape the brutal first mate, Heinrich the Bull. Although his father was a sailor and his mother an English fisherman's daughter, Jarl has a strong fear of the sea, partly because of seeing a man washed overboard in rough weather and partly because the mate has sent him aloft when he was sick and dizzy. Goaded beyond endurance, he throws hot stew at the mate, giving him an excuse for denying the boy the right to go ashore when they get to port. In addition, when they plan to butcher the pig, an animal for which Jarl has developed some affection, the mate insists that the boy be present and, when he himself knocks down the fence and lets the pig escape, blames Jarl. He stamps on Jarl's hand and, for punishment, makes Jarl clean the hated coal stove every morning, a task that cuts deeply into Jarl's already insufficient sleep. The boy endures his treatment without complaining but refuses to be subdued and quietly makes plans to leave the ship secretly. On several different occasions, Jarl acts decently to aid someone, even though he puts himself in jeopardy by doing so. He is a typical young adventure-story hero, but comparatively well developed and convincing.

JASMIN (Truss*, Jan, Douglas & McIntyre, 1982; Atheneum, 1982), growing-up story in which a sixth grade girl in Dandron, Alberta, Canada, of the late twentieth century tries to escape her personal and family problems by running away to live alone in the wilderness. As eldest of the eight Stalke children, Jasmin Marie Antoinette, 11, does most of the housework and caring for her siblings while her mother cuddles the latest baby and watches television. In their two-room rural house, where the children all sleep in the loft, there is no place for Jasmin to do her homework or to keep her few treasures. When mischievous Nathaniel, 8, gets retarded Leroy*, 10, to play Tarzan and Leroy knocks Jasmin's science project sweet potatoes from the loft window sill into the yard, she breaks into rare tears and, fearing that she will not be promoted from the sixth grade, she decides to run away. Taking with her only her red nightgown and her patchwork quilt made by her now dead grandmother, a small bag of new potatoes, and a slim, leather-bound book of poems she once found, she sets off at night while the family sleeps, heading westward toward the forest and mountains. She doesn't realize that Leroy, disturbed because he has made her cry and unable to communicate his contrition, starts after her. During the night she is scared by coyotes and a bear, which she frightens off by quoting poetry, but the next day she finds a small cave, dry and cozy, screened from view by a curtain of pine branches. Below is a rivulet where she can get water and store her food, where she can be like the subject of her favorite poem, "Meg Merrilies" by Keats, living "as she did please." At home, the search for the missing youngsters is delayed because their parents think they are together. Jasmin spends six days alone, living on only a few potatoes and berries, amusing herself by modeling animals from the riverbank clay—a porcupine, coyote, bear, and a cougar killing a doe—all creatures she has watched during the week. She discovers unsuspected artistic skill, survives a terrible rain and hail storm, which washes away her clothes except the nightgown, hides from a searching helicopter, and gradually sinks into a feverish lethargy. She is found by a young couple, artists named Hana Townsend and Jules Airlie, who live in an isolated log house and have heard from the Royal Canadian Mounted Police about the missing children. They help her and treat her concerns with respect. Jules persuades her to design a habitat for her clay animals for the science and art fair to replace her ruined project, and Hana draws her picture in her red nightgown. Since they have no phone and are cut off by high water, they feel no rush to make her whereabouts known, but they gently build her self-image, then tell her that Leroy is also absent. Jasmin decides to go home to find him, and they signal a searching helicopter, which returns her to her family. With her siblings, Jasmin hunts for Leroy and finds him in a cellar under an abandoned house. After Hana and Jules talk to the school principal, he promotes Jasmin to junior high. Her project wins second place at the fair, and Hana's picture of her, also entered in the fair, is much admired by her family and even by the boy whose project wins the first prize. Although Jasmin's confidence that she can live in the wild with no tools or supplies seems naive for a girl depicted as highly intelligent, and the ending piles good fortune on her unbelievably, the story progresses with good pace and strong suspense. Jasmin's troubles and the family relationships, particularly between her and Leroy, are interesting and believable. Can. Ruth Schwartz.

JASMIN STALKE (*Jasmin**), Jasmin Marie Antoinette, 11, competent over-worked eldest child in the large Stalke family. Though Jasmin is embarrassed by the fancy names her mother chooses for her children, by their two-room house surrounded by rusting cars and other junk, and by the reputation for general shiftlessness of her parents, she is fond of her family and devoted to her retarded brother, Leroy*. With great patience, she has talked to Leroy and tried to explain things, actually doing more for him than her loving but ineffectual mother. Jasmin does not discover her own artistic ability until, alone in her hideaway, she begins modeling animals, but she remembers watching her grandmother sew and do beautiful handwork. In the end, her friends Hana and Jules have offered her a place in their home to get away from the family now and then, and her father is dividing the loft with partitions so she can have her own room.

JEAN (*The Keeper**), girl whose left arm has been smashed in an accident and therefore, since she is not much good at day-to-day work in the primitive village, has become a senior learner. In the superstitious climate of the village, she is looked upon with suspicion because many of the post-nuclear survivors suffer from radiation sickness and children born to them are often deformed, even several generations after the bombing. Since people think of the sickness as a plague, they fear that they may catch it from its victims, and they are even unwilling to spare Jean, an accident victim, because of her arm's resemblance to a birth deformity. Her own mother is one of the most intolerant. Hurt and embittered Jean turns for understanding and help to Michael*.

JELLYBEAN (Duder*, Tessa, Oxford, 1985; Viking, 1986), realistic novel of family life set recently in Auckland, New Zealand. Although sometimes she is lonely and jealous of her mother's music, Jellybean (Geraldine) Waite, 10, is proud of her divorced mother, Anna-liese, a talented cellist who plays with orchestras and ensembles, performs mostly in the evenings, leaves Jellybean with baby-sitters, and spends many hours practicing. One night when Anna's ensemble is playing at a restaurant and the baby-sitter falls ill, Jellybean goes along and sits at a table while the group performs. A bearded man in a dark suit, who says he is a musician named Gerald Matthews, sits down beside her. They converse agreeably, and she confides that she hopes to become a conductor. Later she learns that he was a cellist for seven years with the Orchestra of the Royal Opera House at Covent Garden in London. When his wife fell ill, they came to her native New Zealand, where she recently died. Gerald is to audition for the orchestra, but he has played little for four years and fears he will fail. Weeks pass without much incident. Jellybean becomes engrossed in listening to music and plays at conducting at home. One morning in August during spring holidays, she accompanies her mother to the dress rehearsal of *The Nutcracker*. Because they are late, Anna runs ahead, leaving Jellybean to get herself into the concert hall. She gets lost outside, then finds an entrance, blunders backstage, and finally ends up in the orchestra pit, where she crouches near Gerald. She feels conflicting emotions of jealousy, anger, and joy, and especially deep interest since the conductor is a woman, Frederica Wilton. In a long passage, Jellybean pretends she is a mouse disrupting the concert by frightening the musicians and confusing the dancers. Afterward she learns that Gerald passed the auditions and that he and her mother are friends. Quite unexpectedly Jellybean gets her chance to conduct publicly. At the annual school concert, the woman conductor who led *The Nutcracker* appears. She has learned of Jellybean's ambition and invites her to lead the pieces the musicians know she knows and loves, "Dance of the Sugar Plum Fairy" and "Waltz of the Flowers," and as encores, "Russian Dance" and "Grand Pas de Deux." Jellybean is so elated at how well the pieces go that she runs off to the playground to savor the joy by herself. While she is sitting in the swing, Gerald joins her and brings her up to date on family history. He and her mother had been friends while they were students in London and had planned to marry. Things went awry, and she returned to New Zealand where she married Jellybean's father, a violist, who fell in love with another orchestra member and divorced Anna before Jellybean was born. Anna joins their conversation and suggests a trip to London, where she and Jellybean can attend concerts and where perhaps Jellybean can meet her father who now plays in the Royal Opera House Orchestra. Gerald hopes to accompany them. The use of the present tense throughout strengthens the third-person limited point of view, which is so sharply restricted to Jellybean's perspective that the narrative has the intimacy of first person. The details of rehearsals and especially of the hustle and bustle of the ballet practice make the world of the musicians and dancers startlingly real and believable, although Jellybean's confusion backstage seems overdone for comic effect. The revelation of Gerald's relationship with Anna is not unexpected but satisfactory. Anna's decision to vacation in London at this particular time seems contrived, especially since there is some suggestion of a resumed romance between her and Gerald. Though the plot moves unevenly and the story is many times interrupted by Jellybean's innermost thoughts and reactions, the relationship between Anna and Jellybean is convincing and strong. The unconventional family situation is warm and rewarding for both, and the world of music is presented in unpretentious descriptions that convey a deep sense of the satisfaction a strongly held interest or talent can bring N. Z. Govt. Short List.

JEM FLETCHER (*Hebe's Daughter**), steady, hardworking youth. He is very unhappy at Ironlatch, where his stepfather, Jake Hallam, is "the leader of the biggest gang of smugglers" on the east coast of England and where Jem must slave to earn his keep. He longs to recover the inn that his father once owned and that Hallam has sold. At first he is truculent and hostile toward Liz Pollard because she says that she is of the gentry, but eventually he warms to her. Years later, after she returns from France, Liz discovers that Jem is prosperous, dresses in fine clothes, and runs the inn called the Privateer in Hastings. Though she spurns his offer of a job as a housekeeper, he remains her friend and helps her when Petit-Jean* falls ill. Jem is the stereotypical youth who succeeds because he is virtuous and hardworking.

JIMMY JASPERS (*The Halfmen of O**; *The Priests of Ferris**; *Motherstone**), conniving, old gold prospector, who influences the action on several occasions, most notably by kidnapping Susan, chopping down a bridge so that Cling cannot reach the children, and killing Cling's much-dreaded Bloodcat. In *The Halfmen of O*, he is described stereotypically and comically as "an ugly old man" [with] "a big rough nose, coloured with veins, a drooping lower lip, all wet with spit and yellow with tobacco, and loose skin under his chin, like a turkey's wattles." He speaks in a kind of "down under" backwoods dialect: "Yer better tell me, sonny, else I'll bash yer." In the other two books, he is less comic in behavior but still impulsive and somewhat irascible. He is one of the few characters in the three novels who stands out as an individual.

JOE SPECKLEDHAWK (*Winners**), Jordy Threebears's Blackfoot maternal grandfather. A silent, little old man of seventy, he wears his hair in short braids and was once a rodeo champion. Joe is determined that Jordy go to school because while in prison he discovered that most Indians there were illiterate, or semi-literate. As he becomes more involved in the boy's life, Joe grows closer to his Indian neighbors and loses some of his hatred and distrust of whites. He is one of the better developed characters in the story.

JOHN BAINS (*Shantymen of Cache Lake**), Ottawa boy who with his younger sister, Meg*, takes the job of cook's helper in a logging camp to support his mother and younger siblings. At fourteen, John is not as robust as his sister nor as assertive, and at first he is ambivalent about the union activity, worrying about the correctness of challenging authority. When Hardy* fines him unjustly and some of the men stand up for him, he begs them not to fight and says he'll willingly accept the fine, thereby winning their contempt and causing them to shun him. After the collapse of the log chute, which kills Tim McGuire, he becomes a strong and eager union supporter, and in the attempt to walk to Ottawa, he is the main force that helps Cameron* survive. John is a more convincing character than his sister.

JOHN OF THE "SIRIUS" (Chadwick*, Doris, ill. Margaret Senior, Nelson, 1955), travel novel for middle-grade readers about the first voyage of settlement to New South Wales in 1787, headed by Arthur Phillip, who became the first governor. The action starts in an English village where John, probably about ten, and his younger sister, Sue, learn that they and their mother are to accompany their marine father on his next trip, this time to Botany Bay, which John knows of from reading about the travels of Captain Cook. They sail on the man-o'-war *Sirius*, flagship for the eleven vessels, some of which carry convicts. Evidently the only children on the *Sirius*, they are soon favorites of the carpenter, Chips;

the cook, Cookie; the young midshipmen; and even the Commodore, captain Arthur Phillip. Their first stop is at Teneriffe, in the Canary Islands, where the governor sends John a gift of mulberries, with which Cookie makes a pie. As they cross the equator, John is initiated by King Neptune, rather more gently than are the older sailors and marines for whom it is the first crossing. They next stop at Rio, Brazil, where John falls overboard trying to catch an orange thrown by a Portuguese gentleman and is saved by his friend, Midshipman Dan. He also makes friends with Martin, a boy about his age traveling on the *Friendship*, one of the transports in their group, and together they explore and meet the Captain of the Fort, a portly gentleman who collects butterflies. He also loses his dog, Gyp, leaving him on land when he returns to the ship, but that evening, seeing him swimming wearily, gets Midshipman Dan to help haul him aboard. In Rio they also attend a church service, where Martin's baby brother is christened, and Sue gives her favorite doll to a little convict girl. The small fleet then heads for Capetown, where they live ashore with a Dutch family, and John has a number of mild adventures with Martin. Soon after, the Commodore decides to go on ahead in the *Supply*, taking also the *Friendship* and two other vessels to find and prepare a site for the settlement. He takes John with him as a cabin boy. On board John learns to work conscientiously, enjoys his first Christmas away from his family, and suffers through a severe storm. In January, 1788, they arrive at Botany Bay, where John goes ashore carrying the box of trinkets with which the Commodore dispels the hostility of the black men, but they find no spot suitable for a settlement. John and Martin are both in the boat with the Commodore when he goes to Port Jackson, named but not explored by Cook. They find a river and a harbor suitable for a large settlement, which the Commodore names Sydney Cove. On January 26, when the Commodore takes possession of the place in the name of George III, John hoists the flag on the newly raised flagpole. He looks forward to eating soup made from the hopping animal he and Martin have seen and to a life full of interest in the new land. The novel has no plot, just a series of incidents, many of which come from actual records of this voyage, although John is fictional. The attitude of the adults to his sometimes mischievous behavior is extremely tolerant, not too convincing considering the period and the usual discipline aboard naval ships. In tone the book seems to come from an earlier period than the 1950s, and the grimmer details of life aboard ship are omitted. Aust. Bk. of Year Highly Com.

JONES, BENJAMIN (*The Brown Land Was Green**), manager for Mr.* Archibald Blake, John Webster's supervisor, and the novel's villain. Before the novel begins, he came to Australia as an army lieutenant and dreamed of setting himself up as a landed man. Unfortunate experiences with the Aborigines turned him so much against them that he now considers them barely human, usually refers to them as ''varmints,'' and kills as many as he can. As a character, he is overdrawn and described tritely and melodramatically: ''Hate narrowed his eyes to slits'' and the corners of his mouth twitched, ''shivering the loose wrinkles of dark skin like waves over a muddy bed.''

JOSH (Southall*, Ivan, Angus, 1971; Macmillan, 1972), tense novel of a visit by a modern Australian city boy to the remote town founded by his great-grandfather some one hundred miles from Melbourne. Although his cousins have told him great stories about the place, Josh Plowman, 14, has never been to Ryan Creek, partly because his mother doesn't want to join the family rush to butter up Aunt Clara, the only remaining Plowman in the town, in hope of inheriting her wealth. Josh finds his great-aunt abrupt and censorious. In the morning he is appalled and furious that she has unpacked his bag and taken his book of poems, private writings he protects carefully from prying eyes. His anger when she admits she has read them starts them off on a bad footing. In the next three days he suffers scorn and mean tricks from the local youngsters, who make snide remarks about his aunt but pretend to adore her. Only fat, somewhat simpleminded Laura Jones makes friendly overtures and, despite his protests, jumps from the bridge, a highly dangerous trick, to impress him. At the insistence of his aunt, the boys invite him to play in a cricket match with a team from Croxley, a nearby town. Hoping to edge him out, Bill O'Connor insists that he wear proper whites. Before time for the match Josh encounters Rex, Bill's younger brother, and he discovers some complicating factors: Laura has been lying and saying that he chased her up to the bridge and forced her to jump off; Aunt Clara has been spending her money to send all the brighter youngsters in town off to high school and letting families live free in the houses she owns; Rex blames Josh and his cousins for coming and sponging off her; and Rex is losing his position as wicketkeeper because Josh is entering the cricket game. Back at his aunt's house, he finds that Bill has deliberately borrowed whites for him from someone much shorter and twice as heavy, so that even with them pinned up he looks ludicrous. Roused to real fury, Josh confronts Bill, shrilly accuses him, and starts a fight, which he is losing badly when it is broken up by the schoolteacher, who is to act as umpire for the match. Josh is told that they will accept him dressed in his own clothes, but if he won't play, Bill will not be allowed to play either, and Bill's team will boycott the game. Josh refuses to let them pressure him and locks himself in his room. He decides that he will walk home. He leaves a note and sneaks out, but by the dam pond he is waylaid by Harry Jones, who beats him up for his treatment of Laura, among other things, and obscurely for worrying Aunt Clara. Josh doesn't fight back until Harry tears the poems, which Josh has taken with him. Harry tries to protect him when both cricket teams converge on him and tear off his clothes, bounce him in the brush, and throw him into the pond, where he almost drowns, because he can't swim. The Croxley team, pulling him out, suddenly turns on the Ryan Creek kids, and a terrific battle ensues, with Josh crouching in the middle, kicked by both sides. He is rescued by the schoolteacher, who, with Aunt Clara, takes him to the doctor. The truth has come out. His aunt says that the kids are all ashamed of themselves and want to make it up to him by a new cricket match and a picnic in his honor. Josh finally is able to assert himself and retain a bit of self-respect by insisting that he is walking home, starting in the morning. This is an initiation story, and Josh is clearly meant to triumph in the end. He is characterized as a sensitive boy, a poet, who brings on part of his troubles by his impulsiveness and his clumsiness. The hostility of the local kids is presumably explained by their feeling of obligation to Aunt Clara and their resentment at having had to entertain his cousins on previous occasions, but the antagonism seems extreme and too sudden. Much of the story is told in inner monologue, which starts at such a pitch of tension that it is wearying and loses effectiveness before the really strong scenes on the third day. Carnegie Winner; Cont. Classics; Fanfare.

JOSHI, NIHARIKA, writer in India whose novel *The Golden Buddha** (CBT, India, 1982) won Second Prize in the 1981 Children's Book Trust of India competition. A lively, suspenseful detective story involving the recovery of a priceless Tibetan artifact, the novel has its source in the historical flight of the Dalai Lama into India after the Chinese invaded Tibet. *The Mystery of the Fake Arjuna** (CBT, India, 1984), another novel about idol smuggling, placed second in the 1982 competition.

JOURNEY BEHIND THE WIND. See *BEHIND THE WIND*.

JOURNEY TO JO'BURG: A SOUTH AFRICAN STORY (Naidoo*, Beverley, ill. Eric Velasquez, Longman, 1985; Lippincott, 1986), realistic novel of home and community life set in contemporary South Africa. Their gold-miner father dead of coughing sickness, their mother employed as a maid in distant Johannesburg, Naledi, 13, her younger brother, Tiro, 9, and little sister, Dineo, live with their grandmother and aunt three hundred kilometers west of Johannesburg in an unnamed village, which, according to the map in the front of the book, lies near the Botswana border. Since Dineo has been suffering from a fever and seems near death, Naledi persuades Tiro to accompany her to Johannesburg to inform their mother of her plight. On their own, the two set out with provisions given them by a neighbor girl, a couple of sweet potatoes and a bottle of water. They trudge the dusty red earth road to the tar highway, then through a small town, always keeping a lookout for policemen, who, they know from conversation, are dangerous. When they pass an orange orchard, a young worker chances a whipping to give them fruit to eat and an old shed to sleep in that night. The next morning, a friendly truck driver, bound for the city, picks them up and takes them to Johannesburg. He gives them money for the bus to the Parktown sector, where Mma works, because he says it's much too dangerous for them to walk there. When they innocently almost board a whites-only bus, they are saved from trouble by a young woman named Grace Mbatha, who also offers them shelter for the night. They take a non-whites-only bus and soon arrive at the large, pink house where Mma works. When Mma's Madam coldly insists that Mma care for her little girl that night while she and her husband attend a party, the two children go to Grace's house, experiencing on the way a police "pass raid," during which blacks are arrested and herded into a van for violating the law that says they must at all times carry identification. At Grace's house they learn that her older brother emigrated to an unnamed foreign country after being imprisoned for demonstrating for black rights. The next morning they meet Mma at the train station and return to their village. Mma hires a car to take Dineo to the hospital, and Naledi accompanies them there. They must wait hours in line along with many other parents and ill people; Mma endures the delay with patience. One woman's baby dies before they see the doctor, and the grief-stricken woman carries the tiny body out wrapped in a plastic bag. The doctor hospitalizes Dineo and tells Mma to come back for her in three days. When Mma brings the little girl home, Dineo is much improved, but Mma must return immediately to Johannesburg. If Mma does not get back by the time Madam has said she must, Mma will lose her job and, without a good reference from this employer, she will not be able to get another position. Mma leaves worrying about the debt to the hospital and about how to provide the fruit, vegetables, and milk the doctor says Dineo needs to thrive. Naledi is discouraged but hopeful. She would like an education and takes courage from knowing that Grace and others like her have the same aspirations and are working to improve conditions for blacks. She realizes that her journey to Johannesburg has been a valuable learning experience. The characterization is minimal, scenes are undeveloped, and dialogue sounds stilted and contrived to instruct the reader. Since the author does so little with Naledi's character and fails to exploit incidents adequately, it is hard to feel much sympathy for Naledi as a person, and she remains a type. Whites are uniformly presented as unfeeling and abusive and blacks as abused and suffering. Style and narrative technique are naive, and the book often sounds like a reading textbook. Thinly veiled sociology, it gives middle and later elementary readers some idea of the problems produced by apartheid. Naledi seems older than thirteen in the illustrations. Glossary. Sequel is *Chain of Fire*. Child Study; Other.

JOY REGAN (*Take the Long Path**), mother of David, originally from Yorkshire, a disorganized, dithering woman whose energies go mostly to keep the boy from antagonizing her husband and to deflect Bob's* anger at the boy. David thinks she is badly misnamed until, when Bob is out of the house, she dances the *pois*—a traditional Maori dance—twirling a ball on the end of a string, and seems to come to life. There is a strong parallel between Joy and the penguin Mabel, both seemingly unfocused and ineffective, yet both managing to protect their offspring. It is only when David tells her about the mother penguin, who is trying to care for her chick after her mate is killed, that Joy is able to let David know that Bob is not his real father and suggest that she married him to have support when David's father died. Even then David cannot ask whether his real father was Maori, though he is quite sure and begins to remember things from his early childhood, pet names and Maori words, that confirm his suspicions.

JULIE (Taylor*, Cora, Western, 1985), story of a young girl blessed and plagued with second sight, set in farming country near Red Deer, Alberta, Canada, in modern times. Julie (Juliet), ten when the culminating action occurs, is the seventh child of Will and Alice Morgan. Small and dark, she differs from her large towheaded siblings in personality as well as in appearance. At three, she often entertains them with stories that they consider highly imaginative but obviously seem so real to her that her mother becomes worried and reprimands her sharply, baffling Julie and creating strain between them that never quite disappears. Only when her mother takes her to see a neighbor who tells fortunes in tea leaves, Granny Goderich, does Julie find a kindred spirit. While Granny is talking of her son, George, who was killed many years before in a train accident that she had foreseen, Julie is attracted to a purple jar among the cluttered bric-a-brac on the sideboard, and Granny remarks that Julie sees George's ashes and asks her mother if she knows that Julie is "sensitive." Uncomfortable with the idea, Alice hustles Julie away, but the child remembers the smell of geraniums in the Goderich home. When she is five, a quieter and more solitary child then ever before, she suddenly smells the overpowering odor of geraniums again. Knowing that her mother is upset by her "imaginings," she secretly begs her father to take her to see Granny Goderich, and indulgently he agrees, only to discover that the old woman has suffered a stroke and fallen on her parlor floor. While her father summons help, Julie sits with Granny, who tells her that she knew she would come, and then she assures Julie that they share a gift, which she should not fear. Before the ambulance takes Granny away, Julie climbs up and gets the purple jar, Granny's "treasure," she tells her father, and tucks it in beside the old woman. School is not as difficult as she has dreaded, for she has learned to keep quiet about her special insights and she makes a friend of the librarian, a woman considered a terror by all Julie's siblings. Her gift recurs on three more major occasions, once when she foresees the grain shed burning in a lightning storm, once when her mother is undecided about whether to travel to Victoria to see the aunt who raised her, and Julie, by pretending to read her tea leaves, convinces her that she should go before the aunt's death, and most importantly when she is ten and foresees her father's tractor accident. Julie seems to see the Egyptian Ship of the Dead sailing slowly across the fields and at the same time smells her father's work shirt. Without pausing, she climbs on the stallion Diablo, considered unridable, jumps the corral fence, and streaks head-long down the road. Her mother, having watched with horror from the kitchen window, pursues her in the truck, and when she arrives at the tipped-over tractor, Julie is already trying to dig her unconscious father from beneath it. Together they scrape away the sand from the bank beneath his body, and Alice pulls him out while Julie holds the tractor still with her concentrated gaze. As a neighbor lifts him into the truck bed, Julie at last looks away, and the tractor rolls the rest of the way down the hill. At home, she runs to her favorite tree in the pasture and fiercely declares that she will not let him die. Later, learning that his heart stopped briefly during the operation but started again, she realizes that she is beginning to control her gift and no longer fears it. Although the book can be considered fantasy because of the element of extrasensory perception, the rest of the story is highly realistic, with good scenes of family life and descriptions of the natural features of the farm. In the context, Julie's gift is convincing because her father's grandmother was considered a seer and is interesting because she does not understand and grows to be afraid of it, and she sees it bring concern and disapproval from her mother. The secondary characters are not highly developed but are more than types, and Julie herself is well depicted, a strange but appealing little girl. Can. Council Winner; Can. Bk. of Yr. Winner.

K

KANGA (*By the Sandhills of Yamboorah**; *The Roan Colt of Yamboorah**), lone, hardbitten old dogman for the Yamboorah cattle station or ranch in South Australia, who has been a friend of sorts to the odd-job boy. As the boy says, "Me an' you have always been sort of mates." He recognizes the boy's need for Rags, and in giving up the pup he spells the end of his own useful life as a dogman. In *The Roan Colt* he appears only briefly, but he is important to the plot because he has the knowledge and patience to doctor animals and fellow workers.

KAPLAN, BESS (1927–   ), born in Winnipeg, Canada; journalist and author. She worked in various factories from 1943 to 1951, when she was married. Her writing career began with a weekly column, "The Better Years," based on her experiences raising her four children, a column that she continued for five years. For three years, from 1973 to 1975, she was editor of *The Jewish Press*, and much of her writing has reflected the heritage of her parents, who fled a pogrom in the Ukraine in 1921, and her grandparents, who were killed in the Ukraine when their village was burned during the Holocaust years. *Corner Store** (Queenston, 1976; *The Empty Chair*, Harper, 1977), her first novel, is the story of a Jewish family in Winnipeg, which was a runner-up for the Max and Greta Ebel Memorial Award and received honorable mention from the Canada Council. Kaplan has received a number of other honors, among them the Centennial Award in 1972 from the Winnipeg branch of the Canadian Author's Association for her story, "Rainy Day." She has also written stories for the *Toronto Star Weekly*, for various Canadian magazines, and for the Canadian Broadcasting Company.

KASPER, VANCY, contemporary Toronto, Ontario, Canada; journalist, poet, and novelist, whose imaginative writing pursues sociological themes. Runner-up for the Max and Greta Ebel Memorial Award, *Always Ask for a Transfer**

(Schoolhouse, 1986), was inspired by an article Kasper read that reported that school children consider foster children inferior socially. The book tells of a brother and sister who have been placed in a series of unsuitable foster homes and find acceptance and self-esteem with an elderly immigrant Greek couple. She has also published a book of poems, *Mother, I'm So Glad You Taught Me How to Dance* (Williams, 1986) and another novel, *Street of Three Directions* (Overlea, 1988). Kasper's ancestors emigrated to Toronto from the New England states in the early 1700s and had a strong influence on the history of the region. She is the great-granddaughter of Joseph Shepard of Toronto, in whose living room the Upper Canada Rebellion of 1837 was planned.

KATE CHANT (*The Changeover**), mother of Laura* and Jacko. She is a sympathetically drawn figure, warm, loving, disorganized, at times torn between her needs as a woman and her responsibilities as a mother. Divorced, Kate barely makes ends meet on her salary as the manager of a local bookshop. When Kate allows Chris Holly to spend the night, Laura's resentment of the young librarian grows, but Kate is at that point too worried about what is happening to Jacko to pay much attention. Later her attention returns to Laura, and she cautions her daughter against Sorry* Carlisle. Married at a young age herself, she frets about Laura's growing relationship with Sorry. At the end, Kate and Chris are contemplating marriage.

KATH HUON (*Cannily, Cannily**), mother of Trevor, a good-natured young woman who dresses like a gypsy and has chosen with her husband to follow the fruit crops and live in a caravan for the fun and interest of such a life. At some stops she sets up as a seamstress, sewing the sort of hippy garments she herself wears. When Trevor decides to join the team that plays Australian football, not the American variety but still a rough sport, she is doubtful, worried that he might be hurt, but she doesn't object to his decision, and she helps him buy the necessary shoes and uniform from a secondhand clothing shop. Like Buckley*, she willingly gives up their roaming lifestyle when she reads Trevor's story and sees how hard it is for him to have no stable home.

KATHY GILSON (*The Spirit Wind**), five-year-old sister of Jill and Curly, who attaches herself with devotion to Jarl* Hansen after he prevents Ned Ganger from stealing Jill's horse. In that skirmish, she dances around the combatants yelling, ''Hit him, hit him.'' Her trust in Jarl is fortunate when they are attacked on the wheat stack by the Bull and Ned Ganger, since she does exactly what he tells her to do, hides in the grain bin of the old harvester and stays there, despite the mouse that scares her and the heat that makes her pass out. Rescued by Nunganee*, she tells the story between sobs, but she soon indulges her flair for the dramatic by repeating it eagerly for Jill and again for Curly. She is self-important and slightly spoiled, a well-drawn figure.

KATZ, WELWYN WILTON (1948–   ), born in London, Ontario, Canada; teacher, textbook consultant, researcher, and writer of fantasy novels for children. After earning her B.Sc. degree in mathematics and a Diploma in Education from the University of Western Ontario, she taught mathematics in high school for seven years and was a textbook consultant and researcher in social science, computer science, and applied mathematics before becoming a full-time writer. Her novels reveal her strong interest in prehistoric peoples. *Witchery Hill** (Groundwood/Douglas, 1984; Atheneum, 1984), which takes place on the island of Guernsey near the Trepied Tomb, is a fast-moving novel of witchcraft and magic that was runner-up for the Canadian Library Association Children's Book of the Year Award. *False Face** (Groundwood/Douglas, 1987; McElderry, 1988), included on the short list for the Governor General's Literary Award, winner of the Max and Greta Ebel Memorial Award, and runner-up for the Canadian Young Adult Award, is the dramatic story of how an evil influence pervades an area after the discovery of Iroquois false face masks. *The Third Magic* (Groundwood/Douglas, 1988; McElderry, 1989) improvises upon Celtic myth and Arthurian traditions. Her first novel was *The Prophecy of Tau Ridoo* (Tree Frog, 1982), in which five brothers and sisters pass through a cupboard and enter a strange world controlled by an evil force. She has also published *Sun God, Moon Witch* (Groundwood/Douglas, 1986) about the threatened destruction of a prehistoric stone circle. Critics cite her careful craftsmanship, skillful blending of universal themes as maturation into the magical contexts, ability to create atmosphere, and vigorous, literate style.

KAUR, SIMREN (1940–   ), born at Nabha, Punjab, India; writer of short stories, novels, and non-fiction for young people. After studying at Waverly Convent, Mussoorie Hills, she earned her Bachelor's Degree from Isabella Thoburn College, Lucknow. She is married to a general in the Indian Army and has been trekking and mountaineering with him extensively in the Himalayas, an area that provides the setting for her adventure novel, *Mystery of the Missing Relic** (CBT, India, 1986), which won the Children's Book Trust first prize for fiction. She has also won a Children's Book Trust first prize in the natural history category. Her other published works include a book for younger children that was made into a film by the Children's Film Society, India, and a book of short stories published under the pseudonym of Sim Mesha. She makes her home in the thick jungles of the tribal belt of Chota Nagpur near Ranchi.

THE KAZIRANGA TRAIL (Datta [Dutta*], Arup Kumar, ill. Jagdish Joshi, CBT, India, 1979), action-filled detective novel in which three enterprising, persistent, and resourceful schoolboys bring a ring of six rhinoceros poachers to justice. Events take place in and near the Kaziranga wildlife sanctuary on the Brahmaputra River in Assam, India. Dhanai, 14, whose father is with the Kaziranga Tourist Department, and his two long-time friends, twins Bubul and Jonti, 13, sons of the village headman, are enjoying a summer vacation jaunt in the reserve on Makhoni, their elephant, when they come upon the carcass of a rhinoceros that had been trapped and slain for its horn. Deeply alarmed, they immediately report to Mr. Neog, the district forest officer, whose assistant is Phukan, head forest ranger. Neog listens carefully to their report of finding a clue, a footprint with a missing right big toe, and informs them that this is the latest in a series of such crimes obviously being perpetrated by a clever ring to whose identity they previously had no clue. He also tells the boys that he thinks someone in his own organization has been providing the poachers with information about Forest Service efforts to bring them to justice. When Phukan dismisses their story and efforts to help, the reader has a clear tip-off as to the identity of one of the culprits. The boys continue their involvement through a series of well-paced episodes built around such conventions of the genre as knives with warnings attached cast through windows, nocturnal spyings, and overheard conversations. The twins are captured by the poachers, but Dhanai manages to evade them by a hectic flight through the forest on Makhoni. Phukan is knifed by the head poacher, but he tells the authorities where the twins are held before he dies. In a grand climax at the jungle hideout involving the Forest Service, villagers, and poachers, the boys are rescued, the evildoers captured, and the escape of the head poacher ironically prevented by the fortuitous appearance of a huge rhinoceros from a small nearby lake. The boys are choral characters, barely distinguishable from one another, and the villains and good fellows are similarly typecast. The language is easy enough for beginning readers, often clichéd ("They knew the area like the palms of their hands."), and sometimes stilted ("A strange silence prevailed."), and there is some humor. The accent is on action, which is plentiful and well paced, and there is a strong appreciation and respect for the natural beauty and wildlife of the region. CBT of India, First Prize.

THE KEEPER (Faville*, Barry, Oxford, 1986), futuristic fantasy set about five generations after a nuclear holocaust has destroyed the entire population of the northern hemisphere and almost all of the people in the southern. In New Zealand, descendants of the survivors live in small, primitive villages, like that of Big Lake on the northern shore of Lake Taupo, or as loners, who wander singly or in small groups. They are often deformed from genetic effects of radiation and have been driven from the villages. In Big Lake, Michael*, 17, has been told that his parents died of radiation sickness when he was three. Michael was raised by the teacher, Charles Clinton, and has become a senior learner, one of a few (mostly handicapped) young people, whose job is to copy pre-holocaust books of science, medicine, engineering, and other practical skills for future generations. The story is told in entries from a journal Michael is secretly keeping. These entries alternate with sections written by Mr. Clinton, who has discovered the journal and, without letting Michael know of his find, is allowing him to continue it. To get aid in a tiger hunt, a group including Michael goes to the nearest village, Mud Flats. The Mud Flats teacher, dying of radiation sickness acquired many years before when he explored a bomb site, sends for Michael and bequeaths to him some books and a map to an underground bunker where guns and ammunition have survived. When the men of the two villages fail to destroy the tiger, Michael, his friend Andy, 19, Jean*, a fellow learner whose left arm was damaged in an accident, and Ora, a free-spirited Mud Flats girl attracted to Andy, set off together and manage to kill the animal by a combination of intelligent reasoning and good luck. Their success arouses the hostility rather than the gratitude of the other hunters. On their return to their village, the Mud Flats hunters discover that loners have moved in, peacefully but firmly no longer content to be outcasts. There is some fighting. Michael is summoned to a council of elders during which a Mud Flats hunter demands the map that the dying teacher said he gave to the boy. Michael pretends ignorance and gains time by saying he will search through the books for it. After consulting Mr. Clinton, he and Andy start at once, secretly, to try to reach the weapons and destroy them before they can be used to add a new, horrible dimension to the conflict with the loners. The boys narrowly avoid an ambush of men from their own village, who obviously foresaw their aim and started ahead of them. They must pass close to the volcano, which is smoking and rumbling. With considerable difficulty, they find the bunker and kick in the door, just as a tremendous eruption jolts the earth. Almost immediately they are surrounded by men from Big Lake and Mud Flats village who have followed them. Before they can be killed or taken prisoner, the eruption increases and molten lava begins to flow toward them. Michael runs, gasping in air almost too hot to breathe, trips, and loses consciousness. He is rescued by Luke, a hairy, toothless loner, and cared for by a woman named Sarah and her husband, Honi. Recovered, Michael is set on his way by Honi, who talks in riddles but, before parting, suggests that there are islands in the ocean to the north where one might settle. In his own village, Michael is seized to be executed for treason. Paul*, one of the senior hunters who has always been sympathetic to him, helps him escape and join Jean and Andy. Later, Ora accompanying them, they travel northeast toward the sea. A final passage by Mr. Clinton tells briefly of Big Lake Village being taken over by loners. The novel is fast paced, with plenty of suspense and strong themes of the need for acceptance and intelligence as opposed to bigotry and superstition. The characters are not highly developed but are adequate for their roles. Although the picture of life even generations after nuclear bombing is grim, the story is generally hopeful that generosity of spirit and respect for art can survive. N. Z. Govt. Winner.

KELLAWAY, FRANK (1922–), Australian librarian, educator, occasional farmer, and novelist. He received his B.A. degree with honors from the University of Melbourne after having served during World War II in both the Australian navy and the English navy, in Darwin and on a minesweeper in the Mediterranean Sea. At the university he won the Alexander Sutherland Prize for English Language and Literature. He has been a school teacher, farm worker, abalone diver, and owner-manager of a farm and orchard in Eldorado, Victoria. He has also been a lecturer at Preston Institute of Technology, Preston, Victoria, and has served as a librarian at the Wangaratta Regional Library Service in Victoria, for the city of Warrnambool, Victoria, for the School of Architecture at the University of Melbourne, and at Heidelberg Regional Library, Heidelberg, Germany. He has published poems and stories in periodicals in Australia, England, and the United States and has written plays and novels, among them *A Straight Furrow* (Cassell, 1960) for adults, and *The Quest for Golden Dan** (Cheshire, 1962; Angus, 1962) for young people. This adventure story is set in the gold fields of Victoria in the 1850s and concerns—along with a kidnapping, the gaining of a fortune, numerous attacks, and several fortuitous rescues—the changing perceptions of self as a boy matures.

KELLEHER, VICTOR (MICHAEL KITCHENER) (1939–   ), born in London, England; university English teacher, novelist, short story writer. He went to Zambia while in his mid-teens and later attended the University of Natal, South Africa, graduating with a B.A. in English. After teaching in London, he studied for a diploma of Education at the University of St. Andrews in Scotland, later returning to South Africa, where he attended Witwatesrand University in Johannesburg. He received his master's degree and doctorate at the University of South Africa, Pretoria. After teaching at both these universities, he emigrated with his wife to New Zealand, where he taught English at Massey University, then moved to Australia where he has taught at the University of New England in Armidale, New South Wales. His first two novels for young people are fantasies set in a world of clans and monsters, featuring a youth named Tal, *Forbidden Paths of Thual* (Kestrel, 1979) and its sequel, *The Hunting of Shadroth* (Kestrel, 1981), both exploring the nature of violence. The first won the Australian Young Readers' Book Award and the second was runner-up for the same award. His third novel for young people, *Master of the Grove** (Kestrel, 1982), is also a fantasy, this one set in a medieval world of witches and weapons of power, with a young protagonist who suffers a series of ordeals before finding his rightful place in society. It won the Australian Library Association Book of the Year Award. *Taronga** (Kestrel, 1986), a futuristic post-holocaust fantasy set in the Sydney zoo, has a protagonist who communicates mentally with animals. It was commended for the Book of the Year Award. Other titles by Kelleher include *Papio* (Kestrel, 1984) and *The Green Piper* (Kestrel, 1984). He has also published a novel and short stories for adults.

KENDRICK (*Sea Menace**), villainous Yankee who plots to seize Sydney, Australia, and hold it for his own personal gain. An elegantly dressed, handsome man, he is shrewd, cruel, and ambitious. He lures other whalers to his ship by having a whale lashed alongside, then saying his barrels are full of oil and offering to give the whale to the approaching ship. At the last minute his hiding crew runs out the guns and boards the unsuspecting whaler, thereby taking it with little damage to add to his fleet.

KERRI BUCHANAN (*All the Proud Tribesmen**), Firecrest Island youth. Kerri was given to Miss Alice Buchanan when he was about a year old, the most beautiful gift the islanders could think of to give her for living among them and serving them for so many years. Kerri is a sincere, conscientious youth, loyal and loving, whose main problem outside that of the evacuation is whether or not to try for a scholarship as Miss Buchanan desires. With dignity and trepidation, he goes to boarding school in Queensland and finds that his roommate treats him well and acts as his advocate. He takes a little mild hazing and accepts with good nature the boys' nickname of Tar, short for Tarzan, realizing it really. means that they regard him as one of them and appreciate his athletic ability. Kerri is a winning figure, a memorable protagonist.

KIDNAPPING AT BIRPUR (Bhatty*, Margaret R., ill. Subir Roy, CBT, India, 1985), fast-moving realistic detective novel of a kidnapping in Birpur, India, in the 1980s. Sarkoo, a bony, limber, glib, ten-year-old street boy, gets a job as a gardener's helper at the palatial home of Mr. and Mrs. Dobe, the wealthiest citizens in Birpur. Spirited, fun-loving Sarkoo soon becomes the companion of Bharat, 9, the Dobes' timid son, who has been crippled by polio and is confined to a wheelchair. Jugnoo, a dark, sinister, beaked-nose man, who likes to show off his skill at sleight of hand, enlists the aid of the Dobes' ex-chauffeur, Raghuvir, to kidnap Bharat for ransom. Both boys are carried off to an abandoned Buddhist cave-monastery in the mountains. When the ransom pickup goes awry and the chauffeur is captured, Jugnoo instructs the three members of his gang to eliminate Raghuvir and transports the boys on foot and by train to the city of Vadodara, where he takes refuge with his uncle, a cunning jewel thief named Modarya. Modarya soon employs all three in his shoplifting scams, along with his sour wife and pretty, unwilling ward, Devaki, 16. A note Devaki helps the boys send home to assure the family that Bharat is safe, the capture of the other gang members by the Birpur police, and the clever detective work of local Inspector Jagat lead to Jugnoo's apprehension. Jagat concludes correctly that a certain street juggler who writes with his toes the words "Hari Om Hari Om" (we are all friends) on a pavement or wall near the scene of jewel thefts may be Jugnoo and that the beggar boys seen near him may be the missing youths. Several weeks after their abduction, the boys are joyfully welcomed home. Although offered the opportunity for an education, Sarkoo returns to the streets, a free spirit who intends to stay that way. Most characters and situations are stock for the genre. Jugnoo is stereotypical in appearance and behavior, even engaging in blood-sacrifice rituals as further evidence of his villainy. Sarkoo remains loyal to Bharat, even though he could easily escape, and his return to the streets seems appropriate to his independent character. The book has many exciting moments, some humor, and several well-depicted scenes, among them the village fair where Jugnoo fire walks and his gang picks the pockets of the crowd and the scene where Modarya cleverly shoplifts jewels. Class structure is another interesting aspect, with the Dobes' patronizing Sarkoo, for instance, and the presentation of the hill people as "tribals." CBT of India, First Prize.

KIEWA ADVENTURE (Aldous*, Allan, Oxford, 1950), realistic novel set mainly in the Kiewa Valley of New South Wales, Australia, in the 1940s, in which two children rescue the crew of a crashed plane and clear their father's name of an embezzlement charge. John Shapley, 11, and his twin sister, Ric (Erica), are both angered and baffled when their accountant father is wrongfully accused of stealing a ten-pound note from the safe at the firm where he works in Brisbane, then convicted, fined, and fired. Although Ric suspects their father's co-worker, charming Dick Halmer, a man also eligible for the promotion Mr. Shapley has been promised, John stoutly defends Halmer because he is a good cricket player and seems such a decent sort. Mr. Shapley takes a job as a truck driver in the remote Kiewa Valley where a series of dams are being constructed to provide electric power. Soon Mrs. Shapley and the twins join him. The children are much impressed by the beautiful mountain scenery and are told, in long passages of dialogue with various adult residents, how the dams and the hydroelectric plants work, how to catch trout in the river, and, eventually, how to ski. One prominent adult is "Mac" Macpherson, who has traveled and worked in many parts of the world and various professions. When winter comes, weekends are spent mostly at the ski hut high on the mountain. Mac proves to be adept at skiing and also at first aid. Not long afterward, John and Ric and their friend from school, Judy Barton, are skiing within sight of the clubhouse when a plane swoops out of the clouds and crashes just over the crest from them. John shouts to the girls to get help while he starts off to see if there are any survivors. Before he reaches the plane, a mist descends, and for a few minutes he is panicky, knowing that on these high plains it is certain death to be caught out in a storm. He stumbles on the furrows in the snow caused by the plane, however, and follows them to the crash site. To his surprise, when he shouts and bangs on the door a voice answers. Though the door is jammed, he manages to climb onto the front of the plane and break a window to get in. There he finds the pilot with a foot caught and broken and a navigator badly hurt. Recognizing the symptoms from having watched Mac, John applies a snow compress to the chest where a broken rib has punctured the lung, finds blankets in the freight compartment to keep the men warm, with a crowbar levers out the pilot's foot and helps him splint the ankle, and figures out a way to build a fire in a drum so that they can survive the bitter storm that descends on them. To their mutual surprise, the pilot, Dave Monger, turns out to be a former RAF officer who flew with John's father. When the storm eventually clears, they make a huge signal fire outside with gasoline-soaked wood, and the skiers, including John's father who has been summoned, arrive to carry out the wounded men. The story, which the newspapers have played up, has an unfortunate consequence: police arrive to arrest Mr. Shapley on the charge of large-scale embezzlement from the firm where he previously worked, a crime discovered after he left. Monger takes upon himself the job of proving Mr. Shapley's innocence. When Ric repeats her suspicious about Dick Halmer, Monger and John call upon him and catch him altering the company books. Monger also recognizes him as a small-time racketeer he once met during the war. Though they will now live again in Brisbane, where Mr. Shapley has been reinstated and promoted in the company, John and Ric plan to return to Kiewa for vacations and perhaps someday to live. Clumsily written and slow moving, the book has very little action until three-quarters of the way through, then piles on events in unconvincing abundance. The characters are stock types and the tone is dated. The setting, however, is well evoked and dominates the other elements, giving a good picture of the rugged and beautiful landscape. Aust. Bk. of Year Com.

KIT QUAYLE (*The True Story of Lilli Stubeck**), narrator, friend of Lilli and Dorothy* Malone. His friendship with the girls is not adequately motivated to receive so many details about Lilli. He encounters her about town while she is scrounging, sees her in school, and visits once at her house and she once to his. Mrs.* Stubeck begs at his house and steals fruit there, but that Lilli should send him her diary after she leaves town when they have had only a Platonic relationship does not seem believable. Kit is a bland character, an almost faceless narrator. At the end he gets the job on the local paper that Devlin* had, a convenient situation.

KLEIN, ROBIN (1936–   ), born in Kempsey, New South Wales, Australia; writer of stories, poems, plays, and novels mainly for children. Her humorous, realistic, short novel *Penny Pollard's Diary** (Oxford, 1983), about the friendship between a non-conformist ten-year-old girl and an elderly woman resident of a nursing home, was highly commended for the Australian Children's Book of the Year Award. Klein previously received the Australian Junior Book of the Year Award for *Thing* (Oxford, 1982), a picture-book story. Klein left school at age fifteen and held various odd jobs, married young (and later divorced), and became a painter and craftworker. After publishing *The Giraffe in Pepperell Street* (Hodder, 1978), a picture-book story, she turned to full-time writing. More than two dozen books of different types have followed, among them *Snakes and Ladders: Poems about the Ups and Downs of Life* (Dent, 1985; Merrimack, 1986); other books about Penny Pollard including *Penny Pollard's Letters* (Oxford, 1984) and *Penny Pollard in Print* (Oxford, 1986); more picture-book stories like *Brock and the Dragon* (Hodder, 1984), *The Princess Who Hated It* (Omnibus, 1986), and *Thingnapped!* (Oxford, 1984), the sequel to *Thing*; novels for younger readers like *Junk Castle* (Oxford, 1983); *Halfway across the Galaxy and Turn Left* (Viking, 1985), a novel of science fiction; and some young adult novels, including *Laurie Loved Me Best* (Viking, 1988). She has also contributed to the New South Wales *School Magazine* and the publications of the Victoria Department of Education. She won a Senior Fellowship Grant from the Arts Council of Australia Literature Board.

KO-IN (*The Ice Is Coming*; Behind the Wind**), wise and powerful man-like spirit of the mountain. He assists Wirrun in securing the stone of power that Wirrun uses on various occasions and also helps Wirrun in other important ways. The stone of power is a large quartz crystal that for years has lain hidden in a cave on Ko-in's mountain. Enclosed in a bag of coarse net and suspended from Wirrun's belt as he travels, it enables him to fly and protects him against hostile creatures. Ko-in is eloquent and authoritative, and Wirrun refers to him as Hero, just why is unclear.

KRISTLI'S TREES (Dunham*, Mabel, ill. Selwyn Dewdney, McClelland, 1948), warm, humorous, realistic novel of family life set on a farm in Mennonite country along the Conestoga River near Kitchener, Ontario, Canada, in the mid– 1900s after World War II. This almost plotless story ambles along good-naturedly, spanning about two years in the life of earnest, naive, occasionally mischievous Kristli (Christian) Eby, 7, and includes his serious-minded, patient Doddy and his gentle, solicitous Mommy, both of whom strive diligently to raise the boy as a strong Mennonite so that he will not "run with the world" like his much older brothers and sisters, who have left for the city, and his almost grown-up older sisters. The theme of physical and spiritual resources making for happiness and a good life binds together the episodes. It is exemplified by the trees of the title, which refer both to the maples Doddy plants for Kristli down by the river, one on each birthday, and to the Eby family tree of staunch, hardworking Mennonites. Every day Kristli feeds his colt and his calf, fetches eggs, and plays with Hundli the dog. He attends the one-room school down the dirt road, and sometimes he and Hundli walk over to the big white house where Groszgroszdoddy (great-grandfather) lives to listen to the old blind man's stories about how the Ebys came to the area from Pennsylvania. The book's most exciting incident occurs when the Conestoga River floods in April. Although Kristli has been warned to stay away from the swollen stream, he overhears his father talk about how the "deifel" in the river has stolen some pigs and decides to go see for himself. He is swept downstream by the raging waters to the nearest village. When he recovers, he is delighted to learn that his parents have invited his cousin, Mannie Stauffer, to visit. They pick Mannie up at the family reunion that summer, a joyful event to which they are taken in the sedan of "worldly" son Pete and where they see daughter Lizzie, a nurse, with her young doctor boyfriend. Once home, naughty Mannie exerts a bad influence on Kristli. To raise himself in Mannie's esteem and to satisfy his own urge to see a circus "elly-fant," Kristli steals admission money from Groszgroszdoddy's secret money drawer. When the deed is revealed, Doddy makes them stay home from the circus, and Mommy marches them down the road to return the money. Chastened, Mannie adopts a more wholesome attitude, and Kristli decides he should pay more attention to his inner "Ai! Yai!" voice that warns him when he is inclined to err. The attraction of this book, intended for young readers, lies in its affectionately and picturesquely described scenes of Mennonite life and beliefs, gentle humor, abundant dialogue with just enough dialect to be convincing and enhance the local color, and the author's remarkable ability to make little things important without sentimentality, didacticism, or melodrama. Kristli's activities and ways seem typical of any boy his age; yet his reactions and thoughts are distinguished by his upbringing and hence he rises above type. The great-grandfather is an especially memorable character. Can. Bk. of Year Winner.

KROB (*Master of the Grove**), young man who comes to the cave of Obin asking to be taught the ways of the Witch People. Although he sees that Krob has great natural power, Obin also sees his arrogance and refuses to give him lessons. Krob sits for days just down the slope from the cave, not eating, drinking, or sleeping. On the fifth day, at Asti's insistence, Obin relents, and they carry Krob to the cave and nurse him. Thereafter, Obin lets him live in a hut below the cave and learn with Asti for three years. When Obin finds him attempting to open the alcove that holds the Warden's Staff, he sends him away. Later Krob returns, kills Obin, and steals the Staff. This he uses to take control of the Circle of the Grove, turning the other members into dead-eyed automatons, and plans to make war upon the Council of the plains, and thereby to control the whole land. Krob is an orphan who seems to have no emotions, only ambition. In the end, having bound his whole being into the power of the Staff, he turns old and withered when it is destroyed and stumbles away over the edge of the cliff to his death.

KUSHNER, DONN (1929–   ), born in Lake Charles, Louisiana; microbiologist, violinist, and author of inventive and moving fantasies for young people. He received his undergraduate degree from Harvard University and his doctorate from McGill University. For several years he worked as a research scientist for the Forest Insect Laboratory at Sault Sainte Marie and for the National Research Council of Canada, but from 1965 on he taught at the University of Ottawa. In addition to one book and a large number of articles on his scientific specialty, he is the author of several novels for children. *The Violin-Maker's Gift** (Macmillan, 1980), a legend-like story, tells how a simple act of kindness to a bird gives an ordinary instrument maker the skill to produce violins that sing with a human voice. It is winner of the Canadian Library Association Book of the Year Award. *Uncle Jacob's Ghost Story* (Macmillan, 1985), is about how an immigrant is changed from a rationalist by the appearance of childhood friends who died of typhus. In *A Book Dragon** (Macmillan, 1987), a medieval dragon, shrunk to insect size, finds and protects his treasure, an illuminated manuscript of the Book of Hours, through the centuries to modern times. It is the winner of the National Imperial Order of the Daughters of the Empire Award and received honorable mention from the Canada Council. Kushner's novels have been commended for their beauty of language and sophisticated themes embodied in apparently simply stories.

L

LADY KEZIA BUTLER (*Come Danger, Come Darkness**), wife of the surgeon at the penal colony on Norfolk Island off Australia. Lady Kezia has a horse of which she is very proud and asks that the young convict, Corny* Stack, a former groom, be allowed to care for it. She also influences the story by eliciting from Paddy Paul Cannon the information that Otter has been planning Corny's escape. She is a useful and likeable if type character.

LANCE DUCHARME (*Let It Go**), good looking, talented teenager, more than half Cree Indian and proud of his heritage. He and his father have lived alone for ten years since his mother, Anne-Marie* Charbonneau Ducharme, left to become a country-western singer. Although Mike can be demanding and has in the past occasionally been abusive, Lance is devoted to him and agrees to go with his mother only to save his father from the humiliation of a court custody hearing. In his love of nature and skill at drawing wild things, Lance borders on the stereotype of the Noble Redman, but in his misery over his mother's abandonment and his confusion and anger when she comes back, he transcends stock characterization. A symbol of his reconciliation with his mother is the St. Christopher medal she gave him on the night she left when he was five, which he discards in fury when she reappears and which he is again wearing as he dresses to go home to the ranch.

A LAND DIVIDED (Hayes*, John F., ill. Fred J. Finley, Copp, 1951), historical adventure novel set in 1755 on the shores of what are now Nova Scotia and New Brunswick, Canada, dealing with the events leading to the deportation of the Acadians from the district and the French and Indian War. Michael Harvey, 14, son of a captain at Fort Annapolis who has married an Acadian, and his cousin, Pierre Duchene, 14, have grown up together and are close friends, equally at ease speaking French and English. Returning in his dory one foggy night from his cousin's house, Michael crashes into the getaway boat of the malcontent, Lucien Vaudreuil, who has just set fire to the anchored English schooner waiting to take an expedition led by Captain Harvey to Fort Lawrence on Chignecto Bay just across the Missaquash River from French-held Fort Beausejour. When news comes back that his father has been captured, Michael and Pierre set out in their sailboat, the *Anne*, to try to rescue him, with the blessing of Michael's mother and her brother, Henri Duchene, Pierre's father, who has mixed sympathies but personally likes Captain Harvey. Their adventure involves the aid of Thomas Pichon, an English spy, the wounding of Michael by an Indian arrow, the meeting of Michael's uncle, Archer Harvey, who heads an English expedition aboard the *Siren*, the destruction of Fort Beausejour, and more captures and escapes than a reader can keep straight. Their homecoming, with Michael's father, is marred by the news they bring that all the Acadians who did not earlier take unconditional oaths of allegiance to the English king are to be transported so far away that they will not be able to return or to aid the French forces and that their homes are to be destroyed. The evacuation of Annapolis must be directed by Captain Harvey and includes his wife's family, though Acadians who have married English soldiers are exempted. Pierre chooses to go with his family, though Uncle Archer has sworn him in as part of the crew of the *Siren* and he could stay. Michael helps them pack and depart, and he sees great suffering as the Acadians, many of them unprepared because they refused to believe the harsh order, try to get their aging relatives and little children aboard the transports, and he grieves when he watches the cabins and barns set afire. Since he is so lonely without Pierre and cannot go hunting or fishing because the area is full of Acadian snipers, his father arranges a job for him keeping the night fires going in the fort. One night he sees a shadowy figure approaching the fort, then disappearing. He follows and discovers a secret passage that leads into the old French well in the fort's courtyard. He also discovers a bomb set against the side of the munitions storehouse and sees Vaudreuil running back toward the well. Thinking fast, Michael grabs the bomb and throws it down the well. He is injured by the flying stones as it explodes, but he saves the fort. The tunnel collapses and Vaudreuil presumably is buried. When the *Siren* returns with Pierre once again aboard and Uncle Archer agrees to take Michael, too, the boys are together again and look forward to a future when Pierre can return to Annapolis to live. Too many events are included in one novel, any of which might make a good and convincing story but together change a dramatic period in history into an implausible adventure. The number of daring rescues and fortunate escapes strains credulity, and the deportation of the Acadians, which tears families from their homes and causes death and suffering to many with mixed loyalties, becomes just another incident. The characters are mostly types, particularly evil Vaudreuil and noble Uncle Archer. The action, however, is fast and exciting. Can. Gov. General's Winner.

LAST CHANCE SUMMER (Wieler*, Diana J., Western, 1986), sociological problem novel of a twelve-year-old boy who, having run away from numerous foster homes, is given one last opportunity in the group home run by Carleton*

Jenner at the edge of the badlands of Alberta, Canada. Marl Silversides, whose one strong attachment is to his Family Services social worker, Cecile* Martin, is the orphan son of an alcoholic, evidently part Indian, and, though intelligent, he suffers from a birth defect that gives an Oriental cast to his features and affects his ability to read. He has become a "ripper," one of the children who slash their own arms or legs in times of stress. Rather than return him to Ryerson, the juvenile institution that Marl dreads, Cecile takes a chance and persuades Carleton to allow Marl to work as the tenth boy on his farm. On the first day Marl is assigned to hoe the garden with Topo*, 13, a big, angry boy who goads Marl into attacking him with a hoe. In the nick of time Goat*, 14, the oldest boy on the farm, intervenes and slams Marl against a shed, saving the younger boy but making Topo determined to seek revenge. Carleton, an Englishman, has great good will and considerable skill at handling his tough charges, but ten boys, all with emotional problems, are too many for one man, aided only by the middle-aged cook, Vilda*. Having witnessed the scene in the garden, he asks Goat to befriend Marl. On impulse, Carleton decides to take all the boys to see the Badlands in his Volkswagen bus, with Vilda reluctantly accompanying them. Len, a junior con artist, needles Goat into stealing the bus and taking Marl and two others for a joy ride, leaving the adults and five boys stranded. They are soon apprehended, but harm is done when Vilda, upset and nervous, insults Topo. Carleton refuses to press theft charges but insists on knowing whose idea it was. When Len, backed by the other two boys, blames Goat, Marl speaks up, insisting that it was all of them. Carleton puts them to work the next day cleaning, waxing, and polishing the bus, and through the work together Marl and Goat become closer. Their growing friendship infuriates Topo, who has overheard Carleton asking Goat to look out for Marl and resents this special treatment. When the police on invitation tour the farm, Topo lures Marl into the bus to get high by breathing typewriter correction fluid. Marl is discovered passed out, is revived by the policemen, and is assigned by Carleton to write a report on "The Abuse of Common Household Products." The punishment seems light to the other boys, but to Marl, who has kept a secret of his inability to read, it is horrifying. Goat, checking to see how he's doing, forces the admission from him and solves the problem by reading aloud from the encyclopedia and spelling words as Marl writes painfully. Carleton, realizing that ten is too many boys, decides that Topo, who has never really fit in, should go back to Ryerson. Shocked and furious, Topo blames Marl and announces before the other boys that Goat is being nice to Marl at Carleton's request. Marl is devastated. He runs blindly into the night as Goat attacks Topo. After Vilda helps Carleton pull them apart, she firmly tells him that Topo is acting up because she hurt his feelings and that they need more help to control the boys. Goat pursues and finds Marl, and he proves his sincerity by showing him what he always keeps concealed, the scars of old beatings that cover his body. Marl persuades Goat to go with him to Carleton and protest Topo's return to Ryerson. Because he has approached Cecile to help him run the farm, Carleton backs down and gives

Topo another chance. Although predictable in plot, the book does an excellent job of characterizing the various main boys and of convincingly evoking their anger and hurt that is masked with toughness. The three main adults are also well drawn. The tone of tension alternating with exhaustion is alleviated by brief touches of happiness and humor to keep the whole from being entirely negative, but although the ending is upbeat and hopeful, there is no assurance that all will now be well at the farm or easy for Marl in the future. Can. Ebel Winner.

LAURA (*Always Ask for a Transfer**), Willy's* ten-year-old sister. She is an assertive youngster, whose feminist views amuse Yota* Bazos, her foster mother, and startle Dino*, her foster father. She speaks them with a charming smile and so much unassuming confidence that she never raises Dino's ire, and he ends up respecting her spunk. Although it seems strange that Laura does not figure out that Willy's money must be going to their father because he has managed to locate his children everywhere else they have lived, she is a pleasingly depicted figure.

LAURENCE, MARGARET (1926–   ), born in Neepawa, Manitoba, Canada; reporter and free-lance writer of novels, short stories, and non-fiction. She is a 1947 graduate of United College, Winnipeg, and has lived in Vancouver, England, Somaliland, Ghana, Crete, Greece, Palestine, India, Egypt, and Spain. Her wide travels have formed a background for her books, among which are *A Tree of Poverty: Somali Poetry and Prose* (Eagle, 1954); *This Side Jourdan* (McClelland, 1960), a novel that won the Beta Sigma Chi Award; *The Prophet's Camel Bell* (McClelland, 1963), which was reprinted in the United States as *New Wind in a Dry Land* (Knopf, 1964); and *A Jest of God* (McClelland, 1966) a novel that won the Governor General's Literary Award and was produced in 1968 as a film titled, *Rachel, Rachel*. She has received many awards for short stories, some of which were collected in *The Tomorrow-Tamer* (McClelland, 1963). Her book for children, *The Olden Days Coat** (McClelland, 1979), a fantasy for middle readers, was a runner-up for the Canadian Library Association Book of the Year Award.

LAURENS BECK (*Callie's Castle**), painter, paperhanger, stepfather of Callie Cameron, whom he treats with the same affection he does his own children. Although not a demonstrative man, he is very family oriented. A Danish emigrant to Australia, he works hard to fix up the big old Victorian house and is very proud of his handiwork. He also is very proud of having acquired a historic Cadillac, which he intended to restore and show. When he gets the idea of building a stairway to the cupola, he sells the car for the money. Callie protests and tells her mother not to let him do it, but Heather responds that selling it is "part of being a father, for him" and that "Grandpa* [Cameron] says we're not to spoil it for him [Laurens] by arguing over it." Providing for and making his family happy are of the utmost importance to Laurens.

LEDWARD, MR. (*The Lieutenant**), acting surgeon, one of the nineteen men in the open boat. With very little knowledge of medicine and no supplies at all, he is unable to do much for the suffering men and is in fact ill himself with fever and dysentery for much of the terrible trip. He was taken on the *Bounty* journey mostly because the surgeon was so far gone with drink that he could not usually act, and became acting surgeon when the regular surgeon died. He has a horror of amputation, which he has never performed but which is the standard treatment in the British navy of the eighteenth century, and he cringes when the more experienced seamen tell him of the barbarous practices common on the vessels.

LEE JETSON (*Starbuck Valley Winter**), holder of the trapping permit on land that adjoins Don Morgan's trapping area, a silent, suspicious-acting man who has a bad name in the community. At first, he seems to be spying on the boys and even shoots a warning shot at them to try to scare them away, but when Don challenges him, he admits that he has a mine in the area, and he is afraid they might try to steal his claim. He tells them the story of how he innocently killed a man in Montana in a dispute over a mine, out of which he was tricked. Eventually he proves to be a good friend.

THE LEFT OVERS (Spence*, Eleanor, Methuen, 1982), lighthearted sociological problem novel set about the time the book was written in the town of Millbrook, Australia. Barnfield, the big, old foster home Auntie Bill Wilson runs for the department that oversees homeless children, is to be torn down to make room for a freeway. Four children, the last residents and hence the "left overs," as they term themselves, set out to find a place where they can be together: their leader, serious Drew, 11; pretty, aspiring model and dancer Jasmine, 10; chubby James, 9; and little Donna, 8, called Straw because she is often the "last straw" in behavior. Since the children have only the Christmas holidays in which to find new parents, Drew quickly earns money delivering newspapers to put an advertisement in the local paper, but no one answers it. Jasmine suggests that they improve themselves so as to be more attractive to potential parents, and they begin by putting James on a diet, an effort he staunchly resists. While they are at Beachwood House, a place for foster children while their house directors are on vacation, Drew puts a notice in a news agent's shop window, which is answered by Mick Mulvaney, who owns a print shop, and the children's hopes are up. A good-hearted man, Mick doesn't have room for them but says he might be able to help some other way and starts by taking the children and Auntie Bill out for hamburgers. Back at Barnfield, while helping Auntie Bill clean out files, Drew discovers tickets to the "Noon-with-Neil Show," a television variety and talk program in Sydney, and he takes the children there. When the camera pans the audience, he holds up a sign asking for a home, and Neil promptly interviews the children. Auntie Bill is deluged with letters about them, but again nothing develops. Then, ironically, Drew discovers that what James and Jasmine really want is to return to their mothers, their own special people, and sends off letters to their homes without telling the children. In a short while, their family difficulties are sufficiently resolved so that the two can go home. Straw, the department decides, will live with Auntie Bill in her next position. Drew is happy for the others but both disappointed and resigned when he learns that the department will send him to Fairlee House. Once there, he learns that he has a person of his very own, too, because Mick plans to take him on weekends. At the very end, Drew wonders to Mick whether or not James's being half Aborigine, Jasmine's being half Chinese, and Straw's being slow had anything to do with their not being able to find a home together. While earlier the reader learns that Drew is considered emotionally disturbed, this is the reader's first indication that others also may have problems that make them hard to place. This is a touching novel of love and caring within an unconventional family situation. The abundant humor of situation and especially of dialogue keeps the story from seeming sentimental and didactic. Since the book is almost all dialogue, the pace is very fast, and much of the humor comes from the children's often naive attempts to understand their world and their candid discussions about changing it. Aust. Bk. of Year Highly Com.

LEROY STALKE (*Jasmin**), Leroy Lorne Raphael, 10, retarded brother of Jasmin, who devotedly follows her everywhere, understanding much of what she says to him and trying to talk. When he has ruined her science project sweet potatoes, he realizes that she is very upset, and when the drug that he has been given to calm him wears off and he discovers that she is gone, he sets off in the night to find her, soon becoming soaked, exhausted, and lost. He is an albino, with weak eyes easily hurt by sunlight. He has a stocky build and short legs, and a tongue that frequently lolls out of his mouth. When Jasmin finds him, he is hiding in the cellar of an abandoned house, eating mice that a cat has brought him. At the end, social workers have persuaded the family that he should go to a special school for the mentally impaired. At the science and art fair, he recognizes the picture of his sister and says his first coherent word, ''Jasmin!''

LESTER (*Underground to Canada**), young, strong mulatto slave ''with speckly skin and angry eyes,'' who escapes from the Riley plantation. Because he is alert, intelligent, and determined, and, unlike most slaves, can read a little, Massa Ross gives him the instructions for getting to Canada along the Underground Railway. Although he and Adam are captured shortly after the little group reaches Tennessee, both escape again. When last seen, Lester is proudly working at a hotel in St. Catharines as a porter.

LET IT GO (Halvorson*, Marilyn, Irwin, 1985; Delacorte, 1986), realistic novel of two teenaged boys maturing and coming to understand their troubled parents set in Alderton, near Calgary, Alberta, Canada, in the 1980s. Red-haired Red (Jared) Cantrell, 14, narrates the story of his friendship with Lance* Ducharme,

15, an artistically talented boy more than half Cree Indian, whose father, Mike, manages the big Silverwinds ranch. The boys are inseparable, but each has a secret. Red's older brother, Greg, the apple of his father's eye, became involved with drugs and is now in a coma in a nursing facility, unable to recognize or respond during the weekly family visits. To protect his younger son, Red's father has taken a job as the sole police officer in Alderton and has almost suffocated the boy with his constant surveillance and stringent rules. Lance's secret is that when he was five, his mother left to become a country-western singer. Red is astonished at Lance's violent reaction when they see a good-looking new Nashville sensation, Anne-Marie* Charbonneau, on television, with the announcement of her coming concert in Calgary. Several days later, Red is waylaid by a woman in an expensive car whom he recognizes as Charbonneau and who tells him she is really Anne-Marie Ducharme, Lance's mother. Against his better judgment, Red tells her that he and Lance plan to ride to the Cliffs, a narrow pathway between a fence and a steep drop. They find her waiting, blocking the path on a borrowed horse, and rather than talk with her, Lance plunges his horse down the precipitous bank in a wild ride that tests even his skill. After the incident he hardly speaks to Red, starts skipping school and flunking tests, and begins to associate with teenaged troublemakers, mostly Randy Borowski, a spoiled boy who drives a white Corvette and sells marijuana. Some days later Red comes upon Lance selling marijuana behind a school building. They fight, Lance runs away, and Red catches up on a bridge, where Lance, staring down into the water, tells him of the night his mother left and the pain of waiting for her to return, and he finally sobs out the hurt that he has bottled up for years. They are startled by the approach of the white Corvette. Randy, obviously high on something stronger than pot, demands the money from the sale, sees a police car in the distance, and thinks he has been set up. Holding a switchblade to Red's throat, he forces both boys into his car and drives one-handed at a crazy speed to a mountain cabin, where he announces that he will kill Red. Lance jumps for the knife, and Red ends the frantic scramble by knocking Randy on the head with a chunk of firewood. Lance's hand, however, has been so badly cut that he needs expert medical help. They stuff Randy into a root cellar under the floor, pull a heavy table over the trapdoor, and leave in the Corvette for Calgary, with Red driving and learning as he goes. Lance tells Red his real trouble: his mother is seeking custody and has a good chance of winning it in the hearing set for the next day. To spare his father the humiliation, Lance has decided to go with her. While they wait at the hospital for the specialist, Red tells Lance about his horror of drugs because of Greg and his guilt that he didn't tell, even though he knew his brother was using them. When his father arrives, Red tells him the truth, is surprised that he shows understanding and even admiration, and is persuaded to be honest with the police. Later he is present when Anne-Marie comes and Lance tells her he will go with her if he can go from the hospital, without returning to the ranch. The next day Anne-Marie picks up Red to help her get Lance's belongings. At the ranch they see the many drawings of wildlife Lance has made, in particular one of an eagle, flying wild and free, with the words below, "If you love something, let it go." Anne-Marie leaves, taking only the eagle picture and letting Lance stay with his father on the ranch. The characters and their actions are well drawn and believable, and the tensions between the boys and their parents keep the plot taut. As a narrator, however, Red is too perceptive and inclined to analyze situations in mature vocabulary to be convincing as a fourteen-year-old, and the intended young audience, having been shown in good scenes, might be insulted to be told the meaning of the action at such length. Can. Council Hon. Ment.

LET THE BALLOON GO (Southall*, Ivan, ill. Ian Ribbons, Methuen, 1968; St. Martin's, 1968), brief novel of an Australian cerebral palsy victim who achieves the right to compete in the rough and tumble of life without excessive protection. John Clement Sumner, 12, though highly intelligent and imaginative, has never participated in neighborhood play or any active games because he is spastic. He is subject to sudden attacks during which he cannot control his arms and legs or even his speech, episodes that end in violent shaking. In his imagination, however, he is a competent hero, doing great deeds to impress Mamie van Senden, 9, whom he admires, or soundly beating up Sissy (Cecil) Parlow, a classmate with whom he often quarrels. When John's over-protective mother must drive into Melbourne for a day of meetings, she intends to take him with her as usual, planning to leave him in the car in a basement parking area most of the time. He protests and, for the first time ever, she agrees to leave him alone. Aware that her husband thinks that she should stop shielding John so much yet torn by her fears and her long habit of watching his every movement, she leaves with a long set of prohibitions—don't run, don't use the stove, don't let any other children in to play—but she doesn't think of specifically forbidding what he has longed to do, to climb the gum tree in the yard. At first, overwhelmed by the choices open to him, he tries nothing and is on hand when his mother calls from Melbourne to check on him, but then the desire to see from high up in the tree is too great. Even starting to climb is a tremendous effort for him, since the first branch is fifteen feet above the ground and he must haul his father's heavy ladder from its rack under the back verandah, drag it across the lawn, and prop it against the trunk, all feats far beyond any he has yet tried. He gets stuck half way up the ladder, unable to make his muscles push him upward or even to let go and slide to the ground. Gradually, he works his way up the ladder and then up the tree, fifty feet from the ground. There he exults as he looks down on the town around him, until someone notices and soon a crowd clusters below the tree, thinking the boy is in trouble. John calls to them to go away and he will get down all right, but the only one who believes him is Sissy Parlow, who points out that John always stammers when he has an attack and that he is talking without difficulty now. The policeman, Constable Baird, though afraid of heights, feels that it is his duty to rescue the boy, so he pretends that the other people have gone away and starts up the tree. At first he speaks soothingly to John, but before he reaches the boy his foot gets jammed in a crotch. Panicky, he snaps at John and shouts to those below to call the fire department rescue crew from Melbourne and to alert the boy's parents. Sissy Parlow volunteers to climb up with a rope, but the constable angrily rejects the idea. Feeling betrayed, John makes some rude remarks, then deliberately climbs down, unlaces Constable Baird's bootlace so he can get free, and continues to descend until he loses consciousness and falls. He wakes to discover that he is scratched and bruised, that he has slept seventeen hours, and that his parents, having re-evaluated their way of treating him, have decided to let him try to stand on his own feet, even if it means bumps and more serious risks. The title comes from a remark an understanding stranger once made to John when he was having a shaking attack, "A balloon is not a balloon until you cut the string and let it go." John's zealous mother and his excessively meticulous father are stock figures, and Sissy Parlow's unconfessed desire to be John's best friend, though it offers hope for the future, is not entirely plausible, but John himself, with his imaginary heroic actions, his natural resentments, and his great desire for freedom, is believable and well drawn. The tone, often frantic, is appropriate for John's tremendous effort and overwrought emotions. Aust. Bk. of Year Com.; Choice.

LETTY WILKINS TRUELANCE (*Longtime Passing*; Once there was a Swagman**), loyal, deeply religious wife of Edwin*, loving mother of Mark*, Patsy*, Ella*, Boo, and Teddy*. She had a pampered upbringing and finds life at Longtime* very hard at first, but she gradually learns bush survival. After the Truelances move to Longtime, the novel focuses on her, but later the emphasis shifts to Edwin and other members of the clan. In *Swagman*, Letty appears as a chunky, practical, hardworking farm woman. A likeable figure, she is roundly and dynamically created.

LIDDLE-MA LORENNY (*Devil's Hill*; Tiger in the Bush*; The Roaring 40**), affectionately called so by her husband, Dave*, and children because she is a big, husky, good-natured woman. She is sensible and practical, used to making the most of life in the wild and sharing the work and problems of her husband, who lovingly and respectfully calls her "mate." She cleverly finds ways of handling strong-willed Sheppie* and brash Iggy*, without making them feel put down and of building Bron's* and Badge's self-esteem. For example, she throws Badge the rope with which they capture Brindle. This raises his spirits because he had been left behind to mind the girls and was sure that he would miss the excitement of capturing the cow.

THE LIEUTENANT (Bennett*, Jack, Angus, 1977), subtitled, *An Epic Tale of Courage and Endurance on the High Seas*, a historical adventure of the four-thousand-mile voyage in an open boat led by Captain Bligh after he and eighteen men are put off HMS *Bounty* by mutineers on April 29, 1789, although his name is given only in as afterword and the ship's name is mentioned only as the last word of the fictional text. The story starts as the ship disappears over the horizon, leaving the ill-assorted group in an overloaded boat with few supplies, somewhere east of Tofoa. The lieutenant, the deposed captain of the ship and now captain of the launch, sets a course for Timor, the Dutch colony that he considers the closest safe place to land. Among the eighteen who have chosen to go with the captain rather than stay on board with the mutineers is the botanist, Mr. Nelson*, an educated man, slight of build and of delicate health, ill-suited to the hardships they endure. The story is seen mostly through the alternating point of view of these two, though sometimes the thoughts as well as the words of other characters are reported. At their first stop, on Tofoa, they get some water and breadfruit from the natives, who then turn hostile and stone the boat, killing the fine old, uncomplaining quartermaster, John Norton. After that they pass a number of islands but dare not stop, though some of the men are grumbling dangerously, particularly John Fryer*, the sailing master, and William Purcell, the ill-humored carpenter. The captain is well aware of the dislike of most of the men, and he admits to himself that he is making mistakes, acting too schoolmarmish and insisting on discipline even under the extremely uncomfortable and increasingly hopeless circumstances, but he sees it as the only way to get the boat to its destination. Nelson and Ledward*, the acting surgeon, and old Lawrence Leboque, the sailmaker, all become ill with fever and dysentery. The meager supply of ship's biscuit has weevils and the salt pork is maggoty. At first they run through heavy seas and continual rain and spend much of their energy bailing, but later the glaring sun nearly broils them alive. A few times they kill birds or catch fish, which they eat raw, and when they get inside the reef they are able to stop at an inlet and make a stew of oysters and sea grass, but they dare not stay long for fear of the natives. The captain worries about the court martial that he will have to face for having lost his ship and about whether he has set the right course, but he determinedly keeps himself from dwelling on the events that brought about the mutiny. The antagonism of Fryer and Purcell and a few of their cohorts erupts at a stop that the lieutenant later names Sunday Island, and he faces down the disgruntled men and keeps his precarious command, with the strong support of William Cole, the boatswain. Finally, after more than a month of sailing under nearly impossible conditions, they sight Timor and, close to starvation, skins scarred from sunburn, clothes in rags, they head for the Dutch harbor of Coupang. The afterword tells what happened later to the captain and to all the crew members who could be traced. Descriptions of the hardships are graphic and much is told of the deplorable conditions aboard the British naval ships of the period, mostly through the memories that some of the seamen relate of the floggings and amputations, the almost inedible food, the press gangs and the "quota boys"—usually work house orphans impressed into the service—the withholding of pay, and official neglect. The lieutenant is depicted as an admirable figure, though not a likeable one. In an unusual stylistic pattern, the story shifts frequently into present tense, a technique that is effective in making the danger and misery immediate and striking. Aust. Bk. of Year Com.

LILA (*The Village by the Sea**), eldest of the children in the poor village family and the one who shoulders the responsibility for her sick mother and her younger siblings. Perhaps twelve or thirteen, she has left school and works constantly to try to feed the family. Lila is stoic, but she is strongly aware of the beauty around her and takes time from her grueling work to scatter flowers on the sacred rock in the sea near their hut and to watch the birds and the waves. Unlike Hari*, she does not dream of ways to change their fortunes but only tries to meet the day to day challenges.

LILLIPILLY HILL (Spence*, Eleanor, ill. Susan Einzig, Oxford, 1960; Roy, 1963), novel of family life in New South Wales, Australia, in the 1880s, concerning the adjustment of an English family to its newly inherited home at Barley Creek, fifty miles north of Sydney. Although Rose Ann, 10, and Aidan*, 13, are at first unhappy, and their mother, Mrs. Wilmot, deplores the uncouth servants and villagers and the lack of proper schools, Mr. Wilmot likes the area and Harriet, 12, is fascinated by their new home, known locally as Lillipilly Hill. A lively, uninhibited girl, she contrives to slip away from bookish Aidan and pretty, proper Rose Ann and meet the Barley Creek schoolteacher, Mr. Burnie, persuading him to call upon her father and assure him that Aidan can receive proper tutoring for a scholarship to Sydney Grammar School and the girls can get learning suitable for them in his school. After Mr. Burnie's call, the Wilmot parents decide to give the place a six-months' trial. Escorted to and from Barley Creek by their maid of all work, Polly, a local hired girl much too familiar and outspoken for Mrs. Wilmot's taste, the three start school. Harriet, befriended by tough, competent little Dinny* O'Brien, is immediately happy; Rose Ann, popular because she is so pretty and sweet, soon adjusts; but Aidan, who haughtily ignores the other children and speaks only to Mr. Burnie, is disliked and taunted. Hulking Paddy Tolly torments him, and Aidan does not stand up to him. Harriet explains the problem to Charles Farmer, the other boy bound for grammar school, and Charles, a cheerful, lively boy, volunteers to provoke a fight, so that Aidan will be forced into action, but Aidan runs off. That night, miserable and humiliated, Aidan decides to run away from home. In a swamp, he runs into a dog ready to spring and a rifle-toting boy aiming at him. The dignity that has alienated his schoolmates impresses this boy, who takes Aidan to his cave home. In the morning the boy, Clay* Stewart, 16 or 17, offers to guide him, but Aidan sees the beauty of the cranes at dawn and changes his mind, inspired by his admiration for Clay to face his schoolmates again. After school, he offers to fight Paddy, but the bigger boy backs down. Later, he helps Barley Creek win the trophy at a cricket match and is fully accepted at last. During the autumn holidays Dinny suggests that Harriet go with her to Winneroo, five miles away, where her father works in the lumber mill. Harriet knows that it will be forbidden if she asks but decides to go anyway. The girls have a wonderful time at the beach and get a ride part of the way home with old Mr. Bentley, a landholder and mill owner, who offers to help Mr. Wilmot plan his farm. On her return, Harriet is in deep disgrace and confined to the house for a month. She decides to be extra good so that her mother will give up the idea of returning to England so that the girls can be properly raised. Aidan, however, enlists her to help him warn Clay, assumed to be a bushranger and the target of a local posse. They have not counted on the recent flooding, and crossing the swamp at night, Aidan leaves Harriet, who is chilled and exhausted. He meets another group, led by Charles's father, also bent on rescuing Clay. Later they find Harriet barely conscious, but she recovers rapidly and this time is not blamed or punished. The Wilmots employ Clay to help plant orange trees provided by Mr. Bentley, and the prospects for staying in Australia are good. Most of the action is seen through Harriet's eyes, though for some passages the point of view switches to Aidan. The frustration of an energetic, imaginative girl confined to the role thought proper by her conventional mother in the late nineteenth century is well evoked without being falsified by late twentieth-century attitudes. Other aspects of life in Australia of the period, as well as the physical beauty of the Barley Creek area are also well depicted. Aidan, with his self-tormenting conscience, is likewise well drawn, but his involvement with Clay and the older boy's story are not as convincing. Aust. Bk. of Year Com.

LINDSAY, HAROLD A(RTHUR) (1900–   ), born in Adelaide, Australia; writer of fiction and non-fiction on outdoor and anthropological subjects. As a boy he spent much time in the bush, and when an adult he settled on a farm in South Australia, though he also explored extensively for material for his writings. During World War II he instructed Australian and American sailors, soldiers, and airmen in bush survival. After the war much of this information was published in *The Bushmen's Handbook* (Angus, 1948). He became a full-time writer, producing radio scripts, more than 3,000 articles and 150 short stories for newspapers and magazines, and several novels for adults, among them *The Red Bull* (Hale, 1959) and *Sweeps the Wide Earth* (Hale, 1960). With Norman B. Tindale*, curator of anthropology at the South Australian Museum, he wrote two children's novels: *The First Walkabout** (Longmans, 1954), a historical adventure about how the Aborigines first came to Australia that was named Australian Children's Book of the Year, and *Rangatira** (Reed, 1959; Rigby, 1959; Watts, 1959), another historical adventure, which relies on known facts about Polynesian migrations in the 1200s and was commended for the Book of the Year Award. They also collaborated on a book of non-fiction, *The Australian Aborigines* (Angus, 1963; Jacaranda, 1963). By himself Lindsay published *The Cruise of the Kestrel* (Rigby, 1960), another novel for young readers.

LISA (Matas*, Carol, Lester, 1987; *Lisa's War*, Scribner, 1989), historical novel set in Copenhagen, Denmark, during the German occupation of World War II and culminating with the mass evacuation of Danish Jews to Sweden at Rosh Hashanah in September, 1943. Bright, assertive, fun-loving, Jewish Lisa, 12, tells the story of how her life changes when the Germans take over Denmark. Awakening early one April morning in 1940 to the sound of airplanes, she soon learns that Denmark has surrendered. Her father, a surgeon, and her mother, a university English teacher, are apprehensive since they have heard about the abuse of Jews in Germany. They try to go on with their normal lives, and for a while Lisa finds that her life with school and friends remains much the same. Her brother, Stefan, 14, however, is furious about the invasion and joins the Resistance. On the other hand, cousin Erik and his parents feel that the stories of German discrimination against Jews are unfounded. More from romantic impulse than conviction, Lisa blackmails Stefan into letting her aid the anti-Nazi effort and, although she knows her parents would disapprove, distributes anti-Nazi leaflets on streetcars. As life grows harder for the Danes under the German occupation, Lisa becomes more and more involved in the Resistance. The beginning of the end comes on her fourteenth birthday, the day of her first big dance, when German soldiers barge into the operating room at her father's hospital and kill, among others, a woman about to give birth. Lisa's father saves the baby, and the family unofficially adopts little Sarah. Shortly they also acquire Susanne, Lisa's best friend and the daughter of Gentile dance hall owners who are slain when the Germans bomb the hall for playing American swing music. Susanne, who also works for the Resistance, remains mute from shock until she kills an informer. Events come to a head in 1943 on Rosh Hashanah morning, a Friday. Father phones from the hospital that the family must go on "holiday," a code expression that indicates that a roundup is imminent. Lisa promptly informs as many family friends as she can, even taking the train to the country to warn Erik's relatives. Many Jews take refuge in the psychiatric wing of the hospital, and many others are hidden by Gentile friends. As soon as possible, they are evacuated by boat by Danish freedom fighters, Jew and Gentile. Lisa's people leave on Sunday night in tense, action-filled scenes. Lisa and Stefan stay behind as lookouts and are themselves almost captured. They get away in a rowboat that almost submerges before they are picked up by a Swedish destroyer. Lisa tells her story directly and simply, partly after the fact and partly as it happens but always in present tense, a technique that gives the story immediacy, heightens the tension, and underscores the horror, irrationality, and drama of events. Lisa's verbal economy and focus on major events do, however, create some problems. One wonders, for example, how Lisa becomes so adept with guns, since her training is never described, and how she, her brother, and Susanne could be so deeply involved in Resistance activities without arousing tension within the family and suspicion among the Nazis, especially since the father is prominent in his field and the mother is an intellectual who would probably be under surveillance. The characters are one-dimensional, scenes have power, and the generosity of the Danish Gentiles and the bravery of the evacuators in the face of such tremendous odds come through strongly. Can. Bilson.

LISA'S WAR. See *LISA*.

LISTEN FOR THE SINGING (Little*, Jean, Clarke, 1977; Dutton, 1977), realistic novel of family and school life with girl's growing-up and problem story aspects set in Canada in 1939–1940, sequel to *From Anna*. The Soldens, emigrants to Toronto from Germany five years earlier—understanding, warmhearted, literary Papa Ernst, a grocer, his wife, capable, retiring Mama, and their five children—are a close and loving family. Anna, the youngest at thirteen or fourteen and the story's focus, feels especially near to Papa and to Rudi, the elder son, a university student outstanding in math. When Britain declares war on Germany, Rudi yearns to enlist, but the family disapproves, and they also worry about Papa's sister, Tania, who lives in Germany. As she has poor eye sight, Anna's main concerns, however, revolve around starting high school. Gretchen, her elder sister, helps her locate rooms the first day, as later does her first friend, warm, kind Maggie de Vries, with whom she shares a locker and through whom she meets the other two girls who make up her "gang," bubbly, pretty Suzy Hughes, a cheerleader, and strong-minded, assertive Paula Kirsch, their leader. The year brings good times, like shopping trips, and Anna gets along fine in most of her courses, especially English, but has trouble with Mr. McNair, the math instructor. When Rudi, who takes an interest in her now that she is beyond the kid stage, tutors her, she blossoms in that subject, too, and at year's end she is encouraged by her teachers to consider attending the university. Mr. Lloyd, the history teacher, presents a continuing problem: he bullies students with German names. Anna keeps cool and discovers, to her surprise, that he is responsible for her exams being typed in large letters. She thanks him and makes more discoveries—that he also has limited sight and that his disability and the loss of a brother in Germany in World War I have made him short-tempered and shy. Henceforth the two have a quiet friendship. Rudi and Gretchen teach her to dance, and Rudi gets her hair cut in a fashionable, new style. An ongoing problem for the family and their friends, among them the Schumachers, physician Franz and his wife, Eileen (who had been Anna's teacher, Miss Williams, in the Sight-saving Class in *From Anna*), is anti-German sentiment and their own ambivalent feelings about their homeland. Rudi's enlistment, on the heels of Tania's disappearance along with her old Jewish father-in-law, brings even more trauma for the family. Mama collapses and takes to her bed, staying there until Anna stoutly insists that she should be ashamed of her bad behavior. Further difficulty occurs when Rudi is blinded in an accident during basic training. Mustered out in early fall and home again, he becomes despondent and isolates himself in his room. Anna, with Mrs. Schumacher's help, interests him in talking books, then eases him into Braille and gradually whets his appetite for continuing his schooling. At the end, she realizes that she has developed confidence in her ability to cope with problems and believes that the Soldens can have a good future. As in the first book, characters are drawn in the most basic strokes. The only one the reader gets to know well is Anna, and passages about her vision difficulties often have an instructive and encouraging tone. The plot is loose and uneven, and Rudi's blindness, in particular, seems tacked on and contrived didacticism. Like many girl's books, the novel is highly introspective, much concerned with Anna's innermost feelings and aspirations, and this is its main strength. Another is the warm and personal relationship within the family. Style flows and emphasizes words of touch and sound, and vocabulary and grammar are more mature than in *From Anna*. The result is pleasant, wholesome reading for pre- and early teen girls. The title comes from a speech by Mr. Appleby, school principal, who encourages his students in an assembly to "warm the world the way the mother bird warms her egg" and admonishes them "to listen for the singing," even before the egg is hatched. This becomes a kind of slogan for Anna. Can. Council Winner.

LITTLE BROTHER (Baillie*, Allan, ill. Elizabeth Honey, Blackie, 1985; Methuen, 1988), historical novel set for four months in Kampuchea (Cambodia) during recent hostilities. As they are racing through the forest to escape from Khmer Rouge soldiers at Big Paddy, where they have been forced labor, Muong Mang, 18, the son of a doctor and a dancer, draws the fire so that his younger brother, Muong Vithy, 11, can get away, and then disappears. The rest of the novel focuses on plucky Vithy's harrowing flight to the Thai border where he hopes to find Mang. He arrives at Phnom Penh, the ruined and deserted capital, where a garishly dressed youth, who calls himself the King, feeds him and shares with him his cellar "palace," which is crowded with an incredible hodgepodge of gleanings. The King smuggles him aboard a truck loaded with supplies from a Red Cross ship and headed for Aranyaprathet, the closest Thai town. Vithy rides the truck across the Tonle Sap River for some distance, until it tips and he is dumped out. He runs off, encountering a cyclo (bicycle rickshaw) boy, who takes him to a scrapyard, where he fashions a bike of sorts, and then sets off to cover the remaining one hundred fifty kilometers. He meets many people with gaunt faces and hunted looks. About forty kilometers from his destination, an old woman seizes his bike, but an old man gives him a ride on a bullock cart and a coconut to eat. Near his destination, he hears shots and comes upon a fallen teenaged girl, whose wound he staunches with moss. Dawn finds them stumbling into the refugee camp near the Thai border. He has been two hard weeks on his way. At Nong Samet, or 007, as the Thais call it, an Australian doctor, Betty Harris, helps the girl (who expresses no gratitude to her or Vithy), and an American worker takes Vithy on an unsuccessful hunt for Mang. Vithy is then taken to a hospital camp, where with other refugee children he lives in the house of a woman called Ponary, works around the hospital, and helps translate for English-speaking refugees because he knows some English. When Vithy has given up hope. Dr. Harris, whose term of service is up, invites him to return with her to Sydney. There a gaunt stranger, who turns out to be Mang, awaits him at airport customs, and the two brothers are joyfully reunited. Found wounded and almost dead, Mang was brought to Australia and operated upon by skilled neurosurgeons who saved his life. The ending leaves questions. At what point does Dr. Harris discover that Mang is still alive? When they arrive in Australia, the reader knows she has known that Mang would be there. How much does Mang's being alive have to do with enabling Vithy to emigrate? Why hasn't Dr. Harris told Vithy that his brother is alive? Keeping the information from him seems unnecessarily cruel. The story offers many suspenseful scenes, and the sense of danger, the destruction, and the desolation in the war-torn country seem very real. The Americans and Australians though types are not idealized, and Vithy's fear of soldiers, his loneliness, and his inability to trust come through strongly. The story of what happened to Vithy's family at the hands of the Khmer Rouge is told gradually through his thoughts as he is fleeing and in a story to Dr. Harris. Although unevenly paced, the book is a straightforward, unmelodramatic account of the devastation of war and the hardships children suffer in one. The story is all Vithy's, but the King is a memorable figure. Aust. Bk. of Year Highly Com.

LITTLE BROWN PICANINNIES OF TASMANIA (Fletcher*, Jane Ada, ill. Margaret Senior, Sands, 1950), highly illustrated historical story not much more than a picture book in length set among Tasmanian Aborigines at the time of Abel Tasman's arrival in 1642. Events revolve around informed speculation on the native way of life, looked at mostly from the children's point of view, and concentrate on food gathering. The little girls, whose leader is Weetah, a child distinguished from the others only by her greater daring, chase a wombat and discover a cave that becomes a temporary home for the tribe. The boys hunt kangaroos and capture a snake, which they look forward to as a delightful meal for the men, but which gets away while they are horsing around. After the inland food resources give out, the group burns the land to enable it to replenish itself and moves to the shore. Here two important events occur. A storm washes in the carcass of a large whale, which provides plentiful food for many days, and, while seeking opossums, the girls spot two sailing ships put in at their bay. The people hide, believing the ships to be devils, and cower in fear when the guns boom as the Dutch flag is planted on the shore. As the ships depart, the point of view shifts to Tasman, who records his discovery in his log book. The story is lively with activity and dialogue. The details of food gathering and family life, like caring for the younger children and the sex roles, seem plausible, and there is no hint of instruction. An expository prologue gives information about these ancient people. Many native terms, explained in a glossary, add to the credibility. Aust. Bk. of Year Highly Com.

A LITTLE FEAR (Wrightson*, Patricia, Hutchinson, 1983, Atheneum, 1983), fantasy novel rich in atmosphere of place and emotion set mostly in a swampy region in the contemporary Australian countryside. The story starts in a pleasant rest home, Sunset House, where her daughter has arranged for old Mrs.* Tucker to live out her days in what the younger woman considers peace and comfort. An intelligent, sturdy, hardworking farm woman accustomed to taking care of herself and making her own decisions, Mrs. Tucker detests the place. No one knows, however, that when her brother, John Bright, died, he left to her his isolated cottage on Broad River in another state. Mrs. Tucker steals away to the empty, rusty-roofed place on a ridge above the swampy flats lining the Broad River, gets herself a dog for company and protection, hires an errand boy, and settles in, rejoicing quietly in the dignity that independence brings. Trouble soon comes from the Njimbin*, who lives in the fowlhouse. A sly and cunning gnome, he resents her presence and mobilizes the area's indigenous creatures of land and water for what soon accelerates into a war over possession of the place, an unrelenting conflict that grows in intensity and acrimony. The Njimbin tricks Hector*, the water-wary dog, into the rowboat and tows the terror-stricken animal far downriver; harries the chickens and gives their mash to the rats; burns up the rat traps Mrs. Tucker sets; and plants dozens of frogs in her house, among other acts of spite and trickery. Mrs. Tucker consults Ivan, the errand boy, who assumes that foxes or similar creatures are at work, and fires warning shots into the ground at what he considers strategic places, including, as it happens, the Njimbin's storehouse, an act that so infuriates the gnome that he sends a plague of midges against the old woman. At this point, Mrs. Tucker, now aware of the identity and formidableness of her adversary, capitulates. She informs her daughter of her whereabouts and cleverly manipulates her into agreeing to sell the Bright land and buy another less isolated property. She has proved that she can still take care of herself and deserves to be independent and self-determining as long as she is physically able to manage. Before she leaves the Bright place, she sets fire to the "maggoty old fowlhouse," leaving the Njimbin with a hollow victory. Careful attention to creating the feel of timeless mystery and the physical appearance of the area, the painstakingly developed and sustained tension between two equally determined, aged adversaries, the occasional touches of humor, much irony, skillful characterizations that extend even to the "maggoty," slow-witted rats, the ironic, thoroughly satisfying conclusion, and the bold yet understated style make for a spellbinding story about courage and coming to terms with life that avoids the preachiness and sentimentality of many contemporary novels about the aged. Aust. Bk. of Year Winner; Boston Globe Winner; Carnegie Com.; Fanfare; Young Observer.

LITTLE, (FLORA) JEAN (1932–   ), born in Taiwan; prolific Canadian writer of realistic psychological and physical problem novels in family settings. She was born with limited sight, the daughter of medical missionaries. After the family returned to Canada, she attended regular and special schools, becoming an avid reader and developing an interest in writing. After earning a degree in English literature from the University of Toronto, she worked with handicapped children in the United States and Canada and turned to full-time writing after she published her first novel, *Mine for Keeps* (Little, 1962; Little [U.S.], 1962). It tells of a girl with cerebral palsy whom mainstreaming in school forces to confront her fears. Since then, Little has published more than a dozen novels, several books of poems, including *When the Pie Was Opened* (Little, 1968) and *Hey World, Here I Am!* (Kids, 1986; Harper, 1989), and her autobiography, *Little by Little: A Writer's Education* (Viking, 1987). Among her novels are *Home from Far* (Little, 1965; Little [U.S.], 1965), in which a family that has just lost a child in an automobile accident takes in as foster children two half-orphans; *Take Wing* (Little, 1968), where a family copes with a mentally retarded son; *Look Through My Window* (Fitzhenry, 1970; Harper, 1970), about the problems and pleasures of a blended family; and *From Anna* (Fitzhenry, 1972; Harper, 1972), about the partially sighted daughter of German immigrants to Canada just before World War II. *Mama's Going to Buy You a Mockingbird** (Viking, 1984), which revolves around the death of a father, was Canadian Children's Book of the Year and a Ruth Schwartz selection. *Listen for the Singing** (Clarke, 1977; Dutton, 1977), which continues the story begun in *From Anna*, was a Canada Council Winner. Little's books excel in portraying family relationships and are well paced. She has also received the Vicky Metcalf Award from the Canadian Authors' Association for a notable contribution to literature for children. Almost blind, she has lived in Guelph, Ontario, the "Riverside" where most of her stories take place.

LITTLE PAT CONNELL (*The Seventh Pebble**), dreamy, earnest little lame boy. The book's title comes from Little Pat's habit of arranging six small stones in rows, one for each member of his family. At the end, while the family waits for the bus, he puts a seventh one in line, which he says stands for the baby that Maeve is going to have. After the Connells board the bus, the wife of the storekeeper on whose step he has arranged the stones scornfully sweeps them away.

LIZA (*Underground to Canada**), slave girl of about twelve. The daughter of a Baptist minister and a slave at the Riley plantation when Julilly arrives, she becomes Julilly's friend and shows her how things are done on the place. She is a hunchback, crippled, and terribly scarred from repeated beatings that Sims, the overseer, has given her because she tried to escape. Julilly helps her fill her cotton sack so that Sims won't beat her even more. Even though she is presented as easily tired and not nearly as strong as Julilly, she manages to hold up quite well on the trip. She demonstrates the inhumanity of pre–Civil War slavery.

LONGTIME (*Longtime Passing*; Once there was a Swagman**), a rugged, forested region in the Blue Mountains of New South Wales, Australia. In *Longtime Passing*, it is the sacred area of the Daruk Aborigines, the most holy portion being the Place* of the Stone Giants. In a kind of preface, Teddy* Truelance tells how Longtime was discovered by whites. Alexander Bell, son of a British army lieutenant during the Australian development period, is curious about how Aborigines manage to travel through the mountains when whites cannot. He trails a lubra (Aborigine woman) along the Aborigines' secret route and unwittingly is responsible for her death. From hiding, he watches as the elders crucify her because they think she betrayed them. The Truelances enter the area by the route she and Bell used many years earlier.

LONGTIME PASSING (Brinsmead*, Hesba, Angus, 1971), biographical, historical novel set in Longtime* in the Blue Mountains of New South Wales, Australia, outside Sydney just after World War I. The story covers about twenty years in the lives of the Truelances, chiefly of Edwin*, the eldest of four sons, who pioneer in the forested uplands that were once the sacred preserves of the Daruk Aborigines. The story is told years later by Teddy* (Edwina), the youngest of the four daughters and one son of Edwin and Letty*. Missionaries in Java when their second child and first daughter, Ella*, is born, Edwin and Letty are advised that the sickly baby needs a cooler climate. Edwin persuades his three brothers, Vance*, Sean*, and Merlin, to accompany him into the uninhabited uplands of Australia and stake out farms. Although Merlin continues as an itinerant piano tuner, the other three develop homesteads. Edwin's being Wangerra, on the flatlands between his brothers' mountaintop sites. The novel focuses on Edwin's family, but also keeps track of the other three brothers. Edwin, Letty, Mark*, about five, Ella, and baby Patsy* live in a rude bark hut for some months and then in a rustic board house. Years of hard work, difficulties, and good times follow for the family, which adds first Boo and then Teddy to its number. God-fearing, idealistic, impulsive Edwin tackles his responsibilities with characteristic enthusiasm, while pampered Letty accepts with goodwill the role of a pioneer wife. Edwin has uncertain success in raising turnips, and the sawmill the brothers start flourishes until the Depression, when Edwin peddles lamps for a living. Vance moves to the city and marries, while Sean takes over Vance's house and has a family. Later the lumber business revives, but a forest fire destroys the mill and Sean's house and narrowly misses Edwin's home. After automobiles are available, Edwin buys a truck and operates a rural mail route. Though the family must contend with threats from dingoes, failed crops, torrential rains that render roads impassable, and limited medical services, they thrive and feel that cities offer unnecessary conveniences. They enjoy occasional visits from family and neighbors, and a traveling circus with an elephant named Betty performs for Teddy's birthday. Teddy reports humorous incidents as well as serious ones: Black Dog stealing a leg of lamb; Mark and Edwin being driven from a tent at night by swarms of ants; and Darling, the family raven, tearing to confetti the summons to call father to account for shooting at surveyors plotting a highway through the region. After tutoring in bush correspondence lessons at the kitchen table, one by one the children leave for school in the city, and the book ends with Teddy's departure. Farms now dot the area, and the highway means car and truck traffic. Both Edwin and Teddy regret the passing of an era and sense that "progress" (Edwin calls it seeking fairy gold) threatens what hundreds of years and nature have kept intact. The novel excels in character revelation, details of pioneer life, descriptions of nature, and its warm and sympathetic picture of a close-knit family. It suffers from diffusion, insufficient tension, and too many figures and incidents inadequately developed. The author fails to identify the narrator at the beginning, nor does the reader ever learn how Teddy acquired so much information. The tone is serious, though warm, but not somber. The introduction about the Aborigines catches the reader's attention and is the only really suspenseful part of the book. Themes include doing one's best, family love and support, and respect for the land. Though overly ambitious, the novel is a memorable picture of the development of a significant portion of the vast continent. A companion novel is *Once there was a Swagman** (Sweeney* Mulligan). Aust. Bk. of Year Winner.

LORD ERIC (*The River Kings**), tall young deckhand on the Murray River riverboat, the *Lazy Jane*. Eric has a cultured English voice, courteous manners, and more education than the other men of the crew. He explains to Shawn that he came to Australia because "there'd been a bit of trouble back home," and he takes a special interest in the boy. Before the *Lazy Jane* catches fire and explodes, he receives a letter from England, obviously telling that the "trouble" has been solved or forgotten, and he plans to go home at the end of the next trip.

LOST IN THE BARRENS (Mowat*, Farley, ill. Charles Geer, Little, 1956; *Two Against the North*, Scholastic, 1956), adventure and survival novel set for about six months in the mid–1900s on the Barrens of Canada, a thousand miles north of Winnipeg, Manitoba. Jamie Macnair, 18, an orphan living with his Uncle Angus, a trapper, and Awasin, a Cree Indian youth, accompany a small band of Chipewyan Indians, led by Chief Denikazi, north by canoe to caribou country in early summer. Denikazi's people are near starvation, and the object of the trip is to secure enough meat to survive until fall when the caribou migrate south again. The journey is hard and dangerous, taking the little band through treacherous rapids and difficult portages and into the territory of the dread Eskimo, the ancient enemy of the Cree and Chipeweyan. Instructed to wait at a certain place while the men go on to accomplish the mission, the boys become impatient, and Jamie persuades Awasin to travel upstream to investigate the Great Stone House, a ruin of which they have heard. Against his better judgment, Awasin agrees. Their canoe wrecked at a rapids and most of their gear lost, the youths find themselves forty miles from the rendezvous and dependent on ingenuity for survival. After investigating the Great Stone House, which turns out to be a Viking ruin, they trudge laboriously overland in an unsuccessful attempt to intercept the Chipewyans. Alone, three hundred miles from home, they face rapidly coming winter on the treeless, windswept, soon-to-be-frigid plains. They construct a stone igloo, catch and preserve meat and fish, prepare garments from skins, gather berries, and render fat. While exploring, they luckily happen upon a secluded valley with stands of sturdy timber and a live stream. They struggle to erect a small cabin in Hidden Valley and gradually move their accumulated stores from the igloo to the cabin, first by packing them and then on a sled they build that is pulled by two huskies they have rescued and tamed. Ticklish moments abound, among them raids of wolverines and an attack by a grizzly, but Jamie's ingenuity and Awasin's experience combine to provide answers to most problems, including the terrible feeling of isolation and monotony that sets in when the blizzards begin. After Christmas, the youths take advantage of a break in the weather to leave for home, an ill-advised enterprise because both soon suffer from severe snow blindness and are ill for three days. Intending to return to Hidden Valley, they stumble on an igloo built as a temporary shelter by Peetyuk, an Eskimo youth, who takes them home to his family. To the boys' surprise, they are treated very hospitably. Peetyuk is traveling south to join his white father's people near the Macnair place, and the Eskimos take all three boys south. A grand reunion follows since the boys have been given up for dead, and, after six harrowing months on the Barrens, both Jamie and Awasin are delighted and relieved to be back home. The boys are distinctly characterized, their personalities gradually revealed by events. The sense of adventure in unknown and far-off places is exceedingly high, there is never a dull moment, with events following one another with more cause than is usual for this kind of book, and as a result the story stands out as a splendid example of the adventure-survival genre for its sheer excitement and human-against-nature tension. The book is also exceptional for the generous and clear detail with which the author recreates the setting, the difficulties, and the day-to-day activities that enable the boys to stay alive. The Indians are sympathetically and unstereotypically presented. Can. Bk. of Year Winner; Can. Gov. General's Winner.

LOVE, DAVID (Case*, Dianne, ill. Mario Sickle, Maskew, 1986), novel of black family life and a boy's difficulties growing up in the Kamp, a shanty town of the Cape Flats, near Cape Town, South Africa, in the period of its publication. The first-person narrator, whose name, Anna Jantjies, is not given until the last page, tells of the problems of her fourteen-year-old half-brother, David, mainly with her father, Dadda, a gardener and odd job man who has a terrible temper, drinks too much, and holds himself aloof from his neighbors. They live in a one-room shack Dadda has built, where Anna sleeps across the foot of her parents' bed and David sleeps on cardboard on the floor. Mamsie works for a white family in Hout Bay, leaving before first light and returning after dark. Anna takes care of Baby, her infant sister, although she has not yet started school. David, who is small for his age, has two good friends, Buddy J., a fat, not very bright neighbor, and Oupa, an older boy with deformed legs. Together they roam the area near the Kamp, sometimes peering into the windows of homes where television is going, sometimes walking to the nearby lake where they rummage in garbage cans for food discarded by picnickers, with Anna tagging along, and David often carrying Baby. David rescues a three-legged puppy being drowned in a bag, names it Stumpy, and adopts it, although Dadda hates dogs. When Dadda catches David smoking, he beats him with his fists until the boy is bleeding, and when Dadda discovers items that David has stolen, he runs away with Stumpy. Anna is heartbroken and, when David comes back while Dadda is working, follows him and Stumpy to a camp of poor shanties and junked cars surrounding a large bonfire, where people come and go all night, a hangout for thieves and petty criminals. She spends the night shivering by the fire, and the next day David takes her home. Dadda beats Anna with his belt for leaving Baby unattended, and he almost kills David. For a while David lives at home and goes back to school, but a new conflict arises when Stumpy has four puppies. For several days, David keeps them concealed. When Dadda discovers them, he is angry but tries to be fair, saying that they can keep one male puppy but must get rid of Stumpy and the others. Their efforts to sell the puppies are futile. When the pups get into some of Dadda's seedlings, his temper erupts, and he kicks Stumpy viciously. David defies him, Dadda hits him, and, as the bleeding boy picks up the injured dog, shouts at him not to set foot in the house again. Anna follows David, and they spend the night on sand dunes near a cemetery, with David cradling Stumpy in his arms. The next day they hitchhike to the SPCA, only to find that Stumpy has been dead for hours. With Oupa and Buddy J., they bury her. Buddy J. takes Anna home, but David stays away. Anna finds it difficult to eat or sleep. After weeks, police contact the family. The next day a social worker brings David home, much subdued, though he confesses to Oupa that he made good money delivering drugs and buried his savings in his ''manager's'' yard. Detectives come and pressure him until he tells them his manager's name. He fears reprisals and worries about his coming trial. Although it is his first offense, he is sent to a ''place of safety,'' evidently a reform school, for two or three years. Through the social worker's intervention, the family moves to a council house in Lotus River, with three bedrooms and running water. The last page is a letter from David to Anna, written a year after the trial, in which he says he is glad that she likes school and tells of an injured cat he has adopted. It is unclear whether or not the reader is to assume that David is reformed and that, in their improved living conditions, he and Dadda will be able to get along when he returns. The strength of the book lies in the portrayal of David, whose quiet defiance drives Dadda to extreme anger, and in Anna's continued devotion to her half-brother. The deplorable living conditions, the heat, and the cold are well evoked, but there is no suggestion of the protests and police brutality associated with the black sections of the country. Young Africa.

LOVE MAGNET (*The Sun Horse**), arrowhead that pierced the throat of an Indian girl of the Sun Tribe of Forgetful Valley when she thrust herself in front of her true love to save his life. Made of some strange, powerful metal, it became the sacred, magical, protective talisman of the tribe.

THE "LOYALL VIRGINIAN" (Finkel*, George, Angus, 1968; *The "Loyal Virginian,"* Viking, 1968), historical novel of events in Virginia Colony and England from 1644 to 1649 as related some twenty years later by a planter, Roger Bolynge, with emphasis on the struggle between Parliament and King Charles Stuart. After his betrothed, her father, and mother are slain by Indians, Roger joins other settlers in annihilating the Indian town on the Potomac River and capturing the chief, Opechancanough. Indian power beaten, the settlers look forward to more prosperous times. Parliament, however, has severely restricted trade with the colonies, and Roger proposes that they raise and outfit a sunken Dutch vessel and trade their tobacco themselves. *De Drie Gebroeders* is accordingly renovated, renamed the *Loyall Virginian* (a term that also obviously applies to Roger), and sets sail in the spring of 1647 for Europe under the captaincy of James Kinnear, Scots survivor of a shipwreck, with Roger as captain general and his cousin, Henry Byrd, as supercargo. They trade in Spain and in Bordeaux, where they also meet William Carey, an enigmatic figure in the service of King Charles, currently a prisoner of Parliament. At Leith in Scotland, they acquire as a guide a soldier of fortune, Geordie Hay, trade handsomely in wool, and stay the winter with a Dales family, the Dugdales, whose daughter, Celia, Henry later marries, and whose Highlands niece, Moragh MacDonald, becomes Roger's wife. Carey enlists their aid in rescuing the king, a prisoner on the Isle of Wight, but the attempt in February, 1648, fails because the king refuses to cooperate. Later Carey enlists Roger in fighting against Parliament. Roger assembles a band called Bolynge's Graycoats, which are thoroughly defeated along with other partisans. Sad and somewhat bitter, they flee northward with the Dugdales to safety in Scotland, planning to return to Virginia as soon as possible. The next spring, after learning of the beheading of King Charles, they sail homeward, certain that the political unrest in England will continue for years. A broad canvas, the book is so filled with details of fighting and political discussion that is projects more the flavor of text than story. The numerous characters play parts necessary for the meager plot. Oliver Cromwell makes a brief appearance to engage Roger in a discussion about political theory. Rory MacDonald, a kinsman of Moragh, a proud and ruthless man for whom clan is the most important, provides a perspective on how society should be governed that contrasts with those of both the Royalists and Parliament. The style is slightly archaic in sentence structure and vocabulary. Action scenes abound, and plentiful details recreate the period. The book's strongest feature is the impression it gives of the turbulence in England, the conflicting philosophies, the shifting loyalties, the potential for violence, and the general instability of life. Aust. Bk. of Year Com.

THE "LOYAL VIRGINIAN." See *THE "LOYALL VIRGINIAN."*

LUATH (*The Incredible Journey**), large, red-gold Labrador retriever, a young dog, who is devoted to his home and master. Not nearly so adjustable as the other animals, Luath tolerates the attentions of John Longridge, who is keeping them during the Hunter family's absence, but he does not reciprocate with affection. When he decides to start for home, he persuades the other two animals and leads them with sure instinct in a direct line, and at natural obstacles like the river, where he swims across several times to encourage the others; he is responsible for their progress. He is constantly hungry and arrives in much worse condition than the other two.

LUKE ANDERSON (*Shadow in Hawthorn Bay**), 19, tall, capable son of the ne'er-do-well Andersons of Hawthorn Bay on Lake Ontario, Canada, the only adult in the family with courage and a sense of responsibility. Luke first encounters Mary Urquhart as she is tramping through the woods toward Hawthorn Bay and gives her a ride in his horse-drawn cart. On the way he informs her that the Camerons have left the area, and she realizes that Duncan is dead. Luke leaves her in the care of imperious Julia Colliver, the miller's wife, where she stays for several days until she recovers from the shock. Then she goes to the Andersons' cabin to help care for the family, since Mrs. Anderson is ill and suffering from the effects of alcoholism. Luke is a paragon of dependability, good for Mary and the plot, and represents desirable settlers.

LUNN, JANET (LOUISE SWOBODA) (1928–   ), born in Dallas, Texas; Canadian editor, lecturer, and writer for children. The daughter of a mechanical engineer, she was educated in Vermont, New York, and New Jersey, studied at Queen's University in Ontario, and became a Canadian citizen in 1963. She lives on the shore of Lake Ontario where her award-winning novels are set. In *The Root Cellar** (Lester, 1981; Scribner's, 1983), chosen as the Canadian Library Association Children's Book of the Year, an American orphan girl living with Canadian relatives enters a root cellar and finds herself in the nineteenth century, where she seeks a Canadian youth who has run away to fight in the American Civil War. A strong historical novel framed by fantasy, it appeared on the Honor List of the International Board on Books for Young People for 1984. *Shadow in Hawthorn Bay** (Lester, 1986; Scribner's, 1986) is a historical novel in which a Scottish girl with second sight "hears" her emigrated sweetheart calling her from Canada and journeys to Upper Canada in search of him. A vivid picture of life in Canada among immigrants from Scotland and refugees from the American Revolution in the early nineteenth century, it won the Canada Council Award, the Canadian Young Adult Award, the National IODE Award, and the Canadian Library Association Book of the Year Award. She has also published *Larger Than Life* (Porcepic, 1979), stories about Canadian real-life heroes; *The Twelve Dancing Princesses* (Methuen, 1979), a retelling for which she received another Library Association Book of the Year Award; *Double Spell* (Martin, 1968; *Twin Spell*, Harper, 1969), a novel in which twins are pulled into Toronto's past; *Amos's Sweater* (Groundwood/Douglas, 1988) and *Duck Cakes* (Groundwood/Douglas, 1989), picture-book stories; and with her husband a history of Prince Edward County in Ontario. She has been an editor for Clarke

Irwin and Company, Publishers, and a writer in residence for the Regina Public Library in Saskatchewan, written scripts for the Canadian Broadcasting Company and articles and short stories for periodicals, and received the Vicky Metcalf Award from the Canadian Authors Association for her total work for young readers.

LURIE, MORRIS (1938–), prolific Australian writer of mainly humor and short stories for adults, who also writes for children. His novel *Toby's Millions** (Viking, 1982), a lighthearted farce with satiric overtones, was commended for Australian Children's Book of the Year. He has written several stories published in illustrated form, like *Arlo the Dandy Lion* (Collins, 1971; McGraw, 1971), *The Story of Imelda, Who Was Small* (Oxford, 1984; Houghton, 1988), and *The Twenty-Seventh Annual African Hippopotamus Race* (Simon, 1969; Collins, 1969), and a collection of short stores for children, *Night-night!* (Oxford, 1986). He has also published numerous short stories, an autobiography, and collections of anecdotes and satire for adults.

M

MAADA (*Raven's Cry**), sister of Yatza, the heir to the chieftaincy of the Haidas, presented as a proud and beautiful princess. In keeping with Haida matrilineal practice, Maada's son is Yatza's heir. Like other Haida women, after she has a son, she becomes more assertive in speech and manner and demands her prerogatives as a chieftainess. These traits lead to her death in a vividly described scene when American sailors trade with the Haidas. They care nothing for the rights of the Indians and slaughter Maada and her small son, though both are defenseless. With her last breath she encourages her people to resist. She was an actual historical figure, whom Haida history obviously remembered as heroic. The story of the shipboard and shoreside battle on June 16, 1791, that resulted in her death as well as those of many other Indians is related in an Old New England ballad. The novel is an attempt to give "the other side" of the story.

MACDONALD, CAROLINE, New Zealand editor and author of science fiction and fantasy novels for young people. She grew up in Taranaki, New Zealand, has worked as an accountant, and, more recently, as an editor for a university press in Australia. Her first novel, *Elephant Rock** (Hodder, 1983), a sensitive time-slip fantasy, won the New Zealand Esther Glen Award. She was granted the Choysa Bursary for Children's Writers, during which time she wrote *Visitors** (Hodder, 1984), an absorbing story of a boy who is contacted by beings from outer space through his television screen. It won the New Zealand Government Award. *The Lake at the End of the World* (Hodder, 1988), has also been highly honored. Macdonald has also written a picture book, *Joseph's Boat* (Hodder, 1988).

MACKAY, CLAIRE (1930–   ), born in Toronto, Canada; social worker and novelist. She is a graduate of the University of Toronto and studied further at the University of British Columbia and the University of Manitoba. Her novels typically deal with conflicts that the teenage protagonists must face and moral choices they must make. Her first, *Mini-Bike Hero* (Scholastic, 1974), concerns a boy with a passionate interest in mini-bikes, an interest that he must conceal from his father. This has been followed by two sequels, *Mini-Bike Racer* (Scholastic, 1975) and *Mini-Bike Rescue* (Scholastic, 1982). In *Exit Barney McGee* (Scholastic, 1979) the conflict is triggered by the remarriage of a boy's mother, a change that prompts him to run away to find his alcoholic father. *The Minerva Program* (Lorimer, 1984) stars a girl who lacks self-confidence until she is chosen for a special computer class. *One Proud Summer** (Women's, 1981), which Mackay wrote in collaboration with Marsha Hewitt*, is a departure from her usual subject matter, for it is about the 1946 strike in a Quebec textile mill. It won the Ruth Schwartz Children's Book Award and received honorable mention for the Canada Council prize.

MACKENZIE, WILLIAM LYON (*Rebels Ride at Night**), historical figure who led the Reformers, a group of settlers and city workers opposed to the corruption and high-handed practices of the leading Toronto citizens in the 1830s. Mackenzie is shown as a charismatic speaker, a fearless fighter for justice, but such a poor organizer that no provision has been made to supply his followers and no other realistic plans are made. Frank Sanford also sees Mackenzie in his printing shop, where he is quietly absorbed in writing and setting up his newspaper, surrounded by books, a gentle, thoughtful man.

MAGPIE ISLAND (Thiele*, Colin, ill. Roger Haldane, Rigby, 1974; Collins, 1975), short realistic animal novel set at an unspecified modern time on an island off South Australia. The story, based on research into the ways of the Australian magpie and told in retrospect by a knowledgeable, perceptive human, is quickly summarized. A young magpie, called Magpie, is caught by an intense north wind while he and some other magpies are attempting to drive an eagle from their area. He is deposited on an isolated island on the edge of the fishing grounds where he manages to survive. One day a tuna boat, the *Windhover*, captained by practical, capable Benbow Bates, puts in to mend nets. Benbow's son, Benny, 10, spots the bird sitting lonely and dejected in a she-oak, and a year later, at Benny's suggestion, the *Windhover* returns with Mate to ease Magpie's loneliness. A period of bliss follows for the two birds, and the island rings with Magpie's song. The following spring Magpie and Mate await the hatching of two eggs, when one day Mate is caught in the updraft of a spotter plane that buzzes the island and is killed, her body thrown into the sea. When they return and find Magpie alone, Benny's father advises against another try at supplying the bird with a companion, saying simply that the bird seems destined to be alone, as are some people, that his boat will not come here again because they will be fishing to the east, and that they should view the bird as a symbol, the "everlasting picture of the one against the world." The straightforward linear plot employs little dialogue and then only by the father and the son. The narrative is liberally laced with descriptive passages whose sensory diction vividly pictures the rugged island and makes the reader feel the weather of the changing seasons and the bird's isolation. Magpie is not anthropomorphized or sentimentalized. The writer occasionally speculates on motives ("Perhaps they [the magpies] thought he [the eagle] was coming to rob them of their food. . . . ''), and the loneliness, affection, and other emotions attributed to the bird would be those easily deduced from appearance and behavior. A legendary quality comes from the mostly somber tone and from the introduction of the symbolism at the end, but the dialogue projects a contemporary note, and occasional humor, almost incongruous given the circumstances, also lessens the old-legendary mood: "He was marooned. A castaway. Robinson Crusoe Magpie." Late twentieth-century attitudes toward wildlife would dictate another conclusion and would suggest at least another try at helping the bird if not by the fishermen then by the wildlife service. Possibly an interdict against buzzing would be issued and another magpie would be introduced on the island. Magnificent full-color, full-page and two-page wildlife paintings and smaller black-and-white drawings liberally interspersed throughout the text make this an especially attractive book. Aust. Bk. of Year Com.

MAHY, MARGARET (1936–   ), born in Whakatane, New Zealand; librarian and prolific writer of fiction for children and adolescents. Educated at the University of Auckland, she received her diploma of librarianship in 1958 and became director of School Library Services in Christchurch, N.Z., until 1976, and then children's librarian at Canterbury Public Library. Now a full-time writer, she has created scripts for television and films as well as written stories, novels, and poems for young readers. A story her father told about a lion lingered in her memory and eventually formed her first published book, the picture storybook *A Lion in the Meadow* (Dent, 1969; Watts, 1969). In rapid order, the Watts company published several of her other stories in picture-book form. Some four dozen books followed, stories for picture books, collections of short stories, longer stories for beginning readers, and novels of fantasy and the supernatural for middle and teenaged readers. All show lively imagination, the courage to be different, a liking for the bizarre in character and incident, and a spirited command of language. Two novels received the Carnegie Medal: *The Haunting** (Dent, 1982; Atheneum, 1982), an amusing story for middle readers that also won the New Zealand Esther Glen Award of the New Zealand Library Association, in which a shy eight year old receives frightening telepathic messages; and for teens, *The Changeover: A Supernatural Romance** (Dent, 1984; Atheneum, 1984), which also appears on the Fanfare and *Boston Globe–Horn Book* Honor lists. It is a suspenseful and surprising account of a girl who uses her latent supernatural powers to save her younger brother from demonic possession. Mahy's other publications include *The First Margaret Mahy Story Book: Stories and Poems* (Dent, 1972), which also received the New Zealand Esther Glen Award; *The Catalogue of the Universe** (Dent, 1985; Atheneum, 1986), a tightly knit realistic story that revolves around a girl's search for her father, which was named to the Fanfare list of notable books; *Aliens in the Family* (Methuen, 1986; Scholastic, 1985), a science fiction novel; *The Tricksters* (Dent, 1986; Atheneum, 1986), a suspenseful story about a family on holiday visited and threatened by three sinister young men; *Memory** (Dent, 1987; McElderry, 1988), an engrossing novel about the unlikely friendship between a troubled teenaged boy and an elderly woman with Alzheimer's disease that won the Young Observer Teenage Fiction Prize; the nonsensical farce *The Blood and Thunder Adventure on Hurricane Peak* (Dent, 1989; McElderry, 1989); and *The Tin Can Band and Other Poems* (Dent, 1989).

MAJOR CALDWELL (*Family at The Lookout**), old retiree from the British army who lives in an isolated house in the bush and raises bulldogs. Strongly prejudiced against foreigners, he is not even civil to the decent Vermeers, and he has cut himself off from his own son because the young man works for the United Nations. He is also scornful of artists, whom he considers unmanly, but he respects Mark for defending his father. In two crises, when Lindy sprains her ankle and in the bush fire, the Major, though about seventy, works doggedly to aid the Weatherall family. His respect for Joss Vermeer's hard work and his rapport with dogs begins to break down his prejudice against the foreign-born, and Bill Weatherall's efforts as a volunteer fire fighter shake his convictions about artists.

MAJOR, KEVIN (1949–   ), born in Stephenville, Newfoundland, Canada; teacher and writer. He was graduated from Memorial University in St. John's and began teaching high school in small Newfoundland towns. He compiled his first published work, *Doryloads* (Breakwater, 1974), an anthology of Newfoundland fiction and poetry, to provide his students with material about their own history and culture. In 1976 he gave up full-time teaching to write and soon established a reputation as a realistic and honest chronicler of teenage life and trauma on his home island. Of his first five novels, four have won major recognition. *Hold Fast** (Clarke, 1978; Delacorte, 1980), a story of a fourteen-year-old boy displaced from his rural home by the death of his father to live with a domineering uncle in the city, was a winner of the Canadian Book of the Year Award, the Ruth Schwartz Award, and the Canada Council Prize. *Far from Shore** (Clarke, 1980), about family disintegration after the father must leave the island to get work, won the Young Adult Book Award and received honorable mention for the Canada Council prize. *Dear Bruce Springsteen** (Doubleday, 1987), uses a more generic setting and concerns a teenager who finds solace in writing to his musical idol when his parents are separating and divorcing. It was named a runner-up for the Young Adult Book Award. *Blood Red Ochre* (Doubleday, 1989) has also been critically acclaimed. Although Major's novels have been controversial and have even been banned in some places for their blunt language and frankness about sex, drinking, and drug use, they do not exploit these concerns sensationally and are notable for their inventive style and convincing use of Newfoundland speech patterns.

MAMA'S GOING TO BUY YOU A MOCKINGBIRD (Little*, Jean, Viking, 1984), realistic problem novel with boy's growing-up story aspects set in Riverside, Ontario, Canada, for six months about the time of publication. In June, the Talbot children, responsible Jeremy, 11, the protagonist, and little tagalong Sarah*, 7, go to stay with prim, bossy Aunt Margery Talbot at the family lakeside cottage while their sixth-grade teacher father, Adrian, is hospitalized for an important operation. Both are puzzled and distressed when they hear that their father has a "fifty-fifty chance." When their mother, Melly*, and Adrian join them at the cottage, Jeremy in particular is disappointed because Adrian is too weak and tired to spend time with him, though they do view an owl together, birding being a shared interest. Adrian also shops for a small polished stone owl that he presents to Jeremy and that the boy cherishes and names Hoot. One rainy day, when the four are alone in the cottage, Dad confides to the children that he has cancer, and a little later, he asks Jeremy to befriend Tess* Medford, one of his former students who is Jeremy's age, because he says that he won't be back. He says that Tess is a gifted singer, is lonely, and is in need of a friend. Jeremy rejects the suggestion, continues to feel left out and unneeded, and asks again for a dog, though he knows that's impossible. When, however, the owner of the trailer park nearby comes with two abandoned kittens, Dad sees to it that Jeremy gets the little dark one and Jeremy names it Blue. Back in Riverside, Adrian is hospitalized again, disrupting the children's routine. Jeremy also finds school uncomfortable sometimes because the students' attitudes show that they know that Adrian is dying, and one teacher asks tactless questions. Gradually, however, he forms a friendship with Tess, which deepens after he helps her drive off three bullies who are tormenting a calico kitten and she finds Blue when the kitten runs away. He learns that she feels unwanted because her mother abandoned her, leaving her with her Grandpa. Jeremy copes manfully with the funeral, though afterward he goes through a cantankerous period. Then Melly announces that she's going back to school to finish her degree, that the children will have to help more with everyday tasks, and that they will have to move to an apartment. When Tess's Grandpa's upstairs apartment becomes vacant, the Talbots move in. The two families soon merge, Sarah almost immediately adopting Grandpa as her own, and Grandpa helping Melly occasionally with the cooking and "grandfathering" them all. Jeremy takes an interest again in bird-watching and helps Tess fit in better in school, where she gets an alto solo in the Christmas program. The story ends on Christmas morning, with Jeremy filling Melly's stocking with several small but very personal items. The Talbots miss their father but are trying to have good lives without him. The family's attempts to come to grips with the loss of their father are sensitively presented, unsentimental, non-didactic, and completely believable. The conversation is natural, and the home scenes are vividly typical of an educated, upper middle-class family. The reactions of friends and relatives toward terminal illness and death seem typical. Jeremy's character exhibits the big-little perspective of the pre-adolescent. His on-off feelings for his little sister, his avoidance of Tess and the subsequent guilt, his understanding and acceptance of what his parents are experiencing and yet his need to be a little boy are naturally and perceptively presented. Jeremy and Tess's problems are ineptly knit, and for a while the focus of the story shifts to Tess, whose problems serve to help Jeremy to deal with his. Hoot obviously symbolizes Adrian's love, and the title signifies the mother's new position now that the father is dead. Can. Bk. of Year Winner; Can. Ruth Schwartz.

MANLEY, RUTH, Australian specialist on Japanese folklore and author of fantasies. As she was deeply interested in Japanese culture, Manley returned to university studies in middle life to study the Japanese language and became especially interested in the folklore and mythology, which she describes as "the richest, the most diverse and fascinating in the world." Her first novel, *The Plum-Rain Scroll** (Hodder, 1978), which won the Australian Book of the Year Award, is an episodic quest story employing characters from this mythology in a lighthearted, often humorous way. Sequels are *The Dragon Stone* (Hodder, 1982) and *The Peony Lantern* (Hodder, 1987).

THE MAP-MAKER: THE STORY OF DAVID THOMPSON (Wood*, Kerry, ill. William Wheeler, Macmillan, 1957; St. Martin's, 1958), fictionalized account of the life of historical David Thompson, "the greatest land geographer the world has ever known." The son of a poverty-stricken Welsh widow, in 1784 at the age of fourteen David leaves the London boarding school for promising boys he attends for an apprenticeship with the Hudson Bay Company in Rupert's Land on Hudson Bay in Canada. He soon shows the resourcefulness, intelligence, loyalty, bravery, and love of adventure that will result in an outstanding career. At age sixteen, he accompanies an expedition up the Saskatchewan River to establish Mountain House trading post among the Cree, and at age seventeen he heads an embassy of six men to the warlike, independent Piegans and spends the winter with the Indians by himself. Shortly thereafter, he learns geographical science under surveyor Philip Turnor and conceives the ambition, eventually fulfilled, of mapping British America. His apprenticeship over, he signs on with the Hudson Bay Company as a bona fide employee and establishes posts and finds a shorter route to fur-rich Lake Athabaska with the help of Chipewyans, among other responsibilities and feats. David leaves the company at the end of his second term of service, having completed thirteen years, and joins their chief competitor, the North West Company, with whom he spends the rest of his active career, becoming a full partner. He locates the forty-ninth parallel, now the boundary between the United States and Canada, and opens several posts in west and northwest Canada. He marries Charlotte Small, the half-Indian daughter of a trader, and she and their children accompany him on his extensive travels. The culmination of his career is the discovery and mapping of the Columbia River, though he is disappointed that John Jacob Astor's Pacific Fur Company ship arrives at the rivers' mouth before he does. During the War of 1812, he accepts a commission as an officer, then settles at Terrebonne, Quebec, where he prepares a trading map that provides the details of over a million and a half square miles of territory and surveys the eastern boundary of Canada from the St. Lawrence River to the Lake of the Woods west of Lake Superior. In his late fifties, Koo-Koo-Sint, "the man who looks at stars," as the Indians call him, retires to do private surveying in Williamstown, Ontario. In later life he suffers from poverty and blindness but still prepares a narrative of his explorations before dying in Montreal on February 10, 1857, at age eighty-seven. Based upon Thompson's own journals and other writings, the novel catches the attention well at the beginning and has some exciting and well-drawn scenes, as when David staves off a Piegan attack at Kootenay House near Lake Windermere. For the most part, however, the author seems so intent on tracing every trip and including every worthwhile contribution David Thompson made to science and the opening of the west that the book reads more like history than either biography or fiction. Characterization is minimal; the author tells the reader how to feel about David rather than showing what he is like. The many historical figures with whom David associates, both explorers and company executives, are so underdeveloped that they are mere names. Descriptions of the territory David traversed are often loving and vivid, and the reader catches the man's incredible devotion to his work and the difficulties and hardships he and other explorers and traders faced from both humans and nature. Can. Gov. General's Winner.

MARILLA CUTHBERT (*Anne of Green Gables**), elderly owner, with her brother, Matthew*, of the farm called Green Gables in Avonlea on Prince Edward Island. Marilla is a stern, proper, no-nonsense woman, who is determined not to spoil Anne* Shirley or indulge her whims. Marilla is conscious of appearances and wants the approval of her friends and neighbors, but she also has a strong sense of fairness and sometimes takes Anne's part even against her friends. Occasionally she is too strict and frugal, for example, not wanting Anne to go to "concerts" (readings and recitations) and to dress in the new fashion, but she gradually sorts out what is important from what is insignificant and is gratified to see Anne develop into a responsible and respected young woman able to earn her own living. Marilla is one of the best developed figures in the novel, and she appears in many outstanding scenes.

MARION (*Displaced Person**), teenaged girl whom Jamie has found and taken in. Although she argues bitterly with Jamie, she is very dependent on him and at first not too willing to let Graeme share their life. On their last night together, she tells Graeme about her past, of growing up in a conservative family, hating school, dropping out at fifteen, running away from home, getting in trouble with the law, and ending up in a Salvation Army farm not far from the city. The next morning she is gone, just as Jamie was gone earlier. They have developed no theory about where things or people go when they disappear from Limbo, but Graeme finds himself in his own home with no memory of the experience, so perhaps Jamie and Marion have also returned to the real world.

MARK GUNNING (*The Sun Horse**), eleven-year-old orphan who goes to live with his uncle and aunt in western Canada and makes friends with Giselle* Martin. Mark is a spirited youth, who courageously stands up to taunts at school and who gets the idea of looking for the fabled Sun Horse. Mark's fear, resentment, and reluctance to live with relatives he hardly knows are convincing in the first part of the book, but after that events and figures lose credibility.

MARK KERR (*To the Wild Sky**), eleven-year-old brother of Colin*, asked to Gerald* Hennessy's birthday party as a courtesy, even though he is about three years younger than the others. A hyperactive, noisy boy, Mark often annoys grown-ups and older children, and Jim Butler, the bush pilot taking the group to the Hennessy sheep station, spots him immediately as a potential troublemaker and promptly makes him tow the line. Mark is the only boy who isn't a great admirer of Carol* Bancroft, who has treated him scornfully. He is the first one to wake on the beach and to spot Jim's body, but he is afraid to say anything about it. At the end, he is with Jan* Martin when the stick she has been patiently twirling begins to glow, and he feeds it dry grass to start the fire. Because of his age difference from the other youngsters, Mark represents a different attitude toward their accident, with less realization of the potentially fatal situation and more sense of adventure.

MARK TRUELANCE (*Longtime Passing**), Edwin* and Letty's* eldest child and sober, serious, responsible only son. Ironically, Edwin, who is characteristically open and generous, fails to see Mark's good qualities and often belittles him. Mark perseveres, however, becomes a surveyor, and later returns to the mountains to join the family business. The author leaves undeveloped the story potential of the tension between father and son, probably sticking to biographical fact.

MARNA (*Master of the Grove**), old Witch of Sone, who manipulates Derin, erases his memory, makes him lame, and accompanies him on a quest to find and rescue his supposed father, Ardelan. She continually derides Derin, making him believe that he has been self-centered, lazy, and ungrateful all his life and that he fled when the soldiers attacked their upland home rather than try to defend his father. She vacillates from grumbling bad temper to cunning, with rare gestures of affection, and she resists telling Derin more than the bare details forced from her. She does, however, appear to feel genuine grief at the death of Obin, and she detours on their journey to take warnings to isolated communities of woodlanders, urging them to stay hidden in case of major war and so to remain outposts of sanity in a mad world. She admits that she was once Obin's student and that he turned her away for being too violent and ambitious until she learned humility. The staff that Derin uses as a crutch, a minor staff of power, she stole from Obin. In the end she accompanies Derin to the cave to teach him and Asti the knowledge of the Witch People.

THE MARROW OF THE WORLD (Nichols*, Ruth, ill. Trina Schart Hyman, Macmillan, 1972; Atheneum, 1972), serious time and quest fantasy that begins and ends in the world of reality in the late 1960s. Responsible, accommodating, teenaged Philip is spending the summer with his adopted cousin, reserved, self-willed Linda, and her parents at their lakeshore cottage in a remote forested area. One day the youths discover what appear to be the ruins of a castle on the lake floor. Determined to explore, Linda persuades Philip to accompany her on a night rowboat excursion during which they encounter a merman. Unable to find their way home, they spend the night on the beach and awaken in the morning to find themselves by a lake in another time dimension. Herne, a kind hunter dressed in skins, takes them upstream in his carac through a ghostly, marshy woods. Leading them is a mysterious Power embodied in the form of a large, gray wolf. Separated from Herne by the Power, the youths continue upstream in the carac until it runs aground. They go by foot to a hollowed-out tree, within which is the palatial dwelling of Ygernac, a mysterious personage who appears aged and haggard and tells them that she is Linda's half-sister. She informs Linda that both are the daughters of Morgan the Enchantress, a witch who was slain by the powerful Kyril, king of the land, but unlike Ygernac, Linda is half-human, the daughter of a mortal huntsman. Ygernac says that if they secure for her the Marrow of the World, an indigo-blue substance that will make her young again, she will send them back to their own dimension. The quest leads them to the underwater city, where once Morgan had her palace and which is now inhabited by the Merpeople, to brigands, from whom Herne rescues them, and to the dwarfs who live in the mountains. One dwarf leads Linda far inside the mountains to the deep desolation of eternity where the dwarfs keep the precious Marrow. Realizing that Linda's inherited powers of sorcery are enabling them to overcome obstacles but are also making her susceptible to the witch's evil, Philip flees for help to King Kyril. Kyril advises Philip, who arrives just in time to rescue his cousin from death at the hands of Ygernac, who needs Linda's blood to activate the Marrow. Philip destroys Ygernac with fire, the only element she cannot withstand, and decides to return to the world of reality. Linda has come to see that she has depths of compassion and love inherited from her mortal father that bind her to the world of humans and also returns. Both awaken on the bank of their lake. Linda thinks that the experience was a dream, but Philip has marks on his wrists from Kyril's grip that indicate otherwise. Folklore and modern fantasy motifs are woven into the story, but the characters are the types usually found in the genre, and the plot seems strained, filled with coincidence, and thesis oriented. Events move rapidly, however, and the formal dialogue supports the far-off-time atmosphere. The theme is obvious: the triumph of good, as exemplified by the power of love and selflessness, over evil, as represented by disregard for life, abuse of power, and selfishness. Although he is otherwise colorless, the story is told from Philip's vantage point, and the author conveys Philip's feelings adequately. Can. Bk. of Year Winner.

MARTIN, DAVID (1915–   ), born in Budapest, Hungary; Australian writer of prose and poetry for both adults and children noted for his sympathetic treatment of those considered different from mainstream society. After receiving his education in Germany and serving with the International Brigade in Spain during the Civil War and as a foreign correspondent, he settled in Australia and turned to writing full time. His earliest publications were poems and novels for adults. The best known of the fiction, this one also appreciated by younger readers, is *The Young Wife* (Macmillan, 1962), a novel about a Greek woman in Melbourne. His first juvenile book, *Hughie*** (Nelson, 1971; St. Martin's, 1971), was commended for the Australian Book of the Year Award. About racial discrimination against Aborigines, it grew out of real incidents and situations he observed when he lived in a small settlement in New South Wales where his wife taught in a rural school. After *Hughie* came a dozen more books for young readers, one of poetry, the others novels. His novel *The Chinese Boy* (Hodder, 1973; Brockhampton, 1973) deals with the plight of Chinese gold miners during the gold rush in New South Wales in the 1860s, and *The Man in the Red Turban* (Hutchinson, 1978) concerns an Indian peddler in rural Australia in the 1930s, both ethnic groups alienated from larger society. *Mister P and His Remarkable Flight* (Hodder, 1975), a novel about a plucky pigeon, made the short list for the Book of the Year. His writings stress the importance of hard work, friendship, and perseverance. For adults he also wrote plays, short stories, and non-fiction on film, television, and travel.

MARTIN GRACE (*Cannily, Cannily***), the biggest boy in the class, who shares a seat with Trevor Huon. Since he lacks only a few days of being old enough to go to the other school, he has been left behind by most of his friends and, although he is large enough to be good on the team and to hold his own with the other boys, he is lonely. He is genuinely baffled by Trevor's lack of response to his insults and derision and his unwillingness or inability to defend himself in kind. In his own home, it is apparent that his father has ambitions for him in sports that he does not share wholeheartedly. Gradually he gains respect for Trevor's stubborn determination and almost becomes a friend to Trevor, as much of a friend as anyone in the country town.

MASTER OF THE GROVE (Kelleher*, Victor, Kestrel, 1982), sword-and-sorcery fantasy set in a medieval culture in an unspecified time and world. When Derin, 14, wakes and finds himself in the snow, his head bruised from a blow, he can remember nothing of his past. With difficulty, since his right foot will not bear his weight, he makes his way out of the woods to the smoldering ruins of a farmhouse, where an old woman with long unkempt hair, dressed in a ragged cloak, greets him bitterly, accusing him of running away rather than staying to help protect his father. Grumbling and berating him for lifelong laziness and selfishness, she grudgingly tells him that she is Marna*, who came to help care for him when his mother died some twelve years before and that his father, Ardelan, an upland farmer, has been captured and pressed into service by the soldiers of the Council. When Derin calmly decides that he must follow and try to rescue his father, Marna produces a crutch, which she says is his, and with a show of unwillingness says she will go with him. He picks up an old, long-bladed dagger, rusty with its edges badly hacked, a poor weapon but the best he can find among the rubbish of the burned house. Gradually, as they flounder through deep drifts and labor to the south, she tells him bits, never full explanations or much about his own past, but enough so that he can piece together the situation; an ancient enmity between the Council of Iri-Nan, on the plains, and the Circle of the Grove, in the mountains, has erupted and a devastating war threatens as occurred many years in the past. When peace finally came, the ruler, Wenborn the Wise, arranged that war could only be declared by unanimous vote of either group, each made up of ten members bound by sacred oaths, but that only nine should be known. The tenth should always remain secret and living apart, so that war could not come again to the land. Something has obviously disturbed that equilibrium, though Marna will not voice her suspicions as to what that might be. Together they go through a series of exciting adventures involving strange, blank-eyed bowmen, a search for an ancient sword and staff of power, a villain named Krob*, the discovery that the Wiseman Obin has been killed in his cave, and the meeting with his great-granddaughter, a beautiful witch girl named Asti, and various captures and escapes. The action culminates in the Circle of the Grove, of which all members are like zombies except Krob. He tells Derin that Marna has deceived him about everything in an effort to get the ancient staff for herself, and he almost convinces Derin by reversing the spell that she put on him to make him lame. Derin doubts Krob's accusations, however, and in a final confrontation pulls out his own dagger, which proves to be the true Sword of the Kings and which destroys the Staff. The dagger is consumed in the effort. With the great symbols of power gone, Krob has lost his control and the zombie-like people wake up. Derin realizes that Marna has deliberately kept him ignorant of the true purpose of their journey, to destroy the staff and the sword, because Krob could read his mind at a distance, and that his own crutch is a staff of power, smuggled along with the Sword of the Kings into the Grove with his ignorance as a shield against Krob's mind probing. Back in the uplands, Derin helps Ardelan rebuild the house, then slowly realizes that his place is in the cave, where Asti is waiting for him, since he is the successor to Obin as tenth member of the Circle of the Grove. Although it is highly derivative of Tolkien novels and others of the genre, the story is compelling and the action keeps the reader's interest, with an urgent tone and good concrete detail of the journey's difficulties. Some of the loose ends are not well tied up; what was Derin's life before the attack in the snow? Does he ever get back his memory, which was stolen by Marna? How does he happen to be the tenth member of the Circle? Only two characters, Derin and Marna, are well developed, Marna being the more interesting. Aust. Bk. of Year Winner.

MATAS, CAROL (1949–   ), Canadian novelist for children who lives in Winnipeg, Manitoba. She received the Geoffrey Bilson Award for Historical Fiction for Young People for *Lisa** (Lester, 1987; *Lisa's War*, Scribner's, 1989), a novel about the mass evacuation of Danish Jews to Sweden during the German occupation of Denmark in the fall of 1943. Its sequel is *Jesper* (Lester, 1989; *Code Name Kris*, Scribner's, 1990). She has also published *The DNA Dimension* (Gage, 1982), *The Fusion Factor* (Fifth, 1986), *Zanu* (Fifth, 1986), and *Me, Myself, and I* (Fifth, 1987).

MATHINNA'S PEOPLE (Chauncy*, Nan, ill. Victor G. Ambrus, Oxford, 1967; *Hunted in Their Own Land*, Seabury, 1973), historical novel set in Tasmania mainly among the Poynduc tribe of the Toogee people of the western part of the island. It traces the events of the some one hundred fifty years that lead up to their extinction from the time the Dutch arrive under Abel Tasman in 1642. The Stone Age Poynducs live satisfying lives. They are close to nature, their spirits, and one another and are secure in their ancient customs and beliefs. One day Chief Wyrum, exploring the eastern mountains, spots what looks to him like whales with butterfly wings on their backs, which swim toward shore and then leave. He reports the phenomenon in dance and song at a *korobarra*, a tribal gathering for the full moon, a story-dance that lives on in legend among the tribes. A little later some members of the Loonty, a neighboring people, also see the ships and men who land and plant a strange stick with some kind of cloth affixed to the top. Generations pass without further incident, and when Wyrum has long been dead, the Poynduc learn of another landing of the *num*, as the whites become known. The story now follows the fortunes of a young Poynduc, Towterer, who grows to manhood hearing about how the *num* are growing numerous. He observes them one day by a lagoon killing swans and chopping down trees, which are sacred to his people. When Towterer's father objects, they kill him and others with their "magic sticks." Towterer marries a young woman from a neighboring tribe, Wongerneep, becomes chief, and tries to live a normal existence. The English, however, send "the good white man," as some tribes call him, George Augustus Robinson, to move the Aborigines to Wybalenna (Flinders) Island, off the north shore of Tasmania. Towterer and his people resist for months but are finally hunted down. Misery awaits the Poynducs on Wybalenna. They suffer from cold, inadequate or improper food, unsanitary living conditions, disease, and culture shock. Their pleas to be allowed to return home are rejected with scorn and ironic assertions of surprise that they are not delighted with the homes provided for them. One daughter dies, and Towterer and Wongerneep have another, whom Robinson ironically names Mary. After Towterer, now called Romeo, and Wongerneep, renamed Queen Eveline (names the two hate) die, the new governor of what is now known as Van Dieman's Land, Sir John Franklin, and Lady Franklin take Mary in and rename her Mathinna, or "necklace." Mathinna soon dies, too, but leaves behind a reputation for sweetness, gentleness, and kindness. Soon there are no Tasmanian tribespeople alive. The impact of this quietly told, intensely tragic story comes from the reader's knowledge that, though fictionalized, the basic facts are true for much of the information comes from Robinson's own journal. The plot is slow, sometimes tedious, and unbalanced. The several main characters are undeveloped and almost interchangeable, and barely two pages are given to Mathinna. The descriptions of Aborigine ways and beliefs are vivid and completely believable as presented, and the point of view is unerringly that of the native people, making this a bitter indictment of their treatment. Sharp irony pervades many scenes and increases the tragedy of this account of the demise of a once proud and dignified people. Aust. Bk. of Year Com.

MA TREGARREN (*The Devil's Stone**), about twenty-one years of age, fond stepmother of Emma Rose and Lauralei Tregarren, solicitous mother of little Patrick, and loving wife of Father Tregarren. An Irish orphan girl of about nineteen, she met her husband while they were on the boat emigrating from the British Isles to Australia. She had hoped to find a job as a serving girl or dairy maid but married him instead. Although she feels intimidated by the wilderness, she never complains, works very hard, and manages their survival when Father leaves for the gold fields. She has another baby, little Sarah, while he is gone. She gives birth to Sarah while Lauralei fetches a neighbor woman to help and is assisted by Emma Rose. At the end, she is considerably more self-assured, her many responsibilities having matured her. She is a strong woman and the most interesting character in the novel.

MATTHEW CUTHBERT (*Anne of Green Gables**), elderly owner, with his sister, Marilla*, of the farm called Green Gables in Avonlea on Prince Edward Island. He sensibly sometimes intervenes between Anne* Shirley and Marilla. He urges Anne to apologize to Mrs. Rachel Lynde for losing her temper and being saucy, and the passages in which he insists Anne have more fashionable dresses, with puffed sleeves, and arranges for the fabric and sewing are among the most memorable in the book. Matthew is steady, hardworking, warmhearted, reliable, and loyal to a fault. He keeps the Cuthbert money in the local bank because that is where the Cuthberts have always put their money, even though he knows that the bank is on the brink of ruin. When the bank fails and he realizes that all their money is gone, he has a heart attack and dies. His death is a hard blow for Anne because she loves him very much. Matthew is a winning figure, a good contrast to Marilla and ballast for Anne.

MATTINGLEY, CHRISTOBEL (1931–), born in Adelaide, South Australia; librarian, social worker, author best known for her books for eight-to-ten-year-old readers. Her father's work as a civil engineer moved the family a number of times, from the seacoast of South Australia to Sydney, to Tasmania. Mattingley was educated at Presbyterian Ladies College at Pymble, New South Wales, at The Friends' School in Hobart, Tasmania, and at the University of Tasmania. She studied further at the Public Library of Victoria Training College and later served as a librarian in Canberra, in Latrobe Valley, Victoria, in England, and at schools and colleges in Adelaide. Her many publications include picture books, plays, works of non-fiction like *Survival in Our Own Land: Aboriginal Experience in South Australia, 1836–1985* (Wakefield, 1986), and some novels for older children, among them *New Patches for Old* (Hodder, 1977), a story about problems of immigrants, which arose from her work for the Department of Immigration when the end of World War II brought a wave of displaced persons to Australia. Her most popular books, however, have been domestic adventures of young people like *Windmill at Magpie Creek** (Hodder, 1971), in which a farm boy overcomes his fear of heights. It was highly commended for the Book of the Year Award. *Worm Weather* (Hamilton, 1971), received favorable mention for the same award, and both it and *Emu Kite* (Hamilton, 1972) were reprinted in the Young Australia Enrichment Readers.

MCFADYEN, ELLA, born near Sydney, New South Wales, Australia; journalist and author for children. After her schooling, she contributed nature articles and verses to Sydney papers, wrote for *The Red Cross Record* during World War I, and then wrote for children and young people for the Sydney *Mail* for twenty years. *Pegmen Tales** (Angus, 1946), the lively fantasy adventures of a family of peg (clothespin) people, began as a daily serial, was dramatized for radio, and was commended for the Australian Children's Book of the Year Award. *Pegmen Go Walkabout* (Angus, 1947), its sequel, *Little Dragons of the Never Never* (Angus, 1949), *The Wishing Star* (Angus, 1956), *The Big Book of Pegmen Tales* (Angus, 1959), selected adventures from the previous Pegmen books, and *Outland Born, and Other Verses* (Aust., 1911) are among her other publications.

MCNAIR, W(ILLIAM) A(LLEN), Australian author of *Starland of the South** (Angus, 1950), which was highly commended for the Australian Library Association Book of the Year Award. It is an informational book, thinly disguised as fiction, about the constellations and planets of the southern hemisphere and the myths associated with them. Illustrations show the night sky with mythological figures.

MCRAE, RUSSELL (1934–), Canadian high school English teacher in Thunder Bay, Ontario, whose novel about life among contemporary teenagers in a small community in northern Ontario, *Going to the Dogs** (Viking, 1987), received honorable mention for the Governor General's Literary Award.

ME AND JESHUA (Spence*, Eleanor, Dove, 1984), historical novel set in an unnamed land that sounds like ancient Palestine, mainly in the years Jesus would have been nine to twelve. Late in life, Jude Bar Asaph tells how he meets and becomes very close to his father's sister's son, Jeshua Bar Josef (probably Jesus). Jude begins his account with stories told to him by his grandfather, Yakim, about family history, then skips to his own boyhood. Impulsive, dreamy Jude is the second child of the three sons and three daughters of a well-off merchant in the Town of Branches (probably Nazareth). Loving Aunt Miriam, understanding, hardworking Uncle Josef, and gentle, good-humored, bright Jeshua, 9, arrive, having lived for some time in Egypt, and move in with Jude's family until Josef can fix up a woodworking shop. Jude and Jeshua, an only child, soon become fast friends. They attend school together, where Jeshua proves apt, and go on trips to the Great Lake (Sea of Galilee?) and into the mountains with Josef for wood, where they are appalled to observe Roman soldiers slaughtering an entire camp of rebels against Rome. When he thinks about it, which is only now and then, Jude is perplexed about the "strange and uncomfortable" rumors about Miriam and Jeshua, in particular, that Josef isn't Jeshua's "real" father. The little family thrives, but Jeshua must quit school to help Josef in the shop. The plot ambles along with mostly mundane details and Jude's ponderings and descriptions of everyday life, but because so much emphasis is placed on a boy's being fitted for his life's profession, tension grows as both boys approach coming-of-age and the Passover trip to the City of the Holy Mountain (probably Jerusalem) when Jeshua is twelve. While Jude likes writing, words, stories, and maps and may become a writer or scribe, Jeshua says he wants to "make people well, and give them food, and be there when they need someone" and that his "father" will tell him how he can manage this. The story culminates with Jeshua's visit to the temple (as described in the book of Luke). When Jeshua tells Jude he has been in his father's house, Jude takes this to refer to King David. The story stops at this point, but in an epilogue, Jude reiterates his deep affection for his cousin. The author never gives the historical identity of the characters, nor is there a map to help with locations. The account is essentially episodic, since the mystery about Jeshua's parentage is mentioned periodically, but unity is achieved by the careful focus from Jude's youthful, uninformed point of view and the ironic understanding of the informed reader. The author never sentimentalizes the Holy Family, and the family is presented as very close to one another, but somewhat isolated and accepted only for what Josef contributes to the community. If Jeshua seems a little too good, a characteristic Jude ironically even discusses with him, his behavior might be explained as typical of many singletons. Some episodes seem false or forced. On one occasion, when Jude gets lost while fleeing from Roman soldiers, hides in the cellar of an abandoned house, and gets locked in, he prays fervently. Jeshua discovers him, explaining that his "father" heard Jude's prayer and sent him to rescue Jude. The author carefully preserves Jude's point of view, revealing him to be an intelligent, articulate if naive youth, growing to manhood in a turbulent era of whose issues he is only dimly aware. The story gains most of its force, however, from its vivid depiction of the times, which are drawn in clear and plentiful detail. The reader gets a strong impression of the geographical, sociological, and political environment, of, for example, the importance placed on family and honor, the dominant position and importance of males compared to females, the intense hatred of the Jews for the conquerors and the rulers chosen by the conquerors, and the hustle and bustle of the City of the Holy Mountain compared to the slower pace of the Town of the Branches. Aust. Bk. of Year Com.

MEAN HUGHIE (*Angel Square**; *Up to Low**), boyhood neighbor of Dad*, a man notorious for his brutality and his physical strength. One of the pastimes in the district is telling Mean Hughie stories. It is generally agreed that the meanest thing he ever did was to hit his little girl when she got in front of the harvesting binder causing her arm to be cut off. He and his wife, Poor Bridget, have a passel of younger children, all of whom disappear at the sight of their father. When it is apparent that he is dying of cancer, Mean Hughie buys supplies at the store and disappears, holing up to die at the deserted farm known as the old Ramsay Place. The Hummer, who is his half-brother, somehow knows his hiding place and directs Young Tommy and Baby Bridget there. They arrive as he is dying, already lying in the coffin he has built for himself. His rough apology to Baby Bridget for hitting her is convincing in the bizarre situation. He appears briefly in *Angel Square*.

MEG BAINS (*Shantymen of Cache Lake**), younger sister of John* Bains who, with him, becomes cook's helper in a remote logging camp. At thirteen, Meg is physically stronger than her fourteen-year-old brother and much more assertive. At the shanty she adjusts more rapidly than he to the grueling work, is more enthusiastic about the union organizing activity, and is insistent that she not be confined to work inside the camboose but share both the indoor and outdoor jobs with John. In the second strike, when Hardy* threatens Cameron* with a shotgun, Meg calmly steps in front, walks up to the huge foreman, and takes the gun away from him, counting on his knowledge that the entire camp of some forty men will go berserk if he shoots a young girl. Nothing is said in the novel of the difficulties a girl (and the woman cook) might have living in a single room with all these men, the lack of privacy, the embarrassments and possible sexual threats. Meg is a lively but not very convincing character.

MELLING, O. R., author of a fictionalized retelling of the story of the ancient Irish hero, Cuculann*, in *The Druid's Tune** (Kestrel, 1983; Penguin, 1984). Two modern-day siblings from Toronto are carried backward in time by a haunting melody and become embroiled in the wars between Ulster and Connaught over the fabled Brown Bull of Cuailange. A blend of high action, humor, intrigue, and poignancy, the novel received the Canadian Young Adult Award. Melling also wrote *Falling Out of Time* (Viking, 1989).

MELLY TALBOT *(Mama's Going to Buy You a Mockingbird**)*, wife of Adrian. His death produces the novel's main problem. Generally a loving and patient mother, Melly helps to cushion the tactless remarks of her sister-in-law, Aunt Margery, toward the children, since, before Adrian dies, Aunt Margery is over-protective of him and quick to find fault with the children. Melly flies off the handle, however, when tired or tense. She does more than anyone else to get Tess* to see that she really is wanted. She is a convincing and likeable character, a foil for Aunt Margery.

MEMORY (Mahy*, Margaret, Dent, 1987; McElderry, 1988), realistic psychological and sociological problem novel set for about a week in the contemporary New Zealand city of Colville. Jonny (Jonathan) Dart, 19, is a tap dancer and former child star with his sister, Janine*, of television commercials. After an argument with his father, a troubled evening at a bar, and a disagreement with the police on the fifth anniversary of Janine's death of a fall from a cliff into the sea, Jonny goes to the home of the parents of Bonny* Benedicta, Janine's best friend whom he has not seen since Janine's funeral. Jonny has been increasingly haunted by memories of Janine's death and wishes to clarify his impressions of that terrible incident by talking with the only other witness. When Bonny is not at home, a guest gives Jonny a lift to an inner-city taxi stand, where he passes out. He comes to at about three in the morning, sick and aching, and encounters in a supermarket parking lot an old woman wearing a hat like a crimson chamber pot and pushing an empty grocery cart. To insure her safety, he accompanies her to her home in the old Tap House at 113 Marribel Street in a derelict part of the city. Cheerful, friendly, senile Sophie* West, 86, lives without family or friends in wretched squalor, with more cats than Jonny has ever seen in one place. He stays with Sophie for several days while he recovers from his night at the bar. Three times he attempts to leave, and each time he is drawn back by the need to insure her well-being. Although he finds that she is terribly forgetful and often either doesn't bother to dress or gets her clothes on wrong, she likes company and enjoys serving tea, though she always forgets to add the herb. She speaks with pride about her dead husband and seems to think that Jonny is a cousin with whom she had apparently been in love many years before. He discovers that someone called Spike is preying upon her, extorting money ostensibly for rent, and that someone is stealing household items. He thinks that it may be Nev* Fowler, an old school acquaintance of shady character. He also discovers that Bonny Benedicta lives next door, now a serious university student. She suggests he contact a social worker, who says Sophie appears to exhibit the classic symptoms of Alzheimer's disease and promises to look into her situation. Jonny invites Bonny to dinner and unsuccessfully attempts to seduce her, having some notion that power over her body will also give him power over her mind and hence clarify his memories. One night Jonny overhears Nev and two henchmen planning to rob Sophie. He jumps down from Sophie's balcony upon them as they stand on the pavement below, injuring himself and incapacitating them long enough for the police to intervene. As the hectic scene sorts itself out, Bonny tells Jonny what he has longed to hear: his sister's death was indeed an accident for which he was not to blame. Six weeks later a new Jonny returns to Sophie's. He has come to terms with his parents, taken a temporary job as a construction worker, and resumed dancing lessons. He decides to move in with Sophie because he needs a place where he can be independent in order to work out his new life and she needs someone to watch over her until suitable arrangements can be made for her. Bonny agrees to watch out for Sophie, too, and Jonny hopes for a romantic relationship with Bonny. This a richly textured story of two odds-out people, one obsessed with memories, the other trying to hold on to them. It is complicated by numerous flashbacks of Jonny's befuddled recollections and by Sophie's muddled remarks, and as in a detective story, small details assume importance. Much of the book's interest comes from the bits and pieces of Jonny's past that flash through his head and are reported in italics, from Sophie's and Jonny's conversations, humorous in their non sequiturs and literal misunderstandings, and from Sophie's dementia-induced antics, that are both funny and pathetic. The urban setting gives a strong sense of the decaying inner city, and the abject squalor in which Sophie lives is made equally palpable. Sophie's dementia is never sensationalized, discussed didactically, or satirized, and she is so winningly drawn that she steals the book. When first met, Jonny is bruised, battered, and reeking of liquor, on a self-destructive course, his unlikeableness tempered only by his love for his dead sister. The decency and capacity for affection that have motivated his quest become the qualities that lead to his redemption, and in devoting himself, even though reluctantly, to Sophie's problems, he wins the reader's approval and liking. The plot's over-reliance on coincidence is more than compensated for by a vigorous, sensory style and by the skillful characterizations that create a plausible cast out of a conglomeration of eccentric figures. Young Observer.

MENIRU, TERESA, Nigerian author of *Unoma** (Evans, 1976), a brief, episodic novel of a village girl whose father, cheated because he is illiterate, vows that all his children will learn to read, even his daughter, and of her trials and adventures in getting an education. It won the Children's Literature of Nigeria First Prize for the Best Book in English for Ages 8–12. It was followed by a sequel, *Unoma in College* (Evans, 1981). Among her other writings are *The Bad Fairy and the Caterpillar and Other Stories* (Evans, 1971) and *The Melting Girl and Other Stories* (Evans, 1971), both English language reading books for non–English-speaking students.

MERCHANT, EVE, South African author of *Ghamka Man-of-Men** (Tafelberg, 1985), historical novel of a clan leader of the great Khoi-Khoin nation that once dominated southern Africa, set in the late fifteenth century when the earliest European navigators, Bartolomeu Dias and Vasco da Gama, came in contact with the people. The novel, which won the Sanlam Prize for Youth Literature, is the result of extensive research into records of the period.

MEREDITH BRENT (*The Green Laurel**), warmhearted, buoyant, generous friend of the Somerville girls. She goes from one interest to another, never settling on anything for long, a "poor little rich girl," with roots but still essentially rootless. Meredith and her brother, Richard*, are unconvincing characters, contrived to comment on contemporary life and values and act as foils to the Somervilles.

MICHAEL (*The Keeper**), senior learner in Big Lake village and, as the most intelligent of the young people, apparently destined to become the next teacher. He is an orphan, his parents having been murdered when he was three years old because his mother had a deformed arm, although he does not know this grim fact and thinks that they died of radiation sickness. Michael was saved at that time and raised by Mr. Clinton, the teacher. Because he does not take part in the hunting, which mostly supports the village, Michael is looked upon with some scorn by many of the villagers. Through observation and reading he has become something of an expert on natural history. With his knowledge and Andy's practical skills, plus the aid of both Jean* and Ora, the young people seem to have a good chance of surviving on their island. In his comment on Michael's journal, Mr. Clinton speculates that the boy may be attracted to Jean because her crippled arm reminds him in some way of his mother's deformity, and he also concludes that Sarah and Honi, who care for Michael in the loners' settlement, are probably his maternal grandparents. Michael is a figure who represents the importance of intelligence, tolerance, and respect for literature even in a society reduced to superstition and primitive living conditions.

MIDNITE: THE STORY OF A WILD COLONIAL BOY (Stow*, Randolph, ill. Joan Sandin, Macdonald, 1967; Prentice, 1968), rollicking tall tale and talking animal fantasy set from 1866 to 1870, in which several pet animals make their master the most famous bushranger in Australia. After his parents die and leave him with a cottage, orchard, and five domestic animals, Midnite, a good-natured, slow-witted youth of seventeen, takes the suggestion of Khat, his wise and handsome Siamese, that he become a bushranger. He and the animals move to Hidden Valley, where they outfit a cave as a hideout. The first night, while Midnite sleeps, Dora the cow bushranges thirty-one head of cattle, Red Ned the horse bushranges thirteen horses, Gyp the dog seventy-six sheep, and Major the cockatoo a boxful of rings, brooches, and other jewels. Since Midnite is depressed because the animals have done all his bushranging for him, Khat arranged for him to hold up the coach of portly Judge Pepper, engineering the whole maneuver from the bushes and giving rise to the legend that clever Captain Midnite has a Siamese confederate. When Midnite becomes bitter because his pocket is picked by Judge Pepper's traveling companion, Trooper* O'Grady, Khat convinces

Midnite to vent his anger by robbing, and soon Captain Midnite's gang becomes legendary. Ladies swoon upon hearing his name, Queen Victoria insists that he be captured, and O'Grady is assigned to the case. For a while Midnite eludes all attempts to capture him because he wears sheepskin shoes that leave no tracks, is masked, and rides his very swift, clever horse, Red Ned. Three times he is caught and remanded to the great grey jail by the sea, the first time because he and Khat become drunk tasting wine (which Midnite swears never to touch again), the second time by O'Grady disguised as a hairy grandmother, and the third time when Midnite is betrayed by his love, Miss Laura Wellborn. Each time the animals resourcefully ''spring'' him. Since Laura knows where the hideout is, the gang leaves Hidden Valley and moves one thousand miles inland to the desert, which Midnite names after Victoria and where he finds a huge chunk of gold, prospects, and becomes a millionaire. Calling himself Mr. Daybrake, he is so socially accepted that Queen Victoria invites him to her palace. Realizing his true identity, she orders him to stop stealing, because it is wrong, and to go home. Midnite (Daybrake) does, intending to woo Miss Laura again, and withdraws his sixteen million pounds from the bank. Trooper O'Grady holds up his coach and takes it all. The animals step in again, woo Laura for Midnite, and, when she still proves intractable, bashful Midnite finally finds the courage to stand up to her. They are married on his twenty-first birthday, after which they repair to his mine in Daybrake, where Captain Midnite and his gang, now including Laura, live happily ever after in wealth and comfort. This consistently entertaining, fast moving romp is completely without serious purpose, improvising cleverly on the Robin Hood–western outlaw–folktale traditions with never a dull moment. The characters are all twists on familiar types, Victoria is gently satirized, Khat is a brilliant sidekick strategist, and the author's witty style adds to the humor. Aust. Bk of Year Highly Com.

MIMI (*The Ice Is Coming**; *Behind the Wind**), an indigenous Australian spirit, one of the shy, frail, sticklike beings with sharp opossum-eyes and large, floppy ears that live in the cavernous, windswept rocks in northern Australia. Easily frightened and temperamental, the Mimi sneezes when she is annoyed and hisses when displeased. She provides some humor and occasionally influences the action, as well as contributing to the sense of place and atmosphere. Although she appears, she has no significant function in *Behind the Wind*.

MINISTER (*An Older Kind of Magic**), earnest official in charge of parks, who feels helpless before Sir* Mortimer Wyvern's plan to turn part of the local Botanical Gardens into a parking lot. One afternoon he goes to the gardens looking for ''hope and belief,'' encounters Selina* Potter, and, when both are shut in after hours, goes along with her wishes to depart surreptitiously through the fence. After they leave, the spirit beings frolic in their wake, giving a hint that they will eventually triumph over commerce and the area will remain in the public domain.

THE MIN-MIN (Clark*, Mavis Thorpe, Lansdowne, 1966; Macmillan, 1969), realistic sociological and psychological problem novel of contemporary family life set in the desert of southern Australia for about two weeks. The story begins at a siding of the Trans-Australian Railway among a settlement of fettlers, workers who maintain the line. Sylvie*, 14, and Reg* Edwards, 11, live with their ill mother, pregnant with her sixth child, and their troubled, often irritable father, who drinks too much and has brought his family from Sydney to this remote outpost for reasons unknown to the children. Finding her home situation intolerable and receiving no encouragement to continue the education she so much desires with Clive* Scott, the inspired young teacher at the local one-room school, Sylvie decides to run away to her friend, Mrs. Tucker, who lives with her family on the outstation of a sheep ranch. She persuades Reg, in trouble again for vandalizing the schoolhouse, to accompany her. They hop the goods (supply) train to the Gulla Siding an hour away and then trudge for three days twenty tortured miles through the desert to the Tucker station. One night, Reg sneaks out and cuts the telephone line to hinder pursuit. Although Mr. Tucker lets the children know that he intends to inform the authorities as soon as he can, the Tuckers—father, mother, and three sons—otherwise receive the children warmly. Mrs. Tucker makes Sylvie a decent dress, and the girl enjoys feeling liked and appreciated for herself alone. Fractious Reg, however, chafes under Mr. Tucker's sharp eye and strict rules. Foiled in an attempt to steal away to a friendly Aborigine, he settles in and gradually comes to enjoy a new sense of self-worth, earning praise for small successes. The cut phone line and then a rare torrential rain keep the Tuckers from returning the children right away. Later at the hearing, the children discover that their father had served time in jail for embezzlement and took the railroad job to leave behind his past. Reg is remanded to a boys' training school, but, when Mr. Edwards implores Sylvie to help him keep the family together, she reluctantly agrees but insists that they move to where she can go to school. She has acquired greater self-esteem and confidence about the future, which, like the Min-Min, a kind of Aborigine will-o'-the-wisp, keeps beckoning and retreating but lures her on anyway. The Tuckers seem too good to be true and too deliberately contrasted with the Edwards family. In spite of their morally questionable behavior, Sylvie and Reg are sympathetic characters. The rigors of their desert trek come through well, and the conclusion, if overly tidy and preachy, works satisfactorily given the options. The description of the Tuckers' life often appears intended to inform young readers about conditions in the outback. Aust. Bk. of Year Winner.

MIRYAM CARLISLE (*The Changeover**), mother of Sorry*, daughter of Winter, members of an old and established family whose land has been gradually absorbed by urban sprawl. In an attempt to protect their property, she and her mother, both witches, decided to raise a "cone of power" over their area. To do this they needed the help of a third witch, and Miryam decided to have a baby. When Sorry turned out to be a boy, disappointed Miryam put him out to foster parents who abused him. Ironically, however, Sorry had inherited her powers. Miryam helps Laura through the ritual that makes the girl a witch. Miryam and her mother are flat and unconvincingly depicted, but they and Sorry contribute most of the story's Gothic elements.

MISPLACED PERSONS. See *DISPLACED PERSON.*

MISS DALGLEISH (*The True Story of Lilli Stubeck**), wealthy spinster, Lilli's guardian. She is a cultured, well-traveled woman who is used to having her own way. Her big house is filled with statuary and paintings and her library with fine books that she encourages Lilli to read, some of which she shares with Kit* Quayle. Miss Dalgleish is a complex figure, a woman who can be cruel yet amazingly generous. She and Lilli are much alike, intensely loyal, proud, stubborn, self-contained survivors.

MISTER LEE (*The Year of the Currawong**), gentle, melancholy old Chinese man, the oldest inhabitant of Currawong Crossing. He lives in a dilapidated hut with a rusty iron roof just down the hill from the old silver mine, which he claims. He enjoys having the children to tea and showing them his quartz crystals and insists that the mine is rich. He putters about, intent on his own purposes and generally oblivious to external happenings. It is discovered that his father was a laborer there in the early part of the century. Although at the end of the story, the mine becomes public property, Mister Lee is assured the right to work it for as long as he wishes to, and the land on which his hut stands is declared legally his. He is an interesting, sympathetic character.

MITCHELL, (SIBYL) ELYNE (KEITH CHAUVEL) (1913–   ), born in Melbourne, Victoria, Australia; author best known for her popular Silver Brumby series of about a dozen wild horse stories that are based on her wilderness exploring in the Australian Alps on skis and horseback. Educated at St. Catherines School in Melbourne, she lived in England during World War I, while her father, General Harry Chauvel, served with the British forces. The war over, she returned to Australia, married Thomas Mitchell, a rancher, member of the Victoria Parliament, and Australian ski champion. They made their home on the Upper Murray River among the Snowy Mountains of the Australian Alps. She learned to ski, and the couple traveled extensively on ski trips and went on skiing adventures in their own remote and isolated region as well. Her first book, *Australian Alps* (Angus, 1942), arose from a winter spent exploring in the Snowy Mountains. When her husband was called up in World War II, she ran the ranch, recording those experiences in *Speak to the Earth* (Angus, 1945), and writing articles. More non-fiction followed and also two novels and a screenplay for adults. Her mountaineering resulted in more than a dozen novels for young readers, most of them about wild horses. Her first children's book, *The Silver Brumby** (Hutchinson, 1958; Dutton, 1959), written to provide her older daughter with reading to supplement her correspondence school lessons, was highly commended for the Australian Children's Book of the Year Award. It was followed by *Silver Brumby's Daughter** (Hutchinson, 1960; *The Snow Filly*, Dutton, 1961), also commended for the award, and several more in the Silver Brumby series. She also wrote *Winged Skis** (Hutchinson, 1964), a mystery-adventure with a sports setting that was highly commended for Book of the Year, and *Jinki, Dingo of the Snows* (Hutchinson, 1970), another wildlife story. In a slightly different vein is *Light Horse to Damascus* (Hutchinson, 1971), which is based on her father's World War I war stories about a horse in his regiment. For adults she has also written *Chauvel Country: The Story of a Great Pioneering Family* (Macmillan, 1983), *Discoverers of the Snowy Mountains* (Macmillan, 1985), and *The Lighthorsemen* (Penguin, 1987), an adaptation of a screenplay.

MONTGOMERY, L(UCY) M(AUD) (1874–1942), born in Clifton, Prince Edward Island, Canada; author whose girl's growing-up novel, *Anne of Green Gables** (Page, 1908) has classic status and was named to the Touchstones' list of important books by the Children's Literature Association (International). Montgomery's own life seems to have provided at least some of the prototype for proud, spunky, lively, nature-loving Anne* Shirley, one of the best-drawn and most memorable heroines in literature. After the death of her mother when she was two years old, Montgomery lived with her maternal grandparents in their farmhouse. She studied at Prince of Wales College in Charlottetown, P.E.I., and at Dalhousie College in Halifax, and became a teacher. She took time off to care for her grandmother, then joined the Halifax *Daily Echo*. All the while she wrote, publishing short stories and poems. *Anne of Green Gables*, her first book, was four times rejected by publishers before being accepted by L. C. Page of Boston. It sold well enough for Page to request a sequel. By the time of her marriage in 1911 to Ewan Macdonald, a Presbyterian minister, she had published three other books, among them a collection of short stories, *The Story Girl* (Page, 1911), and the sequel, *Anne of Avonlea* (Page, 1909). Before her death in Toronto, she had published altogether two dozen books, including six more about Anne; several about a heroine named Emily Starr; two novels for adults; many short stories and poems; and non-fiction. She was elected a fellow of the Royal Society of Arts and inducted into the Order of the British Empire, both in 1935.

MOON AHEAD (Greener*, Leslie, ill. Wm. Pene Du Bois, Viking, 1951), science fiction novel set in Australia and en route to and on the moon, presumably in the 1950s. Noel Durand, 15, and his father, Frank, an Australian cattleman, are hosts to Sam Halloway, 15, and his father, Brock, Americans on a camping trip from Mumjiga Station in western Queensland to the Devil's Rings, a group of meteoric craters at the most remote edge of the Durand ranch. To their astonishment, they discover bustling activity, a set of buildings, and a shiny tower, which they later learn is a space ship ready to be launched toward the moon. When they try to ride off but are quickly captured by men in trucks, they learn that this is a project of BEAMS (British-Empire-American Moon Society), kept secret because a sinister Group X is hoping to beat them to the moon and annex it for their own selfish purposes. A recent accident has left them three men short and, when they cannot procure immediate replacements, they persuade the two fathers to join the expedition, since Frank is an astronomer with flight navigation training and Brock is a radar specialist. The two boys stow away, but just before the launch they reveal themselves to the project leader, British Professor Adrean Rumbold, known as Professor Spitfire, who has foreseen their prank and keeps them aboard because they are both ham radio experts and will be valuable on the ship, which is conveniently equipped for eight. The other expedition members are the joint leader, Dr. Clifford Bruno of Princeton, a cosmic ray expert, Bill Blair, a cameraman, and Lance Raymond, a closemouthed character in charge of pyrotechnics. During flight Noel, while testing his suit in the airlock, opens the outer door and is sucked out into space where he seems to be doomed to die but re-establishes contact with the ship through a radio connection in his suit and is picked up again. On the moon, while they are exploring, their moon vehicle falls into a dust-filled crater, burying them, but Noel digs out and rescues the others except Sam, whom they cannot locate. Just as they are about to give up, a "moon creature" appears. It turns out to be a human in a different sort of space suit, a member of Group X, which has arrived on the moon shortly after the BEAMS ship landed. They dub the creature Mr. X, learn that he has saved Sam but has been marooned by his own group, which launches the other ship but miscalculates and is doomed to extinction in space. Mr. X turns out to be a famous German scientist believed to have died in a concentration camp, who has been forced to work with Group X, but has duped it. He joins the BEAMS team on the return trip. The book is clumsy in style and slow in plot. Characters are differentiated in only the most superficial ways: Sam is always wisecracking, Prof. Spitfire, who has an artificial leg, keeps his hands in his pockets. They continually exchange questions and lectures, so that a reader gets far more information than most want in fiction, probably accurate at its time, although some of it has been outdated by the actual moon flights. The main interest of the book now is in comparing fifties' science fiction ideas to current space travel. Fanfare.

MORICE, STELLA, New Zealand author of *The Book of Wiremu** (Angus, 1945), a gently humorous episodic novel of a young Maori boy, notable for the evocation of the undemanding, accepting culture in which he is growing up. It has been republished in many editions.

MOTHERSTONE (Gee*, Maurice, Oxford, 1985), fantasy novel set in the Tolkienesque mythical otherworld of O, in the series that includes *The Halfmen of O** and *The Priests of Ferris**. Susan Ferris and Nick (Nicholas) Quinn, cousins, on their way back to Earth after the overthrow of the tyrannical priests in *The Priests of Ferris*, are captured in the connecting cave by renegade priests. The leader of the priests, vicious Osro*, intends to use the children as hostages in his effort to become king. He has discovered directions for making a dread Weapon of a death-ray nature that he is sure will render his enemies (the good side) incapable of defeating him. With Susan's help, Nick escapes downriver and by great struggle and considerable luck conveys to the current ruler, Kenno, what he knows of Osro's plans and about the Weapon. The ruling Council of O then prepares to fashion their own dread Weapon from the same directions, which they discover in the O archives. Nick, Soona (Kenno's daughter), Jimmy* Jaspers, Ben the Varg (bear), and Birdfolk go off to rescue Susan. Helped to escape by a disaffected follower of Osro, Susan makes her perilous way across burning sands, through a dense, exotic jungle, and over terrible hot springs. She is saved from pursuit by a Bloodcat, a vicious, red, panther-like creature she had once helped. She tames the Bloodcat by creating a series of mind-slide-pictures of the time that she had helped the creature, in the book's best scene. Accompanied by Thief, her name for the Bloodcat, she makes her way to the coast, where cave Stonefolk inform her that Freeman Wells, revered patriarch of O, had hidden the secret of destroying the Weapon on the island of Furthermost far to the south. No details of Susan's journey there are given, and the reader next sees Nick and the other good people on shore striving to reach her, some enemies hot on their trail. They capture one, a Hotlander youth, who is gradually tamed, whom they name Aenlocht, and who they later learn is destined along with Soona and Susan to save O from the Weapons. They make their way by barge with the help of Seafolk to Susan's island, where stands Freeman Wells's house. There Susan finds a stone through which comes Wells's voice predicting the end of the present order if the Weapons, one of which the men of O also now possess and threaten to use in retaliation against Osro, are not destroyed. He tells them to warn Osro and Kenno about the destructive effects of the Weapons, a mission that Nick unsuccessfully attempts, and to go to the Moth- erstone in the palace of O. In support of this is an old song-story Soona knows that indicates that she, Aenlocht, and Susan are to be the saviors of O. With two new stone Halves, teardrop shaped rocks, they reach the dome of the Moth- erstone. Further complications ensue before Susan can give the Halves to Soona and Aenlocht, who eventually set them in place, an act that destroys the Weapons and also changes the two youths into Neanderthals. The book ends with the hope of a better future for O and Susan and Nick preparing to return to Earth. The book is filled with incidents and action, but coincidence abounds, the plot has gaps, and situations are not always logical. For example, in one short paragraph, while he is fleeing from Osro, Nick "was beaten with water, half-drowned," then almost immediately "sat in the branches like a helmsman and watched for a chance to jump ashore." Characters and incidents are exaggerated with the distortion of the animated film, everything is on the surface and sensationalized for effect, and the parallel with the late twentieth-century arms race is very obvious. The land of O possesses no geography except in the most general terms, and it is never clear why Susan and Nick should be the deliverers of O.N.Z. Govt. Short List.

MOWAT, FARLEY (MCGILL) (1921–   ), born in Belleville, Ontario, Canada; editor and writer of fiction and non-fiction for adults and children. He received the Canadian Library Association Children's Book of the Year Award and the Governor General's Award for *Lost in the Barrens** (Little, 1956; *Two Against the North*, Scholastic, 1956), a story of adventure and survival set for six months in the mid–1900s a thousand miles north of Winnipeg. Outstanding for its sheer excitement and clear, generous details of setting, difficulties, and survival techniques, it won the Junior Book Award of the Boys Club of America and nomination for the international Hans Christian Andersen Award. During his childhood years, Mowat roamed the prairie and traveled with his parents in their trailer through plains and mountains, developing a love for the outdoors and wildlife. After service in the Canadian Army during World War II, he attended the University of Toronto to study biology. While there he conducted research on wolves and caribou as a special project for the government. This work gained him the background and inspiration for a short story and his first book, *People of the Deer* (Little, 1952). A non-fiction work about the decline of the Inuit of the Barrens, it focused attention on the plight of the Eskimos and Indians and shaped the course of his life. Since then his writings have addressed anthropological and ecological concerns. While most of his books are for adults, he also wrote others for children. The autobiographical *Owls in the Family* (Little, 1961) is the amusing, action-filled account of Mowat's own experiences as a boy with various household pets in Saskatoon, Saskatchewan. *The Black Joke* (McClelland, 1962) is about piracy in Newfoundland during the Depression, and *The Curse of the Viking Grave* (McClelland, 1966) takes the characters of *Lost in the Barrens* on a search for Viking treasure. *The Dog Who Wouldn't Be* (Little, 1957), which formed the basis for *Owls in the Family*; *Never Cry Wolf* (McClelland, 1963), also autobiographical; and *A Whale for the Killing* (McClelland, 1972) are books written for adults, but which young people enjoy. Mowat has written scripts for television and contributed many stories and articles to anthologies and periodicals. He also received the Vicky Metcalf Award from the Canadian Authors Association for significant contribution to children's literature.

MR. ARCHIBALD BLAKE (*The Brown Land Was Green**), the wealthy, absentee owner of Kammoora sheep station. Although at first it seems he will be painted as callous and exploitive, the Webster family find him fair and caring. He inherited a fortune, doubled it in Van Dieman's Land (Tasmania), and doubled that sum in shrewd investments in Australia. Small, round, good natured, gentlemanly, he realizes that he has not given the time and attention to Kammoora that he should have and thus Benjamin Jones* was able to take advantage and make bad decisions. Mr. Blake is a representative figure.

MR. ERNEST HAWKE (*An Older Kind of Magic**), bearded, young advertising man, almost a caricature of the rising businessman, except that he has a soft heart for animals and likes children for themselves, not just as potential consumers. He understands the power of public protest. The magic he acquires the night of the comet produces the appearance of a demonstration and is an important factor in saving the gardens.

MR. JO CREASEY (*Bush Holiday**; *Bush Voyage**), hefty, jovial man Martin Haddon meets in *Bush Holiday* on the train from Melbourne to the bush. Mr. Creasey spins yarns about notorious bushrangers, or bandits, which thrill the boy, and carries a seemingly unlimited supply of candy in his copious pockets. At one stop he is arrested by police for receiving stolen goods, but he appears at Tangari, insisting that everything is fine. Martin and the reader never learn whether or not he is guilty of some misdeed. In *Bush Voyage*, he takes Martin and Penny* on a trip down the Murray River on his storeboat, the *Bunyip*, and is consistently responsible and good company. Mr. Creasey is a likeable if dubious character, an interesting "huff and bluff" sort.

MR. QUAYLE (*The True Story of Spit MacPhee**), the lawyer whom Grace Tree hires to help her adopt Spit* MacPhee. She has been advised to seek his services because, although she is Catholic and he is Protestant, he is known to be fair and to champion the working man. He speaks with a pronounced English accent, is manipulative on behalf of his clients, and is thorough to a fault, although he assumes a casual air. His stubborn persistence and quick thinking win the case. The book's title comes from his story at the hearing before Judge Laker about Spit and Fyfe* MacPhee's life together. He is a type important to the plot.

MR. RONALD DREW (*Blue Above the Trees**), teacher who establishes a selection in the Great Forest of South Gippsland near the Whitburn place but fails as a homesteader. His failure contrasts with William* Whitburn's success, which is mostly due to the labor of his several sons. At Old* Jesse's suggestion, Mr. Drew hires Simon* Whitburn to show him the land he later selects, paying the youth two pounds for his time and labor, one of which the boy uses to buy Sarah's* rocker. The task whets the boy's appetite for surveying as a career. Mr. Drew is a flat and faceless figure.

MRS. ANGELA CHASE (*The Catalogue of the Universe**), mother of Angela May's father, Roland Chase. When she encounters Angela in Roland's office, she takes a keen interest in the girl. For some time she has been yearning for grandchildren, Roland having produced none legitimately. This attitude is ironic because Roland himself exhibits little interest in the girl. Ironically also, Angela May is named for her grandmother, Roland having suggested the name to Dido*, Angela's mother. Mrs. Chase is both elegant and tawdry, her outward appearance paralleling her character, which is genteel and refined on the surface but ruthless and opportunistic underneath. As a mother, she is a foil for both Dido May and Tycho* Potter's mother.

MR. SMERTZER (*The Racketty Street Gang**), one of the few developed characters in the novel. He is a sensible, practical man, a loving father to Anton, and a good husband. He keeps secret the information that he was once charged with being a war criminal. When Anton brings the Racketty Street Gang home for cake, he tells the boys stories about his war experiences. He seems unusually eager to discuss the war with them, given the circumstances, but functionally his stories lay the foundation for later plot developments.

MRS. STUBECK (*The True Story of Lilli Stubeck**), Lilli's mother, who dies near the end of the book. A large, loud, strong woman, seemingly the opposite of Matty, her husband, who is small, weasely, and very quick to abuse his children physically. She often calls at houses in town to demand food or necessities, seeming to feel people should give her what she asks for simply because they have it and she doesn't. When she returns in ill health to St. Helen to find Matty jailed for theft and her other children gone, Lilli leaves Miss* Dalgleish and takes care of her without any hesitation. Later, Devlin* takes care of her and Jackie*, her youngest son, until her death. Lilli is much like her mother, proud, self-assured, and a survivor by whatever means.

MRS. TUCKER (*A Little Fear**), canny old farm woman, who battles the Njimbin*, a sly, unscrupulous gnome, for ownership of the area she has inherited but he has lived in for time out of mind. At first, she admits that her mind is not as sharp as it once was and thinks that she may be imagining things or not remembering correctly what she herself has done. Later she concludes that supernatural forces are at work. She is presented as a tall—almost six feet— large-boned woman, with white hair "twisted into an upside-down ice cream-cone on top of her head." She is a thoroughly convincing, consistently interesting, sympathetic protagonist, one the reader does not forget.

MURRA (*Behind the Wind**), one of the Yunggamurra, water- or river-spirits of northern Australia. In *The Dark Bright Water*, Wirrun finds her in a cavern deep underground, a "silver water-spirit with a song to trap men," brings her out, smokes the magic out of her, and makes her his wife. She is mischievous and vivacious, loves him, and is loved in return. She can never understand why he occasionally works for money as a white man, something he does when he needs to buy things like clothes.

THE MYSTERY OF THE FAKE ARJUNA (Joshi*, Niharika, ill. Mrinal Mitra, CBT, India, 1984), realistic detective novel set from late August to early October in contemporary India and involving characters from *The Golden Buddha**:

Detective Inspector K. D. Rao, who focuses on smuggling of idols and is known as ''The Crab'' because he always gets his man; and schoolchildren Pinku and Ranjat Johri and their Lhasa apso dog, Chili. The story begins in Almora with fifteen-year-old Jiwanti, a schoolgirl who is also a librarian, the Johri children, and several friends, who look forward to two events: the school election in which Jiwanti's brother, Bhoovan, is running for president, and the governor's visit to the city. Simultaneously in New Delhi, a clever thief named Billu, a member of an international ring of idol smugglers headed by blue-eyed, ruthless Jericho, makes plans to steal a priceless idol of Arjuna, the famed archer of Hindu legend. Billu pretends to be a film maker, photographs the idol, and prepares two fake copies of it, one of which is cracked in an unsuccessful attempt to steal the idol. Then he learns that the idol will be taken with other recently discovered artifacts for display at the museum and library in Almora during the governor's visit. Billu takes his bogus company to Almora, where he awaits an opportunity to substitute the sound fake for the original. In Almora he films various local events for his supposed documentary, under the pretense of helping Jiwanti toward a film career, and makes a wax copy of her key to the room where the idols are stored. He creates a diversion during the election and secures the original. Before he gets to Delhi, Jiwanti happens to fall in with him, still intent on her career in films, overhears a conversation between him and confederates that reveals his true intentions, and is taken captive. She is discovered by Chili the dog, who fetches the children to release her. On the case by this time, K. D. Rao has followed clues that bring him to Almora, and with Jiwanti's information, traces Billu to Delhi, where he rounds up the entire gang but discovers that the recovered idol is a cracked fake. Jiwanti then confesses that she and the children had switched that one for the original before Billu left for his rendezvous with Jericho, and thus the original is safe. Characters, incidents, and language are conventional for the genre, and the plot depends heavily upon coincidence. Billu is the stereotyped, greedy, manipulative villain, and Jiwanti the easily deluded adolescent with romantic notions. Glimpses of school life add interest, and there is some sense of the problems girls from the lower classes, like Jiwanti, have in getting an education and in resisting the attempts of their parents to marry them at an early age. That Jiwanti should have a key to the small room where the priceless idols are stored is hard to accept, but substituting the fake for the real idol at the end adds an unexpected twist to the plot, which is action filled, exciting, and fast paced. CBT of India, Second Prize.

MYSTERY OF THE MISSING RELIC (Kaur*, Simren, ill. Jagdish Joshi and Mrinal Mitra, CBT, India, 1986), adventure novel set in the Himalayan mountains near the border of Tibet in an unspecified time. When Zangbo, who seems in the illustrations to be between eight and twelve, discovers a stranger sleeping in the barn of their isolated farm and shows his father, Wangyal, the gold locket set with a glowing white stone that the stranger drops, the two take it to Ang Chook, the teacher, who lives near the river. This wise man identifies it as a holy relic stolen from the Buddhist monastery at Chizi-Chu Gompa, the abode of the Buddha of the Thousand Smiles, and tells them that it is their duty to take it back. The two obediently set off on a long and perilous journey, accompanied by their Lhasa apso terrier, Zing Zing Bar. On their first night they encounter the robbers of Sing Phu, who take Zangbo as a hostage, but he cleverly escapes and is reunited with his father. They join a mule train that will pass through Bara Lacha La pass and near Chizi-Chu Gompa. Also with the caravan is Norbu, a trader, who catches sight of the beautiful relic and becomes possessed by a desire to own it. Shortly before they reach the monastery, Norbu secretly departs, taking his own mules and horses and the relic, which he has stolen from Zangbo, so that the boy and his father arrive, after many hardships and near disasters on the trail, at their goal but without the reason for their journey. The head lama hears their story and sends them with a silent monk as a guide on a shortcut over the mountains to Yargil, a town close to Tibet, in hopes of cutting off Norbu before he can cross the border and sell the relic. There Zangbo fortuitously controls a frightened horse, thereby saving the life of the Lady of Patseo, a rich powerful woman, who befriends them. Aided by her men and by Tashi, an innkeeper who once was a lama at Chizi-Chu Gompa but who left after the relic was stolen while he was supposed to guard it, they find Norbu, are captured and escape, chase him to the border where they overtake and overpower him, and return with him to the Fort of Patseo. There Norbu escapes again, takes Zangbo as a shield, and demands that the precious relic be traded for the boy. Zing Zing Bar dashes in and bites Norbu's leg, creating a diversion during which the boy escapes. Norbu leaps up and climbs to the ramparts of the fort, where he loses his footing and crashes to his death. The book ends with the suggestion that there will be further adventures in the return of the relic and the seeking of the lost Patseo treasure, obviously opening the way for a sequel. Despite the title, the mystery element is minimal and action the chief characteristic of the plot. So much happens in fewer than one hundred pages that there is little space left to develop characters, setting, or theme, though Zangbo is depicted as brave and obedient, and reverence is a major element in all the good people. Brief descriptions of steep mountains, icy paths, and deep chasms keep the physical setting in focus, while references to foods and customs give some sense of the exotic culture of the high Himalayas. CBT of India, First Prize.

N

NAIDOO, BEVERLEY, South African teacher and writer, who came to England at the age of twenty-two to study at the University of York. She has since taught in elementary and secondary schools. *Journey to Jo'burg: A South African Story** (Longman, 1985; Lippincott, 1986), her first book of fiction, received the Other Award and the Child Study Award. It tells of the difficult and disappointing trip of two black South African children to fetch their Mma (mother), who works as a domestic, to help their ill baby sister. The idea for the book rose out of discussions at meetings of the Education Group of the British Defense and Aid Fund for Southern Africa. The book is sociological in orientation and coincides with the group's purpose of raising the consciousness of the world to the suffering caused by apartheid and of working for a free, racially equal society. Its sequel is *Chain of Fire* (Collins, 1989; Lippincott, 1990). With the Education Group she has also published *Censoring Reality* (1984), an examination of non-fiction books on South Africa for young readers. *Free as I Know* (Bell, 1987) is an anthology of literature in English that she has edited for school use.

NARGUN (*The Nargun and the Stars**), dangerous, primeval being that looks something like a huge, gray boulder, monstrously cold, born of earth, and moved by basic, rudimentary instincts. Disturbed in its age-old lair in Victoria, it made a slow, lumbering passage on tottering, stumpy limbs to northern Australia, where it settled down on a mountainside on the Wongadilla sheep run owned by Charlie* and Edie* Waters. It is never accepted by the other primeval creatures who have lived for eons in that region. Loud noises and alterations to the landscape anger it. It is attracted by fire and emits high-pitched, weird screams at night that echo over the landscape. On an excursion into the hills, Simon Brent unwittingly and ironically traces his name in the lichen that velvets its sides, thinking it is a stone. The author dramatically catches the Nargun's tremendous potential for destruction.

THE NARGUN AND THE STARS (Wrightson*, Patricia, Hutchinson, 1973; Atheneum, 1974), suspenseful fantasy, especially rich in atmosphere, which improvises upon Australian Aborigine folklore. After his parents die, young Simon Brent goes to live with his mother's middle-aged second cousins, Edie* and Charlie* Waters, a brother and sister who operate a five thousand-acre sheep run called Wongadilla in the mountains of northern Australia. Still grieving, a little resentful, somewhat apprehensive about life in the hills, Simon gradually learns to appreciate his cousins' quiet, homely ways and the rich heritage of the land. While exploring the isolated uplands, he encounters mischievous, harmless, primeval spirits of the earth and waters, among them the self-important, commanding Potkoorok*, who lives in the swamp not far from the farmhouse; the Turongs, elfin beings who inhabit the trees and push into the Potkoorok's swamp a road grader whose work has annoyed them; and the flighty Nyols who guard within their mountain lair the bulldozer stolen from the men who have been clearing the mountainside of trees. He also becomes aware of the Nargun*, a huge, gray, destructive, rocklike being that moves about at night. Angered by the workers' activities, the Nargun kills a sheep, causes various other difficulties, and eventually even threatens the lives of the Waters family. After several unsuccessful attempts at restraining or diverting the creature, Charlie and Simon seek help from the Potkoorok, who sends Simon to the Nyols, where he discovers the missing bulldozer. Hoping to lure the Nargun inside the mountain, Charlie and Simon again seek aid from the Potkoorok, who with Simon enters the mountain through his hidden underground watery passageway. Using magic, he frightens the Nyols into leaving their lair. On the rumbling old farm tractor, Edie and Simon hold the Nargun's attention while Charlie enters the Nyols' cave and starts the bulldozer. Events build to an exciting climax as the Nargun vents his anger by destroying the tractor and then laboriously shifts his vast bulk into the cave and attacks the bulldozer, causing an explosion that brings tons of stone and earth down upon himself. The Nargun has returned to the elements from which he came, and Wongadilla is safe again. Rich characterizations of humans and otherworld beings, an inventive, suspense-filled, well-paced plot, in which motivations are not always clear but in which tension grows steadily and the interactions of humans and primeval spirits is made thoroughly credible, combine with a vividly realized setting and a distinctive style for a dramatic, highly convincing, and unique fantasy. Aust. Bk. of Year Winner; Fanfare.

NED BURNEY (*The Roaring 40**), wild boy of Port Davey, nephew of Harry* Burney, the old recluse. He was marooned at remote, isolated Port Davey as a small child with his mother when Harry's boat, the *Thora Ann* foundered. When Mrs. Burney left to get help and apparently died in the bush, the boy lived in a hidden cave. He regularly goes off into the bush, apparently to commune with God and nature and, although he can't make sentences, he sings the hymns his mother taught him, among them, "There wuzza green hill far away. . . . " He hoped for rescue when Flinty and his two brothers, fishermen, arrived. They happened on the *Thora Ann*, fixed her up, and renamed her the *Roaring 40*. They abused the boy for sport, physically and psychologically, dressing him up as a saloon entertainer in an old top hat, suspenders, and trousers, teaching him dance hall songs, like "Show me the way to go 'ome . . ." and making him perform for them in exchange for much-needed supplies like matches. Ned is a pathetic, grotesque figure when found, frightening to the Lorennys and Vik, only gradually becoming sympathetic as Badge slowly wins his confidence and helps him learn to trust people.

NELSON, MR. (*The Lieutenant**), frail botanist who is one of the nineteen men in the open boat. Through much of the four thousand mile voyage, Nelson keeps his sanity by writing an imaginary journal, describing the events and his thoughts about them. A decent, educated man, he is well aware that physically he has less chance of survival than most of the men, and he suffers from fever and dysentery for much of the trip, but he keeps his spirits up and supports the captain in his decisions, though he longs for good food, dry clothes, and the pleasant, safe life he left in Kew Gardens.

NEV FOWLER (*Memory**), hoodlum. When they were in school, Nev often bullied Jonny Dart, taunting him about his tap dancing and even threatening to knife him. When Jonny encounters Nev in the pub near Sophie* West's house, Nev calls him "Chickie" from the Chickenbits television commercials starring Jonny and his sister, Janine.* Jonny stands up to Nev for the first time. Later Jonny prevents him and two pals from robbing Sophie. Jonny's leap from the balcony upon them though melodramatic is redeeming; it both saves Sophie and leads to Jonny's discovery that he did not cause Janine's death. Nev is a type figure who nevertheless plays an important part in the plot.

NICHOLS, (JOANNA) RUTH (1948–   ), born in Toronto, Ontario, Canada; author best known for her fantasy novels for children and young people. Her first full-length book, written at age eighteen and published three years later, was *A Walk Out of the World* (Longman, 1969; Harcourt, 1969), in which children transported to another dimension strive to restore the rightful rulers to the throne. It was an American Library Association Notable Book. *The Marrow of the World** (Macmillan, 1972; Atheneum, 1972) employs a similar plot structure to work out personal problems of identity and life direction. A Canadian Children's Book of the Year Winner, it moves with tension and rapidity. Her other books include *Song of the Pearl* (Macmillan, 1976; Atheneum, 1976), a fantasy for teenagers; *The Left-Handed Spirit* (Macmillan, 1978; Atheneum, 1978), a historical novel set at the time of Marcus Aurelius; and *Ceremony of Innocence* (Faber, 1969), an autobiographical novel for adults. She received an honors B.A. in Religious Studies from the University of British Columbia in 1969, an M.A. from McMaster University in 1972, and her Ph.D. in Western

Religious Thought in 1979, also from McMaster. She has also published *The Burning of the Rose* (St. Martin's, 1989).

NIGHT RACE TO KAWAU (Duder*, Tessa, Oxford, 1982), suspenseful sailing adventure novel with family story aspects set about 1980. Early Friday morning, impulsive Dad (Nick Starr), a teacher, bounds up the stairs to the attic bedroom of his daughter, intense Sam (Samantha), 12, to announce that that night the Starrs will participate in the night sailing race to Kawau Island up the Hauraki Gulf north of Auckland, New Zealand, an annual event in the area for fifty years. Their boat, the old, reputable *Aratika*, once belonged to Dad's father, William, who taught Dad to sail, and the Starrs have now sailed together as a family on long vacations for about five years. Practical Mum (Louise) is none too keen on this trip, however, her intuition warning of trouble, but Dad has engaged a young crewman and is sure that with the help of the two younger children, Jane, 10, and Jeremy, 9, the family will manage nicely. Problems start even before they depart: rushing Jeremy to the hospital to repair a head cut makes Mum late and irritable, their bacon and egg pie for dinner burns, and, even though the crewman never shows up (a family emergency, they learn later), Dad insists on sailing, and Mum gives in. After the tension of reaching the starting point on time is over, they settle down to enjoy the trip, which the calm weather promises will be pleasant. Particularly enthusiastic are Dad and Sam, who revel in the beauty of the colorful sails and admire the expertise of the skippers. They soon raise the spinnaker to make better time and to please old William, whom Sam has spied watching them from a nearby hill, and eat a satisfying meal of fish and chips. After sundown, troubles resume and multiply. The wind changes suddenly to an unexpected northerly. While lowering the spinnaker, Dad is somehow knocked unconscious, leaving Mum and Sam, who have never navigated alone before even in daylight, to get them all safely to Kawau. Because Mum isn't strong enough to handle the engine, the trip must be entirely by sail. Sam stifles her panic and pitches in, mostly with a will, but sometimes with anger and bitterness, steering, helping with sails, whatever needs to be done. The two experience cold, hunger, increasing fatigue, and fear and realize their lack of knowledge and inexperience handicap them. With great difficulty, they get dad into a bunk, lower the big sail, avoid colliding with other boats, and navigate narrows. They anchor, somewhat after midnight, at Bosanquet Bay across Kawau Island from their destination, because Dad is hallucinating and needs a doctor quickly, a decision Mum makes unilaterally to Sam's disgust. She sends Sam and Jane in the dark on foot across the hilly island for help—a sometimes terrifying experience for imaginative Sam—at Mission House Bay. They arrive to find no boats there because of the northerly and the house closed. Despairing, they encounter a ranger in early morning who quickly arranges for help. Saturday midmorning finds Dad awake and lucid and on his way to the hospital for X-rays and observation and William arriving to help sail the *Aratika* home. The emphasis is on action and trouble at sea, and, although events are overforeshadowed, suspense runs very high. This is also an account of interpersonal relationships within a loving family accustomed to doing things together. Circumstances dictate reversed roles, which add to the tension. Sam gives orders to Mum, for example, when Mum's weariness and worry keep her from functioning, and Jane, who usually manages to weasel out of responsibility, takes over in order to get herself and Sam across the island. With some resentment toward Dad, Mum complains to Sam about not being instructed for such eventualities but also realizes that she has not pushed hard enough to get instruction. There are some other interesting commentaries about sex roles in sailing. Dialogue is especially apt and catches the flavor of typical family life. Characters are conventional but appropriate for the plot. The sense of being aboard a boat is strong because of the liberal use of nautical terms (explained in a glossary) and the careful descriptions of boat handling and equipment. N.Z. Govt. Short List.

NJIMBIN (*A Little Fear**), sly and cunning gnome, as ancient as the land itself, who has lived for eons among the ridges, woods, and swamps near the cottage that old Mrs.* Tucker has inherited from her brother. Once the Njimbin had made a good living off the land, but the coming of humans changed his way of life and made hunting harder. When Mrs. Tucker arrives, he has been living quite comfortably in the fowlhouse near the cottage. He sets out to drive her away by playing tricks upon her. At the end, she leaves, but his victory is an ironic one because the reader last sees the old woman preparing to burn down the filthy old fowlhouse before she goes.

NKWALA (Sharp*, Edith Lambert, ill. William Winter, Little, 1958), historical novel of an American Indian boy of the Spokan tribe evidently before the coming of the white men or the use of horses, set in what is now northern Washington State and British Columbia. In his twelfth year, Nkwala, like the other boys of his people, goes out alone for a four-night period to pray and sing to Day Dawn, the children's god, seeking a name and a guardian spirit. Although he repeats his efforts again and again, overcoming his fear and testing himself with ever more difficult feats of endurance and skill, he is not sent a dream or a song or any special happening to reveal his name and spirit and allow him to join the adult men of the tribe. So often is he alone at night in his chosen spot that a small coyote begins to frequent his camp and to share his food. Drought drives his people north, toward Soiyus, the Meeting Place (now Osoyoos), where they hope to find members of the Salish nation and to spread the word that they come peacefully and temporarily, until the rain comes. At the Meeting Place, they find that no Salish have been in the area for months and their shaman senses the presence of ghosts, frightened and weeping, many of them children. He cannot lead the children's spirits "over the white sky trail" because they are too timid to go with a man. Then Bright-Star, Nkwala's mother, bravely volunteers to stay with the shaman through the night, singing lullabies and rocking an empty cradle, to comfort and reassure the spirits so that they may be led to their rest. Nkwala finds a half-starved dog, obviously from the massacred village, which attaches itself to him. Running-Elk, the chief, directs that they fortify the caves in the bluff above the lake of the Okanagon as a place of retreat in case of attack. With the tribe settled in its new home, Nkwala again goes off on his lonely vigil. Alone in the high spot of his choosing, he hears a coyote and almost answers its call before he realizes that it is not a real coyote but an enemy scout. He runs to give the alarm, so that almost all the Spokans are able to climb to the caves. Seeing that a diversion may give time for the last older and weaker ones to scramble up the ladders to the fort, he throws armloads of pitchy branches and dry twigs onto the fire, then dances around it, singing and shouting. Although the Okanagon warriors are wild for revenge against those who they think murdered their women and children, the chief recognizes the dog and argues that it would not make friends with people who killed his master. The diversion gives time for Running-Elk to parley and to point out that the Okanagon and the Spokans are both part of the ancient Flathead tribe, therefore brothers, and by right can share hunting grounds. The Okanagon chief agrees and seals the pact by saying that Nkwala will be his son, to replace the one murdered in the village. In a matter of such importance to the tribe, Nkwala cannot protest or weep, and he dares not seek out his own parents for fear of weakening. At the celebratory feast, the shaman tells a story, the tale of the night when the brave Bright-Star sang to the spirits of the slain Okanagon children. When the Okanagon chief demands that she be brought forth, he sees that she has been weeping. In payment of his debt to her, he gives her back her son. Nkwala is painted with the red flame of courage and the bright flame of the council fire, the two guardian spirits he has discovered, and he is declared no longer a child. In the picture of the way of life of these western tribes, the book is probably as accurate as it is possible to be about any group in the far past, at least concerning their living style, initiation vigils, way of travel, and tribal organization. The Spokans are pictured as very peace loving and family oriented, and they speak in formal diction, all aspects that may be more speculative but make an interesting story and allow for some character development. A brief glossary helps locate places and explain terms. Can. Bk. of Year Winner; Can. Gov. General's Winner.

NOBBY (*The House that was Eureka**), son of Mrs. Oatley, the despot*, by a first marriage. He is in love with Lizzie Cruise, who lives next door in the attached house also owned by his mother, and sides with the Cruise family in the conflict over their eviction. After he has been spotted by police with the gun pointing down from the balcony, he runs down the stairs and crawls through the legs of the police and defenders fighting in the living room to get to the scullery in the back, where Lizzie helps him hide the gun in the stovepipe of the water heater in the corner cupboard. In his flight he has not stopped to defend Mick Cruise, who is being battered by the police, and he blames himself for cowardice the rest of his life. After the incident at Eureka House, as it is called, Nobby leaves for the outback, giving his mother an assumed name with which to write him and to send on messages from Lizzie. The vindictive woman keeps the letters from both the young people. For fifty years Nobby has wandered, until, a man in his seventies, he takes a room near his old home, unsure whether he wants to re-establish relations with his mother. From there he hears the noise of the simulated eviction riot for the videotape. When Nobby learns of his mother's duplicity, he accepts her contrition and actually is glad to know that Lizzie died loving him.

NOEL CAVENDISH (*The House that was Eureka**), grandson of the despot*, Mrs. Oatley. Noel is odd looking, small, thin, and pale, with dark hair which he stubbornly wears long; he plays the harmonica or talks constantly in a sardonic, wise-cracking style, punctuating his conversation with wild laughs. Since his timid mother has always worked outside the home, he has been brought up mostly by his grandmother, who was unsympathetic and often abusive, and now that she is bedridden and unable to talk he sometimes gets back at her by writing impertinent remarks on her soft, erasable slate or by serving her cold oatmeal uneaten at breakfast for her lunch, just as she used to do to him. Noel has long suffered a recurring nightmare of shooting down at a mob of people, of running and crawling through a riotous scene, a series of actions that happened to Nobby*, his uncle of whom he has never heard. As the time-slip takes hold of him and Evie, he seems destined to act out the dream by merging with Nobby. Noel is a little younger than Evie and is still in school, though he frequently skips it.

NORMAN, LILITH (1927–   ), born in Sydney, New South Wales, Australia; librarian, editor, and author of novels for children and of local histories for adults. After her education at Sydney Girls' High School, she held a variety of positions before becoming children's librarian at the Sydney Public Library and a member of the editorial staff of the New South Wales Department of Education *School Magazine*. In 1978, after publishing four books, short plays, and a reader for children, she turned to full-time writing. Her novels commonly unfold within a family situation. In her best-known book, *Climb a Lonely Hill** (Collins, 1970; Walck, 1972), a suspenseful story commended for Australian Children's Book of the Year, a brother and sister find hidden reserves of strength to survive in the barrens of New South Wales. *The Shape of Three* (Collins, 1971; Walck, 1972) involves twin boys switched in a hospital nursery, while *My Simple Little Brother* (Collins, 1979) tells of the humorous misadventures of a boy who takes expressions literally. *The Flame Takers* (Collins, 1973) and *A Dream of Seas* (Collins, 1978) are fantasies. The former concerns an acting family whose members suddenly lose their talent, and the latter improvises on the selkie theme (a legendary seal-man) among present-day Australian surfers. For adults she wrote a series of books of history and non-fiction published by the city of Sydney.

NUNGANEE (*The Spirit Wind**), old Aborigine who tries to save Jarl* Hansen from having to return to the *Hootzen* by calling up the spirit wind to wreck the ship. Although he has lived among the whites far from his own people for many years, he is still a firm believer in the tribal ways and carries with him the death stick that he once prepared and over which he sang the curses that caused another man to die in that dim past. Since that time he has been on the run, working in cattle stations and moving on at the slightest hint of a pursuer. After Jarl saves him from drowning and helps capture the outlaw, Nunganee testifies in court and sees the brutality of the mate, Heinrich the Bull. He believes that the only way to save the boy is to destroy the ship. Therefore, he sharpens his death stick and chants the proper incantations over it, then jerks it backward toward the ship, cursing it and calling the spirit wind. To his surprise, the wind comes up much sooner and stronger than he anticipated, does indeed wreck the *Hootzen*, and nearly kills Jarl, Jill Gilson, and most of the ship's crew that reach the island.

NYBERG, (EVERETT WAYNE) MORGAN (1944–   ), born in Thunder Bay, Ontario, Canada; teacher and writer. Nyberg received his B.A. degree from the University of British Columbia in 1966 and his teacher's certificate in 1978. He has been an instructor in creative writing at Douglas College, New Westminster, British Columbia, and in English as a second language at Vancouver Community College and at the University of Aveiro, Portugal. He has also taught in the American high school in Quinto, Ecuador, and at the University of British Columbia. Among his many honors are several Canada Council grants, second prize in the Canadian Broadcasting Company Literary Competition in 1979 for *Mark, a Memoir*, and the Governor General's Literary Award for *Galahad Schwartz and the Cockroach Army** (Groundwood, 1987), a fantasy for middle-grade readers. His book of poems written in four voices about the Indian wars of the 1870s, *The Crazy Horse Suite* (Intermedia, 1979), has been produced as a stage play, as a radio drama, and, with music by composer Stephen Chatman, as a musical theater piece. Nyberg divides his time between Surrey, British Columbia, and Ecuador.

O

OBORO (*The Plum-Rain Scroll**), girl whom Taro meets when she and her pet panda, Tama, arrive at the inn at which he works in the company of a group of traveling players. Taro thinks she is conceited and overbearing, and the two often bicker. He thinks she doesn't know her place, and she thinks he's trying to control her. She is clever and decisive and, adept at a kind of karate, gives a good account of herself in skirmishes against evil Lord Marishoten. Taro wonders why some people they meet address her as "princess" and is truly amazed to learn that she really is the Mikado's grandniece and entitled to call herself Cherry-Blossom Princess. She had joined the traveling players while running away from home to avoid having to go to live with a prissy aunt who she is certain would try to make her over into the aunt's idea of a lady. Oboro is one of the most interesting figures in the novel because the author withholds information about her true identity until the end of the novel and because she is so strongly drawn.

O'BRIEN, KATHERINE, born in Australia; New Zealand author for children. When she was a child, she lived on her grandfather's farm in the Southland, the southernmost point of New Zealand's South Island. This area is the setting for *The Year of the Yelvertons** (Oxford, 1981), winner of the Esther Glen Award. In the novel, a sister and brother help an old man prepare for a visit from London cousins. O'Brien has made her home in Wellington.

THE OCTOBER CHILD (Spence*, Eleanor, Oxford, 1976; *The Devil Hole*, Lothrop, 1977), sober, instructive novel about the problems of a contemporary Australian family with their autistic son. The five Mariners—Robert, an easy-going storekeeper; Beth, his loving wife; Kenneth, 12, athletic and outgoing; Adrienne, 7, companionable and adaptable; and responsible, artistic Douglas*, 10, from whose vantage point events are seen although he does not tell the story—live in the coastal village of Chapel Rocks an hour from Sydney, where the family is liked and respected by friends and neighbors. The Mariners look forward to a baby in October, never suspecting how drastically their lives will be changed. Little Carl is exceptionally good looking, but right away his behavior seems different. He cries a lot and does not respond to the family's loving overtures. Only Douglas's singing (he has a remarkable soprano) evokes a positive response, and that only seldom. Soon Beth must devote most of her time to the intractable, destructive child, who bites, kicks, scratches, screams, and breaks whatever he lays his hands on, setting the family's nerves on edge and horrifying the neighbors. The family and Beth in particular cling tenaciously to the idea that Carl is just slow to develop. Helpful and affectionate Douglas is most often called upon to assist with chores and Carl. So Carl can go to a special school, the parents sell the house and move to Sydney. Kenneth especially resents the move, seeks companionship elsewhere, and eventually joins a religious commune. Douglas has the opportunity to study at a music college, but he almost misses his audition because Carl breaks through the yard fence and runs away and Douglas must search for him. When Carl wrecks the tiny room Douglas has outfitted as a studio and then bites him when they are returning from a visit to the playground, Douglas has had enough. He abandons the boy, then relents and calls home. In despair and anger, he goes to his music teacher's house, where he encounters Carl's teacher. She sympathizes with him, encourages him, and points out that, in spite of all the trouble Carl has caused, Carl's disability brought Douglas to Sydney and enabled him to study music. At the end, the situation remains dark because there seems to be no solution to the problem of what to do about Carl. Events seem intended to teach about autism, and the book makes better sociology than fiction, but Douglas is well drawn, and one can hardly help feeling sorry for this unfortunate family, whose lives have been so disrupted, who are bewildered and defensive about Carl, who are unable to find much of any help, and who recognize that all they can do is try to do the best they can for themselves and the son whom they love and want even though he is a terrible burden. Aust. Bk. of Year Winner.

O'DEA, MARJORY (RACHEL) (1928–   ), born in Melbourne, Victoria, Australia; novelist, teacher, and civil servant. Beginning in 1974, she was project officer with the Department of Science of the Australian Public Service. Prior to that, among other positions, she was senior history mistress at Ruyton Church of England Girls' Grammar School in Kew, Victoria, lecturer in scienomics at the Australian National University, special assistant to the chief biographer with the Commonwealth Scientific and Industrial Research Organization (CSIRO), and assistant to the Joint Parliamentary Committee on Foreign Affairs and Defense and Senate Standing Committee on Securities and Exchange. She has published *Six Days Between a Second** (Heinemann, 1969), a fantasy novel with an environmental theme that was commended for Australian Book of the Year, and *Of Jade and Amber Caves* (Heinemann, 1974), and has contributed to such journals as *The Australian Quarterly* and *The Australian Journal of Science*.

THE OLDEN DAYS COAT (Laurence*, Margaret, ill. Muriel Wood, Mc-Clelland, 1979), brief time fantasy set in a Canadian village partly in the modern era and partly two generations earlier. Sal, 10, bored and depressed because she and her parents are spending Christmas at her grandmother's house instead of at her own city home, amuses herself by looking through old photograph albums in Gran's shed. Then she tries on a navy blue coat with a hood and a red wool sash that she finds in an old trunk. After a dizzy spell, she finds that Gran's house and other nearby buildings have disappeared, although the old church still stands across the road. As she walks down this road, a girl about her age comes by in a horse-drawn sleigh and offers her a ride. Without quite lying, Sal manages to stall off questions from the girl, who introduces herself as Sarah from New Grange Farm. The two girls discover that their families both have the custom of the Early Present, one gift that the children are allowed to open before Christmas Day. Sarah shows Sal her Early Present, a wooden box with a Monarch butterfly carved in the lid. When Sarah asks her to come meet her parents, Sal, who realizes that the old-fashioned coat has taken her back in time, is frightened because she might have to remove the coat and reveal her blue jeans. Just then the horses are startled by falling icicles and, as they rear, the box is knocked from Sarah's hand. Sal jumps down to retrieve it and, after handing it back, takes the opportunity to slip out of the coat and toss it into the back of the cutter. She finds herself again in the shed, with the coat beside her. That same day she chooses for her Early Present the gift from Gran, which turns out to be the Monarch butterfly box which was given to Gran when she was ten-year-old Sarah and has been cherished throughout the intervening years. Although it is illustrated with soft-textured realistic pictures and is hardly more than picture-book length, the story is presented as a very short single-episode novel for readers Sal's age or a little younger. It is simply written and predictable, but with enough detail and development of Sal's emotions to be satisfying as an undemanding introduction to time fantasy. Can. Bk. of Year Runner-Up.

AN OLDER KIND OF MAGIC (Wrightson*, Patricia, ill. Noela Young, Hutchinson, 1972; Harcourt, 1972), fantasy novel of magic and folklore set one winter week in the 1960s in the inner city of Sydney, Australia. Three schoolchildren, Selina* Potter, perhaps ten, who "believes in mysterious things" and from whose vantage point most events are seen, her bossy, practical older brother, Rupert, about twelve, and their friend, timid, half-orphaned Benny* Golightly, also about twelve, play every day after school by the fishpond in the botanical gardens near the business buildings in which they live. The siblings live in the Department, the building of which their father is the head caretaker, and Benny lives over his father's magic shop not far away. One Thursday afternoon, Selina, off by herself, notices that the boys have been joined by two more boys who soon mysteriously disappear. These are the first of several sightings of little brown and gray manlike spirits by the children and grown-ups as the time of the thousand-year comet draws near. Unknown to the children, Sir* Mortimer Wyvern, business mogul, plans to railroad through the city's ruling body a scheme to secure part of the gardens for parking. Later the children overhear a conversation in the Minister's* Department office that the issue will be decided at a meeting on Tuesday night, the very time the comet is due. The children make friends with Mr.* Ernest Hawke, an advertising man, who stars them in a commercial for Crackle-Crunch candy bars. He says that he has learned that Sir Mortimer controls the men who will attend the meeting. Events climax Tuesday evening when the comet appears, and indigenous Australian spirits, among them Nyols, Bitarrs, Net-Nets, and Pot-Kooroks, become active. They kidnap Sir Mortimer and take him to their underground cavern, where they make sport of him and cause him to miss the important meeting. Mr. Hawke discovers that he can work magic and brings alive department store dummies, who demonstrate against the parking plan. Since Sir Mortimer fails to appear at the meeting and the demonstration seems to indicate intense public disapproval, the plan is dropped. Some days later, the children discover a stone statue in a secluded part of the gardens that looks like Sir Mortimer. The botanical gardens are safe, and the old, indigenous spirits have proved their strength. The children have distinct personalities, and the atmosphere of mild suspense is well sustained. Because much of the book describes the children's activities in the gardens, at home, and in their neighborhood, the inner-city setting and their way of life is vivid and convincing, a strong picture of middle-class urban domesticity. Careful foreshadowing prepares the reader for the magic portions at the climax, but that Sir Mortimer should be quite literally "spirited away" and turned to stone, and then simply given up seems farfetched, as do some of the other magical occurrences. The setting of the bustling commerce in the concrete city sets in relief the power of the spirits of the earth to affect events. Aust. Bk. of Year Highly Com.

OLD JESSE (*Blue Above the Trees**), father of the innkeeper on the track to the Whitburn selection. A former sailor, he is colorful in appearance and loquacious. He tells Simon* Whitburn about the early explorers of the region and whets the boy's appetite for an education. Old Jesse also teaches Simon about the forest and its creatures. Simon enjoys his company, but William* Whitburn says that Old Jesse is a meddler.

OLD MARJORIE (*Bush Holiday**), pipe-smoking bunk-hut cook at Tangari, who lives with her big, black dog, Prince, in a little hut attached to a corner of the larger hut in which Martin Haddon, Bill* Macleod, and Uncle* Luke stay. Penny* Macleod says Old Marjorie "isn't very right in the head" but "adores Dad [Mr. Mccleod]," who generously indulges her idiosyncrasies. Though she is opinionated and sees the world in a completely different fashion than everyone else at Tangari, Martin feels at ease with her. A vividly drawn character, if an eccentric type, she adds interest to the novel and illuminates the Macleod family.

OLD TAMA (*Take the Long Path**), elderly Maori who appears in the cave above where the penguins nest and eventually is revealed as David's grandfather. He wears an old-fashioned dark blue pinstriped suit, frayed and shiny, a grubby waistcoat, and a shirt with no collar. Because David knows his stepfather is antagonistic toward Maoris and would make trouble if he knew one was living in the old cottage or the cave—even though he doesn't own the land—David keeps quiet about this new friend, whom he calls Old Tama because the man calls David Young Tama and says any name will do for him. He sees in David, despite his blond coloring, a resemblance to his dead son. When the boy flees to him at night, Old Tama helps him to see that it is time to ask his parents questions about his origin and he also helps him understand that he has been using his silence to provoke his stepfather and force his mother to come to his defense. He seems to have unusual ability to calm and tame the penguins, and he says confidently that he will see that Mabel takes care of her chick. His tale of Tarewai is more real than a story to David. In the end, David believes that he was the ghost of his grandfather, who took "the long path" to the dark, then returned to see the family *Oha* fulfilled.

OLWEN (*The Guardian of Isis**), elderly, white-haired, green-skinned Keeper of the Isis Light, daughter of the first keepers and of Earth stock. After her parents died, the Guardian* changed her appearance and gave her green, reptilian skin impervious to Ra's rays so that she could live anywhere on Isis. The President had once been in love with her, and Jody's Grandfather was a mischievous boy when she knew him. She is warm and loving, and Jody never finds her reptilian nature repulsive. She tells him the story of what happened on Isis after the people arrive and before he was born. She is less outlandish than many science fiction characters.

ONADIPE, KOLA, Nigerian writer, educator, economist, lawyer, publisher, and businessman. Among his publications for young readers is *Around Nigeria in Thirty Days** (Natona, 1981), in which three schoolboys spend their holidays traveling around their country in order to learn firsthand about its beauty and diversity. It received first prize for the Best Book in English for Ages 13–18 from the Children's Literature Association of Nigeria (CLAN). His *A Pot of Gold** (Natona, 1980), a story of friendship between two girls of different economic backgrounds intended for younger readers, was named in 1983 the best book in the English language by the Nigerian National Council for Arts and Culture.

ONCE THERE WAS A SWAGMAN (Brinsmead*, H. F., ill. Noela Young, Oxford, 1979), autobiographical realistic novelette about the Truelance family, companion to *Longtime Passing**. It covers three days at their home, Wangerra, in Longtime*, a "somewhere-nowhere kind of place" in the Blue Mountains of New South Wales. All the Truelance children are away at school, except for

Boo, maybe eleven, and the youngest sister, Teddy*, 9. Times are hard during the Great Depression, and Father (Edwin*) peddles lamps to make a living. One autumn day he leaves on a sales trip, as he departs reminding Teddy to look after Rhony, the "wicked old" family cow, which often "gets the wanders." Boo rides off on a ten-mile overnight jaunt to Kurrijung Brush for her weekly fiddle lesson. Left with Mother (Letty*) and missing Father, Teddy feels lonely and sorry for herself until, while they are hoeing carrots, a white-whiskered, humpbacked, old swagman (tramp) arrives, with bedroll and billy, wearing a "cabbage-tree hat" and a "smile [that] disturbed his whiskers," with a mottled cattle dog, Bones, at his heels. In return for meals and a bed in the old bark-tree hut, Mr. Mungo Brodie chops wood, builds the wood pile, and helps hoe and harvest carrots. Teddy thrills to the stories he tells, half-believing he's a gnome, and picks up the eerie tune he sometimes whistles and sings about Jim Crow, who, Mr. Brodie, says, represents time. A heavy mist moves in, and when Teddy goes to milk Rhony, as usual, she finds her gone. She searches the paddock, finds the hole where the cow got out, and goes after her, mindful of Father's orders and Rhony's importance. She follows her instincts, then catches some faint tracks and the far-off tinkle of Rhony's bell through the fog, and picks her way through the trees. Realizing she is lost, scared and tearful, she keeps calm even when she tumbles precipitously down and hits water. She whistles Mr. Brody's tune and soon gratefully hears his whistled response. He and Bones fish her out and take her home. Ironically on the way they encounter Rhony, also on her way home. The next morning, sun shining, Mr. Brodie announces he'll move on. He leaves singing the last verse of his song for Teddy in "his crackly, breathy voice." Unusual turns of expression, the strongly evoked natural beauty of the rugged region, the warm, accurate family relationships, the austere, hill way of life, the social class distinctions and protocol evident in the relationship between Mother, a landed person, and the wandering swagman, the gentle humor, and the economical, rich characterizations make this book a small gem. Aust. Bk. of Year Highly Com.

ONCE UPON A FOREST (Bhatt*, Kavery, ill. Mrinal Mitra, CBT, India, 1986), group adventure novel set in modern times in the Palali Game Reserve of India. Six young people survive several days of a wide variety of near disasters in a wild forest and rescue their adult leader by keeping calm and acting bravely. Uncle Dev (Captain Devendranath) takes his thirteen-year-old twin niece and nephew, Viji and Vinay Chandra, and their family friends, Dilip Gonsalves, 14, his plump little sister, Laila, 9, Smita Parekh, 13 (a spoiled girl who thinks mostly of clothes), lively Soorie Sampath, 9, and Soorie's black and grey dog, Chow, for a weekend camping trip to the game reserve. At the entrance he takes a wrong turn, on the mistaken advice of Vinay, who has been in the park before, and instead of reaching the camping area they find themselves as dark descends at the end of a narrow road unable to turn around. Leaving the youngsters in the Land Rover, Uncle Dev sets out on foot to find the campsite. After waiting a long time, Dilip and Soorie take the flashlight and discover that Uncle Dev has fallen into a pit, breaking his leg and injuring his head. The others help haul the large man from the pit—no easy task—and Viji, a level-headed girl who has always been interested in her father's medical books, splints his leg. For the rest of their adventure Uncle Dev slips into and out of consciousness and is unable to advise them. A series of life-threatening problems occur. First Soorie, then Smita and Vinay, and finally Dilip are chased by a mad wild buffalo. Vinay, who has saved Smita by throwing his shoes to distract the beast, steps on a piece of glass, badly injuring his foot. Laila and Soorie nearly eat some poisonous berries. Laila develops a fever. Two men who have been illegally cutting trees approach the group and reluctantly agree to take the youngsters back to civilization if they leave Uncle Dev behind to die, an offer they indignantly refuse. Smita, leaving the injured Vinay, comes upon a poor village at the edge of the preserve and gets help, first for the boy and then to carry Uncle Dev on the makeshift stretcher to a main road where they hope to get help. In the meantime, the two men encountered in the forest show up in the village, which they have been terrorizing. When Vinay protests, they knock him out, tie him up, and take him with them. At the main road, once again in the dark, the youngsters stop an army truck fortuitously driven by a major from Uncle Dev's battalion, who takes them all to the hospital in Dalitpur. There Dr. Chandra, a neurosurgeon, summoned to operate on the injured man, arrives with the three other fathers. Vinay has been dumped, still tied hand and foot, out of the jeep on a desolate stretch of road. Although he passes out from the fierce sun, he wakes in the cooler evening, manages to worm his way onto the road, and attracts the attention of a young just-married couple, who drive him to the police station. The villains are caught, the village people rewarded, Uncle Dev recovers, and the children plan another camping trip for the next year. Like most books of this subgenre, the novel provides more catastrophes and near-disasters than are entirely plausible, and the youngsters develop predictably: Smita, though unsuitably dressed for the wilderness and unused to doing practical chores, turns out to have unexpected stamina and good sense; Vinay, though impulsive and over-imaginative, is also brave and self-sacrificing; Laila, usually a pest to her older brother, comforts neglected Soorie and cheers all the others by sharing the sweets she has smuggled in her pack; Viji, the one most aware of their real danger, controls her emotions when she is tempted to panic. The pace is lively. In some places the text could use editing to correct some subject-verb disagreement and non-idiomatic usage, but the story is full of action and interesting detail. CBT of India, First Prize.

ONE PROUD SUMMER (Hewitt*, Marsha and Mackay*, Claire, Women's 1981), historical novel concerning the 1946 strike in the textile mill at Valleyfield, Quebec, Canada, which belatedly won union recognition and better conditions for the mostly French-Canadian workers. After the death of her father in a mill accident, Lucie Laplante, 13, must leave school for the weaving room of the

Montreal Cottons (MOCO) mill, part of Dominion Textiles Ltd., where her mother works and her grandmother slaved for many years until her health was broken. A bright girl who has been the pride of the nuns at school, Lucie is called stupid and clumsy by the crude foreman, Angus MacGregor, who bullies and sexually harasses the younger women. For each mistake, MacGregor levies a fine, until Lucie has almost no take-home pay. The long hours and hot, dangerous conditions in the mill depress her, but her friend, Anette Laroche, 16, encourages her and confides to her the secret that the union, headed by her father, Gerard, is planning a strike after agreeing for years to work without protest to aid the war effort and then waiting vainly a year for conditions to be improved. Because most of the bosses are English and wealthy while the workers are French and poor, the labor problems are exacerbated by conflicts of social class. When Colonel Kirk, the manager, refuses to negotiate, the union calls a mass meeting that even Lucie's mother attends, although she fears being out of work with her aging mother and several children younger than Lucie to support. The overwhelming sentiment is to strike. Lucie finds the first months of the summer exciting and pleasant, even the hot hours on the picket line being preferable to the stifling mill. The management imports non-union workers to re-open the mill and break the strike. The church and the provincial police support the management, and workers who try to prevent scabs from entering the gates are clubbed. Only the mayor of Valleyfield is on the workers' side, refusing to allow the jail to be used to hold arrested workers. Tension comes to a head on August 13 when the company imports many more scabs and gets a contingent of provincial police to convoy them. The crowd erupts into a riot. The strikers throw stones and chase the scabs. Running to get help for a boy bleeding from a police club, Lucie feels a heavy hand on her shoulder and finds that she is under arrest by MacGregor, now a company guard. She is taken to an isolated shed, where he tries to trick her into giving incriminating information about her mother and friends in the union, threatening rape if she refuses. MacGregor is distracted by the arrival of Emilie Bouchard, a girl not much older than Lucie who has in the past responded to his advances to get favored treatment. While Emilie flirts with him, she secretly signals Lucie to escape, then kicks Mac-Gregor, locks him in the shed, and rides Lucie on her bicycle back to the mill gates, admitting that she has been ashamed of succumbing to MacGregor in the past but was so afraid of him that she dared not stop. Despite fears that MOCO will in some way trick the Valleyfield people, an election solidifies the union's standing and the workers return to still terrible conditions and low and discriminatory wages, but with hope and some opportunity to improve their lot. With a few exceptions, the characters are simply functional and not highly developed. The most interesting is Lucie's grandmother, who tells her about past labor struggles, keeps a scrapbook of events during the ninety-six day strike, and even joins some of the demonstrations despite being partly crippled from years in the mill. Working conditions sound more like those of a hundred years earlier but are convincingly documented. The action, strong descriptions of mill work, and a sense of outrage keep the book interesting, although it is frankly written to support a social thesis that workers' rights must be respected. The fictional text is followed by photographs of the actual strike, by a long historical note telling of the events on which the book is based, and by a bibliography on the subject. Can. Council Hon. Ment.; Can. Ruth Schwartz.

O'REILLY, BERNARD, Australian author of *Wild River** (Cassell, 1950), an adventure novel set in northern Queensland, which was highly commended for the Australian Library Association Book of the Year Award. It concerns the discovery of uranium and attempts of desperate men to steal the mining claim staked by the ranching family that is responsible for the find.

ORWIN, JOANNA, New Zealand writer for children of novels about the Maoris and of publications for the New Zealand Forest Service. Family holidays at Lake Roto-iti, Nelson, when she was a child, inspired her love of her country's bush and landscape. She worked as a plant ecologist, after earning a degree in botany. Her scientific background and her interest in archaeology come together in *Ihaka and the Prophecy** (Oxford, 1984), a book about an ancient Maori youth with strong artistic talents which was named to the short list for the New Zealand Government Award. She has also published *Ihaka and the Summer Wandering* (Oxford, 1982) and *The Guardian of the Land* (Oxford, 1986).

OSRO (*The Priests of Ferris**; *Motherstone**), renegade priest of O, who seeks to become king and leads a rebellion against Kenno's government. He is painted with the exaggerated villainy of the animated cartoon, snarling and dealing out blows almost indiscriminately, a power-mad megalomaniac. Once employed at the Temple, he played the role of a clown, acting the fool for seven years while the mad High Priest ruled. During that time, Osro discovered the directions for fashioning the Weapon, a kind of death-ray instrument with which he later plans to conquer O.

OTTLEY, REGINALD (LESLIE), born in London, England; man of many trades, mostly dealing with cattle ranching in Australia and the South Pacific, writer of many novels, chiefly for young people. He was educated at St. Mary Magdalene's Church of England School, London. During World War II he served in the Australian Remount Corps. He has been a seaman, farm worker, cattle drover, horse breaker, race horse trainer, and property manager in Australia, a cattle ranch manager in Fiji and New Caledonia, and has worked for the British Colonial Administration in Guadalcanal, Solomon Islands. His wide-ranching experience is reflected in his trilogy, *By the Sandhills of Yamboorah** (Deutsch, 1965; *Boy Alone*, Harcourt, 1966), *The Roan Colt of Yamboorah** (Deutsch, 1966; *The Roan Colt*, Harcourt, 1967), and *Rain Comes to Yamboorah* (Deutsch, 1967; Harcourt, 1968), novels of an orphan boy on an isolated cattle station near the desert of South Australia. The first of these was highly commended for the

Australian Book of the Year Award and was chosen for the *Choice* magazine list of books for an academic library and the Lewis Carroll Bookshelf; the second was commended for the Book of the Year Award. Also commended for the award was *The Bates Family** (Collins, 1969; Harcourt, 1969), a story of a family of drovers who herd sheep and cattle for hundreds of miles in the Australian outback, living a nomadic life. Among Ottley's other books set in Australia are *No More Tomorrow* (Collins, 1972; Harcourt, 1971), about a swagman who trudges the barren stretches with only his dog for companionship, and *Jim Grew of Moonbah* (Collins, 1970; Harcourt, 1970), a story of a boy who helps his mother run a sheep station. Ottley's New Caladonia experience provides the setting for *Giselle* (Collins, 1968; Harcourt, 1968).

OVER THE BRIDGE (Hill*, Deirdre, ill. James Hunt, Hutchinson, 1969), holiday adventure story of an Australian boy who saves an old trolley car from the scrap heap, set in the period of its publication. Bob Burrow, 11, has always been fascinated by the "trams," and regularly waits after school at the nearby terminus where the cars to his suburb reverse and return to the city. His friends among the drivers, in particular Stan, let him change the signs and adjust the poles to the overhead wires. He knows all the cars and is especially fond of 273, an older model with beautiful woodwork and a shining brass rail. He is upset when he learns that the bridge over which the trams pass has been declared unsafe and is to be closed to traffic. At first the trams from the city stop at the far side to let the passengers walk across the bridge, and old 273 picks them up on the suburban side, but there is talk of retiring the older trams and instituting a bus line. Bob is also worried about his best friend, Don White, whose father has been ill and is moving the family to farm land that he owns in the forest, intending to build a house and raise their food. Bob talks it over with his friend, Ted, caretaker of the golf course, who lives in a little house built right into the side of the cliff. He learns that Ted has a wife and son now living with relatives, and that if Ted can get a job rebuilding the bridge, he can rent a real house and bring them to live with him again. Stan tells Bob that old trams are sold for their value in scrap, about fifty dollars, and Bob is determined to buy 273 and keep it in his back yard. Although his father reluctantly tolerates a billy goat named Pop Eye that Bob has obtained for free, he refuses to have a tram in the yard or even to let Bob spend his own money on it. Bob, however, doesn't give up and thinks of ways to double the twenty-five dollars he has been saving for a bike. He gets a part-time job at the grocery store, and he and Don attempt to explore the old boat long grounded near the shore in the bay, hoping to find brass to sell, and salvages an antique ship's lamp, which he eventually sells to his father's boss, a collector, for ten dollars. He tries to get the paper route that Don must give up, but since he doesn't have a bike, it goes instead to Bruce Baker, a boy he doesn't much like. His antagonism to Bruce erupts on the night that 273 is taken across the now condemned bridge. Stan has tipped him off that it will be driven back at midnight, and he has sneaked out alone to see it, having promised not to tell anyone. Bruce and his gang, however, have somehow learned and are up to their favorite sport of swinging the suspension bridge, hoping to derail the tram. Enraged, Bob races onto the bridge and attacks Bruce, only to be apprehended with him by the police. Ted talks them out of arresting Bob. He learns that the transportation department will sell 273 for $100, after it has been stripped of its wheels and some mechanical parts. Ted, who has been working for Mr. White at the farm, gets Bob to give Pop Eye to the Whites. When his father drives them with Don to the farm, the boys see a house made from a tram car, and persuade Mr. White that this is the perfect solution to a temporary housing problem and will make the family split-up to various relatives, which they have all been dreading, unnecessary. Bob is delighted that 273 will not be scrapped and plans to spend his money on a bike so he can ride out to see Don. The story is unpretentious and plausible. Bob's single-minded obsession with the old tram rings true, as does his continued hope, against all evidence, that his father will change his mind. The other characters are functional but undeveloped. Old 273, however, is described lovingly and becomes almost a living creature to the reader, as it is to Bob, and though the solution is predictable, it is not too farfetched. Aust. Bk. of Year Com.

P

PACK UP, PICK UP, AND OFF (Taylor*, William, ill. Alan Howie, Price, 1981), realistic novel of community life in a sheep-raising area of New Zealand in the 1980s with the added complication of a sheep-stealing mystery. Charlie Thomson, 13, tells of the first day he and his sister, Carey, 11, and little brother, George, 8, start in the one-room school at Tahiwi, Hawkes Bay, having walked the three dusty miles after the school bus deliberately passed them. Although the teacher, Mr. Hughes, is welcoming, he overhears one of the older boys sneering, "Dirty rabbiter kids." Before the day is over he has to settle with the sneerer, Scuffer (Bobby) Fletcher, whose father owns a very large sheep ranch, not with a real fight but with a single punch to the jaw, for which Mr. Hughes reprimands him without much conviction. Throughout the next few weeks, a number of incidents reveal that the community looks down on the Thomson family because Charlie's father, Stan, is hired by the local Rabbit Board to hunt and exterminate the rabbits, animals that have become terrible pests. The Thomson family's life has always been one of "pack up, pick up, and off" variety, sometimes in a city where Charlie's father works as a mechanic for a time. Stan always returns to rabbiting because he loves the land and, having no money to buy a place, settles for the house and paddock provided by the local board. Carey quickly makes a best friend of Marlene Spencer, is invited to spend a weekend at her house in town, and is crushed when the invitation is rudely withdrawn. Mr. Fletcher calls at the house and pointedly discusses his recent loss of sheep, clearly with veiled suspicion and warning. When the erratic driving by Gus, the older Fletcher boy, causes an accident that could have killed the Thomson children and is called to account by Mr. Hughes, the Fletchers' enmity toward the family grows. Mr. Fletcher and three policemen arrive and arrest Stan for sheep stealing. The evidence, a dead carcass in his car trunk and several Fletcher sheep in his paddock, seems uncontrovertible, and he has no alibi. Moreover, he has a criminal record, having killed a sheep he thought was due him as wages after a dispute with a ranch boss when Charlie was a baby. Determined to clear his father, who he knows is innocent, Charlie tries to puzzle out who could have framed him. On the Tops, a vast spread of eroded highland bordering the Fletcher acreage, he shelters from rain and sees, to his surprise, a bundle of fresh sheep skins in an old shepherd's hut. He enlists Carey's aid and when they return together the hides are gone. More significantly, they find a place in a deep gully near the Fletcher fence where sheep have obviously been slaughtered and skinned. They decide to check every day. In the meantime, Uncle Mick, who has helped Stan out of difficult situations before, arrives and puts up bail, Mrs. Spencer calls with soup and biscuits and such patronizing comments that Mrs. Thomson has difficulty keeping her temper, and Mr. Hughes calls with his wife and baby and such sincere sympathy that the whole family is touched. Before the trial date, the children see three men in the act of butchering sheep and hauling the hides to the shed. To their amazement, one of the men is Gus Fletcher. Their father alerts the police and Mr. Fletcher, who arrives shortly with a shotgun, and they are able to surprise the thieves still in action. The community rallies to show its contrition, but the Thomson family has had enough of Tahiwi, and packs up, preparing once again to pick up and be off. The mystery is predictable, with one-dimensional villains, but the picture of community and family life holds the reader's interest, and the physical setting gives the story freshness and a sense of reality. N.Z. Govt. Short List.

PAPA (*Corner Store**), Jake Devine, keeper of a small neighborhood store in Winnipeg of the 1930s. Impatient and hot tempered, he has frightened his own children and driven away many of his customers, thereby increasing his financial problems, his worry, and his irritability. He is an immigrant from Russia, where as a boy he saw his own mother killed in a pogrom and narrowly escaped himself. After Mama's death, he tells Becky* that he doesn't want to marry again but mustn't insult the well-wishing relatives who bring old maids for him to inspect, and she feels betrayed when he responds to Miss Sylvia* Cohen, having taken literally his joking statement that he might think of it in ten years or so. With Sylvia's financial help and her self-assured but tactful management, he becomes much more approachable and Becky begins to think, for the first time, that he really loves her.

PAPERNY, MYRA (1932–   ), born in Edmonton, Alberta, Canada; journalist, teacher, writer. Daughter of a Jewish Russian emigrant, she lived as a child in Alberta and British Columbia and received her B.A. degree from the University of British Columbia. The next year she received an M.S. in journalism from Columbia University and has worked as a free-lance reporter for the *Vancouver News Herald* and other newspapers and magazines. She has taught creative writing at Mount Royal College, Calgary, and at the University of Calgary. Her first novel, *The Wooden People** (Little, 1976), is about the puppet theater created and run secretly by a family of children in a small Alberta town of the 1920s in defiance of their stern, domineering father. It won the Children's Book Award given by Little Brown publishers and the Canada Council Prize. Her second book, *Take a Giant Step* (Overlea, 1987), set during World War II, also deals with father-child conflict, this time between a boy violin prodigy and his father, who will not let him play ball or ride a bike lest he injure his hands. A later title is *Nightmare Mountain* (Overlea, 1988). Paperny has been criticized for weak plotting but praised for expertly evoking setting in time and place.

PARK, (ROSINA) RUTH (1922?–   ), born in Auckland, New Zealand, and educated at St. Benedict's College and the University of Auckland; editor, journalist, and writer best known for her dozen books for adults, mostly novels, who has also written more than thirty novels and stories published in picture-book form for children. Before marrying D'Arcy Niland, a journalist, playwright, and author, in 1942 and becoming the mother of five children, she had established herself as a journalist and editor, holding positions with the Auckland *Star*, *Zealandia*, and Sydney *Mirror*. After publishing a half-dozen novels for adults from 1948 to 1961 and winning the Sydney *Morning Herald* prize for her first, *The Harp in the South* (Angus, 1948; Houghton, 1948), she wrote adventure stories for young readers set around the Pacific. The first of these, *The Hole in the Hill** (Ure, 1961; *Secret of the Maori Cave*, Doubleday, 1964), was commended for Book of the Year by the Australian Children's Book Council. Her fame in children's literature, however, came with her Muddle-Headed Wombat stories published in picture-book form that originated in a radio program, *The Muddle-Headed Wombat* (Educational, 1962; Angus, 1963), and twelve others. Later commended for Book of the Year were *Callie's Castle** (Angus, 1974), about a girl's need for space of her own, for younger readers, and *Come Danger, Come Darkness** (Hodder, 1978), a historical adventure novel for older readers set among the convicts of the Norfolk Island penal colony. Her most highly regarded book for young readers is *Playing Beatie Bow** (Nelson, 1980; Atheneum, 1982). It was Book of the Year Award Winner and *Boston Globe–Horn Book* Winner and was named to the Fanfare list by the editors of *Horn Book*. An engrossing historical novel in a time-travel fantasy framework, it takes a modern Australian girl back to Victorian Sydney.

THE PARKHURST BOYS (Beames*, Margaret, ill. Susan Opie, Mallinson, 1986), historical novel that takes place in London and southeastern England, the high seas, and New Zealand in the early 1840s. Unable to bear the ill-treatment meted out by the abusive boarding school to which he has been sent by his stingy uncle, Mr. Murgatroyd, orphaned Charlie (Charles) Blackiston, 10, runs away to London. He is befriended by a ten-year-old orphan street urchin who calls himself Joss (Joseph) Brown and lives by his wits. When Joss is caught stealing an orange and Charlie is taken as an accomplice, the two are remanded to Parkhurst Prison on the Isle of Wight for reforming. After two years they and ninety other boys from twelve to nineteen years of age are sent to Auckland,

New Zealand, to begin new lives there as apprentices to settlers, their sentences commuted. Jammed four to a bunk in the hold of the *St. George* (an actual ship), Charlie and Joss have a mostly uncomfortable, often unpleasant voyage, experiencing harrowing seas, especially around Cape Horn. They arrive at Auckland glad to be alive and hopeful for better times but also surprised and let down by the austerity of the primitive settlement. Before they departed from England, Charlie slipped a message for his older sister, Muriel, to a kindly Quaker woman on the dock. She delivered it to Mrs. Murgatroyd, but Muriel never received it because the aunt burned it. Auckland and its environs are sparsely populated, and the apprenticeships promised the boys simply do not exist. Captain Rough, the historical harbormaster, greets the boys pleasantly but can do little for them. Eventually Joss is hired by a kind carpenter, Mr. MacAllister, and his solicitous wife, recent settlers, who treat him like a son. Charlie, however, fares much less well, being taken by a milquetoast liveryman, Mr. Watchet, and his termagent, domineering wife, who belittles and berates Charlie at every turn and overworks him badly. Unable to bear being treated like a slave, Charlie runs away to the harbor, where a drunken gun runner named Crowder promises him a job in the copper mines on Great Barrier Island, then tosses him off his boat for being too small to be useful. Charlie manages to swim to a nearby island, where he falls in with Maoris, who take him on an island voyage and then back to their mainland home up the coast from Auckland. Charlie ironically becomes the slave of Rewa, the son of the chief, Potere. Rewa calls Charlie Mangu, which means black, as a joke, and the two boys become inseparable friends, Charlie even saving Rewa's life after he falls over a cliff and is almost crushed by a tree the men have felled to sell to a white sawyer. After about four months, Charlie's sister, Muriel, and her husband, a merchant shipowner, arrive on a trading trip, Muriel having learned of Charlie's whereabouts from Mrs. Murgatroyd, who confesses on her deathbed to destroying the letter Charlie had left for Muriel. Searching for Charlie, Muriel encounters Joss, who happens to overhear a waterfront conversation about a white boy among the Maori between Crowder and a sailor. Suspecting that Crowder intends to kill Charlie lest Charlie tell authorities that Crowder tried to drown him, Joss trails Crowder up the shore to the Maori village and intervenes in the nick of time to save Charlie's and Rewa's lives. In the scuffle, Crowder falls, hits his head on a rock, and dies. The Maori return the children to Auckland, where Joss is made the MacAllister apprentice and, actually nameless, chooses to call himself Joseph Charles (after Charlie) Parkhurst (because the Prison gave him a chance at a better life), and Charlie prepares to sail home to England with Muriel and her husband. Although the story employs the conventions and fast pace of the Victorian melodrama, its tone is that of the serious historical novel, and events are broadly historical. The author is sparing with detail, but enough is said about conditions in the prison, at the school, and on shipboard to give the impression of how terrible they must have been. Excitement abounds, the climax scene being especially taut. The characters are one-dimensional and stock. Even Charlie and Joss are barely distinguishable. Charlie is presented as small and fair, and Joss is a freckle-faced, ginger-haired cockney. Class distinctions are less defined than probably would have been the case, and Joss, definitely of the street, is a sympathetic figure. So are the Maori, who are shown as exotic but basically good, and the author informs the reader in an afterword that in some instances the transported boys did in fact run away to the natives rather than endure the bad treatment they received among the often suspicious and abusive settlers. N.Z. Govt. Short List.

A PASSAGE TO ANTARCTICA (Salwi*, Dilip M., ill. Sujasha Dasgupta, CBT, India, 1986), realistic novel of a recent scientific voyage from Goa, India, to the Antarctic. Schoolgirl Neha tells how during Christmas vacation she accepts an invitation from Uncle Sahai, a scientist and her father's closest friend, to accompany him and his son, Ajai, to the Antarctic aboard the scientific ship, *Dakshin Samrat*. During the voyage and after their arrival at the subcontinent, Uncle Sahai and other scientists instruct the children about flora or fauna encountered, experiments being conducted, and the importance of the subcontinent for space exploration, mineral resources, and the like. Both Neha and Ajai are eager to learn and ask intelligent questions. After a bout of seasickness, they explore the ship, and Neha discovers in the library a book entitled *I am Antarctica*, which she includes in its entirety in her narrative. Written in first person from the point of view of the subcontinent, it gives the history of its discovery and development and an overview of its potential. The children participate in the Neptune ceremony at the equator, experience the discomfort of the Roaring Forties, sight a humpback whale, visit a small, abandoned whaling station, and spot a huge iceberg. They learn how an ice breaker works, celebrate Christmas aboard ship by exchanging gifts, and drift through the deep, blue idyllic polynia. They land on the Queen Maud Land side near the Russian camp and fly by helicopter to the Indian station, Dakshin Gangotri. They are pleased to find that the permanent camp has every modern convenience for the scientists to live comfortably while conducting their work. A small mystery provides some spice. The furtive, bearded man Neha has spotted aboard ship hovering nearby turns out to be a scientist who had been asked to keep an eye on her. She meets him officially when she accompanies another scientist by snowmobile to an outlying laboratory. Dr. Dias takes her to visit a woman scientist, Mohini Auntie, who is conducting research on seals. On the way back to the main station, the two get lost in a sudden whiteout and are saved when Neha spots the station through the mist. For her courage she receives a special commendation at the New Year's Day awards ceremony. Their three-day visit completed, the children fly back to Goa and home, delighted to have proved that children "are as good as adults in facing the harsh conditions prevailing in the [southernmost] continent." Although this book received its award as non-fiction, it satisfies the requirements for fiction since the plot and the characters are invented and the book works like fiction. Indeed, an introductory note calls the book "a science fiction." While this statement supports classifying the book as fiction, it is nevertheless an unusual use of the term, since the information presented is factual according to contemporary scientific knowledge, except that the whaling station and the Indian colony do not exist as described. Characters and incidents are undeveloped, and allusions, idioms, sentence structure, and speech rhythms are peculiarly Asian Indian and evoke a special interest for their own sake. The book is purposely didactic and conveys a great deal of interesting information about the Antarctic. CBT of India, Second Prize.

PASTURES OF THE BLUE CRANE (Brinsmead*, H. F., Oxford, 1964; Coward, 1966), realistic novel of family, neighborhood, and farm life with girl's growing-up aspects, set in Australia in the mid–1900s. Imperious, self-centered, calculatedly charming Ryl* (Amaryllis) Merewether, 16, and her independent, free-spirited grandfather, Dusty* Merewether, meet for the first time in Melbourne at the reading of her father's will. To their surprise, they inherit equal shares in a small, rundown farm near Murwillumbah in northern New South Wales. Although she despises both Dusty and the farm, Ryl sets about making the place habitable according to her teenaged, boarding-school standards. Dusty grudgingly grows to admire her spunk and persistence, and she comes to appreciate his attachment to the scenic region with its views of the sea and the majestic blue crane that struts across the pastures. She names the place Geebin Farm after the exotic creature. Friends help them: Clem and Rose* Bradley, who invite them to dinner and extend labor and advice; Perry* Davis, a reliable university student, whose kinky hair betrays his South Sea Island (blackbird*) ancestry and arouses ambivalent feelings in Ryl; Glen* Dynon, a handsome student son of the local pharmacist, who introduces Ryl to area youth. Sensing that Dusty thinks his life has been wasted, she decides to "make something of him" by encouraging his interest in cattle raising and developing a banana plantation with Perry's help. Two main problems confront her: solving the mystery of who her mother was and why her father and Dusty had a falling out and preventing the town council from requisitioning the hill upon which the house stands for a water tower. As the latter problem winds down, Ryl discovers that the source of the disagreement between her father and Dusty lay in her mother's background. She learns that her mother was the granddaughter of old Ki, a blackbird and Perry's great-grandfather, that she herself is South Sea Island in descent, and that Perry is her brother. At the end her family and Perry bury old Ki; the town purchases Ki's farm for the water tower; Perry plans to continue his education with the proceeds from the sale; Dusty is content with his new life; and Ryl savors the sense of family, looks forward to attending the university, and likens herself to the blue crane, a wandering creature always lured back to warm, welcoming, beautiful Geebin Farm. Characters are obvious contrasts, and the mystery of Ryl's parentage is overforeshadowed. Ryl and Dusty change believably, and, if stock, events sustain attention well. The themes of neighborliness, cooperation, closeness to the soil, and racial tolerance cannot be missed, and dialogue is extensive and dates the book. The strength of the story lies in its keen sense of community and vivid evocation of natural setting. Aust. Bk. of Year Winner.

PATCHETT, MARY ELWYN (OSBORNE) (1897–), born on a cattle station on the Queensland–New South Wales border, Australia; prolific author, most notably of animal stories for children, many of them set in Australia. She was educated at New England Girls' School, Armidale, and Church of England Girls' Grammar School, Sydney. For five years she worked as a journalist in Sydney before going to England, where she has made her home for many years. Although she has published a number of science fiction novels about interplanetary flight and undersea exploration, she is best known for her stories about animals, the first of which was *Ajax, the Warrior* (Lutterworth, 1953; *Ajax, Golden Dog of the Australian Bush*, Bobbs, 1953), based on her own childhood in the bush. A series known as "the Brumbies books," starting with *The Brumby* (Lutterworth, 1958; *Brumby, The Wild White Stallion*, Bobbs, 1959), deals with a boy's efforts to protect the wild horses of Australia. Some critics have listed *Tiger in the Dark* (Brockhampton, 1964; Duell, 1966), story of a quest in the outback for the supposedly extinct Australian marsupial Tasmanian wolf, as her most successful book. Her novel of the pair of dingoes, *Wild Brother** (Collins, 1954), was originally published for adults but was highly commended for the Book of the Year in children's fiction. Her animal novels have been praised for their accuracy and lack of sentimentality.

PAT REID (*A Handful of Time**), Patricia Reid, after whom Ruth* Reid ironically named her daughter. Pat (later called Nan) is a domineering mother to Ruth and a bossy, opinionated grandmother to Patricia Potter and Patricia's Grant cousins. In the fantasy portions of the novel, Pat indulges her sons but is an obstinate, controlling, and hateful mother to Ruth, holding firmly to a double standard of conduct for her children. The reason for her behavior is not given, but perhaps the sudden death of her sweetheart on the eve of their wedding, the man who gave her the watch Patricia finds, and Pat's immediate marriage to his brother, a much older, conservative, patriarchal man have some bearing on the matter. In the modern dimension, Pat (Nan) disapproves of Ruth's having a profession. Pat is the most intriguing character in the novel.

PATSY TRUELANCE (*Longtime Passing**), second daughter of Edwin* and Letty* Truelance, pioneers in Longtime* in Australia. Patsy is a strong-minded individualist, stubborn and unyielding. She is often at odds with her mother. In one of the book's most memorable scenes, Mark* accidentally cuts off the end of one of her middle fingers, and Edwin rushes her to a doctor in Richmond.

PAUL (*The Keeper**), one of the senior hunters in Big Lake village, a short, wiry, restless man, who quietly acts as a mentor to Michael* and Andy, though he shows sympathy for them only when other villagers are not present. After

Michael has been in the loners' settlement and looked closely at Luke, he recognizes a resemblance between the hairy, toothless man and Paul, despite superficial differences, and later Paul admits that they are brothers. His parents, having produced a deformed daughter when Paul was still a boy, left him in the village but went with Luke to join the loners, intending to send the older boy back later. Luke, however, chose not to return, and he and Paul have communicated secretly. Mr. Clinton, the teacher, says that Paul looks out for Michael because he has something on his conscience, and it is hinted but never explicitly stated that Paul may have failed to prevent the murder of Michael's parents when he could have acted or perhaps was one of the villagers who killed them and repented later. After the four young people leave the village, Paul travels a long way to trace them and learns that they are probably living on one of the sea islands to the northeast.

PEARCE, FRANCES, born in Peak Hills, New South Wales, Australia; teacher and writer, with Helen Granger* under the pseudonym Helen Frances, of *The Devil's Stone** (Omnibus, 1983). A substantial historical novel with modern realistic and fantasy elements, involving Aborigine beliefs, the story won the Australian Children's Book of the Year Award. Pearce studied at the University of Sydney and the Australian National University, where she met her husband, a New Zealander. She lived in England and France and was a university teacher before her two daughters were born. For a dozen years before the book was written, she was an orchardist in the Adelaide Hills, the locale of *The Devil's Stone*.

PEARSON, KIT (KATHLEEN) (1947–   ), born in Edmonton, Alberta, Canada; librarian and writer for children. She received a degree in English at the University of Alberta, her degree in Library Science at the University of British Columbia, and an M.A. in Children's Literature at the Center for the Study of Children's Literature at Simmons College in Boston, Massachusetts. A librarian in Vancouver, B.C., she published her first novel, *The Daring Game* (Viking) a boarding school story, in 1986, and her second, *A Handful of Time** (Penguin; Viking) the following year. Canadian Library Association Children's Book of the Year Winner and commended for the Max and Greta Ebel Memorial Award, it tells how a young girl gains perspective on her parents' divorce when she is transported back in time to her mother's generation and takes a sharp look at the role of women and relationships between mothers and daughters. Her third novel, *The Sky Is Falling* (Viking, 1989), concerns a British brother and sister evacuated to Canada during World War II. She has also written many reviews and articles for periodicals.

PEGMEN TALES (McFadyen*, Ella, ill. Edwina Bell, Angus, 1946), fantasy adventure involving anthropomorphized clothes-peg (clothespin) dolls, beginning on a sheep station beside the Macquarie River in modern Australia. In the spring young Peter and his cousin Joan from Sydney lay out Pegmen's Run, a miniature station close to the river, and with clothes pegs secured from the washerwoman, fashion Dan Pegman, the head of the family, his mother, maternal, wise Mrs. Peg, and his younger brother, nice but often feckless Nobby. When a flood comes, the children put the Pegmen on Joan's play ark, and thereafter the Pegmen have amazing adventures on the river and ocean as full-sized humans, many of which revolve around the antics of a lazy, lying, mischievous, sometimes bad monkey named Pongo, who has stowed away. The adventures are transmitted to the human children each night in dreams by the White Cockatoo, the magical Maker-of-Dreams that lives by the river. As they float about, Mrs. Peg serves as cook, Nobby and Pongo as crewmen, and Dan as the captain, whose heroes are Lord Nelson and Captain James Cook. The adventures follow rapidly, with no causal sequence, and take them ashore to seek gold, of which Nobby finds nine huge nuggets and makes them rich, and to rescue sheep from the flood and little woods animals from hunters, whom they repel with coconuts shot from a toy cannon now also full-sized. They are visited by a Platypus, engage in a mock jousting tournament, and snare a shark, which takes them for a wild sea-ride to Sydney Bay, where ashore Pongo causes a multitude of troubles. When winter closes in, the Pegmen visit the South Pole. Simultaneously, Peter's and Joan's lives have changed, with school and other interests, and when the Pegmen battle pirate Henry Morgan for his treasure and Nobby calls on Peter for help, Peter barely recognizes Nobby's voice, since the White Cockatoo has been weaving him other dreams. Back at Pegmen's Run, the Pegmen discover the run still ruined by the flood. Mrs. Peg realizes that the children are growing up, and Dan plans further voyages for his family. The peg characters are distinctly drawn, the children less so, and life aboard the ark is enticing and homey with such amenities as delicious pickles and strawberry jam for tea. The swift-paced episodes are consistently entertaining with action, comedy, and mild suspense, and the tone is quaintly lighthearted, cozy, and optimistic, all problems overcome through such traditional values as cooperation, hard work, and perseverance. Aust. Bk. of Year Com.

PENNY MACLEOD (*Bush Holiday**; *Bush Voyage**), freckled, happy, long-legged tomboy, half-orphaned daughter of the owner of Tangari, about twelve. Assertive, decisive, she is used to taking care of herself and having her way. In *Bush Holiday*, she introduces Martin and Steve Duke, and thus Steve and Martin's mother marry. In *Bush Voyage*, she capably cares for the abandoned baby, an unlikely circumstance since Penny has had no experience with babies. She is likeable, if a type, and interesting and appropriate for the plot.

PENNY POLLARD'S DIARY (Klein*, Robin, ill. Ann James, Oxford, 1983), humorous realistic novelette about an Australian schoolgirl's friendship with an elderly resident of a nursing home written as diary entries spanning almost two weeks' time. Penny Pollard, 10, a strong-willed, obstreperous, horse-loving tomboy, resents having to accompany her class on a visit to a local nursing home. Once there, she slips away unnoticed while her classmates sing and play their recorders to entertain the residents, sneaking out to the garden where she encounters old Mrs. Edith Bettany, in her way just as rebellious and non-conformist as Penny. Mrs. Bettany tells Penny about her problems with an unsympathetic matron, about her dead husband, Albert, who was a blacksmith and who, Penny soon notices, Mrs. Bettany often forgets is dead, and about her youth on a little farm in the bush with her ten brothers and sisters. She shares Penny's interest in horses and knows a good deal about them. On a later visit Penny learns more about the old woman, including that she has been in the home for twelve years and in all that time has not been back to the house in Boronia Road where she lived so long with Albert. The following Saturday, Penny takes Mrs. Bettany on the bus to Baronia Road, where they shop in the mall and find businesses and parking lots where her cherished landmarks were and an empty lot where her house once stood. Penny finds one of Mrs. Bettany's beloved geraniums still alive, digs it up with her jackknife, takes it home, and pots it as a gift for the old woman. Penny learns that the following Tuesday is Mrs. Bettany's eighty-first birthday. She and Dad and Mum plan a celebration. Mum prepares Mrs. Bettany's choices for dinner—Maryland chicken and lime inter-planetary missiles for dessert— and a cake with eighty-one candles. As a special birthday present, Dad enlarges a newspaper photo of Mrs. Bettany and her family in front of their house dated circa 1920. The diary stops abruptly with Mrs. Bettany remarking that she is sorry that she has nothing to give them in return and leaving the reader to wonder whether or not the friendship will bring about any permanent change in the life or personality of either Penny or Mrs. Bettany. Although too detailed with conversations and action to be a true diary and not cohesive enough to be a proper novel, the story exerts a certain pull through its richly drawn protagonist and skillfully counterpointed old woman. Penny's fix-ation for horses and dislike of her too good classmate named Simone seem genuine, as does her mother's desire for Penny to be more like Simone. Similarly Mrs. Bettany's matron would like her to conform more. Social comment about ageism and nursing homes is subtly but eloquently made. The style has some of the usual characteristics of a diary—omitted words, missing punctuation, and misspellings—but these often seem like affectations. Most of the humor is of the broad fourth-grade type; for example, Penny's mother complains that the school permission form has manure on it, not knowing that Penny hid it in her boot. Anyone familiar with nursing homes would recognize accurately described conditions, and Mrs. Bettany, though individually drawn in character, is typical in situation of many residents. The book is attractively decorated with drawings of horses, equine trappings, and antiqued photos. Aust. Bk. of Year Highly Com.

PERRY DAVIS (*Pastures of the Blue Crane**), student of agriculture, who drives a taxi on the side, great-grandson of old Ki, a South Sea Islander. Oth-erwise white in appearance, he has crinkly black hair that puts Ryl* Merewether off at first. He is reliable and a little self-righteous and preachy but can always be counted upon for help. As a character, Perry verges on the stock.

PETER MURPHY (*The Druid's Tune**), distant, taciturn young farmhand and Druid priest, Peadur Murrich in the ancient period. Too conspicuously inscrutable and mystical as a character, Peter is searching for his identity and inadvertently transports himself and the two children back in time. He has longed to go there but could not until the three, the two children and he, accidentally form a sacred triad. Through giving of himself he finds himself, apparently one of the book's themes, and at the end he returns to the ancient time frame, having through his experiences somehow become a harper.

PETER NEUFELD (*Days of Terror**), second son in the Neufeld family, the one from whose vantage point most events are seen though he does not tell the story. Not exploited much as an individual by the author, he does have a small conflict with Father over his drawing, which the elder Neufeld thinks frivolous. He is primarily responsible for Katya during raids, and he provides for Otto when he flees to the Neufelds' house for refuge, keeping his activity secret.

PETIT-JEAN (*Hebe's Daughter**), French orphan boy, whom Liz Pollard finds in the inn in Esterel in Normandy. A foundling, Petit-Jean is tiny for his age of about eight, pale, bony, and fearful. He often cries in his bed at night because he is cold, hungry, and overworked. Liz shows a special interest in him and takes him with her when she flees the mob during the French Revolution. He remains in her care during the rest of the book. At the end, he has recovered from his respiratory infection, and nutritious food, loving care, and the security of a good home have transformed him into a normal youngster. He now insists that he is English and later calls himself John Petty. Though a type figure of romance, he is interesting in his own right and also serves to point up Liz's generosity and persistence.

PHIPSON, JOAN (MARGARET FITZHARDINGE) (1912–   ), born at Warrawee, New South Wales, Australia; sheep rancher and novelist. During World War I she lived in India and started school in Bombay. She later went with her mother to England but returned to Australia on a troop ship and attended Fresham School, Mittagong, New South Wales, where she worked for three years as a librarian and printer. Later she worked in Sydney at a radio station as a secretary, then a copy- and scriptwriter. During World War II she spent two years as a telegraphist in the Women's Australian Air Force (WAAF), then married and went to live on a sheep ranch in central New South Wales. Most of her early books reflect this ranch life, including *Good Luck to the Rider** (Angus, 1953; Harcourt, 1968), which was an Australian Library Association Book of the Year Award winner; *It Happened One Summer** (Angus, 1954; *Six and Silver*, Harcourt, 1971), which was highly commended for the same award;

The Boundary Riders (Angus, 1962; Harcourt, 1963), which was named to the *Choice* magazine list of children's books for an academic library; *The Family Conspiracy** (Angus, 1962; Harcourt, 1964), which was both a Book of the Year Award winner and on the *Choice* list; and its sequel, *Threat to the Barkers** (Angus, 1963; Harcourt, 1965), which was commended for the Book of the Year Award. All are essentially novels of family ranch life. Her later books have developed stronger plot lines and more narrative tension, as in the case of *The Cats** (Macmillan, 1976; Atheneum, 1976), a novel of a kidnapping where the tables are turned when the young hoodlums who have seized two teenage brothers are threatened by huge cats that occupy the isolated house where they hold their captives. It was commended for the Book of the Year Award. Among her many novels for young people, some critics have called *A Tide Flowing* (Methuen, 1981; Atheneum, 1981) Phipson's most moving book. It is a psychological study that examines the trauma of a young boy who was the only witness to his mother's suicide.

THE PIGS ARE FLYING. See *PIGS MIGHT FLY*.

PIGS MIGHT FLY (Rodda*, Emily, ill. Noela Young, Angus, 1986; *The Pigs are Flying*, Greenwillow, 1988), amusing fantasy of a journey into another world set in an unspecified place not long ago. Rachel, perhaps seven, in bed with a cold, longs for excitement. To cheer her, her father's friend, Sandy, a smiling, bearded sign painter, makes her a felt-tipped pen picture in which, pajama clad, she rides a unicorn while pigs cavort in the sky above. He also tells her that "nothing you can imagine is totally *impossible*." Shortly after he leaves, she finds herself riding a golden-horned unicorn, while numerous plump, pink pigs dip, dive, and somersault in the sky above. The unicorn deposits her at the door of a pleasant, little white house that belongs to an elderly couple, cranky Bert Beddoes and his nervous, forgetful wife, Enid, who persists in calling Rachel Grace. Grace, Rachel eventually learns, is their niece, who disappeared twenty years earlier during another flying pig storm. Enid and Bert soon conclude that Rachel has come from Outside, an event that occurs about every ten years, and has been brought Inside by the peculiar weather known as a grunter because of the effect it has on pigs. Grunter intensity is measured on a UEF (Unlikely Events Factor) scale from one to ten. Depending on the force of the UEF, personalities change, mechanical devices malfunction, and people simply wander off or disappear. Although they treat her kindly, the day and a half that Rachel spends with the old couple is filled with anxiety about getting home. At his suggestion, Rachel and Bert hurry to town (before the next grunter comes) to determine how an Outsider called Alexander, who worked at the local bank, got Outside again. A promising clue arises when they learn that just before he disappeared in a grunter, Alexander left the library hastily after reading a book of rhymes. They acquire the book and leave the library just before "pig-up" in the next grunter, accompanied by a new young librarian, Miss Rider, and rush home where Bert and Enid discover that Miss Rider is their long-lost Grace and Rachel discovers in the book a rhyme that goes "Outsider jump / On a pig. . . . " Concluding that this is the way to leave Inside, she does so just as the grunter breaks. Back home, she discovers that Sandy is the Outsider Alexander. The reader is left to decide whether events actually occurred, perhaps caused by the flask of UEF brought back by Sandy, or were Rachel's imaginings inspired by Sandy's picture. At any rate, Rachel has learned that the impossible is indeed possible. The parallels to *Alice's Adventures in Wonderland* and to *The Wizard of Oz* are obvious, but the story is much shorter and less complex in concept and structure than they. The author delineates the setting with care, and the basic idea is intriguing, although the descriptions of what happens during pig-ups seem overdone. The humor is sometimes too adult for most of the middle elementary age readers at whom the book is aimed, while at other times it seems overly farcical, employing broad slapstick and rude names like "Dr. Pimplebottom" for comic effect. Characters are one-dimensional types or caricatures, and men seem better able to cope with the UEF disturbances than women and are less outlandishly drawn. The first and last chapters, which present realistic family scenes, are particularly pleasant with warm interpersonal relationships and authentic-sounding dialogue. Numerous black-and-white line drawings support the setting and characterization and help to make this a pleasantly entertaining story for the eight-to-eleven-year-old age range. Aust. Jr. Bk. of Year.

PIONEER SHACK (Birtles*, Dora, Shakespeare, 1947), realistic family novel with elements of the disowned relative, school, and success genres. When, perhaps in the 1930s, Mr. Graham, a lawyer, suffers an accident of undisclosed nature that leaves him an invalid, Mrs. Graham closes their comfortable, rambling city house and moves her now poor family to a shabby, rented flat in a suburb of Newcastle, New South Wales: Elsa, 15, John, 13, and Roslyn, perhaps seven. Elsa dreams of elevating the family fortunes by redeeming a parcel of land that Mr. Graham had inherited from his grandfather and building a small house on it. The Grahams have never seen the land, but they have learned that it will be sold in a tax sale. One Sunday, the children walk over the area where Elsa thinks the lot lies and encounter elderly Grandfather O'Neil, who helps them find the surveyor's pegs. Mrs. Graham remains skeptical, however, and besides they lack the money to pay the taxes. Days pass with little progress toward realizing the dream, but gradually other people become involved in Elsa's plans: Ron Hunt-Johnson, 16, scion of a socially prominent family, who boards with the Grahams while he takes courses at the local technical college, and Marge Tennant, a school friend of Elsa who eventually even enlists her father's help. Although Elsa knows they must hurry, since some local businessman also wants the property, she must study for exams and even takes a little time out to socialize. She finishes at the head of her class, and even Marge, normally the class clown, does unusually well, their association proving beneficial to both girls. The girls decide to attend the tax sale, and, if they don't have enough money to redeem the land themselves, intend to bid up the price. They sneak out on the rainy, dismal sale day, Elsa bolstered in spirits by the fortuitous receipt of fifty pounds from Grandma Spence, who had disowned Mrs. Graham when she married but who has maintained a long distance interest in the children. It turns out that Marge's father has been the mysterious antagonist interested in the property. As soon as he discovers that Elsa wants the land, he arranges for her to redeem it and also buy the two adjoining parcels, all for forty-five pounds. Just before the Christmas holidays start, Mrs. Graham informs the family that Mr. Graham must enter the hospital for an extremely serious operation. While Roslyn stays with an aunt, the others camp out on the land and start construction. Work goes well for Mr. Tennant sends men to do the beginning tasks, and the youths quarry stone and mortar walls with a will. Grandma Spence even visits the site, pleased at Elsa's resourcefulness and now aware of the importance of family unity. She joins the celebration on Christmas Day at the Tennant home, and everyone rejoices that Mr. Graham's operation has gone well. Grandma Spence displays a keen interest in the building project and the next day lays the foundation stone, inscribed with the words "Pioneer Shack." The family's future in their soon-to-be-completed small but adequate country house seems secure. Elsa is a winning and convincing heroine, if too carefully contrasted with the usually scatterbrained Marge. Other figures are sketched in bold strokes, a conglomeration of types conventional for this kind of story. The plot moves rapidly with plenty of interesting, well-paced if stock incidents, and coincidence abounds—Elsa's essay on her ideal home wins a contest just as their funds are at their lowest ebb; Grandma Spence's change of heart comes at just the right time, among other incidents. School scenes—the girls' lively interchanges and the play in which Marge acts as a comic Prince Charming, for example—are vivid and convincing, the episodes of family life and the building seem accurate, and the author uses dialogue generously and skillfully. The result is an enjoyable if dated story of genteel upper middle-class life. Aust. Bk. of Year Com.

PIWAS (*River Runners**), Naskapi Indian woman. In one of the novel's most memorable episodes, Piwas kills by a clever ruse the wolverine that has been raiding their small store of food. She tells Pashak to chew a piece of caribou meat, which she then rolls up into a small ball, inserting into it a long, slender sliver of caribou bone. After freezing the ball, she rubs it with fish roe to destroy the human scent and then throws the ball into a clump of trees a short distance away. The wolverine finds the meat ball, devours it, and dies when the bone sliver punctures its heart.

PLACE OF THE STONE GIANTS (*Longtime Passing**), a group of massive, man-shaped monoliths, sacred to the Australian Aborigines. They stand at the edge of a ridge in Longtime* in the Blue Mountains of New South Wales. Edwin* Truelance tells Teddy*, his daughter, that the Daruk tribe believed that the mountains were sacred, that the stones were the most holy place in the range for them, and that the Daruk thought that those who destroyed Longtime and its sacred places would in time destroy themselves. At the end of the book he fears that "progress" may cause their belief to come true.

PLAYING BEATIE BOW (Park*, Ruth, Nelson, 1980; Atheneum, 1982), time fantasy that begins and ends in Sydney, Australia, in the 1970s, which involves aspects of the modern problem story genre, and in which the fantasy portion is period fiction. Rebellious, sharp-tongued Abby (Abigail) Kirk, 14, feels angry, resentful, and confused when her mother returns to her estranged husband, Abby's father. An antique crocheted collar Abby finds in a neighbor's ragbag and a strange little furry-headed girl, whom Abby sees wistfully observing playground children in a scary game called Beatie Bow, transport Abby back one hundred years to 1873 Sydney. There she is befriended by the Bows and the Talliskers, an immigrant Orkney family: Samuel* Bow, who suffers "spells" from a Crimean War wound; fierce Beatie*, 11, his daughter, the furry-headed girl; warmhearted Dovey* Tallisker, his niece of about eighteen; and firm, loving Granny* Tallisker, his mother-in-law. Granny identifies Abby as the long-awaited Stranger who will help the family perpetuate its precious Gift* of second sight. A family prophecy specifies that one member will die (the family is sure that this will be sickly Gibbie* Bow, 9, the son recuperating from typhoid fever), and one will be barren. Granny expects cousins Dovey and Judah Bow, 18, a seaman, to marry and continue the Gift. Although Abby finds herself warming to and admiring this family that has so lovingly taken her in, she runs away, trying to get back home, and is captured by thugs who take her to a bordello, from which she is rescued by Judah, when Granny's Gift locates her. Realizing that to return to her own time she needs both the help of Beatie, who insists that she will not lead Abby back until Abby fulfills her function, and the crochet, which Granny has hidden in Dovey's hope chest, Abby awaits the event that will release her and hides for Dovey's sake her growing love for Judah. When Mr. Bow has a spell and sets afire his confectionary shop over which the family lives, Abby bravely rescues Dovey, the chest, and Gibbie. Having obviously fulfilled the Stranger's function, she is led back by Beatie to her own time (what Beatie calls Elfland). Her months with the kindly Victorians have given Abby new perspectives on both family and romantic love. She comes home more composed in spirit and more sensitive to her parents' needs and feelings and accepts their reconciliation. After four years of living abroad, the Kirks return to Sydney, where Abby meets the brother of the neighbor from whom she got the crochet, Robert Bow, who bears a striking resemblance to Judah from 1873. Abby discovers that Robert is descended from Gibbie, through whom, contrary to Granny's expectations, the Gift was transmitted, to be inherited in this generation probably by little Natalie, Robert's niece. While some of Abby's behavior and adventures seemed strained, her entrance and exit from the nineteenth century awkwardly handled, and the plot overly convoluted, intense Beatie and imperious Granny win the reader's attention and sympathy. The other characters, if types, are strongly realized and appropriate, the matter of the Gift is skillfully worked out and sustained to the very end, the mystery of why modern children play a singing game about Victorian Beatie provides unity, and the question of how Abby will get home to modern Sydney provides considerable suspense. The author knits past and present together well with respect to Abby's personal problems and portrays life in the 1870s among the working classes of the old harbor city so vividly that the contemporary story seems bland by comparison. Scottish dialect contributes authenticity. The reader is left to ponder why Abby rather than Natalie becomes the protagonist and instrument of the prophecy. Aust. Bk. of Year Winner; Boston Globe Winner; Fanfare.

THE PLUM-RAIN SCROLL (*The Plum-Rain Scroll**), magnificent lost scroll almost as old as Japan, decorated with beautiful paintings of the plum-rain, "the first gentle, misty rains of spring." On the scroll are written the secret of immortality, the secret of turning baser metals into gold, and the Unanswerable Word, an utterance of such tremendous power that it renders enemies weak.

THE PLUM-RAIN SCROLL (Manley*, Ruth, ill. Marianne Yamaguchi, Hodder, 1978), lighthearted fantasy of adventure and magic set in Idzumo (Japan) during the samurai period and improvising on indigenous folklore. Earnest foundling Taro, 13, is odd-job boy for managerial Aunt Piety and bombastic Uncle Thunder at an inn in the village of Akashi. He becomes involved in preventing evil Lord Marishoten from securing the ancient, lost Plum-Rain* Scroll, with which Marishoten can usurp the Chrysanthemum throne, and from kidnapping Aunt Piety, who is a magical fox-woman and the only one who can read the scroll. Taro's cohorts are powerful and wise Prince Hachi, the most famous and noble warrior in the land and nephew to the Mikado, and an assortment of ironic, comic, and incongruous figures: Hiroshi, a ghost who stutters and insists that there is a clue to the scroll's location in a poem that he cannot remember; Beni, a lizard-skinned Roof Watcher and the fierce protector of the Lady Azumi, who keeps the magical sword, Murakumo, one of Japan's greatest treasures; Oboro*, the sharp-tongued, tough-minded Cherry-Blossom Princess; and a huge, bright blue *oni* (ogre) called Tsuki the Terrible, who is kind and gentle, loves poetry, and often reminisces about his mother. Each of these seemingly mismatched traveling companions, and some others, contribute to the success of the enterprise. Among many difficult situations, the companions are imprisoned in a dungeon by Lord Marishoten's serpent woman and later tumble into a pit that turns out to be the underground kingdom of the dreaded King of the Freaks, who is himself friendly but whose terrible-tempered queen flies into rages and enchants those who displease her. The travelers sometimes enjoy exemplary hospitality, in one instance in a beautiful secluded valley from Nature in the form of a man, whose pet is a striking green dog made of grass. When Hiroshi recalls the critical poem, they realize that their destination is the imperial city of Miyako. Although their spirits are dampened by a report that Prince Hachi has died and that Lord Marishoten has captured Aunt Piety in her silver fox form (later proved erroneous), they forge ahead, aided variously by the magic sword and by sundry beings they encounter, like Tsuki's Medusa-oni sister, who turns their evil opponents to stone. After Taro learns in a dream that the scroll is in the palace, they go there, meet the Mikado, a gentle, kind man, and search the place without success. Uncle Thunder, who is obsessed with the desire to produce fireworks, experimentally detonates a firecracker that demolishes one side of the Mikado's parlor, and the scroll is found in the rubble. The climax reached, events occur quickly. Lord Marishoten appropriates the scroll but disregards Aunt Piety's warning against exposing it to the sun and soon finds that it is devoid of writing and hence worthless. As Marishoten is about to execute Piety, Hiroshi pronounces a Word of Power that temporarily turns the evil leader and his followers to ice. Prince Hachi arrives with his calvary and casts Marishoten and his minions into prison, and Aunt Piety concludes the story by attempting to make an island to grace the lake by the palace. Her magic goes awry, as usual, and she creates Mt. Fuji instead. The novel has enough action and excitement for two books. It is almost all plot, and scenes follow one another in rapid succession, are generously motivated by coincidence, and in most instances could easily be interchanged. Conversation abounds, much of it "patter" or comic bickering, and conveys information about Japanese customs and beliefs. It is difficult to remember clearly the large cast of superficially developed characters, and Lord Marishoten is presented as a conventional villain. Some figures echo characters from well-known fantasies, like Beni who recalls Gollum in Tolkien and the Freak queen who strongly resembles Carroll's Queen of Hearts. Certain aspects of Japanese culture come through strongly, like the emphasis on politeness and courtesy, respect for ancestors, authority figures, and the aged, reverence for the gods, and modesty and self-deprecation. Although the characters go from one seemingly impossible situation into another, the comic humor and light tone make it difficult to take the problems seriously. The reader remains distanced from events as in an adventure novel and never doubts that the heroes will eventually triumph. Sequels. Aust. Bk. of Year Winner.

THE POCHETTO COAT (Greenwood*, Ted, ill. Ron Brooks, Hutchinson, 1978), brief novel containing stories within the story, all told by Patrick, known as Pochetto, the Clown with the Thousand Pockets, to Samantha, known as Sam, daughter of the bear trainer, Henry, known as Great Friedrich. Told entirely in dialogue, the frame story cleverly reveals the child's unhappy relationship with her father, who wants her to learn to dive through fire, as her deceased mother, Madame Miracle, did, and with Renata, manager of the circus, who is training her. Although Patrick is alcoholic, on the skids, and eventually is fired, he is understanding and able to cheer Sam and to give her advice and courage to follow her ambition to become a clown. Among the stories told by Patrick is that of Fillipe, costume boy for the actor Rollo, who, in trying to fill in for unconscious Rollo, makes such a ludicrous substitute that the audience roars with laughter, and Fillipe finds his vocation as a clown, wearing an oversized coat and billing himself as Pochetto, which means "pocket." Each of his stories features the Pochetto coat. In one the king's jester is sent away to find a new toy for the prince to substitute for the acting games he loves, presumably to make the prince more interested in serious studies, actually to banish the jester from the court for a while. After much wandering, he comes upon a maker of marvelous models of ships. He buys one of a Roman galley, which, carefully wound, will row itself out into a pond, turn around, and row back. When he returns to court, however, the king's chancellor pays no attention to the jester's instructions, roughly overwinds the key, and spoils the delicate mechanism. The prince furiously throws the galley into the pond, and the jester is permanently banished. He gives his costumes to the prince and returns to live with the maker of the marvelous model boats. In another story, a clown who has lost his knack for making people laugh regains it by eating fruit from the Saporene tree. The yellow half of this apple-like fruit is very sour, the red half wonderfully sweet. To enjoy the red half fully, it is important to eat of the sour golden half first. Before Patrick leaves to go live with a retired magician, Mario the Magnificent, he gives Sam his Pochetto coat and starts her on her own imagining of stunts to make an audience laugh. Rather than interrupt the action, the stories told by Patrick form the main part of the novel. The primary interest, however, is in the character of the old clown, not too sweet and not able to make Sam avoid the role as a diver through fire but giving her hope and direction to find her own vocation eventually. One story, in which he tells his frightening dream of a circus directed by animals, reveals his own fear and insecurity. Aust. Bk. of Yr. Com.

PONNY THE PENGUIN (Basser*, Veronica, ill. Edwina Bell, Aust., 1948), animal story for younger children, obviously designed to tell them facts about the life of Adelie penguins. Mr. and Mrs. Penguin are delighted when their egg hatches to become a very hungry daughter, whom they name Ponny. When her appetite becomes larger than the amount that her father can carry in his gullet for her, the parents leave her with the older females, the Auntie Penguins, who watch the youngsters in their day nursery, while they both fish for food. There Ponny ventures too far away and is attacked by Claw, a skua gull, but is saved by two aunts who rush to her rescue. As she grows up her parents take her to the waters edge and push her in, and soon she is an expert swimmer and can catch more shrimp than any of the other chicks. The fun of swimming, riding ice-crafts, and breaching or leaping from sea to ice is made dangerous by the presence of Fang, the sea leopard that lives under the ledge of the ice and snaps up any careless penguins until he is snapped up himself by a killer whale. One day the penguins begin to gather and form squads to practice drills in preparation for their long swim from the rookery to winter quarters on the ice pack. There Ponny and the other young penguins stay for more than a year until, as the second spring approaches, they are mature enough to swim back to the breeding grounds. Ponny, who is an excellent swimmer, is among the first to arrive, but she worries that she is too fat to attract a mate. However, a handsome young male penguin approaches and drops a stone in front of her, a penguin proposal of marriage. Soon they have made their nest, a round depression in the ice bordered with small stones to protect it from flooding. Peter, Ponny's mate, is kept busy driving off other males who try to attract Ponny away from him or to steal his stones. As more and more penguins arrive, the rookery becomes crowded and fights are frequent, but Peter stays close until Ponny has laid two eggs. Then, not having had time to eat for two weeks, they take turns going for food. In a momentary lapse of attention to the eggs, while Ponny is driving off a stone thief, Claw swoops down and impales one of the eggs on his sharp bill. Though sad, both Ponny and Peter take better care of the second egg, and the story ends as their daughter emerges from the shell as hungry a little chick as Ponny was. Although the Penguins live in their natural setting and follow patterns of their kind, they are pictured to have human language and emotions. Mr. Penguin tells Ponny stories, and later she gossips with the other females and complains about the irresponsible men. As natural history for the very young, it is a pleasantly written story, but it seems dated in its approach. Aust. Bk. of Year Highly Com.

POPPY RICHARDSON (*Going to the Dogs**), Billy Mackenzie's girl friend. Poppy lives in Lac du Bois, a town not far from Nugget, Billy's home, and where her father is production manager of the Kimberly-Clark paper mill. Poppy is beautiful and very much in love with Billy, whose professions of love she does not quite trust until she becomes pregnant and he says that they should marry. She is very much afraid of displeasing her parents, in particular her father, who has cowed his family into behaving just as he wants. When she discovers that she is pregnant, informs her parents, and decides to go with Billy to Toronto, she is astonished to see that her mother gains a new confidence in herself and stands up to Mr. Richardson as she has not done before. Poppy is a credible figure, a good character complement for Billy.

POTKOOROK (*The Nargun and the Stars**), golden-eyed, green-skinned, sly, temperamental, self-important, frog-like creature that lives in a swamp near the farmhouse on Wongadilla sheep run. He has been friends with Charlie* and Edie* Waters, the owners, since they were children. The Potkoorok first warms to Simon Brent when the boy returns to the swamp the body of a frog that has been run over by a road grader. The Potkoorok is a distinctive, imaginatively conceived being, both humorous and imposing.

A POT OF GOLD (Onadipe*, Kola, Natona, 1980), a brief realistic novel of family life and friendship set for a few weeks in an unnamed city in contemporary Nigeria. Two eight-year-old girls, Jumai Audu, whose single mother sells plantain to earn their living, and Lola Anum, whose parents are wealthy, live at opposite ends of a short street. They would like to be friends, but Lola's status-conscious mother vehemently insists that Lola should not associate with one not of their "class." Mr. Anum, on the other hand, supports Lola, asserting that Jumai is a good girl and being poor doesn't indicate unworthiness. With his approval, the two girls meet after school and walk together to Lola's house and sometimes Lola visits at Jumai's. When Lola fails to appear for several days, Jumai investigates and discovers that her friend is very ill, of a disease that turns the skin yellow. Nothing that the doctors do helps. Jumai's mother gives Jumai some ointment from a pot given to her by her mother. Mrs. Audu is sure that the medicine that has come down in the family can cure the little girl. Jumai sneaks into Lola's house and rubs her body with the ointment. Within six hours the pain is gone, and in another six hours Lola's color is restored. The doctor is amazed, rubs some on other patients with the "yellow touch," and when they also recover, he contacts a drug company that markets the drug worldwide as Jumaimycin. Even though Jumai and her mother receive substantial returns from the sales, Mrs. Anum continues her animosity toward them. The reason for her behavior comes out when one day, Mrs. Audu tells Mr. Anum her story. She and Mrs. Anum, both from poor families and left orphaned, were close friends until Mrs. Anum deceitfully took a job as a housekeeper for a wealthy widower intended for Mrs. Audu and subsequently married him (Mr. Anum) and gave birth to Lola. Mrs. Audu married the only other available bachelor, a drunkard teacher, who subsequently abandoned her and Jumai, leaving them in proud poverty. Confronted with the story, Mrs. Anum admits her hostility toward the Audus arose from guilt and shame. The two women are reconciled, Mrs. Audu marries the director of the drug company, and the two girls continue their friendship. The characters exist for the plot. Mrs. Anum is an obvious villain, one time reviling Jumai as "swine," and the plot uses the conventions of the "virtue will be recognized and right will out" form. Although the print is small, the style employs easy language and uncomplicated sentence structure. The book seems intended for the eight-to-ten-year-old reading set to promote the traditional values of hard work, virtue, and compassion for the less fortunate as well as, ironically, recognition that life can hold unexpected twists and turns and the lack of validity of "class" distinctions based purely on economics. Except for the names and a few practices, the setting gives little sense of the area, and the story could take place in almost any city. Nigerian Natl. Council.

POWELL, LESLEY CAMERON (1924–   ), born in Kawakawa, New Zealand; teacher, author, and journalist. After a career as a high school teacher from 1945 to 1960, she served as editor of the Helensville, New Zealand, *Leader* from 1964 to 1969 and then taught at Kaipara College in Helensville. She received the New Zealand Esther Glen Award for *Turi: The Story of a Little Boy** (Angus, 1963; Paul's, 1964), a short novel about a modern Maori child who is given to his grandmother in his infancy to take care of her in her old age. She has also published *Centennial History of Okaihau, 1868–1968* (Okaihau, 1968). A contributor to such publications as *Weekly News* and *Metropolitan*, she has made her home in Helensville.

POWNALL, (MARJORIE) EVE(LYN SHERIDAN), born in Kings Cross, Australia; historian and writer. She grew up in country towns, including Kiama along the South Coast, Windsor on the Hawkesbury River, and Muswellbrook in the Hunter Valley. She attended North Sydney Girls' High School and has worked in publishing, reviewed for country newspapers, and acted as children's book editor for the *Australian Book News*. Her interest in writing began after her marriage, partly to satisfy her children's need for books. She started *The Australia Book* (Sands, 1951), a social history, when her son became interested in a book of United States history and she could find nothing comparable about Australia. It was winner of the Australian Book of the Year Award. From the research for that book on the period of Governor Bourke in Sydney she wrote a novel, *Cousins-Come-Lately** (Shakespeare, 1951), which was highly commended for the same award. Besides writing two picture books, numerous short stories and scripts for radio, and two texts for primary school, she has written a number of histories of Australia, including *The Singing Wire: The Story of the Overland Telegraph* (Collins, 1973), *Australia's Federal Parliament* (Wentworth, 1974), and a history of Australian pioneer women that was republished in many editions.

PRETTY GIRL (*Sweetgrass**), Blackfoot Blood girl, 13. Pretty Girl hopes to marry a certain young warrior, but her father marries her instead to an older man who is able to provide a larger bride-price in horses. Pretty Girl takes his decision in good spirit, as befits a well-brought-up Blackfoot girl. Although she has to work very hard in her new husband's tepee, she accepts that fate without complaint, too. She and her unborn child die in the smallpox epidemic.

THE PRIESTS OF FERRIS (Gee*, Maurice, Oxford, 1984), Tolkienesque otherworld fantasy, middle book in the series about the land of O, which also includes *The Halfmen of O** and *Motherstone**. One year after the events in *The Halfmen of O*, a crippled boy called Limpy, about fourteen, arrives on Earth. His mission is to bring Susan Ferris and Nick (Nicholas) Quinn back to O, where one hundred years, or "turns" as the O people calculate time, have passed since Susan placed the two stones called Halves on the Motherstone and ended the rule of the wicked Halfmen. The land of O has now fallen into the clutches of evil priests who invoke Susan's name to support their reign of terror. Susan and Nick immediately agree to accompany Limpy, who was crippled as a result of a fishing accident when he was small. Their quest becomes twofold: to overthrow the priests and to rescue Limpy's sister, Soona, about to become an unwilling sacrifice in a periodic ritual. Once through the tunnel connecting Earth and O, the three are pursued by priests (who dress in skintight white suits by day that reverse to black by night and wear necklaces of human bones) with man-killing hounds, which they escape with the help of Seeker, a member of the Stonefolk, who shelters them inside his cave on a cliff. They then add to their group Dawn, a fur-covered Woodlander, who gives them more details about the evil, new reign and takes them to another Woodlander, who gives them a message from their old friend Jimmy* Jaspers. In his letter written years earlier, Jimmy urges them to contact him at Mount Nicholas. Helpful Birdfolk transport the party in special down-lined nests—something like shopping bags—through the air for two days over extremely rugged terrain and deposit them at a pass in the mountain range. The group trudges over a glacier where they encounter Vargs, huge blue-white bears that Jimmy's letter had told them not to fear. Susan communicates their friendly intentions to the Vargs through a series of mind-pictures. Accompanied by Vargs, they continue to Mount Nicholas and find in a cave where the bears go to die Jimmy Jaspers and his friend, Ben the Varg, both encased in columns of ice and in a state of suspended animation. (Jimmy would now be perhaps 150 years of age in Earth time.) Using the axe he found at the foot of Jimmy's column, Nick chips away the ice first from Jimmy and then from Ben, and gradually the two revive. The little party then makes for the Temple, which is the seat of the evil government and where Susan intends boldly to confront the High Priest with his misdeeds. After many adventures, they arrive. Susan steals away one night, climbs the cliff with the help of special sticky gloves made of stone-silk, finds Soona, and is herself captured by the priests. She is surprised to find that the High Priest looks and acts like a harried schoolmaster, but she is also horrified that he reveals the sharp, devious, and malevolent mind of a madman. He decides to sacrifice both girls to impress the populace and sets a Bloodcat to guard them. Nick and Dawn, meanwhile, have sought the help of the Birdfolk, and all arrive just in time. Deserted by his guard, the High Priest loses his confidence and in one last demented attempt to impress the people and maintain his rule, he launches himself from the cliff and falls to his death. Their mission to end the tyranny of the priests and save Soona accomplished, Susan and Nick prepare to return to Earth. The plot is causal only in its broadest outlines because most episodes merely succeed but do not depend on one another, and events and characters have the proportions of an animated cartoon. Overwriting is common, and sensationalism appears at every turn. Even Susan and Nick, who seem a little more mature than in the first book, are one-dimensional, "virtuous hero" types. Some concepts are inventive, for example, the nests for transporting passengers and the stone-silk gloves, but on the whole the story is filled with the exaggerations and grotesquerie of the form. The intention, of course, is to provide thriller entertainment of an easily grasped, superficial sort, and as such the book succeeds admirably. N.Z. Govt. Short List.

PROFESSOR ASH (*A Book Dragon**), elderly alcoholic who has retired from his university position and spends his time reading and dozing in Mr. Gottlieb's bookshop. The old professor is the only one who sees Nonesuch, the tiny dragon, in the shop. He persuades Samson, the boy who works in the bookshop, that a friendly spirit has come to their aid and suggests that each night they leave a different book open on the bookstore table for the spirit to peruse at night. Nonesuch especially enjoys the *Booke of Martyrs*, which details the deaths by fire of Bishops Ridley and Latimer, a scene that his grandmother has told him she witnessed. In the morning, the professor and the boy find the pages turned, but they admit that it may have been the wind. Professor Ash also reinforces the cosmic theme by quoting a myth that some dragons are thinking of destroying the universe but refrain because it would make other dragons, who still live among humans, unhappy.

PUK-WUDGIES (*Boori**), a tribe of little men, small in stature but very sturdy, who speak with the voices of small birds and who fight with cudgels. They have the power to slip through sand or what has been sand, including stone. Cousins to the marsupial moles, they live underground in the dark dunes and always travel in companies like the red ants. They love to work mischief, mostly by night, because they cannot stand sunlight. In their admiration for the bullying of their leader, Puk, they are almost comic creatures.

Q

THE QUARTER-PIE WINDOW (Brandis*, Marianne, ill. G. Brender a Brandis, Porcupine's Quill, 1985), substantial historical novel about the settlement of York (now Toronto) in Upper Canada (now Ontario) with girl's growing-up story aspects. Events take place during two months in 1830 beginning in early October, when recently orphaned Emma Anderson, 14, an intelligent, responsible, perceptive girl from whose viewpoint events are seen, and her quiet, impassive younger brother, John, 10, come to live with their father's half-sister, Mrs. Harriet McPhail, the dignified, austere proprietor of a genteel hotel. Emma finds her aunt cold and domineering, if capable, and is very disappointed when her aunt puts her to work as a chambermaid, especially since she had looked forward to an active social life. John becomes an errand boy for Mr. Blackwood's livery stable, and both children sleep in the hotel attic, whose saving grace for Emma is its small quarter-pie window. Although she has to work long hours, she applies herself diligently and wins approval from her employer, guests, and other servants, in particular Mrs. Jones, the cook, who mothers her. Emma is hurt and puzzled by her treatment and by her aunt's desire to keep the children's relationship to her a secret. Emma makes a few friends among the guests: Miss Morgan, a pleasant young schoolteacher from New Hampshire; Major Charles Heatherington, a retired English army officer; and his wife, Jane. Several matters help to unify the ambling plot. First, Emma's attempts to find out about her parents' background result in her discovery that her mother, a chambermaid at the Anchor Pub, was pregnant by the pub-keeper when she married Emma's father. Second, Emma becomes interested in Miss Morgan's proposed school, helps her get the place ready for pupils, and then must decide whether or not to accept Miss Morgan's offer of a position as a housekeeper. Third, and most compelling are the events involving the Heatheringtons. When Emma learns that they intend to buy her parents' farm from Mr. Blackwood, to whom Mrs. McPhail has sold it, that he is asking an exorbitant price, that he has misrepresented the place to them, and that Mrs. McPhail also stands to profit handsomely from the deal, she informs the Heatheringtons and incurs Mrs. McPhail's wrath. The

Heatheringtons buy the place nevertheless, but at a fair price, and at the end, having married off their fractious, spoiled daughter, Caroline, whose behavior also provides some tension, to an army officer, settle on the farm before winter. Emma has grown more self-sufficient, and she and Mrs. McPhail have acquired a grudging respect for each other. Emma decides to remain at the hotel and is pleased to be given occasional duty at the lobby desk. Some questions are left unanswered. Emma discovers little about her parents and what she does learn seems to have little effect on the rest of the story. Little is learned about Mrs. McPhail, who is the most compelling figure in the book. Her relationship with the mysterious Mr. Blackwood remains unexplained, as are those with some other ambivalent characters. The reader never learns how Mrs. McPhail achieved prominence in York and became well-off and why she does not want people to know that she is the children's aunt. The symbolism of the quarter-pie window is never exploited. The large cast consists of an interesting mix of mostly undeveloped characters. John is almost always on the fringes. Best are the picture of everyday life and work in the hotel from the servants' vantage point and the many views of the growing, bustling city, also seen through the activities and from the standpoint of an observant, courageous girl on the verge of womanhood. The novel is the sequel to *The Tinderbox*. Can. IODE Natl.; Can. Young Adult Winner.

THE QUEST FOR GOLDEN DAN (Kellaway*, Frank, Cheshire, 1962; Angus, 1962), adventure story set in Victoria, Australia, in 1855, among the diverse population in the newly discovered gold fields. After a sea journey from England, which he shared with his parents and the family of Dr. Hans Schiller, Dan Jones, 12, goes ashore, becomes separated from the others, and is kidnapped for his beautiful voice by an itinerant musician called Blowfly Joe, who dyes his blond hair, paints his skin black, and teaches him to sing, passing him off as an Ethiopian, Othello Ben Assim, and making it seem that Dan Jones has drowned. They entertain at the better-class taverns where Joe drinks too much, then gravitate to the roughest dives. Several times Dan tries to escape, only to be caught and threatened. One night when Joe drinks more than usual and falls asleep in a pub, Dan climbs into the wagon of a Jewish trader, Abraham Caro, concealing himself with the help of Caro's daughter, Ruth, about his age. After he is discovered, the Caros treat him kindly, even nursing him when he becomes ill. At their arrival in Beechworth, one of the larger mining communities, Caro finds a physician, who turns out to be Dr. Schiller, and Dan is reunited with the Schiller children, thoughtful Sebastian, 12, and pretty Gretchen, 14, but his own parents have not kept in contact with the Schillers. As Dan recovers and gains strength, he continues to live with the Caros in a shop that they have bought, and, he, Sebastian, and Ruth become an inseparable trio, while Gretchen gets a job in the bank. On an outing, Dan is attacked by three big, tough boys led by Bottler Wishart, and the younger children are almost overcome before a local miner known as the Swizzler intervenes. As their friendship with the Swizzler develops, they learn that he is a Norwegian really named Arne Sturluson, that he lost a fortune when the bank burned, and that he has since become almost a recluse in his neat little house. Since working his claim alone is slow and exhausting, the children help by hauling the buckets full of gravel from the shaft and transporting it to the stream with their pony cart. Hearing Dan's story and knowing that he needs money to find his parents, Arne proposes that he give them one-third of his claim. With his part, Dan buys a fine chestnut mare that he names Goldy. Arne has their contract legally written and recorded and, without their knowledge, makes a will leaving the rest of his claim and his property to Dan. A short time later he dies, apparently of a heart attack. The Swizzler's hoard, hidden in an old mine shaft, turns out to be far more than suspected, for the claim was thought to be played out, and although they are attacked by Bottler and his gang, the children get it all safely into the bank. Locally Dan becomes known as Golden Dan. Now well financed, he sets off on Goldy to find his parents. On his way to the McIvor diggings, he is overtaken by two bushrangers trying to steal Goldy, but they are scared off. Both badly injured, Dan and Goldy make their way to an isolated farm of Bert and Susan Rowan, where they are nursed for some weeks. During this period Dan's father, who hears of Golden Dan and hopes that his might be his son, is searching for him, and the two miss each other several times on the road until they finally meet in the bar at Bendigo. Dan, who at McIvor has come upon Blowfly Joe almost dying of malnutrition and too much brandy, gets medical aid for his former captor, and he and his father are soon reunited with his mother and friends at Beechwood. Throughout his adventures, Dan is plagued by a feeling of unreality, wondering if he is actually the same boy who came from Kent and feeling sometimes huge and sometimes very small. Only at the end does he understand that this is a normal part of growing up. Although the characters are not highly developed and the plot contains enough action for several novels, some of it, like inheriting the Swizzler's fortune, highly unlikely, the book has much to recommend it, especially the descriptions of life in Melbourne and in the mining camps, which, in a preface, the author says came from a book written by William Kelly, published in 1857. The physical setting, as in many Australian novels, is also a strong point. Aust. Bk. of Year Com.

R

A RACECOURSE FOR ANDY. See I OWN THE RACECOURSE!.

THE RACKETTY STREET GANG (Evers*, L. H., Brockhampton, 1961), realistic mystery-detective novel set not long after World War II in Sydney, Australia, in a working-class area near the harbor. Sober, responsible, teenaged Anton Smertzer and his German immigrant parents move to Racquetier Street. Anton soon joins the Racketty Street Gang, which also includes clever, inventive Prof, the leader, conciliatory Ben, and cheeky, clowning Stanley. The boys become curious about why the two men, Tommo and Spider, they see about the boatyard never work on the orange-hulled boat there and always angrily order them away. Anton has a personal mystery, too: why his father does not want to be photographed. Events bring these two seemingly unrelated matters together. At the town dump gathering material for snorkeling equipment, the boys discover Tommo and Spider collecting old trunks. Then Anton's father encounters a floor cleaner at the bank, addresses the man as Evans*, and says Evans is an Australian he met in Crete during the war. Evans, however, steadfastly denies knowing Mr.* Smertzer. Later, while snorkeling off the forbidden area, the boys discover under the water trunks filled with what appears to be dirt. The workmen capture Ben and call the police, but he escapes and disappears. Anton recognizes the pilot of the black boat that puts in as Evans. Later Prof deduces from these and other clues that the three men have tunneled from the boatyard into the nearby bank and plan to rob the vault. That rainy Thursday night, the day before payday, the boys slip through the underground drain to where Prof thinks the tunnel lies, are captured by the workmen-robbers and Evans, and are taken in Tommo's truck to the dump, where they are imprisoned in an old refrigerator. They are released just as their air is running out by Ben, who has been hiding in the dump, and return to alert Anton's father and the police. During the shootout, Mr. Smertzer convinces Evans to surrender, and Evans admits that he does know Mr. Smertzer from the war and agrees to testify that Smertzer is innocent of the war crimes of which he had been accused. Now heroes, the boys look forward to receiving reward money, and the Smertzers await a happier future in their adopted country. Though the plot offers few surprises and here and there events seem forced and overly dependent on coincidence, skillful foreshadowing and careful pacing result in a gripping, always interesting narrative. There is some humor, though mostly contrived for effect, and plenty of action. Mr. Smertzer's war stories add texture and interest and are well integrated with the robbery part of the novel. No information is withheld from the reader, who can detect along with the boys. The author excels at creating the moment, and the style is more literate than usual for books of this genre. Aust. Bk. of Year Winner.

RAFFERTY RIDES A WINNER (Woodberry*, Joan, ill. author, Parrish, 1961), realistic novel set in the mid-twentieth century in the village of Bo-ambee on the Pacific coast of Australia, third in a series, following *Rafferty Takes to Fishing* and *Floodtide for Rafferty*, which tell of a Yorkshire boy about ten years old who is transplanted into the fishing community where his grandfather, Robert, lives. Having been in Bo-ambee almost a year, Rafferty has made several good friends, his "mate," Billie, a lively, always hungry ten-year-old, and the red-haired twins, Paul and Bob, somewhat older, and has almost mastered Australian slang and fishing jargon. Rafferty is scraping the hull of his grandfather's beached boat, the *Merlin*, when all three friends converge upon him with news. Billie has seen a poster for a circus coming to town; Paul eagerly tells that the butcher has offered them a pound each to take his mob of horses out to his fattening paddock; Bob says that the doctor will sell them his sailboat, the *Gay Adventure*, for sixty pounds, if they can raise that much by the following Wednesday. Although their pooled resources are about four pounds, they are optimistic. By combining their efforts on the *Merlin*, they earn a pound, and they set off for a wild ride on the horses, none of which will tolerate a saddle and which only the boys ever try to manage. Mission accomplished, they are swimming in a pool nearby when they notice smoke and sneak up the hill, still naked, to overlook Old DiddleO "cooking his worm," making moonshine. When they spot the Sergeant, the village's only law enforcement officer, Billie whistles a warning and the old man dumps his still into the pond and is discovered by the Sergeant calmly fishing. Later DiddleO finds Rafferty and Billie and gives them five pounds for warning him. Still a long way from sixty pounds, the boys enter all their pets in the Church Ladies Auxiliary Pet Show, with disastrous results and no prize money. Discouraged, they consult Robert, who suggests that they set up a limited company, with a goal of eighty pounds, the sixty purchase price plus twenty for necessary repairs to the *Gay Adventure*. The boys promptly sell ten-dollar shares to Robert, Beano, his right-hand man on the *Merlin*, Tommy the cook, and another adult, thereby acquiring half the needed money. To get the rest they work extremely hard netting fish, and see the Co-op truck leave with their boxed catch, confident that they have made it. Later they learn that the truck has been wrecked and the whole Bo-ambee catch lost. When the circus comes, Rafferty and Billie meet one of the circus men who rides a little donkey around town ringing a bell to drum up trade. They volunteer to take over the job and earn two tickets. At the show the master of ceremonies brings out Gentle Annie, the bucking donkey, and offers one hundred pounds to anyone who can ride her for one minute. Rafferty thinks that it is the little animal they have been riding all day and quickly volunteers. He clings to the wildly careening beast for one minute and twenty seconds and wakes up in the hospital. Billie, with great foresight, times the ride and forces the circus to pay up, backed by irate townspeople. Though in pain from a concussion, a broken arm, a broken collar bone, and several broken ribs, Rafferty is happy and agrees to rename the boat the *Southern Rose*, a compromise between the *White Rose* that Billie has suggested and the *Southern Cross* that Bob had chosen. While the series of incidents is unlikely and the characters are not well developed, the story gives a strong feeling for the isolated fishing community and the small-town life there. Particularly interesting is the use of Australian dialect and slang terms. Sequels. Aust. Bk. of Year Winner.

RANGATIRA (Tindale*, Norman B., and Lindsay*, Harold A., ill. Douglas F. Maxted, Reed, 1959; Rigby, 1959; Watts, 1959), substantial historical adventure novel of the Polynesian migrations in the southwestern Pacific in the 1200s. When wise old Rehua, sole survivor of an attack on his island, arrives at their island of Hawaiki (Homeland, or Dreamland) in his canoe after a long solo voyage and tells of a fair land far to the southwest called Aoteraroa, the chief asks him to design a canoe and guide a voyage to this area to ease the pressure on their overcrowded island. Thirty men and women and four youths, among them Maui and Kura in their early teens, embark with Rehua as chief. After a month's harrowing voyage, they sight a mountainous but plenteous land, settle on a pleasant inlet, and call their settlement and tribe Tere-Moana after their canoe. They prosper, in spite of almost continuous difficulties with hostile Manianga people. In time, Maui becomes their leader. He and Kura marry, have a son, Perere, and four more children, and are happy, but Kura longs to return to Hawaiki for a visit. Story interest shifts to Perere, who becomes husky in frame like his mother and resourceful and imaginative like his father. He enjoys exploring the surrounding seas by canoe and has a magnificent singing voice. On one trip he and six friends round the northern end of Aoteraroa and sail down the west coast, where they encounter strangers from an island called Lanaii led by a youth named Huloa, who also has wanderlust. Huloa has a kind of sea chart made of thin sticks and seashells, which shows the location of islands and the direction of winds and currents. The two parties together sail to the west where they land on the coast of Australian, then go on to another island, where they discover a single family marooned there for years, among them the lovely Marama, with whom Perere falls in love and woos with song. They return to Tere-Moana, and soon Perere and Marama are married. By this time the Tere-Moana tribe has grown numerous and prosperous, but Kura still dreams of visiting Hawaiki. Just as preparations are about to begin for the trip, a runner brings news of another attack by the Manianga. Marama has a baby boy and thinks it would be better for the tribe to go to the island on which she grew up and Kura agrees, but they soon realize that too many canoes would be needed for the journey to be feasible. Many are killed in the battle, and Perere becomes the next chief. The tribe continues to prosper under his leadership. The last chapter skips ahead many years to Kura's death. A great-grandmother, the matriarch of the tribe, and the only one of the original settlers of the Rangatira (highborn) rank left, she is much venerated, and her passing is greatly mourned. An epilogue says that there is a place on the North Island of New Zealand sacred to the Maori where the canoe of the settlers lies buried and is marked by a headstone made of the anchor stone. Characters are one-dimensional and exist to serve the plot, and except for Maui, Kura, Perere, and Kehua they are mostly names, and even they are familiar types. Efforts to give them individuality are often clumsy. The plot serves as a vehicle for conveying possible history, and while action scenes are exciting, there is little attempt to build suspense, and the story lacks a proper climax. The book is memorable, however, for its clear descriptions of the native way of life, and details of canoe building, survival at sea, making weapons, domestic life, and the like are clear and fascinating. Descriptions of the terrain show appreciation for the natural life of the area. The style makes use of some Polynesian words, and appended are a glossary and extensive notes about the history and culture of the Maori. Aust. Bk. of Year Com.

RAVEN'S CRY (Harris*, Christie, ill. Bill Reid, McClelland, 1966; Atheneum, 1966), historical novel of the decline of the Haida Indian nation focusing on the matrilineal Stastas Shongalths, whose chiefs bear the ceremonial title of Edinsa, beginning with their first contact with white traders in 1775. Young Yatza, following tribal custom, comes to live with his mother's Eagle phratry (clan group) in their village on the north coast of the Queen Charlotte Islands off British Columbia, Canada. While preparing for a potlatch, he and his uncle, Chief Edinsa, spot a "flying canoe," a white trading ship, are taken aboard, and are presented by the Iron Men with a Thunderstick and an Axehead. A dozen years later another ship arrives and extraordinary trading takes place with the Iron Men—three hundred sea otter cloaks and pelts at a chisel per skin. Numerous contacts ensure, some of them tragic. When the British *Queen Charlotte* puts in, Yatza's sister, Maada*, chieftainess of a neighboring band and mother of the next Eagle Edinsa, receives gifts, as the Indians deem appropriate. Two years later, however, the captain of a Boston ship, the *Lady Washington*, flogs her husband and another chief and cuts their hair, in the Indians' eyes extreme indignities. When the *Lady Washington* puts in two years later (1791), the Haidas' revenge attack goes awry, and they are slaughtered, including Maada and her young son, the Eagle heir. In retaliation, Maada's husband attacks another ship and decapitates the crew. Yatza, now Edinsa, urges his people to remain true to the old ways and especially to keep alive the traditional Haida artistic skills, celebrations, and seasonal activities. When, in 1830, his heirs are killed in raids,

Yatza starts to groom young Gwai-gwun-thlin as Edinsa. In 1840, he dies and Gwai-gwun-thlin succeeds him. By this time, New England whalers arrive regularly, and a Hudson Bay Company fur trading post has been established on the mainland among Haida traditional enemies, the Tsimshians. Gold is discovered in 1850, first in Haida territory, then in Salish country south of Vancouver, bringing an influx of gold seekers, and trouble is constant. Freely distributed ''firewater'' results in strife with whites and among Indians. Chief Edinsa exhorts his people without avail to keep the peace and stay away from the gold fields. Smallpox breaks out in the gold fields, spreads northward, and decimates the people, until only one thousand are left of the ten thousand of first contact. The Haidas feel shamed by the disasters and compensate for their feelings of unworthiness by giving elaborate potlatches and raising enormous totem poles. Tuberculosis strikes, and problems with alcohol persist. In 1876, the Rev. Mr. Collison arrives, and one of Edinsa's sons becomes a Christian, but the heir to the chieftainship, Tahayghen, known among whites as well as Indians as a highly talented carver, and his chieftainess-to-be strive to keep alive the traditional artistic skills. Hearing that another smallpox epidemic is imminent, Mr. Collison vaccinates the people, who, since they survive, convert to Christianity in droves. When, in 1884, a law prohibiting potlatches is passed, Edinsa capitulates, too, accepting baptism as Albert Edward Edenshaw and taking a position as peace officer under the Crown. When he dies, only six hundred of his people remain. The new Edinsa (Tahayghen, now also Christian and known as Charles Edenshaw), and his wife strive to maintain regal dignity. He continues to use his artistic skills, and his carvings in polished slate are much in demand. When he dies of consumption in 1920, his heir, Charles Gladstone, renounces the succession. The book then skips ahead to Gladstone's grandson, Bill Reid, of the Raven phratry and the novel's artist, who feels strongly called at the age of twenty-eight to become an artist and develops a workshop where he revives and popularizes the ancient arts of the Haida. A highly crowded canvas, the book projects the tone of fictionalized history more than the tone of a proper novel. Of the very large cast of characters, most of whom are historical, only the three chiefs stand out, and they are almost indistinguishable from one another. Because the book covers so long a period of time, the author has no room to develop incidents, but some, such as the attack in which Maada is killed and that in which the second Edinsa bravely saves the crew of an American ship, are memorable. Details of Haida life and thought are related in sufficient quantity to point up the Haida tragedy, and the insatiable greed of the whites, their utter lack of desire to understand the Indians, and their total disrespect for the Indians as human beings comes through strongly. Can. Bk. of Year Winner.

RAZZELL, MARY (1930–), Canadian author of a number of young adult novels. *Snow Apples** (Groundwood/Douglas, 1984) is a story of a girl from a struggling family on the British Columbia coast who becomes pregnant, has a secret self-induced abortion, and manages through her strong determination to keep her emotional balance and get into nurses' training. It received honorable mention for the Canada Council Children's Literature Prize. Its sequel, *Salmonberry Wine* (Douglas, 1987) is about her first few months of nurses' training. Both books are realistic in their gritty details and develop both the protagonist and minor characters into convincing figures. A later title is *Night Fires* (Groundwood/Douglas, 1990). Razzell is also author of a brief non-fiction book, *The Secret Code of DNA* (Penumbra, 1986).

REBELS RIDE AT NIGHT (Hayes*, John F., ill. Fred J. Finley, Copp, 1953), historical adventure novel set in Toronto and the countryside immediately north, dealing with the revolt in 1837 of the Reformers, a group of settlers and city workers led by William Lyon Mackenzie*. After his father's death, Frank Sanford, 16, comes to Toronto to take a job as a stevedore at Feighan's Wharf, hoping to earn enough money to pay the five years' back taxes he has been informed are owed on the farm. He is disturbed to find a neighbor, shiftless Shamus Quigley, working on the wharf and remembers that Shamus worked on the farm for nearly a week after his father's death, a period during which his father's tax receipts disappeared. His boss at the wharf, big Duffy Douget, is friendly and helpful and finds him a room in the warehouse at the edge of the wharf where he can stay rent free. Duffy is frankly a Reformer, one of the faction led by Mackenzie, Toronto workmen who side with the settlers in opposition to the government controlled by a group of wealthy men known as the Family Compact. One hot day, as they wait for a steamship to dock, a boy cavorting on the wheelcage slips and falls between the dock and the ship. Frank, an expert swimmer, dives in and saves the lad. He is nonplused to learn that the boy is Clifford Webb, son of the lawyer, Adam* Webb, who so coldly informed him that his land would soon be forfeit for nonpayment of taxes. Frank is amazed when one night Adam Webb calls at his room in the warehouses, ostensibly to thank him for saving his son's life but also to explain that, though he works for some of the prominent government figures, his real allegiance is to Mackenzie and his Reformers and to admit that tax records were altered by bribery so that Shamus, who is a spy for the Family Compact, can be granted the Sanford land as a reward. As Webb leaves the warehouse, a shot rings out, and he drops. Frank rushes out to see what has happened, and is apprehended by the police as he bends over Webb's body with a gun in his hand. Frank ends up in handcuffs, badly beaten by the police, being marched through the streets to the jail, but he is rescued by men from Feighan's Wharf. For hours he runs through the city in the cold rain, chased by lantern-carrying crowds, finally realizing that the one place he will not be looked for is the fine Webb home on the north side of the city. Mrs. Webb and Clifford welcome him, and the next morning Mrs. Webb gets the authorities to drop the case. Clifford, who is almost sixteen, accompanies Frank back to the wharf and insists on being allowed to take a job on the crew. The two boys become fast friends and are involved in numerous other adventures, all involving either Frank's conflict with Shamus or the activities of the Reformers. Adam Webb, who was not seriously hurt, sends both boys north on horseback to find Mackenzie and warn him that thugs hired by the Family Compact are going to start fights at his meetings and that Shamus is to attempt assassination. On their way back they are jumped by Shamus, taken captive to the Quigley farm, and shut in a back room for five days. Word of a rescue party approaching makes Shamus and his brother leave, and Frank searches the house thoroughly and finds the missing tax receipts. Before they get back to Toronto, the rebellion has begun prematurely and, without good organization, soon frizzles and ends with a government attack on Montgomery's Tavern, in which many rebels are killed. Shamus, exposed as a spy, is forced to flee to the United States, and Frank is pardoned along with Duffy in a deal struck by Adam Webb. In the end he is being sent to Upper Canada College along with Clifford. A brief epilogue sees them twelve years later, both partners in Webb's law firm, considering the changes that have pardoned all offenses in the 1837 uprising and allowed Mackenzie to return to Canada. The action packed into the novel would serve for several, but it is consistently interesting, with a wealth of historical detail, all well integrated into the fast-paced plot. Frank is an almost unbelievably skillful fighter, swimmer, and fencer, and Clifford is the stock sidekick, less talented but devoted. The best-developed characters are Mackenzie and Adam Webb, both of whom remain somewhat enigmatic. Can. Gov. General's Winner.

REES, (GEORGE) LESLIE (CLARKE) (1905–), born in Perth, Western Australia; journalist, author of many books for both adults and children. He spent much time as a boy camping and hiking in the country near Perth, on islands off the coast and in the Darling Ranges. He worked for many years on *The West Australian*, then in London, and in Sydney, as a drama critic on *The Sydney Herald*. He has written radio documentaries and edited and produced plays for the Australian Broadcasting Commission. His writings for adults include travel books and drama criticism. For children, he has written half a dozen adventure stories starring Digit Dick, the first being *Digit Dick on the Barrier Reef* (Sands, 1942). Better known are his animal stories, brief illustrated novels of fictionalized natural history, among them *The Story of Karrawingi the Emu** (Sands, 1946), *The Story of Kurri Kurri the Kookaburra** (Sands, 1950), *The Story of Shadow, the Rock Wallaby** (Sands, 1948), and *The Story of Sarli, the Barrier Reef Turtle** (Sands, 1947). *Karrawingi* won the first Australian Book of the Year Award in 1946 and the other three have been commended or highly commended for the award. He has also written some exciting adventure stories, among them *Danger Patrol* (Collins, 1954), set in New Guinea, and *Panic in the Cattle Country* (Rigby, 1974), a mystery about cattle in the outback that were found slaughtered with huge, tearing wounds. With his wife, Coralie Clarke Rees, a writer who died in 1972, he wrote a number of non-fiction books for adults. *Hold Fast to Dreams: Fifty Years in Theatre, Radio, Television, and Books* (Alternative, 1982) is a book of his memoirs.

REG EDWARDS (*The Min-Min**), Sylvie's* younger brother, 11. A rebellious, sneaky, young tough, his anti-social acts repeatedly get him into trouble. Warned that one more escapade will result in reform school, he decides to run away to the city, but Sylvie talks him into accompanying her to the Tuckers' place. He adopts a superior attitude toward her, even though her efforts see them safely to the Tuckers. At the end, he hopes that he can get a job at a station, where he can put his considerable energy to good purpose. Reg is round and dynamic, as much a victim of unfortunate circumstances as a creator of them.

RICE, ESME, Australian author of *The Secret Family** (Angus, 1948), a sensitive story of a girl's problems in adjusting to a new stepmother and learning to share her secret interest in puppets. It was highly commended for the Australian Library Association Book of the Year Award.

RICHARD BRENT (*The Green Laurel**), elder brother of Meredith* and the friend of the Somerville girls. Bright and self-assured, he changes ambitions and interests easily and appears to have no particular purpose in life. The author implies simplistically that his aimlessness is the result of his father's absence. Richard becomes involved with the street kids who damage Mr. Somerville's carnival train. He eventually sees where right lies and identifies the boys who are responsible. His behavior allows the author to make a point.

RICHLER, MORDECAI (1931–), born in Montreal, Quebec, Canada; writer renowned for his adult novels, short stories, and essays. Of these, he is probably best known for *The Apprenticeship of Duddy Kravitz* (Deutsch, 1959), an autobiographical comic satire of a boy growing up in Montreal's Jewish ghetto in the 1940s. The novel is enjoyed by adolescents, has been used as a literature text in Canadian high schools, and was made into a popular film. Richler's reputation as a writer for children comes from *Jacob Two-Two Meets the Hooded Fang** (Knopf, 1975). A comic dream fantasy about family life, it won the Canadian Library Association Children's Book of the Year Award and the first Ruth Schwartz Children's Book Award. It features a child who repeats himself in order to get attention and has been adapted for film and stage. It has received mixed reactions from critics, some of whom characterize its humor as fourth grade, excessive, and strained, while others call it a modern classic. Its sequel is *Jacob Two-Two and the Dinosaur* (Knopf, 1987), in which Jacob receives as a gift a small lizard that grows into a huge diplodocus. A graduate of Sir George Williams College (now University) in Montreal, Richler has been writer-in-residence there, has contributed extensively to periodicals, and lives in Surrey, England.

RILEY, LOUISE (1904–1957), born in Calgary, Alberta, Canada; librarian and novelist. She attended St. Hilda's School for Girls, Calgary, McGill University, the University of Wisconsin, and Columbia University, and was a Fellow of the American Library Association. Her first book for children, *The Mystery Horse* (Copp, 1950), has been praised for integrating the details of small-time ranch life into the story. Her two other books for children, *Train for Tiger Lily** (Macmillan, 1954) and *A Spell at Scoggin's Crossing* (Abelard, 1960) are both fantasies with train settings and involve the same character, Gus, the Black porter who works second-class magic for a group of children. Though highly imaginative, they have been criticized for failing to weld together elements of magic and reality in a convincing manner. *Train for Tiger Lily* was the winner of the Canadian Library Association Book of the Year Award. Riley also wrote a novel for adults, *One Happy Moment* (Copp, 1951).

THE RIVER KINGS (Fatchen*, Max, ill. Clyde Pearson, Hicks, 1966; St. Martin's, 1968), boy's growing-up story of a runaway who works on a turn-of-the-century riverboat in southeastern Australia. Inspired by a swagman's tales of the Murray River, Shawn, 13, leaves his abusive stepfather on their marginal farm and hides away in the cart of a Syrian hawker, who takes him a hundred miles north to the river. There he gets a job on the *Lazy Jane*, an old broad-beamed, shallow draught riverboat owned by Cap'n* Elijah Wilson and crewed by Praying Jack, the mate, Silent Sam, the fireman, Angus, the Scots engineer, Charlee*, the Chinese cook, and Lord Eric, the educated English deckhand who helps Shawn compose a letter to his mother. At Wentworth they pick up the barge master, a huge man known as Tiny, who steers the towed barge. When a boy from a rival boat, the *Lady Mabel*, picks a fight with Shawn, crew members from both boats join a wild free-for-all, broken up only when Charlee comes hurtling toward the combatants shrieking and swinging his meat cleaver in circles around his head. Life on the river is described in a series of anecdotal incidents. They run into Red Morgan, a Murray River pirate or bum, who steals or begs tea and flour from the boats in return for information about snags and sandbars ahead. When Cap'n Elijah spots a missing rope from the *Lazy Jane* in Morgan's rowboat, he throws the pirate's billy, which Charlee has just filled with scalding tea, at the boat, where it douses Morgan and falls into the river, an incident that earns the *Lazy Jane* an implacable enemy. The river is full of characters, including one fisherman known as Mallee Ned, a man so dirty that riverboat men who buy his fish are careful to stay upwind of him. When the *Lady Jane* delivers a gleaming copper mail order bathtub to Mallee Ned, the whole crew insists on hanging around to see the first bath. The tub, however, has been placed on a sloping bank, and it slides with its nude bather gently down into the water, where it floats into the path of a steamer, alarming the passengers, and capsizes in the wake. On a more serious occasion, the *Lazy Jane* races the *Lady Mabel* upriver to a station where a big cargo of wool is waiting, beating the much newer boat only by taking a dangerously shallow channel known as a "gap." Another time, three outlaws board the riverboat, threatening to throw Shawn into the boiler if the men do not cooperate and burning the boy's face badly in a demonstration of how they would proceed. Charlee comes to the rescue by spilling fat on the deck to make footing treacherous, then charging out of the galley and knocking one outlaw overboard, while the quick thinking crew members overpower the other two. At a stop near a new settlement of irrigated fruit orchards, Shawn takes a nude swim, misjudges the current, and is saved by a girl on horseback, Mary Thompson, who rides in and pulls him out. He is so embarrassed that he is an easy target for her blackmail deal: her silence if he will tell her about the river and write letters to her. They carry a load that includes ammunition when Cap'n Elijah surprises Red Morgan stealing one of the chickens kept on board. The captain knocks the thief overboard and adds a string of rich insults. That night Morgan sneaks back, starts a fire on the boat, and slips off downriver. Despite valiant attempts to fight it, the fire reaches the cargo, and it explodes, demolishing the old *Lazy Jane*. The others drift off to jobs on sheep stations or other riverboats, but Shawn declares that he will stay with Cap'n Elijah. The captain persuades him that the days of riverboats are almost over and that he should take the offer of Mary's father to stay and work at his orchard. Though there is little tension in the plot, the book is rich in incident. The characters are mostly eccentrics, interesting in the context, and the sense of place is well developed. Shawn's acceptance by the men is perhaps too effortless, but it suits the tone of the story—easygoing, amusing, and good natured. Aust. Bk. of Year Com.

RIVER MURRAY MARY (Thiele*, Colin, ill. Robert Ingpen, Rigby, 1979), brief novel of family life on a fruit farm on the Murray River in South Australia in 1929. Mary Agnes Baker, 11, lives happily with her parents at Gum Flat Farm, across the river from Pimpoota, one of the first irrigated holdings taken up by Soldier Settlers, World War I veterans. A lively, freckled child, Mary works willingly on Water Day, her father's turn to tap the irrigation channel, helps her mother pick the Sultana grapes, and stokes the fire under the tank of water mixed with caustic soda in which her father dips them before spreading them to dry into raisins. She rows across the river to get groceries and hears the men on the hotel verandah talking of bad times and depression, but she is more interested in meeting her old friend, Abel Stenross, in his ancient riverboat, *Backwater Bessie*. She doesn't tell her parents that she has twice seen a large tiger snake with an odd kink in the end of his tail down at the landing, partly because the beauty of the creature impresses her. She regrets her silence when old Snap, their big "galumphing" dog comes crawling home, dragging his hindquarters, which are paralyzed by snakebite. She and her father row him across in the dinghy to the doctor, who doubles as a veterinarian. Snap recovers, but a series of near disasters follows. Mary's father gashes his arm, the Christmas tree catches fire from the candles, the price of fruit falls so low that they can hire no help at picking time, and hail ruins much of the crop and damages the trees and the grape vines. As another grape harvest arrives, flood waters rise, driving all sorts of animals and crawling creatures into the barns and stables and even onto the verandah. A large tiger snake with a kink in its tail glides across the kitchen floor, startling Mary's mother so much that she drops the can of gasoline she is carrying, splashing some of it onto the hot stove. Mary sees the explosion and the burst of fire, and she beats at the flames with a wet towel, then wraps it around her mother's shoulders, putting out the flares in her clothing. Since her father is absent, Mary takes the dinghy herself and starts for the doctor across a river she no longer recognizes, now spread out and covering trees and the Pinpoota wharf. Before she realizes it, she has been caught by the current of the flood and whisked downstream in what seems like a great rushing sea. Then she sees the *Backwater Bessie* cautiously feeling her way upstream. Mary manages to throw her rope to Abel's helper as she is being swept past, and with difficulty he pulls her close enough to help her scramble aboard. Abel steers the boat over the wharf and the loading yard and then halfway up the hill, right in front of the Pimpoota Hotel. They pick up the doctor and recross the river, landing in the garden outside the kitchen door. After the doctor has attended to Mary's mother, whose burns fortunately are not very serious, it is too dark to risk recrossing the river full of snags and floating debris, so the men settle down to passing the bottle of port and telling tall tales. In the morning, the river has fallen so much that it has stranded the *Backwater Bessie* in the vegetable garden. Abel, who has slept on the boat, surveys the situation with equanimity. "It had to happen vun day," he says. "Very old she vos, and already leaking." He says he will always have his own room now when he comes to visit them. The boat up on the hill, kept painted by Mary and her children and grandchildren, becomes a landmark, showing the unbelieving how high the flood waters once came. The story is easygoing, mostly without a strong plot or tension, but it keeps the reader's interest with sharp details of farm life and of the violent and unpredictable weather of South Australia. Mary is a spunky child, and her relationships with the adults, particularly Abel and her father, are handled skillfully. Aust. Bk. of Year Com.

RIVER RUNNERS: A TALE OF HARDSHIP AND BRAVERY (Houston*, James, ill. James Houston, Atheneum, 1979; Penguin, 1981), novel of adventure "based on true events" and set among the Naskapi Indians of subarctic Quebec, Canada, for about a year in the late 1940s. Andrew Stewart, not quite sixteen, travels by ship in late spring north to Fort Chimo, where he has secured a position as an apprentice clerk at the trading post. He soon learns his tasks and makes friends with Pashak, a capable, knowledgeable Naskapi youth, who introduces him to his relatives and to Naskapi ways. In early November, the factor at the fort orders the boys to lead a party of packmen into the interior to establish a trading post. The overland journey on snowshoes taxes Andrew's strength of body and character, and, although often left behind and sometimes near despair, he manages to use the unwieldy footgear and bear his share of the burden. After about a fortnight, still some thousand miles north of the St. Lawrence River, they come upon the extended family of the old Naskapi, Mium-scum, into which Pashak's sister Wapen has married. The Indians predict a very hard winter because caribou, the mainstay of their diet, are already scarce. After observing the shaman Cut* Cheek's shaking tent ceremony for fetching game, weathering a bad storm in Mium-scum's lodge, and enjoying his hospitality, Andrew's party continues to Ghost Lake, where they construct a cabin and prepare to receive furs. Although the packmen urge them to return with them to Fort Chimo, the boys elect to remain and are left to their own devices. True to prediction, the ensuing months of terrible cold almost claim their lives, and except for lucky catches of fish and the assistance of another almost starving family group into which another sister of Pashak has married, they would most certainly have starved or frozen to death. Traveling with the Indians, they come upon a small herd of caribou, all of which they slaughter, only shortly to lose most of the meat to a wily wolverine. The wolverine is later slain by one of the women, Piwas*. They visit mountain folk and come away with birch bark that they later use to repair a canoe and experience more harrowing episodes with the weather and the environment. They again come upon Mium-scum's family and Cut Cheek, half-dead from starvation, and save their lives. When spring seems imminent, they head north by river to Fort Chimo, an agonizing journey down the turbulent, almost unnavigable stream. Both have proved themselves in the wilderness, and Andrew is adopted into Pashak's family and decides to remain another year at the fort. In spite of flat, stock, and faceless characters and a less than credible plot made up of a string of loosely connected episodes that could easily be interchanged, the story offers plenty of first-rate adventure reading. The action moves fast, complications are sufficient and well spaced for holding power, and the story also gives a limited but still significant view of life in the Far North and the Indian culture there. The setting is so strongly depicted, less by description than by effect, that it almost becomes a character in its own right. Can. Bk. of Year Winner.

THE ROAN COLT. See *THE ROAN COLT OF YAMBOORAH*.

THE ROAN COLT OF YAMBOORAH (Ottley*, Reginald, ill. Clyde Pearson, Deutsch, 1966; *The Roan Colt*, ill. David Parry, Harcourt, 1967), sequel to *By the Sandhills of Yamboorah**, telling of the boy's love for a lame colt and the efforts of a number of the ranch people to save it. Set, as was its predecessor, in the early 1930s at Yamboorah, a cattle station near the desert of South Australia, the story starts perhaps a year later, since Rags, the boy's dog, is no longer a puppy but still not a full grown dog. The unnamed boss tells the boy to unpack the crate in his car carefully and to follow the directions enclosed. The boy discovers a new saddle, with bridle, stirrups, a tin of oil, and instructions for oiling the leather. He is astonished when the boss tells him that it is time for him to learn to ride and that the saddle is for him. Ross, the overseer, delegates the stockman, Joe, to teach the boy, which he does with no sentimental concern for the pain involved. At first the boy tries to soothe his chafed legs with the saddle oil, but old Kanga*, the dogman, returning briefly from the bush, suggests that used motor oil has "got the sting burnt out of it," and the boy finds that he is right, though the blackened oil stains his pants. By the time of the horse muster he is riding well enough to be included, along with Alici and Maheena, the Aborigine girls who help the cook, Mrs. Jones, in the kitchen but who ride as if they were born on horses. They share with the cook a soft spot for the boy. At the horse roundup, the boy first sees a magnificent roan colt that limps because it has a deformed hoof. He is appalled to learn that the boss and Ross plan to shoot the animal, though with Kanga's skill and patient treatment the condition might be cured, a solution that they think is too expensive in time and effort to be practical. The night before Ross and the stockmen ride out to a distant part of Yamboorah, Alici and Maheena, wearing Aborigine feather shoes, tie sugar sacks padded with hay onto the colt's hooves and lead him to a secret hideaway. Although Ross and the boss are puzzled and both suspect that the boy is involved, the ranch work can't be interrupted, and the men ride out. The terribly hot weather breaks in a thunder storm, which starts a grass fire. The boy dashes after Alici and Maheena, who are running toward the fire, hoping to free the colt from the scrub-fringed gully where he is hidden. Although they manage to pull away the brush barrier blocking the gully entrance, the fire almost reaches them, and they are confused in the smoke. Then the boss appears, having ridden out to get them, pulls the boy onto his horse, and gives the extra one he is leading to the girls. He then rides through the flames toward the homestead, followed by the colt and Rags. A torrential downpour saves them all. Realizing that almost everyone on the ranch, including the Aborigine stockmen and Mrs. Jones, have been trying to save the colt for the boy, the boss concedes defeat and agrees to give Kanga a chance to cure the hoof, promising the horse to the boy when it is no longer lame. The novel has a low-key plot, with emphasis on life of the isolated cattle station, the work, the heat, and the unspoken concern of the hard-bitten men, the Aborigine girls, and the overworked cook for the boy. There are also scenes of the boy helping the girls rob a bee tree, of his trying to catch the goanna, a four-foot-long lizard, which is stealing the eggs laid by Mrs. Jones's chickens, and of Ross saving the mail carrier when his half-wild team runs away. The two girls and the Aborigine stockmen, all of whom speak dialectal English, are treated with respect and are shown to be an integral part of ranch life. Aust. Bk. of Year Com.

THE ROARING 40 (Chauncy*, Nan, ill. Annette Macarthur-Onslow, Oxford, 1963; Watts, 1963), realistic adventure novel with well-sustained mystery story aspects, one in the series about the Lorenny family of the Tasmanian bush. Badge (Brian), 12, has been staying with Uncle Link and Aunt Florrie, relatives of his father, Dave*, at their farm while he attends country school with their supercilious son, Sam*. Homesick and insecure, Badge welcomes the summons home to help with old Harry*, the bush recluse, who must be taken to the hospital in Hobart. Harry cared for, Dave decides to take Badge on a long-delayed prospecting trip to remote Port Davey along with Vik* Viking, a huge, outgoing, veteran prospector, who hopes to find the lump of gold as big as a baby's head supposedly hidden there. The hike through the dense and rugged bush proves arduous, but Badge enjoys the company of the men and the stories they tell about the area, and he thrills to the hearty giant's rich singing voice. A tremendous surprise awaits them: they discover a wild boy, monosyllabic, extremely frightened, fleet, scowling, naked, a little older than Badge yet almost completely ignorant of the outside world, untrusting because evidently he has been abused by a seaman named Flinty. He talks to the birds, lives off the meager land and rich sea, sings hymns, and calls himself Ned*. Badge gradually wins the boy's confidence, and the two enjoy romps together while the men prospect. When Ned spots Flinty's boat coming, the three depart hastily for home, taking Ned with them. Ned spooks at first at everyone, except little Sheppie*, Uncle Link's young daughter, with whom he soon becomes close friends. On the way home, Badge is able to read a label that Ned keeps about his person and that curiously bears old Harry's name, Henry Burney. Gradually more information about Ned is revealed. Flinty and his brothers, known to the east coast fishermen as shiftless and hard drinking, suddenly become so affluent that they buy a fine fishing boat, the *Roaring 40*. They have mentioned finding a boy at Port Davey too "dotty" to rescue, apparently Ned. Then Ned gives warm and gentle Liddle-ma*, Badge's mother, an old "baccy" tin that contains a letter written by his now dead mother. Ned is discovered to be Harry's presumed dead nephew, who was shipwrecked and marooned at the bay for many years. At the end Badge deposits Ned with old Harry at his bush hut. The reader wonders how Ned and Harry will manage, but evidently the proceeds from the sale of the *Roaring 40*, once Harry's boat, are theirs. Although Badge is the protagonist, interest focuses on Vik, Harry, and especially Ned, whose mystery builds gradually and is deftly maintained. Flinty never appears but is powerfully drawn as the villain because the reader sees him through Badge's sympathetic and often horrified reporting to Vik and Dave of what Ned manages to tell him about the fisherman who mistreated him physically and psychologically. The conclusion seems sentimental—Ned singing a hymn on an outcropping by Harry's hut—and Badge too abruptly sees the virtues of schooling. The warmth and closeness of the Lorennys are a great plus in the story, the conversations sound real and make good use of colloquial idiom, and the descriptions of the valley and bush evoke a strong appreciation for the area's unspoiled, natural beauty. Previous novels about the Lorennys are *Tiger in the Bush** and *Devil's Hill**. Aust. Bk. of Year Highly Com.

ROBIN AND THE HAWK (Bulsara*, C. N., ill. Jagdish Joshi, CBT, India, 1982), animal story of anthropomorphized birds in which a young robin helps a community of birds drive off a hawk that has been terrorizing them. Robin, having grown up in a loving family, sets off to seek his fortune in the high mountains. He comes to Happy Valley, where he stays at the inn run by Mr. and Mrs. Sparrow. He learns about the village, where the preacher is Father Parrot, the barber is Mr. Mynah, the nursery school manager is Miss Crystal

Crow, and Mr. and Mrs. Canary run the tailor shop. It seems such a pleasant place that he asks the mayor, Mr. Woodpecker, for permission to stay, which is granted but with the grave warning, "Take care of yourself." He soon learns what brings an air of sorrow to this beautiful valley. An enormous hawk dives into the public square and seizes little Charles Pigeon in his claws of steel. Robin learns that these raids have become a regular part of life in the village, and he carefully selects a site for his home, in a strong tree only a short distance from the public square. Although there is no public show of mourning, he senses the grief and tension that this predator causes the village. To bring some cheer, he whistles an enchanting melody, and soon all the birds are dancing in the square. The sound of such merriment enrages the hawk, who plans to end it by removing the source of the music. He dives on the square but Robin cleverly eludes him. The next night the hawk again dives, but the nimble little bird leads him to his tree, which he has booby-trapped with false twigs and leaves, so that the hawk falls and bruises himself. The birds, delighted to have won a round in the battle, vote to continue dancing in the evenings but to keep their young out of the way. In the ensuing days, the hawk wrecks many of the village homes, but he does not capture Robin. Determined to repay the village for its kindness, Robin decides to sacrifice himself, and when the hawk next raids he deliberately walks to the center of the square and lets himself be seized. The hawk plans to torture Robin before eating him, and the brave bird responds with a song, which is heard in the village. His courage so impresses the other birds that they organize a rescue, dropping stones on the hawk and freeing Robin. The hawk, bruised and battered, leaves the area and the birds have a celebration dance, with Robin, recovered from his ordeal, supplying the music. The theme, that strength lies in unity, is stated explicitly by the mayor. It is not clear just how Robin's sacrifice would have saved Happy Valley if the birds had not banded together. This brief and simple story is highly illustrated with pictures that are strangely much more realistic than the text. CBT of India Second Prize.

ROCKY BARBIZAN (*Going to the Dogs**), Billy Mackenzie's best friend. Abandoned by his parents at an early age, he was raised by his fanatically religious Catholic grandmother. Expelled for disobedience from Catholic school, he enters public school where he also does poorly, drops out, and eventually takes a job with an area drug dealer, which involves cloak-and-dagger escapades. Rocky is an only marginally credible character.

RODDA, EMILY (JENNIFER ROWE) (1948–), Australian editor and novelist. Her first two novels for young readers both received the Australian Junior Book of the Year Award. The first one was *Something Special** (Angus, 1984; H. Holt, 1989), a deftly humorous short fantasy for the eight-to-eleven-year-old age range about a little girl who gets involved in her mother's rummage sale. Her second winner was *Pigs Might Fly** (Angus, 1986; *The Pigs Are Flying*, Greenwillow, 1988), a clever, lighthearted fantasy with mystery aspects about the power of the imagination, in which a girl is transported to a place where storms cause pigs to fly. She has also published *The Best-Kept Secret* (Angus, 1988; H. Holt, 1990), about a magical carousel ride. Rodda also writes mysteries for adults under her real name of Jennifer Rowe, among them, *Grim Pickings* (Allen & Unwin, 1987). She and her husband, also in publishing, have made their home in Sydney.

ROLAND, BETTY (1903–), born in Kaniva, Australia; dramatist and novelist. Her childhood was spent in rural areas, and she attended Church of England Girls' Grammar School in Melbourne. Early in her career she wrote *The Touch of Silk*, a play performed by the Melbourne Repertory Society and many amateur companies, and also many radio plays. She also wrote for a weekly paper, *Girl*, mostly serialized adventure stories. Her first book for children was *The Forbidden Bridge** (Bodley, 1961), a simple but appealing story about a young boy on a sheep ranch. The same boy is the protagonist in *Jamie's Discovery** (Bodley, 1963), *Jamie's Summer Visitor** (Bodley, 1964), and *Jamie's Other Grandmother* (Bodley, 1970). The first three were either commended or highly commended for the Australian Library Association Book of the Year Award. Her mystery for young people, *The Bush Bandits* (Landsdown, 1966), concerns the smuggling of rare birds and animals from a wildlife sanctuary. She has also written novels for adults and travel books on the Greek island of Lesbos and on Sydney.

THE ROOT CELLAR (Lunn*, Janet, Lester, 1981; Scribner, 1983), fantasy with historical novel aspects that starts in the present and takes the protagonist back in time to the American Civil War. When her globe-trotting grandmother dies, self-absorbed, lonely, orphaned Rose Larkin, 12, is sent from New York City to live with her Aunt* Nan, a writer, and Uncle Bob Henry, a game warden, and their four boys in their big, old house on an island in Hawthorn Bay off the northern shore of Lake Ontario, Canada. On her arrival, she sees superimposed on the dilapidated house an earlier, well-kept dwelling, and a little old woman with an ''apple-doll'' face greets her by name, says she's Mrs. Morrissay, tells her she must do something about refurbishing the house, and disappears as suddenly as she had materialized. Rose has other visionary manifestations, and the next evening she follows Mrs. Morrissay into the yard, where she enters an old root cellar and finds herself back in the spring of 1862. She meets and makes friends with the hired girl of the Morrissay's, the 1862 occupants, Susan* Anderson, 12, and Will* Morrissay, 13, their son, and in just a few minutes feels completely at ease. Back in the twentieth century, she discovers that she can enter the root cellar dimension when the nearby hawthorn tree casts its shadow in a certain way. She enters again and finds that Will and Susan are now in their mid-teens and that Will left in 1864 for the United States to join the Union forces as a fifer. Now it is August, 1865, the war is over, and Lincoln is dead, but no one has heard from Will. She persuades Susan to join her in searching for Will and becomes the leader of a quest that over the next several weeks takes them from Canada to New

York City to Richmond, Virginia, and back again. They sail to Oswego, New York, where they discover that Mrs. Jerue, Will's aunt, has had no news of her son, Steve, who had joined the Union Army with Will. At the local fort, they learn that Steve was wounded at Cold Harbor and that both boys were last seen at Richmond. They head for Washington, hoping to find them in a hospital there. In New York in a scene that strains credulity, Rose faints when she realizes that Grand Central Station does not yet exist, recovers, and for the first time wishes she were back with the noisy yet comfortable and sturdy Henrys. In Washington, they search the hospitals in vain. Then as a last resort they visit Arlington Cemetery, where they encounter Will, thin, haggard, wiser about war, and guilt-ridden over Steve's death. After he tells his lengthy story, which includes a good deal of historical information about the Richmond campaign, the girls persuade him that, since Steve is dead, Will is no longer bound by his promise to stay with Steve, and all head home. They arrive as a terrible rainstorm hits the region. When she sees the root cellar flooded, Rose despairs of getting back to her dimension, plunges into the water anyway, and comes up relieved to discover that it is the evening of the day she left. Grateful to be home after the trying war events, Rose tries harder to fit in with the Henrys and in school. About a week before Christmas, she decides to give the family an old-fashioned holiday dinner. Although she studies up on the dishes, things go awry, but a grand feast appears anyway, and Rose knows it is really Susan's doing. She shares her story about the past with the Henrys, who believe her. Alone in the kitchen afterward, Rose converses with Susan, who she now learns married Will and is the old Mrs. Morrissay who welcomed her on her arrival at Hawthorn Bay. She resolves to make the house beautiful again as it was when she met Susan in Susan's dimension. The time shifts are awkward, and the dialogue sounds unnatural, but the mid–1800s dialect of Will and Susan seems appropriate. Though individualized, the Henrys are almost choral characters, and Rose herself is an older Mary of *The Secret Garden*, a book that ironically she deems a most precious possession. Will's disillusionment as a result of his experience seems genuine, and Susan's deep concern for him and her moral uprightness are fitting to her character as presented and to the period. Why Rose should be so determined to find Will is not clear. We are told that she thinks him attractive, but the author does not exploit her awakening sexuality. It is not clear why the root cellar should be her portal of entry into the Civil War dimension when the Morrissays can enter Rose's dimension through the house. The realistic, problem, girl's growing-up frame story of the unhappy adolescent who changes through involvement in a larger endeavor seems trite, and the historical portion is the most compelling part of the book. It gives some sense of the war and good views of the period and the Canadian attitude toward events. Can. Bk. of Year Winner.

ROSE BRADLEY (*Pastures of the Blue Crane**), neighbor and friend of Ryl* and Dusty* Merewether of Geebin Farm. She first informs Ryl that Ryl's mother was part South Sea Islander and granddaughter of old Ki, Perry* Davis's great-grandfather, and that Perry is really Ryl's brother. Rose is an interesting, if stock, character who plays a vital role in the plot.

ROY, THOMAS (ALBERT), Australian writer whose novel *The Curse of the Turtle** (Bodley, 1977; Collins, 1978) was commended for the Australian Children's Book of the Year Award. Set among Aborigines in northeastern Australia in the late 1940s, it has been praised by critics for its carefully escalating suspense and its sympathetic and accurate picture of the Australian native peoples. Roy also published *The Vengeance of the Dolphin* (Bodley, 1980).

RUBENSTEIN, GILLIAN, born in England during World War II; Australian editor and novelist. She attended boarding school in England, visiting occasionally at her parents' home in northern Nigeria. She was graduated from Oxford University where she developed a strong interest in theater. She later took teacher training at the University of London. She has worked as an arts and entertainment editor on Chambers' *Encyclopedia Yearbook* and as a film critic for the *Sunday Australian*. She lives in Adelaide with her husband and three children. Her first book, *Space Demons** (Omnibus, 1986; Dial, 1988), was commended for the Australian Children's Book of the Year Award. An action-filled science fiction novel, it tells of the dramatic fight for life of some children who, addicted to computer games, are pulled through the video screen and encounter terrifying space creatures.

RUNAWAY TO FREEDOM. See *UNDERGROUND TO CANADA.*

RUTH REID (*A Handful of Time**), Patricia Potter's mother, a successful and popular television commentator. When the novel begins, she and her husband are planning to get a divorce. The fantasy part of the story gives insights into her character. She grew up playing second fiddle to her older brothers, who were encouraged to develop their talents because they were boys, while she was expected to be attractive and agreeable, marry, and raise a large family. Ruth early decided to "show them all," won a scholarship to college, devoted herself to her career, and had little to do with the Reids henceforth. As an adult, she still shows a need to be in charge and serves as a foil for Aunt Ginnie Grant, her maternalistic younger sister. Ruth and her controlling mother, Pat* Reid, are the most interesting figures in the novel.

RYL MEREWETHER (*Pastures of the Blue Crane**), Amaryllis Merewether, 16, daughter of an Australian lumberman whose business was in New Guinea. Ryl has grown up in boarding schools and has no sense of family. Through fixing up Geebin Farm, she learns to reach out to others, particularly Dusty*, her grandfather. At first she dislikes the South Sea Islanders of the region, but her association with Perry* Davis and her success with the farm produce a strong sense of self-worth and appreciation of people for what they are. Ryl is a convincing, well-developed character.

S

SACCO, BARTHOLOMEW (*A Book Dragon**), shoemaker and locksmith who owns a shop on the hill next to Mr. Gottlieb's bookshop. Once engineer on a ship torpedoed during the war in the North Atlantic, he rescued his parrot and broke his leg jumping into the lifeboat. As a consequence, he walks with a limp. Sacco is a socialist who was once elected, by default, to the city council. He has many friends among taxi drivers, policemen, reporters, and minor city officials, and, when Mr. Abercrombie begins to harass the three store owners on the hill, Sacco is able to get information and to thwart some of his schemes. His theory about Mr. Abercrombie's disappearance is that the devil himself carried the exploiter away. Much of Nonesuch's information about the neighborhood comes from Sacco's parrot.

SADIE TREE (*The True Story of Spit MacPhee**), daughter of Grace and Jack Tree and Spit* MacPhee's only friend. Sadie is shy, overprotected, especially by her father, and a loner like Spit. Grace encourages their friendship because she realizes that since the Trees live on the river Sadie should have survival skills that Spit can teach her. Sadie learns to assert herself, and she quietly persuades her father to sign the application to adopt Spit. Sadie is a foil for both Spit and Ben Arbuckle, Betty's timid son.

SALTWATER SUMMER (Haig-Brown*, Roderick L., Collins, 1949; Morrow, 1948), adventure novel set one spring and summer in the mid–1940s among fishermen on the British Columbia coast north of Vancouver, Canada. Don Morgan, not yet seventeen, is the proud owner of the *Mallard*, the fishing boat he bought with money he earned trapping and hunting in *Starbuck Valley Winter**. He heads north from Vancouver with his pal, Tubby Miller, crewing, and soon encounters Red Holliday, captain of the *Falaise*, a capable, friendly man of about thirty, and his army buddy crewman, Tom Moore, an educated man whose "head isn't right" because of his experiences in World War II. Don and Tubby fish on their own for a while, and Don patches up a quarrel between two stubborn

Irish handloggers (timbermen) who have disagreed over whether their bay should be called Canada or Killarney and have been communicating by talking to their cat, Babe. The boys gradually move northward and arrive at Pendennis Island, trolling for salmon. They encounter Red and Tom again and enjoy the company of the many fishermen there. Don is pleased with the seaworthiness of the *Mallard* but disappointed by his small catches and turns surly, and Tubby leaves for another job. During a birthday party on another boat, someone questions Don's skill at hunting, and the next day he goes ashore and shoots a buck, though he is aware that it is out of season. Arrested, he counts himself lucky to get off with a stern lecture and a twenty-five dollar fine. During a social gathering among the men, feeling runs high against the Japanese fishermen, but Tom Moore speaks up, for the first time in a group, and delivers a long, moralistic anti-prejudice speech. This marks a turning point in his character, and he assumes a new competence. The turning point in Don and Tubby's relationship comes when the *Varga Girl*, moored next to the *Mallard*, explodes. While Don rescues its crewmen, Tubby moves the *Mallard*, and the two settle their differences. A sudden storm leads to the book's most exciting episode. An elderly ex-farmer, Jake Heron, called Old Cowbells, is caught offshore in his dilapidated boat and is rescued under Tom's direction. Amid twenty-foot waves and with Don manipulating lines and Tubby at the wheel, Tom leaps to the *Blue Grass* and heaves Jake aboard the *Falaise* just before the old boat sinks. When the cohoe run fades and winter approaches, the boys return to the gulf. The summer has been financially successful, but Don has discovered that he is no longer enthusiastic about fishing. He sells a half-interest in the *Mallard* to Tubby, who seems suited to the water, and looks forward eagerly to trapping and hunting again. The characters are drawn in broad strokes and are typical of the adventure story genre. Also conventional are most of the incidents, which seem devised to present the protagonist with opportunities to excel and exemplify moral and practical values. Tom is the stereotypical war hero who makes a miraculous recovery, and Red is an example of the mature, knowledgeable, caring adult who serves as a fine role model. Tubby and Red are described as natural sailors, but we actually see little of their skill. The fishermen are choral characters, either upright and skilled or inept troublemakers. The story is mainly fast-moving plot. Most of the story is told from Don's point of view (though not by him), but occasionally it deviates to alert the reader about what might happen next. The sense of the power and majesty of the sea is strong, and Don is allowed to see a glimmer of the ecological impact of hunting, trapping, and fishing on the environment. Usually the talk of eddies and tides is just enough to provide the necessary setting, and only occasionally does nautical talk impede understanding and hold up the story. Can. Gov. General's Winner.

SALWI, DILIP M. (1952–), born in Ratnagiri, Maharashtra, India; science journalist and writer of fiction and non-fiction books on scientific topics. Since earning his undergraduate and graduate degrees in science from the University of Delhi and a diploma in journalism, he has been on the staff of the *Science Reporter*, a widely circulated science monthly that he currently edits. Although he also writes for adults on science and technology for newspapers and other magazines, he started his career by writing on science and creating science puzzles for *Children's World*, a magazine published by the Children's Book Trust of India. He has since written more than 800 articles, 20 short stories, and a dozen books on scientific topics. His *A Passage to Antarctica** (CBT, India, 1986) won second prize in the Children's Book Trust of India literary competition in 1985. This realistic novel of a contemporary expedition from Goa, India, to the southernmost continent is written with careful attention to scientific detail. He also won a Children's Book Trust Prize for *Our Scientists* (CBT, India, 1986), a collection of biographies of Indian scientists, and the prestigious Sanskriti Award for science journalism in 1986.

SAMANKWE AND THE HIGHWAY ROBBERS (Ekwensi*, Cyprian, Evans, 1975), adventure story set in Nigeria, presumably in the late twentieth century. Samankwe, probably ten to twelve years old, is designated to accompany his Uncle Silas, a well-to-do trader, from his home in San Pedro to Benin, carrying on the bus a suitcase full of money while his uncle carries an identical suitcase containing a smoke bomb in an effort to thwart the highway robbers so common in the country. The bus driver is late and then stalls so that they will have to travel after dark. Further suspicious events delay them and when they are well away from towns, they are stopped by a tree trunk across the road. The bus is invaded by four masked men. According to their plan, Uncle Silas pushes the button to open his suitcase and set off the smoke bomb, only to discover that the cases have been mixed up and his is full of money. Samankwe presses the button on his suitcase and in the smoke and confusion stumbles away into the forest. In the morning he finds a wounded man, one of the robbers who introduces himself as Tijani Ahmadu Okafor and tells Samankwe how he became involved with the highway bandits and how he now wishes to be free from them. The boy persuades him to go to the police, confess, and offer information about the other robbers in return for clemency. Samankwe runs ahead toward the road, hoping to stop a truck and get help for the wounded man, but he is captured by another robber named Man Pikin, who gives him some food and takes him to the robbers' headquarters in the forest. There he is locked in a room from which he can watch the leader, Black Diamond, and all that goes on in the clearing outside, including a conjuring ceremony to insure their continued freedom. He sees the arrival of a woman, Alhaja, who is known as the Chief Planner. He also sees the bus on which he was traveling arrive with the stolen suitcases. The police, who have found Tijani, surround and raid the robbers' headquarters. Samankwe comes out of hiding and tells his story. Later he testifies at the robbers' trial and is present at their public execution. When the firing squad shoots and Black Diamond is not hurt, the huge crowd believes that he is bulletproof and panics. The robbers are taken back to prison, and it is discovered that the soldiers were firing blanks. The officer in charge is tied to a stake and shot. Three weeks later Black Diamond, along with the other robbers, is again shot, this time with live bullets, before a crowd of fifty thousand, many of whom, having bet on his immortality, lose money and are disappointed when he is killed. Some weeks later, Uncle Silas appears, having been wounded in the attack on the bus, wandered in the bush for some time, and eventually recuperated in a hospital. Although the story is almost all plot with very little development of character or setting, the final chapter is devoted to statements of morals by Samankwe and his mother: thievery does not pay and never carry cash when you travel. The dialect, which is limited almost entirely to the use of ''tha's'' for ''that is'' intermixes with rather formal English and is thus not convincing. The most surprising element to Western readers is the relish with which the public executions are described. Nigerian Ife, First Prize.

SAM LORENNY (*Devil's Hill*; The Roaring 40**), Badge's* spoiled cousin. In *Devil's Hill*, he comes reluctantly to live with his Tasmanian bush relatives. He soon shows that he looks down upon their bush life and often speaks with admiration of the city, distinctly false pride since he lives on a farm on the other side of the Gordon River from Badge's home. During the search for Brindle, the lost heifer, Sam comes to enjoy the challenge of the bush and the satisfaction of doing his share in bringing about a successful enterprise. In *The Roaring 40*, he reverts to his old superior attitude toward Badge, while Badge stays with Sam's family to attend country school. As a character, Sam borders on being a type.

SAMUEL BOW (*Playing Beatie Bow**), tall, middle-aged man who runs a confectioner's shop in Sydney, Australia, in 1873. Usually muddled, Samuel is the ruin of what had once been a handsome soldier. His deeply scarred head and crossed eyes are the result of a head wound during the Crimean War. Particularly after drinking rum, he thinks that he is back at Balaclava fighting the ''Rooshians.'' Then he grabs his scimitar from the wall and rushes from his shop, attacking anyone unfortunate enough to be in his path. When Abby Kirk first enters the 1873 time frame, Samuel is having one such ''spell.'' Samuel is a pathetic figure, who is treated with compassion by constables and neighbors, a loving kindness that impresses Abby greatly.

SARAH TALBOT (*Mama's Going to Buy You a Mockingbird**), Jeremy's little sister. A lively child, she follows Jeremy around while they are at the lakeside cottage and has many problems with Aunt Margery because she doesn't fit her aunt's ideas of how a little girl should behave. Unlike Jeremy, she cries about her father's death, an action that makes Jeremy wonder whether she loved their father more than he did. When she loses her beloved doll named Fiona and Jeremy thoughtlessly tells her that she wouldn't have lost it if she took care of her things, she swipes Hoot, the polished stone owl Adrian gave to Jeremy before he died. Later she returns it, and Jeremy puts it in their mother's stocking on Christmas morning. Sarah first accepts the Medfords as family, soon calling Mr. Medford Grandpa. Sarah is well drawn, typical yet individualized.

SARAH WHITBURN (*Blue Above the Trees**), enduring wife of William* Whitburn, mother of Simon* and several other children, English immigrants to the Great Forest in Australia. A small, sensible woman, she disagrees with William's strongly held desire to emigrate to Australia, but she still loyally supports him. Her quiet assertiveness keeps the family intact. She intercedes about the rocking chair, for example, insisting that it be kept, and she speaks up to William about letting Simon go to school. On the few but important occasions that she asserts herself, William quickly defers to her judgment. She is a strong influence and a well-depicted, never sentimentalized maternal figure.

SCOTT, BILL (WILLIAM NEVILLE SCOTT) (1923–), born in Bundaberg, Queensland, Australia; bookseller, publisher, editor, writer. He was educated at Caboolture State Primary School and served in the Royal Australian Navy during World War II. During the 1950s and 1960s he worked as a publisher and editor, then became a full-time writer, with a strong interest in Australian folklore and social history. In his two books for young people, *Boori** (Oxford, 1978) and its sequel, *Darkness under the Hills**, he uses characters and motifs from Aborigine mythology, reshaped with respect. Both are essentially hero tales and employ a fittingly serious and sometimes lofty style. Both were highly commended for the Australian Library Association Book of the Year Award. He has also published books of short stories, verse, and non-fiction for adults and edited several anthologies of poetry, Australian ballads, songs, and folklore. *Tough in the Old Days* (Rigby, 1979) is an autobiography.

SEA MENACE (Gunn*, John, ill. Brian Keogh, Constable, 1958), rousing sea adventure set in 1807 off the east coast of Australia. In the barque *Thomas**, Paul Harris, 19, is traveling with his uncle and guardian, Charles Britton, and his cousin, Ian*, to make a home in New South Wales. When the ship founders in a storm, they escape in a boat with three seamen, thin, melancholy Black, wiry O'Neil, and Carter, a talkative older sailor. They pick up three survivors, including Captain Graham, who has become deranged and dies a short time later. The eight others row toward land for four days before Black's mind snaps, and he is restrained with difficulty. Soon thereafter they sight a sail and are picked up, somewhat reluctantly, by what appears to be a whaler commanded by a well-dressed, sinister Yankee named Kendrick*. The survivors soon learn that they are really prisoners aboard a pirate ship that uses its whaling rig as a decoy to lure other ships within attack distance, but they suspect and soon confirm a greater villainy in the making: Kendrick on his own privateer, with three captured whalers, plans to storm and capture the settlement of Sydney. To lure the men-of-war out of the port, he plans to set Paul and Ian adrift in the longboat near Sydney harbor, with the story that the *Thomas* was set upon and sunk by pirates, and to keep Britton as a hostage. In a skirmish with a whaler, the boys escape, are captured, escape again, and are recaptured, but Kendrick sticks with his plan, only deciding to keep Ian as a second hostage and to send a trusted seaman with Paul. To get supplies they go to a pirate's secret base in Tasmania where the men from the *Thomas* are locked in a jail hut. Kendrick's ward, a red-haired American boy about Paul's age named Patrick Harding, is assigned to care for their needs, but he soon reveals that he is himself really a prisoner. With Patrick's help, they attempt a daring escape by taking a launch with the hope of sailing to Hobart, from where they can send a fast ship with a warning to Sydney. Their plan fails when they go aground and are retaken, but they have tied Patrick so that it will seem that he was with them involuntarily. Kendrick sticks to his plan, but before they reach Sydney, they take a Dutch merchantman, and Paul and his friends plus a skeleton crew are put aboard it. With Patrick's aid, they throw a man overboard, and when a boat is lowered to pick him up, overpower the rest of the meager crew. Since it is clear that they cannot sail the ship with only their few men, they find a sandy beach and ground it, hoping to walk to Sydney in time to raise the alarm. Ian, Peter, and the two other seamen set out ahead, leaving Paul, Patrick, Britton, and the now half-mad Waters, the surgeon's mate, camping on the shore. When they sight a sail, Waters frantically spreads the fire to signal it, though the others try to restrain him, rightly guessing that it is the *Sussex*. Waters is killed in the fire, but the others are again taken by Kendrick, who assumes that the four missing men were also killed and who now treats Patrick as a prisoner. They sail to Sydney and, as they approach the harbor, Black unlocks their prison quarters, having joined the pirates but repented. As the ship comes to the narrow harbor entrance, they jump overboard and swim for shore, with Paul first starting fires at several points on the ship. The *Sussex* is intercepted by men-of-war warned by Ian, and it blows up. Sydney's Governor Bligh (Captain Bligh of *Bounty* fame) gives Paul, Ian, Britton, and Patrick grants of land beyond Parramatta, a settlement to the west, and the seamen are given comparable grants of money. The number of daring escapes and recaptures strains credulity, but the fast pace obscures the implausibility. The violent history of piracy in early nineteenth-century Australian waters and in the colony of New South Wales makes a good background for the swashbuckling tale. The characterization is adequate, but the strength of the story lies in its action. Aust. Bk. of Year Winner.

SEAN TRUELANCE (*Longtime Passing**), Edwin* Truelance's younger brother, who, after returning from World War I bitter and disillusioned, discovers new possibilities for happiness at Longtime* in the Blue Mountains of Australia. A partner in the Truelance sawmill, he often makes surprise visits to Edwin's family. He marries after being in the mountains several years, and his wife, red-haired, cheerful Aunt Alanah, adapts quickly. She gives the Truelance girls piano lessons and brings some culture to the area.

THE SECRET FAMILY (Rice*, Esme, ill. Pixie O'Harris, Angus, 1948), school and family story that centers on how a Melbourne, Australia, schoolgirl adjusts to a new stepmother, set in the years just after World War II. Ariel Strong, 14, although well liked by her classmates, has learned to keep a barrier of reserve between her private thoughts and the outside world because her mother is dead, Mrs. Murphy, the housekeeper, has become increasingly cross and dissatisfied, and her busy father, George*, forgets her existence for days on end. Since she saw a Punch and Judy show when she was eight, Ariel's secret comfort and interest has been in puppets for whom she has invented stories and who have become her surrogate family, at first crude stick puppets with paper faces but gradually more sophisticated marionettes, as she has learned to manipulate their strings and carve wooden heads and hands. She keeps all her secret family, as well as a puppet stage she has built, locked up from Mrs. Murphy's prying. Her father suddenly announces that he is planning to be married the next month in Sydney, so she must buy a new dress. With the help of a dressmaker who was her mother's friend, Ariel and Mrs. Murphy select a yellow silk suit, and Ariel takes the overnight train to Sydney, very apprehensive about meeting Priscilla, her prospective stepmother. To comfort herself, she takes a couple of her puppet heads in her purse. Priscilla's sister Lillian, an artist at whose apartment she is to stay, takes her to a marionette show by the Steleviskis, a family Lillian recognizes as one that she stayed with in Europe before the war. To Ariel's delight, they are invited backstage for a warm reunion. She tells Frank Steleviski about her marionettes, and he invites her to visit them when they take the show to Melbourne. The rest of the wedding is something of a happy blur to Ariel: the yellow suit proves to be perfect and Priscilla is pretty and friendly. Although the changes at home with Priscilla are mostly for the better and Ariel finds it a new experience to have her father around so much, she maintains her reserve. Pointing out that girls need some privacy, Priscilla even keeps Ariel's father from insisting that she open the locked cupboard in which she keeps her marionettes, but the well-meaning stepmother unwittingly creates a major problem by claiming for a studio the old shed that George once converted into a workshop and that has become Ariel's special place, where she can be by herself and do her carving and painting. The strain in the family comes to a head when Ariel leaves while her parents are out to keep her date with the Steleviskis in their flat. When she shows her puppet heads to Hans, a famous sculptor, he offers to teach her carving free. Although she has never had to ask his permission to come and go in the past, her father is annoyed that she has gone into the city on her own, and he sends her from the table in disgrace. In the next weeks, even though Ariel is polite and Priscilla tries by humor and vivacity to ease the tense atmosphere, their relations remain strained. It is not until Ariel's play is published in the school magazine that her secret activities are revealed, and she astonishes her parents by performing a marionette show for them and begging that she may take lessons from Hans. Amazed and delighted, they agree, and the future looks brighter for all of them. The story of the family problems, occurring despite each member's trying to show good will and understanding, is interspersed with chapters and scenes from school. It is somewhat implausible that Ariel's father would surprise his daughter with a stepmother and expect their first meeting to be at the wedding, or that Priscilla, a woman of good sense, would have allowed this to occur. Also, Ariel's multiplicity of skills—she is a fast runner, a good playwright, and an expert though untaught artist—are unlikely and date the book as from a less realistic era, but the difficulties of her family in adjusting to its new pattern are convincing and interesting. School scenes, though less compelling, are believable and lively. Aust. Bk. of Year Highly Com.

THE SECRET FRIENDS. See *TANGARA*.

SECRET OF THE MAORI CAVE. See *THE HOLE IN THE HILL*.

SEGUN, MABEL D(OROTHY) (1930–), born in Ondo, Nigeria; writer, editor, educator, and government official. The daughter of a village minister, Segun attended schools in Akure and Lagos and University College in Ibadan. She has held various positions as a teacher and administrator, including service as vice-principal of the National Teachers College in Lagos and research fellow for the Institute of African Studies, University of Ibadan. She has been deputy permanent delegate of Nigeria to UNESCO; chief federal inspector of education, Federal Ministry of Education, Lagos; editor of *Modern Woman* in Lagos and for Silver Burdett and Harper and Row publishers; and president of the Children's Literature Association of Nigeria (CLAN), among many other positions. Her writings for children seek to promote such traditional African values as patriotism, unity, and perseverance. *Youth Day Parade** (Daystar, 1984) recounts the efforts of a group of multi-ethnic Nigerian students to win the annual parade prize. Her first book, it received honorable mention for ages eight to twelve in the CLAN book competition. Her other publications for children include another school novel, *Olu and the Broken Statue* (New Horn, 1985), her autobiographies, *My Father's Daughter* (African Universities, 1965), and *My Mother's Daughter* (African Universities, 1987), and *Under the Mango Tree* (Longman, 1980), two volumes of verse she collaboratively edited. She has also written poems and essays for adults.

SELINA POTTER (*An Older Kind of Magic**), younger sister of Rupert Potter and playmate of Benny* Golightly. Selina's stubbornness impels her to try to save the botanical gardens from being made into a parking lot. She is kindhearted, particularly to animals, and her attempt to find a safe place for the body of a crushed lizard brings her to the attention of Mr.* Ernest Hawke. Selina is a foil for both Rupert and Benny.

SENGUPTA, ABHIJIT, author in India who wrote the realistic novelette, *The Story of Panchami** (CBT, India, 1986), about how a brother and sister rescue and make a pet of a wounded seagull. His second full-length story, the book was awarded second prize in the India Children's Book Trust competition of 1985. His first novel was *The Man from Sundarbans* (CBT, India, 1981).

SENGUPTA, POILE (AMBIKA) (1948–), born in Ernakulam, Kerala, India; writer of fiction and non-fiction for adults and children. After earning her undergraduate and graduate degrees with high honors in English from Delhi University, she taught at a women's college in Delhi and began writing. In 1969 she initiated a humor column for children, ''A Letter to You,'' in *Children's World*, a monthly published by the Children's Book Trust of India. Her novel, *The Exquisite Balance** (CBT, India, 1987), a science fiction mystery about a visitor from outer space who becomes marooned on earth, received second prize in the 1986 Children's Book Trust of India writers' competition in collaboration with UNICEF on the theme of gender equality. She has co-edited a series of spelling books, is a frequent contributor to *Target*, another prominent New Delhi children's magazine, and has published the story for a picture book, *How the Path Grew* (CBT, 1988). She is married to a senior civil servant and teaches English at a high school in Bangalore in South India. In 1984–1985, she studied Children's Literature at Carleton University, Ottawa, Canada.

THE SEVENTH PEBBLE (Spence*, Eleanor, ill. Sisca Verwoert, Oxford, 1980), realistic novel of family and community life set from August, 1938, to January, 1939, in semi-rural Hollybush Flat, three hours by train from Sydney, Australia. Life changes dramatically for Rachel Blackwood, 11, daughter of the local physician, when the Irish Connell family, a mother and five children, move into the abandoned old Turner place overlooking Tin Can Creek. Rachel gains a new best friend in lively, imaginative, talkative Bridget, just her age. The Connells are Catholic, a matter of significance in this entirely Protestant community. The girls visit back and forth, Bridget often with Little* Pat, 5, lame from polio, in tow. Bridget maintains that the Connells are descendants of Irish royalty and that her father is an engineer who will soon re-open the old area shale mine, but Rachel realizes that the Connells are very poor, that Mrs. Connell is terribly overworked, and that they are scorned in the community as ne'er-do-wells and Catholics. The friendship grows in spite of Mrs. Blackwood's frequent requests that Rachel not spend so much time with Bridget. They sit together at school, where Bridget does satisfactorily and brainy Dermot, 14, who plans to become a priest, and Little Pat take top honors. They bail brash Timmy, 9, out of trouble, especially after he raids the kitchen for goodies during the local ladies' tea party, to which kind Mrs. Blackwood has invited Mrs. Connell. Assisted by Dermot, they build a clubhouse at the junction of the river and the creek, and then all the children, including Rachel's older brother Daniel*, home from boarding school and with a crush on beautiful Maeve Connell, 16, band together for a joyful mock battle that levels the little bark and twig hut. Bridget invites Rachel and other classmates to an ineptly conducted birthday party, at which she receives a beautiful new bike from her absent father and uncle. The book moves toward its climax when dogs attack Little Pat's pet lizard, Larry. Pat grabs Larry and runs for refuge into the deserted mine tunnel, where the children find a secluded pool and subsequently create a grotto with Rachel's doll, Isabella, as a kind of patron saint. In rapid succession come two scandalous pieces of news: Mr. Connell is a convict and has escaped from the work farm, and Maeve is pregnant, probably by local rowdy Billy Finch. The children locate Mr. Connell in the tunnel, and before long he is arrested. Feeling runs high against the Connells, local bullies taunt them and stone their house, and the family leaves as quietly as it came, heads high but huddled together for security on the outgoing bus. Almost simultaneously Rachel, who has some idea now of how religious prejudice works, discovers that she is Jewish on her father's side, makes some connection between what has happened in Hollybush and current events in Europe, and announces that she is Jewish. Except for Bridget, who is a much stronger personality than Rachel, the children are differentiated only in broad terms, and the adults are conventional types. Curiously, Rachel shows little regret at the Connells' departure. The book is almost all conversation, mostly among the children, and the point of view is so skillfully handled that the reader senses strains, tensions, and subtle nuances that the children do not. Thus the violence that afflicts the Connells near the end of the book, while unexpected to Rachel, does not surprise the reader or the Connells. The revelation of Dr. Blackwood's ancestry and Rachel's announcement seem superfluous and are not knit well into the Catholic-Protestant problem, which is enough to sustain the story. The author creates a very strong sense of the pre–World War II period— the Shirley Temple craze, radio programs, Hitler's speeches, the reaction of the young men to talk of war in Europe, references to Chamberlain and the Depression, and the like. Equally strong is the sense of normal children at play, and while the tone is serious as a whole, some humor arises from mild calamities as well as from Bridget's attempts to explain beliefs that she doesn't really understand and Rachel's attempts to understand what seem to her exotic ways. The claustrophobic effect of the isolated, ingrown community is supported by the hot summer weather; the intense drought broken by torrential rains enhances the religious tension. The title refers to the number of people in the Connell family. Aust. Bk. of Year Com.

SHADOW IN HAWTHORN BAY (Lunn*, Janet, Lester, 1986; Scribner, 1986), historical novel set in Scotland and Upper Canada at Hawthorn Bay on Lake Ontario in 1815–1816 among immigrants from Scotland and refugees from the American Revolution. Plain, strong-minded Mary (Mairi) Urquhart, 15, gifted with second sight and the ability to heal, runs away from her Highlands home, convinced that her beloved cousin, Duncan Cameron, whose family emigrated to Canada four years previously, is calling for help. She arrives at the small pioneer village of Colliver's Corners on Hawthorn Bay after a hard two-months' journey and is bitterly disappointed to learn that Duncan is dead and his family is on the way back to Scotland. Helped by generous neighbors, she settles in the Camerons' tiny cabin, intending by weaving and assisting the local school-teacher to keep herself alive and to earn money to pay for her passage home. She is sustained by her love for Duncan, her firm belief in the Old Ones, and her powerful will to survive. She also feels a strong antipathy for the woods of Canada, which are so different from her beloved Scottish hills and glens. Nightmares about Duncan persist, his voice continues to call her, and her frequent premonitions prove beneficial in various ways, among others in saving the lives of little Polly Pritchett from a barn fire and of young Henry Anderson from drowning. Consistent and unselfish help comes from Henry's older brother, Luke*, 19, who provides food and other articles and whose proposal of marriage she refuses, although she appreciates his concern and affection. When, however, the schoolchildren, to whom she has told old stories of magic and strange happenings, turn against her, and even Henry, who has been living with Mary because his mother drinks and his older brother, Sim, beats him, refuses to stay with her any more, the future looks so bleak that she seeks consolation from Duncan at the pool in the bay where he died. The dark shadow in the water that she takes as his exerts so strong a force that she almost throws herself in, but at the critical moment she realizes with horror that Duncan had committed suicide. She then realizes that Duncan had always been selfish, immature, and devious, a dark force in her life. She decides to put him in the past (Luke had urged her to stop loving a "deader"), sees the Canadian forests as welcoming instead of threatening, accepts Luke's proposal, and prepares with further help from friends and neighbors to begin life anew in this new land. The plot flags during the winter, and the resolution of Mary's personal problems seems abrupt in view of the strength of her convictions as presented. Nevertheless, the conclusion is acceptable because both Mary and Luke are so sympathetically drawn. Considerable tension rises from Mary's relationship with Duncan, and the setting in Canada has great immediacy. Without didacticism, the author includes information about Scottish animosities and those of the American wars that resulted in the emigrations to Canada in the late eighteenth and early nineteenth centuries. The people of the little community are tied together by common needs, though the farms are separated from each other by several miles, and the ethic of neighborliness has tremendous force. Although most of the characters are easily recognized types, they serve the plot adequately and offset Mary. A potentially interesting figure brought briefly into the story and then dropped is Owena, a Mohawk Indian woman, who shows Mary some of the herbs of the region. Scottish dialect and Canadian backwoods speech add stylistic interest, and there is a keen appreciation for the area's natural beauty. The themes that cooperation and a stout and cheerful heart can overcome obstacles and make for a brighter future and that one must sometimes make the best of circumstances appear subtly and undergird this substantial, well-textured story about a little-known period in world history. Can. Bk. of Year Winner; Can. Council Winner; Can. IODE Natl.; Can. Young Adult Winner.

SHANTYMEN OF CACHE LAKE (Freeman*, Bill, ill. with photographs, Lorimer, 1975), historical novel concerned with lumbering in the 1870s in the Ottawa Valley at Cache Lake in what is now Algonquin Provincial Park of eastern Ontario, Canada. After the funeral of their father, who was ostensibly killed by a falling tree while working for the Percy Lumber Company, John* Bains, 14, and his sister, Meg*, 13, are hired as cook's helpers in the camp where their father died. They travel for several days from Ottawa to the shanty at Cache Lake with a teamster, who gives them some tips on getting along in the camp and hints that their father's death may not have been an accident and that the foreman, Hardy*, may have been responsible. At the camboose shanty at Cache Lake, a one-room building that is kitchen, dining room, and bunkhouse for all the workers except the foreman and the clerk, they are welcomed. The cook, Mrs. Ferguson, who runs the camboose with a firm hand, is kindly, and they soon settle into the exhausting work, but Hardy, a huge man with a violent temper, drives them hard, and MacInnes, the self-important little shanty clerk, tries to intimidate John into spying. Because their father had been the main voice for forming a union, those at the nucleus of the organization, including the quiet, thoughtful Cameron*, fiery Tim McQuire, and Mrs. Ferguson, assume that the youngsters will be part of their group. Meg is immediately enthusiastic, but John has reservations because he strongly feels that bosses should be obeyed. Besides Hardy's brutality, the men object to the way they are building the chute down which squared timber will be floated to bypass the rapids and waterfalls to the calmer river water below. Hardy's plan is quicker, but it is unsafe, as is proved on the first windy day when it collapses, injuring several of the men, including Cameron, and killing Tim. The accident completely changes John's attitude and galvanizes the men of the shanty into calling a strike, which fails after they are forced to camp in the bitter cold with no shelter or supplies. Hardy lets most of the workers return but fires Cameron and the Bains children. The three begin the long trek to Ottawa, but because Cameron's leg was injured in the chute collapse, they must turn back to Cache Lake. John sets off ahead, leaving Meg to care for the injured man and keep a fire going. When John arrives, exhausted, the men ignore Hardy's protest, welcome him, and send a sleigh to pick up Cameron and Meg. Hardy tries to force them out, but the anger of the men and Meg's accusation that he killed their father suddenly make him back down. The men discuss leaving as a group, but they know that without a completed chute to transport the season's cut timber Percy Lumber Company would go bankrupt and they will never be paid. They decide to ignore Hardy, build the chute in their own, safer way, and wait to strike until Percy himself comes. As the big spring flood, which will provide water to carry the timber downriver, is almost due, Percy arrives in a cutter. Mrs. Ferguson and the Bains children load the big sleigh with food, bedding, tent canvas, and other essentials and get it out of camp undetected. The second strike, undertaken with these supplies and in far better weather, is quite different from the first, and they demand that both Hardy and MacInnes be fired and that Percy recognize their right to bargain directly with him. In a fury Hardy attacks Cameron, drags him up onto the spillway of the log chute, and is choking him when John scrambles up to defend his friend. When Hardy turns to attack him, John kicks him off the chute onto the rocks sixty feet below. Percy, seeing that it is the only way to avoid bankruptcy, accedes to their demands. They work feverishly to finish the chute before the spring flood, and John and Meg join the men on the log drive back to their home in Ottawa. Although the plot contains a number of improbabilities, mostly concerned with Meg's part in the work and life of the camp, and the characters are one-dimensional, the novel gives a vivid picture of the hardships and grueling work of the lumbermen of the period. There is a great deal of information about the methods of lumbering, the way the workers lived in the isolated camps, and the final drive of the logs through several lakes and down the river. The illustrations are actual photographs from the period showing the camboose, the loggers, and the various stages of getting timber to market. Can. Council Winner.

SHARP, EDITH LAMBERT (1917–), born in Manitoba, Canada; writer and director of the Okanagan Summer School of Fine Arts. She grew up in Penticton, British Columbia, and studied at both the Vancouver School of Art and the Smithsonian Institution in Washington, D.C. Author of only one book for children, *Nkwala** (Little, 1958), she was the recipient of a large number of awards, including the Diploma of Merit from the Hans Christian Andersen award committee in Luxembourg, the Canadian Governor General's Medal, and the Little Brown of Canada Award. *Nkwala* is a historical novel of a boy of the Spokane tribe before the coming of the white men and his struggle to complete his vision quest and to aid his people. It has been praised for its historical accuracy and strong evocation of setting, what is now northern Washington State and southern British Columbia. She also published a play, *The Little People of Crazy Mountain* (Nelson, 1963), as well as short stories, articles, and book reviews in periodicals and for the Canadian Broadcasting Corporation.

SHEILA BRARY (*Snow Apples**), sixteen-year-old who survives, despite a background of poverty and family strife, an unfortunate love affair, pregnancy, and a self-induced abortion, to find a hopeful future in nurses' training. Pretty and bright, Sheila has more inherent assets than do her four brothers, but her grim mother, seeing in her some of her father's qualities, burdens her with nothing but blame. Sheila is realistic enough to accept life's difficulties and determined enough not to settle for a marriage that will trap her in a situation almost like that of her mother. In the end, the reader can be confident that she will not let herself be sexually exploited again but cannot be sure that her capacity for freely giving love has not been crippled by her experiences.

SHELLEY, NOREEN (WALKER) (1920–), born in Lithgow, New South Wales, Australia; artist, broadcaster, editor, novelist. She was educated at the Methodist Ladies' College, Burwood, New South Wales, at Sydney Teachers' College, and at Sydney Art School. She taught elementary school in Sydney and lectured in art at Sydney Teachers' Training College and Abootsleigh College, Wahroonga, New South Wales. For two years in the 1940s she wrote children's programs for "Children's Session" and "Kindergarten of the Air" for the Australian Broadcasting Commission, and for twenty years she was the assistant editor and editor of *School Magazine* in Sydney. Her early publications were mostly illustrated story books for young children, including a number starring Piggy Grunter. Her first novel for older children, *Family at The Lookout** (Oxford, 1972), a story of family life with mystery aspects, won the Australian Book of the Year Award. *Faces in a Looking Glass* (Oxford, 1974) was listed as worthy of mention for the same award. It is also a mystery and family story with the main element being the kidnapping of a baby in which the young protagonist is both a witness and a suspect. *The Other Side of the World* (Angus, 1977) is about an English boy who must stay for six months with his grandmother in Sydney. Shelley also wrote and published a number of plays for children and a collection of myths.

SHEPPIE LORENNY (*Devil's Hill**; *The Roaring 40**), Soolvie, little cousin of Badge. About five years old in *Devil's Hill*, she has the fixations and peculiarities of one her age. Crazy about horses and dogs, she insists on being called Sheppie because, with her thick, unruly brown hair, she looks a little like a sheep dog. She discovers the tunnel through which the children reach the back side of the mountain, and she also finds Brindle's calf, and promptly names it Merle from the sound the tiny creature makes. She is about a year older in *The Roaring 40*, where she seems immature for her age.

SHOOTING THROUGH (Taylor*, William, Reed Methuen, 1986), realistic problem novel set in the mountains of New Zealand about two runaway boys from a "remand," or juvenile detention home, in the city, presumably in the 1980s. August O'Malley, 13, half Maori, and Jon-Mark Cowan, 13, low-achieving youngest in an affluent white family, have teamed up and, despite the distance, rain, cold and hunger, have made it to an old sawmill town near Turangi that Jon-Mark remembers from a holiday trip. There they are found by Boss, a large man who supervises forestry operations in the area. After Boss arrives Pinkie Wirihana, a nurse and farmer of Maori descent, who rides a contrary mare called Hoiho. Jon-Mark cheerfully admits that he is uncontrollable, but August refuses to tell what trouble landed him in the home. Soon they are installed with sleeping bags on the floor of Boss's isolated cottage, with meals at Pinkie's tiny cabin, where Nanny, her old Maori aunt, welcomes them, calling August by the Maori name, Akuhata. Boss precipitates a crisis by insisting that they both write their parents. August points out that he can't write his Daddy, who "shot through" when he was little and hasn't been heard from since. He willingly writes his Mum, sending love and directions to find money he has saved if she needs it, but Jon-Mark, pressured to start, breaks into sob and admits that he can't read or write. Pinkie helps him by printing out his dictation and letting him copy it. In the next few days, the boys explore the area, get lessons in riding reluctant Hoiho, watch from a hideaway while a group of schoolchildren visit the ghost town, and generally come to terms with their problems. Jon-Mark, at first greatly excited to shoot Boss's gun and kill rabbits, decides it is not much fun. August, although he is sickened by the idea of hurting animals, admits that he was arrested for killing three cats that belonged to a woman in their neighborhood who spied on welfare recipients and reported his mother if she has an "uncle" living in the house. Before they are ready to admit that they should go home, Boss is arrested for growing a little marijuana in the isolated area. Out on bail, he confesses his stupidity and insists that he and Pinkie, who is pregnant, marry before Christmas. The next morning the Cowans arrive by car to get the boys, having picked up August's mother on the way. The book ends with the prospect that Jon-Mark will try to learn to read and mend his ways, that August may persuade his family to move to this area where he can work for Boss, and that the boys will spend their holidays with Boss and Pinkie. Although this end is a little too pat (will the Cowans be as understanding when they know of Boss's drug charge and that Pinkie's baby will be born shortly after their marriage?), the characters of the boys are well developed, and the dialogue rings true. Descriptions of the mountains, the decaying ghost town, and Pinkie's tiny house are vivid, and scenes of the school group, with Emery, the constant troublemaker, are funny. N. Z. Govt. Short List.

THE SILENT ONE (Cowley*, Joy, ill. Hermann Greissle, Whitcoulls, 1981; Knopf, 1981; Random of Canada, 1981), legend-like story of a deaf-mute boy in the Fiji Islands whose friendship with a great white turtle inspires fear among his fellow villagers. As a newborn infant, Jonasi is found by the men of the copra boat alone in a canoe far from any land and is brought to the island. Old Luisa, who has just had a stillborn child, considers the new baby a gift from the God of the Church, a sign that he has forgiven her for praying to Degei, the ancient Snake God, for more children, and she adopts him as her own. But the baby proves to be deaf and unable to learn to speak. As he grows older, some of the villagers shun him, afraid of his strangeness and suspicious even of his great skill at fishing, which often feeds the village in times of scarcity. Only Aesake, son of Taruga Vueti, the chief, who has been to school in Sevu, understands Jonasi's condition and befriends him. When Jonasi is twelve, all the village men set off to hunt wild pig, taking even his brother Samu and other boys his age but rejecting Jonasi. He goes disconsolately out onto the reef on his raft and spots a marvel, an all-white turtle whose shell gleams like a pearl. At first, he thinks that he will catch it and present it to the chief when the men are exulting over their wild-pig catch, but when he grabs its shell, planning to turn it over and make it helpless, it dives deeply so that he has to release it. Grieving that he has lost this treasure, he returns to his raft, only to have the turtle surface and follow him. Giving up the idea of catching it, Jonasi returns each day to the reef and finds the turtle, gradually making friends with it, until he can stroke its neck or hold on to its shell and be towed through the water. He keeps its existence a secret, but one day Aesake and Samu follow him, and he fights, actually threatening Aesake with a knife, to protect the turtle. The chief's son realizes the relationship between Jonasi and the turtle and binds Samu to secrecy, but Samu tells a friend, and the distrust of Jonasi deepens to a fear that he is consorting with a devil. He is even waylaid by three men who intend to force him to lead them to the white turtle, but the chief rebukes them. Then a terrible hurricane hits the village. The chief sends Aesake to Ramatau to beg for help from their chief, but he finds there a government man with a red beard surveying the islands to see what emergency help is needed. Delighted, he returns to his village without having shamed his people by begging and with the promise that the Redbeard will arrive in two days, just before returning to Sevu. In his absence, one man, evidently hunting for the white turtle, has been mauled and killed by a shark, and even Vueti sees that some of the people blame Jonasi. He summons Luisa and tells her that she must accompany Jonasi to Sevu on the Redbeard's boat, to stay with her married daughter until a copra boat comes again, and Aesake will also go to speak for his father to get the boy into the school for the deaf. As they cross the lagoon, Jonasi spots the white turtle and tries to leap over the side, but Aesake prevents him. When the Redbeard sees the turtle, he tries to get the men on the boat to catch it, but they think that it is a demon and will not move. Annoyed, the Redbeard seizes his gun, and Jonasi dives, holds to the shell, and is towed away. At first the Redbeard thinks that he is attempting to catch the turtle, but when it dives he becomes worried. Though they circle the area, searching, they never see Jonasi nor the white turtle again. Legends grow up in the islands about the Silent One and his albino turtle. The novel captures Jonasi's bafflement and hurt at the way the villagers treat him and his delight with the white turtle. It is also a strong picture of life on a Figi island. Despite the concrete details and characterizations, the tone is predominantly that of a legend. N. Z. Govt. Winner.

THE SILVER BRUMBY (Mitchell*, Elyne, ill. Ralph Thompson, Hutchinson, 1958; Dutton, 1959), horse novel, in which the horses speak among themselves and with other wild creatures but are not otherwise anthropomorphized, set in the Snowy Mountains of New South Wales in southeastern Australia at an unspecified time but probably in the mid-twentieth century. In the shadow of the granite Ramshead Range near Crackenback River during a terrible spring storm are born to Bel* Bel, a creamy brumby (wild mustang), a colt that she names Thowra, meaning wind, and to her companion wild mare, Mirri, a chestnut Mirri names Storm*, both the sons of the mighty stallion, Yarraman. The two foals grow sleek, strong, knowledgeable, and cunning. The four horses rejoin

Yarraman's herd, where bold, quick, and often mischievous Thowra early incurs the enmity of Arrow, a chestnut bully the same age, observes Yarraman battle The Brolga, a rival stallion, and with the others barely escapes a brumby roundup. When the colts are sturdy two-year-olds, they head off on their own, though Thowra and Bel Bel never forget one another as mare and colt usually do, and, after again escaping capture by a man on a black horse (men are presented as cunning, dangerous, faceless evils), Thowra and Storm become clever loners, like their mothers, and Thowra's reputation for beauty and, in particular, elusiveness and cunning grows until it has achieved legendary proportions and reaches the ears of the wild horses as well as of the humans. Thowra becomes known as the ghost horse who can appear and disappear at will. His creamy coat with silver mane and tail blends with the forest and mountain shadows, and he can travel without leaving tracks. When Thowra attracts a small herd of three greys, a bay, and two browns from among The Brolga's mares, he and Storm part, Thowra retaining the greys, Storm taking the others, but now and then the two stallions run together for friendship and safety. Gradually, three intersecting conflicts appear involving Arrow, The Brolga, and the local stockmen. After numerous skirmishes with Arrow, Thowra faces the bigger horse down, and, in a terrible battle, tricks him into leaping over a cliff to his death. Thowra has several run-ins with The Brolga, too, but Bel Bel advises him to wait until he has attained full strength before fighting for supremacy with the older, often tested stallion. When the two finally do meet in a showdown, over a creamy mare named Golden*, Thowra's cunning and superior speed ensure his victory, and he is acknowledged as the king of the hills. The third problem is the more alarming. Stockmen persist in attempting to capture him, especially after he lures away Golden, a tame mare, and has a creamy filly by her. He escapes numerous times, recaptures her and her baby from a stockman, then even outwits a black (Aborigine) tracker who is also after a black mare, Lubra, a former racehorse that has joined Storm's herd. The book's climax comes with a great hunt for him and Golden, in which he takes his creamy mares to a secret valley that he has found, puts the rest with Storm's horses, and leads the men on a cunning but exhausting chase away from them all. Hard pressed, he leaps over a cliff to elude the most tenacious one, the black tracker, and, although the reader never learns whether or not he survives the precipitous jump, the reader is told that rumors of a cream and silver ghost horse continue to circulate in the hills. Although it seems farfetched to believe that the horses and even Thowra himself have heard of the creamy brumby's legends and that the horses can understand human talk, the story is otherwise completely credible. The details of the horses' lives are clearly presented and woven interestingly into the fabric of the story, the ways and habits of the horses described as though by a well-informed and sympathetic observer. The many movements of the herds are confusing in spite of the map, but otherwise the action, excitement, and conflict combine skillfully with a winning protagonist for a top-notch animal adventure story that carefully avoids sentimentality and melodrama. Sequels. Aust. Bk. of Year Highly Com.

SILVER BRUMBY'S DAUGHTER (Mitchell*, Elyne, Hutchinson, 1960), horse novel true to nature except that the animals speak (but never with humans), understand human speech, interact and speak with such other animals as kangaroos and wombats, and reason logically. This sequel to *The Silver Brumby** is set in the same area, the Snowy Mountains of New South Wales in southeastern Australia, and also deals with the horses' efforts to remain free. Thowra, the cream and silver brumby, or wild horse, has somehow survived the great leap that concludes the previous book and has built up a small herd that he secludes in Secret Valley. One day he is traveling the mountains with his equally striking daughter, Kunama, which means Snowy, when they spot two hooded skiers, a father and son, the elder of whom vows to catch Kunama some day. They also spot an elusive young black stallion, a loner they later learn is Tambo who sometimes travels with the herd of Storm*, Thowra's bay half-brother. Much of the story, which lasts from spring to early winter, deals with Kunama's growing desire to be with Tambo, whose rival for her is a persistent chestnut called Spear. She steals out to be with him, they roam the hills, and Tambo and Chestnut fight battles over her. Eventually Thowra kills Spear because he is troublesome and represents a possible threat to the safety of Thowra's herd. Kunama is properly impressed with the need to keep the valley secret from even other horses because they are creamies and hence much coveted by men who might be led there unwittingly by other horses. On an excursion out, however, she is spotted by the skiers who eventually drive her into a wooden enclosure and retain her in spite of her attempts to flee. She is broken to a halter and saddle by the son. She senses his strong affection and admiration for her, and these qualities in addition to his expertise enable him to keep her as long as he does. After the cattle roundup in the fall, when winter truly sets in, he realizes that she is miserable and needs her kind and frees her. She goes back to the brumbies, where she is trumpeted home by Thowra, Tambo following behind her. Both will join Thowra's herd in Secret Valley. Tension remains high throughout the novel because the author keeps the reader aware of the threat from humans who yearn in particular to catch Thowra, now called a ghost horse, and the filly of his line. The silver-gray kangaroo, Benni, who has hay fever and sneezes often, provides a little comic relief and also advances the plot with information useful to the brumbies. The style is occasionally awkward and clichéd ("This was a terrific fight," and Thowra runs with "wind's speed.") The author's knowledge of and sympathy for the brumbies contributes conviction, and the descriptions of the mountains, rocks, cliffs, and even the storms evoke the natural splendor of the area and are a special feature of the book. Others in series. Aust. Bk. of Year Com.

SIMON WHITBURN (*Blue Above the Trees**), third son in the William* Whitburn family, English settlers in the Great Forest of South Gippsland in Victoria. Simon longs to become a surveyor, but since he knows how much his father needs him, he doesn't leave the farm until his father releases him. He does, however, often become impatient with hard-driving, penny-pinching William. He is furious when William wants to cut the trees that grow in the lyrebirds' part of the forest. When Simon's axe fells a tree that topples on William, Simon feels guilty even though his brothers assure him that the wind caused the accident. Simon is a well-drawn protagonist, a foil for his older brothers and for his sister Clarissa*. His independence comes gradually.

SINHA, NILIMA, educator in India, author of numerous novels, short stories, and books of non-fiction for young people. She was educated at the Convent of Jesus and Mary and received her B.Sc. in Home Science from Lady Irwin College. She has made her home in New Delhi. For ten years she taught primary classes at Bluebells School and Notre Dame Academy in Delhi and Patna, and founded a nursery school in New Delhi. In 1979 she won first prize in a national competition for children's fiction with *The Chandipur Jewels** (CBT, India, 1979), a fast-paced adventure and mystery novel for middle-grade readers. Two sequels starring the same three children have also won prizes, *Vanishing Trick at Chandipur** (CBT, India, 1984) and *SOS From Munia, the Emerald Crown*, which is scheduled to be published by the Children's Book Trust. *Adventure on Golden Lake** (CBT, India, 1986), which won the second prize given by the Children's Book Trust, is a novel about a kidnapping and international espionage. Another of her adventure novels, *Adventure Before Midnight* (CBT, India), was selected for the Black Raven List at the Bologna Book Fair. In addition to picture books, she has written numerous prize-winning stories and a cassette tape script, and has edited collections of stories. Mrs. Sinha writes in Hindi as well as English.

SINHA, SAROJINI (1922–), born in Rangoon, Burma; social worker in India, writer for both adults and children. She earned a bachelor's degree in education and a master's in history, and as a social worker has been interested primarily in the welfare of women and children. She organized a primary school for children, which later became a high school, and more recently has been a member of the managing committee of the Anand Vihar School, Bhopal, India. She is also treasurer of the Family Planning Association of India, Bhopal Branch. Mrs. Sinha has traveled widely in Europe and the Far East, and she has visited Canada and lived briefly with a family in Vermont under the Experiment in International Living Programme. She has published at least nine books for children, three of which have won prizes in the national competitions for writers of children's books held by the Children's Book Trust. *A Pinch of Salt Rocks an Empire* (CBT, India, 1985) won second prize in the non-fiction category, while *The Return Home* (CBT, India, 1989) won first prize in the history section. Her historical novel concerning the Sepoy Rebellion against the East India Company in 1857, *The Treasure Box** (CBT, India, 1982), was winner of the third prize in the fiction category. Her short stories and articles for adults have been published in leading magazines and newspapers in India, and some have been broadcast over BBC World Service, London, England. Two of her books were serialized in *Women's Era* of New Delhi.

SIR MORTIMER WYVERN (*An Older Kind of Magic**), unscrupulous, avaricious businessman for whom commerce is paramount. He schemes to get a portion of the Sydney, Australia, botanical gardens for a parking lot to ease the pressure on downtown shoppers. While inspecting one of his construction projects somewhere in the city, he is kidnapped by indigenous spirits and thus misses the meeting where the fate of the gardens was to be officially sealed. After the Nyols return him to the gardens, he encounters a dog, which the comet has given the ability to talk. When the dog speaks to him, Sir Mortimer is turned into a stone statue that stands in an out-of-the-way part of the gardens. Sir Mortimer obviously functions as a representative of materialism.

SIX AND SILVER. See *IT HAPPENED ONE SUMMER.*

SIX DAYS BETWEEN A SECOND (O'Dea*, Marjory, Heinemann, 1969), fantasy novel set in the 1960s near Canberra, Australia, involving real and fabulous animals that talk and interact with humans. When the four Collard children, David, 12, Barbara, 10, Genevieve, 7, and Peter, 5, play hide-and-seek in a grove near Lake Burley Griffin, they encounter a gryphon who says his name is Burleigh. Burleigh tells them that basilisks (creatures that are half cock, half snake) have moved into the lake and are polluting it and threatening to poison the city's water supply. He enlists the children in an elaborate scheme to drive the basilisks out of this world and into the second of the series of worlds that are wrapped around this one. The entrance into the outer worlds lies at any place where humans have dammed or forded a river. Most of the action of the story takes place by Cotter dam near the lake. Since the gryphon not only tells the children what the problem is but also how to defeat the basilisks, the story's interest lies in how the children manage to carry out his instructions. He directs the two girls to capture unicorns, which they do with silken threads. Careful, maternal Barbara captures the irascible Onegar, and literal-minded, regal Genevieve seizes accommodating Bucephalus. The unicorns are needed to locate dolphins and bees, creatures that the basilisks hate. While Genevieve, Bucephalus, and Peter seek dolphins, David, Onegar, and Barbara seek bees. Armies of dolphins and bees, headed by a fabulous fighter bee, Mandrokles, ambush the basilisks as they come downriver to poison the water at the dam and herd them into a crack leading to the outer worlds. The whole enterprise takes six days of outer layer time but only a second of time in the real world. On the whole the fantasy seems strained and ecologically didactic. As in most stories in which children are called upon to save the world, no clear reason appears for their being given such an important task. Characters are numerous and not well fleshed, but the author has provided a cast list at the beginning of the book that helps to keep them straight. The basilisks, of which there are two kinds, aeriids (flying) and pedestriids (walking), are overdrawn as villains, the internal strife between the two groups is not well motivated, and the leader of both groups, Chaunterclasp, a pedestriid, is typecast as a murderous, unscrupulous tyrant. The plentiful action, shifting point of view, details of preparations, resourcefulness to overcome mild calamities, social commentary, and humor that arises from dialogue and interpersonal relationships hold the reader's attention. Aust. Bk. of Year Com.

SLAVE OF THE HAIDA (Andersen*, Doris, Macmillan, 1974), historical adventure novel set among the Native Americans of the Canadian Pacific Northwest in the eighteenth century. A band of marauding Haida from the north raid his village and kidnap proud Kim-ta, 14, and his little sister, Seagull, children of a Salish chief. Seagull becomes the slave of the chief of a Haida village who is also the father of the young man who becomes Kim-ta's master, kind and understanding Duan. Duan lives with and will become the heir and successor of his mother's brother, Gi-tin, the cruel, proud, and extremely ambitious man who is chief of another Haida village. Determined to become the wealthiest man in the islands in furs, coppers, blankets, and slaves, he prepares to hold a potlatch, a ceremonial feast during which many gifts are given to impress everyone with his power and wealth. After an unsuccessful escape attempt results in a terrible beating, Kim-ta fits in and accompanies the band to search for salmon and otter and to trade with the Tsimshian, where he is almost traded for a copper. He is present when the Iron Men (white traders) come trading for otter skins. After Kim-ta has been a slave for about a year, Gi-tin plans one last raid for slaves before winter sets in. Duan, who sympathizes with Kim-ta's desire for freedom, takes Kim-ta along so that he can escape if possible. The group is about to raid a Salish village, not Kim-ta's, when they are hit by fire from a cannon left by the British. Kim-ta makes it to shore, where he is soon captured by these people and then taken south to his own village. There he is exchanged for the Salish chief's daughter who coincidentally has been a slave of Kim-ta's father. Although he is happy to be with his own people again, Kim-ta knows it will be hard to erase the stigma of having been a slave. Characters are easily recognized types, and Kim-ta matures as expected. Incidents are also conventional, although the exchange of slaves is an unexpected plot twist. The relationship between Kim-ta and Duan might have been exploited further, as well as that between Kim-ta and his former slave on Kim-ta's return. The book is best for its clear and enlightening picture of life among the Haida from the standpoint of a slave to the wealthiest of the upper class. The class system, the rivalry among the tribes, sex roles, religious beliefs, food acquisition and preservation, commerce with the whites—the sociological background—give a general sense of what life was like. According to an author's note at the end of the novel, a cannon was left among the Salish by the British for protection against the Spanish, and slaves among the coastal tribes were an important part of the economy and remained slaves for life, unlike among some tribes where they were often adopted or allowed to intermarry. Can. Bk. of Year Runner-Up.

SMUCKER, BARBARA (CLAASSEN) (1915–), born in Newton, Kansas; Canadian teacher, librarian, and author of novels about the problems of minorities. After graduating from Kansas State University in 1936, she taught high school English and journalism for a year, then worked on a small Kansas newspaper, where she met her husband, Donovan Smucker, a Mennonite minister. When he accepted a post at the Mennonite Conrad Grebel College in Waterloo, Ontario, in 1966, she emigrated to Canada, where she studied further at the University of Waterloo and became a children's librarian at the Kitchener, Ontario, Public Library and then head librarian at Renison College, Waterloo. *Underground to Canada** (Clarke, 1977; *Runaway to Freedom*, Harper, 1978) arose out of her keen interest in the progress of the civil rights movement. It describes the exciting flight from slavery in Mississippi to freedom in Canada of two girls who are helped by Alexander Ross, a real-life figure associated with the Underground Railway. In 1978, the Children's Book Centre cited the novel as one of the fifty best Canadian children's books, and it was runner-up for the Canadian Children's Book of the Year Award. More highly regarded by critics is *Days of Terror** (Clarke, 1979; Herald, 1979), which received both the Canada Council and the Ruth Schwartz awards. A solid historical novel, it relates in considerable detail the events that led up to the emigration from the Ukraine to Canada of German-speaking Mennonites during the Russian Revolution. Her first two novels also focus on Mennonites: *Henry's Red Sea* (Herald, 1955), about the perilous flight of Mennonites from Russia to Paraguay after World War II, and *Cherokee Run* (Herald, 1957), about Mennonite settlements in Oklahoma. Dealing with Native Americans are *Wigwam in the City* (Dutton, 1966; *Susan*, Scholastic, 1978) and *White Mist* (Clarke, 1985). About still another minority is *Amish Adventure* (Clarke, 1983), set on a Waterloo farm. *Jacob's Little Giant* (Viking, 1987), about the domestic adventures of a small Mennonite boy, is intended for an early elementary-age audience.

SNOW APPLES (Razzell*, Mary, Groundwood/Douglas, 1984), realistic novel of a girl's coping with her own developing sexuality and coming to terms with her strained family life, set in British Columbia, Canada, at the end of World War II. Among five children, Sheila* Brary, the narrator, is the only girl and the one on whom her bitter mother, Agnes, is hardest, accusing her of being "just like her father," Frank*. When her two youngest brothers are both thrown from a half-wild horse and badly injured, Sheila gets help from Helga Ness, a widow locally thought to be crazy, and the girl's competence wins her the approval of Dr. Howard, the physician at Hobson's Landing, the nearby community. Later, Sheila is shocked that her mother expects her to quit school and get a job to help out the family. Although her brothers are encouraged to continue their educations, her mother says that hers won't matter because she is a girl.

Helga, however, refuses to sell Agnes some land that she covets unless Sheila is allowed to finish high school. A new neighbor asks Sheila to babysit and tries first to seduce, then attack her. Her brother Paul, enraged, sets off to defend her honor but comes back disgusted, having been convinced by the man that she had been ''asking for it.'' A job as a maid for a summer family named Lawson turns out to be a continual effort to escape Mr. Lawson's wandering hands. At the same time she is much attracted to a young man, Nels Bergstrom, who is helping build a house for her mother on the land that she has bought from Helga. They date and soon are a steady couple. Nels is possessive, not wanting her to drink or smoke, although he does both himself, and objecting when she takes the boat into Vancouver to go to the dentist. Sheila goes out with a young deckhand who has suggested meeting him and has a nice time, but Nels (who has also dated in her absence) is furious. After they make up, they have intercourse for the first time, as much from Sheila's desire and need for love as from Nels's urging. When she is late getting home, her mother goes to the Bergstrom home, makes a scene, and demands that Nels either marry Sheila or leave her alone. He never speaks to her again. When her father is discharged from the air force, he works in mining at Williams Lake. The regular allotment checks are replaced by occasional letters from him containing a little money, never enough. Sheila helps support the family with earnings from a Saturday job in Dr. Howard's office, and her mother goes on welfare. When her father returns and demands that the land, which his wife paid for with money saved from the allotment checks, be put in his name, she tells him to leave. The family manages to survive. Sheila graduates from high school, already realizing that she is pregnant. She finds a room in Vancouver and a job at a drive-in restaurant and contacts her father. He is quite casual and cheerful about her problem. He meets her at a run-down hotel, along with a blond he says is his new wife, although he has not divorced her mother. He gives her some capsules from a pharmacist and he tells her they should solve the problem, and he and the blond go out. Sheila wakes up horribly sick and disoriented and eventually finds her way to the boat and back to Hobson's Landing. There she heads for a meadow near Helga's home, where she has a miscarriage with terrible pain. Afterwards, Helga takes care of her gently and firmly and gets her back on the boat without anyone seeing her. Later she learns that Nels has married. She doesn't see her father again. Although she has saved as much money as she can, she doesn't have enough to start nurses' training, into which she has been accepted. Reluctantly she puts it off for another semester. Then her mother tells her that she has sold her most treasured possession, her piano, to get Sheila the money to start in training. Sheila feels guilty and then miserable for being so ungrateful. Later her brother Tom, two years her junior and a good stable boy who has been working in the mines all summer, tells her that the money is from his savings. This is a story of the problems of a family that lacks communication and of girls in a society that refuses to recognize their needs and normal desires. The frankness with which it describes both Sheila's sexual yearnings and the agony of her self-induced abortion is unusual. The double standard of the times is shown for the outrageous unfairness it was, without the feminist overkill of many novels. The writing is uneven. Helga is not entirely convincing. In one section the narration skips to present tense illogically, and one of the episodes with Mr. Lawson fails to ring true, but the characterizations of Sheila and both her parents are sharp and memorable. Can. Council Hon. Ment.

SOMERSET, DAVID, author of *Barney and the Eels** (Price, 1981), a realistic novel of neighborhood life for younger readers that was on the short list for the New Zealand Government Children's Award.

SOMETHING SPECIAL (Rodda*, Emily, ill. Noela Young, Angus, 1984; H. Holt, 1989), brief fantasy in a realistic setting about a used clothing stall at a school money-raising fete, set somewhere in Australia in recent times. Sam Delaney, perhaps eight to ten years old, has been helping her mother, Lizzie, organize the boxes and bags of clothing deposited at their house. She especially admires a red satin dress, which her mother agrees must have been somebody's "Special," a favorite garment that seems to suit its wearer perfectly. While Lizzie takes their lively baby, Toby, for a bath, Sam dozes among the racks of clothes and is startled to see a lady in the corner, dancing in the red satin dress. A few seconds later, a grey-haired woman steps out in a green-and-black triangle dress and introduces herself as Miss King. She is surprised to find herself all dressed to teach school, although she has been retired for years, but when Sam suggests that the dress is the cause, she assures the girl that it is a very ordinary dress, though so convenient and practical that she wore it year in and year out. Then an old man rises from the chair across the room, stretches, and points out that good fabric like that in his tartan dressing gown lasts for years. He is somewhat confused because his daughter-in-law, Cynthia, gave the gown away, although he liked it so well that his own daughter called it his second skin. The lady in the red dress joins the conversation, confiding to them that she wore it to her twenty-first birthday party and to the dance where she met her husband. While they are talking, a nosy, bossy woman in a houndstooth check suit is rummaging through the boxes, telling them at the same time how suitable the houndstooth check garment was at the office where she was a supervisor. Sam tries to stop her from messing up the neatly folded garments, and at her shouts Lizzie comes in. The others are gone, and Lizzie assumes that Sam has been dreaming. They find a pair of silver dancing sandals, left behind, Sam knows, by the lady in the red dress. The next day at the fete, Sam helps at the Pre-Loved Clothes booth where each of these "Special" garments finds a new owner. Miss Wilkinson, who taught Sam in the infant's class, sees the value of the green-and-black dress and buys it. A girl in blue jeans falls in love with the red satin dress, so Lizzie and her partner let her have it at a reduced price. A wealthy, aggressively rude woman tries to talk down the price of the houndstooth check suit, but Lizzie says sweetly that if she doesn't have enough money for it, they will understand and accept whatever she is able to give, thereby so insulting the woman that she pays twice the marked price and stomps off. The real triumph occurs just before they close, when a friend of Sam appears with the old man of the tartan dressing gown and introduces him as Mr. Maxwell, her grandfather. Sam immediately dives for the dressing gown, already folded in one of the boxes to be given away. Mr. Maxwell is delighted to have his "second skin" back and remarks that at his age one doesn't question miracles. Lizzie surprises Sam with a gift for helping with the clothes, the pair of silver slippers which she knows Sam has coveted, just because they are so pretty. The fantasy element, about which Sam is certain yet unable to explain to her parents, is well handled. Family and neighborhood relationships show a deft touch. The book is for younger but not beginning readers. Aust. Jr. Bk. of Year Winner.

SOPHIE WEST (*Memory**), senile old woman who brings together Jonny Dart and Bonny* Benedicta. Very forgetful, she often takes things that belong to other people, like the milk and the mail from the next-door neighbor. When Jonny finds a letter belonging to Bonny among Sophie's things, he learns that the girl he is searching for lives next to Sophie. Both comic and pathetic, Sophie is strongly drawn and memorable.

SORRY CARLISLE (*The Changeover**), Sorensen Carlisle, 16, a witch. At school he is an almost exemplary student, polite, well organized, satisfactory in his studies, and a good athlete. At home, he affects a different appearance, wearing a black dressing gown or caftan and many rings, seeming altogether less good, Laura Chant thinks, than at school. Much less self-assured than he seems, he has trouble accepting his witch nature, but at story's end he has come to terms with it. He decides to devote himself to ecological causes and takes a position as trainee for the wildlife division. After Laura becomes a witch, Sorry and Laura are able to communicate telepathically. Sorry sensibly warns Laura against vindictiveness in dealing with Carmody Braque. Through Laura his human side grows and hence also his abilities as a witch.

SOUTHALL, IVAN (FRANCIS) (1921–), born in Canterbury, Victoria, Australia; engraver, airman, prolific writer of novels and non-fiction for both adults and children. He attended Surrey Hills State School, Chatham State School, Mont Albert Central School, and Box Hill Grammar School, but when he was fourteen his father died and he left school to help support the family. He became a copyboy at the Melbourne *Herald* and then a photoengraver. During World War II he served with the Royal Australian Air Force, an experience that contributed background information for many of his stories and is told in detail in the autobiographical *Fly West* (Angus, 1974; Macmillan, 1975). His earliest books for children were a series of superficial adventure stories about a flyer named Squadron Leader Simon Black. His more serious novels began with his development of group adventures, in which he follows several different characters caught in some disaster—bush fire, flood, truck accident, plane crash—showing how different personalities react to a tense and usually life-threatening situation. Of these, *Hill's End* (Angus, 1962; St. Martin's, 1963) was named to the *Choice* magazine list of books for an academic library; *Ash Road** (Angus, 1965; St. Martin's, 1966) and *To the Wild Sky** (Angus, 1967; St. Martin's, 1967) both won the Australian Book of the Year Award; and *Finn's Folly** (Angus, 1969; St. Martin's, 1969) was commended for the same award. Others of his novels are more psychological studies, following a sensitive protagonist in a high state of tension through a situation that another sort of youngster might take in his stride, as in *Bread and Honey** (Angus, 1970; *Walk a Mile and Get Nowhere*, Bradbury, 1970), which was a Book of the Year Award winner. Also of this type are *Josh** (Angus, 1971; Macmillan, 1972), his most honored novel, which won the Carnegie Award and was named to the *Horn Book* Fanfare list and to the list of Contemporary Classics; *The Fox Hole** (Methuen, 1967; St. Martin's, 1967), which was commended for the Book of the Year Award; and *Let the Balloon Go** (Methuen, 1968; St. Martin's, 1968), called by some critics his most successful book because the sense of struggle and emotional tension fits its protagonist, a cerebral palsy victim. It was commended for the Book of the Year Award and named to the *Choice* list. Southall has also written several novels for adults and a large number of non-fiction books for both adults and children.

SOUTHWARD HO WITH THE HENTYS (Hill*, Fitzmaurice, Whitcombe, 1953), historical novel of the establishment of the first permanent settlement in Victoria, Australia, at Portland Bay in November, 1834. All events and almost all characters are true. When gentleman farmer Mr. Thomas Henty of West Tarring, Sussex, England, breeder of the finest merino sheep, decides to sell Church Farm and emigrate to Swan River on the west coast of New Holland (Australia) where he has purchased 80,000 acres unseen, his tenants, the Halls— Will, Will's wife, and their ten-year-old twins, Judy and Jim (who tells the story)—eagerly agree to accompany him on the promise of excitement and a farm of their own. Part of the advance group, they set sail in the spring of 1829 on the Henty ship, *Caroline*, with three Henty sons, stock, supplies, and the children's pet merino ewe, Captain Tuffems, who will eventually be the progenitor of the Halls' own flock in Australia. The trip on the very crowded ship is uneventful except for the equatorial initiation and a terrible gale that hits east of Cape Town. Disappointment greets them at Swan River; the Henty land is forested and hence unsuitable for grazing, and there are no roads and only shacks. Leaving one son to make what he can of the place (he becomes a prosperous trader and merchant), they sail on to Van Diemen's Land (Tasmania) and rent a large farm at Cormiston up the Tamar River, an area they soon come to love. In 1832 Mr. Thomas Henty (the elder) arrives, intending to sell the unsuitable land and file for free land in Van Diemen's Land, both of which prove impossible. Jim decides to go to sea, joins the *Thistle*, which, as things turn out, puts in with Mr. Edward Henty (a son) at Portland Bay, a whaling post. Mr. Edward, who has been searching for suitable grazing on the continent, immediately sees the area's possibilities and convinces his father to settle there. They establish the first permanent settlement in 1834, an area ironically thought free but which, after expending considerable labor and financial resources in development, they are forced by the government to buy. Both the Hentys and the Halls prosper. The Halls are happy with their farm and look forward to a bright future with a flock comprised of descendants of Captain Tuffems. The fictitious Halls are a warm, sympathetic family, if obsequious to the Hentys, and undoubtedly mirror their historical counterparts. The Hentys are presented as determined and enterprising, as history says they were. The book is almost all dialogue and is lively with details of sailing, settling, and coping, although one never gets the feeling that they will not be successful. The characters exist for the plot, and the accent is on historical events. The book's strength lies in its clear picture of the difficulties that the emigrants faced stemming from the terrain and government regulations. An introduction and foreword give historical background. Aust. Bk. of Yr. Highly Com.

SPACE DEMONS (Rubenstein*, Gillian, Omnibus, 1986; Dial, 1987), action-filled science fiction novel with psychological problem story aspects set in an unspecified city in the late twentieth century. Life offers new possibilities for excitement for spoiled, arrogant, manipulative Andrew Hayford, 12, when his physician father returns from a conference in Osaka, Japan, with a new computer game about demons and rockets. Andrew soon entices several friends into playing it with him, the first of whom is meek Ben Challis. When they are actually pulled through the screen into the game world, both realize that this game may be dangerously different. About the same time, Andrew realizes his parents' marriage has gone sour, his anti-social behavior intensifies, and he gradually becomes more and more abstracted from everyday life. Each of the other youngsters who plays the game has problems, too: Mario Ferrone, who bullies his younger brother and is fast on the way to becoming a hoodlum; and Elaine Taylor, a motherless gymnast whose ne'er-do-well father changes jobs so often that they have never had a settled life and who is viciously harried by a girl classmate. Although Ben hesitates about continuing the game, Andrew points a gun, which has materialized out of the screen into his hand and sends Ben into the game where Andrew watches him being stalked by space demons. Andrew enlists Elaine's help to bring back Ben, provoking her into pointing the gun at him because he now realizes that the game feeds on hate. Elaine's self-hatred carries her into the other dimension, too, and after a tense struggle with the ferocious demons, they terminate that stage of the game and return to Andrew's room. Andrew and Mario strike up a friendship of sorts over the game, which appeals to Mario who also suffers from low self-esteem. Both boys thrill to the danger of the hunt and chase in the other world. All game participants have also begun to notice strange and menacing cracks or splinters of shadows following them, slivers of darkness that become larger whenever they are arguing or feeling angry or hostile. They come to see that their hatred also contributes to the formation of these demons. As the children associate more with one another, however, over the game and in school, they discover the reasons for their anti-social behavior and also see that the only way to terminate the game is to respond with positive feelings instead of hatred and to follow the game's internal, cryptic instructions exactly, the most significant being, at the critical moment, to lay aside the guns that they feel are necessary for defense. Elaine is the first to insist on this, and as a result she and Andrew make Mario the champion demon hunter and "defeat" the game, which then erases itself, leaving the diskette of the space demons game totally blank. At the end, the reader, like the participants, is left to ponder if there ever was any real danger in the other world or whether the game was simply programmed to end when it does. The children behave better because of their experiences, however. Elaine realizes that she can make decisions on her own and considers living in a foster home. Mario sees possibilities for friendship with his younger brother, and Andrew informs his mother that he knows that his father has left them, for the first time verbalizing the problem that has nagged him. Ben realizes that he doesn't always have to be a follower. The children are obviously used as foils, and their behavior is exaggerated for effect. The several families are in various states of dysfunction and represent a typical school community. The parents are more sympathetically presented than the children, who are pretty awful for the most part, and the teacher, Mr. Russell, is humane, inventive, and patient under the most trying circumstances. The space scenes are filled with action, excitement, and tension, all of which are pointed up for the reader by the suspense of wondering whether or not the children will ever be able to return to their dimension or will be compelled by their hatred to fight forever the space demons within the screen. As in most science fiction, the obvious message dominates. Aust. Bk. of Year Com.

SPEAR AND STOCKWHIP: A TALE OF THE TERRITORY (Graves*, Richard H., Dymocks, 1950), realistic novel of the western type with mystery elements set for one year in northern Australia beginning in September, 1946. "I," a youth who calls himself William Flint, is nicknamed Stones, and hints at a past problem. He and four friends his age, steady, redheaded Tom Brinsley, impulsive Snowy Jansen, half-caste Darkie* Johnson, and cutup Joker Payne, sign on with respected old drover, Chikker Jackson, to take a mob (herd) of 2,400 malnourished Herefords from the drought-stricken village of Sleepy Hollow in eastern New Queensland one thousand miles to the rich pastures of the Laurance Estate on the Roper River on the west coast of the Gulf of Carpentaria in the Northern Territory. Stones, who claims to be an orphan, joins the expedition for the good money, adventure, and hope of having his own outfit some day. He gets a letter of permission from old German immigrant hotelkeeper, Mr. Schusmann, whose story of his runaway childhood broadly hints at Stones's past and who presents Stones with a new saddle for his newly acquired horse, Tiger, as a send-off gift. Stones soon discovers that the saddle has been replaced by an identical one with four long narrow tin cans attached. He virtuously leaves the cans unopened and places them for safekeeping at the hotel desk. He also overhears a conversation between a rough, scar-faced, red-haired man named Gillespie and a dark "Dago" concerning a delivery of some sort. Jackson and the boys leave Cartref Downs, their mob in a sorry state, and have a difficult hundred miles before arriving at pasturage across the Burdekin River. Near Cloncurry a dogger (dingo hunter) who calls himself Imrey and is discovered to be a cohort of Gillespie, rides up on a saddle identical to that of Stones. Believing it to be his, Stones switches saddles, and days later the boys discover papers in the lining indicating that Gillespie and his companions are cattle thieves, out to steal Jackson's mob. The conflict proceeds with expected complications; Gillespie incites Aborigines against them and the mystery about the saddles deepens. Jackson's crew must guard the cattle against Gillespie as well as help them through hostile terrain. Action abounds: Darkie shoots a huge dingo called Red Robber and gains a tidy bounty, Snowy wins the big horse race at Cloncurry, and in the Barkly Tablelands they stay overnight at the plantation of another old German immigrant, Gustav Feldman, who turns out to have run away from home along with Mr. Schusmann and who believes that Mr. Schusmann is dead. In Aborigine country, Chikker is wounded by a spear from an unknown assailant and dies, leaving Tom in charge. When the boys backtrack to investigate, they discover that a black threw the spear but was accompanied by a white. Sensing an imminent hijacking, they proceed carefully through the forested highlands, fending off an attack of blacks, surely incited by Gillespie. Stones shoots a black in the leg, Baroopa, whom they nurse to health and who becomes their friend and expert tracker. When they reach a point from which they can scan the plains, they observe a camp of rustlers—Gillespie's bunch—rebranding stolen cattle. The boys are instrumental, mainly through creating a stampede, in apprehending the thieves. After four more days of excitement, including a flood, they arrive at the Laurance Estate, with the mob safe and in good shape. They are flown to Darwin to testify against Gillespie and his gang, who are convicted of thieving and running brands. When he testifies, Stones virtuously gives his real name, Gerald Wilkinson, and admits that he has run away from his home in Brisbane. The authorities then enlist the boys' help in apprehending Gillespie's boss, a smuggler of gold, opium, and hashish (the contents of the four tins), a fat man named O'Halloran, and do so in an exciting, action-filled scene at his airstrip south of the Laurance Estate. The boys then retrace their overland journey, are reunited with their families, inherit Chikker Jackson's estate of 24,000 pounds, and are made a gift of Gustav Feldman's plantation in the Tablelands. Darkie's mother speaks forcefully to the boys' need for more education in order to make a go of their business, and all agree with her sensible suggestion. Action and excitement abound, the scenes are well drawn, and the book's pace maintains interest well. Adults are stock characters, but the boys, though obvious types, are carefully individualized and foil one another for a pleasing mix. Descriptions of the countryside and of handling the stock are given in sufficient detail to strengthen the rather conventional story, and a sense of the vastness and wildness of the territory comes through strongly. Although it is difficult to believe that five boys with only minimal experience in stockhandling could accomplish the drive with so few problems, and that the authorities would give them so much responsibility in apprehending known criminals, the plentiful action and carefully planned complications skillfully obscure those plot implausibilities. The author has a tendency to overwrite and sentimentalize, in particular the elderly Germans, and the villains are drawn with such conventional strokes that one recognizes their ilk immediately. Racial and ethnic biases might offend late twentieth-century readers. Aust. Bk. of Year Com.

SPENCE, ELEANOR (RACHEL) (1927? 1928?–), born in Sydney, New South Wales, Australia; librarian and writer highly regarded for her realistic novels of family life and of history for readers ages eleven to fifteen. She received her B.A. in English from Sydney University and taught at Methodist Ladies' College for a year. After training as a librarian, she served with the Commonwealth Public Service Board in Canberra before her marriage to John Spence, an engineer, and then for two years with the Coventry City Libraries in Coventry, England. Her work there sparked her interest in writing for children, and in Australia again, she wrote a series of stories for the Australian Broadcasting Company and began work on *Patterson's Track* (Oxford, 1958), a mystery-adventure that became her first published book. More than a dozen novels followed, making her one of the best-known Australian children's writers. Two books were named Australian Children's Book of the Year: *The Green Laurel** (Oxford, 1963; Roy, 1963), a contemporary story about a family forced to settle in low-cost housing; and *The October Child** (Oxford, 1976; *The Devil Hole*, Lothrop, 1977), about a family's problems with their autistic son. Seven novels were commended or highly commended for the Book of the Year Award: *The Summer in Between** (Oxford, 1959), a girl's growing-up story with a background of domestic adventures; *Lillipilly Hill** (Oxford, 1960; Roy, 1963), in which an immigrant girl in rural New South Wales defies Victorian conventions; *The Year of the Currawong** (Oxford, 1965; Roy, 1965), in which several children determine the ownership of an abandoned mine; *A Candle for Saint Antony** (Oxford, 1977; Oxford, 1979), about a friendship between two youths suspected of being homosexual; *The Seventh Pebble** (Oxford, 1980), which explores religious prejudice in a contemporary community; *The Left Overs** (Methuen, 1982), about four children who search for a real home when their foster home is closed; and *Me and Jeshua** (Dove, 1984), a novel of friendship between two cousins, one probably Jesus, who live in an unidentified country resembling ancient Palestine. Among her other titles are *The Nothing-Place* (Oxford, 1972; Harper, 1973), a novel about the problems of deafness, and *The Switherby Pilgrims* (Oxford, 1967; Roy, 1967) and its sequel, *Jamberoo Road* (Oxford, 1969; Roy,

1969), both historical novels dealing with settlers in New South Wales in the 1840s. Spence was a teacher of the handicapped at the School for Autistic Children in Sydney and in 1978 received a Churchill Fellowship to study residential facilities for the autistically handicapped.

THE SPIRIT WIND (Fatchen*, Max, ill. Trevor Stubley, Hicks, 1973; Methuen, 1973), adventure novel of a boy who jumps ship in South Australia from a sailing vessel in the early twentieth century. Jarl* Hansen, 14, an orphan, has been so abused by the brutal mate of the *Hootzen*, a man known as Heinrich the Bull, during the voyage of the ancient iron square-rigger from Norway to Australia, that he throws hot stew at his tormentor. The mate, who controls the ship, vows that he will teach the boy a lesson and denies him the right to land when they reach port. Genuinely afraid, Jarl lowers a crude raft he has tied together over the side and lets himself down into the shark-infested waters. He swims, pushing the raft, until he gets well away from the ship, then climbs on and tries to propel the cranky craft toward the shore. He comes upon an old Aborigine named Nunganee*, whose fishing net has been invaded by a giant ray, and, with his leg caught in a rope, is being pulled underwater. Jarl swims to his boat, manages to cut the rope, and hauls Nunganee aboard. The old man takes him to his hut, gives him food, and hides him in a brush-covered hollow when he hears horses approaching. The visitors are three local ranch children, Jill Gilson, 14, her brother Curly, 9, and their little sister, Kathy*, 5, who have come to spread the news that Ned Ganger has broken out of jail and that Nunganee may be wanted to help track him. Watching them from hiding, Jarl sees a man slipping through the bushes toward Jill's horse. Heedless of his own safety, Jarl jumps from cover and grabs the outlaw's leg. In the ensuing scuffle he is considerably battered, but Jill clobbers Ganger with a chunk of wood, and Nanganee ties him up. Although Australian law clearly demands that Jarl be returned to the ship, the Bull is so abusive in court that he turns the local people into partisans for Jarl. Mr. Gilson suggests that Jarl be placed in his custody while he consults with the Norwegian consul in Adelaide. Furious, the Bull is determined to get the boy back. He takes beer to Ganger at the jail window and makes a deal to help him break out and get him out of the country aboard the *Hootzen* in exchange for his help in kidnapping Jarl. They hide out near the Gilson farm, waiting until only little Kathy is there with Jarl, who is working on the wheat stack. For a while Jarl fights off both men by knocking them down with bags of wheat directed through the short chute, but when they coordinate their efforts with a ladder and a pig net, they capture him. Kathy is found hiding by Nunganee. As soon as Jill arrives, Nunganee commandeers her horse to track and follow the kidnappers. When her horse comes back riderless, Jill slips out and rides to Nunganee's hut where she finds the old man, who has been knocked unconscious by the Bull. His boat is gone, but they see a wisp of smoke from a usually deserted island and, taking a fishing boat, set off to investigate. A strong wind, which Nunganee believes he called up by Aborigine incantations, almost capsizes them. In the meantime, Ganger has taken Jarl in Nunganee's boat to the island, where he has a hut, to wait until dark just before the *Hootzen* sails. Jarl has broken away and started a signal fire. A terrible storm sweeps into the bay, breaking the *Hootzen* from anchor and driving it against the rocks. Jarl, Nunganee, Jill, and even Ganger save most of the men, but the Bull is not among them. Hunting for other survivors, Jarl comes upon the mate and tries to get him to the hut, but the Bull, crazed by the storm and his anger, attacks Jarl and slips into one of the blowholes through which the water is being forced like a great spout. When the storm abates and they return to the mainland, the *Hootzen* is a total wreck. Mr. Gilson has received permission for Jarl to remain in Australia in his care. Nunganee burns his "singing stick" with which he called up the spirit wind to wreck the ship and save the boy. Fast action is the main element of the novel, though the characterization is more than adequate, of Jarl and Nunganee in particular. Scenes on the ship and on the island in the storm are especially strong, and the rallying of community support for the boy in this sparsely populated area is handled well. Aust. Bk. of Year Highly Com.

SPIT MACPHEE (*The True Story of Spit MacPhee**), Angus MacPhee, obstreperous, defiant orphan whom do-gooder Betty Arbuckle seeks to adopt and who is finally placed with Grace, Jack, and Sadie* Tree. Spit prefers going barefoot and half-clad, speaks in a shout, and often spits, the latter two habits copied from his half-mad grandfather, Fyfe* MacPhee. Spit is a well-rounded protagonist, a boy whom circumstances have molded into a self-sufficient, responsible, capable youth with a good sense of values and of his own worth.

STARBUCK VALLEY WINTER (Haig-Brown*, Roderick, ill. Charles DeFeo, Collins, 1944; Morrow, 1943), adventure novel set in British Columbia, Canada, in the 1930s. Don Morgan, 16, has done fairly well fishing during his summer out of school, and he is willing to help on his Uncle Joe's farm where he lives, but his real desire is to spend the winter trapping and to earn enough money to buy the *Mallard*, a boat big enough to make fishing a serious vocation. After Don builds a waterwheel to pump water to the farmhouse, Uncle Joe gets a permit to trap in the country of the Shifting River, one of the tributaries of the Starbuck River, with permission for Don, who is too young to qualify for a permit, to run the trapline for him. Despite the objections of his Aunt Maud, Don scouts the proposed area, finding the cabin in poor repair and the country dark and gloomy. The man whose claim adjoins his and whom he has been warned about, Lee* Jetson, pays him a visit that seems threatening. He is relieved when his friend, Tubby Miller, decides to spend the winter with him. They repair the cabin and set their lines with little success at first, but they have high hopes until Tubby cuts his foot severely with the ax. Afraid to leave him while he goes for help, Don gets him into the canoe and starts down the flooded river in a harrowing trip, shooting rapids and even riding over the falls, until the canoe hits a snag and capsizes. Don is able to get it to shore, but both boys are soaked, night is approaching, and it is a long distance to the big log jam beyond which is Tubby's skiff. After he has built a fire, left Tubby a supply of wood, and managed to bring back the skiff, Don finds Jetson caring for Tubby. The man, whose tracks they have found around the cabin so often they know he has been watching them, helps get Tubby below the last log jam, then leaves Don to take him the rest of the way in the skiff. In the next few days, Don helps his uncle by trapping three cougars that are threatening his cattle and visits Tubby, who is recovering in the hospital. When he returns to the mountains, Don finds Jetson's cabin and challenges him for spying on them. Jetson admits that he has because he has a mine, and he has suspected Don of prospecting since his father was a miner. He freely advises Don of better ways to trap marten, and they part, their differences resolved. When Tubby recovers and rejoins Don, he is still suspicious of Jetson and is barely civil when the man visits them. Some time later, however, when Tubby fails to return in a snowstorm, Don enlists Jetson's help, and they track him down to where he has left the trail to escape wolves and get him to shelter in time to save him. Thereafter, the three of them stalk the two wolf packs that are feeding on the deer in the vicinity, and in an exciting night hunt Don manages to kill all six in one group, while Jetson and Tubby kill four of the others. With these skins and the bounty for killing wolves, Don has enough money to buy the *Mallard*. When he returns to Bluff Harbor, however, he learns that the boat has been sold. He is disconsolate until he discovers that Aunt Maud has bought it to hold for him until he can sell his skins and buy it. The descriptions of poling up the river in the canoe and of the adventures in the wild country are exciting, and the hunting and trapping exploits are believable. In a more conservation-conscious era, the wanton killing of wolves, wolverines, cougars, and other animals, now known to be growing rare, may be less acceptable than when the book was written. Character development is not strong, but the fast-paced action keeps the reader's interest. Sequel. Can. Bk. of Year Winner.

STARLAND OF THE SOUTH (McNair*, W. A., ill. William R. Taplin, Angus, 1950), informational book about the constellations that appear in the sky of the southern hemisphere and the myths attached to them, thinly disguised as fiction. Beth and David, of indeterminate ages, are two farm children of New Zealand. Their Uncle Michael, visiting from Australia, begins to tell them of the stars that they can see from their veranda in the autumn with the story of the centaur and the wolf. He continues with the story of Jason and the Argonauts, Orion, and various other related myths. In December the family travels to Australia, where they visit Uncle Michael in Sydney and hear more stories, including those of Pegasus and of the signs of the zodiac. In August Uncle Michael visits again in New Zealand and tells them of the stars visible in the southern winter, among them Bootes the Ploughman or Herdsman and the Scorpion. He ends by telling them about the planets, the differences between the stars seen in the northern and southern hemispheres, and the twenty brightest stars, with more scientific explanations than previously. The book is almost entirely in question and answer form, with brief introductions to each section describing the children's activities. There is no characterization beyond David's preference for the more exciting stories and Beth's tendency to cry at the sad ones. Included are star maps of the entire sky in autumn, early summer, and winter, and numerous detailed pictures of individual constellations with the mythological pictures drawn in black and the stars in white against a blue background. The myths are told briefly, without much detail. Aust. Bk. of Year Highly Com.

STARLIGHT IN TOURRONE (Butler*, Suzanne, ill. Rita Fava Fegiz, Little, 1965), short realistic novel of community life set in the village of Tourrone, Provence, France, just after World War II. Grandfather's stories of how in his youth the entire village participated in an annual Christmas Eve march to the dilapidated chapel on the hill overlooking the town to bestow gifts on the Virgin and Christ Child inspire his four grandchildren, Michel, Pierrette, Anne Marie, and Patrice, and two friends, Teresa and Jeremie, to revive what they feel was an exciting and valuable old custom. Michel, the organizer, assigns each of the children a task, and much of the story tells how they enlist the villagers and make preparations for the big event. Grandmother helps with costumes, and Madame Zoppi offers cream and butter. Several villagers provide music, but Grandfather grumps. Father Chrisophe is too dispirited from his war experiences and his cousin, Marthe, too busy with running her large farm to look beyond their own problems, but even they eventually catch the children's enthusiasm. The greatest problem involves finding a Virgin and Christ Child. In the old days, the baby was played by the newest infant in town, whose mother acted as Marie. When Teresa's sister, who has been planning to bring her baby for a visit, is unable to come, it seems that the pageant will lack its stars. Coincidentally, at the very time, Jean Sebastian, Marthe's younger brother, estranged from his family and now fallen on hard times, decides to return to Tourrone. He arrives with his young wife and their new baby just in time for Marie and little Jean to serve as the Marie and Jesus for the March. This uncomplicated story of how several determined, confident children inspire their disheartened village avoids sentimentality and condescension and projects a certain charm. Although Jean's return seems too fortuitous, the activities and attitudes of the children are thoroughly convincing, and the villagers, if conventional types, are likeable and appropriate. Smudgy, loosely drawn black-and-white illustrations underscore significant happenings and contribute to the atmosphere of homely warmth and simple miracle. Fanfare.

STEELE, MARY, born in Newcastle, New South Wales, Australia; teacher, researcher, and writer. She grew up in the country town of Ballarat and received her M.A. from Melbourne University and a teaching diploma from London University. She has taught English at Melbourne and Monash Universities, has worked in a primary school library, and does free-lance research. She has reviewed children's books for the *Australian* and has contributed articles to various publications. *Arkwright** (Hyland, 1985), a short, lively, amusing talking animal fantasy about the adventures of a giant anteater and an old salt named Captain Chilbain in his retirement seaside cottage, was named Australian Junior Book of the Year.

STEVE (*The Green Laurel**), leader of the Blackbutt Hill Outcasts, a group of six youths whose families emigrated from Europe to Australia after World War II. They have formed the club for the purpose of encouraging one another to get an education and earn money to move from the low-cost housing settlement as soon as possible. A formidable youth, Steve opposes developing the library because having one implies permanency. When the library is vandalized, suspicion falls on him. He runs away but later returns to identify the real culprits. His return exemplifies facing up to issues and acting morally. Steve and his Outcast friends are essentially faceless, choral characters.

STEVENSON, WILLIAM (HENRI) (1925–), born in London, England; journalist, film producer, author of one novel for children. During World War II he was a carrier fighter pilot in the Royal Navy Air Service, becoming a lieutenant commander. He received his B.A. degree from Ruskin College, Oxford, in 1948, and became a correspondent for the London *Sunday Times*, the *Toronto Star*, and the Canadian Broadcasting Company. In the next fifteen years he worked in Peking, Hong Kong, New Delhi, and Kenya and was a war correspondent in Korea, Indochina, and Malaya, with added assignments in Moscow, Cairo, Tokyo, Warsaw, and Kabul. He has also been a director for Five Continents Film Corporation, Toronto, and a filmer and producer of documentaries for the National Broadcasting Company and Commonwealth Research and Development Corporation. At one time he was an aviation adviser for the Pan-Africa Research Institute, and used his knowledge of Africa for his novel, *The Bushbabies** (Houghton, 1965; Hutchinson, 1966), a story of a thirteen-year-old English girl who sets off across Kenya with her father's African headman to return her pet bushbaby to its natural home. It was named to both the *Horn Book* Fanfare and the *Choice* magazine lists of outstanding children's books and was filmed in 1970. Stevenson has also written biography for adults and a number of books on travel and current events.

STORM (*The Silver Brumby**), the chestnut brumby (wild horse) that is Thowra's partner from birth, his soul- and playmate and staunch companion and helper throughout his life. Storm is strong and sturdy and is especially noted for his kindness. As a character, he foils Thowra.

STORM BOY (Thiele*, Colin, ill. John Baily, Rigby, 1963; Angus, 1964; Rand, 1966), brief, poetic story of a boy growing up on the South Australia coast in the mid-twentieth century. At the death of his mother when he is four, Storm Boy moves southeast from Adelaide with his father, Hideaway Tom, to the

ninety-mile beach. There they live in a shack, fishing and shunning people except
for their nearest neighbor, an Aborigine known as Fingerbone Bill, whose shack
is a mile from theirs, and for occasional trips up the Coorong River to the nearest
town, Goolwa, for supplies. To prevent Storm Boy from getting lost, the men
set a big timber upright in the sand for a landmark, and the boy happily wanders
the beach and learns about nature from Fingerbone. Occasionally, this idyllic
life is interrupted by hunters, campers, or poachers in the bird sanctuary near
their stretch of beach. One day when he is ten or eleven years old, Storm Boy
sees three young men wantonly destroying some pelican nests and smashing the
eggs in them. He finds three tiny pelicans alive, which he takes home. Two are
fairly strong, and he names them Mr. Proud and Mr. Ponder, but the third is
very weak and must be nursed carefully. When the bird lives, Storm Boy names
him Mr. Percival. All three become pets, but since he cannot feed three hungry,
growing birds, Hideaway insists that they must be taken in their boat far into
the sanctuary and released to care for themselves. The next morning Mr. Percival
is back and soon becomes a constant companion to Storm Boy, even retrieving
a ball like a dog. Hideaway teaches him to fly out with a fishing line and drop
it in the sea. In a bad storm a tugboat goes aground near the shack, and they
are able to send Mr. Percival out with a fishing line, which can then be fastened
to a rope and pulled in so that the crew can attach a bosun's chair. They save
all six men aboard, and in gratitude, the captain proposes to send Storm Boy to
boarding school in Adelaide. Since he can't take Mr. Percival, Storm Boy refuses.
The next season, a couple of hunters, angered because Mr. Percival keeps
warning the ducks of their presence, shoot the pelican. Storm Boy, heartbroken,
holds the bird until it dies, then buries it, and announces that he is ready to go
to Adelaide. The slight book handles many of the conventions of the pet story
without undue sentimentality and strongly evokes the vastness and solitude of
the setting. Illustrations by John Schoenherr in a 1978 edition add to the sense
of beauty and mystery. Aust. Bk. of Year Com.

THE STORY OF KARRAWINGI THE EMU (Rees*, Leslie, ill. Walter Cunningham, Sands, 1945), realistic animal story set in Australia in the days when
white men were beginning to fence and cultivate the land and after the introduction of trucks, presumably in the early twentieth century. It follows the life
of one emu, Karrawingi, from his hatching out of one of fourteen olive-green
eggs tended by his father, Baramool, until he escapes back to the wild after
having been captured for a zoo. Life for the young emus is hazardous. Two of
Karrawingi's siblings are carried off by eagles. A number of the flock, including
Baramool, are killed by blacks, who ingeniously attract the birds by appealing
to their curiosity. The emus leave their seaside feeding grounds and resettle in
the mountains. Occasionally they see white men building the railroad, but at
first they are not bothered. Karrawingi, now a handsome full-grown young male,
is attracted to Warree, and they go off together to build a nest in which Warree
lays a record eighteen eggs. Karrawingi soon drives Warree off the nest and sits

on the eggs, but two white men appear, scare him away, and take all the eggs, knowing that one emu egg equals about eight hen's eggs. Continued fencing and settlement activities drive the emus further inland to less productive land, where Karrawingi must fight off a dingo and become leader of the flock. As the dry season limits their food, the emus begin to break down fences and raid the crops, even chasing the sheep for sport. Farmers disturbed by the resulting loss of grain and lambs team up for a big emu hunt, even though the herds are protected by law. Karrawingi escapes the terrible slaughter but falls into a pit trap and is captured for a small town zoo. After some time of this safe but boring existence, he is bought by a big city zoo and is being transferred in a stock truck when emus appear running in the road ahead, keeping pace with the truck for miles. The sight and sound of the birds excite Karrawingi, and he drums and stamps until one of the emus swings out in front of the truck, causing the driver to swerve, catch a wheel in a rut, and overturn the truck. Karrawingi is thrown out but not seriously injured, and he joyously runs across the country at the head of the new flock. The story is fictionalized natural history, only slightly longer than a picture book and illustrated with several handsome, full-page paintings and numerous smaller drawings. Although the author attributes thoughts and emotions to the birds, he does not otherwise anthropomorphize them. Aust. Bk. of Year Winner.

THE STORY OF KURRI KURRI THE KOOKABURRA (Rees*, Leslie, ill. Margaret Senior, Sands, 1949), fictionalized natural history of the introduction of the laughing Australian bird, native of New South Wales, into Blackswanland of Western Australia in the early twentieth century. Kurri Kurri, which means "the very first," is the smallest of three chicks of Kuringai and his mate, Kinkoona, their hatching announced by unusually loud shrieks of laughter from the father and the friends and relations of the kookaburra colony. In a short time Kurri Kurri, the first hatched and liveliest of the three, has caught up in size with his siblings and has tempted his sister, Kareela, out to the front of the nest, where a giant goanna, a lizard nearly five feet long, sees them and starts his climb of the gum tree to catch them, only to be driven off just in time by the alerted parents. Soon the father bird begins giving his chicks lessons in laughing, one at a time, an exercise that attracts the attention of a young female chick nearby named Karloo, which means "water." When the father is ready to give lessons in flying, Kurri Kurri must wait for third place, and before his turn comes he is captured, as is also Karloo, by a man, then taken by sea on a long journey to the home of Mr. Hensman in Blackswanland. There, as his son, Jerry, watches, Mr. Hensman clips the ends of Kurri Kurri's flight feathers and turns him loose in the yard, but Karloo seems so close to death that he just sets her gently on a heap of dry leaves. Jerry feeds both birds, and soon Karloo becomes strong enough to flutter off, leaving Kurri Kurri alone. He gradually adjusts, enjoying the dead mice the humans provide for him and making friends with the family dog, but he does not laugh. Then one day a group of magpies attacks him in force. Mrs. Hensman drives them off with a broom and carries the bleeding and shaken kookaburra into the kitchen where, after he becomes calm again, he gives his first full-throated laugh. After a year and a half during which his wings are clipped but not so much that he can't flutter around in the bushes, his laugh is answered one day by that of Karloo. Although he tries to warn her away, he cannot help answering her. When the dog knocks a wooden picket loose in the fence, Kurri Kurri flutters out and then from shrub to shrub after Karloo. She feeds him and encourages him to fly until his wings grow. They decide to make a nest in the forest, but the first year Karloo lays no eggs. As they become more at home, they learn to kill the snakes they encounter and to catch rats and mice. The second spring Karloo lays three eggs, the beginning of a colony that spreads throughout Blackswanland. The kookaburras, which are a species of kingfishers with a short body and heavy bill, are anthropomorphized with human speech and emotions, but the details of their laughter-like calls, their nests, and their habits are true to nature. The story is meant to be a pleasant way to introduce rather young children to an unusual bird. Aust. Bk. of Year Highly Com.

THE STORY OF PANCHAMI (Sengupta*, Abhijit, ill. Subir Roy, CBT, India, 1986), realistic novelette set in a village in contemporary India. Happy days follow for Mithun, about twelve, and his younger sister, Ruma, when they rescue and tame a seagull that has become entangled in Mithun's red box kite. They name the bird Panchami because they acquired it on Basant Panchami, the day that marks the arrival of spring in India. They care for its damaged wing, nurse it back to health, and become fond of it in spite of its aggressive tendencies. At first Mithun keeps it in a bamboo cage that he makes especially for it, releasing it only on a tether, but eventually it flies free and responds to its name when called. Although Panchami brings the children much pleasure, it causes some problems too. It dominates the family cat, Pushy, swipes fish that their mother has cleaned, and upsets the teacher with its squawking. The biggest problem concerns Asman Hawk, the ornithologist who lives nearby. Since the bird bore a tag with Hawk's name on it, the children know that it is his property, at least for study, but since they regard him as somewhat mad, they are careful to keep the bird secret from him. In late winter, almost a year after they find Panchami, they accompany their father by bus on a pilgrimage to the Ganga (Ganges) River delta. There Panchami mingles with a flock of gulls, almost responds to Mithun's call, then chooses to remain with its kind. Mithun feels some consolation when his father reminds him that he had learned much from the bird and that Panchami is only following "the law of nature." Mithun is grateful for the good times he had while the bird was with him. None of the characters is developed beyond what is necessary for the simple plot. The relationship between the siblings lacks definition, and the two are almost carbon copies of each other. The reader has ambivalent feelings about the relationship between the children and Asman Hawk. Hawk is seen through the children's eyes as abrupt and scary, and he has a hawk that he sends out to hunt other birds for him. On the other hand, he has banded the gull and appears to be knowledgeable and respected in his field. Morality and common decency would dictate, however, that the children at least inform him that they have the bird, and indeed their father tells them to contact the man, but they do not obey. At the end, Hawk seems to have been aware that they have the bird, but the moral problem is left unsolved. There is some sense of Indian family and neighborhood life, and colloquial terms and modes of expression contribute to the atmosphere. The result is a pleasing story of two children's attachment to an unusual pet. CBT of India, Second Prize.

THE STORY OF SARLI, THE BARRIER REEF TURTLE (Rees*, Leslie, ill. Walter Cunningham, Sands, 1947), fictionalized natural history relating the life story of one of the giant turtles native to the barrier reef of Australia. Sarli hatches about two inches long among dozens of other little turtles in a hole in the sand, just above the high-water mark. After two days she breaks free, fortunately waiting until nightfall when the seabirds have gone off to their nests. She escapes the gulls, the shore crabs and other dangers that kill many of her fellow nestlings on their first vital journey down the beach to the water. For seven days she needs no food. She then discovers shoots of seaweed that she considers lovely and soon learns to catch and eat small fish. For her first year she stays among the colorful corals in the shallow water of the cay where she hatched, but by the time her upper shell is about eight inches long she is ready for the demanding journey to the Outer Reef. After swimming for six days she sees the coral columns, known as niggerheads that mark the reef. There she meets Sappoo, one of her own brothers, and together they escape sharks that are preying on larger turtles, though a small piece of Sarli's fore flipper is bitten off. Three years later Sarli encounters her first humans, tourists who ride turtles for fun. She is sunning herself on a sandy beach when she feels a great weight on her back. She heaves herself forward, struggling back into the lagoon where she is able to shed her rider and dive deeply to get away from the terrifying creatures. Her next encounter is more dangerous. Again tourists invade the beach where she is sleeping, and two of them turn her over on her back, then amble off. Helpless, she suffers for five days, unable to right herself while the scavenger birds wait for her to die. She is saved by a cyclone that raises the sea level enough to float her off into the boiling surf, where she can quickly flip over and ride currents into deeper seas. In another eighteen months she is thirty-six inches long and still growing. She often finds herself with other green turtles in the shelter of the Outer Reef, among them Awati, a male who is attracted to her. He is caught, however, by natives who have fastened a line to a suckerfish and allowed it to swim among the turtles and attach itself to his back. Patiently they wait until he is tired out by trying to free himself from their gentle pull on the line and then draw him up to the canoe, where they can harpoon and kill him. Soon Wurli, another male, takes Awati's place as Sarli's companion. When she is a hundred miles from land in the deep ocean, she suddenly knows that she must return to the coral cay where she was hatched. Despite the dangers of sharks and other sea creatures and of the surf on the ocean side of the Outer Reef, she swims night and day, floats across the reef at high tide, and continues the thirty miles to her own beach. There, as her mother did, she pulls herself up the sand above the high-water mark, digs several holes, abandoning any where she strikes something hard, until she has a round hole about six inches deep, beneath which she scoops out an egg pit and lays 130 eggs. Ten times that summer, she returns, makes another hold, and lays another batch. On her last visit she again encounters humans, these from a turtle canning factory. As they try to turn her over, however, she rakes one with the sharp nail on her fore flipper and gets away. And so she continues to live for many years, no longer growing after her twelfth summer and not laying eggs every year, but swimming in the lagoons, among the coral of the Outer Reef, and in the great ocean beyond. The beautifully illustrated book is frankly didactic, telling the life story in attractive prose with vivid descriptions of the plant and animal life that Sarli encounters but without anthropomorphizing her beyond the emotions an observer might deduce from her behavior. Although the story is meant for younger children, the style is not extremely simple and it is not condescending in tone. Aust. Bk. of Year Com.

THE STORY OF SHADOW, THE ROCK WALLABY (Rees*, Leslie, ill. Walter Cunningham, Sands, 1948), fictionalized natural history concerning the small, kangaroo-like wallabys of the Australian mountains. At two or three months old, Shadow, a wallaby baby, or joey, is being carried in his mother's pouch when she is chased by rock-throwing humans. Hindered by the weight of the joey, she is almost caught until she forces Shadow to tumble out and hide in a hollow log. Throughout the afternoon and the long, cold night he cowers, but he comes out in the morning, although his legs are hardly strong enough to support him. His mother returns, having escaped her pursuers, and he gratefully returns to the warm, dark comfort of the pouch. Gradually he emerges for longer and longer periods until his legs gain strength and he can hop, eat grass, and play with Tuft, another joey his age. Tuft, however, is crushed and eaten by a carpet snake, one of the most feared predators in the wallaby colony. Shadow makes a new friend, Lillypilly. His curiosity leads him to explore a shady gorge, although his mother has warned him never to go there. In the unfamiliar territory he is attacked and bitten by a fox but is able to get away. Emboldened by this escape, he wanders further into the valley, eating the rich vegetation and enjoying his freedom. He meets a walleroo, a cousin of sorts, larger and heavier than a wallaby, and explores a cave where he sees bats. Following the distress cries of an animal, he comes upon a rabbit in a trap and watches curiously while a man kills it and mimics the cries to lure a fox from the brush. The blast from the man's shot at the fox stuns Shadow, and when he wakes he is being carried by the tail with intense pain. He bites and claws at the man's leg. Thinking that the wallaby is dead, the man believes he has been bitten by a snake and drops Shadow, who hops off at top speed toward the rocky heights of home. He returns to find that his mother has given birth to a new joey, a tiny hairless female who struggles unassisted until she reaches the mother's pouch. In the next months, Shadow grows and tussles with the other young males until the old male of the group, his father, becomes interested in Lillypilly. He attacks Shadow savagely. Although he is larger than Shadow, he is now aging, and after a fierce battle he is driven off. Shadow and Lillypilly mate and look forward to the birth of their joey. The simple story is told in seven brief chapters, illustrated with nine full-page color paintings and numerous line drawings. Although the wallabys talk to each other and are endowed with some human emotions, they are otherwise treated as wild animals. Descriptions of their lives, of the other animals Shadow encounters, and of the flora and topography of the area are detailed and interesting. Aust. Bk. of Year Highly Com.

STOW, (JULIAN) RANDOLPH (1935–), born in Geraldton, Western Australia, the son of a barrister; teacher, novelist, and poet for adults who has also written works for children. His spirited and witty tall-tale novel of an Australian bushranger, *Midnite: The Story of a Wild Colonial Boy** (Macdonald, 1967; Prentice, 1968), was highly commended for Australian Children's Book of the Year. After receiving his B.A. from the University of Western Australia, he worked as an anthropologist's assistant in Northwest Australia and in New Guinea and lectured in English at the University of Leeds, England, and the University of Western Australia. His more than a dozen publications for adults include several books of poems, pieces for the musical theater, and a number of novels, including *Tourmaline* (Angus, 1963) and *The Suburbs of Hell* (Secker, 1984). He also edited the periodical *Australian Poetry*.

THE STROLLERS (Beake*, Lesley, Maskew, 1987), realistic sociological problem novel about strollers (street children) in contemporary Cape Town, South Africa. Almost plotless, the story focuses upon the homeless black youths' struggles to survive in the hostile, often violent atmosphere of the inner city. Earnest, intelligent Johnny Xhashan, 12, the *laatlammetjie*, or last and final of the eight sons of his Ma, a laundress for a white woman, flees the arguments in his poverty-stricken home. Although he yearns for an education, which Ma is always haranguing him to get, he can't tolerate the crowded conditions at the school, where the overworked teachers are unable to give such problem learners the attention they need. Johnny runs to the streets, where first he falls in with *bergies*, a motley group of usually drunken adult beggars and pickpockets led by the much feared woman known as Kaatjie se mob. In his haste to evade a police raid, Johnny falls, hits his head, and is found by the gang of children to which his friend, film and video-game fanatic, glue-sniffing Abel Blou, 10, belongs. Abel's strollers also include little Mesana, 8, for whom Johnny develops a brotherly fondness and who is the best of them all at "getting things," that is, begging. The gang is made up of two older boys, cousins, and two older girls; frail, thin, wasted Finkie, a younger boy who coughs almost constantly, and tall, scowling Kosie, the leader until he leaves for Johannesburg after being accused by one of the dreaded Spider Men mob of informing to the police. Johnny then becomes leader, by default rather than inclination. They live, like other strollers, by raiding trash cans, begging from passersby and at houses, sleeping under cardboard and bushes, passing time with stories and sniffing glue or sampling bottles, evading police and older mobs, a tightly knit little family that shares everything and looks out for one another. Warned by Abraham, a gaudily dressed, foppish Spider Man—who ironically turns out to be one of Johnny's missing brothers—of a pending police raid, Johnny leads his little family of waifs first to a cave on the side of the mountain overlooking the city, then back to the streets because they feel more at home there. On Saturday night while the children are playing video games, Kaatjie's mob causes trouble. The other children manage to flee before the police come, but Johnny is taken. Mesana and Abel summon help from strollers and mobs, and at his hearing Johnny has so many who declare themselves his "family," including, of course, Abraham, that the magistrate remands him to their custody. At summer's end, Finkie's health has deteriorated so badly that Johnny and Mesana take him to the hospital in a cart provided by Kaatjie, where they leave him. Johnny has by now gained a new perspective on freedom and responsibility, understands his mother better, and elects to return home, taking Mesana with him. A clear picture of the children's way of life, their loving concern for one another, and the sights and sounds of the city combined with some humor (Johnny's gradually swelling family at the hearing, for example), much poignancy, an understated style, and often urgent tone offset the flimsy plot and result in a powerful account of survival within an unconventional family. Young Africa.

SUE CLARK (*Climb a Lonely Hill**), half-orphaned girl marooned with her brother, Jack*, on the Australian desert. Sue can be sensibly assertive, once insisting that Jack practice with the rifle before he wastes all the ammunition. The children learn to talk to each other and to look for the other's good points, new experiences for them because of their chaotic home situation, and, when Sue confides to Jack that she would like to become a teacher, Jack begins to think more seriously about what he might do with his life. Sue is a round, likeable figure, a good contrast to her at first less responsible and resourceful brother.

THE SUMMER IN BETWEEN (Spence*, Eleanor, ill. Marcia Lane-Foster, Oxford, 1959), girl's growing-up novel in the context of neighborhood adventures set in the village of Kenilworth, Australia, at the time of publication. The summer between the end of primary school and the beginning of high school looks drab for Faith Melville, 12. Her long-time playmate, her younger brother, Jamey, 10, has found a close friend in Brian Bailey, whom Faith considers a troublemaker, and she has come to regard her best girl friend, Betsy, as too obsequious and acquiescent for her lively mind and expanding horizons. She finds just the right companionship in idea-filled Pauline Selby. Pauline has come to recover from whooping cough during the Christmas holidays with her aunt and uncle who live just across the paddock from the Melvilles. Uniting the various episodes are two interlocking story strands, the problem of the mysterious disappearance of the prize peaches belonging to Mr. Melville, a headmaster and hobby horticulturalist, and, most importantly, the matter of Faith's relationship with the community children. The first problem is solved when Faith discovers that a tramp has stolen the peaches and not Jamey and Brian as she had feared. The second revolves around the suggestion of Pauline, an aspiring actress, that they form the Kenilworth Literary and Dramatic Club. They build a clubhouse and invite the neighborhood children to join. Betsy suggests that Faith, an aspiring writer, write a play for them to perform. Mrs. Melville thinks that the play, about the history of Kenilworth, is good enough to be performed as part of the C.W.A. (Country Women's Association) annual fundraiser. The children are elated, but difficulty arises over casting. When the lead role, which Faith covets, goes to Colleen Bailey, Faith quits the club in a huff. For some days she is aloof and gloomy, too proud to apologize or make up. To give her something else to think about, Mrs. Melville arranges for her to spend a day with her Aunt Elizabeth in Sydney. The episode provides a pleasant interlude in the story as they shop for school clothes and attend *A Midsummer Night's Dream*. When Aunt Elizabeth remarks that good plays endure while an actor's contribution is ephemeral in comparison, Faith realizes that what she really wants to do is write, not act, and finally she admits to herself that Colleen is superior in the part. Pauline helps her to rejoin the club by seeking her advice about a production problem. After a few minor complications, the grand performance is held for an audience of over one hundred enthusiastic supporters. Faith has learned that one must identify and develop one's strengths and swallow one's pride and ambition for the common good. The book reflects the conventional family and community situations and attitudes of the "unreal realism" of children's books of the 1930s and 1940s. The characterization is minimal for the most part, the adults are uniformly helpful, patient, and wise (the ones who save the day at crucial moments), the girls are occupied with "girl things," and the boys are assumed to be nonliterary and superior in technical matters. Best are the portrayal of Faith—who changes believably—the optimistic tone, the fast pace, and the clear sense of community life. Aust. Bk. of Year Com.

THE SUN HORSE (Clark*, Catherine Anthony, ill. Clare Bice, Macmillan, 1951), fantasy novel of adventure and magic that begins and ends in the world of reality of the mid–1900s. After his parents die, Mark* Gunning, 11, goes to live with his aunt and uncle, Bessie and John Gunning, on their ranch at Rainbow Flats in the mountains of western Canada. He makes friends with Giselle* Martin, 11, a French-Canadian girl whose father has been presumed dead since he failed to return from a trip into the mountains in search of the Sun Horse, a fabled palomino stallion said to roam the hills. The children join a local forest service guide on a camping trip into the area, and, exploring on their own, enter secluded Forgetful Canyon. When a terrible storm hits, they find shelter in a cave, where Giselle is awakened by a talking bat. The children follow the bat into a rose-colored cave and watch costumed Indians perform sacred dances. They come out into Forgetful Valley, a place of magic, talking animals, nature spirits, the Sun Indians, and assorted beings human and otherwise. They meet kindly Michael, a sourdough, who informs them that Mr. Martin lives nearby, as does Old Beard, a prospector who has also been missing for some months. Michael takes the children first to visit Old Beard, who has drunk the valley water and so has no memory of his previous existence and cares for nothing but his gold mine, and then to Mr. Martin, who can no longer remember Giselle or his life outside the valley because he also drank the water. Numerous strained, unconvincing fantasy incidents follow in rapid succession, which take the children from one set of strange characters and situations to another. Among others, they receive help from the Flame-Lighter Woman, a kindly comic witch who lights the marsh gas and fabricates for them a magical sky rope, and an Indian medicine man who prepares a magic potion. The children eventually destroy the terrible Thunderbird that has been terrorizing the Indians and has stolen their powerful Love* Magnet. The grateful Indians return to Mr. Martin his two mares, which have been running with the Sun Horse, now the Indians' special mount, and which in the spring will bear the Sun Horse's foals. Mr. Martin, Michael, and the children then return to Rainbow Flats and resume their normal life. The fantasy section of the novel is an often confusing concoction of disparate elements drawn from European story and Indian lore lamely welded to the realistic story. The ending seems abrupt, the characters are types, the incidents are underdeveloped, the pacing is poor, the tone is condescending, and the dialogue is stiff and unconvincing. The early, realistic portion of the novel holds promise as a problem story in a family context, and Mark's relatives seem convincing and likeable in the few passages in which they appear. The author, however, abandons the potential for dramatic involvement that placing a lonely, resentful youth into a situation of which he is understandably apprehensive offers and abruptly casts the characters and the reader into the contrived, poorly motivated, overly long fantasy. The descriptive details, however, are vivid and engaging. The result is the kind of occasionally moralistic, innocuous entertainment that is more typical of the earlier part of the twentieth century than the fifties. Can. Bk. of Year Winner.

THE SUN ON THE STUBBLE (Thiele*, Colin, Rigby, 1961), novel of family life on a farm in South Australia, evidently in the 1920s, a humorous and nostalgic view, mostly following the activities of Bruno* Gunther, 12, youngest son in a large German-Australian family. Looking back, in a brief frame in which he is starting out for boarding high school in Adelaide, Bruno remembers the good times and the funny times, most of them involving fiery-tempered Dad*, Marcus Gunther, who is always sure he is right, even when proven wrong. Some of the episodes center on Bruno's personal misadventures: he catches an opossum and releases it proudly in the kitchen, sure that the family will applaud, only to have the room nearly wrecked and Dad badly scratched in the ensuing chase; smoking after school he and a couple of friends are surprised by a neighbor, Ted Knightley, who keeps them talking until the cigarette Bruno has quickly stashed in his pocket burns a hole in his coat; he and his friend, Ernie Geister, dam the creek on the property, and when the dam breaks it floods the neighbors living downstream, washing away three piglets; he is sent to dump the trash after the school year-end party and interrupts his teacher, Miss Gent, and Ted Knightley in a tender moment; later, when he tries to recreate the moment with Louise Obst, she thinks he is probably sick. His relationship with Miss Gent, who becomes Mrs. Knightley, is one of mutual understanding after he explains that his initials, with his middle name, Untermeyer, give him the nickname of Bugsie and she confesses that in boarding school her initials gave her an equally unappealing nickname. The most hilarious episodes involve Dad. He decides to sink a well and succeeds in blowing up the water tank. He buys a car, after years of resisting, and carefully stops at exactly five hundred miles, as directed by the dealer, to drain the oil, even though it is on a deserted stretch of road in the broiling heat. Because he has scornfully had nothing to do with automobiles, he does not realize that he should replace the oil, and when the engine seizes, he and Bruno walk for miles through sand and dust, the sun beating on their backs. To get even with the thief who is helping himself to logs from their enormous woodpile, he booby-traps a few choice pieces with gelignite and discovers that the culprits are Aunt Emily and Uncle Emil in Adelaide. A piece of the firewood that they have surreptitiously stowed in their car at each visit to the farm blows up as Dad warms himself by their fire. Collecting rabbits from his traps one night, Bruno comes upon thieves loading some of Dad's sheep into their truck. Alerted, Dad sets off to stop them and is so outraged that he loses the element of surprise and the thieves make a getaway, with the sheep cascading out of the still-open back of the truck on top of Dad, who can only shout in both English and German as he waves his fists. Some months later, however, Bruno is helping his aging grandfather home from a distant paddock in a storm, and as they find shelter in a cave, another person stumbles in whom Bruno recognizes as one of the sheep stealers. As the thief lunges for the boy, Grandpa calmly hooks his ankle with his hoe, then knocks him out with the hoe handle. Together, they drag the man to his truck, and Bruno, who has never driven before, steers them in a wild ride right into the nearest village of Nagapalee. Less exciting but just as interesting are the incidents of farm life: the butchering of the pig, the joys of Christmas Eve and Christmas, the "tin-kettling" for the newlywed teacher and Ted Knightley. Although the novel is all in the third person, much of it has the ring of remembered times and people, not only irascible Dad and timid Mum, who always sees danger in any proposed change, but also twinkly eyed Grandpa, who thoroughly enjoys watching his son's temper flare up, and various other family members and neighbors. The general tone is one of good-natured humor, with even the disasters treated lightly. Aust. Bk. of Year Com.

SUPER BIKE (Brown*, Jamie, Clarke, 1981), realistic sports novel about motorcycle racing in the Montreal, Canada, area. Neil Hackett, high school student, has been doing badly ever since his mother married A. L. Dunlop, a hard-driving businessman who seems to have no understanding or sympathy for his stepson. Neil sneaks out of the window to see his girlfriend, Marsha, and together they attend an auction of a defunct car dealership. Impulsively Neil buys a racing bike that was taken in trade, a Ducati 900 Super Sport that needs repair. The one rival bidder introduces himself afterwards, Gord Wenig, a mechanic who used to own the bike and traded it in on a truck for his motorcycle shop. Neil wheels the Ducati home and faces his worried mother and angry stepfather. To his surprise, Dunlop makes a deal with him: he can keep the bike if he will improve his grades, get a job to support it, and keep his records on a businesslike basis. With the help of Gord, Neil repairs the machine and gets an appreciation for the care and precision that must go into every detail of a racing bike. He even gets his friend, Marc Capa, a local barber of Italian extraction, to call Rome for him to order a rare part. Marc's artistic daughter, Carol, a classmate of Neil, comes over to watch him work on the bike and goes with him and a friend when he finally tries the bike out at the deserted race track at Sanair. He breaks it in carefully, according to Gord's instructions, but is bitten by the racing bug and soon is going to all the local races with Gord and his girl friend, Kate, a champion racer, and once with Marsha, who is soon bored by the sport. Since his job at the garage takes much of his time and the racing the rest, Neil sees little of Marsha, and at the big graduation dance she leaves without him. He gets drunk and has to be driven home in his stepfather's Cadillac. After that he concentrates on racing and gets his picture in the paper as he wins a qualifying race. Then he damages his bike the next day on a rain-slick track. Discouraged, he is grateful for Carol's invitation to spend a day with the Art Club in the country, but Marsha learns of his date and deliberately schemes to make him break it. Neil cannot get Carol to listen when he tries to apologize. The newspaper publicity has impressed his stepfather, who announces that he will be Neil's manager. Immediately he begins to get some free Ducati parts, free oil and gas, and as Dunlop starts coming to races with him and talking to other racers and sales representatives, soon becomes well known on the circuit. Dunlop also insists that Neil get into better shape physically and puts him on a running and exercising program. The relationship between the two improves, and Neil starts to call his stepfather A.L. As the season progresses, Dunlop sees that Neil may eventually have a chance to be part of the national Team Canada amateur circuit. At the final race of the season, there is again rain and on a crucial turn a bike turns into Neil, causing him to swerve, and another hits him from the back, knocking both racers off the track. Though his bike is damaged, Neil gets back on and gamely finishes the course, thereby assuring his third place, while Gord gets second. To his delight, Carol has come with her father to watch and seems inclined to forgive Neil for his past blunders. The main interest in the book is in the bikes themselves—the repairs and tests and the races, which are described in exciting detail. Readers who are not motorcycle enthusiasts may find this too much for the thin plot, but the book does give an idea of the intense interest and dedication of those racers on the circuit, and dispels some of the image of motorcycle riders as hoodlums. The style is staccato with many sentence fragments, which is quite effective in the action scenes but becomes rather tiresome in the parts that deal with family relationships and romance. The characters are not much developed, and some, like Dunlop, are far from believable. Can. Young Adult Winner.

SURGEON'S BOY (Sutton*, Eve, ill. Fiona Kelly, Mallinson, 1983), episodic historical adventure novel set in Sydney, Australia, and New Zealand in the early 1840s. After the death of his wife and a falling out with her landed gentleman father, Doctor Jim Fenton and his son, Jamie, 14, who tells the story, emigrate from England on the brig *Diana*, which belongs to Jim's friend, Captain Steve. At Sydney pirates seize the brig and head for the Bay of Islands off New Zealand. Almost there Jim and Jamie slip overboard at night and swim to Kapiti, an island whaling station where they are taken in by burly, red-haired Red Billy Bassett, the master, and his Maori wife, Kiri. Jim is soon busy tending to the various ailments of the settlers and whaling men, and, when word comes from the mainland that Kiri's brother, the chief's son, has been shot in a battle with a hostile tribe, Jim works along with the tribal *tohunga* (medicine man) to heal him. They learn that the local surgeon, Doctor Mac, is believed to be dead, lost in the hills. Jim and Jamie return by schooner to Sydney, and a host of adventures follow. They connect with Captain Steve, and Jamie gets ample opportunity to view convicts at hard labor and along with other travelers beats off bushrangers who attack their coach. Back at the Bay of Islands settlement of Kororareka, they have more skirmishes with ruffians, doctor more Maori, recover the *Diana*, and then go on to Port Nicholson (Wellington), which is still so primitive a settlement that they must sleep in the sand on the shore. Jim tends a Maori chief with chicken pox and vaccinates the Maori against a threatened smallpox epidemic. Doctor Mac appears, wearing a wooden leg, his own leg having been amputated after a fall in the mountains. He and Jim decide to go into practice together. Jamie chooses to stay in New Zealand for a while and plans to return to England to study medicine. The book's strong points are its plentiful action and its clear if limited sense of the rigors and tensions of the settlement in Sydney, the harsh life and desperate attitudes of the convicts, the whaling, the native part of New Zealand, and the current medical problems and methods. The scene in which Jim and the tohunga treat the Maori youth is especially good, with Jim displaying strong respect for the tohunga's methods and inquiring about his ways of healing. The characters are minimally developed, coincidence abounds, the dialogue is lame, and the style is often clichéd, but the entertainment value is high and Jamie is a sympathetic if unrealistically brave hero. N. Z. Govt. Short List.

SUSAN ANDERSON (*The Root Cellar**), the Morrissays' hired girl. Rose first sees her making the four-poster bed upstairs in the Henry house and thinks she's real. She later learns that Susan also materializes as the old woman, Mrs. Morrissay. Rose meets her as Susan, age twelve, when she goes into the root cellar. Kind, sensible, steady, accepting, Susan has a calming effect on Rose. Susan later marries Will* Morrissay and becomes mistress of the house in which she was a hired girl, the house that over a hundred years later the Henrys buy. Susan contrasts well with Rose.

SUTTON, EVE (LYN MARY BREAKELL) (1906–), born in Lancashire, England; New Zealand teacher and writer for middle-grade children. She was educated at Goldsmiths' College, University of London, and taught primary school in Lancashire until her marriage in 1931. She and her family emigrated to New Zealand in 1949, and she became a citizen in 1955. She received the Esther Glen Award of the New Zealand Library Association for her historical adventure novel of nineteenth-century emigrants from England to New Zealand, *Surgeon's Boy** (Mallinson, 1983). Among her other novels of adventure intended for able younger readers and slower older readers are *Green Gold* (Hamilton, 1976), *Tuppenny Brown* (Hamilton, 1977), *Kidnapped by Blackbirders* (Mallinson, 1984), and *Valley of Heavenly Gold* (Mallinson, 1987). For younger readers she wrote the illustrated storybook, *My Cat Likes to Hide in Boxes* (Hamilton, 1973; Parents', 1974).

SWAGMAN (*The Year of the Currawong**), elderly wanderer, descendant of the Irishman who was killed in a quarrel over the ownership of the mine. When the Swagman passes through Currawong with his dog, Smoke, he usually spends the night in the abandoned inn, the Silver Bell. There he happens to meet Alex*, who is spending the night there on a dare because the place is said to be haunted by the ghost of the murdered man. His claim to the mine proven legally as a result of the children's investigations, the Swagman settles in Currawong to realize his dream of raising chickens. He is an individualized character, distinctively and convincingly drawn.

SWEENEY MULLIGAN (*Longtime Passing**), proprietor of the sometime hostel Drover's Kip at Longtime* in the Blue Mountains of Australia. An old resident of the region, he meets the four Truelance brothers, Edwin*, Vance*, Sean*, and Merlin, when they come looking for land to claim. He is one of many minor characters in the novel who contribute to its rich tapestry and are one of its most charming features. They are also one of its faults, since they are poorly integrated into the action.

SWEETGRASS (Hudson*, Jan, Tree Frog, 1984; Philomel, 1989), historical novel of Indian life from 1837–1838 in south-central Alberta, Canada, more concerned with character than events and focusing on the life of women in the

Blackfeet confederacy. The story starts in the spring as Sweetgrass, 15, a Blackfeet Blood, is gathering strawberries with her best friend, Pretty* Girl. Sweetgrass, who tells the story, yearns to be accepted as a woman and, in particular, hopes that her father will betroth her to tall, capable Eagle Sun. She envies Pretty Girl, married at thirteen to the mature warrior, Five Killer. Her Grandmother* and her Almost-Mother* (stepmother), Bent-over-Woman, must often urge her to do her work and consider her spoiled by her father, Shabby Bull, who indulges her because she is his only daughter, and she is continually and childishly at odds with Otter, her just younger half-brother. Much of the book concerns her private thoughts and conversations with Pretty Girl or her girl cousin, Favourite* Child, about women's work, relatives, Eagle Sun, and the possibilities of marriage. Excitement ensues when the Assiniboin attack unexpectedly, the annual buffalo hunt occurs, and the Blackfeet bands come together to celebrate the Sun Dance. Sweetgrass is bitterly disappointed because her father does not betroth her at the Sun Dance and learns that he thinks her too immature for marriage. When news of smallpox arrives, the Sun Dance is cut short, and the bands disperse. The following winter turns very hard, and food runs low. Two days after Shabby Bull leaves to seek food, the disease strikes their tepee, and the baby and Little Brother die. When Bent-over-Woman and Otter get sick, Sweetgrass cares for them as best she can. Although she works terribly hard, is often discouraged and frightened, and wolves kill the horses, she persists in her duties and gathers roots, bark, and the like and even fishes, a source of food ordinarily despised by the Blackfoot. On the seventeenth day after her father's departure, a Chinook arises, and Shabby Bull returns. He reports that he, too, has had the illness and that most of their relatives and friends are dead, including Grandmother and Pretty Girl. Sweetgrass feels that she has not lived up to tribal expectations, especially since she gave her family fish for food and threw away so many illness-soiled buffalo robes. When she apologizes to her father, to her surprise he compliments her. She accepts his praise with the quiet dignity befitting a Blackfoot woman. The book ends with Sweetgrass and Favourite Child gathering strawberries the next spring, the horrible year of the smallpox not forgotten but thankfully in the past. Sweetgrass has proved that she is capable of doing women's work and confidently expects that this year her father will arrange her marriage to Eagle Sun. The plot moves unevenly and somewhat artlessly to the climax, the characters remain types, and the style is sometimes that of a primer. The strength of the novel lies in its detailed and convincing picture of the daily lives of Blackfoot women. Sweetgrass is likeable and grows up believably, and her friends are different enough from her and each other for a pleasing character contrast. Grandmother and Almost-Mother provide foils from their respective generations. The tension between Sweetgrass and Otter seems typical, and their reconciliation and new appreciation of each other resulting from the terrible time of the illness seem reasonable. Can. Bk. of Year Winner; Can. Council Winner; Can. Ebel Runner-Up.

SYLVIA COHEN (*Corner Store**), the schoolteacher Aunt* Leah brings as her candidate to be Papa's* new wife, the second Mrs. Devine. Sylvia is from the same Russian village as Aunt Leah, but she has been in Canada since she was a little girl and seems much more at ease with English and modern ways than most of the relatives. She is not beautiful, but nice looking with a forthright manner and, it is soon apparent, much greater tact and understanding of people than Papa. After they are married, she insists that the family use some of her own savings for an unprecedented vacation, a week at the beach of Lake Winnipeg. She also takes over the accounts at the store, rearranges the stock, writes polite collection letters (saving Becky* the hated task of trudging to neighborhood doors and asking for something on account), persuades Papa to be tactful to trying customers, and generally steers the operation toward greater profitability. With Becky she is very patient, helping the girl make the difficult transition to accepting her as a stepmother.

SYLVIE EDWARDS (*The Min-Min**), daughter of a fettler (worker on the Trans-Australian Railway). Sylvie is intensely loyal to her family. She is a caring, loving, maternal child, who resents not being given what she feels is proper recognition for her hard work in keeping the household going. She also rebels against her father's verbal and physical abuse. She is thrilled when Mrs. Tucker shows her how to make herself attractive. One reason that the magistrates release Sylvie is that she appears to be clean and well kept. Sylvie is a likeable, well-drawn, dynamic figure.

SYRED, CELIA (MARY) (1911–), born in Gloucestershire, England; Australian novelist for older children and teenagers. Trained at the Royal College of Art in London and at Cheltenham School of Art, she taught art in colleges and art schools from 1934 to 1955. She came to Australia on a visit and stayed, soon thereafter deciding to fulfill a long-held ambition to write for children. Her first novel, *Cocky's Castle** (Angus, 1966), a family story of how cousins try to save the homestead, is most notable for its convincing family relationships. It was highly commended for Australian Children's Book of the Year. Also commended for Book of the Year was *Hebe's Daughter** (Hodder, 1976), a lively, broad-canvas, eighteenth-century melodrama for teenagers of the vicissitudes of beautiful, red-haired Elizabeth Pollard, daughter of an actress. Her other publications include *Baker's Dozen* (Angus, 1969), *An Innkeeper* (Oxford, 1970), *A Printer* (Oxford, 1971), and *The Shop in Woolloomooloo* (Hodder, 1983). She married a farmer and lived in Bowral in the southern highlands of New South Wales, the setting of *Cocky's Castle*.

T

TABITHA PALMER (*The Haunting**), a brown, plump child, who always has something to say and who considers everybody's business hers. She is an aspiring writer and jots down in her notebook whatever she thinks might provide material for her projected masterpiece. Her bossiness and curiosity are a trial to the family, and her stepmother, Claire, gently tries to rein her in. She is bouncy and lively, and she sincerely cares about her family. She is the first one to discover that something special is going on with Barney, and she takes it upon herself to help him. She exemplifies the theme of acceptance.

TAJALLI (*The Curse of the Turtle**), leader of the Oona tribe of Aborigines in Cape York Peninsula, upon whom Jack* Brent looks down and patronizingly calls Charley. Tajalli is a strong leader, self-assured and decisive. He is angry when Jimmy Brent, Jack's son, violates tribal ways but has confidence that Jimmy is sympathetic and can be trusted. Tajalli gives his father, Tirkalla*, and his mother the *barata*, a secret poison used by the Aborigines for mercy killings. At the end, he helps Jimmy dig the well, and, after the Brents move, he looks forward to more friendly relations with them.

TAKE THE LONG PATH (De Hamel*, Joan, ill. Gareth Floyd, Lutterworth, 1978), novel that walks a thin line between realism and fantasy, set on the Otago Peninsula near Dunedin, on the South Island of New Zealand, dealing with Maori traditional beliefs as they affect a boy of the late twentieth century. David Regan, 11, keeps to himself his strong interest in the yellow-eyed penguins that nest between his father's small sheep holding and the beach. He also keeps from his father his friendship with his schoolmate, Hemi* Waka, since quick-tempered Bob* Regan has a strong antagonism toward the Maori and especially the Waka family, with whom he has had a land dispute. David's favorite penguin is Abel, a banded bird with a feckless mate, Mabel. Although David works as hard as he can with the Maori shearers, his father is dissatisfied with him, continually sneers at his small size, accuses him of daydreaming and shirking, and hints that it is time he learned some "home truths." David's mother, Joy*, acts much like Mabel, always flustered and dithering, trying to mediate between her blustering husband and her son, who retreats into silence. Early one morning David hears a penguin shrieking but goes back to sleep, only to be filled with remorse when he discovers that it was Mabel, distraught because Abel has died, injured by a shark. Next time he goes to check, David finds that her nest has been transported to a cave above its old site, and an old Maori man is watching over her and digging for something lost, a family thing, he says. Although Hemi doesn't seem to know about the old man, David sees him frequently and learns that his son, who left the area for Auckland, has died. Now he must himself handle the *Oha*, the family obligation to fulfill the wishes of a dying ancestor. The old man calls David Young Tama, meaning lad, and says that although he has fair skin and hair, he reminds him of his son. Because he avoids giving his name, David calls him Old* Tama. The old man tells him the story of Tarewai, a Maori hero. As a boy, his ancestor, Tama, rescued Tarewai, tended him in that very cave, and later accompanied him to retrieve his *patu*, a whalebone weapon, from his enemies at Harbour Cone, at the tip of the peninsula. The Oha is to find the hidden or lost patu. Living the story as it is told, David seems to experience the incident in which the original Tama, trying to save the patu, is chased over the cliff and falls, arms outstretched, onto the rocks below. Various clues and things that his mother says finally make David realize that Bob is his stepfather, and he suspects that his real father was Old Tama's son. Hemi, who is intensely interested in ghosts, tells David that if a Maori dies before passing on the Oha, he has one chance to return after he has taken "the long path" to the northern tip of New Zealand, where the spirits leap off into the sea, and he will come back as an ordinary looking person, though unable to eat or sleep. Remembering how Old Tama will never take the biscuits he offers, David wonders. He feels compelled to go to Harbour Cone and search a ledge high on the cliff. There he finds a partially buried whalebone patu, and with great difficulty he gets back to the top as heavy rains create landslides along the edge. He runs through the rain back to the cave, only to find it deserted except for Mabel's chick. As he cuddles the little penguin, a landslide blocks the mouth of the cave, leaving only a small opening. Mabel, unable to get to her chick but hearing it, starts shrieking, and David's mother, now calling him by his Maori name, Rawiri, comes to find him. Although many clues indicate that Old Tama is a ghost, a realistic explanation is possible for everything that happens. David's discovery that he is half Maori is predictable but interesting because it comes as a relief to him and seems to presage better relations with his stepfather, whom he begins to understand and whose expectations he no longer feels he has to meet. All the main characters are well developed, the sense of place is strong, and the Maori beliefs are presented with respect. A glossary of Maori words and a reference bibliography are included. The illustrations include three helpful maps. N. Z. Esther Glen.

TAL AND THE MAGIC BARRUGET (Wuorio*, Eva-Lis, ill. Bettina Ehrich, Nelson Foster, 1965; World, 1965), lighthearted fantasy set on the Mediterranean island of Ibiza, in the mid-twentieth century. Tal (Talfryn), 8, lives happily with his artist father and the old woman who cares for him and the house, Bruja* Vieja, an affectionate name that means "old witch." When his father leaves to find him a new mother, Tal is depressed, knowing he will be expected to pick up his clothes, bathe even when it is too cool to swim, and eat green vegetables, and he is not sure that he wants another person in their cozy arrangement. Bruja Vieja suggests that what they need is a Barruget, a sort of elf or brownie that does the work for its master. To catch a Barruget, she says, they need a black bottle. They go to the Hill-of-the-church-that-fell-into-the-sea, where there are relics from old Roman ruins, and in a cave, under layers of old seaweed, they find a black bottle that Bruja Vieja seems to remember will be there. The next step is to find a sweet-scented flower that lasts only a moment. Tal knows that such a vine grows by an old bridge where he and his father often wash their hair. He and the old woman go by moonlight through the sleeping village, cut a flowering piece of vine, stuff it into the jar, and pop a cork in the neck. The next morning Tal wakes to find Bruja Vieja washing clothes, and he quickly uncorks the black bottle to release the Barruget. A small, mostly green creature emerges, grows rapidly to nearly Tal's height, and loudly demands, "WORK OR FOOD WORK OR FOOD." Faster than Tal can think of jobs, the imp completes them and is back demanding more. To distract him Bruja Vieja cooks ten kilos, about twenty-five pounds, of rice. He wolfs down this enormous meal and starts munching on the chair legs before Tal makes up an effective incantation to get him back into the bottle. Before releasing him the next day, Tal talks to his friends, Jamie the fisherman and Creu the builder, both of whom have a lot of heavy work to be done. Tal demonstrates by having the Barruget clean his own boat, wash the sails, scrub the decks, and empty the bilge. From then on, the creature works all over the village, pulling a big sunken boat to shore, making bread for the baker, hauling materials for Creu, repairing the roads, painting houses—any job that Tal tells him to do. Because Creu, who is much respected in the village, accepts and trusts the strange helper, the other villagers do, too, and all contribute fish and other food to satisfy his enormous appetite. When Tal gets a telegram saying that his father is bringing home a new mother "for your approval," Tal finds that he is reconciled and, simultaneously, the Barruget stops shouting and starts talking to him. He says that his name was once Thomas, a spirit brought centuries before in a black bottle from a cold land. Tal gives him his freedom and goes to meet his father. The matter-of-fact acceptance of the voracious worker makes the story plausible, and clever touches, particularly in the relationship of Tal and the old woman, bring the story out of the ordinary run of fantasy for younger children. Fanfare.

TANGARA (Chauncy*, Nan, ill. Brian Wildsmith, Oxford, 1960; *The Secret Friends*, Watts, 1962), realistic novel of family life and friendship with fantasy and adventure story aspects, set on a Tasmanian sheep ranch deep in the bush in the contemporary period. Little Lexie Pavemont, about eight, also called Snowy because of her silvery gold hair, lives in the rugged outback at the foot of the Tiers range with Daddy, a widower, her brother, Kent, about eleven, who is mostly away at boarding school in Hobart, their housekeeper, Terkie, and Terkie's elderly aunt, who is also Lexie's tutor. A lively, imaginative child, Lexie particularly enjoys conversations about her great-great-aunt Rita Pavemont, another snowy-haired child whose girlhood picture hangs by the dining room table. Rita is said to have played with an Aborigine girl named Merrina (shell) and to have gone into a decline and died after the government rounded up the natives. Rife in the area, however, are rumors that natives are still living snug in the mountain fastnesses. When Daddy, Terkie, and the aunt go to Hobart on business, Kent takes Lexie to stay with friends, Andy and Beth Malley, an elderly couple who have a cabin under the Tiers. Kent explores with Lexie in a chasm called Blacks' Gully. While he is in the depths and she is alone above, she spies a little black girl playing on the rocks amid ferns. She keeps the sighting secret, and during the weeks that she stays with the Malleys she returns regularly to the place, accompanied by sluggish Uncle Podger, the Malleys' aged dog. There she plays with a woolly-haired, naked, spirited Aborigine girl, about her age, named Merrina. Merrina is curious about Lexie's clothes, especially zippers, and as she becomes more confident of herself with Weehta, as she calls Lexie, she tells her about Aborigine ways and beliefs (curiously, Merrina has no trouble with English), and even takes her to meet her family. Terror puts a sudden end to their pleasure together when one day the tribe is gathered in the gully. Two cruel, white faces appear on the cliff above, and the cracking of guns reverberates through the peaks. Merrina urges Lexie to flee and then disappears. A while later Andy and Mr. Pavemont find Lexie lying senseless on the cliff. She regains consciousness but remains dispirited and vague for days. After some weeks, she confides in Kent, then falls into a deep, deep sleep, awakening refreshed and happy for the first time since the incident. When Kent is seventeen and Lexie fourteen, Kent and his pal Cray camp on the Tiers near the gully. Cray is injured, and Kent goes for help and disappears. When search parties fail to locate him, Lexie senses Merrina calling her and goes to the gully by herself, where she finds Kent, injured but safe, he says, through Merrina's help. The two then observe Merrina calling her dead loved ones, as the Aborigines used to, by gazing into a small fire. After they all disappear into a mist, the brother and sister agree that they will never tell anyone what they know about Blacks' Gully. The fantasy and realistic stories are not well knit, and the reader is left to puzzle about what happened—did Lexie actually meet modern Aborigines or was she caught in a time warp—and ponder the meaning of it all. One carries away the impression, supported strongly by a few passages where the author gives history of the Aborigines, that the book has a didactic purpose—to raise consciousness about the way whites have treated this nearly extinct people. Lexie and Merrina have depth, and suspense is minimal until Kent and Cray disappear. The novel's chief power comes from its depiction of setting and life among the Aborigines and on the ranch. Descriptions of the physical environment are so clear that they evoke a very strong appreciation for the natural beauty of the rugged, isolated area. The scenes in which the two girls interact are lively with details. The title is an Aborigine word that means "let us set off again." Merrina says this when she is about to introduce Lexie to another experience or to try something new, exciting, or possibly even dangerous. Aust. Bk. of Year Winner.

TAO (*The Incredible Journey**), wheat-colored Siamese cat with chocolate-brown front paws and face and blue eyes. Aloof and independent, Tao is nevertheless devoted to the old bull terrier, Bodger*, and so follows when the young retriever leads them on their long journey across largely uninhabited country. Skilled at hunting, the cat supplies Bodger with enough food to keep him going and saves him by bluffing a mother bear when the dog has collapsed from exhaustion. Although Tao has two life-threatening experiences, being washed down the river and being stalked by a lynx, he arrives in excellent condition, untired and well fed despite weeks in the wilderness.

TARONGA (Kelleher*, Victor, Penguin, 1986; Hamilton, 1988), futuristic fantasy set in and near Sydney, Australia, two years after a nuclear holocaust has destroyed the northern hemisphere and the resulting chaos has broken down technology and civil order in the lands south of the equator. Ben, 14, sneaks away from Greg, a brutal young man with whom he has been living since his parents were ambushed and killed while trying to escape. Greg has been forcing Ben to use his gift of Calling, a mental communication with animals, to lure prey into range of his rifle, and Ben has become filled with guilt at this betrayal of the trust of the wild animals. Hoping that order may have returned to Sydney, he heads for the city. In the smoking ruins of a farm, he finds a small cattle dog whose scratching in a shed leads him to a well-stocked hidden cellar. He takes a bicycle and his backpack full of supplies, rehides the entrance, and sets off again accompanied by the dog. On the way he is several times set upon by survivors gone wild, each time escaping when the dog, at his Call, attacks and distracts his assailants. In the ruined city he is less fortunate. The dog is killed, and Ben is captured by a roaming gang headed by Chas, a young thug who wears a balaclava to hide his hideously disfigured face. Chas plans to assault and take over the old zoo, Taronga, where a well-armed group is living, feeding on the excess animals, the fences and gates rigged with alarm systems. Ben is to be pushed through a hole in the fence as "bait" to distract the tigers and other great cats, which are loosed at night to guard the grounds, until the gang can enter undetected. Inside Ben senses the great tiger, Raja, and his mate, Ranee, and wards them off by sending a mental danger signal, but he is saved only by a young Aborigine girl, Ellie, who soothingly calls the animals away and, amid the screams as invading gang members are killed by the huge cats, takes him to the former restaurant, now the main office of the Taronga group. There he meets Molly, the heartless leader, and her chief lieutenant, Steve, who are persuaded to let him live only because Ellie points out that he can control the tigers, releasing and caging them as she cages and releases the non-predatory animals, thereby eliminating the short but vulnerable period between. Soon Ben sees that, despite the beauty of Taronga, the group there is no better than Chas's gang, although he loves Ellie and the animals. Realizing that Chas's group or some other organized hoodlums will eventually break in and that Molly plans to kill all the animals rather than let anyone else have them, Ben and Ellie formulate a plan to set the two groups upon each other, meanwhile freeing all the animals to make their way into the now almost deserted mountains and wilderness. Many will be killed, but some will survive to make all of Australia a kind of nature preserve, a huge Taronga, an Aborigine word meaning "water views." The way that they accomplish this is a tense, grisly, fast-paced story, full of sudden twists and surprises. At the book's end, the two young people are heading for the burned-out farm and its hidden storage room, with the idea of going from there to the deserted dry regions to the west, where they may survive safe from people. Not all the details stand up to close scrutiny. How, for instance, are all the animals fed with no supplies coming into Taronga? There is no explanation for Ben's unusual gift of Calling. The most moving scenes have to do with the contest of wills between Ben, who must control and cage Raja, and the fiercely independent tiger who first hates Ben, then gradually comes to emphathize with the boy. Aust. Bk. of Year Com.

TAYLOR, CORA (LORRAINE) (1936–   ), born in Fort Qu'appelle, Saskatchewan, Canada; teacher and writer. Taylor was graduated and received her teaching certificate from the University of Alberta and taught at the Duffield School in Duffield, Alberta, before devoting her time fully to writing. Her first book, *Julie** (Western, 1985), is about a girl with psychic powers, both a blessing and a curse to her. It won the Canadian Library Association Book of the Year Award and the Canada Council Prize. Her second book, *The Doll** (Western, 1987), is another fantasy about a young girl who, through the intermediation of a doll, returns to the time of her great-great-grandmother's journey with her family to a homestead in Saskatchewan. It was the winner of the Ruth Schwartz Award. Both have been praised for evoking a sense of the prairie setting and the psychology of the young protagonists. Taylor has also written musical plays and has contributed articles and stories to various magazines.

TAYLOR, WILLIAM, New Zealand teacher, novelist, and writer of short stories, plays, and non-fiction. Two of his novels for young people have been included on the short list for the New Zealand Government Award, *Pack Up, Pick Up, and Off** (Price, 1981), a story about the life of a family hired to exterminate the rabbits that are pests to sheep ranchers, with mystery story aspects, and *Shooting Through** (Reed Methuen, 1986), about two runaways from a reform school who hide in an old sawmill ghost town and, with the help of a local couple, learn to face their problems. Taylor lives in the central North

Island town of Ohakune with his two sons. Among his other novels for young people is *My Summer of the Lions* (Reed Methuen, 1986). He has also published several novels for adults.

TEDDY TRUELANCE (*Longtime Passing*; Once there was a Swagman**), Edwina, the narrator of *Longtime Passing* and the youngest child of Edwin* and Letty* Truelance. Almost indistinguishable from her sisters, who are all adventurous and opinionated, she does seem to have her father's ear in a way that the others do not. Like him she grasps the significance of the Place* of the Stone Giants, and her musings at the end of the book about the passing of Longtime* are both didactic and sentimental. She seems to be an accurate reporter of family history and deeply loves the land and mountains. In *Swagman*, she is an imaginative schoolgirl of nine. She seems more real in the third person account of *Once there was a Swagman*.

TEMBO MURUMBI (*The Bushbabies**), African companion and protector of Jackie Rhodes on their hundred-mile, week-long journey through the bush in Kenya to return the pet bushbaby to its home area. A tribal warrior and a former soldier in the colonial army, he has been more recently headman for Game Warden Rhodes in Kenya's Rift Valley and a lifelong friend to the Rhodes children. Though used to taking orders from the whites and subservient to Jackie in her usual environment, he assumes leadership when they get into the jungle; yet he loses much of his confidence when he is temporarily without his ancestral war club. A mixture of wisdom and naiveté, he has an exaggerated respect for Jackie's ability to swim and to read maps, but he saves her repeatedly by his knowledge of the jungle from wild animals, fire, flood, and other dangers.

TENNANT, KYLIE (KATHLEEN TENNANT RODD) (1912–1988), born in Manly, New South Wales, Australia; editor and author best known for her novels for adults based on her experiences while living and traveling among the unemployed and disadvantaged during the Great Depression. Most acclaimed of these are her first book, *Tiburon* (Currawong, 1935), which received the S. H. Prior Memorial Prize for best Australian novel of 1935, and *The Battlers* (Macmillan, 1941), which won the Australian Literary Society's Gold Medal. At an early age, she acquired the name Kylie, which means boomerang, and all her books were published as Kylie Tennant. She left school at sixteen, and, after various jobs, she attended the University of Sydney for a short time. She traveled extensively in Australia, gathering materials for her books, once with her son Benison to the Torres Strait Islands, an area that subsequently provided the setting for *All the Proud Tribesmen** (Macmillan, 1959; St. Martin's, 1960). This story about the natives there was named Australian Children's Book of the Year and is her most highly regarded book for young readers. For children she also wrote *Long John Silver* (Associated, 1954), an adaptation of the film by Martin Rackin; *Trail Blazers of the Air* (Macmillan, 1966), in the Great Stories of Australia series of which she was general editor; and plays, including *John o' the Forest, and Other Plays* (Macmillan, 1950), in response to the request of her husband, L. C. Rodd, a headmaster, for dramatic material for his students. She wrote a popular history, *Australia: Her Story* (Macmillan, 1953), and several other novels and biographies for adults.

TERRY KENDALL (*The Year of the Currawong**), Maria Theresa, called so because Professor Kendall was writing a paper on Austria when she was born. She discovers Mister* Lee, setting the plot in motion, takes the lead in finding out who has fenced the mine property, and is secretary of the Currawong Mine Preservation Society. She likes to write, but realistically her work is not very good, though she does win a contest. She is an interesting, winning character, convincingly drawn.

TESS MEDFORD (*Mama's Going to Buy You a Mockingbird**), tall, gangly, cynical school friend of Jeremy Talbot. She feels that her mother abandoned her because she was illegitimate. Melly* Talbot, Jeremy's mother, tells her that she was in the hospital having Jeremy at the same time that Tess's mother was having Tess and that Tess was definitely wanted, both by her mother and by Grandpa Medford. Tess has a fine singing voice, and Jeremy helps her to feel comfortable about sharing her talent with the class and to win a part in the school choir. Tess is not wholly convincing as a character, and the friendship that develops between her and Jeremy lacks credibility, given their characters as presented and their ages.

TETACUS (*The Whale People**), Atlin's grandfather on his father's side. A wise and respected old man, once a great whaling chief in his own right among the Hotsath Indians, Tetacus teaches and advises Atlin, especially after the death of Atlin's father, Nit-gass, Tetacus's son, in domestic affairs and in relations with other tribes. When the tribe nearly starves after Nit-gass's death, Tetacus takes to the canoes again, even though he is old and weak. Like the other characters, he never rises above being the stock figure of the Indian adventure story genre.

THIELE, COLIN (1920–   ), born in the Eudunda Kapunda district of South Australia; educator, prolific playwright, poet, and novelist for both adults and children. He grew up in a German-speaking community of sheep and wheat raising just north of the Barossa Valley, a rural and small town area that forms the setting for a number of his novels for children, the largely humorous *The Sun on the Stubble** (Rigby, 1961; White Lion, 1974), *Uncle Gustav's Ghosts* (Rigby, 1974), *The Valley Between** (Rigby, 1981), and the more serious *The Shadow on the Hills* (Rigby, 1977; Harper, 1977). He attended Kapunda High School, an hour from his home by train, and Teachers' College in Adelaide. During World War II he served in the Royal Australian Air Force in northern

Australia and New Guinea. He returned to teach at Port Lincoln on the Eyre Peninsula. In the following years he wrote hundreds of programs for radio, including plays in prose and verse, features, documentaries, talks, school broadcasts, and children's serials, winning first prize for a radio play in the Commonwealth Jubilee Literary Competition and in the radio feature section for a documentary, *The Golden Tide*, the story of wheat in Australia. A number of his novels have rural settings other than the German community of his youth, among them *February Dragon** (Rigby, 1965; Angus, 1966; Harper, 1976), a novel about a bush fire, and *River Murray Mary** (Rigby, 1979), a story of family life in the fruit-growing region along the river. Others are more highly adventurous, like *Blue Fin** (Rigby, 1969; Harper, 1974; Collins, 1976), about a struggle for survival on a tuna boat wrecked by a water spout, and *Fire in the Stone** (Rigby, 1973; Harper, 1974; Penguin, 1981), a story of mystery and danger in the opal fields six hundred miles north of Adelaide. Some of his books are brief, essentially highly illustrated short stories, notably *Storm Boy** (Rigby, 1963) and *Magpie Island** (Rigby, 1974; Collins, 1975), both with birds, realistically portrayed, as prominent characters. Among his many honors, he won the Australian Book of the Year Award for *The Valley Between*, and all his other books listed here have been commended, highly commended, or specially mentioned for that award.

THE *THOMAS* (*Sea Menace**), old barque that founders off the east coast of Australia. In addition to fifteen passengers, she carries locked below decks some seventy convicts, who drown despite the last-minute effort of the mate to free them by opening hatches.

THREAT TO THE BARKERS (Phipson*, Joan, ill. Margaret Horder, Constable, 1963; Harcourt, 1965), family novel with mystery aspects, set in New South Wales, Australia, at the western edge of the central tablelands near the town of Bungaree, sequel to *The Family Conspiracy**, starting about a year later, sometime in the mid-twentieth century. Everyone in the Barker family is pleased when the stud or thoroughbred ewes, for which Jack, 21, has been working and saving, arrive, since they are all especially fond of Jack, who is more even-tempered and sensitive than their father, more interested in sheep raising, and more likely to make a success of their marginal ranch. Robbie, 10, takes it upon himself the job of riding out to the distant paddock, where they are placed because the grass is best there, to check on them since sheep thieves have been stealing stock in the area. The others offer to help. Edward, 14, and his friend, Garry, spend a rare summer afternoon together fishing for *yabbies*, or crayfish, and on their way back are given a ride by Bill Morrison, an older boy who is a hero to Garry, in his red MG, which he drives with reckless speed. Returning late that night from selecting a stud ram to complete his prize breeding stock, Jack, Edward, and sensible Lorna, 15, discover a place where a large sheep truck has backed up to a fence and a flock of sheep have been herded close and loaded. A little further up the road they pass the red MG half hidden at the road's edge, and the next day their neighbor is missing nearly three hundred sheep. Later Edward and Garry take shelter from a storm in a deserted house and discover Bill and his friend, Keith, and two other youths planning their operation of spotting likely flocks in isolated places for a big concern of sheep thieves. Edward and Garry manage to talk their way out by pretending that they think Bill and his friends are hunting for gold, but they are much shaken by the brutality shown to Edward's dog and the threats of accidents to their farm or families if they tell of the meeting. Other clues show that Bill has designs on the new sheep in the Back Willow pasture, and Keith shows up with the stock agent, having wangled the ideal job as his assistant. When he leaves, Edward's dog has disappeared. That night Edward sneaks out, rides to Bungaree, searching for his dog. He is trapped by Bill, then bargains his way out by agreeing to make sure that the sheep are in the Back Willow paddock on Thursday. When he finally returns home, dead tired, he confesses everything to Jack, who has been up all night hunting for him. Jack arranges with the police to trap the thieves. When the trap is sprung, one of the men gets away and heads up the gulch for the hills. Edward and Garry, bent low, cut across the hillside, intercept him, and manage to hold him, one clinging to his neck and the other to his legs, until the police catch up. Edward's dog is discovered in a shed, where she was shut by accident, has had water from an old tank, and has given birth to six puppies. Although the many family anecdotes are rather slow and labored, the story of the sheep theft arises naturally out of the ranching circumstances, and the solution is both believable and exciting. The entire family's devotion to Jack and rather condescending patience with their father is a telling bit of characterization. The view of girls reflected in Lorna's position as a spectator and Belinda's as a figure of fun dates the novel. Aust. Bk. of Year Com.

TIGER IN THE BUSH (Chauncy*, Nan, ill. Margaret Horder, Oxford, 1957; Watts, 1961), realistic novel of family life set in a secluded, rugged valley in the Tasmanian bush at an unspecified time but perhaps in the 1950s. The episodic story focuses mostly on naive, earnest Badge (Brian) Lorenny, 11, youngest child of hardworking, perceptive Dave* and sensible, capable Liddle-ma*, and younger brother of Lance, away at school in Hobart, and strong-willed, brash Iggy* (Isobel), about fifteen and also usually away at school. Years earlier, Dave happened on the hidden valley while prospecting for gold and settled there with the encouragement and help of his brother, Link, never registering his claim and both families maintaining silence about it all these years. The makeshift house grew to accommodate the family, and the Lorennys have had a satisfying if hardscrabble life, free and independent in their unspoiled wilderness. The few supplies they need are brought laboriously over The Wire, a kind of metal bridge Dave and Link built over the Gordon River. From the bridge, a path called the Zig-Zag leads "right off the map" to the Lorenny place. Events start in the spring when Iggy simply decides to come home. Most ensuing scenes are routinely domestic, but two assume importance later—Dave reads in the newspaper Iggy brings that scientists intend to search for the Tasmanian tiger, and Iggy and Lance, home on holiday, encounter a "hatter," who they learn is Harry*, an old fellow "gone bush." After Lance returns to school, Iggy and Badge set off for Harry's place with needed supplies. Harry takes a liking to Badge and in the evening ushers the boy to a hidden pool where they watch a Tasmanian tiger come out and drink. Near Christmas (summertime), Uncle Link turns up with Russ Lorenny, zoologist son of a brother who emigrated to the United States, and an American scientist called Doc. Badge accidentally drops information about the tiger. Torn by guilt and shame, Badge worries, then comes up with a scheme to save the beast and enlists Harry's and Iggy's help. Iggy takes the two scientists to Harry's place, where they photograph what they think is the tiger's footprint but is really only that of Harry's huge wombat, Zircon. The scientists leave Lorenny valley in elation, only later detecting their error. Badge is relieved that the tiger remains undiscovered. He feels better about himself and ranks higher in the esteem of his siblings. The Lorennys are richly and subtly drawn, and the warm, loving, and supportive family relationships are among the novel's most attractive features. The emphasis is on character and interpersonal ties rather than plot, and much interest comes from the detailed descriptions of the rugged area and of the family's difficult life, from humor of conversations, and from Badge's naiveté. The colloquial speech adds to the sense of place and to the credibility of the family. Sensory images abound, often appropriately homespun and presented in interesting diction. This is an engrossing book, with a serene charm that comes from its picture of a simple life with emphasis on the basic virtues of faith in self, hard work, education, family togetherness, and decency. The glossary of Tasmanian terms is an asset. Companion books are *Devil's Hill** and *The Roaring 40**. Aust. Bk. of Year Winner.

TIKTA'LIKTAK: AN ESKIMO LEGEND (Houston*, James, ill. James Houston, Longman, 1965; Harcourt, 1965), realistic novelette of an Eskimo youth's struggles to survive in the hostile environment of frozen tundra and ice-filled seas in the Far North at an unspecified time. Late in a very hard winter, Tikta'liktak, about eighteen, is searching for food for his starving family when the patch of ice on which he stands breaks away from shore and he is carried out to sea. Stifling his terror, he eats a bird he has killed and makes a small snowhouse for shelter against the bitter wind. The little floe carries him to a larger one, which he quickly tests with his harpoon and gratefully boards. A lean raven he adeptly snares is his only food, after four days he nears despair when he sights a familiar island on the horizon, granite-hilled, barren, deserted Sakkiak. Bravely summoning his strength, he bounds the ice pans until he reaches shore, where his struggles to survive continue. Once he is so near defeat that he makes a stone coffin, lies down in it, and waits for death, harpoon, knife, and bow at his side. He falls asleep and awakens with a strange but welcome sense of hope, and soon afterwards he has a vision of a seal that is so lifelike that he flings his harpoon toward the water and impales one. His circumstances now take a turn for the better, though some hazardous times follow, for example, when a great white bear attacks him. He fashions a rude boat of sealskins and one foggy morning crosses to the mainland in his unwieldy craft, narrowly escaping a bull walrus. After a two days' walk, he arrives at a cave known to his people as "The Place of the Beautiful Stones," whose floor is covered with smooth white pebbles and shining red stones, a few of which he takes along. More walking brings him to his family's camp, which he approaches cautiously so as not to frighten them, since he is sure that they think he's dead. Indeed, he arrives on the very day that they have decided to give away his clothes to neighbors. The story has something of the tone of legend, since the author does not exploit the boy's emotions, elaborate upon his predicaments, place the story in time, or develop the descriptive passages much. The kind of detail Houston employs— descriptions of Tikta'liktak himself, how he uses his tools, how he uses skins or snares creatures, and so on, are more typical of fiction, though less developed than usual for that genre. The cave scene seems extraneous, since it is not tied in with the rest of the plot, and the circumstances of his arrival home are too coincidental. The best part of the book concerns Tikta'liktak's efforts to survive, and, even as understated as the story is, considerable tension occurs there. Can. Bk. of Year Winner.

TINDALE, NORMAN B. (1900–), Australian anthropologist and writer of fiction and non-fiction for adults and children. Beginning in 1926, he was curator of anthropology at the South Australian Museum. He was a Carnegie fellow and traveled and studied in Europe and the United States. Fluent in Japanese, he served in the Royal Australian Air Force and with United States Military Intelligence during World War II. In 1956, he was awarded the prestigious Verco Medal by the Royal Society of South Australia for his contributions to science. He collaborated with Harold A. Lindsay* on several books for young readers that draw heavily on his knowledge of the early inhabitants of Australia and Tasmania. The first of these, *The First Walkabout* (Longmans, 1954), follows a group of Negritos on their migration from their home in the forests of Southeast Asia into Australia and Tasmania and was named Australian Children's Book of the Year. The second collaboration, *Rangatira* (Reed, 1959; Rigby, 1959; Watts, 1959), commended for Book of the Year, is a historical adventure about Polynesian migrations in the southwestern Pacific during the 1200s. Together they also wrote a book of non-fiction for children, *The Australian Aborigines* (Angus, 1963; Jacaranda, 1963). For adults Tindale wrote several non-fiction books.

TIRKALLA (*The Curse of the Turtle*), aged Aborigine of the Oona tribe, who has been imprisoned for many years by the whites. A staunch, proud, dignified traditionalist, he escapes and returns to Oonaderra because he does not want to die in prison. He drinks barata, a secret poison used by the Aborigines for mercy killings. After his death, a drought sets in that worsens the second year, leaving the region so arid that human as well as animal life is threatened and raising fears that the curse will wipe out everything in the area.

TOBY'S MILLIONS (Lurie*, Morris, ill. Arthur Horner, Kestrel, 1982), comic novel set one recent year just outside of London, England. One autumn Saturday morning, while digging in his vegetable garden what he hopes will be a "completely-out-of-sight hole" extending all the way to Australia, schoolboy Toby Willoughby, ten and three-quarters years old, uncovers three musty, worn, and rotting chests full of pirate treasure. After an assessor from the British Museum estimates that the treasure is worth twenty-three million pounds, the Willoughbys are besieged by reporters, photographers, television crews, autograph hunters, and assorted gawkers. Although Toby's mother, Flora, an inveterate organizer, joiner, and do-gooder, seems satisfied with being the center of attention in the village, especially with the history society, his father, Percival, a bookworm and executive for a merchant bank in London, yearns to acquire something spectacular, like a helicopter, or maybe a fleet of them. He and Toby's school friends are disappointed when Toby just plays with the treasure in his room and buys only a modest magnifying glass called a Genuine Bug Viewer. When Percival, a commuter, becomes depressed with having to take the "silly old 8:12" every morning, Toby tries in various ways to humor him. He buys him his very own railroad carriage (car), a shining red and brass Victorian one with Willoughby on it, but Percival soon misses his crossword puzzle chums in the regular car. Then Toby provides the family with their own marquee (tent) in the zoo so his father won't have to fight traffic to take the family to visit, but sightseers and media personnel pester them there, too. Toby hires a balloon to take them to Aunt Kate's at Christmas, but the balloon goes astray and dumps them in France. He hires the *Spanish Main*, a cutter like the ones pirates used to ply the Cornish coast, for his father's holidays, but Percival just sits around and reads while the captain tells Toby pirate tales and teaches him knots. When Flora and Toby decide to live on the ship permanently, Percival finally gets his wish. Toby buys a helicopter to carry him back and forth to London. Percival's boss, however, complains about the noise that the helicopter makes, and Percival suddenly realizes that everything Toby has bought or provided with the treasure has been to make him happy, while all he has done is complain or immerse himself in books. Ashamed, he resigns his job and flies back to the ship, arriving just in time to rescue his family from a sudden storm. The Willoughbys go home and settle down, Percival to a bank job in the next village to which he can ride his bike and Flora to write a book called *Toby's Millions*. One year after he discovered the treasure, Toby decides the Willougbys do not need the money to be happy, buries the three chests in the big hole, and plants an apple tree over them which in due time bears golden fruit. The obvious message of this moral fable is tempered by the humor, slapstick, and action. All the characters are distorted for effect, the most normal being agreeable, practical Toby. These include Judge Anderson, who falls asleep while Toby's father carries on in his attempts to convince the magistrate that the treasure belongs to him not Toby; Englebert Foss, official treasure expert; Baggy, the inept balloon driver; Cecil Benedictus, Toby's tutor; and Captain Nathaniel Spade, the ultimate salt. The pace is quick, the author's voice is intimate, almost gossipy in tone, the satire and social comment are genial but astute, and the dialogue is extensive and convincing. Aust. Bk. of Year Com.

TOM WALSH (*False Face**), half-orphaned classmate of Laney McIntyre. After his Iroquois father was killed by a drunken driver, Tom's white mother moved to London, Ontario. Tom hates the place and scorns his mother because she is white. She, however, yearns for his affection. Their situation is similar to that of Laney and her mother, except in reverse. When Tom returns to the reserve for advice about the big false face mask and is himself scorned as white for living in London, Tom realizes that his judgments about people have been based on appearances. He taxes Alicia McIntyre, Laney's mother, with prejudice when she is about to use the mask to destroy Ian McIntyre, her ex-husband, and Laney. Tom is scorned by his classmates because he is Indian, and Laney is scorned by Rosemary, her sister, because she associates with Tom. Tom is presented as an unusually gifted artist, whom a famous artist invites to exhibit in a renowned gallery, a situation less than convincing. Tom is a stock figure but one that works in the story as a foil for Laney.

TOPO (*Last Chance Summer**), tough, angry thirteen-year-old boy who resents the new boy, Marl Silversides, at the Jenner farm and causes much of the trouble for Marl. Topo is hurt and angry by being left out when five of the boys steal the bus and when Vilda*, the cook, says that it would be better if he had never been born. When she tries to make amends with a plate of cookies, he knocks it out of her hands and slams the door. Later he overhears her talking to one of her own children over the phone, realizes that she is in pain herself, and lets her apologize to him. He is a foil to Goat*: where Goat is a loner, sad and weary, deliberately shut off from friendship, Topo is emotionally raw, ready to flare up and explode at the least slight or hurt. His relief that he has not killed Marl and the younger boy's protest to Carleton that Topo should not be sent to the reform school begin to soften his attitude, and there is a suggestion of hope that he will gradually fit in at the farm.

TO THE WILD SKY (Southall*, Ivan, ill. Jennifer Tuckwell, Angus, 1967; St. Martin's, 1967), adventure novel of a plane trip in the 1960s from a town on the edge of Lake Ooleroo in New South Wales, Australia, to somewhere on a tropical sea coast, probably Molineaux Island in the Gulf of Carpentaria, detailing how a group of youngsters meet disaster in the air and after they crash. In the *Egret* Jim Butler, bush pilot, picks up Gerald* Hennessy and five of his school friends to take them to Gerald's home at Coonabibba, a huge sheep station west of the River Darling for his fourteenth birthday party. None of his guests has Gerald's money or social pretentions. There is no friendship between attractive Carol* Bancroft and Jan* Martin, who really doesn't want to go to the house party and knows that she has been asked because her twin, Bruce*, is Gerald's good friend. Colin* Kerr, the most intelligent and intellectual of the group, is saddled with his rambunctious younger brother, Mark*, for whom he feels responsible. Jim is preoccupied with a strong wind that is pushing him northward and an approaching sand- and rainstorm, and he climbs to try to fly above the weather. Then, with no warning, he has a heart attack and dies. Gerald, who has flown a few times with his father or Jim at his shoulder, is momentarily paralyzed. Jan helps him drag the dead body away, get into the seat behind the controls, and pull the plane out of its dive. With his limited experience, he doesn't understand all the instruments and is unaware that Jim was veering south to compensate for the wind. For the next six hours he flies the *Egret*, at first hoping to find Coonabibba or at least another homestead where he can try to put down, though he has never landed a plane. Then, as the storm strikes he tries to maintain a northerly course to avoid mountains until he can see again. He climbs above the clouds and keeps flying desperately as darkness reaches them. By moonlight, he spots a break in the clouds and drops down to discover that they are over water. Just as the fuel runs out, he sees a shoreline and puts the plane down, miraculously avoiding boulders, a few feet from land. Only Bruce, who has a badly sprained ankle, is hurt, but Gerald is so emotionally exhausted that he can't move. Colin strips to his underwear, attaches the rope that Jan finds to a strut, and swims through the chin-deep water to wrap the other end around a boulder. With the rope to guide and steady them, he and Jan get the others to shore, and they all fall asleep exhausted. They wake to find the *Egret* broken up and the beach surrounded by tropical vegetation. They bicker and waste effort throughout the day. For a short time they seem to reach agreement as they bury Jim's body, which has washed ashore. Carol discovers a sea wall and a long-abandoned settlement with the date 1874 carved over a door, and Jan, who is good at history, thinks that it must be the settlement of a religious sect that settled on the waterless Molineaux Island in the Gulf of Carpenteria in that year and four years later were all dead of some mysterious illness. Soon they are arguing and splitting up, Gerald insisting that they stay at the scene of the crash and Bruce insisting on making a raft and trying to reach the mainland. As the book ends, the older boys have followed a flock of ducks flying inland heading, they hope, for water, while Jan, angrily twirling a stick as she has on and off all day in an effort to make a fire, gets a whisp of smoke and, with Mark's help, teases it into a flame. The pattern of a group of youngsters on their own facing disaster, which Southall has used frequently, works fairly well in this novel, but there are some weaknesses. Although the open ending offers hope, the author has weighted the odds against them by drawing the personalities as unable to cooperate, with no effective leader. The flight itself is gripping in its intensity, where the frantic tone is appropriate. The same tone is less effective before the takeoff and during the day on the beach. It seems unrealistic that, with five of the six at least thirteen years old and all of them thirsty, they would not realize that finding water should be their first priority and improbable that they would waste their time and energy on other efforts. Aust. Bk. of Year Winner.

TRAIN FOR TIGER LILY (Riley*, Louise, ill. Christine Price, Macmillan, 1954; Viking, 1954), fantasy set in Canada in the mid-twentieth century. Five children are the only passengers of the sleeping car attended by the porter, Gus (Augustus P. Wallingford), who is also a Master of Magic Second Class. Duncan is mostly preoccupied with his fine white calf, Prince Rupert, which has just won a blue ribbon at the fair from which they are all evidently returning, and his intelligent collie, McRoberts, who guards the calf in its baggage car. His sister, Cathy, is also a lover of animals. Her friend, Victoria, is a maternal type, devoted to caring for her younger brother, Benjie, and somewhat subservient to her older brother, Mark, who is a practical realist. After a night on the sleeping car, they wake to find themselves in Tiger Lily, a signpost in an expanse of green, rolling hills. The engine is no longer with them, but fortunately the dining car is. It soon becomes apparent that Gus has transported them to this place by magic as an answer to Victoria's wish that they "could stay on this train for days and days." Gus has the boys paint an enormous circle with a silvery fluid, within which Gus's magic will work and they will be safe. If anyone crosses the edge of the circle, a bell in the car will ring loudly. Cathy's wish is for a wild colt, which happens by with its mother. Benjie's is to turn into a duck and learn to fly, a goal he achieves briefly. An old cowboy named Seven U O'Leary wanders by on his ancient horse, Lightnin'. He tells the sad story of how a magic belt, which made both him and Lightnin' young again, has been stolen from him by an old woman who runs a store not far away. Since then he has been living in a shack within the circle with Lightnin' and a white pig he calls Queenie. All the children decide to go to the store to investigate and are surprised to see not an old woman but a young one. Cathy realizes that she must be wearing the magic belt, but before they can figure out a way to act on this suspicion, the woman has stolen Prince Rupert. With the help of McRoberts and Gus, they jockey her into the circle where Gus's magic is strong, force her to give up the belt, and punish her by having her turned temporarily into a gopher, which McRoberts chases. In the morning they discover that Seven U is old again. His belt is missing, and so is Queenie. When they get to the store again, they find it being run by a round, fat man in a white apron named Smiley McQueen, who admits to having taken the belt to bargain with the old woman, a witch who turned him into a pig. He has captured her and returns the belt to Seven U, who sets off on Lightnin', both young again. After the children are asleep that night, the car is again attached to the train and rushes off across the prairie. The story is pleasant but fanciful, without the control of a fantasy pattern. Although each person is shown to exhibit a specific quality (Mark is skeptical, for instance;

Gus talks in pretentious language), the characterization is shallow. Can. Bk. of Year Winner.

THE TREASURE BOX (Sinha*, Sarojini, ill. Subir Roy, CBT, India, 1982), historical novel set mostly in Delhi, India, in 1857, concerning the Sepoy Rebellion against the East India Company. Govind Prasad, 14, works with his physician father, learning to grow herbs, prepare medicines, and treat illnesses. When it is time for his sister, Champa, 13, who has been married for several years (as has Govind), to go live at her husband's home in Meerut, she weeps so heartbrokenly that her young husband asks Govind to come along for a visit, thinking that his presence will comfort the girl. There Govind learns that the sepoys, or soldiers, hate the English who control them, especially because they must bite open cartridges greased with animal fat forbidden by their religious dietary laws. When the sepoys storm the jail, free comrades who have refused the order, then rampage through Meerut, Govind slips out to watch the excitement and meets Abdul Aziz Khan, a young sepoy whom he knows, who tells him that they are headed now for Delhi to drive out the foreigners. The boy takes the horse of a slain soldier and follows them to the Red Fort. Abdul is wounded in an attempt to capture and powder magazine, and Govind treats his injuries and gets him to the house of his elderly father. At his own home, Govind finds that his father has left for Kanpur, where he will join the patriots. His wife takes the children to the home of her brother in Bulundshahr, leaving Govind, who is ill with the measles, in the care of the servant boy, Bhola, with instructions to join her as soon as he is able to travel. Govind, however, is determined to stay in Delhi, where he and Bhola have various adventures, including a daring rescue of Abdul who has been captured as a spy. They get information that a siege train is on its way and urge an immediate attack on the British camp while it is low on men and munitions. The various leaders of the rebellion, however, bicker among themselves and lose this and other opportunities. Life becomes much more difficult in the city and supplies become scarce. The exits are closely guarded and all loyalists are arrested and shot. One night a freedom fighter named Chintamani, a friend of their father, comes to the house, a hunted man. They hide him until plague infects the city. Since the British, in an effort to control the disease, have ordered the people to leave the city, the boys contrive to dress Chintamani and Govind's brother, who has joined them, as women and to persuade an old woman to use her ancient horse and *tonga*, draped as if it is carrying women in purdah. By suggesting that one of the women is ill, they keep the soldiers at the gate from investigating too closely and make their way to a village where their mother is staying. After they return to ravaged Delhi, Govind persuades an elderly physician who was his father's teacher to teach him, too. A man named Kesar Dev comes with a letter from Govind's father, saying that before he left he hid the money he had saved in the little "treasure box." Govind knows this means a hollow high in the *neem* tree in the courtyard. Kesar Dev also brings news that the father has been killed fighting the British.

Now head of the family, Govind tells no one about the money hidden in the tree, but Kesar Dev continues to stay and learns about the hiding hole from the youngest child. A few mornings later he is gone. Govind climbs the tree and is horrified to find the treasure box empty. He is terribly downcast until Bhola shows him a bag he took from the tree and hid, substituting a bag of small copper coins, which Kesar Dev stole in the night, thinking he had the family treasure. Although the rebellion has failed and his father is dead, Govind is able to repair the family home, bring his wife to live with them, and practice as a physician, still hoping for the eventual freedom of India from foreigners. While a great deal happens, much of it of historical or ethnological interest, the story seems slow because most is told rather than shown and the characterization is weak. Govind is not developed beyond being an adventure-loving boy, and the other characters are flat, often little more than names. The style is aimed at middle-grade children but, unless one is already familiar with the history, it is easy to get lost in the many names and incidents. CBT of India, Third Prize.

TROOPER O'GRADY (*Midnite**), scapegrace policeman who captures Captain Midnite several times through trickery. On their first meeting, he picks Midnite's pocket of the watch and purse that Midnite has just bushranged from portly Judge Pepper. O'Grady later swears to capture Midnite, or "my name is not O'Grady." The governor, who has hired him to capture Midnite, is unaware that O'Grady's real name is Murphy. O'Grady insists that he is Midnite's best friend, and the gullible Midnite believes him, even after he hijacks Midnite's sixteen million pounds. O'Grady acts as Midnite's best man at his wedding to Laura Wellborn, where he pilfers the ring. The character of O'Grady plays cleverly on the Sheriff of Nottingham type of villain.

TROUBLE AT KOLONGIJAN (Dutta*, Arup Kumar, ill. Gita Verma, CBT, India, 1982), realistic novel of mystery and adventure set in the village of Kolongijan in contemporary India. One dark, stormy night during the monsoon season, Moina, 13, is emptying his fish traps on the river that runs through the village when he surprises several men engaged in suspicious business. The village schoolteacher, Debeshwar, the only educated man in the area, summons the elders to a meeting and consults the officer in charge at the nearest police outpost. They conclude that Tularam, the village moneylender who has just been released from prison after a term for theft and extortion, is behind the activity. Debeshwar breaks into Tularam's house one night in search of evidence and discovers that Tularam belongs to a ring headed by the notorious Barua. Debeshwar overhears the criminals plot to lure the villagers away from the embankment while Barua's men plant explosives to demolish the embankment and flood the village. The police set a trap, and Barua almost gets away. He is chased and tripped up by Moina and his pal, Ponakan, and held fast by Cheekah, Moina's dog, until the police catch up. It is learned that Tularam had engaged Barua and his cutthroats to destroy the embankment in order to get revenge on the villagers. Barua agreed to do the job, expecting to acquire the contract to reconstruct the embankment that he himself had destroyed. Although the incidents are typical of the genre and the characters are flat types easily identified as good or bad and described in clichés, the plot grips the reader quickly and holds the attention throughout. Events move fast, and there are no dull moments. The problem of saving the embankment derives naturally from the setting, and Tularam's villainy is equally credible given the large illiterate population current in India. That Debeshwar should be the only literate member of the community and as such be a leader and organizer is also believable. The boys are Johnnies-on-the-spot too frequently, but that and their vital contribution to the unmasking and capture of the criminals are also stock for the juvenile mystery-adventure. The style employs turns of phrase peculiar to India and Indian words that add interest. CBT of India, Second Prize.

TROY PALMER (*The Haunting**), a dark, bony, silent child, good in school and fanatically neat and well organized. Unknown to the family (but not unexpected to the reader), she has magical powers inherited through her dead mother from her Great-Grandmother* Scholar, talents that she tries to use to good ends. For example, she has been conjuring up playmates for Barney, but the rest of the family thinks that they are figments of his imagination. Though she proves to be a witch, the family accepts her and continues to love her, exemplifying one of the novel's themes. She becomes friends with Great-Uncle Cole, a magician.

THE TRUE STORY OF LILLI STUBECK (Aldridge*, James, Hyland, 1984), realistic novel of family and community life set in the country town of St. Helen on the Murray River in Victoria, Australia, during the Depression of the 1930s. The narrator, Kit* Quayle, son of the town lawyer, relates events that begin when he and Lilli are seven and she and her ne'er-do-well, light-fingered family of parents and seven older children, soon to increase by a son, Jackie*, squat in the deserted house called The Point down by the river. Dark-haired, cat-eyed, gypsy-like, abused (her mother disciplines her by ordering an older sister to bite her legs), Lilli soon establishes herself as bright, independent, expert at scavenging and thieving, a staunch antagonist and equally sturdy proponent. Forced into school, she hisses defiantly at classmates and resists instruction. Not amoral but with her own morality, she knifes the town bully for belittling her. Mr. Quayle defends her, and Kit and Lilli form a friendship of sorts. Kit is even invited to dinner at her home, an experience he can barely tolerate. Lilli attracts the attention of Miss* Dalgleish, a wealthy member of the town gentry in her sixties, who hires Lilli to run errands. When the Stubecks leave town, she buys the girl, now eleven, from them for money and no strings attached. Miss Dalgleish intends to be Lilli's Pygmalion in order to have a companion in her old age, and for the next six years the two wage a quiet battle for supremacy. Each yields in certain respects, Lilli on remaining in school and learning proper speech and social graces, and Miss Dalgleish on allowing Lilli to wear knickers instead of bloomers and to come and go over the wooden wall that surrounds the estate. Lilli becomes a fine student, mostly because of Miss Dalgleish's tutelage and her fine library, and an attractive, well-mannered girl, sexually attractive but uninterested in men. When Lilli is seventeen and in her last year of school, the possibility of a struggle between the two women over whether or not Lilli will go to the university is averted when Mrs.* Stubeck, dying, moves back to The Point, with Jackie, now ten, and demands Lilli's services. Lilli's new job barely gets them by, and Lilli encourages Jackie to pilfer. She accepts help when it is given as though it is her due. Unable to get Lilli back, Miss Dalgleish buys The Point and fixes the place up with electricity, plumbing, and furniture. When Miss Dalgleish's housekeeper leaves, Lilli takes her job because it pays more money. Ironically, she is caring for two dying women because Miss Dalgleish, unknown to Lilli, also suffers from a terminal illness. Under the responsibility Lilli blooms, and after Mrs. Stubeck dies, the girl remains at The Point but continues her housekeeping duties for Miss Dalgleish. When Miss Dalgleish descends into her final illness, Lilli returns to the Dalgleish house with Jackie, and it seems that Miss Dalgleish has won. At her death she leaves the house and a generous fund for Lilli with the proviso that Lilli live permanently in her house. A week after the will is read, Lilli disappears, with Jackie and Abraham Devlin*, an eccentric reporter for the local newspaper. Other townspeople think it is a "tragedy" that she cast aside so much, especially "considering where she came from," but Kit thinks that the match is perfect and sees what happened as a "reversion to something indestructible in Lilli that had kept her on her feet" all her life. Although Kit's narrative seems objective and honest and he tells it with just enough suspense to hold the reader's interest, details for which he gets from Lilli, Dorothy* Malone, Lilli's best friend, and Lilli's own diary, he is not completely convincing. His friendship with Lilli lacks the solid foundation that one would expect of a person to whom so many intimate details are disclosed. The novel, which might also be classed as a girl's growing-up story, is rich in characterizations, especially of the two indomitable women, and succeeds in spite of a tendency toward unnecessary eccentricity in minor figures and toward a too studied approach. It is also notable for its vividly detailed tapestry of life in the claustrophobic community where class structure is rigid and important, and tradition dies hard. Aust. Bk. of Year Winner.

THE TRUE STORY OF SPIT MACPHEE (Aldridge*, James, Viking, 1986), realistic novel set in the country town of St. Helen in Victoria, Australia, in the 1930s. Orphan Spit* (Angus) MacPhee, 11, lives with his reclusive grandfather, Fyfe*, by the Murray River in a ramshackle house made from an abandoned boat boiler. Since Spit arrived six years ago, townspeople have worried about his future with the half-mad old clock and watch repairer, especially Betty Arbuckle, a zealous evangelical who deplores Spit's running barefooted and half-clad and growing up like an "African heathen." When Fyfe has a fit and burns down the house and then dies in the hospital, the local policeman places Spit with Betty, whose efforts to reform the boy meet immediate opposition. He promptly runs away to Pental Island, helped with food and supplies by his only friend, Sadie* Tree, daughter of the Catholic family that lives up the river from the MacPhees. Local men contrive to catch him and turn him over to warm and loving Grace, Sadie's mother. Ordinarily unassuming, she unexpectedly intervenes out of pity and genuine liking for the forlorn child. While Spit remains the story's center, the point of view shifts to Grace, who decides to adopt Spit and starts proceedings, against the wishes of her husband, Jack. Betty files a counter-suit, claiming that Spit, Presbyterian by birth, must be raised by Protestants in accordance with a 1928 law guaranteeing the birth religion. The Trees' attorney, Mr.* Quayle, cleverly requests that the Trees be named foster parents. Since Judge Laker is impressed by the Trees and by Spit's preference for them, he grants the petition. After a slow start the plot gradually grows in intensity, and the custody hearing grips both the reader's intellect and emotions. The reader's sympathies are solidly on the side of the Trees, and the 1928 law (which is historical) sets into strong relief the problem of religious prejudice that produced it and that puts religion above the emotional and physical well-being of a child. Most of the characters are types: Frank Arbuckle, the henpecked husband, and Ben Arbuckle, the cowed son, both obvious foils to their Tree counterparts; the sparring, posturing lawyers; and the local policeman determined to do his duty, among others. Betty Arbuckle is an obvious antithesis to Grace, unsympathetically overdrawn for the plot, and the story might have been stronger if she were not so fanatic and stubborn. The Trees are realistically well rounded and dynamic, and Spit stands out as an Australian Huck Finn, determined to run his own life, occasionally wrongheaded but never bad. The author evokes the small town ambience with remarkable clarity, from the naturalistic life by the river to the distinctions between social and religious groups within the town itself. The style employs the detailed, humanistic approach one associates with feature story writing, the vantage point of the omniscient narrator looking back on and assessing events. Guardian Winner.

TRUSS, JAN (1925–   ), born in Stoke-on-Trent, England; teacher and writer. Having won scholarships to grammar school and the university, she received her teaching certificate from Goldsmiths' College, London, and taught for some years in Liverpool and in the British reform school system. In 1957 she emigrated to Canada, where she received her B.Ed. degree from the University of Alberta and did graduate study at the University of Calgary. She has been a teacher and administrator in schools in southern Alberta, an art consultant in the Alberta school system, and a lecturer in drama, creative writing, art, and education at the University of Calgary. In 1974 she was the first winner of the Alberta Find a New Novelist Contest for *Bird at the Window* (Macmillan, 1974), a story of a teenage pregnancy. *A Very Small Rebellion* (LeBel, 1977), a novel based on the struggle of Louis Riel and his métis followers against the federal government, is an outgrowth of a play by the same name first produced in 1974. Her best-known novel, *Jasmin**, won the Ruth Schwartz Award and was named to the *New York Times* Spring List of Recommended Books for Young Readers. It is a survival story of an artistically talented girl who runs away from overwhelming personal and family problems to live in the woods. *Summer Goes Riding* (Douglas, 1987), a horse story, has been praised for giving psychological and sociological depth to the conventional pattern. Among later titles are *Peter's Moccasins* (Reidmore, 1987), a picture book, and *Red* (Douglas, 1988). Truss has also written plays, an opera score, and a book of description and travel about the Canadian Rocky Mountains.

TURI: THE STORY OF A LITTLE BOY (Powell*, Lesley Cameron, ill. Pius Blank, Angus, 1963; Paul's, 1964), episodic realistic novelette set in New Zealand in the mid–1900s. The linear plot follows the first five years in the life of Turi, a little Maori boy. When he is nine months old, his mother gives him to Granny (her grandmother) ''to make her happy in her old age.'' His sister carries him in a backpack across the river to Granny's tiny house, where he is cared for by Granny and his older brother, Heke, who works for Granny and also lives with her. Turi's life with Granny is happy, because he is cherished and well cared for, and most of the story tells of his simple childhood adventures about the house and in the neighborhood. Once he throws a stick at their black hen, and when she falls down, he fears that he has killed her. He rolls downhill while romping with Ahu the dog and tears the new pants a neighbor has just sewed for him. He investigates the stream near their house, and on a trip with Granny to the sea to gather seafood he is frightened by an octopus. At home again, he cuts his foot severely on a shell and suffers a fever. Granny heals the wound with leaves in the traditional Maori way, evoking admiration from the local pakeha (white) nurse. Everyone celebrates when Heke marries kindhearted Rangi in festivities that combine both traditional Maori and Christian aspects. The book concludes with Granny's departure for her brother's house by the sea. She knows that she will die soon and wants to be with her own people and by the sea that she loves so much. Though the prospect of her death saddens him, Turi knows that he must accept the situation, and time and school activities will help to ease the loss. The characters are developed only minimally, and the emphasis appears to be on showing how some Maori have maintained pride in their heritage and knowledge of their traditions while also fitting into the dominant culture. Large clear photographs on almost every page and a glossary strengthen the impression that the book's main intent is sociological. The book's strength lies in its clear depiction of everyday life from the child's point of view. The style uses easy

language and undemanding sentence structure but never reads like a primer.
N. Z. Esther Glen.

TWO AGAINST THE NORTH. See *LOST IN THE BARRENS.*

TYCHO POTTER (*The Catalogue of the Universe**), youth who discovered
at a very young age that people think him ugly. He is short, unathletic, and
brilliant and is a well of information on almost every topic, though he never
flaunts his knowledge. He has loved Angela May for years with a deep, steady,
supportive love. Unusually sensible for a teenager, he believes in letting things
take their course, just as the universe follows its course. Angela affectionately
calls him ''Big Science.'' He is a rounded, attractively drawn character.

U

UNCLE ARION SWALES (*What's the Matter, Girl?**), Anna Swales's favorite uncle, who returns from World War II with his mind gone. He is presented as a fun-loving idealist who indulged Anna, calling her his "fairy princess," and was a little late and naive in associating with girls his age. After he loses his close friend in the war, Arion suffers from severe emotional problems, receives shock therapy, loses his mind altogether, and is brought home to Gran*, his mother, an empty shell of a man. His numerous and varied relatives seem to know about his condition before he arrives but are not able to really comprehend it, and, with terrible irony, they have gathered for a big dinner-celebration in his honor. At the end, he utters a few words that may mean that he recognizes Anna. Arion dominates the book, although he appears only at the end.

UNCLE LUKE (*Bush Holiday**), strange old prospector who lives at Tangari ranch, comes and goes as he pleases, and is a kind of mascot there. His speech is grandiloquent, and his grasp of reality seems weak. He is always in scrapes; for example, Jock Macleod's prize bull, Monarch, falls to his death in a shaft Uncle Luke has dug but not fenced, and he digs for gold in the main street of a nearby town. After the bull dies, Uncle Luke disappears, then returns to Tangari, conveniently shrugging off the incident. He is a likeable if typical eccentric, the male counterpart of Old* Marjorie.

UNDERGROUND TO CANADA (Smucker*, Barbara, ill. Tom McNeely, Clarke, 1977; *Runaway to Freedom*, ill. Charles Lilly, Harper, 1978), historical adventure novel of the Underground Railway focusing on the contribution of the Mennonites in helping slaves to freedom in Canada. The story is set not long after the passage of the Fugitive Slave Act of 1850 in various parts of the United States South and, at the very end, in Ontario. After the overused soil on Massa Hensen's Virginia plantation gives out and he falls ill, he sells his slaves to plantation owners in the Deep South. Julilly (June Lilly), 12, from whose vantage point events are seen, her fellow field hands Lester*, a strong mulatto, Ben, and Adam, and three small children are purchased by a cruel, fat overseer named Sims, and transported over many grueling miles by wagon to Massa Riley's plantation in Mississippi. Before she leaves, her mother, Mammy Sally, tells her to follow the North Star to freedom in Canada, pray, and retain her pride in self and family, words that give her hope over the difficult coming months. The Riley slaves are overworked, underfed, ill clothed, and whipped for the slightest infraction. Julilly makes friends with Liza*, a hunchback her age. When a Canadian abolitionist, Alexander Ross, visits the plantation, pretending to be an ornithologist, he instructs them in escape and survival techniques, gives them directions, and teaches them the password, "Friends with a friend." Lester, Adam, and the two girls disguised as boys run away on a Saturday night. By compass by day and the North Star by night, they follow the Mississippi River north to Tennessee, where they are met by an agent of Ross and transported by wagon to a deserted barn. Soon after, the men are captured, but the girls get away and head for Knoxville. Almost done in by the rigors of the journey and lack of food, they are helped by a German-speaking Mennonite community at Felsheim, Tennessee, continue overland to Covington, Kentucky, where a freed-man named Jeb Brown runs a station on the Underground Railway. He transports them over the Ohio River under the very noses of slave catchers to Cincinnati. Abolitionist Levi Coffin puts them on a train as "dry goods" to Cleveland and the schooner, *Mayflower*, bound for Ontario. At St. Catharines, Ontario, they join Lester and Mammy Sally, who have also managed to escape, but Adam has died of an infection caused by chains. No "fairy tale" ending, the conclusion hints that life in Canada though free may be difficult. Events are based on actual happenings, and Ross and Coffin really lived. The reader gains a limited sense of the slaves' hard lives on the plantation and of the difficulties of reaching Canada. The book's time frame is vague, and the fugitives' arrival seems assured from the outset. Incidents follow rapidly upon one another, and since so much happens suspense is high. Incidents are underdeveloped, however, and sometimes unlikely. For example, the bloodhounds detect Adam and Lester but not the girls. Sims is the stereotypical villainous overseer, and Julilly seems a paragon of strength both physical and spiritual. The style employs much nature imagery. The reader learns about the contribution of the Mennonites, but the story is most notable for its adventure. Can. Bk. of Year Runner-Up.

UNOMA (Meniru*, Teresa, ill. Gay Galsworthy, Evans, 1976), realistic novel of a girl growing up in a Nigerian village and getting an education, despite tradition. When Ikemefuna, treasurer of Okehi village, is cheated by the financial secretary, Okonkwo, because he is illiterate, he feels the insult deeply and decides that all his children shall be educated, even Unoma, his eldest, although girls are not ordinarily sent to school. Unoma proves to be bright and works hard, but she is sometimes absentminded and forgetful. One day, running back to school to find handiwork that she forgot, she hears someone in the headmaster's office. Getting no answer to her call, she fears ghosts and runs home. The next morning she learns that the fee money has been taken from the office. Suspicion among students falls upon her, and she is shunned. The next time that fees are collected, however, at Ikemefuna's suggestion the headmaster hides Unoma's little brother, Chimezie, in his office with directions to ring the school bell if anyone enters and opens the cupboard. All goes according to plan, and the thief is apprehended. Running home from school in a blinding rainstorm, Unoma sees Okonkwo stealing a goat. After the elders fine him, he guesses who was the witness. Later, when he catches her collecting firewood in woods he owns, he chases her, striking her sharply across the calves with a stick, but she gets away without serious harm. Forgetful Unoma leaves her fee money at home and must run back for it, talking a shortcut near the house of the masquerade cult. When she is seen, she runs literally for her life to her father. Wearing his best wrapper, he takes her to the masquerade house, where, standing outside, he negotiates and throws coins until it is agreed that Unoma will be initiated into the organization, thereby obviating the sacrilege of the uninitiated having possibly seen some of the mysteries of the cult. For the scripture examination, which is essential to promotion, she and other members of standard five (a grade) must go to a center five miles from the village, crossing an inlet of Azi Lake on a dangerous foot bridge. Unoma, since she can swim, volunteers to cross first and makes it with ease, but the last boy steps on an unstable center piece and plunges into the water. Unoma dives in and reaches him, but is swept, holding his head above water, by strong currents toward the open lake. By good fortune, they are caught in the roots along the edge, and fishermen are able to reach them by boat and save them. Unoma goes to convent school for standard six. There she learns cooking and often serves her father, convincing him that her education is worthwhile. At the end of standard six, Unoma takes the examinations but cannot imagine that her father will send her to college so that she can become a full-fledged teacher as she wishes. Her uncle, who has heard that she is taking the exams, protests to Ikemefuna that he must be besotted by his wife to consider sending their daughter for further schooling. His anger roused, Ikemefuna declares that Unoma will go to the four-year college if she passes the required examinations. When Unoma takes first place, he is pleased. The story is a simple and naively told progression of episodes obviously intended to encourage the education of girls, but it also reveals much of the social pattern and attitudes of village people, evidently in the late twentieth century. The disparaging remark, "She is only a girl," is repeated by several characters, but women are shown to be clever and competent, and in distress the children cry, "My mother, I'm dead!" Unoma's mother skillfully manipulates her husband's humor, feeding him well and choosing carefully the time to speak about their daughter. A pagan, she prays to her gods and credits them with Unoma's success. Unoma's father, who lives in a separate house and summons his wife and offspring when it pleases him, is a somewhat distant and austere figure to his daughter, but he backs her at all the essential times. Nigeria CLAN First Prize.

UP TO LOW (Doyle*, Brian, Groundwood/Douglas, 1982), novel of a teenage romance that blossoms during a boy's brief holiday in 1950 in Quebec, Canada, a trip that also includes the drunken antics of his father's friend, a reconciliation of the girl with her brutal father, and the father's bizarre death. Young Tommy, the first-person narrator, who is perhaps fourteen or fifteen years old—not yet driving age—and Dad*, known as Tommy, escape from fanatically clean Aunt Dottie, who has lived with them since Young Tommy's mother died, to go to Dad's cabin on his family farm on the Gatineau River. They meet Dad's friend Frank* at the railroad station, where he pulls up in his newly purchased Buick, right into a lamppost. As they travel, with frequent stops during which Frank and Dad drink whisky, gin, or ale and Young Tommy drinks a Coke, the car gets progressively more battered. At each stop someone remarks that Mean* Hughie is dying of cancer. Each time the answer is, "I'll believe that when I see it," and this calls for another Mean Hughie story concerning some feat of strength or depth of brutality of Dad's boyhood neighbor. After about six hours en route, they arrive at the farm, where at least ten of Dad's siblings still live, along with his father, Old Tommy, his one-hundred-year-old grandfather, Crazy Mickey, and his ninety-nine-year-old grandmother, Minnie. There also conversation concerns Mean Hughie, the news that he has disappeared and speculation about what has happened to him. In the morning, Dad sends Young Tommy over to get some bread at Mean Hughie's ramshackle farmhouse from his wife, known as Poor Bridget. He sees again their eldest child, Baby Bridget, a girl with one arm cut off at the elbow in a binder accident when she was very young. Young Tommy has heard the story many times, of how she was reaching out to pick a flower when her father beat the horses, they lurched ahead, and the knives chopped off her arm, of how Mean Hughie hit her for being in the way, then broke off a piece of binder twine and tied it around her arm to stop the bleeding. From the one time he saw her before, Young Tommy remembers the green of Baby Bridget's eyes, shaped like trillium leaves. They pick berries together and go fishing, and a gentle, companionable love grows between them. In the middle of one night, Baby Bridget asks Young Tommy to take her to Old Willy, the Hummer, a hermit known as a healer, whose farm was buried by the lake when a dam was built and who now lives in the old stable, accessible only by water. Baby Bridget says the Hummer promised her a healing, and she knows it is time. The Hummer, who hums along with the power lines, tells them to find Mean Hughie at the old Ramsay Place. Young Tommy rows back up river to the deserted farm, where they find Mean Hughie, emaciated and barely able to talk, lying in a coffin he has built for himself. With his last strength, he tells Baby Bridget that he is sorry to have hit her when she lost her arm, and she says, "It's all right, Pa." She stays with him the few minutes until he dies. Young Tommy, thinking that she is expecting a physical healing of her arm, is afraid she will be terribly disappointed, but then he realizes that she has been healed in a more important way. With the coffin balanced across the gunnels, they are rowing back downstream when a sudden hailstorm hits, and they capsize.

The coffin floats, and they hang onto it until Dad and several of his brothers appear in three boats, hunting for them. The uncles tow the coffin, with Mean Hughie's body floating in it, to Dad's cabin, where Father Sullivan and several of the aunts are waiting. The novel ends that evening, just before Young Tommy and Baby Bridget kiss for the first time. Despite the sweet, low-key romance, which is treated seriously, and the scene of Mean Hughie's death at the Ramsay Place, the predominant tone of the book is humorous, with Young Tommy describing a large cast of eccentric characters in a tolerant, matter-of-fact way. The mixture of superstition, folk wisdom, and Catholicism is an interesting part of the background. The style is brisk and amusing. A companion novel, *Angel Square**, takes place when Tommy is twelve. Can. Bk. of Year Winner.

V

THE VALLEY BETWEEN (Thiele*, Colin, Rigby, 1981), humorous novel of family and neighborhood life in South Australia evidently in the 1920s. Benno Schulz, 13, has just finished his last year of school in Gonunda, a small town in wheat country north of Kapunda, and expects to work full time on his father's farm. The episodic story of his next few months is held together by the feud of two men in the community, terrible-tempered Adolf Heinz, a barrel of a man with a strict Lutheran disapproval of dancing and frivolity, and Jack Ryan, a lean, laughing Irishman, who plays the harmonica, loves to dance, and thoroughly enjoys baiting Adolf. Although Benno's father usually approves of Adolf's attitude, Benno sides with Jack. The first big contest is a race up Jacob's hill, Adolf's horse Prince pulling his sulky against Jack's new Model T Ford, an occasion that brings the whole town out to watch. After losing the first heat, Jack lines up his car backward for the next start, bounces up the hill, swerving to avoid stones, reaches the top well ahead of Adolf, overshoots it and crashes into the waters of Geister's Hole far below. On some occasions Benno is more directly involved. When Adolf, racing to get his wheat into the railroad yard before the one o'clock Saturday closing, forces his way past Jack, he smashes the wheel off Jack's wagon. Benno, helping Jack reload, is an unwilling lookout while Jack removes the pins from both back wheels of Adolf's wagon and uncouples the freight car that holds Adolf's wheat, so that it will not be picked up and taken to Adelaide until Monday. Their major clash comes at the sheep dog trials when Jack, eliminated early, gets Benno to crank his car just as Adolf's dog is at a critical point in the trials, and the Ford lets out a series of backfires that startle and scatter the sheep irretrievably. One evening near the train station, Benno sees someone pushing a flatbed freight truck on which is sitting Jack's new harvester from Adelaide. The man undoes the fastenings on the harvester, intending to tip it off the truck where it will crash down the steep hill and be destroyed. Benno, appearing suddenly, scares the man to step back and roll down the hill in the dark, but this leaves the freight truck on the track in the path of the approaching train. Benno sets his straw hat afire, hoists it on a stick, and runs down the track, swinging it. The train brakes at the last minute, early enough to prevent a derailment but not soon enough to keep the harvester, no longer fastened down, from being knocked off and destroyed. Driving the buggy home later, Benno hears faint cries for help, climbs down a steep slope, and discovers Happy Geister, a slow-witted local youth, with two sprained ankles and bad cuts from a fall. Benno thinks that Happy might have been the man pushing the freight truck. At the ensuing trial, Happy is acquitted for lack of evidence, and later, hearing Adolf gloat, Benno wonders. Incidents of the feud are interspersed with other episodes: the night when a freight car in which Benno's sister, Louisa, and her beau are necking, is picked up and Benno gets Jack to race the train and rescue them before his parents discover their absence; the excursion to the seaside, where Benno is warned for indecent exposure when his home-knit bathing suit stretches; the late evening when Benno, carrying a scarecrow on his bicycle, scares Adolf near the cemetery and causes Jack's team to bolt; the time Benno, using an old carbide lamp for a bicycle light, causes Adolf's team to run away and starts a fire that threatens the wheat crop; the bomb he and his friend make with the rest of the carbide, intending to blast the fish in Adolf's pond, instead causing his bull and cattle to stampede; the railway crash Benno witnesses; the accident on slaughtering day, caused partly by Benno, which results in a broken leg for his father; and other occurrences on the farm or in the small town. The tone throughout is good natured, with the feud and even the accidents and near disasters treated humorously. Benno is essentially moral and well meaning, if often hapless. The distinguishing feature is the picture of the tight-knit, mostly German community, farm life in the early part of the century, and the large Schulz family. Aust. Bk. of Year Winner.

VANCE TRUELANCE (*Longtime Passing**), Edwin's* next younger brother, who builds his house on the mountaintop because he likes the freedom. He marries strong-minded, supercilious Imogen, a Roaring Twenties flapper, who refuses to live there. Vance returns to the city and becomes a successful businessman. The scene in which Imogen, dressed in the latest fashion, visits Edwin's family in their rustic farmhouse has a bittersweet, ironic humor. While she looks down on them as countryfolk, they pity her lack of appreciation for the wild beauty of Longtime*. Although they accept her, she rejects them. The passage is a beautiful contrast in values.

VANISHING TRICK AT CHANDIPUR (Sinha*, Nilima, ill. Subir Roy, CBT, India, 1984), mystery sequel to *The Chandipur Jewels**, opening on a return visit of the three children, Saringa, about 13, Praveen, 12, and Sunil, 10, to the Chandipur palace of their grandfather. The old man, recovered from his long illness, gives a gala party that is attended by Panditji, the village priest, Munshiji, the accountant, Mukhia, the scholarly headman, and Lalaji, a shop owner and moneylender, among others, and at which the main entertainment is provided by Shriman Chhoo Mantar, a stage magician. While all these main people are present, but before most of the guests have arrived, the grandfather shows them a silver urn, presented by Sher Shah Suri, sixteenth-century ruler of India, to an ancestor of the family. The next morning the urn is missing, and Ramu *kaka*, old and trusted servant, is arrested. Urged by his daughter, Munia, a servant girl about Saringa's age, the children set out to find the thief. They search the garden, and because of various clues and events, their suspicion falls on first one, then another, of the guests at the party with only Sunil, who was greatly impressed by the magician's powers, believing that Chhoo Mantar is the guilty party. At the bus stop, as they begin their trip back to their home in Patna, they are joined by Munia, who has been married for several years but never lived with her husband and who has run away rather than be sent to his home before her in-laws learn of the shame of her father's arrest. On the bus also is Lalaji, acting suspicious and guarding a bag large enough to hold the urn. In Patna, Praveen contrives to follow Lalaji and learns that the moneylender and his son plan to catch the steamer the next evening. Sunil, still convinced that Chhoo Mantar has made the urn disappear by magic, enlists Munia to visit the magician and ask him to make the urn reappear. Returning with Praveen to Lalaji's house, Saringa is accidentally shut in a van along with the suspicious bag and carried aboard the steamer, with Praveen clinging to the back. Munia and Sunil, having run in fear from the magician, see Praveen, and Munia impulsively also boards the steamer, which begins its slow journey across the Ganges River. Sunil, sobbing, is picked up by Chhoo Mantar, who has followed in his car and, when all is explained to him, crosses the river in a small boat with the little boy and takes a taxi to the steamer landing. With the help of the magician, the money-lender and his son are apprehended with not only the urn but other stolen antiques they plan to sell across the border in Nepal. Although the plot is highly sensational and predictable, the novel in some ways is more successful than its predecessor because it includes more local color—the streets of Patna crowded with rick-shaws, carts, and vans, the views from the ferry steamer of the busy Ganges River, the crowded vegetable market through which Chhoo Mantar leads Sunil—and its villain has a plausible motive. There is nothing, however, to distinguish the children from their counterparts in England or the United States and the total effect is of imitation rather than true originality. CBT of India, Second Prize.

VERITY OF SYDNEY TOWN (Williams*, Ruth, ill. Rhys Williams, Angus, 1950), realistic period novel set in Sydney, Australia, in the early 1800s while Australia is still a British penal colony. Staunch, resilient Verity Asherton, about twelve, has been living in Sydney Town as the ward of wealthy, diffident merchant Mr. Flintley, and his status-conscious, miserly, domineering wife. When Verity's sea captain father is two years overdue from a voyage and the money he left for her care has run out, the Flintleys arrange for her to live with Farmer Staples and his family in the outback, a good day's journey by wagon.

An understanding, steady, elderly man, Mr. Staples helps her smuggle along her dog, Mr. Rankin, which Mrs. Flintley wants shot. Verity feels at home right away with the farmer and his wife on their hundred-acre place and helps with chores in the garden and the house. She is grateful for the new dress that Mrs. Staples makes for her because her clothes are in tatters, and Humphrey, the accommodating Stapleses' son, treats her like a sister. The whole family appreciate the help and company of Slippery Britter, a young man who has been transported to Australia for stealing a plum pudding. Slippery serves the Staples family loyally and tells them amusing stories. Excitement occurs when Mr. and Mrs. Staples go to help their married daughter, Joan, whose home is endangered by a flood, leaving the children with Slippery at the farm. During the night, bushrangers (runaway convicts who live by stealing and terrorize the countryside) take over the farmhouse, help themselves to food, and set fire to the kitchen house. Mr. Rankin arouses Slippery, through whose wit and courage they escape. About the same time, Mr. Dillon, Captain Asherton's partner, arrives in Sydney Town from London, hoping to restore their failing business. He looks for Verity at the Flintleys, learns that she is at the Stapleses' farm, travels there with Mr. Flintley and an escort of soldiers, and arrives just after the robbers leave and just before Verity, Slippery, and Humphrey return. After a grand reunion, Mr. Dillon takes Verity back to Sydney with him, hires as her personal maid Binny Dibbs, Mrs. Flintley's "assigned maid" (convict), who had befriended Verity while she was living with the Flintleys, buys Verity suitable clothes, and takes her to meet the governor. To cap her joy, Verity's father's ship puts in, concluding a long, adventurous voyage. Captain Asherton and Mr. Dillon reward Slippery for his loyalty and bravery by hiring him as foreman of their Sydney branch. The story holds few surprises, and its slightly formal style, conventional characters, and predictable plot place it among the right-will-out, virtue-triumphs literature of the period. Though unevenly paced, it is consistently entertaining and gives some insights into this period of Australian history. Aust. Bk. of Year Winner.

VIK VIKING (*The Roaring 40**), hearty old giant of a prospector with whom Dave* and Badge Lorenny go "fossicking" for gold. Intelligent, well-read Vik has a strong presence and beautiful singing voice. He once aspired to a career on the stage but chose instead to spend his life in the Tasmanian bush. He is instrumental in bringing the villainous Flinty and his brothers to justice for their abuse of Ned*, the wild boy, and their theft of the *Thora Ann*, which Flinty renamed the *Roaring 40*. Vik is a well-drawn, convincing character, a good contrast for the milder Dave.

VILDA (*Last Chance Summer**), middle-aged cook at the Jenner farm, shaped "like a tired squash" but tough and with better control of the boys than has Carleton* Jenner. Her own children, evidently, have been troublesome, though she doesn't talk about them. Having been raised in the Badlands, she sees no point in the expedition to see the geological formations and does not think it is her job to chaperone the group. Left alone with five boys when the bus is stolen and Carleton walks to town, she is scared of the responsibility and reacts to Topo's* baiting by saying that it would be better if he had never been born, a statement that hits a vulnerable spot with this discarded boy and fuels his already simmering anger. In the end she is instrumental in forcing Carleton to face the truth that he can't handle so many boys alone and defends Topo and saves him from returning to the reform school. She is a vivid and believable character.

THE VILLAGE BY THE SEA: AN INDIAN FAMILY STORY (Desai*, Anita, Heinemann, 1982; Allied Publishers, India, 1983), quiet but moving novel of a family living in poverty in the village of Thul in modern India and of the changes that industrialization of their area promises for their lives. Lila*, the eldest, has left school because her mother is ill and her alcoholic father earns little and drinks that little up each night. She tries to care for their home, her bedridden mother, and her two little sisters and to stay out of the way of her drunken father. Her brother, Hari*, one year younger than Lila, has also left school and helps by clearing space for a garden, catching a few fish with his net, and climbing for coconuts to sell in the market, but their combined efforts scarcely keep the family from starvation. Occasionally they earn a little money by running errands and doing odd jobs for the de Silvas, a wealthy Bombay family whose vacation house, *Mon Repos*, is just across the creek from their hut. The point of view alternates between that of Lila, who toils stoically but with little hope, and that of Hari, who is humiliated by the low status to which they have fallen and who dreams of ways he might change their fortunes. Rumors of a huge fertilizer factory to be built all along their coast bring hopes of jobs, which his friends anticipate, and he joins their talk somewhat skeptically, fearing that labor for all the good jobs will be imported to their area. When he polishes Mr. de Silva's car, the man gives him his Bombay address and suggests that he will give the boy a job if he ever gets to Bombay. Hari hears an impassioned speech about the harm that the chemical factory will do to the village, ruining the fishing, the crops, and the whole way of life of the area, and he joins the men from their village and from nearby towns who go in their fishing boats to Bombay to protest to the government. After the rally, Hari decides to stay in Bombay and get a job. He finally makes his way to the high-rise apartment building where the de Silvas live, but a scornful servant tells him that they have left that day for Thul and sends him on his way. The night watchman, a kindly sort, spots him and takes him to the Sri Krishna Eating House of Gowalia Tank, the lowest of thepoor restaurants in Bombay. There the proprietor, Jagu, gives him a meal and a job helping the two other boys who toil around the clock in the heat and fall exhausted on the benches in the kitchen to sleep. The village boy finds life confined to the eating house stifling and is desperately homesick until he meets Mr. Panwallah, the old watchmaker in the shop next door, who suggests that he sleep in the park and starts to teach him to repair clocks and watches. Their mother becomes much worse and the de Silvas agree to take her to the hospital, which is free, and to pay for her medicines and let Lila work to repay them. When her father returns, drunk, and finds his wife gone, he is furious, berates Lila, smashes the water pots, and stumbles off to the town hospital, where he stays, not drinking. With him out of the way, the three girls get along better than they have before, working for the de Silvas and then, to their delight, for the friend of Mr. de Silva, Sayyid Ali, who comes to stay at *Mon Repos* throughout the monsoon season, when the wealthy family goes away. The monsoon season is a nightmare in Bombay, and Hari decides go home. When he gets back to Thul, with presents for his sisters and his carefully hoarded earnings, he goes to the hospital to bring his much improved mother home. His father, now sober, seems old and grey, and for the first time Hari feels pity for him instead of hatred. When he visits Sayyid Ali to thank him for employing the girls, he finds that it is the same man who addressed the rally. He compliments Hari on his willingness to adapt, to start a poultry farm and eventually a watch-repairing shop. The story is plausible and the main characters believable, but the strength of the book lies in the descriptions of life in both Thul and in Bombay, seen from the point of view of the two young village adolescents, of both the hardship and the beauty of their lives and that of the many people both poor and well-to-do whom they come to know. Guardian.

VILLIERS, ALAN (1903–   ), born in Melbourne, Australia; seaman, writer of novels, stories, and non-fiction about the sea. He attended Essendon High School but left at age fifteen to become a cadet on the barque *Rothesay Bay* and sailed in square-rigged ships in Cape Horn trade. Although he worked for some time on the *Mercury* newspaper in Hobart, the sea has always been his first love and he has returned to it frequently. In 1923 and 1924 he was a member of the modern whaling expedition to the Ross Sea, an experience related in *Whaling in the Frozen North* (Bobbs, 1925). In 1927 he was part of the crew in a race between two four-masted sailing ships from Melbourne to England, an experience related in *Falmouth for Orders* (Scribner's, 1929). Later he went into a partnership for a four-masted barque, *Parma*, which sailed in the Australian grain trade. In 1931 he bought a miniature full-rigged ship and sailed around the world with a group of boys, a story related in *Cruise of the Conrad* (Scribner's, 1934). He has also re-enacted the transatlantic crossing of the Pilgrim Fathers, told in *The New Mayflower* (Scribner's, 1959). His novel of the first factory whaling endeavor in the Antarctic, *Whalers of the Midnight Sun** (Scribner's, 1934; Angus, 1949), won the Australian Book of the Year Award when it was republished in 1949. He has written a number of other novels, compiled collections of sea stories, published a study of Magellan's voyages for the National Geographic Society, and produced books of non-fiction, including *The Way of the Ship* (Easton, 1988), about the square-rigged sailing vessel.

THE VIOLIN-MAKER'S GIFT (Kushner*, Donn, ill. Doug Panton, Macmillan, 1981; Farrar, 1982), brief, legend-like fantasy of how the violin-maker, Gaspard l'Innocent of the Pyrénées Mountains near the Spanish Border in the 1820s, was able to make some instruments that seemed to sing with a human voice. Always a careful craftsman, Gaspard at first makes gaily varnished violins that give out a loud, clear sound, appropriate for the peasant dances and weddings of the district but not distinguished by depth or subtlety of tone. As he passes the toll bridge on his way to the market town, he is always challenged by Matthias, the official toll collector, who makes the most of his petty authority by consulting his list, discussing the rates for various items, and always finding that there is no toll for violins. Gaspard waits patiently during this ritual and usually leaves the man some small tip, but on this occasion he forgets and thinks that he will bring him something from the market on his return. Toward the end of the day, he is startled by a gypsy boy who points out a bird, evidently too young to fly, perched on the wing of an angel on the church portal. Gaspard climbs the wall, a difficult and dangerous feat that leaves the crowd below gasping, rescues the bird, and carries it down inside his shirt. Afraid that he will not be able to look after it and knowing that the toll collector's wife, Babbette, has a knack for raising animals, he gives it to Matthias on his return trip. Later he has second thoughts, as the bird grows more and more beautiful, but Matthias will not trade it back in exchange for a cleverly made wreath or even a violin. As the bird grows, developing gorgeous golden feathers and a scarlet band around its throat, Matthias sets up a booth near the bridge and charges for views of the bird. Gaspard hears tales of its wonders as it begins to talk and even to predict the future, but the violin-maker avoids the booth, not wanting to see his bird exploited. Later Matthias takes the bird touring, dreaming of opera houses and grand ballrooms in Paris. He finds, however, that while the bird always predicts truly, he does not predict on demand, and only the poor, used to being cheated, are willing to pay for such an uncertain chance at information. When Gaspard learns that Matthias has returned to a disreputable inn in his own market town, he goes to see the bird and is shocked at the condition of the golden feathers in the smoky air and at the petty and greedy questions asked. When he learns that Matthias is planning to team the beautiful creature with a band of performing turtles or rats, Gaspard steals the bird. At first he thinks that he will build a new cage in the clear air of his forest and show the bird to only a select few. Later he realizes that he must free it. Before it leaves, the bird tells him to go high into the mountains in the early spring, to look for a plant with a crown of five spiky leaves, and to inlay these in the belly of his violins. Matthias returns to his toll bridge and builds an inn, where he becomes genial rather than officious. Gaspard finds the plant, just enough for a few violins each year, and produces marvelous instruments that sound as if a human soul were imprisoned in the wood. As his violins age, the human voice fades, leaving only a clear, smooth tone, like water flowing over polished rocks, and they are still identifiable by the small bird with outstretched wings carved on the side of each scroll. Can. Bk. of the Year Winner.

VISITORS (Macdonald*, Caroline, Hodder, 1984), science fiction novel set in New Zealand in the 1980s, in which for ten days a boy is contacted by beings from outer space who communicate with him through his television screen. Terry Carpenter, evidently eleven or twelve years old, generally pays attention only to his cat, Mex, and to the television. Since his mother, Margot, and father, Steve, both work long hours, Terry is alone a great deal, a situation that suits him. Coming with schoolmates to see and play video games on Terry's television, Maryanne Rice, who lives next door, a cerebral palsy victim physically deformed and able to speak only with great difficulty, discovers and plays with a box of fossils that Steve once supervised Terry in collecting. In the box is also a piece of stone with glassy, vitreous streaks in it that make a wavy pattern when held up to the light, the only part of the collection in which Terry has any interest. He is bothered by occasional periods when all color drains out of the world around him, a phenomenon that his mother and others don't notice. His television develops wavy red-and-yellow zigzags, for which the repairman can find no cause. Later, to his amazement, it shows him a film as if a spaceship is approaching earth, zeroing in. Finally it focuses on the scene of him collecting the fossils with Steve. In the next few days, it shows him a series of strange pictures, often of an old scientist writing in a freezing room about scenes he views in an "ice-bath," a large pan of frozen water. Eventually Terry identifies him as a teacher of Sir Isaac Newton, writing in the winter of the plague year of 1665. He also sees a girl from some earlier century, who shows scenes reflected in a pool of water and is stoned to death as a witch. His intense interest is almost thwarted when a letter from his teacher prompts Steve to lock up the television sets in his study. Despite bitter weather and a cold, Terry goes out at night to a television store, where sets are left on in the window. He wakes in his room two days later, having collapsed there. His television set is back, and his parents are clearly worried. In his room is Maryanne, to whom he has evidently been talking at great length about seeing her face on the television screen. He tries to tell his mother about what he sees, but she doesn't believe him. Maryanne, however, is interested and, communicating with Terry via the computer attachment to his television as she has never been able to by voice, soon becomes his ally. They speculate about whether the visitors, to whom they refer as "they," are from another planet and what they were trying to get from the early scientist, the girl accused of witchcraft, the men of Stonehenge, and the Australian Aborigine whom they are shown in various scenes. Brief italicized passages let the reader know that "they," incorporeal beings from space, have been trapped for centuries in earth's atmosphere and are patiently trying to get human aid for their release. With a flashlight and a paperweight shaped like a prism, Terry repeats one of Newton's experiments to break up light into a rainbow pattern, and the resulting explosion of color on the screen indicates that they are on the right track. Maryanne realizes that the wavy patterns on the screen and those in the stone in Terry's collection are identical. On the tenth evening, having decided that "they" want to exit this world and somehow need the energy of the pattern to help them, the youngsters take the equipment and the stone outside. The result is an explosion of color in the yard, leaving a burnt patch in the wavy pattern on the grass and apparently freeing the visitors. The experience does not solve all Terry's problems, but he has been drawn out of his apathy and now has a close friend. Maryanne is going to move to a special school, but Steve gives her a computer, so that she and Terry can continue to communicate by letter. The book contains many sharp and perceptive digs at teacher-child and child-parent relationships. The characters of Maryanne and the Carpenter family are well developed, and the gradual tension and fascination of the visitations are well handled in an absorbing plot. N. Z. Govt. Winner.

W

WALK A MILE AND GET NOWHERE. See BREAD AND HONEY.

THE WHALE PEOPLE (Haig-Brown*, Roderick, ill. Mary Weiler, Collins, 1962; Morrow, 1963), realistic novel of community life with boy's growing-up story aspects set for about four years among the Indians of the upper Pacific coast of North America at an unspecified time. Atlin becomes a skillful whaling chief and understanding, diplomatic leader of the Hotsath Indians, a people for whom the whale is the basis of life. Impressed by his son's near success in capturing a huge salmon, highly regarded Nit-gass, chief of the Hotsath, begins training Atlin, 12, to hunt the huge prey. The boy thrills to Nit-gass's skill and savors the joking fellowship among the men. The whaling is good, and Nit-gass holds a potlatch, or feast, in midwinter for neighboring tribes. The boy's training continues throughout the winter, and the close relationship that develops between father and son is one of the book's most pleasing aspects. The following May, Nit-gass's spirit power (*tumanos*) fails him, he drowns while harpooning a particularly large whale, and Atlin becomes chief. His uncle, Tokwit, who had been his father's steersman and spokesman, and his grandfather, Tetacus*, continue his schooling. With Hinak, his slave, best friend, and loyal sidekick, Atlin seeks the spirit power of the Supernatural Shark at Shark Point, but he fails when a storm comes up unexpectedly. The next winter is particularly difficult for the tribe, and starvation threatens. When Atlin visits his father's shrine and sees a vision in which his father's tumanos, a bird, appears, Tokwit and Tetacus predict a splendid future for the youth. He captures a great sea lion near Tsitikat territory but releases it when Chief Eskowit of the Tsitikats claims it. When Atlin gains shark power by swimming in the Shark's Pool, Tetacus proclaims the boy ready to lead whaling expeditions. With his Uncle Kangass's help, Atlin kills a good-sized whale on his first trip. After he kills three more whales, his position as whale chief is secure. Tetacus suggests that he marry and urges that he speak for a daughter of Eskowit as a way of healing the tension between the two peoples. Twice Eskowit rejects Atlin's request. At Hinak's suggestion, Atlin kills a whale, tows it to Eskowit's territory, and offers to turn it over to the village. He claims that Eskowit's whale magic is so strong that he cannot get the creature back to his own village. The hungry villagers eagerly accept his offer, and Eskowit relents, his face saved, and betroths his daughter to Atlin. The youth's tribe acclaims his diplomacy, and he looks forward to a long life as chief of the whale people. The characters are one-dimensional types, and the superficial plot moves at a good pace with plenty of action, excitement, and adventures on land and sea to a not unexpected conclusion. The story gives the author the chance to convey information about the customs, beliefs, and practices of the Indians from the male point of view, an objective he achieves satisfactorily without becoming judgmental or obviously didactic. A bibliography about the northern Indians is included. Can. Bk. of Year Winner.

WHALERS OF THE MIDNIGHT SUN (Villiers*, Alan, ill. Charles Pont, Scribner's, 1934; Angus, 1949), historical adventure novel subtitled, *A Story of Modern Whaling in the Antarctic*, starting in Hobart, Tasmania, at an unspecified date, which appears to be in the first decade of the twentieth century. Ocker Stephens, with two friends, all about fourteen, see a new sort of ship in the harbor, a big, ugly tramp steamer, its decks loaded with machinery. Before they can investigate, they learn from Ocker's brother Alfie, 11, who is uninhibited about asking questions and squirming his way past "no trespassing" signs, that it is a Norwegian whaler called the *Pelagos*, a floating factory of twelve thousand tons, which will be mother ship to six smaller whale chasers, and that it is heading for the Antarctic in hope of establishing an industry there. The three older boys volunteer, looking for excitement and a chance to escape school and their equally abusive and uncaring families. Alfie, too, tries to get a job, but he is turned down because of his age and small size. A thousand miles south of Tasmania, Alfie is discovered hidden in a lifeboat. He is assigned to help the doctor collect specimens and care for them aboard the mother ship. Ocker and his friends suffer from the hard work, mostly shoveling coal, and from the bully, Stonker Doidge, 17, who terrorizes them whenever possible, but Alfie thrives, soon becoming a favorite of most of the men and officers as he scampers all over the big ship, followed usually by Perc', a baby penguin he and the doctor have found abandoned. As they near the Balleny Islands, they sight their first whales and find the drifting ice becoming heavier. Soon they are caught in the pack ice, a situation especially dangerous for steel ships, which can be crushed by the pressure. The *Pelagos* takes the chasers (all called "Pol" with a number) in tow, and the men literally saw a channel out, then dynamite ahead to clear the way for a short distance. After ten days they sight open water on the other side of an archway formed by two icebergs fused together. Although the opening is only slightly wider than the *Pelagos*, Captain Peterson sees that it is their only chance, and they steer through with a bare six feet of clearance on each side. Then they begin to chase and bring in whales, and the boys get their first taste of the grueling work of flensing and trying-out (cooking the fat out) the blubber and whale meat. Ocker and Red Erik, caught in a boat with no oars or way of steering, drift off in a storm so heavy that they cannot see, their clothes freezing on them. They bump into the floating carcass of a whale, which has broken away from the ship, and Erik cuts a hole in the meat, into which they both climb. Three days later, the crew of *Pol III* sights a dead whale, with a human hand protruding from its side waving a flensing knife, and they are picked up. The *Pol III*, with Alfie aboard, is dragged by a huge blue whale for a long distance. Before it can make much headway back toward the mother ship at McMurdo Sound, fog sets in. The *Pol II* has been lost with all hands, and the *Pelagos* has decided to shift to the Bay of Whales, in hope of a calmer anchorage. The *Pol III* has coal enough for only part of that distance to the new rendezvous. It is forced into the Barrier edge by a floating iceberg. Alfie leads the way up the tilted mast to a ledge in the Barrier, and they get some of the supplies off the *Pol III* before she is crunched by a shift of the iceberg. There follows a terrible trip across the ice, during which eleven of the original men give up and die, with only the captain, Alfie, Perc', and Snitch, the dog, surviving to reach the edge of the ice by the *Pelagos*. Their arrival squelches the impending mutiny and puts new hope into the crew, although Captain Peterson is very ill and soon dies. They set off following the whales and discover a passage between the Grahams Islands and Antarctica that brings them out into the Wendell Sea and so to the Atlantic south of Argentina. The Tasmanian boys are sent home on a passenger liner, but Alfie jumps ship in Port Adelaide, determined to return to the sea rather than to school. The novel gives an exhaustive and fascinating picture of the hardships and dangers of this pioneering voyage, with all its mistakes and poor planning and its genuine heroism. The characters, except for Alfie and Captain Peterson, are not developed, and those two not fully. Occasionally some compassionate remark acknowledges the suffering of the whales, but there is none of the modern concern for the destruction of an endangered species. Aust. Bk. of Year Winner.

WHAT'S THE MATTER, GIRL? (Brochmann*, Elizabeth, Fitzhenry, 1980; Harper, 1980), psychological problem novel of a girl's refusal to accept reality set just after World War II in Port Salish, Vancouver Island, Canada. Anna Swales, 13, almost fourteen, tells about the homecoming from the war of Uncle* Arion, her favorite relative and the second youngest son of a very large family. During the six days prior to his arrival, his relatives gather to celebrate. Anna sits lost in reverie on Gran's* front porch, fashioning potato men with toothpicks, reflecting on the things that she and Arion used to do together, rereading his letters home, and daydreaming of good times when he returns. Although other family members, in particular Aunt* Gemma and Anna's older brother, Marsh, drop hints that should warn her, their words make no impression, nor is she daunted that she has received no letter from Arion in a year. She does have some inkling that all may not be right with Arion when she says she blames what happens on Gladys, the waitress who jilted him. She describes her family, revealing them as the upwardly mobile and motley offspring of immigrants. At the big moment, a taxi pulls up, two strangers emerge, dressed in white. One, an attendant, guides the other, mentally deranged Uncle Arion, released from the hospital into the care of his mother. He is white haired, instead of blond, vacant eyed instead of vibrant, and stiff, slow, and stooped instead of young and virile. Anna sweeps to the ground her potato men gift for him, cries, and runs home, refusing to speak to or even look at him. Various family members reflecting different attitudes talk with her, including blowsy Aunt Cessy, who says she's making things worse than they have to be; Aunt Gemma, who accuses her of idealizing Arion; Mom, who says she's not the only one hurt; and Marsh, who shows her letters Arion wrote to him that reveal mental illness. She begins to think of the grief of the others, accompanies Marsh to visit Arion, who actually speaks if incoherently, releases her tension in a torrent of weeping and screaming, deliberately lacerates her hands on a barbed wire fence, and starts to understand that her family and her life will go on whether she accepts what has happened or not. The reader must be alert for subtle psychological touches about the family and Anna that give texture and strength to the book. The author skillfully creates a sense of impending trouble. Anna and Arion are revealed as immature romantics, who avoid reality and find comfort in dreams and make-believe. While Anna is a typical adolescent, Arion is the idealist for whom the reality of war is far too real. The author employs a visual style, and people and scenes seem alive and vivid. Information about the past is revealed gradually and judiciously for optimum effect on the attention, and pacing is studied. The conclusion seems rushed and the wording overly economical. Arion's letters to Anna seem unusually frank, explicit, self-revealing, and earthy for an uncle to write to a child whom he has reprimanded for swearing. The book's high points lie in its homely detail, its non-didactic confrontation of a common war problem, and its well-drawn protagonist and her uncle. Can. Council Hon. Ment.

WHEATLEY, NADIA (1949–   ), born in Sydney, Australia; free-lance writer of both fantasy and realistic fiction. She spent three years in Greece, and two of her novels concern a Greek-Australian family living in the Newtown district of Sydney. In *Five Times Dizzy** (Oxford, 1982), the main problem for young Marika is to get a goat for her aging grandmother who speaks no English and has difficulty adjusting to the culture so different from her native Crete. Its sequel, *Dancing in the Anzac Deli** (Oxford, 1984), concerns the threat by the local underworld thugs to the delicatessen owned by Marika's father, a problem that is solved in part by the girl and the grandmother. The love and understanding between the child and the old woman are among the strong features of both books. Also set in Newtown, where Wheatley has made her home, is her time-slip fantasy, *The House that was Eureka** (Viking, 1985), which alternates between 1931 and 1981, both periods of high unemployment. The house in which the action occurs is the one in which unemployed men barricaded themselves to fight eviction in the 1930s, and two young people of the 1980s find themselves drawn back into that earlier struggle. Historical background for this novel came from Wheatley's bachelor's and master's theses, and contemporary research grew out of her own lengthy periods on the dole and her experiences in the Unemployed People's Union. All three books were commended for the Australian Book of the Year Award and the first two were winners of the New South Wales Premier's Award.

WHEN JAYS FLY TO BARBMO (Balderson*, Margaret, ill. Victor Ambrus, Oxford, 1968; World, 1969), realistic novel set on the island of Draugoy near Tromso, Norway, north of the Arctic Circle, starting shortly before World War II. Through the long, dark winters and the brief, glorious summers, Ingeborg Nygaard, 14, lives a strange, isolated life with her conventional housekeeper aunt, Anne-Sigri Nygaard; her fisherman father, Arne, who speaks to his sister only when absolutely necessary; and Per, the "Wood Troll," a worker of uncertain background who toils all summer, drinks all winter, and carries on an unspoken feud with disapproving Anne-Sigri. Summer brings another worker, Veikko Kapanen, 16, who is helping Arne build a larger boat; he is an optimistic, cheerful boy treated like a son by Arne and doted on by Anne-Sigri. When Ingeborg finds a complete Lappish outfit at the bottom of a trunk in the storage shed and tries it on, her father is infuriated, and they have still not made up when he leaves for the fishing grounds. While he is gone, the Germans take over Norway, and not long after this word comes that Arne has gone down with his boat, sunk by Germans as he was trying to help Norwegians escape to England. The Wood Troll, now under suspicion by Anne-Sigri because he was born in Germany, reluctantly agrees to take Ingeborg to see the Lapps arrive and drive their reindeer across from the mainland to summer pasture on the island. She discovers that her mother was a Lapp, daughter of old Mikkel, the leader of this particular Lapp extended family, and learns something of her story. Trapped with her unsympathetic sister-in-law when her husband was out fishing through the long winter, the young wife missed her own wandering family, and, the two women having quarreled, she set out to find them and died in the storm after giving birth to Ingeborg. For fourteen years Arne has blamed Anne-Sigri. At first the German presence is not oppressive, but soon Veikko makes a plan to take Per and several others youths in the nearly finished boat and to try to escape and join a fighting group. That very night soldiers come, arrest Per as a Jew, kill the stock, and burn the boat and outbuildings as punishment for not reporting him. Veikko and his friends hide out in the mountains. Ingeborg and her aunt survive the winter, but in the early spring Anne-Sigri dies. Alone, Ingeborg manages until early in the winter that she is eighteen. Veikko appears to warn her that, with the Russians invading from the north, the Germans are destroying everything before they leave. Rather than let the Germans burn her house, she sets it afire herself, starts off to find her Lapp grandfather, and nearly dies as her mother did. She spends the winter with her Lapp family and intends to stay with them permanently, but after she gets back to Draugoy, she discovers that Veikko has returned and is rebuilding the farm, and she knows that her future is there with him. A rather slow-starting but well-constructed novel, it evokes the beauty as well as the harsh conditions of the far north. In this setting, the fourteen-year quarrel of Arne with his sister is credible. The hardships of war and the difficulties, as well as the pleasures, of life in the Lapp camp are essential and convincing parts of the story. With the exception of Veikko, who is functional, all of the main characters are well drawn, Anne-Sigri and Per in particular. The end is predictable but does not seem contrived. The title comes from a Lapp proverb meaning something like "when Hell freezes over," jays being nonmigrating birds and Barbmo the unknown region beyond the horizon where other birds go in the winter. Aust. Bk. of Year Winner; Carnegie Com.

THE WHITE ARCHER: AN ESKIMO LEGEND (Houston*, James, ill. James Houston, Longman, 1967; Harcourt, 1967), realistic novel set at an indeterminate time in the Arctic. Because the father of Kungo, 12, has given food and shelter to three starving and half-frozen fugitives, Indians from the Land of Little Sticks to the south whom the three fugitives have wronged attack Kungo's family's igloo, kill his parents, and abduct his sister, Shulu. Kungo manages to escape but swears that he will avenge the terrible deed. A seal hunter finds him half-frozen and takes him home, and for two years he lives with the hunter and his kindly wife. When one evening the hunter tells Kungo about an old man who has a strange and powerful knowledge of men and animals, can draw a bow so strong that no one else can bend it, and lives on a remote island of ice called Tugjak, Kungo decides to go there. The journey is long and taxing and ends with a perilous crossing from the mainland to the island over a tide-threatened ice bridge. On the island he finds the half-blind old man, Ittok, living in a stone house with roof beams made of whale ribs along with his gentle old wife and their earnest helper, a dwarf named Telikjuak. Since Kungo is able, though with great difficulty, to draw the famous bow, Kigavik (the dark falcon), Ittok takes Kungo on as a pupil, and a long period of training begins. When the lead dog, Lao, has half-wolf puppies, Kungo trains them to the sled, and they become his team. When some four years have passed, snow geese fly over. Ittok shoots with Kigavik the great white leader and presents the body to Kungo, saying that these feathers are for a white archer, what Kungo will become, but that the youth must never kill this bird nor eat its flesh, for he bears its name, Kungo meaning goose. Clad entirely in new white garments made by the old woman, he departs with his dog team, the old woman admonishing him that "hatred and revenge follow each other like two strong men piling heaving stones one upon the other until the stones fall, killing both men and perhaps many others." Kungo travels for some days, arriving at a village in the Land of Little Sticks. Still bent on revenge, he angrily challenges the inhabitants, but sudden doubt assails him, and he releases a barrage of arrows that tease and whine but never kill. His arrows almost spent, a woman calls to him—Shulu, his lost sister. She greets him, introduces him to her Indian husband, tells him that she is happy, and invites him to stay. Peace made, he declines the invitation and departs for Tugjak, his happiness bursting forth in jubilant song. The story combines attributes of fiction and oral tradition. The author makes too little of Kungo's desire for revenge, and the sudden self-restraint and reversal are too abrupt to be convincing as fiction. The many details of setting, costume, and daily life awaken a keen appreciation for the Arctic and are more typical of fiction than oral history. The brooding tone, flat figures, and timeless quality seem more appropriate to legend. Can. Bk. of Year Winner.

WHO IS FRANCES RAIN? (Buffie*, Margaret, Kids, 1987), time-slip fantasy set at Rain Lake near Fish Narrows north of Winnipeg, Manitoba, Canada, in which the action alternates between the present day and the early 1920s. Lizzie McGill, 15, returns with her siblings, Evan, a college student, and much younger Erica, to Gran's cabin for the summer holidays, accompanied this time by their mother and her new husband, Tim Worlsky. Both Lizzie and Evan resent their stepfather, a big, friendly, red-bearded potter whom they refer to as Toothy Tim, and they are not even civil to him. Their mother seems to be regretting her second marriage. Only Erica and (to Lizzie's surprise) Gran like Tim. To get away from the family tension, Lizzie takes her canoe to Rain Island, about a half a mile from Gran's cabin, and there she discovers a sunken spot, clearly the remains of an old cabin. Lizzie decides to excavate the site as she has seen done in archaeological films. She finds various artifacts, including a pair of wire-rimmed spectacles that seems to change the scene when she looks through them, showing a well-worn path and a small cabin in the clearing where she has been digging. When she pulls them off, the scene is back to normal. From Gran she learns that the island once had a cabin belonging to a Frances Rain, a teacher who became a prospector in 1911 or 1912 and lived alone on the island until her death in 1925, but Gran seems reluctant to talk about her. Lizzie keeps returning to the island and, against her better judgment, putting on the glasses and even telling everything she experiences into her tape recorder. She sees a tall, black-haired woman in trousers, a big ugly man Lizzie immediately calls the Toad Man, and a thin, pale girl about thirteen years old who wears wire-rimmed spectacles. The woman and the Toad Man argue, and he leaves abruptly. When Lizzie returns to the island, she often sees the girl sketching, and sometimes she herself sits sketching companionably with the girl who cannot see her. Back at Gran's cabin she finds Erica weeping and learns that Tim has gone, evidently finally fed up with the quarreling. Lizzie has her first real confidential talk with her mother and persuades her to go after Tim, who has been taken across the lake by Gran. When they reach the lodge there, they learn that Gran has had a heart attack. Their mutual concern effects a reconciliation between Tim and the mother. That night Frances Rain, the older woman from the island, appears to Lizzie in her bedroom, seeming to be asking something. The next day at Rain Island Lizzie sees the Toad Man arrive, slap the girl, and force her to go with him. Lizzie discovers a diary-sketchbook, wrapped carefully in leather and oilcloth so that it has lasted for sixty years, stuck in a deep crevice. Lizzie puts on the glasses, finds that it is winter and that Frances is very ill in the cabin. She holds the diary open and watches Frances read the entries telling how happy the younger girl was on the island. When Lizzie shows the book to her grandmother, saying that she found it in a tin box in the cabin, the old woman admits that she was Frances Rein's illegitimate daughter who spent a summer with her mother in the cabin, that they had planned to camp out until winter so that their father, a bitter man who lied to both of them about their feelings for each other, would not find and force the girl to return with him. Gran is extremely relieved to know that her mother saw the book and realized that she had been happy during their one summer together. When she was old enough, she returned to the area, taught school as her mother had, and eventually married and stayed. The plot depends too much on coincidence (the finding of the sketchbook after sixty years, for instance) to be entirely convincing. Some of the present-day characters, especially bitter, snobbish Evan, are overdrawn, and others, like Alex, a boy from across the lake whom Lizzie takes into her confidence, are stock and functional. The fantasy scenes, however, are vivid and whet the reader's curiosity while the modern family situation, though predictable, is plausible and interesting. The dialogue is more convincing than in many books for teenagers. Can. Young Adult Winner.

WIELER, DIANA J(EAN) (1961–   ), born in Winnipeg, Manitoba, Canada; short story writer and novelist. Her young adult novel of a group home for troubled boys at the edge of the Alberta badlands, *Last Chance Summer** (Western, 1987), was the winner of the Max and Greta Ebel Memorial Award and has been translated into Danish. Several of her shorter works have been honored, one with the Vicky Metcalf Award in the children's short story category in 1986 and another as winner of the Canadian Broadcasting Company Literary Competition for Children's Literature in 1984. Her novel for adolescents, *Bad Boy* (Douglas, 1989), was also critically acclaimed. Set in Moose Jaw, it concerns the complexities of developing sexuality as exemplified among teammates on a roughhouse hockey team on which one member is homosexual. Wieler has made her home in Saskatoon, Saskatchewan, and more recently in Winnipeg.

WILD BROTHER (Patchett*, Mary Elwyn, ill. John Rose, Collins, 1954), novel of dingoes, the wild dogs of Australia, and of the men in the outlying sheep and cattle stations who threaten or befriend them. When two dingo hunters, brutal Frank and easygoing Harry, almost wipe out a small band, they miss the big lead male, Warrigal, and capture one female pup, which for some strange reason Frank wants to keep alive. Back at the homestead, the pup, which is nearly dead from Frank's mistreatment, is cared for by Steve, the keeper of the storeroom, a bronco rider who has been crippled, and is named by him Shula, a Hindustani word meaning "flame." Gradually Shula responds to Steve's quiet kindness, but when she is nearly grown Frank, on one of his returns to the ranch headquarters, beats her savagely with a heavy bull whip. Steve, though smaller and much lighter than Frank, seizes another whip and duels with the bully, driving him away from Shula and forcing him to drop his weapon. Realizing that Frank will return to claim the dingo, Steve lets her loose, and she joins Warrigal, who has followed the hunters and hung around the ranch, aware of the presence of the pup. Together they roam the hills, moving their lair a couple of times, with Shula learning survival skills from the older male. In the meantime, Steve acquires a kangaroo dog pup which he names Kylie, an Aborigine word for boomerang. He grows into a beautiful, powerful dog, well trained by Steve. Shula and Warrigal are threatened by a bush fire, and in their escape Shula loses her first litter of pups. Some months later, when Frank hears of sheep being killed by dingoes, he and Harry load up with traps and set off, Frank never having given up his vendetta against Shula. Both dingoes are caught in the traps, but Shula is able to tear her foot free and, though injured, escapes. Warrigal is captured alive and sold by Frank to a little backcountry circus. There, though comparatively well treated, he survives in misery until fire destroys the circus and he is freed. He makes his way the long distance back to where he and Shula had their lair, only to find that Shula, lonely and still feeling some attraction to the place where Steve was kind to her, has hung around the ranch, lured Kylie away, and mated with him. Kylie is a strong, well-developed dog but no match at fighting, and Warrigal kills him. Steve, riding out to seek Kylie, finds the place and realizes what has happened. Shula soon gives birth to Kylie's pups, but a flood drives the dingoes from their lair and Shula can carry only one pup. The men from the ranch have set up a temporary camp on the same hill. There Frank hears the pup, and going to investigate, runs into Shula, who with Warrigal drives him away and into the rushing water. He is able to climb onto a small island, along with countless snakes also escaping the flood. The dingoes, following, are swept away but manage to scramble onto a washed-out tree and ride it safely until it lodges against a bank. Steve, seeing all this, first finds the pup, which greatly resembles Kylie, and which he of course adopts, then organizes a rescue of Frank. Despite a good deal of action, the pace is leisurely, with detailed descriptions of the countryside, the strange animals of Australia, the ways of both animals and men in the isolated area. While much of it is told from the point of view of the dingoes, there is no anthropomorphizing and the author is scrupulously careful to point out that nature is neither deliberately kind nor cruel and that animals, though intelligent, do not think like men. Aust. Bk. of Year Highly Com.

WILD DOG FRONTIER (Hatfield*, William, Oxford, 1951), boy's growing-up story set in the Channel Country of southwest Queensland, Australia, not long after World War II. A shortage of ammunition, fencing, and manpower during the war years has allowed the wild dogs, the dingoes, to proliferate until they are a major menace to cattle and sheep. Jerry Barrett has just turned fourteen, the age his father has set before he can use the twenty-two caliber rifle, and he can hardly wait to shoot at one of the marauding dogs. His efforts, however, seem to go wide of the mark, even after long practice with his air rifle. He and his father, Jim Barrett, come upon a ne'er-do-well neighbor, Slessor, moving a herd of cattle made up of some belonging to the big Barara Downs spread and some to Barrett. Before they have the cattle sorted out, Alan Jorrocks, manager of the Barara spread, and Hansen, the local law enforcement man, approach and assume that Barrett is working with Slessor. They refuse to listen to his protests. Furious, Jim beats up Slessor, and he and Jerry ride home disconsolate because the Jorrocks have been the best neighbors and friends on isolated Barrett's Creek. Jerry, however, soon has other interests since Joe Brown, of *Rod and Gun*, to whom he has written of his problems of setting the sights on his gun, comes for a paying visit to get a shot at a few wild dogs. The first half of the book is mainly about his visit, their discussion of guns and sights, and the many dingoes and kangaroos that they kill. The Barretts are also visited by the "sand shifters," a group of scientists investigating conditions in the dry interior, all of whom act like youngsters on an outing, much to the surprise of Jerry, who was dreading a dry, academic group. A severe drought follows their visit and makes the dingo menace worse, because the stock animals are weakened and the dogs more ravenous. When Jerry and his father come upon seven dingoes harrying one of Slessor's cows, literally eating it alive, they put it out of its misery and kill all seven dogs. Slessor and his son accuse them of rustling. They are jailed briefly and a trial is set for the following March. Just days before Christmas Jorrocks and his wife arrive, both full of apologies and loaded with Christmas gifts for the children. Hanson, it seems, had seen through Slessor's frame-up and had pried the real story out of Slessor's son, then taxed Jorrocks for his false suspicions in the earlier incident. When rain does come, it also brings hail the size of a man's fist, then torrents that last for weeks, until their house is an island. Fortunately Jim had earlier taken the bullock cart into town and bought enough supplies to last for months. An airplane drops a note saying that there is a man on a roof upstream twelve miles and suggesting that they take the boat left by the sand shifters to rescue him. Jim and Jerry manage to get to Slessor's house, a trip that takes two days of tremendous effort and several times almost ends in disaster. When they get to him, Jim has to knock him out to keep him from swamping the boat before they can drag him in. Then since he clearly has pneumonia, they row him four miles east to a flat area where the plane can land and transport him to the hospital. Overcome by remorse, Slessor insists on signing a confession. The scientists take Jerry on a flight around the central desert, which is now covered with water for the first time in fifty years or more. One of them promises to design a dam specifically for their land and let Jerry finance the supplies by his bounty on dingoes. Although Jerry is ostensibly the protagonist, the story is really about the Channel Country—the extremes of weather, the wild animals, the difficulty of stock raising, and the beauty of the austere land. Far more technical information about guns is included than the average reader can absorb, and the delight in the slaughter of the wild dogs, with details of their bodies being ripped to pieces by the bullets and spattered in the dust, is disturbing. The characters are flat types. Several younger children in the Barrett family are mentioned, but despite the isolation, which would make younger siblings important either as companions or antagonists, they are given almost no part in the action. Aust. Bk. of Year Com.

WILD MAN OF THE WOODS (Clark*, Joan, Viking, 1985), psychological problem and adventure novel set in the Rocky Mountains west of Calgary, Alberta, Canada, in the late twentieth century. Stephen, evidently a young teenager, goes on an exchange visit to the home of his cousin, Louie Barrows, while their older sisters visit at Stephen's home in Calgary. Although somewhat apprehensive, Stephen finds Louie compatible and Aunt Lise, a former nurse turned weaver, and Uncle Adam, a former dentist turned wood-carver, welcoming if busy and preoccupied with their craft business. Stephen is particularly attracted in his uncle's home to an Indian sun mask, a giver-of-life mask, made by a local Indian named Angus*. Although Louie is not a reader like Stephen, the boys find common interests in swimming in the nearby lake, hiking, and playing board games. Their good time, however, is marred by two local bullies, Willard Soper and Sludge (Edward) Riley, who swipe their towels, harass them with their motorbikes, and cut loose the diving raft. In retaliation, Stephen and Louie let the air out of the motorbike tires, accidentally puncturing one of the tires in the process. Later they row frantically away from Sludge's motorboat, escape on the far side of the lake to a grove hung with many grotesque masks, and manage to scare the pursuing bullies by donning masks and acting out the characters depicted. They are interrupted by Angus, who shows them how he carves his masks in standing trees, tells them a story that seems to be autobiographical, and warns then against the Wild Man of the Woods mask in a cave high on the mountain, a mask that has terrible power. When they return to their boat, *The Explorer*, which belongs to Louie's sister, they find that the bullies have punched a hole in it. With constant bailing they get home, and Uncle Adam helps them repair it, but Louie doesn't tell his father the truth of how it happened. The feud escalates, with both sides trading acts of minor vandalism. Stephen and Louie climb to the cave and discover the Wild Man of the Woods mask. Stephen puts it on and goes berserk, chanting and chasing Louie, who crashes down the mountain. When Angus is not in his tent, Louie races through the grove of masks to the shore, where Sludge and Willard are in their motorboat, evidently contemplating further mischief. All three boys are appalled to see the Wild Man emerge from the woods, brandishing a sword and chanting about blood. As they struggle to start the motor, he comes toward them, and Louie knocks him into the water. Stephen, stunned by the blow but himself once again as the heavy mask slips off, almost drowns and is pulled from the water by Angus. Stephen realizes that he has lost his fear of bullies but has begun to be scared by the potential of violence in himself. In an unconvincing last chapter, Sludge and Willard, both non-swimmers, show up and ask Stephen and Louie to give them lessons in the lake. Because in the episode of the Wild Man mask Stephen seems to be taken over by a power outside himself, the novel could be considered fantasy rather than psychological realism. The main interest, however, is in the way the boy comes to terms with his fear of bullies and learns to stand up for himself. Angus is an enigmatic character, seeming to represent acceptance of and respect for nature, though his story shows that he has been prey to his own violent nature in the past. Sludge and Willard are stock characters. Aunt Lise and Uncle Adam are figures from the sixties who have rejected the city and adapted to a simpler way of life, but they and the red-neck Sopers are not explored in depth, nor is the difficulty that they have had being accepted in the suspicious mountain community. A companion novel about the boys' sisters is *The Moons of Madelaine*. Can. Bk. of Year Winner.

WILD RIVER (O'Reilly*, Bernard, Cassell, 1950), adventure novel set in northern Queensland, Australia, about 1949, involving a discovery of uranium and the skullduggery of evil men who try to learn the location of the lode and file a mineral claim on it before the rightful owners can. The Dawson youngsters, Buller, 16, Jan, 15, and Mike, 13, are returning from Brisbane, where they have lived with an aunt for a year following the death of their mother, to the family homestead at Wild River. Instead of their father, his lawyer meets them, and tells them that John Dawson has discovered a chip of pitchblende, a radioactive ore, in a bowerbird's nest and is hunting for the source. Since word of his find seems to have leaked out and some suspicious characters have been spying around, he wants the children to stay with friends in Ravenshoe for safety. With no intention of being left out of the excitement, the three wire the friends that they are staying in Cairns, then board the train for Wild River. Their compartment is shared by an athletic-looking young man named Rolf, who at first pretends to have been sent by their father to look after them but, tricked by questions from Mike (who gets his ideas from reading Captain Lightning comics), soon reveals that he has never seen their father. Then he threatens them with a revolver and forces them out on the back platform so that they can't pull the emergency cord. As the train slows on an uphill pull, they jump off, hoping to reach an outpost of the neighboring homestead, Weatherly, where they may get food and horses. After a difficult trek through rough terrain, they come upon the camp of the Three Stinkaroos, as they have nicknamed Rolf and his cohorts. Mike and Jan take the three fine saddle horses and a pack pony loaded with sleeping bags and plenty of tinned food. They lead their pursuers on a long chase across the countryside, eventually losing them. They make their way over the hills to their own home, where they see someone who is not their father in the house. Buller sneaks down to investigate and hears the Stinkaroos say that Dawson is down below the gorge and that they are watching to ambush him when he comes out. The Dawsons ride for a hidden canyon they know well, where they camp and, after scouting the area, circle around by the ridges and eventually find their father trying to locate the lode from which the chip of pitchblende came. At the suggestion of Buller, who has heard at school of geiger counters that are loaned by the government to prospectors, John decides to hike out to the horses, ride to where he has left his car, and get one. When he returns with a geiger counter, which was flown out to him at the spot where he left his car, along with an expert to explain how it works, they prospect for some time with no luck, then find a crevice along a narrow ridge to which the machine responds vigorously. The next day they peg and measure off the claim, only to be met by Rolf and the two other men, who keep them prisoners until they can mark the claim with their own peg, then rush off to file on it before Dawson can. At Mike's suggestion Jan and Buller ride to the homestead and sabotage the Stinkaroos' car, as John and Mike go back to reset their peg. On the wild night ride, Buller is thrown when his horse stumbles and is lamed, but Jan rides on ahead, reaches the homestead in time, and smashes the spark plugs. After some other near escapes, they all meet at the pre-established rendezvous where John has left the car and head for town where they will file on the claim and send the constables out to pick up the villains. Although the style is riddled with clichés ("running a desperate race against ruthless men and the relentless hands of the clock"), the fast pace and evocation of the setting keep the story interesting. Attempts at humor, mostly about Mike's propensity for barley sugar and sleep, are feeble, and other characterization depends on stock elements. Aust. Bk. of Year Highly Com.

WILLIAMS, RUTH C., Australian writer for children. The youngest of eight children, she was born in London of an English father and an Australian mother. When she was in her teens, the family emigrated to Australia and settled in Sydney. Her interest in art led to her meeting artist Rhys Williams, whom she married in 1923. She published several short stories, among them *Timothy Tatters* (Bilson, 1946), about a friendly scarecrow. Named Australian Book of the Year was her novel *Verity of Sydney Town** (Angus, 1950), a girl's story set in Sydney and the outback in the early 1800s. Later she published *The Aborigine Story* (Shakespeare, 1955), a book of non-fiction for pre-adolescents.

WILLIAM WHITBURN (*Blue Above the Trees**), determined, stubborn husband of Sarah*, father of the protagonist, Simon*. A big, strong man, he feels that he was destined for farming and deplores his failure as an accountant. He moves his family to Australia to homestead, intending to sell out and buy back the family farm in Devon but remains in Australia. Except for the deep love, steadfast loyalty, and hard work of his family, he probably would have failed. William learns that he must respect his family if he expects respect in return. He is a complex, convincing, and memorable figure.

WILLIE WINOWIE (*Fire in the Stone**), Aborigine friend of Ernie* Ryan, who becomes his partner in the opal mine and who is killed in the explosion. Willie has many of the idealized qualities of a native minority people: an almost psychic sense, ability to see further than whites and to move silently and gracefully, and real stamina despite his slightness of build. Though he lives in the junk heap of the reserve and must cope with his drunken aunt and his mostly idle relatives, he is able to fit into Ernie's life as a courageous friend. Ernie's hope that the reward money may be used to get Willie training so he can leave this dead-end life is frustrated when Willie dies of his injuries from the explosion.

WILL MORRISSAY (*The Root Cellar**), Canadian farm boy who also plays the flute and has a special appreciation for nature. About thirteen years old when Rose* Larkin first meets him, he is fifteen years old and tall when he enlists in the Union forces in the American Civil War, motivated by gallant spirit and by dedication to the cause of freedom. After the fall of Richmond and the death from an infected wound of Steve, his cousin, he feels that the war was no business of Canadians and is disillusioned. He feels that he should have taken Steve to the hospital, even though Steve insisted he not do so, and is riddled with guilt. A complex, intriguing figure, he marries Susan* Anderson, the Morrissays' hired girl.

WILLMOTT, FRANK (1948–   ), Australian author of *Breaking Up** (Collins, 1983), an unusually convincing novel in diary form kept by a fifteen-year-old boy in a disintegrating family headed by two teachers. It was commended for the Australian Book of the Year Award. Other titles by Willmott include *My Dad at Home* (Educational Resources, 1985), a booklet accompanied by a sound cassette, and *Suffer Dogs* (Collins, 1985), a novel.

WILL STOCKTON (*Good Luck to the Rider**), Willhelmenia, stable, practical girl whom Barbara Trevor meets at boarding school, who spends the holidays at Tikera ranch and encourages Barbara to train her horse, Rosinante, as a jumper. From the plains of North Queensland, Will is surprised at the beauty and greenness of the Bungaree district and is interested in all the practical aspects of the sheep ranch. When Barbara's brother, Clive*, makes sharp remarks and sly digs, Will calmly outsmarts him and wins the admiration of Clive's twin, George*.

WILLY (*Always Ask for a Transfer**), 14, foster son of Yota* and Dino* Bazos and brother of Laura*. Willy has been characterized by social workers as "difficult." When fully confident that Dino really needs him at the pizzeria, he pitches in with a will. His realization that Dino has always been fair with him leads him to name Dino as his father when he is apprehended by the police. Dino's accepting him and taking him home from the station leads to their reconciliation. Willy often makes bad decisions under stress, for example, running away when accused of the theft although he knows that Dino is upset because Yota has had a heart attack, and trusting Karl when he knows that Karl is an ego-driven show-off who deliberately breaks school rules. Willy is a likeable and sympathetic figure who rises above the typical.

WINDMILL AT MAGPIE CREEK (Mattingley*, Christobel, ill. Joan Saint, Hodder, 1971), simple story of family life on an Australian farm set in the modern period, in which a family emergency forces a young boy to overcome his fears. Tim Rogers has always admired the giant windmill on the family farm at Magpie Creek, and he is delighted when his father suggests that he climb up with him to check and service it, as he does four times a year. Although Tim is an expert tree climber, he has never been allowed to climb the windmill. Half way up, he hears his puppy, Shadow, yelping below, looks down, and becomes paralyzed with fear. He drags himself up the rest of the way, watches his father check the wheel, and, by thinking of strawberries and cream, manages the even more difficult task of climbing down, but he never asks to go up again, and his father, obviously aware of his fear, never suggests it. For the next two years, Tim is handy and helpful around the farm. One of his regular jobs is to bring the cows from the pasture for milking and to take them back afterward. His biggest trouble comes from the magpies, which nest along the way and in the spring strafe and dive at him, perhaps because of his bright yellow hair. They do not bother his father or mother. He makes a bull-roarer, which he can swing around his head to scare them away, but it makes the cows nervous. One afternoon when he brings the cows in a little late, he is surprised that his father is not waiting to milk them. He does most of his chores before going to the house and finds an ambulance there to take his father to the hospital because he has fallen from a haystack. Tim's mother goes along, leaving the boy to hook the forty-six cows in shifts to the milking machine, take them back to the pasture, hose out the milking shed, collect, wash, and grade the eggs from her two-hundred hens, and drive the tractor into the implement shed. His father, fortunately, has not broken his back but will need Tim's willing help with many of the farm tasks. For some time neither of them mentions the windmill. Then one day his father shows Tim plans for a pump house with a diesel motor, the kind Tim has always scorned on the farm of his friend, Barney. His father explains that without regular service, the windmill will fall into disrepair as have the others in the area. For several days, Tim worries about the windmill, becoming so preoccupied that his parents are concerned and he gets into trouble at school. Then he finds that magpies are building a nest on a crossbar far up the windmill tower. In anger, he starts up, only to be driven back by angry magpies. Since he can't use his bull-roarer while climbing, he decides that he must make a helmet. Pots and pans are too heavy; billy cans cost too much. He buys a large can of ice cream, shares it with the other youngsters at the school, and claims the empty tin for himself. That evening he cuts eyeholes in it and sets an alarm clock under his pillow. In the morning, dressed in heavy clothes and woollen gloves, he starts up the windmill with the ice-cream tin helmet on his head. He sweeps the nest away and climbs onto the platform, where he painstakingly checks the wheel, as he had watched his father do two years before. His father throws away the plans for the pump house and has a new sign painted, the name Tim has always wanted for their gate: Windmill Farm. The picture of life on a farm—

the physical setting, the animals, and the varied tasks—has interest, and Tim's dilemma makes an adequate plot for a brief, low-key story of a warm family for early readers. The style is simple, and the characterization is minimal. Aust. Bk. of Year Highly Com.

WINGED SKIS (Mitchell*, Elyne, ill. Annette Macarthur-Onslow, Hutchinson, 1964), mystery-adventure novel involving ski enthusiasts set for four months in the Snowy Mountains of New South Wales, Australia, in the early 1960s. When James Milton, a government forester, is dispatched to the Kosciusko Park Trust in the Snowy Mountains on a conservation survey, he and his wife, Agnes, a botanist, make an agreement with their son, Barry, 14, to allow him to study skiing under the Austrian professionals there if he will work hard by correspondence school and get his Intermediate Certificate. In addition to Barry's schooling problem, another concern helps to unify the essentially episodic plot that is liberally laced with skiing tours to the hills, races, and instruction in skiing and skiing protocol: the identity of the mysterious lone skier who leaves such elegant trails on even the most treacherous slopes. Encouraged by his instructors, Heini and Johann, and tutored by a new friend, Michael Hastings, 17, who is spending his pre-university holidays there with his family, Barry doggedly keeps at his studies and passes adequately, doing his best not unexpectedly in English, history, and geography, the subjects that Michael likes best. Barry also takes a prize in the New South Wales Junior Ski Championships. The second problem provides thrills for the story and a kind of villain. From the beginning, Barry is reminded by his parents and instructors of a skier's axiom: never ski alone; always keep your companions informed of your intentions and location. But he and his friends and parents early see evidence of a mysterious lone skier, one apparently very skilled, of whose identity everyone seems ignorant. James eventually learns that the man is an engineer named Hugo Henry on special assignment with the Snowy Mountain Authority, and Michael learns that Henry has a reputation for showing off. Heini and Johann insist that the man is potential trouble, especially because the young people are so intrigued by him, viewing him as a romantic figure. Not unexpectedly, near the end, Henry causes another skier to have an accident and break both legs, is himself injured while alone, and endangers the lives of those who rescue him, among them Barry, Heini, and Johann. On a tour with several others, Barry happens to hear Henry's call for help and sights his fire, and a large party pulls off a daring, very difficult rescue on the slopes. At the very end Johann and Heini take the boys skiing again and Johann demonstrates for them "such skiing as this man has never done [because he does not conform]" and reminds them to "remember for always what is foolish, what is brave, what is right, and what is wrong." The incidents are conventional for sports stories, and the characters are stock, developed only in broadest outline, and are obviously foiled. The responsible, caring James is paired with irresponsible, egocentric, exhibitionist Henry; the intellectual, poetry-quoting Michael with the active, athletic Barry; the skillful extrovert Heini, who also sings and yodels, with serious, often moralistic Johann. The accounts of the ski tours, though clichéd and often instructive, are made interesting by the vivid, affectionate descriptions of the terrain and of the skiing that carry the conviction of the author's own experience. The style is sometimes naive and awkward (Barry thinks Michael "a slender boy with a dreamy face, who looked very nice"), and the dialogue is frequently inept. The action scenes are vigorous and exciting. Aust. Bk. of Year Highly Com.

WINNERS (Collura*, Mary-Ellen Lang, Western, 1984; Dial, 1986), realistic psychological and sociological problem novel set on the Blackfoot reservation near Calgary, Alberta, recently. After staying at eleven foster homes in eight years, Jordy Threebears, 15, returns to Ash Creek Reserve on the Canadian prairie to live with the grandfather he hardly knows, Joe* Speckledhawk, a former rodeo star, lately returned from prison for killing the white man who assaulted and murdered his daughter, Jordy's mother. Jordy is scared and perplexed at first, is not accepted by either whites or Indians at school, doesn't understand his whites-hating grandfather, who keeps him at arm's length, and finds his grandfather's aluminum-sided cabin too remote and austere for his liking. Two interlocking matters unite with Jordy's struggle for self-worth to form the plot: Jordy's desire for information about his parents and the horse that his grandfather gives him for Christmas. After Jordy is forced off the road by drunken whites, he runs away to the prairie. Exhausted after two days without food and water, he sees a vision of an Indian rider who utters a single word, Siksika, which means Blackfoot, and then blunders into a cabin. Its owner, old Erasmus* Watermedicine, gets the boy to a hospital. The shock of Jordy's ordeal brings back details of his mother's death, and over time he pieces together the story. Some information come from Mr. Campbell, the Indian agent, who tells him that his father had been a champion rodeo rider and that his mother was thought to be exceptionally beautiful, a "winner." After Christmas, Indian friends build a corral for the horse, a lean, gray mustang mare, and slowly and patiently Jordy wins her confidence. Miss MacTavish, his gym teacher, agrees to teach him to ride providing that he will be the riding companion of Emily MacKenzie, 16, blind daughter of the area's largest rancher. The two young people become staunch friends in spite of the opposition of the MacKenzie foreman, Fred Brady, who Jordy learns later is the brother of the man Joe killed. The MacKenzies fire Fred when he insults Jordy about his Indianness, and shortly thereafter the mare is stolen. Days later Jordy and Mr. Campbell discover her at a rodeo, starved, beaten, and frightened. Gradually Jordy sets about winning her confidence all over again, and Joe makes her a Blackfoot saddle, which to Jordy's delight she accepts. Jordy and Emily enter a fifty-mile Labor Day endurance race and are contenders until Emily falls and cracks some ribs. Though Jordy persuades her to finish the race, their progress is so slow that they come in last. Jordy is encouraged, however, to enter the hundred-mile Hallman Cup Ride near Jasper, and in spite of fierce competition and inexperience, he and his mare lead the pack until he is attacked by Fred Brady. In the scuffle, Fred falls over a cliff. Although he knows that he will probably lose the race, Jordy rescues the man and goes on to win in spite of his lost time, gaining strength to finish by a vision of the same Blackfoot rider who had earlier appeared to him on the prairie. Jordy names the mare Siksika in honor of his people, with whom he now feels a kinship. He has gained self-confidence and pride in his heritage and has proved he can be a winner like his parents and grandfather. Although the plot is clumsily constructed and relies heavily on coincidence and clichéd characters and incidents, it is sometimes suspenseful and exciting, and Jordy elicits sympathy. The vision sequences are jarring and seem too deliberately inserted for effect. The book's strengths lie in its depiction of the austere and impoverished way of life of the prairie Indians and in the contrast between the lives of the whites and the Indians. A double standard of justice exists. No one, for example, seems to have brought to account the men involved in Sarah Threebears's death, and no one attempts to identify the man who steals Jordy's horse (probably Fred Brady). Mr. Campbell, who is sympathetic but white, simply informs Jordy and Joe that he expects to be repaid the one hundred dollars he gave the rodeo man so that Jordy could legally take his mare from the rodeo, an attitude that the Indians have trouble understanding. Can. IODE Natl.; Can. Young Adult Winner.

THE WISH CAT (Chapman*, Jean, ill. Noela Young, with photographs by Dean Hay, Angus, 1966), brief story of a cat that disrupts the life of a family but eventually wins its affection. When Mrs. Lane comes upon a cat on the best blue chair in the sitting room, she does not put it out immediately because she sees that it is a valuable Siamese and thinks that she should keep it safe for the owner who will obviously be looking for it. Margaret Lane, 8, greets the cat joyously, calling her Lisa and announcing that she has come in answer to her very hard wish for a cat with blue eyes. Despite efforts by parents, her grandmother, and her brother, Bill, 10, to dissuade her, Margaret sticks firmly to her certainty that Lisa is her cat, come in answer to her wish. Although they place an advertisement in the newspaper, a notice in the butcher shop, and inquire throughout the neighborhood and at school, only one person comes to claim the cat, and she clearly is not the owner, having lost her cat after Lisa appeared at the Lane home. Lisa is not an easy addition to the household. She demands food whenever the family eats or the refrigerator door is opened, wrecks the laundry room when she is shut in there, insists on watching the children take baths, wakes them all at first light, sharpens her claws on the carpets and furniture, digs in Mr. Lane's prize garden, and vies with Grandma Lane for the blue chair, complaining loudly when she doesn't get her way. Just as they are about at wit's end, Lisa becomes ill from a tick bite. With a good deal of difficulty, they get her to the veterinarian, who gives her injections and keeps her for observation. The house seems so strangely empty and lonely without her that none of the family can sleep except Margaret. When Lisa is well enough to come home,

Mrs. Lane has bought her a special pet basket for a bed, Grandma has insisted that Mr. Lane buy cod-liver oil, condition pills, and vitamin powder, and even Bill is glad to see her back. She soon has the family trained to treat her as she demands, even Mr. Lane letting her nap under his choice azalea. The simple story makes no effort at strong characterization or plot but has humor for anyone who has been adopted by a pet. Skillful pen-and-ink drawings blend well with photographs of a beautiful, aloof, black-faced Siamese. Aust. Bk. of Year Com.

WITCHERY HILL (Katz*, Welwyn Wilton, Groundwood/Douglas, 1984; Atheneum, 1984), fantasy novel of witchcraft and magic set about the time of publication on the Channel Island of Guernsey. Mike Lewis, 14, accompanies his father, author and journalist Robert Lewis, to Guernsey to spend the summer in the villa home of Robert's Vietnam buddy, Dr. Tony St. George, a widower recently married to Janine, a beautiful Guernsey native. Mike soon discovers that, while his father thinks that the marriage is appropriate, Tony's daughter by his first marriage, Lisa, 13, despises Janine and suspects her of witchcraft. Though his father dismisses Lisa's accusation as illogical and the result of jealousy, Mike soon becomes Lisa's ally in exposing Janine's duplicity. Extremely disconcerting events occur. On the night of the Friday he arrives, Mike observes on the hill called Trepied that overlooks the house what he learns is a sabbat, or coven, meeting of witches, at a prehistoric tomb; the owner of the chateau next door, Seton Goth, dies under mysterious circumstances in spite of Tony's efforts to save him; Tony then falls ill of a strange malady, becomes unusually irritable, suffers a stroke, and dies; the house is burgled; the right hand of the chateau owner's corpse is cut off; and witch signs appear. It becomes clear to Mike that Janine and Seton Goth's nephew, Enoch, are competing for control of the local coven, the deciding factor to be the acquisition of a book of magic known as *Vieux Albert*, which turns out to be not a book in the conventional sense but thought-transferred knowledge. He learns, too, that when Seton died, the information passed to Tony, being the only person present at the time. Lisa's life is then in danger from both Janine and Enoch because of the knowledge she has gained. When Lisa, who is diabetic, takes an overdose of insulin in a deliberate effort to induce shock and amnesia, Janine prepares to sacrifice her on Trepied before the coven, but Mike diverts their attention with a series of stunts and saves Lisa's life with a timely injection. Janine and Enoch stab each other to death in a power struggle, and the police break up the coven. Although the plot uses standard conventions of the Gothic novel and the witchcraft thriller, it is constructed with sufficient skill and human interest to avoid sounding trite. The author teases the reader with the conflict between Janine and Lisa—perhaps the jealous stepdaughter syndrome applies, and Janine is the innocent victim of circumstances—and the conflict between Mike and his strong-minded, intellectualizing father seems believable. After the reader realizes that Lisa has been correct about her stepmother, attention focuses on whether or not Janine will destroy Lisa (and possibly Mike) as she has Tony. The idea of information transference by thought has much story merit as does the depiction of the island society. Although the climax at the tomb is both strained and rushed, since Mike's tricks seem too unlikely even for this genre, the atmosphere of tension begins early and is well sustained, and the style is more polished and literate than is usual for the form. Can. Bk. of Year Runner-Up.

WOODBERRY, JOAN (MERLE) (1921–   ), born in Narrabri, New South Wales, Australia; teacher, librarian, writer. She was educated at the University of Sydney, became a teacher for five years, and later studied library science in England. She studied and worked in England and on the Continent as librarian and teacher, and became a lecturer in English at Teachers' College, Launceston, Tasmania. She spent two years working on a fishing boat, an experience that has contributed background for her novels, notably *Rafferty Takes to Fishing* (Parrish, 1958), a story of an English boy transported to live with his grandfather in an Australian fishing village, the first of several about Rafferty, including *Floodtide for Rafferty* (Parrish, 1959) and *Rafferty Rides a Winner** (Parrish, 1961). This last was winner of the Australian Book of the Year Award. Other titles by Woodberry include *Come Back, Peter* (Rigby, 1968; Crowell, 1972), a story about seal pups, *Ash Tuesday* (Macmillan, 1969), *Little Black Swan* (Macmillan, 1970), and *A Garland of Gannets* (Nelson, 1970). She has made her home in Mount Nelson, Tasmania.

THE WOODEN PEOPLE (Paperny*, Myra, ill. Ken Stampnick, Little, 1976), family story of four children who secretly construct and learn to operate mari-onettes, despite their father's opposition to anything theatrical, set mostly in Alberta, Canada, in 1927. Although the Stein children, Lisa, 13, Teddy, 12, Suzanne, 10, and Mike, 7, love their latest home on a lake in British Columbia, their father, a fiery-tempered storekeeper who resents any frivolity and moves his family continually, sells the store and buys another in Chatko Falls, on the Alberta prairie near Edmonton. After a long automobile trip over bad roads, they discover that Chatko Falls is a hamlet without running water or trees and that their home will be above the general store, a strangely shaped amalgam of two buildings joined and painted a violent, shiny purple, soon christened by the townsfolk the Purple Folly. The girls and Mike adjust quickly, but Teddy is determined that he will not be wrenched away from friends again because he will not make any. On a late October day when their parents have gone to Edmonton, Teddy goes to explore a stream, falls in, and returns in the beginning of a snowstorm, just after Lisa has alerted Macnamara, the patrolman, to start a search. Teddy gets pneumonia and their parents have to be summoned back from Edmonton, bringing a doctor with them. Teddy recovers but cannot go back to school and is very demanding and difficult for Lisa until he becomes interested in making a marionette. Because his sister in Russia became an actress and married a performer, Papa has been violently against the stage, so the puppets that the children start making have to be kept secret. Over the Christmas vacation in Edmonton for the Hanukkah festival, Lisa attends a vaudeville show with her cousin Ben and going backstage afterward talks to an old actor who knows about marionettes. He gives her advice and even a beautiful ballerina puppet. The children get permission to use an attic space in the Purple Folly, enlist Tom Barker, a classmate, son of a carpenter, to carve faces and make the moveable joints, and soon are giving secret performances of the plays Lisa writes for groups of town children, telling Mama that the kids come to see Teddy, who is out of school until spring. Their big opportunity comes at the school Easter program, which is an amateur talent night, complete with a twenty dollar prize and a chance for the winner to perform in Edmonton. Each Stein pretends to prepare some other performance while Tom builds a real puppet theater and they perfect the backdrops. Although for a brief time Papa thinks that he will close the store and come to the show with Mama and cousin Ben, who is visiting, and the children almost despair, he is called away at the last minute, and they perform with great success. As prizes are being announced, however, he appears, loudly upbraids them, and starts to herd them out. Only Mama's rare assertiveness lets them claim the first prize before Papa forces them to go home. He straps them all with his belt for deceiving him, promising further punishment, but after their teacher has interceded and pleaded for understanding, he lets them off with a long lecture and even permits them to move the puppet theater to an unused chicken coop behind the store. When Papa announces that Lisa will go to boarding school in Edmonton rather than to the nearest high school by bus, she is devastated, and Teddy admits to her that he plans to run away. Two events intervene. The chicken coop catches fire, and to their astonishment Papa heroically rescues most of their puppets. Mama later confides in them that Papa was interested in the stage before his sister became a performer. Then Papa announces that he has sold the store and bought one in Edmonton, where Lisa can live at home and they can build a new puppet theater. The novel is rambling and clumsily constructed, with the human characters, except for Papa, almost as wooden as the marionettes. The picture of the small town in Alberta in the 1920s is interesting, the book's strongest element, and Papa, the autocratic European father, who moves his reluctant family all over Canada, is memorable. Can. Council Winner.

WOOD, KERRY (EDGAR ALLARDYCE WOOD) (1907–   ), born in New York City; Canadian journalist, broadcaster, scriptwriter, photographer, naturalist, and author of more than two dozen books of fiction and non-fiction for adults and children, some self-illustrated, some illustrated by his wife, many set in the vicinity of his home town of Red Deer, Alberta, and all reflecting his keen interest in the historical development of the area and its flora and fauna. He also published thousands of articles, short stories, newspaper columns, and television scripts. He early decided to become an author and dropped out of school at sixteen to devote himself to his ambition. His first book of juvenile fiction, a collection of short stories called *Cowboy Yarns for Young Folk* (Copp,

1951), appeared after he had published half a dozen books for adults. It was runner-up for the Canadian Library Association Book of the Year Award. Several more books for young readers followed, including *Wild Winter* (Houghton, 1954), a novel based on his own two winters as a teenager alone in the Alberta wilderness; *The Boy and the Buffalo* (Macmillan, 1963; St. Martin's, 1963), about a Cree youth who is adopted by a buffalo herd; and *Samson's Long Ride* (Collins, 1968), about a boy's four-hundred-mile search for his family. He received the Governor General's Award for two books of biographical fiction, *The Map-Maker: The Story of David Thompson** (Macmillan, 1955) and *The Great Chief: Maskepetoon, Warrior of the Crees** (Macmillan, 1957; St. Martin's, 1958), both of which are sometimes classified as biography. In 1963, Wood received the first Vicky Metcalf Award from the Canadian Authors' Association for his contribution to Canadian children's literature. His family moved to Canada in 1909, and he became a citizen in 1973. Deeply interested in ecology and conservation, he helped to establish more than two dozen wildlife sanctuaries across North America.

WRIGHTSON, (ALICE) PATRICIA (1921–   ), born in Lismore, New South Wales, Australia; hospital administrator, editor, and highly acclaimed novelist of works for pre-teen and teenaged readers, four times winner of the Australian Children's Book of the Year Award. After attending St. Catherine's College in Queensland, she held supervisory and management positions in hospitals from 1946 to 1964, and for ten years she edited the Sydney *School Magazine*. She did not begin to write until after her two children were born, publishing her first novel, *The Crooked Snake** (Angus) in 1955. It was a Book of the Year. Twenty years and several novels later, she retired to focus full time on her writing. Almost all her some dozen books have won or been nominated for awards, both in Australia and abroad, and in 1986 she received the international Hans Christian Andersen Award for the body of her work. Critics consider her ability to establish mood seemingly without artifice outstanding. Her earlier books, like *The Crooked Snake, The Bunyip Hole** (Angus, 1957), and *The Feather Star** (Hutchinson, 1962; Harcourt, 1963), are realistic novels of mild adventures and family and neighborhood life. *I Own the Racecourse!** (Hutchinson, 1968; *A Racecourse for Andy*, Harcourt, 1968) exploits a retarded child's belief that he has actually bought the local racetrack. Her later books are fantasies, and of these the most compelling involve Aborigine beliefs, among them the stories linked by Wirrun, an Aborigine youth: *The Ice Is Coming** (Hutchinson, 1977; Atheneum, 1977), another Book of the Year Winner; *The Dark Bright Water* (Hutchinson, 1979; Atheneum, 1979); and *Behind the Wind** (Hutchinson, 1981; *Journey Behind the Wind*, Atheneum, 1981). A separate novel, *A Little Fear** (Hutchinson, 1983; Atheneum, 1983), is Wrightson's most honored book. About a stubborn old woman's struggles with an ancient, indigenous spirit for the right to live in her own small cottage, it received the Book of the Year Award, the Young Observer Teenage Fiction Award, and the *Boston Globe–Horn Book* Award, was commended for the Carnegie Medal, and was named to Fanfare by the editors of *Horn Book*. Some of her other books are *An Older Kind of Magic** (Hutchinson, 1972; Harcourt, 1972), *The Nargun and the Stars** (Hutchinson, 1973; Atheneum, 1974), another Book of the Year Award Winner, and *Balyet* (Hutchinson, 1989; McElderry, 1989), all of which employ indigeneous folklore and a serious tone, and, in quite a different vein, a lighthearted fantasy about a Martian spaceman in Sydney, *Down to Earth* (Hutchinson, 1965; Harcourt, 1965).

WUORIO, EVA-LIS (1918–), born in Virpuri, Finland; journalist, prolific writer for both adults and children. She immigrated to Canada about 1929, and attended schools in Finland, Canada, Sweden, and Switzerland. She was a reporter, columnist, and feature writer for the *Toronto Evening Telegram* and the *Toronto Globe and Mail*, and was assistant editor for *Maclean's Magazine*. She has made her home on the island of Ibiza in the Spanish Balearics, the scene of her brief book for younger children, *The Island of Fish in the Trees** (Nelson Foster, 1962; World, 1962), which was illustrated by Edward Ardizzone and selected by the New York *Times* as one of the best illustrated books of the year, as well as being named to the *Horn Book* Fanfare list. Ibiza is also the scene of *Tal and the Magic Barruget** (Nelson Foster, 1965; World, 1965), a lighthearted fantasy similarly named to the Fanfare list. Also set in Spain are two mystery novels for young people, *Detour to Danger** (Delacorte, 1981), which was a nominee for the Edgar Allan Poe Award for best juvenile mystery, and *Save Alice!* (Holt, 1968), which was named by *Choice* magazine to its list of children's books for an academic library. Wuorio has written a wide variety of other books for children and mystery novels for adults.

Y

THE YEAR OF THE CURRAWONG (Spence*, Eleanor, ill. Gareth Floyd, Oxford, 1965; Roy, 1965), realistic family novel involving some mystery and detection set for about nine months in the village of Currawong Crossing in the mountains about one hundred fifty miles northwest of Sydney, Australia. The Kendall family looks forward with pleasure to moving from the city to the highlands of Currawong when their father, Professor Kendall, accepts a position teaching history at the new university at nearby Macebridge: Alex*, 12, also "mad on history"; Terry*, 11, a budding novelist; Chess, 8, a rock hound; and mother, Janet, a painter. Only Elizabeth*, 14, has misgivings, but even she soon gets caught up in the excitement that awaits them. The children explore and make friends. Terry meets Mister* Lee, an elderly Chinese man who occupies a rude hut at the foot of the hill that dominates the area and upon which stands an abandoned silver mine. Mister Lee claims it and the land around it. Then Alex encounters an aged Swagman*, who says that the property belongs to him. Trouble begins when Chess discovers a man fencing the area. The children learn that the mine area has been sold for a motel, hold a council of war, and form a club, the Currawong Mine Preservation Society, dedicated to saving the place from commercial development. Alex finds an unofficial history that holds that in 1908 the mine became the property of three local men, a Chinese, a Norwegian, and an Irishman, and that in a quarrel the Norwegian, Bransen, killed the Irishman, Sullivan. Later Elizabeth discovers that the mine is said to hold a hidden treasure, and Chess, taking shelter in the place during a sudden shower, discovers a battered tin box in which is an almost illegible old paper. Suspecting that it might be a deed, Professor Kendall takes it to experts who restore it and turn it over to the authorities. Alex suspects that the Swagman is related to the murdered Sullivan, a deduction that proves correct. While waiting for the report on the paper, which turns out to be a deed, the children and neighbors continue plans for a Back-to-the-Crossing Day, for which Alex has written a historical pageant based upon information gained during his investigations. After the celebration, the children learn that the land had been unlawfully sold to the developers by a descendant of the Norwegian, and all is set to rights. Mister Lee retains ownership of his land, Swagman Sullivan gets a little property upon which to live out his old age raising poultry, the Kendalls arrange to build a house on some of the remaining land, and the mine becomes a public reserve, a relic of the romantic past. The children have been instrumental not only in solving a mystery but also in developing community pride. The Kendall children are distinctively and convincingly drawn, neither paragons of detecting virture nor blustering snoops, and the relationships between them, their parents, and their new acquaintances seem genuine. The elderly characters are neither distorted nor romanticized and are presented with the determination and slightly oblique viewpoint of the aged who have sorted out their priorities but are on the fringes of the action. Although the plot makes ample use of conventions and coincidence, the author avoids melodrama, and the freshness of the characterizations keeps it from seeming trite. There is a strong sense of place, with much mention made of trees and birds, an appropriate aspect since most of the action takes place out of doors and the setting is vital to the events. The plot problem is historically valid, and the novel is consistently entertaining and much better crafted than most books of this genre. Aust. Bk. of Year Com.

THE YEAR OF THE YELVERTONS (O'Brien*, Katherine, ill. Gavin Bishop, Oxford, 1981), realistic family novel of friendship and neighborhood life set for one year in the late twentieth century in a farming region on the southernmost tip of New Zealand's South Island. The Barry children, Julie, almost ten, and Neil, 8, enjoy the company of friendly Mr. Mac (Alexander McTavish), the elderly, retired farmer next door. They like running through the paddocks to spend time with him and often accompany their farmer father on business to Mac's home, which fronts on the sea. During holidays one December, Mr. Barry takes them along on his annual trip to buy Mac's excess lambs. To their surprise, they find Mr. Mac's kitchen uncharacteristically tidy and the old man beaming and bustling with the news that his London cousins, Howard and Isobel Yelverton, a brother and sister, are taking a trip around the world and will be in New Zealand the following year. Exuberant with anticipation, the old man embarks on a trip of his own, a campaign to get his rundown place into shape for them, an effort that takes the entire year. It involves clearing out old furniture and tons of rubbish, redoing the yard and garden, painting and papering the walls, fixing the floors, and buying new furnishings, including such items as saucepans, tablecloths, blankets, and coverlets. The children eagerly help, and he solicits their advice about such matters as paint colors and wallpaper patterns. He even hires a handyman, who produces marvelous changes. Each time they visit, the children find him happily and busily engaged in some aspect of the project. Periodic postcards keep him apprised of the Yelvertons' progress on their tour and build suspense about them. In October a card arrives saying that they have reached Australia, which they will cross by railroad to Sydney. A week before Christmas, Mr. Barry takes the children with him on another lamb-buying trip. To their disappointment, Mr. Mac gloomily informs them that the Yelvertons have written to inform him that they will not have time to visit South Island. Two days later, when the children visit him, apprehensive about the effect of the disappointment upon him, they find that they've worried in vain. An assiduous newspaper reader, he has found and answered an advertisement from a family seeking accommodations for the summer on a farm. Not only is he happy that they will be coming, but Julie and Neil share his joy because they will have playmates their age. The book concludes with Neil spotting a sealion, something he had longed to do. Although it is not clear whether or not the old man merely assumed that the Yelvertons would visit him or whether they simply cut their visit short without giving him reasons for the change in plans, this is a mildly suspenseful story for middle-grade readers. The ending about the sea lion seems added unnecessarily, but the ironic plot has enough low-key action and suspense to hold the reader's attention. The children are types but serve the story satisfactorily, and the old man with his lively personality, eager perseverance, and simple stories about the region keeps the center stage. Clear scenes of farm life and affectionate descriptions of the region add to the appeal of the clever story. N. Z. Esther Glen.

YEE, PAUL (1956–   ), born in Spalding, Saskatchewan, Canada; historian, author of poetry, short fiction, articles, and novels. He grew up in Vancouver, received his B.A. and M.A. degrees in history from the University of British Columbia, and has been the archivist for the City of Vancouver. His first book for children, *Teach Me To Fly, Skyfighter! and Other Stories* (Lorimer, 1983), contains four slightly connected pieces set in Vancouver's Chinatown, where Yee spent much of his childhood. *The Curses of Third Uncle** (Lorimer, 1986) is a historical adventure and mystery novel set in 1909 in the Canadian Chinese community in conflict over the efforts of Dr. Sun Yat Sen to overthrow the Chinese emperor, but it is more directly concerned with the changing possibilities for Chinese women in North America. In another book with a historical background, *Tales from Gold Mountain: Stories of the Chinese in the New World* (Groundwood, 1989), Yee tells eight stories of earlier orientals who overcame prejudice and adversity in the Canadian West.

YOTA BAZOS (*Always Ask for a Transfer**), overly plump, warm, genial foster mother of Willy* and Laura* and loving and patient wife of Dino*. With her and Dino, the children for the first time experience a truly loving home. Yota expresses her love with food, kind words, and unconditional acceptance. When she suffers a heart attack, Willy and Dino are forced to come to terms. Willy comforts Dino and is able to tell Dino that he loves him and that his father has been forcing him to turn over his earnings. Though a type figure and sentimentalized, Yota is likeable and functions adequately for the plot.

YOUTH DAY PARADE (Segun*, Mabel D., ill. Duca, Daystar, 1984), short realistic school story set in contemporary Nigeria. Zuma schoolboy Tunde, perhaps twelve, is both pleased and apprehensive when his headmaster puts him in charge of organizing the school's entry in the annual Youth Day Parade. Praised for the honor by his best friend, Audu, and by his proud parents, he lists the major things to be done (getting a new banner, putting the school band instruments in shape, practicing marching, and composing a new school song), calls a meeting of the student body, and forms a central committee of three other boys and a girl. When the headmaster informs him that there is no money for a new banner, Okanima (the girl) takes responsibility for making one using batik and tie-and-dye. Audu supervises cleaning the instruments with lime and wood ash, and Ekpo writes the words for a rousing song and sets them to an old hymn tune. All seems to be going smoothly until practices begin. The schoolchildren miss marching practice and don't take learning the song seriously. Tunde becomes very discouraged and has almost given up when Okanima arrives with the completed banner, a striking flag dyed a lovely blue with "Zuma School" in bold white letters in the center and white stars in each corner. Encouraged by her efforts, Tunde gets the idea of going to the Police College to watch how they conduct their trainee marching. There he runs into a skillful young drum major, wearing, ironically, a Zuma uniform. Tunde learns that he is a new student named Chike and asks him to perform for the parade. Chike's presence so inspires the students that they march as never before. On Youth Day, Tunde and Okanima carry the banner, which elicits loud cheers. Next comes Chike, strutting with his baton. Even the governor claps for them. The Zuma students are the hit of the day and are certain that they will win first prize. This pleasing story, intended as a reader for middle-grade students, offers mild suspense, an engaging problem, an interesting plot twist, an anticipated conclusion, and the theme of perseverance and cooperation ending in success. Nigerian CLAN Hon. Ment.

APPENDIX A: BOOKS AND AUTHORS BY NATIONALITIES

AUSTRALIA

Authors

Aldous, Allan

Aldridge, James

Baillie, Allan

Balderson, Margaret

Basser, Veronica

Bennett, Jack

Birtles, Dora

Brinsmead, H(esba) F(ay)

Chadwick, Doris

Chapman, Jean

Chauncy, Nan

Clark, Mavis Thorpe

Collins, Dale

Davison, Frank Dalby

Evers, L. H.

Fatchen, Max

Fennimore, Stephen

Finkel, George

Fletcher, Jane Ada

Fowler, Thurley

Frances, Helen

French, Simon

Gleeson, Libby

Granger, Helen

Graves, Richard H.

Greener, Leslie

Greenwood, Ted

Gunn, John

Handford, Nourma

Harding, Lee

Hatfield, William

Hill, Deirdre

Hill, Fitzmaurice

Jackson, Ada

Kellaway, Frank

Kelleher, Victor

Klein, Robin

Lindsay, Harold A.

Lurie, Morris

Manley, Ruth

Martin, David

Mattingley, Christobel

McFadyen, Ella

McNair, W. A.

Mitchell, Elyne

Norman, Lilith

O'Dea, Marjory

O'Reilly, Bernard

Ottley, Reginald

Park, Ruth

Patchett, Mary Elwyn

Pearce, Frances

Phipson, Joan

Pownall, Eve

Rees, Leslie

Rice, Esme

Rodda, Emily

Roland, Betty

Roy, Thomas

Rubenstein, Gillian
Scott, Bill
Shelley, Noreen
Southall, Ivan
Spence, Eleanor
Steele, Mary
Stow, Randolph
Syred, Celia
Tennant, Kylie
Thiele, Colin
Tindale, Norman B.
Villiers, Alan
Wheatley, Nadia
Williams, Ruth C.
Willmott, Frank
Woodberry, Joan
Wrightson, Patricia

Books

All the Proud Tribesmen (Tennant, Kylie)
All We Know (French, Simon)
Arkwright (Steele, Mary)
Ash Road (Southall, Ivan)
The Bates Family (Ottley, Reginald)
Beetles Ahoy! (Jackson, Ada)
Behind the Wind (Wrightson, Patricia)
Blue Above the Trees (Clark, Mavis Thorpe)
Blue Fin (Thiele, Colin)
Boori (Scott, Bill)
Bread and Honey (Southall, Ivan)
Breaking Up (Willmott, Frank)
The Brown Land Was Green (Clark, Mavis Thorpe)
The Bunyip Hole (Wrightson, Patricia)
Bush Holiday (Fennimore, Stephen)
Bush Voyage (Collins, Dale)
By the Sandhills of Yamboorah (Ottley, Reginald)
Callie's Castle (Park, Ruth)

A Candle for Saint Antony (Spence, Eleanor)

Cannily, Cannily (French, Simon)

Carcoola (Handford, Nourma)

The Cats (Phipson, Joan)

Children of the Dark People, An Australian Story for Young Folk (Davison, Frank Dalby)

Climb a Lonely Hill (Norman, Lilith)

Cocky's Castle (Syred, Celia)

Come Danger, Come Darkness (Park, Ruth)

Cousins-Come-Lately (Pownall, Eve)

The Crooked Snake (Wrightson, Patricia)

The Curse of the Turtle (Roy, Thomas)

Dancing in the Anzac Deli (Wheatley, Nadia)

Darnkess under the Hills (Scott, Bill)

Devil's Hill (Chauncy, Nan)

The Devil's Stone (Frances, Helen)

Displaced Person (Harding, Lee)

Doctor with Wings (Aldous, Allan)

A Dog Called George (Balderson, Margaret)

Eleanor, Elizabeth (Gleeson, Libby)

Family at The Lookout (Shelley, Noreen)

The Family Conspiracy (Phipson, Joan)

The Feather Star (Wrightson, Patricia)

February Dragon (Thiele, Colin)

Finn's Folly (Southall, Ivan)

Fire in the Stone (Thiele, Colin)

The First Walkabout (Tindale, Norman B. and Lindsay, H. A.)

Five Times Dizzy (Wheatley, Nadia)

The Forbidden Bridge (Roland, Betty)

The Fox Hole (Southall, Ivan)

Good Luck to the Rider (Phipson, Joan)

The Green Laurel (Spence, Eleanor)

The Green Wind (Fowler, Thurley)

Hebe's Daughter (Syred, Celia)

High and Haunted Island (Chauncy, Nan)

The Hole in the Hill (Park, Ruth)

The House that was Eureka (Wheatley, Nadia)

Hughie (Martin, David)

The Ice Is Coming (Wrightson, Patricia)

I Own the Racecourse! (Wrightson, Patricia)

It Happened One Summer (Phipson, Joan)

James Cook, Royal Navy (Finkel, George)

Jamie's Discovery (Roland, Betty)

Jamie's Summer Visitor (Roland, Betty)

John of the "Sirius" (Chadwick, Doris)

Josh (Southall, Ivan)

Kiewa Adventure (Aldous, Allan)

The Left Overs (Spence, Eleanor)

Let the Balloon Go (Southall, Ivan)

The Lieutenant (Bennett, Jack)

Lillipilly Hill (Spence, Eleanor)

Little Brother (Baillie, Allan)

Little Brown Picaninnies of Tasmania (Fletcher, Jane Ada)

A Little Fear (Wrightson, Patricia)

Longtime Passing (Brinsmead, Hesba)

The "Loyall Virginian" (Finkel, George)

Magpie Island (Thiele, Colin)

Master of the Grove (Kelleher, Victor)

Mathinna's People (Chauncy, Nan)

Me and Jeshua (Spence, Eleanor)

Midnite: The Story of a Wild Colonial Boy (Stow, Randolph)

The Min-Min (Clark, Mavis Thorpe)

Moon Ahead (Greener, Leslie)

The Nargun and the Stars (Wrightson, Patricia)

The October Child (Spence, Eleanor)

An Older Kind of Magic (Wrightson, Patricia)

Once there was a Swagman (Brinsmead, H. F.)

Over the Bridge (Hill, Deirdre)

Pastures of the Blue Crane (Brinsmead, H. F.)

Pegmen Tales (McFadyen, Ella)

Penny Pollard's Diary (Klein, Robin)

Pigs Might Fly (Rodda, Emily)

Pioneer Shack (Birtles, Dora)

Playing Beatie Bow (Park, Ruth)

The Plum-Rain Scroll (Manley, Ruth)

The Pochetto Coat (Greenwood, Ted)

Ponny the Penguin (Basser, Veronica)

The Quest for Golden Dan (Kellaway, Frank)

The Racketty Street Gang (Evers, L. H.)

Rafferty Rides a Winner (Woodberry, Joan)

Rangatira (Tindale, Norman B. and Lindsay, Harold A.)

The River Kings (Fatchen, Max)

River Murray Mary (Thiele, Colin)

The Roan Colt of Yamboorah (Ottley, Reginald)

The Roaring 40 (Chauncy, Nan)

Sea Menace (Gunn, John)

The Secret Family (Rice, Esme)

The Seventh Pebble (Spence, Eleanor)

The Silver Brumby (Mitchell, Elyne)

Silver Brumby's Daughter (Mitchell, Elyne)

Six Days Between a Second (O'Dea, Marjory)

Something Special (Rodda, Emily)

Southward Ho with the Hentys (Hill, Fitzmaurice)

Space Demons (Rubenstein, Gillian)

Spear and Stockwhip: A Tale of the Territory (Graves, Richard H.)

The Spirit Wind (Fatchen, Max)

Starland of the South (McNair, W. A.)

Storm Boy (Thiele, Colin)

The Story of Karrawingi the Emu (Rees, Leslie)

The Story of Kurri Kurri the Kookaburra (Rees, Leslie)

The Story of Sarli, the Barrier Reef Turtle (Rees, Leslie)

The Story of Shadow, the Rock Wallaby (Rees, Leslie)

The Summer in Between (Spence, Eleanor)

The Sun on the Stubble (Thiele, Colin)

Tangara (Chauncy, Nan)

Taronga (Kelleher, Victor)

Threat to the Barkers (Phipson, Joan)

Tiger in the Bush (Chauncy, Nan)

Toby's Millions (Lurie, Morris)

To the Wild Sky (Southall, Ivan)

The True Story of Lilli Stubeck (Aldridge, James)

The True Story of Spit MacPhee (Aldridge, James)

The Valley Between (Thiele, Colin)

Verity of Sydney Town (Williams, Ruth)

Whalers of the Midnight Sun (Villiers, Alan)

When Jays Fly to Barbmo (Balderson, Margaret)
Wild Brother (Patchett, Mary Elwyn)
Wild Dog Frontier (Hatfield, William)
Wild River (O'Reilly, Bernard)
Windmill at Magpie Creek (Mattingley, Christobel)
Winged Skis (Mitchell, Elyne)
The Wish Cat (Chapman, Jean)
The Year of the Currawong (Spence, Eleanor)

CANADA

Authors

Andersen, Doris
Brandis, Marianne
Brochmann, Elizabeth
Brown, Jamie
Buffie, Margaret
Burnford, Sheila
Butler, Suzanne
Clark, Catherine Anthony
Clark, Joan
Collura, Mary-Ellen Lang
Day, David
Doyle, Brian
Dunham, Mabel
Freeman, Bill
Haig-Brown, Roderick
Halvorson, Marilyn
Harris, Christie
Hayes, John F.
Hewitt, Marsha
Hill, Kay
Houston, James
Hudson, Jan
Hughes, Monica
Kaplan, Bess
Kasper, Vancy
Katz, Welwyn Wilton

Kushner, Donn
Laurence, Margaret
Little, Jean
Lunn, Janet
Mackay, Claire
Major, Kevin
Matas, Carol
McRae, Russell
Melling, O. R.
Montgomery, L. M.
Mowat, Farley
Nichols, Ruth
Nyberg, Morgan
Paperny, Myra
Pearson, Kit
Razzell, Mary
Richler, Mordecali
Riley, Louise
Sharp, Edith Lambert
Smucker, Barbara (Claassen)
Stevenson, William
Taylor, Cora
Truss, Jan
Wieler, Diana J.
Wood, Kerry
Wuorio, Eva-Lis
Yee, Paul

Books

Always Ask for a Transfer (Kasper, Vancy)
And Tomorrow the Stars (Hill, Kay)
Angel Square (Doyle, Brian)
Anne of Green Gables (Montgomery, L. M.)
A Book Dragon (Kushner, Donn)
The Bushbabies (Stevenson, William)
Corner Store (Kaplan, Bess)
The Curses of Third Uncle (Yee, Paul)

The Dangerous Cove (Hayes, John F.)

Days of Terror (Smucker, Barbara Claassen)

Dear Bruce Springsteen (Major, Kevin)

Detour to Danger (Wuorio, Eva-Lis)

The Doll (Taylor, Cora)

The Druid's Tune (Melling, O. R.)

The Emperor's Panda (Day, David)

False Face (Katz, Welwyn Wilton)

Far from Shore (Major, Kevin)

Galahad Schwartz and the Cockroach Army (Nyberg, Morgan)

Going to the Dogs (McRae, Russell)

The Great Chief: Maskepetoon, Warrior of the Crees (Wood, Kerry)

The Guardian of Isis (Hughes, Monica)

A Handful of Time (Pearson, Kit)

Hold Fast (Major, Kevin)

Hunter in the Dark (Hughes, Monica)

The Incredible Journey (Burnford, Sheila)

The Island of Fish in the Trees (Wuorio, Eva-Lis)

Jacob Two-Two Meets the Hooded Fang (Richler, Mordecai)

Jasmin (Truss, Jan)

Julie (Taylor, Cora)

Kristli's Trees (Dunham, Mabel)

A Land Divided (Hayes, John F.)

Last Chance Summer (Wieler, Diana J.)

Let It Go (Halvorson, Marilyn)

Lisa (Matas, Carol)

Listen for the Singing (Little, Jean)

Lost in the Barrens (Mowat, Farley)

Mama's Going to Buy You a Mockingbird (Little, Jean)

The Map-Maker: The Story of David Thompson (Wood, Kerry)

The Marrow of the World (Nichols, Ruth)

Nkwala (Sharp, Edith Lambert)

The Olden Days Coat (Laurence, Margaret)

One Proud Summer (Hewitt, Marsha and Mackay, Claire)

The Quarter-Pie Window (Brandis, Marianne)

Raven's Cry (Harris, Christie)

Rebels Ride at Night (Hayes, John F.)

River Runners: A Tale of Hardship and Bravery (Houston, James)

The Root Cellar (Lunn, Janet)

Saltwater Summer (Haig-Brown, Roderick)

Shadow in Hawthorn Bay (Lunn, Janet)

Shantymen of Cache Lake (Freeman, Bill)

Slave of the Haida (Andersen, Doris)

Snow Apples (Razzell, Mary)

Starbuck Valley Winter (Haig-Brown, Roderick)

Starlight in Tourrone (Butler, Suzanne)

The Sun Horse (Clark, Catherine Anthony)

Super Bike (Brown, Jamie)

Sweetgrass (Hudson, Jan)

Tal and the Magic Barruget (Wuorio, Eva-Lis)

Tikta'liktak: An Eskimo Legend (Houston, James)

Train for Tiger Lily (Riley, Louise)

Underground to Canada (Smucker, Barbara)

Up to Low (Doyle, Brian)

The Violin-Maker's Gift (Kushner, Donn)

The Whale People (Haig-Brown, Roderick)

What's the Matter, Girl? (Brochmann, Elizabeth)

The White Archer: An Eskimo Legend (Houston, James)

Who is Frances Rain? (Buffie, Margaret)

Wild Man of the Woods (Clark, Joan)

Winners (Collura, Mary-Ellen Lang)

Witchery Hill (Katz, Welwyn Wilton)

The Wooden People (Paperny, Myra)

INDIA

Authors

Bhatt, Kavery

Bhatty, Margaret R.

Bulsara, C. N.

Desai, Anita

Dutta (Datta), Arup Kumar

Joshi, Niharika

Kaur, Simren

Salwi, Dilip M.

Sengupta, Abhijit

Sengupta, Poile
Sinha, Nilima
Sinha, Sarojini

Books

Adventure on the Golden Lake (Sinha, Nilima)
The Blind Witness (Dutta, Arup Kumar)
The Chandipur Jewels (Sinha, Nilima)
The Exquisite Balance (Sengupta, Poile)
The Golden Buddha (Joshi, Niharika)
The Kaziranga Trail (Datta [Dutta], Arup Kumar)
Kidnapping at Birpur (Bhatty, Margaret R.)
The Mystery of the Fake Arjuna (Joshi, Niharika)
The Mystery of the Missing Relic (Kaur, Simren)
Once Upon a Forest (Bhatt, Kavery)
A Passage to Antarctica (Salwai, Dilip M.)
Robin and the Hawk (Bulsara, C. N.)
The Story of Panchami (Sengupta, Abhijit)
The Treasure Box (Sinha, Sarojini)
Trouble at Kolongijan (Dutta, Arup Kumar)
Vanishing Trick at Chandipur (Sinha, Nilima)
The Village by the Sea: An Indian Family Story (Desai, Anita)

NEW ZEALAND

Authors

Beames, Margaret
Cowley, Joy
Dallas, Ruth
De Hamel, Joan
Duder, Tessa
Duggan, Maurice
Faville, Barry
Gee, Maurice
Macdonald, Caroline
Mahy, Margaret
Morice, Stella

O'Brien, Katherine

Orwin, Joanna

Powell, Lesley Cameron

Somerset, David

Sutton, Eve

Taylor, William

Books

Alex (Duder, Tessa)

Barney and the Eels (Somerset, David)

The Book of Wiremu (Morice, Stella)

The Catalogue of the Universe (Mahy, Margaret)

The Changeover: A Supernatural Romance (Mahy, Margaret)

Elephant Rock (Macdonald, Caroline)

Falter Tom and the Water Boy (Duggan, Maurice)

The Halfmen of O (Gee, Maurice)

The Haunting (Mahy, Margaret)

Holiday Time in the Bush (Dallas, Ruth)

Ihaka and the Prophecy (Orwin, Joanna)

Jellybean (Duder, Tessa)

The Keeper (Faville, Barry)

Memory (Mahy, Margaret)

Motherstone (Gee, Maurice)

Night Race to Kawau (Duder, Tessa)

Pack Up, Pick Up, and Off (Taylor, William)

The Parkhurst Boys (Beames, Margaret)

The Priests of Ferris (Gee, Maurice)

Shooting Through (Taylor, William)

The Silent One (Cowley, Joy)

Surgeon's Boy (Sutton, Eve)

Take the Long Path (De Hamel, Joan)

Turi: The Story of a Little Boy (Powell, Lesley Cameron)

Visitors (Macdonald, Caroline)

The Year of the Yelvertons (O'Brien, Katherine)

NIGERIA

Authors

Ekwensi, Cyprian
Meniru, Teresa
Onadipe, Kola
Segun, Mabel D.

Books

Around Nigeria in Thirty Days (Onadipe, Kola)
A Pot of Gold (Onadipe, Kola)
Samankwe and the Highway Robbers (Ekwensi, Cyprian)
Unoma (Meniru, Teresa)
Youth Day Parade (Segun, Mabel)

SOUTH AFRICA

Authors

Beake, Lesley
Case, Dianne
Merchant, Eve
Naidoo, Beverley

Books

Ghamka Man-of-Men (Merchant, Eve)
Journey to Jo'burg; A South African Story (Naidoo, Beverley)
Love, David (Case, Dianne)
The Strollers (Beake, Lesley)

APPENDIX B: LIST OF BOOKS BY AWARDS

AUSTRALIAN BOOK OF THE YEAR COMMENDED

The Bates Family

Behind the Wind

Blue Above the Trees

Breaking Up

The Bunyip Hole

Bush Holiday

Cannily, Cannily

Carcoola

The Cats

Climb a Lonely Hill

Come Danger, Come Darkness

The Curse of the Turtle

Dancing at the Anzac Deli

Doctor with Wings

The Feather Star

Finn's Folly

Fire in the Stone

Five Times Dizzy

The Forbidden Bridge

The Fox Hole

Hebe's Daughter

High and Haunted Island

The Hole in the Hill

The House that was Eureka

Hughie

AUSTRALIAN BOOK OF THE YEAR HIGHLY COMMENDED

Beetles Ahoy!

Blue Fin

Boori

The Brown Land Was Green

Bush Voyage

By the Sandhills of Yamboorah

Callie's Castle

A Candle for Saint Anthony

Cocky's Castle

Cousins-Come-Lately

Darkness under the Hills

A Dog Called George

Eleanor, Elizabeth

February Dragon

I Own the Racecourse!

It Happened One Summer

Jamie's Summer Visitor

John of the "Sirius"

The Left Overs

Little Brother

Little Brown Picaninnies of Tasmania

Midnite: The Story of a Wild Colonial Boy

An Older Kind of Magic

Once there was a Swagman

Penny Pollard's Diary

Ponny the Penguin

The Roaring 40

The Secret Family

The Silver Brumby

Southward Ho with the Hentys

The Spirit Wind

Starland of the South

The Story of Kurri Kurri the Kookaburra

The Story of Shadow, the Rock Wallaby

Wild Brother

Wild River

Windmill at Magpie Creek
Winged Skis

AUSTRALIAN BOOK OF THE YEAR WINNER

All the Proud Tribesmen
All We Know
Ash Road
Bread and Honey
The Crooked Snake
Devil's Hill
The Devil's Stone
Displaced Person
The Family at the Lookout
The Family Conspiracy
The First Walkabout
Good Luck to the Rider
The Green Laurel
The Green Wind
The Ice Is Coming
A Little Fear
Longtime Passing
Master of the Grove
The Min-Min
The Nargun and the Stars
The October Child
Pastures of the Blue Crane
Playing Beatie Bow
The Plum-Rain Scroll
The Racketty Street Gang
Rafferty Rides a Winner
Sea Menace
The Story of Karrawingi the Emu
Tangara
To the Wild Sky
Tiger in the Bush
The True Story of Lilli Stubeck
The Valley Between

Verity of Sydney Town
Whalers of the Midnight Sun
When Jays Fly to Barbmo

AUSTRALIAN JUNIOR BOOK OF THE YEAR

Arkwright
Pigs Might Fly
Something Special

BOSTON GLOBE-HORN BOOK HONOR BOOKS

The Changeover

BOSTON GLOBE-HORN BOOK WINNER

A Little Fear

CANADA COUNCIL CHILDREN'S LITERATURE PRIZES, HONORABLE MENTION

Angel Square
Corner Store
The Curses of Third Uncle
The Emperor's Panda
Let It Go
One Proud Summer
Snow Apples
What's the Matter, Girl?

CANADA COUNCIL CHILDREN'S LITERATURE PRIZES, WINNER

Days of Terror
The Guardian of Isis
Hold Fast
Hunter in the Dark
Julie
Listen for the Singing
Shantymen of Cache Lake
Shadow in Hawthorn Bay

Sweetgrass
The Wooden People

CANADIAN LIBRARY ASSOCIATION AWARDS BOOK OF THE YEAR, RUNNER-UP

The Emperor's Panda
The Olden Days Coat
Slave of the Haida
Underground to Canada
Witchery Hill

CANADIAN LIBRARY ASSOCIATION AWARDS BOOK OF THE YEAR, WINNER

And Tomorrow the Stars
The Dangerous Cove
A Handful of Time
Hold Fast
The Incredible Journey
Jacob Two-Two Meets the Hooded Fang
Julie
Kristli's Trees
Lost in the Barrens
Mama's Going to Buy You a Mockingbird
The Marrow of the World
Nkwala
Raven's Cry
River Runners: A Tale of Hardship and Bravery
The Root Cellar
Shadow in Hawthorn Bay
Starbuck Valley Winter
The Sun Horse
Sweetgrass
Tikta'liktat: An Eskimo Legend
Train for Tiger Lily
Up To Low
The Violin-Maker's Gift
The Whale People
The White Archer: An Eskimo Legend

CARNEGIE MEDAL WINNER

The Changeover
The Haunting
Josh

CHILDREN'S BOOKS TOO GOOD TO MISS (AUSTRALIA)

The Incredible Journey

INDIA CHILDREN'S BOOK TRUST FOR FICTION AND SCIENCE FICTION (INDIA)

First Prize

The Chandipur Jewels
The Kaziranga Trail
Kidnapping at Birpur
Mystery of the Missing Relic
Once Upon A Forest

Second Prize

Adventure on Golden Lake
The Blind Witness
The Exquisite Balance
The Golden Buddha
The Mystery of the Fake Arjuna
Passage to Antarctica
Robin and the Hawk
The Story of Panchami
Trouble at Kolonginjan
Vanishing Trick at Chandipur

Third Prize

The Treasure Box

CHILDREN'S LITERATURE ASSOCIATION OF NIGERIA, FIRST PRIZE

(Ages 8–12) *Unoma*
(Ages 13–18) *Around Nigeria in Thirty Days*

CHILDREN'S LITERATURE ASSOCIATION OF NIGERIA, HONORABLE MENTION

(Ages 8–12) *Youth Day Parade*

THE CHILDREN'S LITERATURE ASSOCIATION TOUCHSTONES

Anne of Green Gables

THE CHILDREN'S RIGHTS WORKSHOP OTHER AWARD

Journey to Jo'burg

CHILD STUDY CHILDREN'S BOOK COMMITTEE AT BANK STREET COLLEGE AWARD

Journey to Jo'burg

COMMENDED FOR THE CARNEGIE MEDAL

A Little Fear
When Jays Fly to Barbmo

CONTEMPORARY CLASSICS LIST

Josh

ESTHER GLEN AWARD (NEW ZEALAND)

Alex
The Book of Wiremu
Elephant Rock
Falter Tom and the Water Boy
The Haunting
Take the Long Path
Turi: The Story of a Little Boy
The Year of the Yelvertons

GEOFFREY BILSON AWARD FOR HISTORICAL FICTION (CANADA)

Lisa

THE GOVERNOR GENERAL'S LITERARY AWARD, HONORABLE MENTION (CANADA)

False Face
Going to the Dogs

THE GOVERNOR GENERAL'S LITERARY AWARD, WINNER (CANADA)

Galahad Schwartz and the Cockroach Army
The Great Chief: Maskepetoon, Warrior of the Crees
A Land Divided
Lost in the Barrens
The Map-Maker: The Story of David Thompson
Nkwala
Rebels Ride at Night
Saltwater Summer

GUARDIAN AWARD FOR CHILDREN'S FICTION

The True Story of Spit Macphee
The Village By the Sea: An Indian Family Story

THE HORN BOOK MAGAZINE FANFARE LISTS

The Bushbabies
The Catalogue of the Universe
The Changeover
Children of the Dark People, An Australian Story for Young Folk
Fire in the Stone
I Own the Racecourse!
The Island of Fish in the Trees
Josh
A Little Fear
Moon Ahead
The Nargun and the Stars
Playing Beatie Bow
Starlight in Tourrone
Tal and the Magic Barruget

INTERNATIONAL READING ASSOCIATION CHILDREN'S BOOK AWARD

The Curse of the Turtle

JUNIOR HIGH CONTEMPORARY CLASSICS LIST

The Incredible Journey

LEWIS CARROLL SHELF AWARD

By the Sandhills of Yamboorah
The Incredible Journey

MASKEW MILLER LOGMAN YOUNG AFRICA AWARD (SOUTH AFRICA)

Love, David
The Strollers

MAX AND GRETA EBEL MEMORIAL AWARD, RUNNER-UP (CANADA)

Always Ask for a Transfer
Corner Store
False Face
A Handful of Time
Last Chance Summer
Sweetgrass

NATIONAL CHAPTER OF THE IMPERIAL ORDER OF THE DAUGHTERS OF THE EMPIRE (CANADA)

A Book Dragon
The Quarter-Pie Window
Shadow in Hawthorn Bay
Winners

NATIONAL COUNCIL FOR ARTS AND CULTURE, FIRST PRIZE (NIGERIA)

A Pot of Gold

NEW ZEALAND GOVERNMENT PUBLISHING AWARDS, BOOK OF THE YEAR SHORT LIST

Barney and the Eels
Elephant Rock
Holiday Time in the Bush
Ihaka and the Prophecy
Jellybean
Motherstone
Night Race to Kawau
Pack Up, Pick Up, and Off
The Parkhurst Boys
The Priests of Ferris
Shooting Through
Surgeon's Boy

NEW ZEALAND GOVERNMENT PUBLISHING AWARDS, BOOK OF THE YEAR WINNER

Alex
The Halfmen of O
The Keeper
The Silent One
Visitors

NIGERIAN IFE BOOKFAIR CHILDREN'S BOOK COMPETITION

Samankwe and the Highway Robbers

NOMINEES FOR THE EDGAR ALLAN POE AWARD BEST JUVENILE MYSTERY

Detour to Danger
Fire in the Stone

RUTH SCHWARTZ CHILDREN'S BOOK AWARD (CANADA)

Days of Terror
The Doll
Hold Fast
Jacob Two-Two Meets the Hooded Fang

Jasmin
One Proud Summer
Mama's Going to Buy You a Mockingbird

SANLAM PRIZE FOR YOUTH LITERATURE (SOUTH AFRICA)

Ghamka Man-of-Men

YOUNG ADULT CANADIAN BOOK AWARD, RUNNER-UP

Dear Bruce Springsteen
False Face

YOUNG ADULT CANADIAN BOOK AWARD, WINNER

The Druid's Tune
Far From Shore
Hunter in the Dark
The Quarter-Pie Window
Shadow in Hawthorn Bay
Super Bike
Who is Frances Rain?
Winners

YOUNG OBSERVER TEENAGE FICTION PRIZE

A Little Fear
Memory

INDEX

axe, 362; forest fire starting, 17; gashed arm, 322; gun runner hits head in scuffle, dies, 288; gun shot, 95; hand caught in trap, 179; head craftsman hurt felling tree, 175; in Tiers mountains, 384; knocked overboard, 31; legs, broken, 16, 30, 31, 41, 279, 436; legs, splinted by girl, 279; presumed, 38; sailing, 179; scalding in shower, 79; school bus, 285; sister's death in fall from cliff, 185, 252; sprained ankle, 114, 238; tallyman,182; thrown from horse, 433; tractor, 195; tree falls on father, 349; truck, freeing emu, 367; twisted ankle, 163; water drum hits foot, 66. *See also* calamities; catastrophes; disasters; illnesses; injuries; wounds

accountants, 182, 412

accusations, 430; aunt of niece of misbehavior with uncle, 18–19; boy of vandalizing library, 365; of attempted murder, 318; of father's murder, 342; of homosexuality, 53; of street boy of informing to police, 372; of theft, 8, 118, 204; of treachery, 100; of war crimes, 108, 262, 313; of witchcraft, 439

acrobats. *See also* actors; actresses; players

acting games, loved by prince, 302

activists, Maori, New Zealand, 33

actors: 301, 441. *See also* actresses; players

actresses, 121, 157, 440. *See also* actors; players.

ADAM WEB, *1*, 318

Adelaide, Australia: early 20th century, 43, 374; mid-20th century, 365; late 20th century, 122, 361

Adelie penguins, 302

adjustments: to father's death, hard, 239; to needs and demands of autistic brother, 98; to new home, 8, 12, 104

Admiralty, Lords of the, 183

Adolf Heinz, 411

adoptions: Catholic family of Protestant boy, attempted, 401; of son proposed, 270; white boy into Indian family, an honor, 324; white family of Maori girl, 33

Adrian Talbot, 239, 251, 334

Adrift, 21

ads, newspaper: for foster parents, 213; seeking farm for summer, 447

advances, technological, prehistoric, 123

Adventure Before Midnight, 349

ADVENTURE ON GOLDEN LAKE, *1*, 349

adventure novels: African jungle, 45; Arctic Eskimo, 391, 426; domestic, 22, 46, 55, 74, 118, 124, 125, 127, 183, 184, 282; emigration, 377; escaping slaves, 405; girl's, various, 157; fantasy, 26, 149, 258, 300, 305, 350, 373, 383; fantasy, folkloric,

35, 82–83; forest fire, 17; group, 1, 17, 74, 278, 394; historical, 9, 70, 81, 209, 217, 287, 310, 315, 318, 356, 361, 405, 422; Indians (Native Americans), 228, 323, 351, 421; holiday, 17, 43, 47, 178, 199, 372; horse, 346, 348; kidnapping, 58; life of Canadian geographer, 240; Melanesia, 6; mystery aspects, 80, 122, 204, 263, 325; New Zealand Maori, 174; outdoor, 331, 362; outlaw, 253, 333; prehistoric, 123; psychological, 431; riverboat, 321; river, ocean, 293; sailing, 268, 331; scientific voyage, 289; sea, 31, 112, 335; skiing, 436; space travel, 257; survival, 58–59, 66, 159, 170, 228, 323, 391; thriller, 58–59; time travel, 99; travelogue, 16; uranium; discovery, 432; western, 358. *See also* adventures; mystery novels; survival novels; war novels

adventures: conveyed to children in dreams, 293; domestic, 12, 22, 46, 91, 119–20, 127, 164, 178, 372, 402. *See also* adventure novels; mystery novels; survival novels; war novels.

advice: from fortune teller, travel while can, 106; of cat to become bushranger, 253; "overcome evil with reason, not with force," 107

adze, of special black stone, 175

Aenlocht, 259

aeriids, flying basilisks, 350–51

Aesake, 345

Africa: late 15th century, South Africa, 133; mid-20th century, Kenya, 45; late 20th century, Nigeria, 16, 333, 406, 448; late 20th century, South Africa, 193, 229, 371

ageism, 225, 293–94

agents, Indian (Native American), 438

age of protagonists:

—seven: boy, 125, 206; girl, 296

—seven to thirteen: group, 440

—eight: boy, 183, 383, 446; girl, 164, 303, 384, 438

—eight to ten: girl, 354

—eight to twelve: boy, 263

—nine: boy, 184, 193, 203; girl, 71, 278

—nine to twelve: boy, 249

—nine to fourteen: group, 278

—ten: boy, 25, 96, 127, 190, 203, 236, 287, 314; girl, 8, 51, 63, 97, 188, 195, 275, 293, 446

—ten and three-quarters: boy, 393

—ten or eleven: boy, 366

—ten to twelve: boy, 333

—eleven: boy, 22, 54, 89, 131, 182, 204, 213, 223, 239, 282, 373, 381, 390, 422; girl, 12, 124, 143, 144, 187, 204, 322, 339, 373; twin girls, 91

climbs: to rescue bird, 417; to service windmill, 435

Cling, Odo, 150, 190

Clinton, Charles, 200

CLIVE SCOTT, *67*, 255

CLIVE TREVOR, *67*, 138, 434

clock repairers, 130, 400

"closed custody," 135

Closer to the Stars, 117

clothes: hippy-type, 198; made from skins, 229; shopping for school, 373; stolen, 55; to be given to neighbors, 392; used, sorted for sale, 354; washed away, 187

clothespins, talking dolls, 292

clowns: aging, 301; bull dog, 32; class, girl, 297; priest plays, 281; school, 181; unable to bring laughter, 302; understanding, 301

Clown with the Thousand Pockets, 301

clubhouses, 43, 80, 339, 373

clubs: among low-cost housing youth, 143, 365; boys form "Supreme Expedition Council," 16; drama, neighborhood children, 373; Racketty Street Gang, 313; school children's, 74, 262; to preserve mine, 445; writing and drama, 13; youth, 165

Club Under Twelve, 54

clues: camera of missing girl, 1; comic book with initial "L," 11; footprint with right big toe missing, 200; green eyes, 60; to location of scroll in poem, 300; various, 313

coaches: abusive, 43, 54; held up by bushranger, 253

coastal towns: Australia, 15, 36, 314; New England, 34; New Zealand, 112

coats: causing time-slip, navy blue with hood, 275; flawed, birthday gift, 19; red, birthday presents, outgrown, 71

Cobbler, Stick to Thy Last, 161

Cobourg Street, Ottawa, 11

cockatoos, pet named Major bushranges jewels, 253

cockneys, boy, 288

cockroaches, army of, 131

cocky, a small farmer, 68

COCKY'S CASTLE, *68*, 380

Cocky's Castle, family homestead, 68

coconuts, shot from cannon, 293

Code Name Kris, 246

codes, "holiday," indicates imminent roundup of Jews, 221

cod liver oil, for cat, 439

Coffin, Levi, 406

coffins: built by dying man, 250, 408; Land Rover becomes, 66; stone, 391

Cohen, Sylvia, 20, 25, 72, 286, 380

cohoe, runs of, 332

cold spirits, Australian known as Noatch, 26

Colemans Creek, Aborigine girl drowns in, 169

Colin Kerr, 186, 242, 395

Collard family, 350

collars, antique crocheted, 134, 140, 299

Collected Stories, 101

collections: of fossils, 418; of insects, 25

Colleen Bailey, 373

college: girl allowed to attend, 407; mother returns to, 239; music, 274; reward for boy, 319

COLLINS, (CUTHBERT) DALE, 47, *69*

Collins family, 43

Collison, Rev. Mr., 317

Colliver family, 232

Colliver's Corners, Hawthorn Bay, Canada, 341

COLLURA, MARY-ELLEN LANG, *70*, 437

colonies: American develop own avenues of trade, 231; British penal, Australia, 70, 72, 413

color: disappearing, 93; draining from world, 418

colts, 47, 138, 324, 325, 346, 348, 374, 396

The Columbia Is Coming!, 9

Columbia River, discovery and mapping of, 241

Columbine Pine, 119

Colville, New Zealand, 251

combat, single, heroic, 100

Come Back, Peter, 440

COME DANGER, COME DARKNESS, *70*, 287

comedians, TV, mayor of Glitterville, 131

comet, thousand-year, 27, 261, 275

comic books: clue to criminal, 11; used as guide, 432

comic novels, 10, 15, 108, 131, 149, 182, 253, 258, 296, 300, 305, 393, 408

Commerce, thought paramount, 350

commercial development: Botanical Gardens threatened by, prevented, 27; children seek to block, succeed, 63, 445

commercials: children in for Chickenbits, 185, 251, 267; children in for Crackle-Crunch candy bars, 276

Commissioners, in Melanesia, 6

committee, to organize parade, 448

Commodore, 191

communes, 159, 274

communication: by mind-pictures, 306; through cat, 332

communists. *See* terrorists

community life: Australia, 15, 30, 41, 55, 70, 90, 192, 297, 309, Canada, 12, 309, 316, 351, 408, 437; New Zealand, 22, 402, 446; Palestine, 249

community life, novels of: 6, 10, 54–55, 74,

decapitations, of whites by vengeful Indians (Native Americans), 316

deckhands, 228, 314, 321, 353. *See also* crewmen

decisions, vocational, 9–10, 12–14, 30–31, 61, 66–67, 141–42, 182–83, 188–89, 231, 241, 249, 251, 287–89, 321–22, 331–32, 352–54

De Drie Gebroeders (ship), 231

deeds, to silver mine, 445

Deep South, feared by slaves for brutality, 405

deer: buck, shot out of season, 332; white-tailed, boy hunts, 170

De Feo, Charles, 362

Degei, Snake God, 345

DE HAMEL, JOAN (LITTLEDALE POLLOCK), *87*, 381

"deifel," in river, 206

Delaney family, 354

Delaware Bay, New Zealand, 174

Delhi, India, 397

delicatessens, 80, 124

delusions, reappearance of dead mother, 25, 71–72

demented persons: Crimean War veteran, 299, 334; doctor, 6; High Priest, 306; Irish hero in combat, 100; Mennonite woman, 19; old Alzheimer's woman, 251; uncle, veteran of World War II, 405, 424; World War II veteran improves, 331, 332

democracy, lost, on Isis, 147

demons: space demons in computer game stalk human players, 357

Denmark, Copenhagen, 221

dentists, 178, 431

Department: office building, 27; social agency, 213

deportation, of Acadians, 210

Depression, English of 1844, 41; Great, 399; low fruit prices, 322; psychological, 170

derailment, prevented, 412

Derin, 242, 244

Dermot Connell, 339

DESAI, ANITA, *88*, 415

deserts: Australia, 49, 66, 123, 181, 254, 255, 324, 372, 430

Desert Saga, 155

de Silva family, 415

desires: boy wants dog, 239; for permanent home, 43, 54; for place of one's own, 51; for safety and comfort of Kew Gardens, 267; to attend Rugby, 3; to be competent hero, 216; to buy fishing boat, 362; to derail tram, 283; to have best friend, 144; to join wife if in death, 26; to own tram, 282; to return to outer space, 109; to return to sea, 423; to train as nurse, 353. *See also* ambitions; wishes

desolation, of eternity, 243

THE DESPOT, *88*, 165, 270, 271

desserts, lime Interplanetary Missles, 294

destiny: birds, to be alone, 236–37; to save O, 150, 259, 305; boy to become white archer, 426

Detained at Her Majesty's Pleasure, 24

Detective Inspector K. D. Rao, 138, 263

detectives: ignores boys' pleas for help with murder, 29; India, 203; member of international smuggling gang, undercover, 29; super-sleuth Lamont Cranston, 11; youthful, 10, 29, 199, 313, 413, 445

DETOUR TO DANGER, *89*, 443

Devaki, 203

developers: unprincipled, 275–76; unprincipled, eaten by dragon, 34

THE DEVIL HOLE, *89*, 273, 360. See *THE OCTOBER CHILD*

Devil on My Back, 168

devils: Aborigines believe live on certain crag, 91; Aborigines believe ships to be, 224; credited with carrying away developer, 331; exorcised, 76; Tasmanian mammal, 90

DEVIL'S HILL, 63, *89*, 90, 326, 391

Devil's Rings, Queensland, Australia, 257

THE DEVIL'S STONE, *90*, 140, 292

"devil's stone," falls from sky in 1880, 91

Devine family, 19, 20, 25, 71, 286, 380

DEVLIN, ABRAHAM, *92*, 205, 262, 400

Devon fishermen, 81

de Vries, Maggie, 222

Dewdney, Selwyn, 206

Dhanai, 199

diabetics, girl, 439

Diablo the stallion, 195

dialects, 62, 162, 314–15, 325, 334, 345. *See also* style, dialect

dialogue: inappropriate, 82; moralistic, 437. *See also* style

The Diamond Feather, 65

Diana (ship), 377

DIANA BARRY, 12, 15, *92*

diaries, 38, 90, 91, 104, 105, 205, 293, 400. *See also* journals; style

diary-sketchbook, found, 427–28

Dias, Bartolomeu, 133

Dick, Astra Lacis, 68

Dick Felton, 179

Dick Halmer, 204

didactic novels: about Aborigines, 76, 247, 384; about Antarctic, 290; about blind, 223; about geographer David Thompson, 241; about Pacific migrations, 316; *apartheid*, 194; Australian Flying Doctors, 95; autism, 273; contribution of Mennonites to freeing slaves, 406; convict transportation, 71; ecological, 350; exploration, 9–10, 183;

Fran Smeaton, 68
Fran the puppy (*The Forbidden Bridge*), 126
Fran the dog (*Jamie's Discovery*), 184
Fran the dog (*Jamie's Summer Visitor*), 185
Franz Schumacher, 222
Fraser family, 73
fraud, over farm in Upper Canada (Ontario), 309
Freaks, King of, 300
Frederica Wilton, 189
Frederick Abernathy, 113
Fred Finn, 121
Fred Hitchens, 157
Free as I Know, 265
freedmen, on Underground Railway, 406
freedom, 73, 351, 372, 398, 406, 417, 429
freedom fighters, World War II, in Denmark, Jew and Gentile, 221
Freedom Sing-out, for Aborigines, 169
Freelove (ship), 182
FREEMAN, BILL (WILLIAM BRADFORD), *129*, 159, 342
Freeman Wells, 150, 259
freight car, uncoupled, 411
French and Indian War, 209
French-Canadians, 11, 279
French, in England, boy, 295
French Revolution, 157, 295
FRENCH, SIMON, 7, 53, *129*
frenzy, black comes upon Cuculann in battle, 75, 100
friars. *See* monks
friends: Aborigine girl and white girl, 384; abused girl and son of town lawyer, 399; American boy and Australian girl, 46; ancient Irish hero, Cuculann, and modern boy, 100; Australian prisoner of war and German soldier, World War II, 108; bar room, 121; bedridden schoolmate and underachiever, 96; blind boy and undercover policeman, 29; blind boy and sighted classmate, 29; "bosom," girls, 13; boy and cerebral palsied girl, 418; boy and dog, 96; boy and girl, 57, 439; boy and "hatter," 391; boy "not anything" and Jewish boy, 11; boy and old man, 276; boy and pelican, 366; boy and tenant girl, 109; boy and street urchin, 287; boy and wild boy, 326; boys, best, 327; boys, mutual interest in music, 87; brother and sister, 372; chief's son and deaf-mute, 345; children and old Chinese man, 256; children and old retired farmer, 446; children and reclusive miner, 311; cousins, boys, become fast, 249; deaf-mute boy and white turtle, 345, 346; derogatory, 54; doctor's daughter and poor girl, 339; English girl and old African man, 45; farm boy and rich boy, 318; father and bank floor

cleaner, 313; foster boy and basketball player, 8; foster, children and printer, 213; four boys in working-class Sydney, 313; four high school years, 222; four Nigerian schoolboys, 16; girl and convict maid, 414; girl and girl, 12, 98, 297, 372, 400; girl and great-uncle, both magicians, 399; girl and librarian, 195; girl and minister's wife, 13; girl and new teacher, 13; girl and nursing home resident, 293; girls, school chums, 133; girl slave and hunchback girl slave, 406; girl and woman potter, 106; hero kills best friend in single combat, 100; imaginative girl, bossy boy, and timid boy, 275; Indian (Native American) boy and blind girl, 437; Indian (Native American) boy chief and slave, 421; Indian (Native American) chief and arrow maker, 141–42; Indian (Native American) girls, 379; Jewish surgeon's daughter and gentile dance hall owner's daughter, 221; London boy and Australian girl, 47; lonely girl and son of dying teacher, 239, 388; migrant boy and local insulting boy, 54, 244; modern girl and mid-19th century girl, 328; mothers, years ago, 304; neighborhood boys and retarded boy, 177; official's son and twin sons of village headman, 199; older boy and younger boy, 116; older brother and younger brother, 358; orphan boy and French-Canadian girl, 373; orphan boy and old dogman, 197; outgoing girl and shyer girl, 92; partially sighted girl student and partially sighted teacher, 222; part Indian (Native American) boy and white boy, 215; poor girl and wealthy girl, 303; poor girl with wealthy youth, 143; Protestant well-off boy and poor emigrant Catholic boy, 52; Protestant boy and Catholic girl, 331, 401; rancher of dead pilot father, 47; relationship concealed from father, 381; retarded boy and racetrack employees, 177; several French village youngsters, 118; ski enthusiasts, 436; slave girl and slave daughter of Baptist minister, 226; spoiled boy and budding hoodlum, 357; station white children and Aborigine children, 41; teenaged boys, 362; town girl and rabbiter girl, 285; troubled boys, 211; 20th century girl and 19th century girl, 98; two-faced, 144; wealthy boy and gardener's helper, 203; white boy and Aborigine boy, 75–76, 122, 168, 433; white boy and Maori boy, 22, 288; white boy and Naskapi (Native American) boy, 323; white boys and half-Aborigine boy, 82; white girl and mixed blood girl, 33; wild boy and farm boy, 277; wild boy and little girl, 326; wild brumbies

kite, box, seagull caught in, 368
KIT QUAYLE, 92, 98, 181, *205*, 256, 399
Ki, the blackbird (South Sea Islander), 290, 294, 329
kittens: calico, tormented by bullies, 239; pets, 178
Kitty Kite, 28
Ki-Yu: A Story of Panthers, 149
Klassen family, 19
KLEIN, ROBIN, *205*, 293
knifings, 200, 399
knights, mock tournament, 293
knitting: to raise money, 115; for school expenses, 174
knives: wielded by drug dealer, 215; with warnings attached, 200. *See also* weapons
knots, captain teaches boy, 393
Knots and Lashings, 141
know-it-alls, schoolboy, 22
knowledge: thought transferred, 439; gained jeopardizes girl's life, 439
Koh family, 7
KO-IN, man of the mountain, 26, 104, 173, *206*
Kolonga, 83
Kolonijan, 398
kookaburras, 367
Koo-Koo-Sint (David Thompson), "the man who looks at stars," 241
Kootenay House, Lake Windermere, Canada, 241
korobarra, Tasmanian Aborigine tribal gathering, 246
Kororareka, New Zealand, 377
Kosciusko Park Trust, 436
Kosie, 372
Kristli Eby, 206
KRISTLI'S TREES, 101, *206*
KROB, *207*, 245
Kroom, Vicki, 159
Kubingi, Laszlo, 9
Kukaku, the Cree Medicine Man, 141
Kunama (Snowy) the creamy brumby, 348
Kungo, 426
Kung the Fluteplayer, 107
Kura, 315
Kuringai the kookaburra, 367
Kurri Kurri the kookaburra, 367
KUSHNER, DONN, 33, *207*, 417
Kylie Bethel, 7
Kylie the dog, 429
Kyril, king of land, 243
Kyrios Graham, 80

"L," clue to criminal, 11
laatlammetjie (last and final child), 371
labels, with name Henry Burney, 326
laboratories: chemist's, 33; Antarctica, 289

laborers, Chinese, 256
labor, forced, 223. *See also* slaves
labor struggles, history of, 280
Labrador retrievers, 231
lacerations, of hands on fence, deliberate, 424
Lady Azumi, 300
LADY KEZIA BUTLER, 71, 73, *209*
Lady Mabel (boat), 321
Lady of Patseo, 264
"Lady of the Lake," 13
Lady Washington (ship), 316
lagoons, whipped by storm, 175
Lagos, Nigeria, 16
Laila Gonsalves, 278
Lake Athabasca, Canada, 240
The Lake at the End of the World, 235
Lake Azi, 407
Lake Burley Griffin, 350
Lake Drumoor, Ireland, 99, 100
Lake of the Okanagon, Canada, 270
Lake Ontario, Hawthorn Bay, 328
Lake Ooleroo, New South Wales, Australia, 394
lakes: dangerous, 407; holiday site, 427; polluted by basilisks, 350; remote, forested area, 243; ruins of castle in, 243; serves as mirror, 100
Lake Taupo, New Zealand, future time, 200
Lake Windermere, Canada, 241
Lake Windigo, Canada, 176
Lake Winnipeg, Canada, 380
Lalaji, 412
lamas: Buddhist, 264; old, one-eyed Tibetan, 137
lamb, leg of, stolen by Black Dog, 227
lameness, induced, 242
Lamont Cranston, radio supersleuth, 11
lamps: kerosene, named Eladdin, 103; peddlers of, 278; ship's, antique, 282
LANCE DUCHARME, 14, *209*, 214
Lance Lorenny, 84, 174, 390
land: Aborigines burn for renewal, 224; clearing, brutally hard work, 30; closeness to, 76, 174; free for filing, Tasmania, 356; redeemed, 298; sacred to Aborigines, 76; unsuitable for grazing, western Australia, 356
A LAND DIVIDED, 156, *209*
land grants, as reward, 336
landladies, 88
landmarks: boat on hill, 323; upright timber in sand, 366
Land of Little Sticks, 426
Land Rovers: man pinned under, 68; mired in sand, 95; stuck in forest, 278; wrecked, 66
landscape, changes in anger Nargun, 265
landslides, 382
Lane Cove River, 73

kookaburras, 367; penguins, 302; turtles, 369; wallabies, 370

naturalists, on global voyage, 183

nature: Aborigine affinity for, 27, 174; appreciation acquired, 3; antagonist, 46, 387; anthropomorphized as man, 300; Australian interior, 42; beauty of coast, 160; beauty of farm in bush, 105; Blue Mountains, New South Wales, 228, 278, 387, 412; bush, appreciation for, 47; Canada, descriptions of loving, 241; Canada, Lake Ontario area, 341; Canadian Arctic, 427; desert, appreciation for, 49, 95; farm, northern New South Wales, 290; functions as character, 24; India, appreciation for, 200; island off Australia, 237; lack of appreciation for the beauty of, 412; land loved by drover, ex-convict, 28; mountain home, 114; New Zealand, 23, 447; North Coast, New South Wales, 44; northern Australian mountains, 266; opal fields, 123; preserves, 68; Prince Edward Island, Canada, 13; Snowy Mountains, New South Wales, 348, 437; southern highlands, New South Wales, 69; Southwest Pacific, 316; Tasmania, 90, 326, 384, 391; Victoria, 31

Nature Studies for School Children, 26

Navy, Royal, 182

Nazareth, Palestine, 249

Nazis: in Crete, 80; in Denmark, 221; neo, in Spain, 10, 89

Ndi, 46

Neanderthals, youths changed into, 259

necklaces, of human bones, 305

NED BURNEY, the wild boy, 155, 266. 326, 414

Ned Fraser, 73

Ned Ganger, 198, 361

ne'er-do-wells: Anderson family, 232; Catholic Irish so regarded, 339; family, 187, 188, 399; father, 48, 357; neighbor, 430; thief, 73

Negritos, earliest Australian Aborigines, 123

Neha, 289

neighborhood life, 354–55, 411, 446

neighborhood life, novels of. See community life, novels of

neighborliness, 90, 143, 178

neighbors: across river, 126; apologetic and contrite, 430; boyhood, 79, 250; busybody, 12; generous, 341; helpful, 31, 63, 290, 445; hostile, 55; hysterical, 121; next-door, 439; potter, helpful, 106; sharp, demanding, 12; shiftless, 318; staunch, helpful, 329; threatening, 362; wealthy, helpful, 416; wealthy, promises job, 415

Neil Barry, 446

Neil Hackett, 376

Nels Bergstrom, 353

Nelson, Lord, 293

NELSON, MR., 218, 267

Nelson, New Zealand, 174

Nelson the bulldog, 114

Neog, Mr., 200

Nepal, 413

nephews: American zoologist, 391; of Mikado, 300; of storekeeper, 5; presumed dead in shipwreck, 155, 326; wild boy of recluse, 155, 266, 326; witch, 439

Neptune ceremony, equator, 289

Neptune, King, 191

Nest in a Falling Tree, 74

nests: bower birds' contains chip of pitchblende, 432; downlined air vehicles, 306; magpies' on windmill crossbar, 435; penguins', 303; transported to cave, 382

Net-Nets, Australian spirits, 276

Neufeld family, 85

Never Cry Wolf, 260

NEV FOWLER, 251, 267

New Brunswick, Canada, 209

Newcastle, New South Wales, 297

New Delhi, India, 263

New England, coastal town, 34

Newfoundland, Canada: seventeenth century, 81; late twentieth century, Marten, 115, 161

New Grange Farm, 275

New Holland (Australia), Swan River, 356

The New Mayflower, 416

New Patches for Old, 248

newsmen. See reporters

New South Wales, Australia:
—late 18th century: Botany Bay, 190
—early 19th century: Sydney, 73, 173, 335
—late 19th century: Barley Creek, 219
—early 20th century: Blue Mountains, 227, 277
—mid 20th century: Bowral, 68; Bungaree, 114, 389; Currawong Crossing, 445; desert, 66; Hollybush Flat, 339; Kiewa Valley, 204; Lake Ooleroo, 394; Merringee, 168; Murray River, 47; Newcastle, 297; North Coast, 43; northern rural, 290; Snowy Mountains, 346, 348, 436; southern highlands, 68; Sydney, 143; Yedda River, 46
—late 20th century: Blue Mountains, 113; Sydney, 7
—named by James Cook, 183

New South Wales Ski Championships, 436

newspapers: ads, cat found, 438; assiduous reader of, 447; boys, 213; father loves, 84; photos enlarged for birthday gift, 294; report unseasonable frost, 173; stories about feral cats, 59

Newton, Sir Isaac, 418

Cretan woman, 80, 124; crippled sailor, 112; dogman on cattle station, 49, 324; eccentric cook, 46, 276; eccentric prospector, 46, 405; ex-farmer fisherman, 332; former pearl diver, 6; fortune-telling woman, 106; frail grandfather, 60; geographer, poor and blind, 241; ghost woman, 328, 378; green boy, 113; imperious grandmother, 152; inspires pioneer boy to education, 276; lame grandfather, 146; Lapp grandfather, 425; lively man, potter, 96, 161; lonely man, 140; man helps refugee boy with food and ride, 223; man "sells" racetrack to boy, 177; man with power to bend Eskimo bow, 426; Maori man, 277, 382; Mennonite woman, 19; mercy killing of, 76, 381, 392–93; mysterious woman, 243; one-eyed Tibetan lama, 137; prospector, 190; recluse, 266, 325; recovered from illness, 412; retired army officer, 238; retired New Zealand farmer, 446; seem genuine, 446; senile woman, takes things, 355; storytelling sailor, 47; sturdy, independent farm woman, 225, 262; survivor of attack on island, 315; swagman, 184, 378, 445; tells stories about Great Forest explorers, 276; wily tramp, 22; wiseman, 35; witchlike woman, 245; woman hates retirement home, 225; woman immigrant from Orkney Islands, 140; woman in nursing home, 293; woman, senile, with Alzheimer's, 251, 355; woman steals refugee boy's bike, 223; woman storekeeper, 396; woman wearing hat like a crimson chamber pot, 251. *See also* grandfathers; grandmothers; grandparents
OLD TAMA, *277*, 382
Old Tommy, 79, 408
Old tram car, 282
Old Willy, 408
"Old Witch," name means, 42
O'Leary, Seven U, 396
Oliver Cromwell, 231
Olu and the Broken Statue, 338
OLWEN Pendennis, Lady, 146, 147, *277*
Olympics, 1960, Rome, 4
O'Malley, August, 344
omens. *See* prophecies; predictions; premonitions; warnings
ONADIPE, KOLA, 16, *277*, 303
ONCE THERE WAS A SWAGMAN, 39, 103, 228, *277*
ONCE UPON A FOREST, 28, *278*
Onegar the baselisk, 350
One Happy Moment, 321
O'Neil, 335
O'Neil, Grandfather, 297
ONE PROUD SUMMER, 159, 236, *279*

1005: Political Life in a Union Local, 129
The One-Winged Dragon, 64
One Woman's Arctic, 45
oni: Japanese ogre, loves poetry, 300; Medusa-like female ogre, 301
On Loyalist Trails, 157
Ontario:
—early 19th century: Hawthorn Bay, 340; Toronto, 309
—mid-19th century: Hawthorn Bay, 328; St. Catharines, 405; Toronto, 318
—mid-20th century: Kitchener, 206; northwest, 175
—late 20th century: Hawthorn Bay, 328; London, 111; mill town, 135; Nugget, 135; Riverside, 239
Oonaderra, "land of the turtle," 76, 181, 392
Oona, god of Aborigines, 76
Oonas, Aborigines, 76, 381, 392
opal fields, Australia, 108, 122
opals: stolen from fire spirit, 35; stolen from mine, 122
Opechancanough, Indian Chief, 231
operating room, German soldiers invade, kill new mother, 221
operations: father's, 298; mother needs, 115; successful, 32
Opie, Susan, 287
opium, smuggling, 359
opossums, 22. *See also* possums
Ora, 201, 253
oral tradition. *See* folklore; legends; myths
orange orchards: Australia, 220; South Africa, 193
oranges, stolen by urchin, 287
orchids, idol hidden in bag of, 138
Ordeal, 69
O'REILLY, BERNARD, *281*, 432
O'Reilly family, 170
ore, radioactive, 432
Oriental evil spirits, 83
Orion, stories of, 363
Orkney people, in Australia, 299
ornithologists: disguise for Abolitionist, 406; neighbor, 368; painter, 113
Oro the baby goat, 178
orphanages: Australia, 213; Canada, 14
orphans: American girl, sent to Canada, 328; baby, World War II, 221; boy, 373, 385, 400; boy, claims to be, 358; boy, goes to Far North to live with uncle, 228; boy, goes to live with middle-aged cousins, 103, 266; boy, lives with uncle and aunt, 242; boy, on cattle station, 49; boy requested, girl sent, 12; boy, sent by uncle to abusive boarding school, 287; boy, street urchin, 287; colt, 138; defiant boy, 362; errand boy, 309; fluteplayer, 107; French boy, 157, 295; girl,

157; gypsy boy, 10, 89; half, 239; half, boy, no father, 46; half, boy, witch, 61; half, girl and boy, 384; half, girl gymnast, 357; half-Iroquois boy, half orphaned, 111, 394; half, sent to uncle, 70; half, siblings, 193, 372; half, timid boy, 275; intelligent boy, 253; Irish girl, emigrant to Australia, 247; man without emotions, 207; Melanesian boy, 6; newborn infant, 345; Norwegian boy on sailing vessel, 186, 361; part-Indian boy, 211; red-haired girl, 12, 14; sister and brother, 309; workhouse, 218; World War II, 221
ORWIN, JOANNA, 174, *281*
Osoyoos, British Columbia, Canada, 269
OSRO the priest, 259, *281*
Otago peninsula, New Zealand, 381
Othello Ben Assim, 310
The Other Side of the World, 344
otherworlds, 149, 243, 258, 305, 350, 357, 373, 418. *See also* medieval worlds, fantasy
Otis Claw, 150
Otis Hand, 150
O'Toole, 182
Ottawa, Canada, ll, 190, 342
Ottawa Valley, Ontario, 342
Otter, 379
Otter Cannon, 70, 72, 209
Otter Roxtell, 159
otters, sea, trade in furs, 316
OTTLEY, REGINALD (LESLIE), 23, 49, *281*, 324
Otto Neufeld, 85, 295
Oupa, 229
Our Scientists, 332
outback: Australia, 23, 55, 271, 413, 428; Tasmania, 154. *See also* rural areas; wilderness
outer space, beings from, 418
Outland Born, and Other Verses, 248
outlaws: Australian, 361; boarding riverboat, 321; famous bushranger, 253
Outside, 296
overdose, insulin, 439
The Overlanders, 29
overseers: cattle station, 49, 324; cruel, of slaves, 226, 406
OVER THE BRIDGE, 160, *282*
owling, father and son go, 139
owls: made of stone, Hoot, 239; stone, taken by little sister, 334
Owls in the Family, 260
owners: ranch, towering, laconic, 46; sheep station, absentee, 41, 191, 260
Oyo Alafin empire, ancient, 16
Oyo, Nigeria, 16

Pacific Fur Co., 241

Pacific islanders, 218
Pacific Northwest, Canada: coast, unspecified time, 421; eighteenth century, 351; twentieth century, 331
Pacific Ocean:
—13th century—southwest, 315
—late 18th century, 217
—mid 20th century: Melanesian Islands, 6
—unspecified time: Fiji Islands, 345
pacifists, Cree Indian chief, 141
pack ice, 422
PACK UP, PICK UP, AND OFF, 285, 386
Paddy Paul Cannon, 70, 72, 209
Paddy Tolly, 219
pageants: Christmas Eve, 364; historical, 445
paheka, white nurse, 402
pain: absorbed by others, 100; from leukemia therapy, 170; in hand from stamp, 61
paint, white, on bandsmen's trousers, 177
painters: father, 212; house, father, 51; mother, 445; of birds, 113. *See also* artists
paintings: Aborigine, 183; missing, 114; of dragons, 33, 40; of plum-rain, 300; of village, 169; valuable ancestral, 68; wild life, 237. *See also* photographs; pictures
palaces: bushranger invited to Queen Victoria's, 254; in cellar, 223; in hollowed out tree, 243; inside mountain top, 147; northeastern India, 60; of grandfather, 412; underwater, 243. *See also* castles; mansions
Palali Game Reserve, India, 278
Palestine, ancient, 249
Palliser, Captain Hugh, 182
Palmer family, 142, 155, 381, 399
palominos, fabled, 135, 242, 373
Panchami the seagull, 368
pandas: Great, or Master, Panda, 107; pet named Tama, 273
Panic in the Cattle Country, 319
Panton, Doug, 417
Paoa, the craftsman, 175
PAPA Devine, 19, 20, 25, 71, *286*, 380
Papa Ernst Solden, 222
Papa Stein, 440
Pa-pee, daughter of medicine man, 141
paperhangers, father, 51, 212
PAPERNY, MYRA, *286*, 440
paperweight, shaped like prism, 418
Papio, 202
Papps, Ernest, 22
parades: annual Youth Day, 448; Anzac Day, 37; in Glitterville, 131; pet, at school for Christmas, 164
parallel, 49th located, 240
paralysis, from snakebite, 322
paratroopers, Nazi, 80
pardons, for rebels, 319
Parekh, Smita, 278

moa named Marmaduke, 164; panda named Tama, 273; penguin named Perc', 422; puppy, 178, 435; raven named Darling, 227; rooster named Samuel, 164; seagull named Panchami, 368; sheep, ewe, named Captain Tuffems, 356; spider named Scary, 164; talking animals, 253; various, 119

pet shows, 119, 164, 314

pharmacists, fifteenth century, 9

Philip, 243

Phillip, Arthur, 190

Phillip Island, convicts shipwrecked on, 70

Phillips, Neil, 124

philosophers, Greek, boy studies, 57

PHIPSON, JOAN (MARGARET FITZHARDINGE), 58, 114, 138, 178, *295*, 389

Phnom Penh, Kampuchea (Cambodia), 223

photographers, amateur, schoolchildren, 74

photographs: albums, old, 275; as illustrations, 439; family, 105; father refuses to be subject, 313. *See also* paintings; pictures

phratries, Eagle, Raven among Haida, 317

Phukan, the ranger, 200

Phyllis Fenwick, 121

physicians: father, 94; German in Canada, 222; in mining community, 310. *See also* doctors; healers; herbalists; medicine men; shamans; surgeons

physicists, renowned, 109

pianists. *See* musicians

piano lessons, in Blue Mountains, New South Wales, 336

pianos: sold, 353; used, 2

piano tuners, itinerant, 227

Pichon, Thomas, 210

picketers: children protesting loss of clubhouse, 80; eviction protesters, 88; textile mill strikers, 280

pickpockets, 203; scapegrace policeman, 253, 398

picnics: "chop," 119; seashore, 164; Sunday School, 13

pictures: girl in red nightgown, 187; girl on unicorn and pigs flying, 296; of lost boat, 155. *See also* paintings; photographs

pidgin English, 62

Piegan Indians, Canada, 240

Pierre Duchene, 209

pies, of gift mulberries, 191

pigeons, seized by hawk, 327

pigs: butchered, 186; farm, 435; in sky, picture of, 296; pink, flying, 296; stolen by "deiful" in river, 206; white, 396

THE PIGS ARE FLYING, *296*, 327

PIGS MIGHT FLY, *296*, 327

pig-ups, storm, 296

pilgrimages, to Ganga (Ganges) River, 368

pillar: girl tied to, 100; Irish hero dies tied to, 100

pilots: dies in air, 133, 395; inexperienced boy, 133, 395

Pimpoota, 322

A Pinch of Salt Rocks an Empire, 349

Pinch the possum, 119

Pine family, 119

Pinkerton family, 126, 184, 185

Pinkie Wirihana, 344

Pinku Johri, 138, 236

pioneer novels: Australia, 30, 41, 227; Canada, 97; Tasmania, 89, 325, 350

pioneers: Australian bush, 291; Australian interior, 41; Blue Mountains, New South Wales, 227; British in Australia, carpenter, 41; Canada, 97, 232, 341; girl lost in fog, 91; Great Forest, South Gippsland, 30, 335, 348; sheepranch, Victoria, 41; South Australia, 90, 247; teacher for, 261; wife of, 335. *See also* settlers

PIONEER SHACK, 29, *297*

"Pioneer Shack," inscribed on foundation stone, 298

pipes, Iroquois, 111

Pippa Buckingham, 17

pirates: based in Tasmania, 336; elegant, cruel, 202; Henry Morgan, 293; in Australian waters, 173; Murray River, 55, 321; North Atlantic, 82; repentant, 336; seize brig, 377; treasure of, 393

pistols. *See* guns; weapons

pitchblende, found in bower, 432

PIWAS, *298*, 324

Pixie O'Harris, 337

pizza shops, owned by Greeks, 8, 93, 434

"The Place of the Beautiful Stones," 392

Place of the Hippopotamus, 45

PLACE OF THE STONE GIANTS, 227, *298*, 387

plagues: frogs, 225; midges, 225; of 1665, 418; radiation sickness, 188; storms, mosquitoes, heat, drought, 123

plains, spirit of, 64

plane crashes: in gulf near land, 42, 56, 395; in snow-covered mountains, 204

planes: buzzes isolated island, kills magpie, 236; crashed, 204, 395; dropping note, 430; rides from Antarctica to India, 289; spotter, 236

planets: in Milky Way, 150; Isis, 146; O, 150, 305; space, non-sexist, 109; stories about, 363

plans: help convict escape, 70; parking, resisted, 276; poor for whaling voyage, 423; secret, to jump ship, 186; to break embankment and flood village, 398; to sell man into slavery, 107; to sell stolen antiques, 413

Portland, Victoria, 41
Port Nicholson (Wellington), New Zealand, 377
Portrait of Peter West, 48
portraits. *See* paintings; pictures; photographs
Port Salish, Vancouver Island, Canada, 423
Portuguese explorers, 134
Portuguese man-o'-war, 25
possum-cord, binds power stone bag, 174
possums: in kitchen, 375; pet, 119; sought for food, Tasmanian Aborigines, 224. *See also* opossums
post cards, about Yelverton world trip, 446
posters: against discrimination toward Aborigines torn up, 169; anti-Jewish, 11
postmasters, 113
potato men, 140, 423
potato patch, refuge from fire, 18
Potere, Maori chief, 288
potions, magic, 374
POT-KOOROK, Australian spirit, 27, 266, 276, *303*
potlaches, 351; among Haida, 317; Hotsath, 421; made illegal among Haida, 1884, 317; planned, 316
A POT OF GOLD, 277, 303
Potomac River, 231
Potter family (*The Catalogue of the Universe*), 57, 262, 403
Potter family (*A Handful of Time*), 152, 291, 330
Potter family (*An Older Kind of Magic*), 27, 254, 275, 338
potters, 96, 106, 161, 427
Potty, disparaging nickname, 152
poverty: blacks in South Africa, 371; family has hard times, 297; family, very poor, 339; in India, 415; sudden, 157
POWELL, LESLEY CAMERON, *304*, 402
power: cone of, to protect property, 255; failure, enables boys to escape, 29; in form of wolf, 243; inherent in mask, 431; inherited, 134; lust for, 147; sought over girl, 251; stone of, 26, 150, 173, 206; utterance of great, 300
POWNALL, (MARJORIE) EVE(LYN SHERIDAN), 73
Poynducs, Tasmanian Aborigines, 246
Poynton, Nina, 25
practices, marching and singing for parade, 448
prairies, Canada, 97, 396, 440
pranks, boy drapes scarecrow in nightgown, 173. *See also* schemes; tricks
Prasad family, 397
Praveen, 59, 412
prayers: for more children, 345; result in rescue, 249; slave mother stresses, 406

Praying Jack, 321
prayer wheels, symbol of identity, 137
preachers, Utopian soapbox, 92. *See also* clergymen; ministers; priests; shamans
predators, hawk, 327
predictions: by bird, always true, 417; hard winter, 323; "progress" will destroy, 298; volcanic eruption, ignored, 6. *See also* premonitions; prophecies; warnings
prefects, school, 61
pregnancies: extra-marital, 82, 92, 340; pre-marital, 136, 303, 309, 345, 353; troubled, 20
prehistoric times: Australia, 123; southeast Asia, 123
prejudice: against Aborigines, 181, 381, 392; against blacks, 56; against Catholics, 339; against foreigners, 238; against Germans, 222; against Germans, World War II, 139; against gypsies, 10; against Indians, 112, 438; against Japanese fishermen, 332; against migrants, 54; against outsiders, 285–86; against poor, 304; against whites, 112, 394; class, 77; racial, 77; racial and ethnic, 360; religious, 11, 52–53, 85, 340, 401. *See also* apartheid; bigotry; discrimination; racism; social classes, distinctions between
Pre-Loved Clothes, 354
premonitions, girl has several, 341. *See also* omens; predictions; prophecies; warnings
President: leader on Isis, 146; of Cascade Valley on planet Isis, 146
press gangs, 182, 218
pretending: boy to be airplane, 96; boys own public properties, 177; girl as mouse disrupting concert, 189
pretenses: convict as sycophant, 178; to make girl a film star, 263
PRETTY GIRL, *305*, 379
pre-white conquest: British Columbia, 269; Washington state, 269
Price, Christine, 396
price, exorbitant for farm, 309
pride, 373; accusation of, 56; community enhanced, 446; in heritage, 438; slave mother stresses retaining, 406
Priestley, Glenn, 8
priests: Druid, 99, 295; evil, 305; kindly Normandy, 158; magician, 134; Quebec, 128, 409; renegade, 259, 281; village, 412; wear skintight white suits and necklaces of human bones, 305. *See also* clergymen; ministers; preachers; shamans
THE PRIESTS OF FERRIS, 132, 151, 258, *305*
Prince Edward Island, Avonlea, 12
Prince Rupert the calf, 396
princess, Hachi, 300

See also apartheid; bigotry; discrimination; prejudice; social classes, distinctions between

Racketty Street Gang, 262, 313

THE RACKETTY STREET GANG, 108, *313*

Racquetier Street, Sydney, Australia, 313

radiation: producing genetic deformity, 200; sickness, parents supposedly died of, 253

radicals. *See* terrorists

radio broadcasts, origin of novel, 26

radio conversations, 95

radios: considered magic, 146; crystal set, 43; shows, historical, "The Shadow," 11

Rae Somerville, 143

RAFFERTY RIDES A WINNER, *314*, 440

Rafferty Takes to Fishing, 314, 440

RAF officer, former, 204

rafts: crude, 361; cut loose, 431; Fiji lagoon, 345; idea for, 42; vehicles for migrating to Australia, 123

rages, queen flies into, 300

Ragged School, 25

Raghuvir, the chauffeur, 203

Rag Lane, London, 157

Rags the dog, 49, 197, 324

raids: for slaves, 351; "pass raid," South Africa, 194; police, 136; police of street people, Cape Town, 371; wolverine, 229

railroads: building of, 366; car, son buys for father, 393; crash, 412; Trans-Australian, 67, 255, 380; yards, 411

Rainbow, 24

Rainbow Flats, Canada, 373

Rainbow Serpent, Aborigine, thought to live in swimming hole, 169

Rain Comes to Yamboorah, 281

Rain, Frances, 427

Rain Island, 427

Rain Lake, Manitoba, Canada, 427

rains: annual called the Wet, 76; continual, at sea, 218; heavy for weeks, 430

raisins, making grapes into, 322

rajas, 60

Raja the tiger, 385

Rakasha, 83

Rakesh, 60

rallies, protest, 415. *See also* protests; riots

Ramatau, Fiji Islands, 346

Ramsay Place, 250, 408

Ramu, 29

Ramu *kaka*, 413

rancher, amateur entymologist, 47

ranches: Alberta, Canada, 215; Australia, 361; bush, 28, 46, 276, 405; cattle, Australia, 75, 95, 181, 257, 430; cattle, South Australia, 49, 197, 324; cattle and sheep, Australia, 428; horse, Australia, 138; sheep, Australia, 114, 125, 138, 179, 184, 434;

sheep, Australia, Carcoola, 55; sheep, Australian interior, 28, 41; Australia, huge, 133, 394; sheep, marginal, 389; sheep, miniature, 293; sheep, New Zealand, 285; sheep, northern Australia, 62, 265, 266, 303; sheep, outback station, 255; sheep, Tasmania, 383–84; sheep, Victoria, 260; Tangari, in bush, 47; western Canada, 373

ranch life, Australia: cattle, 49, 324, 325; sheep, 55, 114, 255, 389. *See also* farm life; sheep ranches; sheep stations; stations

ranch managers: father, 215; former rodeo rider, 14

Randy Borowski, 215

Ranee the tiger, 385

RANGATIRA, 220, *315*, 392

Rangatira, means "highborn," 316

rangers: forest, 200; helpful, 268

Rangi, 402

Rangitoto, ancient D'Urville Island, 175

Ranjat Johri, 138, 263

Rankin family, 170

ransom: demanded for dog, 5 bob, 44; sought by kidnappers, 58, 203; 3 bob, flashlight bulb, and IOU, for dog, 44

Ransome, Arthur, 70

Rao, K. D., Detective Inspector, 138, 263

rapes, attempted, 353. *See also* seductions; sexual harassment

rapids: river, 228; shooting, 362

Rashid, 1

raspberry farmers, 17

rat traps, torn up by gnome, 225

rats: literary, 33; performing, 417

Raven, phratries, Haida, 317

ravens: children enchanted as, 100; pet named Darling tears up summons, 227

RAVEN'S CRY, 154, *316*

Ravenshoe, Australia, 432

ravines: muddy, refuge from fire, 97; near home, 114

Raukawa, ancient Cook Strait, 174

Rawiri, 382

Ray Farlow, 37

Raymond Bradley, 144

rays, giant, 361

RAZZELL, MARY, *317*, 352

reading: inability, 211, 345; learning to, 33; teaching of, 60

realistic novels. *See particular types*

reappearances: boy as old man, 166; scientist thought dead, 258

rebel leaders: bickering, 397; poorly organized, 236

rebellions: adolescent, 136; defeated, 319; planned, 281; premature, 319

rebels, in armed conflict: slaughtered by Romans, 249; Toronto Reformers, 318.

stowaways: on Ark, 293; on space ship, 258; younger brother on whaler, 422

A Straight Furrow, 202

Stranger: identified by Tallisker property, 134; predicted to perpetuate Gift, 134, 140, 299

strangers: bearded cellist, 188; black-cloaked, armed, bejeweled, sinister, 107; dubious reputation, talkative, 46; found sleeping in barn, 263; sinister, 109, 289

Straw, 213

streamers, retarded boy decorates grandstand with, 177

streetcar barn, 11

Street of Three Directions, 198

strength: physical, notorious, 250; physical, rival's, 79

stretchers: carried with difficulty, 122; makeshift, 279

strikebreakers, with guns, 153

strike demands, firing foreman of clerk, 343

strikes: broken, 342; lumbercamp, 52; planned, 280; textile mill, 279

strokes. *See* illnesses, strokes

THE STROLLERS, 24, *371*

strollers, street children, Capetown, 371

Strong family, 132, 337

struggles, moral, 128

Stubeck family, 92, 98, 181, 205, 262, 399

Stubley, Trevor, 361

students: agricultural, 294; all-round, 4; blackbird ancestry, 290; Catholic boys take honors, 339; college, mother, 239; exemplary, 355; girl, partially sighted, excellent, 222; good, 249; honor, 136; medical, 1; music, 189; of wise man, 243; scholarship, 52; skiing, 436; starting high school, apprehensive, 222; technical college, 297; treacherous, 207; university, 33, 222, 251

studios: planned, 337; ruined by autistic boy, 274

Stumpy the dog, 230

Sturluson, Arne, 311

stutterers, ghost, 300

style: almost plotless, 206; appreciation for earth, strong, 174; archaic, slightly, 231; artful diction, 156; Arthur Ransome-like, 44; Asian Indian expressions and rhythms, 30, 109, 290, 369, 399; atmosphere of sea strong, 332; Australian terms, 47, 48, 314; author intrusive, 67; brisk, 409; cartoonish, 132, 182; caricature characters, 150; characterization, rich, 14, 58, 446; character revelation, subtle, 424; clear detail of race-track life and action, 177; cliched, 138, 200, 377, 433; climax exciting, 174, 266, 440; coincidence, dependence on, 42, 48, 174, 200, 252, 298, 301, 364, 377;

colloquial speech, 90, 326, 391; comic humor, 151; conventional characters and incidents, 47, 298, 446; conventions of detective mystery, 30, 138, 200, 263, 399; conventions of 18th century novel, 158; conventions of pioneer stories, 42; conventions of Victorian melodrama, 288; conventions of "virtue winning," 304; crowded canvas, 86, 132, 158, 183, 210, 228, 231, 241, 247, 301, 316, 317, 319, 357; crowded climax and conclusion, 132; dated, 374; descriptive of area, 357; descriptive of nature, 241; details, archeological, 112; details, effective, 374, 401; details, ethnic, 316; details, lively, extensive, 357; details of Aborigine life, 384; details of camping, 44; details of canoe building; 175; details of Cape York life, 76; details of convict life, 71; details of farm life and terrain, 447; details of hunting might offend, 47, 362, 429; details of lives of Indian women, 379; details of Mennonite life, 206–7; details of music world, 189; details of period, 12, 183, 231, 250; details of pioneer life, 31, 228; details of ranch locale, 139; details of setting, 229, 310, 446; details of sheepranch life, 255; details of swimming athletes, 5; details, small, important, 252; details of wild horses' ways, 347; dialect, Australian, 315; dialect, Mennonite, 207; dialect, mid 1800s, 329; dialect, "down under," 190; dialect, Irish and Cornish, 92; dialect, rural Newfoundland, 162; dialect, Scottish, 300, 341; dialogue, almost all, 214; dialogue, apt, 269; dialogue, entirely, 301; dialogue, extensive, 26, 47, 48, 52, 136, 224, 340, 357, 394; dialogue, static, 95; diary, 200, 293, 294; diary entries, interspersed throughout action, 105; diary entries, too polished and detailed, 105; easy vocabulary and simple sentence structure, 403; epilogue, 319; explicit language, 136; family anecdotes, 390; fanciful, 396; fast-paced, 30, 82, 107, 200, 263, 359; flashbacks, 4, 90, 170, 224, 252, 423; formal diction, 270, 414; frame stories, 301; frenetic pace, 151; frequent shifts to present tense, 218; Gothic elements, 61, 256, 439; graphic descriptions, 218; hectic pace and overtense tone, 128, 182; hero-quest pattern, 27, 173; high action, 229, 259, 324, 359, 406, 437; high tension, 138, 348, 358; humor, incongruous, 237; humor, ironic, 14; humorous scenes, 72; hyperbolic, 132, 259; imagery, extensive, unusual, 61; imagery, nature, 406; imagery of light and dark, 171; imagery of touch and sound, 223;

improvises on Robin Hood-western outlaw-folktale patterns, 254; inner directed, reflections and reactions, 189; intense atmosphere, 266; interesting expressions, 17; introspective, highly, 223; ironic, 58, 249, 447; legend-like, 107, 237, 345, 392, 417, 427; leisurely, 90; local color, 2, 92, 206–7, 310, 399, 400, 401, 413; Maori terms, 34–35, 175; melodramatic, 30, 107, 151, 191, 259, 306, 360; moralistic, 14, 17, 243, 332; naive, 379; narrative unmotivated, 64; nautical terms, 269, 332; offensive elements, 360; open ending, 122, 395; overwrought, 193; past tense alternates with present tense, 5; point of view, alternating, 90; point of view, male, 175; point of view, naive, 214; point of view, severely focused to girl's perspective, 189; point of view, sympathatic to blacks, 194; point of view, sympathetic to tribespeople, 247; Polynesian words, 316; present tense, 5, 189, 221; primer-like language and sentence structure, 151; question and answer, 363–64; rich in atmosphere, 225; sailing atmosphere strong, 269; satire, 131; satire on family life, 182, 394; satire on whites, 174; satirical, 132; sensory description, strong, 236–37; sentimental, didactic, 8; setting strongly depicted, 67, 341; short italicized prologues to each chapter, 5; simple vocabulary, 165, 200; social comment, searing, 136; staccato, 377; stereotypes, Chinese cook, 62; stereotypes, cultural of women, 153; stereotypes, Noble Redman, 209; subtle psychological touches, 424; suspenseful, 147, 300; suspense, mild, 276; tall tale, 16; Tasmanian native terms, 224; tense, 27, 171, 174, 314; themes pronounced, 147; third person sharply focused, 105; thrills, 436; two interlocking stories, 90; understated, 221, 225; undeveloped incidents, numerous, 374; unreal realism, 360; visual, strongly, 52; vividly described geography, 326; vivid, sensory, 252; witty dialogue, 58; witty, Hogarthian, 158; wordplay, 107; Yiddish terms, 72. *See also* stories within stories; tone

Subir, 109

substance abuse: breathing correction fluid, 211; marijuana, 115; various, 135

substances: indigo-blue, 342; viscous, 93

substitutions, fake for real idol, 263

The Suburbs of Hell 371

succession, among Haida, renounced, 317

suckerfish, used to catch turtle, 369

Sue, 190

SUE CLARKE, 66, 181, *372*

Suffer Dogs, 434

The Sugar Plum Christmas Book, 62

suicide: boy committed, 341; contemplated by girl, 341; convict leaps from cliff, 70; girl, fifteen, 136; leap over cliff, 306

suitcases: booby-trapped, 333; full of money, 333; stolen, 333

suitors, of father, 20, 25, 72

suits: blue velvet, 155; yellow silk, 337

sulkies, horse drawn, 411

Summer Goes Riding, 402

THE SUMMER IN BETWEEN, 360, *372*

Summerton, South Australia, 119

summons: to help people, 26; torn up by raven, 227

Sumner family, 216

sun: at sea, broiling, 218; erases writing on scroll, 301; Ra, 147, 277

Sun Dance, Blackfoot, 379

Sunday Island, 130, 218

Sun God, Moon Witch, 199

Sung Wu, "slightly enchanted realm" in ancient China, 107

THE SUN HORSE, 64, *373*

Sun Horse, fabled palomino stallion, 135, 242, 373

Sunil (*The Blind Witness*), 29

Sunil (*The Chandipur Jewels*, *Vanishing Trick at Chandipur*), 59, 412

Sun Indians, Canada, 230, 374

Sunny, 70

THE SUN ON THE STUBBLE, *374*, 388

Sunset House, rest home, 225

Sun, Wind, and Coral: Australia's Great Barrier Reef, 62

Sun Yat Sen, 77

SUPERBIKE, 40, *376*

superman, costumes, 182

supermarket parking lot, old woman encountered in, 251

Supermarket Thursday, 62

supernatural, novels of, 61, 111, 155, 225, 266, 275, 381, 383, 396, 427, 439

Supernatural Shark, 421

supplies, lost in canoe wreck, 228

Supply (ship), 191

"Supreme Expedition Council," 16

surfboards, carried inland, 43

surgeons: boy wishes to become, 70; father, Jewish, 221; ship's, acting, 213, 218; ship's, drunken, 213. *See also* doctors; healers; herbalists; medicine men; physicians; shamans

SURGEON'S BOY, *377*, 378

surrenders: of Denmark, World War II, 221; old woman to gnome, 225

surveyors: Blue Mountains, New South Wales, 242; boy's ambition, 348; Canada, 240; Great Forest, 30

Ted (*The House that was Eureka*), 88, 108, 165
Ted (*It Happened One Summer*), 179
Ted (*Over the Bridge*), 282
Teddy Stein, 440
TEDDY TRUELANCE, 103, 217, 227, 278, 298, *387*
Ted Knightley, 375
teenage life, small town, 116, 135
teetotalers, bushranger, 254
telegraph lines, downed, 46
telepathy: Aborigine elders use, 83; mental, 355; mental, with animals, 385
telephone line, cut to hinder pursuit, 255
television: commercials, child stars dance in, 185, 251, 267; father's pleasure, 5; in store window, 418; locked up by father, 418; mayor performs comic routines on, 131; mother, news anchor, 152, 330; mother's pleasure, 3; shows, in Sydney, children attend, 213; used for contact by extraterrestials, 418. *See also* TV
Telikjuak, 426
Tell Me Another Tale, 62
Tell Me a Tale, 62
TEMBO MURUMBI, 45, *387*
tempers: father's, 440–41; girl loses, 13; hair-trigger, 58; mother's, 251
temples: of O, 281; seat of evil government, 306; visit to, 249
tenacity. *See* perseverance; persistence
tenants: of English sheep farmer, 356; shot dead, 29; strike, 165–66
tenderfeet, ranch, 28
Teneriffe, Canary Islands, 191
Tennant family, 297
TENNANT, KYLIE (KATHLEN TENNANT), 6, *387*
Tennyson, "Lady of the Lake," 13
tension, religious, 340
tenth member, always secret, 245
tents: collapsed, 128; in zoo, boy provides for family, 393
Tere-Moana, New Zealand, 315
Terrebonne, Quebec, home of Canadian geographer, 24
terriers: English bull, 32, 176, 385; Lhasa apso, 264. *See also* dogs
terrorists: bully on ship, 422; in village of India, 279; of birds, hawk, 326; underworld, 80
terror, reign of, in O, 305
Terry Blanchard, 86
Terry's Brrrmmm GT, 145
Terry Carpenter, 418
TERRY KENDALL, *388*, 445
TESS MEDFORD, 239, 251, *388*
Tess Moorland, 178–79

Tess Roxtell, 159
testimony: at robber trial, 333; court, 272; of boys convicts cattle thieves, 359
TETACUS, *388*, 421
Te Taniwha family, 163
textile workers, Quebec, 279
Thailand, border of, refugees' destination, 223
Thanksgiving Day, rituals for, 146
theaters: father opposed to, 440; puppet, 441
thefts: accusations of proved wrong, 434; bicycle, 223; Buddhist relic, 264; car, 95; cattle, 430; chicken, 176, 322; composition, 144; contract, 41; emu eggs, 366; family funds, 398; fee money, 407; fishing boat, 414; horse, 437; horse, attempted, 311; Love Magnet, 374; magic belt, 396; manuscript, 33, 40; money and jewels, 73; money from great grandfather, 206; nest stones, 303; opals, 122; penguin egg, by gull, 303; plum pudding, 414; prize peaches, 373; rope from riverboat, 321; Staff of Power, 207; stone owl, 334; "travel bud" stone, 109; unsuccessful, idol cracked in, 263; Volkswagen, 162; Volkswagen bus, 211, 394, 415; white calf, 396. *See also* burglaries; robberies
Their Town: The Mafia, the Media, and the Party Machine, 129, 159
theme parks, proposed to feature anteater and echidnas, 16
thesis, graduate school, on riots of unemployed, 166
They Found a Cave, 63
Thief the Bloodcat, 259
THIELE, COLIN, 31, 119, 122, 236, 322, 365, 374, *388*, 411
thieves: assumed, 66; boy of money from great grandfather, 206; bushranger, 253; Cape Town, South Africa, 371; cattle, apprehended through stampede, 359; clever old tramp steals boy's camping gear, 22; girl, 399; girl encourages younger brother to steal, 400; goat, 407; handicapped boy, 181; hides in hedge, discovered by dog, 138; idols, 263; jewel, 203; joins scientific party for escape, 138; London serving girl, 158; mother, of fruit, 205; of old woman, thwarted, 267; policeman, 254; river pirate, 55; schoolboy at pizzeria, 8; school friend, 39; senile old woman, 355; sheep, 375; son of ranch owner, 286; sought by children, 413; steal household items from Alzheimer's woman, 251; street urchin steals orange, 287; supposed, shunned at school, 407; woodpile, 79, 375; younger brother, 400. *See also* bandits; bushrangers; robbers
Thing, 205
Thingnapped!, 205

About the Authors

ALETHEA K. HELBIG is Professor of English Language and Literature at Eastern Michigan University. A former president of the Children's Literature Association, she has published over one hundred articles in professional journals, such as *Children's Literature* and *The Children's Literature Association Quarterly*. She has also contributed to reference books such as *American Women Writers*, *Writers for Children*, and *Masterplots*.

AGNES REGAN PERKINS is Professor Emeritus of English Language and Literature at Eastern Michigan University. She has published numerous articles in journals and reference books, including *A Tolkien Compass, Unicorn, Children's Literature, Children's Literature Association Quarterly, Writers for Children*, and *Masterplots*. She has also co-compiled three poetry anthologies, two of them with Helbig.